AF323757

FROM CRISIS to RECOVERY

East Asia Rising Again?

FROM CRISIS to RECOVERY

East Asia Rising Again?

Editors

Tzong-shian Yu
Chinese Institute of Economics and Business

Dianqing Xu
Huron College, University of Western Ontario

World Scientific
Singapore • New Jersey • London • Hong Kong

Published by

World Scientific Publishing Co. Pte. Ltd.

5 Toh Tuck Link, Singapore 596224

USA office: Suite 202, 1060 Main Street, River Edge, NJ 07661

UK office: 57 Shelton Street, Covent Garden, London WC2H 9HE

British Library Cataloguing-in-Publication Data
A catalogue record for this book is available from the British Library.

First published 2001
Reprinted 2003

FROM CRISIS TO RECOVERY: EAST ASIA RISING AGAIN?

ISBN 981-02-4434-7

This book is printed on acid-free paper.

Printed in Singapore by Uto-Print

PREFACE

The financial crisis first broke in Thailand on July 2, 1997, and swept the region like a tornado, engulfing Malaysia, Indonesia, Philippines and Singapore, and encroaching upon Hong Kong, Taiwan, Korea, Japan and China. No country in East Asia managed to completely evade its impact. One year later, the far-reaching effects of the economic storm have still not died down in East Asia, and had spread even to Russia and Latin America. All the countries that succumbed to the crisis found themselves facing a sharp depreciation in their currencies and collapse of market stock; these effects have in turn resulted in a decline in exports, a slowdown in economic growth, and a rise in unemployment.

It may be an oddly ironic that these newly-industrializing Asian countries had all maintained a high growth rate for over two decades before 1997, since, within the period of just a few months, prosperity was transformed into depression, and abundance into scarcity. Many well-known and well-regarded large enterprises have gone bankrupt, while the governments concerned still have no effective means of mitigating the impact of the financial crisis. However, it may also be interesting to note that after two years of recession in East Asia, almost all the countries in this region are rising again. In the wake of this sudden onslaught on the economies of East Asia, many new questions have come to light, and are waiting for the right answers, such as: How is it that the Asian countries could have become so weak so as to totally succumb to the financial crisis? What are the real causes of the financial crisis? What policy measures have the affected countries undertaken in order to combat the financial crisis and how effective are they? As for the argument of "hands off policy" vs. "government intervention", which approach is more appropriate for curbing the expansion of the financial crisis? What are the policy implications for solving the problem of financial crisis? Why is East Asia rising again after two-year recession? And so on.

Obviously, the financial crisis in East Asia has not only troubled the government and businessmen but also caused great concern for economists in this region. Mr. Harold H. C. Han, president of the Himalaya Foundation, realized the serious impact of the financial crisis to East Asian countries and asked us to submit a research project on this crisis to his Foundation. At the Meeting of Leading Grant-Making Foundations in Asia and Oceania held on November 20–21, 1998 in Tokyo, he presented our project on the East Asian Financial Crisis to the Meeting and gained the support of all the participants. We then organized a research team, composed of twelve leading economists from the ten East Asian countries, including Thailand, Malaysia, Indonesia, the Philippines, Singapore, Hong Kong, Taiwan, Korea, Mainland China and Japan. We also invited one expert from the United States to be responsible for making an aggregate analysis of the interdependence of this region in the context of a financial crisis.

The first meeting of the research team was held in Taipei in April 9, 1999. All participants discussed the outline very carefully. The team members had a second meeting in Taipei in January 22 and 23, 2000. About one year later, we finished the project.

There are already many research papers and books regarding the Asian financial crisis. However, there are several characteristics that make this book unique, and attractive to many readers.

First of all, labor division among the economists is the most important characteristic of the book, since the author of each chapter is an expert on their own country's economy. They are very active not only in economic research but many of them were also deeply involved in the policy-making process during the financial crisis. They provided a great deal of first-hand knowledge and the latest information on the financial crisis and economic recovery in their country.

Secondly, because all the authors in the book worked on the same framework instead of writing their paper totally independently, it is much easier for our readers to understand what has happened in Asian countries through comparative studies. Even though each paper focuses on one country's case, there is an internal connection among the chapters. All articles in the book discuss the external affects and regional environment during the financial crisis.

Thirdly, the articles in the book not only pay attention to policy analysis but also emphasize economic theory. Many articles in the book challenge the traditional economic theory in international finance.

The potential readers of the book will be professors and graduate students in economics, and economists who work in financial institutions such as the World Bank, IMF, ADB and commercial banks and other financial and international business arenas. In addition, this book is also very important to all economic policy-making officials in either Asian countries or the rest of the world. This book is a very rich information resource for all readers who are interested in Asian economies.

The completion of the research project should be mainly attributed to Mr. Han who initiated the project and fully supported the proceeding of the project. We are also deeply indebted to the foundations, banks and groups, including Himalaya Foundation, Pou Chen International Group, Lin Rong San Foundation of Culture and Social Welfare, Holmsgreen Foundation, Fubon Bank, Toyota Foundation, Chiang Ching-Kuo Foundation for International Scholarly Exchange, Vedan Group for their generous support. Without their support, it would be impossible to successfully focus on carrying out our project.

Tzong-shian Yu
Director
Chinese Institute of Economics and Business

Dianqing Xu
Professor of Economics
Huron College
University of Western Ontario

CONTENTS

CHAPTER 1

AN OVERVIEW
OF THE FINANCIAL CRISIS
IN EAST ASIA

Tzong-shian Yu*

*Chinese Institute of Economics and Business
Rm 10-17, No. 233, Sec. 4, Chung Hsiao East Road
Taipei, Taiwan
E-mail:cieb@ms27.hinet.net*

1. INTRODUCTION

Some two years after the financial crisis first broke out in Thailand, all of the East Asian countries, with the exception of Indonesia, have managed to stage a recovery and are now demonstrating gradual growth. This seems, therefore, an appropriate time to take a retrospective look at the financial crisis and to undertake a comprehensive analysis of the underlying causes and impacts, upon financial systems in particular, and on the economic climate in general. Throughout the past two years, there have been many books, and many thousands of articles, dealing with the crisis from various points of view, but none of these has made any attempt at providing a systematic and satisfactory explanation covering the entire period from

---

*Member of Academica Sinica, Director of the Chinese Institute of Economics and Business and consultant to the Chung-Hua Institution for Economic Research.

economic downturn to recovery. This is a situation that requires rectifying since, naturally, in all of the countries affected by the financial crisis in East Asia, for both governments and citizens alike, this is not only a true story that we have experienced, but also an invaluable lesson for us to bear in mind for the future.

In the introductory chapter of this volume, first of all, we examine the importance of the issue of the East Asian financial crisis from an historical perspective. From the very first signs of the financial crisis, there have been many arguments regarding the causes; we go on to review the various explanations provided, presenting a model used to explore the root causes of the crisis. We also talk about the role of the government in facing the challenge of the financial crisis and the function of the IMF's rescue program. Since many signs indicate that East Asia is gradually recovering from crisis, we would like to explore its reasons. Finally, we explain the purpose and the structure of this volume.

2.   THE IMPORTANCE OF THE ISSUE: THE FINANCIAL CRISIS IN EAST ASIA

During the twentieth century, there have been two major financial crises that have struck on an international scale. The first of these occurred during the period 1929–30, mainly affecting the developed nations on both sides of the North Atlantic, while the second crisis, which struck in 1997 and persisted until 1999, was experienced mainly by the newly emerging economies in East Asia. The important lesson learned from the first financial crisis was the need to construct much more sound financial systems within these developed countries and recognition of the requirement for separation of the business of banks, from dealings in stocks and insurance. The banking system was considered a key financial institution, which, above all, must maintain its independence and soundness so as to protect depositors. It was therefore imperative that the banking system was in a position to be able to avoid the impact of the inherent risks involved in stock market and insurance transactions. The by-product of the 'great depression', which resulted from the first of these financial crises, was J. M. Keynes' "The General Theory of Employment, Interest and Money" (1936), which dominated mainstream economic thought for around four decades. Even now, many governments still prefer to pursue Keynesian fiscal policy to stimulate their sluggish economies.

The two major financial crises have some similarities. Prior to the 1930s, most western nations lacked any form of sound financial system. In the aftermath of the crisis, these countries embarked upon various programs aimed at setting up much more sound financial systems, which would have the capability of meeting various challenges. Therefore, these countries were in a position to withstand the contagion from the second, recent financial crisis in East Asia. Similarly, this second crisis also occurred in countries where financial institutions were still in an embryonic state. When this crisis struck, sweeping quickly across all the newly emerging economies in East Asia, none of these countries were in any position to avoid the contagion.

In short, the first financial crisis forced the developed countries to strengthen their financial systems to create effective barriers against any future potential crisis. As for the recent crisis in East Asia, whether or not strengthening the financial institutions of the newly emerging economics will prove similarly beneficial, depends largely upon the attitude, and subsequent actions, of the various governments. And whether this will also bring about the emergence of a new economic paradigm will depend mainly upon the wisdom of today's economists.

For us, the importance of the Asian financial crisis lies in the lessons we can learn on how to eliminate internal causes and how to avoid external impacts. The former is usually the rootstock of any financial crisis, whilst the latter tends to be the catalyst in bringing about financial crisis. Sound economic fundamentals can clearly help to reduce the potential of future financial crises, but they cannot completely remove the possibility of contagion from any regional financial crises which, theoretically, are transmitted through trade and capital flows, but which, practically, are transmitted by highly modernized communication instruments, such as television, the Internet, and so on. Nevertheless, the means of entry for any regional financial crisis is a country's foreign exchange and stock markets.

During the 1990s, it seems clear that financial economy has gradually become the predominant consideration in the mainstream of the world economy. As a result of general economic liberalization and internationalization, controls on capital movement and non-tariff barriers to trade have both been greatly reduced. This move towards free capital movement and trade transfers results in all the countries within a region becoming closely related and reliant upon each other, thus, a financial crisis in one country can quickly spread to neighboring countries. Furthermore, capital flow and trade flow, are also closely linked together.

It should be noted that as a result of the liberalization of capital movement, international funds have formed a powerful stream, exerting great influence over a country's exchange and stock markets. In any country where the market was comparatively small, the international funds would have the potential for dominance and control of its stock market. When huge amounts of capital flowed in, stock prices would soar; when capital of such magnitude flowed out, the stock market would collapse, virtually overnight. This phenomenon has led to the question: what kind of financial mechanism for an individual country would be able to face the challenge of a financial crisis? Needless to say, so far, no definite answer has been provided. This is why many governments still prefer to maintain some measure of control over their capital movement, and tend to be somewhat reluctant to open up their capital account completely.

However, since financial conditions have become more dynamic, more uncertain and more complicated than ever before, it has become necessary to consider the possibility of setting up a series of financial indicators that will reflect the signals of impending financial crisis, while providing a coherent approach for effectively preventing contagion from external financial crises.

3. VARIOUS EXPLANATIONS OF THE CAUSES OF THE FINANCIAL CRISIS

Since the 1960s, the four so-called 'Asian Dragons', Taiwan, Hong Kong, Singapore and Korea, have all achieved high economic growth, largely propelled by the expansion of their exports and investment, and from the late 1980s onwards, the four so-called 'Asian Tigers', Thailand, Malaysia, Indonesia and the Philippines have also enjoyed rapid economic growth. Their amazing achievements have been described as an "economic miracle", suggesting that they are "making the impossible possible". However, sometimes "miracle" is more an indicator of "good fortune".

When many people in East Asia were removed from poverty and began to become infatuated with the so-called "economic miracle", Professor Paul Krugman's argument seemed to be to "pour a bucket of cold water over their heads". According to Krugman, all of the output growth in Asia could be attributed to the growth of factor inputs, such as labor and capital. In other words, the Asian miracle was more a result of perspiration, rather than inspiration and there was nothing really miraculous about the high growth in Asia at all.[1]

Lewis T. Preston, President of the World Bank also holds a similar argument suggesting that: "the research shows that most of East Asian's extraordinary growth is due to superior accumulation of physical and human capital"[2]. Put simply, the suggestion is that if there were no continuing accumulation of sufficient capital and available labor, the miracle would simply become a bubble. Is it surprising then that the East Asian financial crisis actually occurred, or should we conclude that the crisis is a reflection of the bursting of the Asian bubble economy?

There have been many attempts at explaining the causes of the financial crisis in East Asia, some of which are unreasonable and excessively emotional, and some of which are incomprehensive and lack impartiality. However, all of these arguments are helpful in providing many perspectives for consideration of the cause-and-effect relationship of the financial crisis.

3.1 Sinister Tactics

From this perspective, in view of the rapid development of the East Asian economy over the past twenty years, there would have been a

---

[1] See Yasuhiro Maehara, "Financial Stability in Southeast Asia".

[2] See 'foreword' in the East Asian Miracle: Economic Growth and Public Policy.

presupposition amongst western nations that the East Asian nations could become a great threat to their dominant position in the world economy. In order to eliminate the threat, these rich economies took advantage of the situation by initially investing in the East Asian economy, and then later withdrawing their investments. Once the East Asian countries lacked the operating capital, their economies would become gloomy and even lose their competitiveness in the world market.

3.2 International Speculation

Many international speculators have recently become interested in indirect investment in the newly emerging economies, and through the effective use of valuable information and their huge funds, they are able to penetrate particular capital markets. Since most of these countries have adopted fixed exchange rate mechanisms, or have otherwise linked their exchange rate to the U.S. dollar, the speculators can make short-term investments in their stock markets through such kinds of exchange rate systems. First of all, they create successive rises in the stock prices within these countries, then, as soon as the stocks reach suitably high levels, the speculators sell out all of their stockholdings, creating a sudden drop in prices, and a bursting of the bubble.

3.3 Excessive Devaluation of the Chinese Currency (RMB)

In 1994, due to hyperinflation and over-investment, the government in Mainland China adopted the strategy of "adjustment and control of the macro-economy" taking devaluation measures in the foreign exchange system. Many foreign economists considered that, as a result, the RMB had been over-devalued. This was helpful for the Mainland Chinese economy, since it led to an increase in exports, but harmful for many of the Southeast Asian countries, where continued economic growth relied heavily upon the expansion of exports.[3]

---

[3] This is not supported by the export statistics of the ASEAN countries, refer to Table 1.3.

3.4 The Rapid Depreciation of the Japanese Yen

The relationship between Japan and other East Asian countries is closely linked to trade and capital flows. Many East Asian countries import large quantities of intermediate products and machinery equipment from Japan, whilst producing less goods for export to Japan. Consequently, they generate massive trade deficits with Japan. As the Japanese Yen appreciates against the U.S. dollar, the East Asian economies become prosperous; as the Japanese Yen depreciates against the U.S. dollar, their economies can rapidly decline into recession. Ever since late-1995, there has been a tendency for continuous depreciation of the Japanese Yen against the U.S. dollar, making it increasingly difficult for the East Asian countries to expand exports to the United States, and subsequently leading to economic recession.

3.5 The Collapse of the 'Bubble Economies' of East Asia

Over the past decade, many East Asian economies have been characterized as 'bubbles' in the context of soaring stock prices and sharp rises in the price of real estate. When the level of prices reaches beyond the purchasing power of the middle-income classes, many real estates become inventory, which presents not only an enormous burden upon construction investors, but also results in a rapid rise in bad debts amongst the financial institutions as the real estate companies loans remain unpaid.

3.6 Short-Term Capital Used for Long-Term Investment

In most of the East Asian countries, enterprises have relied upon the various financial institutions to provide them with short-term capital, lending that must be repaid within one year. However, many of these enterprises have subsequently gone on to utilize these funds as long-term investment capital. Clearly, however, once these loans mature, if the debtors do not have sufficient readily available funds to meet repayment of the loans, this will lead them into bankruptcy.

3.7 The Nepotism Between Politicians and Enterprises

In many East Asian countries, very close relationships exist between politicians and enterprises. Engaging in this sort of nepotism provides the enterprises in question with substantial preferential treatment being offered by the government. In concrete terms, the enterprises may be provided with mortgage-free loans from the state-owned financial institutions at preferential interest rates. If the enterprises fail in their investment of these funds, and fall into financial difficulties, the relevant institutions would inevitably find themselves becoming part of the subsequent financial crisis.

These arguments seem plausible, but they cannot provide the whole picture of the Asian financial crisis, either completely or systematically. In some sense, they seem to be consistent with an old Chinese saying, "the blind who touches an elephant", meaning that their impression of the financial crisis is merely partial, incomplete. Nevertheless, no one explanation can provide the answers to the underlying causes of the financial crisis in East Asia.

4.   THE IMPACTS OF THE FINANCIAL CRISIS IN EAST ASIA

4.1 The Initial Impacts of the Financial Crisis on Financial Markets

There are two important indicators, which reflect the initial impacts of the financial crisis on East Asian economies during the period June 30, 1997 to December 31, 1997. One is the change in exchange rates and the other the change in stock prices. Table 1.1 shows that among the ten countries, Thailand, Indonesia, Malaysia, the Philippines, Singapore, Hong Kong, China, Taiwan, Korea and Japan, the worst reactions in each of these indicators were demonstrated by just four of them, Indonesia, Korea, Thailand and Malaysia. In terms of depreciation of currency against the U.S. dollar, in Indonesia the depreciation was 52.3%, in Korea 47.8%, in Thailand 46.1%, in Malaysia 34.9%, and in the Philippines 34.3%. Regarding the change in stock prices, Korea dropped by 49.5%, Malaysia by 44.8%, Indonesia by 44.6%, the Philippines by 33.5% and Thailand by 29.3%.

Since the Hong Kong currency was linked to the U.S. dollar, there was no significant change in its exchange rate, but stock prices there dropped by 29.4%. In China, the RMB was purposely unchanged while the stock prices dropped by 4.4%, the lowest movement amongst the ten countries affected. The Japanese Yen depreciated by 12%, while its stock prices declined by 25.9%. Taiwan was not affected as dramatically from the impact of the crisis during 1997; the Taiwan currency depreciated by 14.8%, and stock prices dropped by 9.3%. In Singapore, the currency depreciation was 14.7%, and its stock prices dropped by 23%. Comparatively speaking, China, Hong Kong, Taiwan, Singapore and Japan suffered least from the financial crisis, whilst Indonesia, Korea, Thailand, Malaysia and the Philippines suffered significantly more during the initial stage of the financial crisis.

Table 1.1 Impacts of the Crisis on Financial Markets

(1) On Exchange Rates

Country	Initial Level	Rate of Change in Exchange Rate (currency units / US$1) Unit %			
	June 30, 1997 (currency unit/ US$1)	Dec 31, 1997 / June 30, 1997	June 30, 1998 / June 30, 1997	June 30, 1999 / June 30, 1997	Jan 5, 2000 / June 30, 1997
Taiwan	27.81	−14.8	−19.0	−13.9	−9.41
Hong Kong	7.75	0.0	0.0	−0.1	−0.38
Singapore	1.43	−14.7	−15.4	−15.9	−13.86
Korea	888.00	−47.8	−35.3	−23.3	−21.76
Thailand	24.70	−46.1	−38.7	−29.9	−33.60
Malaysia	2.52	−34.9	−39.0	−33.7	−35.68
Indonesia	2,432.00	−52.3	−83.6	−64.6	−66.21
Philippines	26.38	−34.3	−37.3	−30.6	−34.38
China	8.28	0.0	0.0	0.2	0.00
Japan	114.6	−12.0	−18.3	−5.5	−24.60

10   *T.-S. Yu*

(2) On Stock Prices

Country	Initial Level	Rate or Change in Stock Prices (Index)%			
	June 30, 1997 level/index	Dec 31, 1997 / June 30, 1997	June 30, 1998 / June 30, 1997	June 30, 1999 / June 30, 1997	Jan 5, 2000 / June 30, 1997
Taiwan	9030.28	−9.3	−16.4	−6.2	−2.0
Hong Kong	15196.79	−29.4	−43.8	11.0	4.2
Singapore	1987.96	−23.0	−46.3	9.1	20.2
Korea	745.4	−49.5	−60.0	18.5	32.3
Thailand	527.28	−29.3	−49.3	−1.06	17.7
Malaysia	1077.30	−44.8	−57.7	−24.7	−24.3
Indonesia	724.56	−44.6	−38.5	−8.6	−6.5
Philippines	2809.21	−33.5	−40.9	1.4	−26.2
China	1306.78	−4.4	−25.5	−4.6	14.6
Japan	20604.96	−25.9	−23.2	−14.9	−10.1

Note: Negative signs of exchange rate indicate depreciation.
Currency: Taiwan - NT$; Hong Kong - HK$; Singapore - S$; Korea - Won; Thailand - Baht;
        Malaysia - Ringgit; Indonesia - Rupiah; Philippines - Peso; China - Renminbi (RMB);
        Japan - Yen.
Sources: Datastream and the Economist.

4.2 Impacts of the Crisis on Economic Activities

4.2.1 On economic growth

The impacts of the financial crisis on economic growth can be seen from Tables 1.2 and 1.3. In 1996, prior to the outbreak of the financial crisis, all ten of these East Asian countries performed well. Even the countries which were most affected by the subsequent financial crisis were demonstrating extremely high growth, for instance, Indonesia's growth rate was 8.0%, in Korea it was 7.1%, in Thailand, 6.7%, and in Malaysia, 8.2%. The initial impact on growth in 1997 was not serious. In comparison to the 1996 figures, there was a definite decline, but only Thailand had a negative growth rate of -0.4%. The remaining countries still managed to maintain positive growth rates. In Indonesia, the growth rate was 4.7%, in Korea 5.5%, and in Malaysia 7.8%.

Table 1.2 Main Economic Indicators of East Asia

(Unit: %)

	Economic Growth Rate				Industrial Growth Rate			Inflation Rate			Unemployment Rate		
	1996	1997	1998	1999	1997	1998	1999	1997	1998	1999	1997	1998	1999
Taiwan	5.7	6.8	4.8	5.5	7.0	3.8	10.9(Dec)	0.9	1.7	0.1	2.7	2.7	3.1(Nov)
Hong Kong	5.0	5.3	−5.1	1.7	−0.8	−8.6	−6.3(Q3)	5.7	2.6	−3.3	2.2	4.6	6.1(Nov)
Singapore	7.0	7.8	1.5	5.5	4.3	−0.5	7.0(Dec)	2.0	−0.3	0.4	1.8	3.2	3.7(Sep)
Korea	7.1	5.5	−6.8	9.2	7.7	−7.1	24.1(Dec)	4.5	7.5	0.8	2.6	6.8	6.4
Thailand	6.7	−0.4	−8.0	4.2	−0.7	−10.0	15.3(Dec)	5.6	8.1	0.3	3.5	5.3	5.6(May)
Malaysia	8.2	7.8	−6.7	4.9	10.7	−11.2	23.1(Nov)	2.6	5.3	2.1	2.5	3.9	1.3(Jun)
Indonesia	8.0	4.7	−13.7	−0.1	13.1	−.−	20.2(Q2)	10.0	77.6	28.4	4.7	5.5	6.4(Feb)
Philippines	6.8	5.8	−0.5	3.0	5.2	−0.5	−11.7(Nov)	5.1	9.7	7.3	8.7	10.05	9.4(Oct)
China	9.5	8.8	7.8	7.2	10.9	8.8	8.8(Dec)	0.8	−2.6	−0.9	3.1	3.1	−.−
Japan	3.5	0.9	−2.8	0.6	1.2	−7.1	5.1(Dec)	2.0	0.2	−0.3	3.4	4.1	4.6(Dec)

Note: Economic growth rate in 1999 is estimated; inflation rate is the rate of change is consumer price index.
Source: The Council for Economic Planning and Development, International Economic Situation Weekly, April 15, 1999, and July 8, 1999.

Although the financial crisis had taken place in 1997, the most serious impact on economic growth throughout the region was not felt until 1998, when most of the East Asian countries experienced negative growth. Korea, for example, dropped by 6.8%, Thailand by 8%, Indonesia by 13.7%, Malaysia by 6.7%, Hong Kong by 5.1%, the Philippines by 0.5%, and Japan by 2.8%; only Taiwan, China, and Singapore maintained positive growth rates. Obviously, almost all the East Asian countries were plunged into serious recession in their economic activities.

4.2.2 On exports

Prior to the financial crisis, all ten of the East Asian countries had high growth in terms of exports, although in comparison to 1995, export growth rates showed a general tendency towards decline in 1996. Of the average export growth rates, in 1996, only Thailand's export growth rate was higher than its recent average growth rate throughout the whole period (1994-1996). In 1997, the growth rates of the four dragons' exports were higher than in 1996, while the growth rates of the four tigers' exports, with the

Table 1.3 Main Economic Indicators of East Asia

	Growth Rate (Real GDP), %		Trade Balance US$ bill (Dec)		Foreign Exchange Reserves US$ bill (Dec)		Growth Rate of Exports (%)	
	1998	1999	1998	1999	1998	1999	1998	1999
Taiwan	4.8	5.4	5.9	11.0	90.3	103.5(Nov)	−9.4	−.−
Hong Kong	−5.1	1.5	−10.59	−5.6	89.6	92.1(Nov)	−7.4	−1.2
Singapore	1.5	5.5	8.4	3.6	74.6	75.1(Oct)	−12.1	0.7
Korea	−6.8	9.2	40.3	24.8	52.0	69.6(Nov)	−2.8	9.0
Thailand	−8.6	4.2	12.1	8.9	28.8	32.1(Nov)	−5.1	6.7
Malaysia	−6.7	4.9	13.9	18.5(Nov)	25.6	29.8(Nov)	−6.9	12.6
Indonesia	−13.7	0.5	21.4	24.0(Nov)	22.7	26.2(Aug)	−8.3	−3.1
Philippines	−0.5	3.0	−0.2	4.5(Nov)	9.2	12.7(Sep)	16.9	18.9
China	7.8	7.2	45.0	29.1	145.2	156.0(Oct)	−.−	−.−
Japan	−2.8	0.7	107.39	98.37	215.5	272.0(Nov)	−7.8	−.−

Source: The Economist (Jan 1999 – Jan 2000).

exception of Indonesia, were much lower than in 1996. China's export growth rate in 1997 was higher than in 1996. Export growth rate in Japan declined by 8.7% in 1996, further declining in 1997 by 0.1%.

It was not until 1998 that the greatest impact of the financial crisis was experienced. Among the ten East Asian countries, only China and the Philippines maintained positive growth in exports and all the remaining countries had negative export growth rates, implying that the currency depreciations in East Asia during 1997 were not helpful in improving the balance of trade within these countries. Accordingly, the argument follows that although the depreciation of a country's currency is a necessary condition for the increase in its exports, it is not a sufficient condition.[4]

Table 1.4 The Impact of the Financial Crisis on Exports

(Unit %)

Country	1994	1995	1996	1990~1993	1994~1996	1997	1998	1999
Taiwan	9.4	20.0	3.8	9.2	10.1	5.3	−9.4	7.2
Hong Kong	11.9	14.8	4.0	15.6	10.2	4.2	−7.4	−1.2
Singapore	30.8	22.2	2.9	17.8	16.8	3.4	−12.1	0.7
Korea	16.8	30.3	5.3	12.6	17.5	7.3	−2.8	9.0
Thailand	22.7	25.1	18.9	18.9	15.5	−1.3	−5.1	6.7
Malaysia	24.7	26.0	6.7	19.8	19.1	−7.2	−6.9	12.6
Indonesia	8.8	13.4	10.4	12.7	10.9	11.6	−8.3	−3.1
Philippines	19.9	31.6	17.5	14.8	23.0	12.2	4.7	18.9
China	33.1	22.9	17.9	19.4	24.6	20.9	0.7	10.0
Japan	9.7	11.6	−8.7	8.4	4.2	−0.1	−7.8	8.0

Note: Growth rate (US$).
Sources: Ross H. McLeod and Ross Gamant (eds.), East Asia in Crisis, p. 23.
The Directorate-General of Budget, Accounting and Statistics, Executive Yuan, 1999.

---

[4] In the second half of 1997, due to the effects of the financial crisis, all of the currencies of the East Asian countries, with the exception of China and Hong Kong, were greatly depreciated. Theoretically, this should have led to an increase in exports during 1998, and yet all of them saw a corresponding decrease in their exports, whilst their growth rates became negative.

Table 1.4 is also useful in verifying the fact that the depreciation of the RMB in 1994 did not harm the expansion of exports in Southeast Asia. In 1994 and 1995, all the East Asian countries had very high export growth rates. Only in 1996 did the export growth rates in all ten of the East Asian countries begin to show a decline.

4.2.3 On inflation and unemployment

Two sensitive economic indicators reflected the impact of the financial crisis. The inflation rate and the unemployment rate have risen. The former resulted from depreciation, while the latter was due to the sluggishness of the economies. Inflation rates have risen amongst two of the four dragons, Taiwan and Korea, while Hong Kong and Singapore have decreased their inflation rates. Since the Hong Kong dollar is linked to the U.S. dollar, it depreciated less, as did the Singapore dollar. The four tigers have different profiles because their currencies have been greatly depreciated, so all of them have a correspondingly high inflation rate.

Unemployment relates closely to economic recession, and as 1998 was the most serious year of the recession, with the exceptions of Taiwan and China, all the East Asian countries have seen an increase in their unemployment rates. These countries have also seen a reduction in industrial productivity and economic growth.

5.   EXTERNAL DEBT AND FINANCIAL CRISIS

The relationship between external debt and economic growth is somewhat complicated. Whether external debt is good or bad for economic growth depends largely upon how we make use of it. For a developing country, usually lacking in capital, external debt plays a key role in the promotion of economic development and during the last thirty years, for example, many East Asian economies have benefited greatly from external debt. Conversely, many of the East Asian countries worst hit by the financial crisis were those that were already saddled with heavy external debt. From the end of 1995 through until June 1997, the sum total of short-term debts in Korea accounted for 68.2%, in Thailand 66.6%, in Indonesia 60.9%, and in Malaysia 52.2%. These countries clearly have too much short-term external debt, which they must repay, together with the accrued interest, within one year. In any country where short-term debt accounted for a large proportion of total external debt, there would be greater sensitivity to changes in financial conditions. In addition, as noted earlier, many of these East Asian countries have taken advantage of short-term lending for use in long-term investments. This is simply the worst high-risk measure they could possibly take.

If the highest proportion of external debt is long-term, then this is mainly used for direct investment, which is helpful for the debtor's economic development. Correspondingly, if most of the external debt is short-term, it is mainly used for indirect investment. The importance of external debt lies not in its absolute value, but in its proportion of GDP. But even if the external debt accounts for a large proportion of GDP, this is still not a sufficient condition for the country to become drawn into financial crisis.

An example of this is Australia where, from 1990 through until 1995, external debts accounted for 46.1 percent of GDP, larger than that of Korea, Thailand or the Philippines. And yet, Australia was able to virtually ignore the penetration of the East Asian financial crisis. If, however, the short-term external debt accounts for a large proportion of total external debt, under a condition of relatively low foreign exchange reserves, this would deepen the financial crisis. This was the case in Korea, which had the largest proportion of external debt, and which also felt the worst effects of the financial crisis. (See Table 1.4).

Among the four Asian tigers, the Philippines had the largest external debt in terms of its proportion of GDP, but it suffered far less than Malaysia, Thailand and Indonesia, as well as Korea. In reality, Korea's external debt was not large in comparison to the ASEAN countries. A further example is Vietnam which has been following market economy policies for about ten years, but which was affected much less by the financial crisis.

The question arises, therefore, if a country is equipped with large foreign exchange reserves, is it in a position to avoid financial crisis? From the

Table 1.5 External Debt and Foreign Exchange Reserves

Country	External Debt (as % of GDP)			Exchange Reserves (as months of imports)		
	1990–95 Avg.	1995	1996	1990–95 Avg.	1995	1996
Taiwan	0.3	0.2	0.1	14.5	11.8	10.3
Hong Kong				9.0	9.1	10.9
Singapore*	7.7	8.0	8.2	6.8	7.0	7.0
Korea	10.0	9.4	11.2	2.8	3.1	2.8
Thailand	22.1	20.1	19.8	6.9	7.0	6.6
Malaysia	32.0	32.2	28.8	5.2	4.2	4.3
Indonesia	47.7	43.4	38.9	6.5	5.6	6.1
Philippines	53.6	50.9	n.a.	3.7	3.5	4.4
China	14.4	15.3	15.0	4.9	8.0	9.1
Vietnam	176.8	122.5	n.a.	1.4	2.2	2.1
Australia	46.1	46.8	n.a.	4.4	3.1	2.5

* 1993–95 average external debt estimated by Singapore Department of Statistics, Dec 1998.
Source: Ross H. McLeod and Ross Gamant (eds.) East Asia in Crisis, p. 26.

figures at Table 1.5, the answer is inconclusive. For instance, Thailand's exchange reserves were equivalent to 6.9 months of its imports during the period 1990-1995, and were larger than any one of the other Southeast Asian countries. Therefore, it follows that Thailand should have suffered much less from the financial crisis, however, Thailand was the one country most affected by the financial crisis!

6. CORRUPTION AND NEPOTISM BETWEEN OFFICIALS AND ENTERPRISES

In general terms, corruption may be a culture of developing countries, but corruption itself is not the main rootstock of financial crisis, although it does have the capacity to weaken the foundation of financial institutions. In East Asia, with the notable exceptions of Singapore and Hong Kong, none of the countries are currently able to avoid corruption[5]. Corruption is viewed as a kind of transaction cost, through which enterprises can enjoy special privileges offered by the government. For instance, most of the governments in the Asian countries still own and run banking businesses. Enterprises can borrow large amounts of mortgage-free capital from the state-owned banks with low interest rates, and since it has become so easy for them to obtain loans, these enterprises usually tend to enlarge their scales whilst ignoring efficiency. Under these conditions, it is impossible for banks to set up a sound supervision system for use in overseeing the debtors' behavior. Therefore, many of the financial institutions involved become too fragile to be able to withstand the financial challenge.

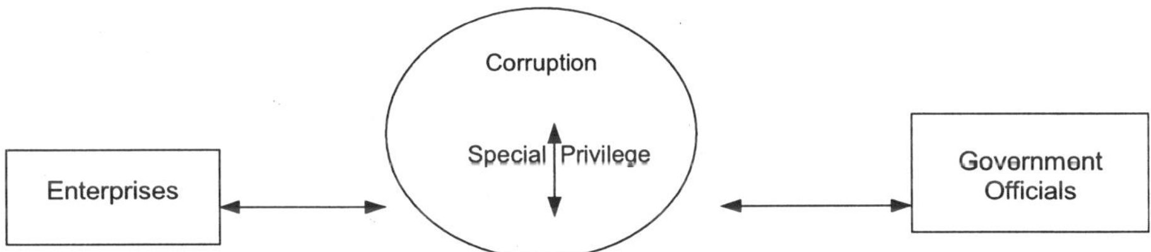

Fig. 1.1 The Black Market Mechanism

Through the operation of the black market mechanism, relevant officials obtain ill-gotten gains from the enterprises while the enterprises themselves are provided special privileges to make money.[6] When the economy becomes sluggish, many debtors do not have the ability to repay their loans, leaving the relevant banks saddled with accumulated heavy bad loans, and thus

---

[5] Prior to the 1970s, Hong Kong also had a serious corruption problem, but since then, corruption cases have been greatly eliminated due to the operation of clean administration.

[6] In some countries, the enterprise would reward the official for the special privilege by offering a high position within the enterprise once he retired from the government. The so-called "corruption, cronyism and nepotism", as popularized on CCN, takes place in most Asian countries: the most serious being Indonesia. This is why, when financial crisis struck, political revolution immediately followed.

extremely vulnerable to financial crisis. When these banks go bankrupt, the government will usually use special measures to rescue them, which causes the problem of "moral hazard".

7.   A MODEL USED TO EXPLAIN THE FINANCIAL CRISIS

Returning to the causes of the financial crisis, as already mentioned, many explanations have been provided. Here, we present a further explanation: the marriage of internal excess investment and external excess

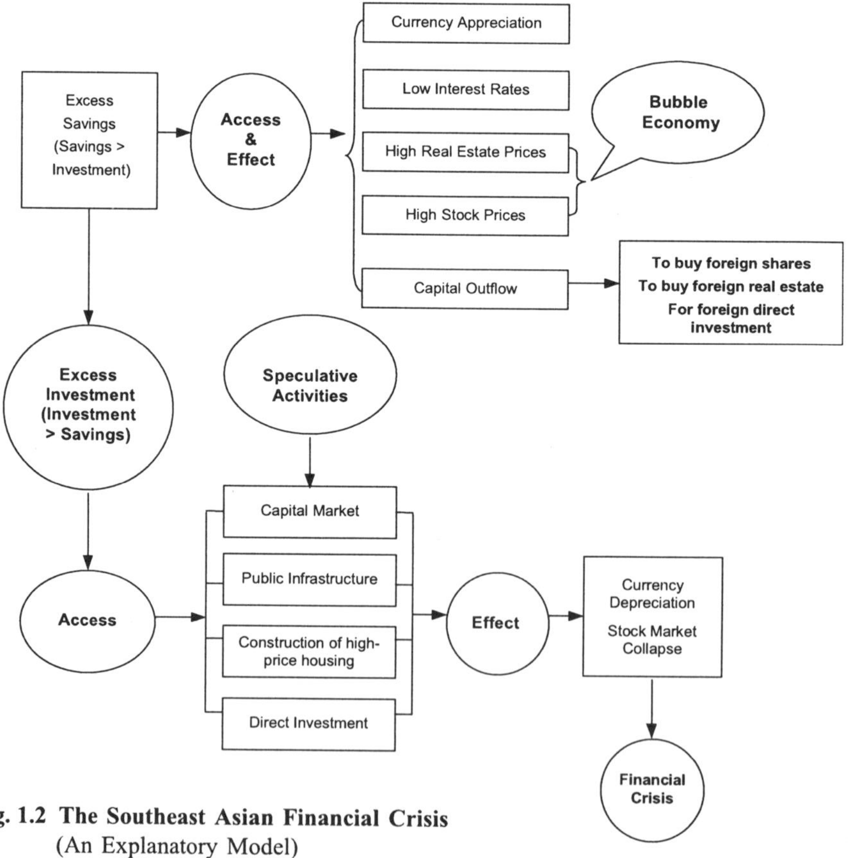

Fig. 1.2 The Southeast Asian Financial Crisis
    (An Explanatory Model)

savings, which is considered to be the main cause of the financial crisis in East Asia, since most of the East Asian countries' excess investments have been financed through excessive external savings. Either of these conditions, excess investment or excess saving, provides a condition for economic disequilibrium. Excess investment would raise inflation and increase employment, while excess savings would produce a bubble economy resulting in unemployment later. In order to increase an understanding of this, a diagram may be helpful.

7.1 Excess Investment

When investments are larger than savings, the result is excess investment. Here savings comprise of domestic savings, and inflow of foreign capital and loans, and loans include both domestic and foreign loans, which in turn, consist of short-term and long-term loans. All the sources of investment can be used in both direct and indirect investment. The former is used for producing goods and services, of which, a large part is used for domestic demand, while the remainder is used for exports. The latter is channeled to the money market, capital market or real estate market.

In the case of any one of the following, financial problems would ensue.

a. Exports continue to decline because of weak competitiveness. This would influence the exporters' repayments to the financial institutions and produce bad debts and subsequent troubles for the financial institutions.

b. Short-term loans are used for long-term investment. It becomes very difficult for the enterprise to adjust its financial account, and again, this would cause financial difficulties.

c. International speculators with huge amounts of capital penetrate the stock market and dominate the change in stock prices. Once the stock prices rise to a high level, the speculator immediately withdraws all of his capital from the market, causing the collapse of the stock market.

d. Investments are channeled to the real estate market causing real estate prices to rise too high, beyond the purchasing power of the middle-income class. It would become very difficult for real estate owners to sell out and, therefore, if the owners have substantial loans from financial institutions, the financial institution themselves would face financial difficulties and go bankrupt.

7.2 Excess Savings

When savings are larger than investment, the result is excess savings. If excess savings were too large, this would create a bubble economy. The examples of Taiwan and Japan can be used here to illustrate this phenomenon.

In the late-1980s, Taiwan enjoyed huge trade surpluses and abundant foreign exchange reserves. Since such huge savings had no inappropriate excesses to absorb, it was natural to use these funds for indirect investment in the stock market and real estate market. Consequently, the stock market soared and real estate prices rose sharply. Many speculators made use of the money earned from the stock market to purchase real estate, further pushing up the price of real estate up until early-1990, when stock prices suddenly dropped, and the bubble burst!

Simultaneously, Japan was also enjoying huge trade surpluses and foreign exchange reserves, which caused both the stock and real estate markets to soar; prior to 1990, Tokyo house prices were the highest in the world, and the stock market was booming. However, by the end of 1990, both of these markets had collapsed.

7.3 A Marriage

As stated earlier, the East Asian countries most affected by the financial crisis were Indonesia, Korea, Thailand and Malaysia. Among these four countries, over the period from 1995 to June 1997, Korea's loans were the highest, then Thailand, Indonesia and Malaysia respectively. (See Table 1.5). Japan, the United States and Germany had provided the bulk of these loans, with Japan in particular providing the largest loans to the four countries, US$112.1 billion to Thailand, US$69.5 billion to Korea, US$66.2 billion to Indonesia and US$26.0 billion to Malaysia. Clearly then, Japan's banks were most affected by the financial crisis, simply because they had made the greatest contribution to East Asian loans.

Accordingly, excessive investment is considered to be the basic cause of the financial crisis in East Asia, with speculator activities being nothing but a fuse. The most important factor is that if the internal excess investment had not been financed with external excess savings, it would not have been possible for these countries to make so much unnecessary investment in real estate and stock markets and to create such a serious financial crisis. On the other hand, if their financial sectors had been sound, the financial crisis would have been diluted to some extent, even if the financial crisis could not have been completely avoided.

As for the contagion of the financial crisis, when it broke out in Thailand, it immediately and quickly swept across Northeastern Asia and all the ASEAN countries. Theoretically, capital and trade flows should have been the channels of contagion; but actually, psychological factors played the most important part in this respect, since the pessimistic psychology caused by the financial crisis occurring in Thailand was reflected in foreign exchange and stock markets creating rapid currency depreciations and dramatic falls in stock prices.

To sum up, it may be reasonable to argue that the outbreak of the financial crisis in many East Asian countries can be considered a marriage of internal excess investment and external excess savings.

8.   THE ROLE OF THE GOVERNMENT

When a financial crisis occurs in the exchange market and stock market, what kind of reaction and attitude should be expected from the government? This issue has caused many debates. One school argues that the government should leave the market alone, and allow the "invisible hand" to automatically adjust the markets accordingly, in other words, government intervention is unnecessary. The alternative argument is that the government should intervene in the markets because they were only destroyed as a result of international speculation and they had subsequently failed to adjust themselves.

An infamous case took place in August 1998, when international speculators made use of enormous amounts of capital to penetrate the Hong Kong stock market. First of all, the speculators bought successively large amounts of stock, pushing up the stock prices until they reached a high level, whereupon they withdrew their capital from the market, offloading all the stocks they held, so that the stock prices dropped sharply. This illustrates the case earlier described, that where the stock market is not sufficiently large, it is easily attacked and destroyed by powerful speculators. And once the market has collapsed, no small investors are able to survive. In order to maintain a free market, in which no one single buyer or seller can dominate prices, it is necessary to have international laws or regulations, which to a large extent are able to eliminate the influence of these speculative activities.

Foreign exchange systems are also an important factor in speculative activities. If a country adopts a fixed exchange rate system, it is very easy for international speculators to take advantage of the system to make huge gains without any foreign exchange loss. If the country were to adopt a floating exchange rate system, the speculators must then run the risk of currency depreciation.[7]

9.   THE FUNCTION OF THE IMF

Following its establishment, many developing countries have benefited greatly from the implementation of programs offered by the IMF. As the financial crisis has affected so many East Asian economies, the IMF has played the role of firefighter. However, these countries including Indonesia, Thailand and Korea, which have each received the support of the IMF, must meet some specific requirements: the receiver should agree to a program of restructuring, which includes macroeconomic, structural adjustment and social policies. The macroeconomic policy includes suggestions on economic policies including contraction of monetary and fiscal policies, and liberalization policy, all of which have been criticized by western economists

---

[7] Before the financial crisis, most Southeast Asian countries had adopted fixed foreign exchange rate systems, which had provided speculators with an opportunity to take advantage of the system to make speculative gains. Since then, they have all adopted managed floating foreign exchange rate systems.

since these economic policies are considered unhelpful to these troubled countries attempting to recover from recession. Rather, they are regarded as the cause of a deepening of their financial crisis instead[8]. Even so, these three countries have adopted the suggestions and have already received more than 77 percent of the promised amount. Among the three countries, Korea has carried out most of the suggestions, as can be seen from Table 1.6.

Table 1.6 IMF's Rescue Program

(Unit: US$ bill)

	IMF Promised Amount (1)	IMF Paid Amount (2)	(3) = (2) / (1)
Thailand	4.0	3.1	77.5%
Indonesia	11.2	8.8	78.6%
Korea	21.1	19.0	90.0%
Total	36.3	30.9	

Source: IMF, International Financial Markets, Dec 1998.

Although the policies have been criticized, the three troubled economies have started to recover, demonstrating growth in their industrial production and exports. So far, Korea has displayed the best achievement in its economic activities, followed by substantial growth in Thailand. Due to political chaos, Indonesia could achieve only slight positive growth. Their foreign exchange reserves have also increased, for instance, Korea now has US$65.42 billion, Thailand has US$32.4 billion and Indonesia has US$26.18 billion, and their balance of trade figures have also greatly improved. An interesting point is that positive growth was demonstrated in Korea from November 1998, in Thailand from January 1999 and in Indonesia from April 1999. It is expected that Korea's economic growth rate for 1999 will have been around 9%, Thailand around 3.5% and Indonesia around 0.1%.

---

[8] In a meeting held in the mid-October, 1998 in Singapore, Jeffrey D. Sachs criticized the IMF's reform plan as undermining Asian economies because it failed to understand the real causes of the financial crisis.

10. EAST ASIA'S RECOVERY

1998 was the worst year of the East Asian financial crisis. The financial markets clearly show that, with the exceptions of Hong Kong and China, all the currencies of the ten countries in this study were seriously depreciated, and in each of the countries, stock prices dropped sharply. From the commodity markets, we know that apart from Taiwan, Singapore and China, which still achieved positive growth rate, all the remaining countries had a negative growth rate.

However, through the readjustment of their financial institutions and the enhancement of their endeavor, most of the East Asian countries have started to improve their economic conditions since early 1999. And from January 2000 on, their currency depreciations have greatly improved, and their stock prices have resumed their increasing tread to the eve of the outbreak of the financial crisis (see Table 1.1). As for their growth rates in 1999, all of them had achieved positive growth rates. For instance, among the most affected countries, Korean's growth rate would be 9.2%, Indonesia 0.1%, Thailand 4.2%, and Malaysia 4.9%, even though some of them have not yet achieved their growth rates as high as them before the crisis (see Table 1.3).

Generally speaking, East Asia has tended to recover, though many of the countries have not yet recovered to the level achieved in 1996, all of them have greatly improved as compared to their economic situation in 1998. It may be ironic to say that none of the economists foresaw the sudden meltdown of the financial markets in East Asia and predicted the recovery of East Asia so rapidly.

The reasons why East Asia can resume its path to growth are interesting to know. Actually, the economic fundamentals of East Asia are not as weak as expected by many western economists, otherwise, it would prove impossible for the region to gain strength again from its depression in two years. The key factor is that most industries in the region are trade-oriented, and their major markets are the United States and the European Union. During the last years, the two regions have maintained high growth so that they have the capacity to absorb the exports with low prices from East Asia. In addition, many of the trade-oriented industries are managed by foreign investors who have no serious financial problems. Even if they had, it is rather easy for them to resolve their financial difficulty. Another equal important factor is that almost every East Asian country has undergone restructuring of their financial institutions. They also have tried to eliminate the nepotism between government officials and enterprises, to make their management more transparent and to reduce their debt and unnecessary investment, which should be helpful for them in regaining their growth.

By the end of 1998, the rising prices of stocks in the U.S. have reached more than 10,000 points, which has caused many people to become worried about the busting of the bubble economy. Correspondingly, many big international funds started to consider the reallocation of their capital in order to avoid the risk of "putting all eggs to one basket". In particular, finding that the financial crisis in East Asia has reached its bottom and was in position to rise again, and not wanting to lose an opportunity, they shifted the direction of their capital movement from the developed area to the newly emerging markets. Since the summer of 1999, all the countries in the region have tended to gradually recover.

So far, East Asia has met two basic requirements for its recovery, that is, the expansion of their foreign trade and the inflow of capital to their financial markets.

11. THE PURPOSE OF THIS VOLUME

The financial crisis in East Asia is almost over; now is the time for us to review the real causes and potential effects of the crisis, and to examine the most important lessons to be learned from the bitter experiences of the past three years. There is an old Chinese saying, "the past that should not be forgotten may serve as a master for the future". This is of paramount importance in exploring the problems of the East Asian financial crisis.

In this volume, we have dealt with ten counties, the four Asian dragons, Singapore, Hong Kong, Taiwan and Korea, the four Asian tigers, Thailand, Malaysia, Indonesia and the Philippines, and two giant countries, China and Japan. We would like to find the answers to the following questions:

(1) What were the real causes of the financial crisis in each country?
(2) What interactions between the countries in East Asia have been created as a result of the financial crisis?
(3) What policies and measures has each government taken for curbing the financial crisis and its effects on economic activities?
(4) How appropriate and how effective have the policy recommendations of the IMF been in the cases of Korea, Thailand and Indonesia?
(5) Is it possible to draw a theoretical framework from the general causes of the financial crisis?
(6) What are the important lessons to be drawn from the experiences of each of the affected countries?

The answer to each of these questions is presented in the final chapter of this volume.

References

Cheng, Chieng Mao. (1999), "An Analysis of East Asian Economies Two Years After the Financial Crisis Outbreak", The Council for Economic Planning and Development: International Economy Weekly, No.1292, 6–29.

Delhaise, P. F., (1998), Asia in Crisis: The Implosion of the Banking and Finance Systems, John Wiley & Sons (Asia).

Greenspan, A., (1999), Controlling Financial Crisis: International Delivered to the World Bank, Conference on Recent Trends in Reserve Management, Washington, D.C. (April 9).

Henderson, C., (1998), Asia Falling? Making Sense of the Asian Currency Crisis and Its Aftermath, McGraw Hill Companies, Inc.

Kapstein, E. B., (1998), "Global Rules for Global Finance", Current History, (November), 355–360.

Kreszner, R. S., (1999) Bank Regulation: Will Regulators Catch up with the Market? CATO Institute, Briefing Papers, (March 12).

Krugman, P., (1999), "The Return of Depression Economics", Foreign Affairs, (Jan.–Feb.) 56–74.

Lee, Cheng, F. (1999) "The Impact of the Asian Financial Crisis on the ROC Economy and Economic Policy Reactions, Economic Review, No. 308, (March–April), 8–17.

Letiche, J. M., (1998), "Causes of the Financial and Economic Crisis in Southeast Asia and the Need for National, Regional, and IMF Structural Reforms", Journal of Asian Economics, Vol. 9, No. 2, 181–192.

Liang, Cheng-King. (1999), "The Prevention and Handling of Financial Crisis in Emerging Markets", Bank Sinopac Quarterly, No. 8, 1–34.

Liu C.Y. and Jia He, (1999), The Asian Countries: Before and After the Financial Crisis, (in Chinese), Taipei: Shongtin Finance and Economics Advisors Co.

Machara, Yasuhiro (1999) "Financial Stability in Southeast Asia", Journal of Asian Economies, Vol. 9, No. 2 (summer), 227–235.

McLeod, R. H. and R. Garnaut (eds.), (1998), East Asia in Crisis: From Being a Miracle to Needing One? London: Routledge.

Morrison, W. M., (1999), China's Response to the Global Financial Crisis: Implications for U.S. Economic Interests. CRS Report for Congress (March 3).

Noland, M, Li-Gang Liu, S. Robinson and Zhi Wang, (1998), Global Economic Effects of the Asian Currency Devaluations. Institute for International Economics, No. 56.

Noland, M., S. Robinson and Zhi Wang, (1999). The Continuing Asian Financial Crisis: Global Adjustment and Trade. Institute for International Economics, Working Paper 99-4.

Quibria, M. G., (1999), "How to Avert the Next Financial Crisis", Economic Review, (Sept.–Oct.) 25–29.

Peng, Huai-nan, (1998), "Asian Financial Crisis", The International Commercial Bank of China, Vol. 17, No. 2, 1–30.

Ranis, G., (1999), "Lessons From Taiwan's Miracle and Crisis", Economic Review, (Sept.–Oct.) 1–24.

The World Bank (1995), The East Asian Miracle: Economic Growth and Public Policy, Oxford University Press.

Walden, B. and S. Rosenfeld. (1992), Dragons in Distress: Asia's Miracle Economies in Crisis, The Institute for Food and Development Policy.

CHAPTER 2

JAPAN

JAPAN'S BUBBLE ECONOMY AND ASIA

Lim Hua Sing

Institute of Asia-Pacific Studies
Graduate School of Asian-Pacific Studies
Waseda University
Sodai-Nishiwaseda, Shinjuku-ku, Tokyo, 169-0051, Japan
E-mail: Limhs@mn.waseda.ac.jp

1. INTRODUCTION

The collapse of the so-called bubble economy in Japan and the long entrenchment of Japan's economy in the doldrums of recession and financial despair can be considered one of the important factors contributing to the Asian financial crisis that erupted in July 1997. Similarly, it is one of the main reasons why the recovery from the crisis is still on an uncertain footing.

Firstly, this article examines the background and causes of the bubble economy, focusing on stock and real estate market issues. Next, it delves into the various government policies (such as monetary and fiscal policies, banking and foreign exchange rate systems and crisis management measures) implemented, their impact and limitations as to re-energizing the economy, discussing them in detail and putting forward criticisms and suggestions. Lastly, it considers the complementary relationship between Japan and Asia and analyses in some detail Japan's role in the recent financial crisis. This part is particularly aimed at examining the potential effects of the so-called New Miyazawa Plan on the nascent economic recovery of Asia.

Despite their high degree of interdependence, the East and Southeast Asian countries have few and weak formal organizations that may help them coordinate their economic policies. Setting up a new international organization or institution among the Asian countries to strengthen economic cooperation in the region is regarded as being an important focal point in the future.

2.   THE BACKGROUND AND CAUSES OF JAPAN'S BUBBLE ECONOMY

The Western nations, led by the USA, put pressure on Japan to let the yen appreciate in the mid 80s. This happened at the G5 meeting held in September 1985 ("the Plaza Accord"). Since then the Japanese currency appreciated rapidly from 242 yen to the US dollar just before the G5 meeting, to 100 yen in June 1994, and later to 80 yen in May 1995[1]. As a result, asset values in Japan in dollar terms, tripled within a decade. The reason behind the move was that the USA suffered from serious "twin deficits" (fiscal and international trade), and wanted to restrict imports from Asia, Japan in particular.

Meanwhile in Japan, asset (stocks and land property) values increased substantially but abnormally from the second half of the 1980s to the end of 1990. It was even referred to as "asset price inflation" or "stock inflation". The situation was characterized by strong increase in asset prices, while prices of commodities and services in general remained stable. The Nikkei Index jumped threefold from approximately 13,000 in January 1986, to approximately 39,000 by the end of 1989. Land prices also tripled during the same period. Table 2.1 indicates that total land prices in Tokyo alone increased from 176 trillion yen in 1985, to 517 trillion yen in 1990. Market

---

[1] Lim Hua Sing, *Japan's Role in Asia*, Times Academic Press, Singapore, 1999, p. 206.

capitalization (total equity of listed companies on the Tokyo Stock Exchange) increased from 160 trillion yen to 478 trillion yen during this period[2].

Table 2.1 GDP, Stock and Real Estate Values

(trillion yen)

Year	GDP	Stock	Real Estate
1985	324	169	176
1986	338	230	280
1987	354	301	449
1988	377	394	529
1989	403	527	521
1990	434	478	517
1991	457	373	504
1992	484	297	428

Note: 1) Stock value represents the total value of partially listed companies by Tokyo Stock Exchange.
2) Real estate value represents the total amount of residential assets in Tokyo.
Source: Noguchi Yukio, Baburu No Keizaigaku (Bubble Economics), Nihon Keizai Shimbun-sha, 1993, p. 23.

Obviously this did not reflect the economic reality in Japan. If we take a closer look at the GDP in Japan, it increased only from 324 trillion yen to 434 trillion yen during the same period. Table 2.1 further shows that both land prices (in Tokyo) and market capitalization (as described above) exceeded Japan's GDP during the 1987–1991 period and the 1988–1990 period respectively. Hence Japan created a "bubble economy" during the period between the second half of the 1980s and the end of the year 1990.

What made the bubble economy possible? The large scale financial deregulation policy implemented since the second half of the 1980s was a major reason. Following the drastic yen appreciation in September 1985, the tempo of the financial liberalization process in Japan escalated and current account surpluses fuelled the liquidity of the market. At the same time, the already huge demand for business offices in big cites in Japan, Tokyo in

---

[2] Noguchi Yukio, Baburu No Keizaigaku (bubble economics), Nihon Keizai Shimbun-sha, 1993, pp. 21–23.

particular, increased significantly. The government could not play any active role as she had fiscal expenditure constraints and was in urgent need to cover deficits incurred by various governmental departments. Under these circumstances, measures pertaining to the privatization of city development projects and deregulation policies were introduced. Later in Autumn 1987, the "Black Monday" incident occurred and this further prompted the deregulation process in Japan[3].

In retrospect, the bubble economy in Japan was partly created by the government. After the second half of the 1980s, the deregulation policies prompted investors to concentrate on land speculation for capital gains, partly because there was no rational land property taxation system. Land prices were pushed further northwards by government sales of state land, in particular land owned by the Old National Railways, at high prices. The Old National Railways (now called JR, for Japan Railways) suffered from serious deficits, before it was privatized. Land owned by the state was sold at high prices to cover part of the railway company's losses. Land prices were hiked up in this way by measures taken by the government.

The low interest rates policy had also contributed to speculative activities on land property in Japan. Up till 1988, this policy of low interest rates policy was still in effect. Bank lending had been concentrated in real estate, construction and loans to finance companies. From May 1989, the government implemented deflationary policies to restrict bank lending in order to curtail the bubble economy. However, bank lending to real estate concerns, the construction industry and finance companies continued to increase. The government was unable to control speculative activities for capital gains on real estate.

3.   UNFOLDING OF THE CRISIS

From February 1990, stock prices in Japan started dipping. At the end

---

[3] Tanaka Naoki, *Saigo No Jyunen, Nihon Keizai No Koso* (Towards the Twenty-first Century — A Vision for the Japanese Economy), Nihon Keizai Shimbun-sha, 1992, pp. 62–64.

of 1989, stock prices reached their highest level and dropped drastically during the following year. Within a year between end of 1989 and end of 1990, stock prices recorded a 40% plunge. The prices went on decreasing, however. The average stock price dropped from 24,000 yen in December 1990, to merely 14,000 yen in the middle of August 1992.

From October 1990, real estate transactions in Japan started decreasing abruptly. In 1991, land prices started dropping. Within one year, from July 1991 to July 1992, residential land prices dropped as shown in the following: Tokyo 15.2%, Osaka 23.8% and Kyoto 27.5%. Except for 1975, land prices in Japan had increased annually since the Second World War. When land prices started to fall drastically from 1991, it was the first time in its history Japan had experienced this.

The total stock market capitalization plummeted by more than 300 trillion yen, from 590 trillion yen at the end of 1989 to approximately 260 trillion yen in July 1992. As early as in summer 1992, the financial sector in Japan was already in panic. Both banks and finance companies had encouraged borrowing, by lending substantially to real estate investors and speculators at high valuations of land price and other collateral. The sudden drop in real estate prices from the very beginning of the 1990s implied that real estate investors and speculators could not pay loan interests, resulting in a precarious situation within the financial sector.

Both city and local banks had lent substantially to individual investors and finance companies. Just before the final collapse of the bubble economy in 1991, the finance companies had outstanding loans amounting to 70 trillion yen, of which approximately 60 percent were real estate loans. Besides, the finance companies were also deeply involved in providing loans to affiliated enterprises that had acquired real estate throughout Japan. Unpaid loan interests and bad debts piled up, which in turn affected the survival of the affiliated enterprises, finance companies, local and city banks. In the end, the bubble economy collapsed and the financial crisis erupted in Japan[4].

---

[4] Noguchi Yukio, op. cit., pp. 22–25; Tanaka Naoki, op. cit., pp. 62–66.

4.   THE GOVERNMENT POLICIES AND ITS IMPACTS

By and large, the government was slow at reacting to the emerging problems. In the following sections the policy reactions to monetary and fiscal policies as well as regarding the banking and exchange rate system are outlined.

4.1 Monetary Policy

The government came close to seriously tackling the bubble economy in 1992. However, as mentioned earlier, as early as from May 1989, the Bank of Japan had introduced a deflationary monetary policy to curtail real estate prices, when they reached an abnormally high level and were spiraling almost out of control. This prompted the increase of a short-term loans interest rate which was aimed at reducing the volume of loans (especially for speculative purposes) extended by banks to real estates buyers. Furthermore, from April 1990, a series of administrative guidelines from the Ministry of Finance, to limit loans for real estate, was also issued. Under such circumstances, speculation in real estate activities should have been curtailed. However due to the following two reasons, the policies did not take effect until later.

Firstly, after the deflationary monetary policy was introduced, stock prices in Japan had continued to rise. Banks agreed that up to 45% profit earned through stocks held by loan borrowers, could be considered as their own capital, hence enabling them greater capacity to borrow more money. In other words, loan borrowers had more borrowing power as long as the value of their stocks kept on increasing. Bank managers could not refrain from lending money to real estate speculators as they thought it was a profitable venture with little risk involved.

Secondly, because the financial liberalization (liberalization of the rate of interest in particular) process was underway, banks were able to accumulate substantial amounts of capital through "free interest rate deposits" (MMC and large fixed deposits), parked in banks by customers. The total amount of these "free interest rate deposits" accumulated by city banks skyrocketed.

The proportion of this type of deposits in city banks' overall portfolio increased from 37.1% in 1998 (by the end of March; same as below), to 47.2% in 1989, to 61.1% in 1990 and to 69.8% in 1991. In the case of local banks, the figure for this proportion was 60% in 1991, and for credit houses, 50% in the same year.

Thus both city and local banks continued to extend loans to real estate investors and speculators directly or through finance houses. It was somehow restricted when the government enforced "controls over loans towards real estate businesses" in April 1990. However, the controls were abolished again in January 1992. There were signs of policy inconsistencies, which implied that the government was undecided as to how the problem of the bubble economy should be tackled, or even at the very least, how to solve the lingering real estate problem.

4.2 Fiscal Policy

Japan is a trading country. The economic development of Japan relies very much on export trade. An export-led growth policy has been Japan's survival mantra, and export industries (particularly automobile, electrical and electronics industries) contributed to a stable currency. The other members of the G5 meeting in September 1985 pressured the Japanese government to appreciate its currency drastically and this had a tremendous impact on Japan's export trade. Japan's export trade was seriously restricted and this also created a high yen stagnant economy soon after.

Countermeasures to a high yen stagnant economy are a low interest rate climate and, in general, an economic stimulus policy. These had already been implemented. As pointed out earlier, low interest rates had prompted speculative activities in real estate. In May 1987, as an emergency economic measure, a supplementary budget amounting to 6 trillion yen (5 trillion yen for public infrastructure and 1 trillion for tax deductions) was introduced. This supplementary budget, together with the "Black Monday" incident happened in autumn 1987, prompting deregulation sentiment in Japan. All this worked as a catalyst for speculative activities in real estate, which fuelled the bubble economy in the country. In other words, the stimulation package, intended to make up for the decrease in economic activity caused by stagnant exports, backfired as the stimulation effect was channeled mainly into the asset markets.

4.3 Banking System

We mentioned earlier that the deregulation of the financial sector had enabled banks (city banks, local banks and credit houses) to accumulate substantial amounts of capital through utilizing the MMC and the "huge fixed deposits" facilities. One serious side effect of this maneuver was the inordinate increase in operational costs. At the same time, bank managers were more inclined to supply lending to speculative activities in real estates for quick returns and possibly better profits. Over the last few years, numerous scandals, relating to illegal loans extended by financial institutions to speculators, unlawful individuals or organizations, have been disclosed.

As described already, the stock market flourished from the middle of the 1980s till February 1990. Centered around big enterprises in Japan, the equity finance companies were in a better position to raise funds, compared to other banking institutions. Within 3 years, from 1987 to 1989, these equity finance companies managed to raise funds amounting to 56 trillion yen out of a total of 58 trillion yen raised. The equity finance companies were not interested in investing in equipment or production, but in the so-called "assets technology", such as the "huge fixed deposits", the "special monetary trust" and the "fund trust".

At the other end, banking institutions encountered difficulty mobilizing funding. They then took two approaches. Firstly, they became more aggressive and looked for speculative investments such as in real estate. Secondly, they switched their loan facilities from big enterprises and manufacturing industries to small and medium-sized industries and, of course, to real estate concerns[5].

4.4 Exchange Rate System

Drastic yen fluctuations have been typical for the Japanese economy. A

---

[5] Noguchi Yukio, op. cit., pp. 35–37.

strong yen has both beneficial and adverse effects on the economy. Yen appreciation contributes to import industries such as the foodstuff, petroleum and natural gas industries. It also contributes to Japan's purchasing power and hence has stabilizing effects on domestic markets. However the strong yen limits exports of manufactured goods such as automobiles, electrical and electronic products to international markets and puts pressure toward outsourcing of industrial activities. On the other hand, yen depreciation reduces Japan's purchasing power and has inflationary effects on the Japanese economy, although it stimulates Japan's export trade and contributes favorably to her international trade balance.

Since the G5 meeting in September 1985, the yen has been fluctuating drastically. The *yen-daka* (yen appreciation) and the *yen-yasu* (yen depreciation) have been major concerns of Japan as well as the world. Japan has been particularly annoyed by the drastic fluctuation of the yen. The Japanese economy has been disturbed by the abrupt changes of Japan-USA currency exchange rates, particularly over the last 15 years. In general, it has been quite flexible and has been quick to adjust to the international monetary environment. This is due to Japan's strong industrial infrastructure and the strengths of numerous manufacturing industries. When the yen started appreciating substantially from September 1985, the Japanese economy was thrown into a chaotic situation, however. Many Japanese believed that 100 yen to the US dollar was the lifeline of the Japanese economy. However, Japan managed to survive even when the yen reached its peak of 80 yen to the US dollar in April 1995.

Presently the exchange rate is about 108 yen to the US dollar (February 2000), but the rate has been on a rising trend lately and this has not worked to the advantage of Japan, as the Japanese economy has just started to show signs of recovery. The Japanese authorities intervened many times by buying US dollars and selling the Japanese yen but all to no avail.

One serious problem is that Japan has lost control of the Japanese currency. Without the so-called Kyocho Kainyu (harmonious interference) with the USA, nothing much can be accomplished by Japan. Although Japan has managed to survive from the "yen shocks", the Japanese economy has remained in bad shape. Recently (24th December 1999), the Bank of Japan

(BOJ) injected US$2.4 billion into the forex market in its yen-selling intervention but only managed to pull the yen from 101.57 to 103.1 to the dollar. The former vice-finance minister Mr. Sakakibara Eisuke suggested that the yen's current level of then 102 should be pulled to the 110 level. In doing so the BOJ should make its yen-selling intervention an "unsterilized intervention", meaning that any excess currency created through intervention by BOJ should be allowed to stay in the market rather than being absorbed via daily money market operations[6].

4.5 Crisis Management

The Government of Japan has pumped in billions of dollars to rescue the country's economy. Public funds have been used to bail out banks and finance houses, to expand construction of social and industrial infrastructure, to reduce income taxes and corporate taxes and to give out promotion (free) tokens to children and the elderly, etc. Initially, the Japanese in general had a very strong objection to using public funds for private purposes, especially for rescuing ailing corporations. After 8–9 years of recession, the Japanese have become indifferent to this government strategy and pay less attention to how public funds are being utilized.

Despite announcing numerous economic rescue packages and pumping billions of dollars into the Japanese economy, Japan Inc. has remained sluggish. Why? Does the Japanese economy have structural defects or cyclical problems?

If the collapse of the bubble economy in Japan were limited to merely cyclical problems, the macro-economic policies pursued (including expansionary demand policies such as tax reductions, public expenditure increases, financial deregulation, distribution of regional promotion tokens or free tokens to children and elderly) should have pulled Japan out from the economic doldrums over these 8–9 years.

After the sluggish economy has dragged on for nearly a decade, with no effective, efficient and consistent policy being implemented to put the

---

[6] Straits Times, 27th December 1999, p. 43; Lian He Zao Bao, 27th December 1999, p. 23.

economy back on track, it has begun to show signs of structural defects, with no easy cures in sight. One of the such defect is evident from the extremely low level of domestic consumption. This is due to the long-term uncertainty over unemployment opportunities (the unemployment rate has now reached 5% and this is the highest rate since World War II) and uncertain pensions scheme (evidently the government will be unable to pay pensions to retirees due to huge fiscal deficits). Tax reductions only encourage the Japanese to save more for the uncertain future. They apparently do not work toward stimulating domestic consumption or to reenergize the domestic economy.

In fact, the Japanese government has come under heavy criticism for not being bold enough to embark on significant reforms of the economy. Instead it has resorted to old-fashioned Keynesian pump-priming in order to keep the economy going. Despite of the fact that enormous amounts of money has been spent the effect have been rather insignificant. The main outcome instead has been an enormous public debt now amounting to 1.3 times the value of the GDP[7].

Various suggestions to break the deadlock have been put forth. Large-scale urban reconstruction projects have been suggested, rather than the general increase of public expenditures (construction of social and industrial infrastructure). By doing so, the declining real estate market could be revitalized and the urban living environment could be upgraded at the same time. In the end, the Japanese economy would be lifted once again from the depths of gloom[8].

It is commonly argued that by taking advantage of a strong yen, through deregulation and opening up of the domestic market and totally amending housing and land systems in Japan, products from overseas could be cheaply imported. The Japanese domestic market could then be expanded and living standards in Japan could be improved.

---

[7] *Asiaweek*, February 21, 2000.

[8] Noguchi Yukio, Nihon Keizai Saisei No Senryaku (Strategies for the Resuscitation of the Japanese Economy), Chukyo Shinsho, 1999, pp. 22–24.

On the other hand, one important aspect that must be taken into consideration here is that the collapse of the bubble economy was related to the restructuring of the financial sector. Solving the problems in that sector can be viewed either as a short-term crisis management problem or a long-run structural reform problem. The Japanese government has been racking their brains on how to settle the problem of bad debts incurred by banks and other financial institutions. The focus of their plan is protecting the depositors (up to a limit), improving the accounting system and making sure that loans are available for reliable borrowers.

However, prices of real estate and stock have continued to fall as the Japanese public in general does not have confidence in the country's economic prospects and have remained largely pessimistic about the direction of asset prices (i.e., real estate and stocks) in the future. (During the last year considerable improvements in the general trend of share prices have occurred but whether this trend is sustainable is still a moot point.) It is argued that in order to prevent future drops in asset prices, improving the outlook of the Japanese economy has become a matter of paramount importance. In the long run, the government undeniably has to create an environment conducive to development of leading industries. In order to do so, Japan has to create a new and healthy financial system, the sooner the better[9].

The Japanese government has recently tried to revitalize the financial sector through carrying out a reform program (the so-called Big Bang) since fiscal year 1997. The reform covers the financial sector as a whole, including banking, securities and insurance and removes restrictions on organizational structures and financial products and services. It also aims at improving the protective rules for customers and providing improved mechanisms for dealing with financial failures. Some institutions had to be closed down or taken over by the state (such as the Long-Term Credit Bank and the Nippon Credit Bank). While these measures are likely to make the financial system more efficient they may not, as such, help boosting the level of demand in the short term. The conventional way to do this is through low interest rates. For over three years now, the Bank of Japan has kept the interest rate very close

---

[9] Ibid., pp. 24–26.

to zero. This has not had much effect, however. The households are too pessimistic to take up new loans, while the excess capacity of many firms discourages from new investment.

Japan is a highly industrialized country and has accumulated numerous advanced technologies. Using its strong technological bases to nurture some new industries should not be a big problem. In fact, new industries have been nurtured all the time. The problem is that under the present gloomy economic environment, bringing up leading industries in time and pull Japan out of the dead waters is obviously a difficult task. In any case it takes time to do so. To follow the example of the USA, using information technology to lead the Japanese industries to engineer a third industrial revolution is a task yet to be fulfilled.

5. JAPAN'S ROLE IN ASIA'S FINANCIAL CRISIS — EFFECTS OF THE NEW MIYAZAWA PLAN ON THE ECONOMIC RECOVERY

Over the last 8–9 years, to the surprise of most people, Japan's economy, as we have seen, has not shown any promising signs of recovery. Actually, the economy has already bottomed out several times, but has not recovered with consistency and dynamism. Nobody could have predicted that this situation would have dragged on for such a long period. Nor could anybody have anticipated precisely when the economy really would bottom out and then start to recover steadily. Japan's economy has lost its direction and is in a state of confusion.

The Japanese government has so far pumped in billions of dollars[10], in the form of rescue packages, in order to put the Japanese economy back on

---

[10]The Japanese government approved another biggest-ever draft budget totaling 84.98 trillion yen to stimulate the domestic economy on 20th December 1999. This brings Japan's National Debt to 364 trillion yen and is if the debt of local governments are included, to a staggering 647 trillion yen — or roughly equivalent to 1.3 times Japan's GDP (*Straits Times*, 21st December 1999, p. 57).

the right track. Despite several attempts, the Japanese economy would at best succeed in acieving a 0.6% growth rate for the fiscal year 1999 and perhaps 1.0% in the year 2000.

In terms of GDP, Japan is the largest economy in Asia (it is about twice as large as that of the rest of East Asia taken together), and the second largest in the world, next only to the USA. Japan's poor economic performance has been detrimental to the economic development of the other Asian countries. Japan's decreasing investment in Asia, especially after 1995, and its diminishing import of manufactured products (machinery and equipment in particular) from Asia in the second half of the 1990s, have contributed adversely to Asia's economic performance. The financial crisis erupted in Thailand in July 1997. Japan's economic collapse and prolonged stagnation in the 1990s contributed largely to the contagious economic malaise that spread to the other Asian countries.

The present strong yen situation in Japan, after the drastic currency appreciation, (US$1 = 103 yen, as on 21st December 1999) stunts the country's recovery. Most of its export industries suffer from the strong yen. Japan has again been put in a difficult situation, as she has to adjust to the new international environment and has to restructure its weak economy. Many Japanese experts estimate that the US dollar should be kept at the 115–125 yen level, for the country to be able to proceed along the path of smooth economic recovery. Japan seems to be in for hard times. The USA believes a "weak" US currency (i.e., against the yen) will continue to benefit its economy, and has no intention of interfering with the currency market. The Japanese government and the Ministry of Finance in Japan have had limited success adjusting the yen level despite continuous interference. Without "harmonious interference" by the USA and Japan, the Japanese currency will not be weakened significantly in the foreseeable future.

The strong yen encourages exports from Asia to Japan. The Asian countries are thus in a great dilemma. They hope for the Japanese economy to recover quickly as well as their exports to Japan to increase. However, it would be preferable that exports to Japan rise because of an economic recovery of Japan rather than because of a strong yen.

The Asian economies have shown some signs of recovery, after the devastating Asian financial crisis. Some critics still question whether the recovery is sustainable, however, since most of the affected countries in Asia have not gone through a thorough industrial and financial restructuring. Some Asian countries may not have learnt their lesson and might have become complacent or too confident. In a way the Asian economies are still vulnerable.

Japan, still in the midst of a possible recovery, is expected to make a contribution also to Asia's economic recovery. The so-called New Miyazawa plan (Shin Miyazawa Koso) originally allocated US$30 billion to assist Asian countries recovering from the Asian financial crisis. This amount has so far been increased to US$80 billion.

It is clear that a quick recovery in Asia is also to Japan's benefit. Economic relations between Japan and Asia are complementary. Japan's economic recovery relies very much on the quick recovery of the Asian countries. Japan dispenses the largest amounts of Official Development Assistance (ODA) of all countries in Asia. Corporations in Asian countries have been suffering seriously from bad debts since the Asian financial crisis erupted and Japan is the most important country extending loans to the rest of Asia, especially to Thailand and Indonesia. Japan would suffer the worst consequences should the Asian countries not be able to solve their bad debt problem. In other words, only when the corporations and banks in Asia have solved this problem are they in the position to repay their loans to Japan (i.e., Japanese corporations, financial institutions and the government).

The New Miyazawa Plan is aimed at helping the Asian countries overcome the Asian financial crisis contagion. In doing so, corporations' bad debt issues must be solved and industrial restructuring must be carried out as smoothly as possible. Loans can be repaid to Japan only when Asia is economically sound. The New Miyazawa Plan is designed to help the Asian countries and Japan can also be benefit in return. Judging from this aspect, Japan's recovery greatly depends on Asia's overall recovery.

The crisis has prompted new efforts at strengthening formalized economic cooperation in Asia. The New Miyazawa Plan could contribute to the formation of an Asian Monetary Fund (AMF). Government officials among the Asian countries unofficially mooted the AMF idea soon after the Asian financial crisis. The USA was quick to respond and opposed the idea of forming the AMF, however. The USA insisted that the AMF should either act subordinately to, or as a supplement the International Monetary Fund (IMF), should the plan materialize. However the initiative for forming the AMF has gradually subsided for now without much fuss.

The USA was less involved in the Asian financial crisis as compared to the previous crises in the Latin American countries, in particular Mexico. From USA's point of view, Latin America is in its backyard while Asia is rather far away. Under the initiative of the USA, the IMF extended loans to, and prescribed deflationary policies for the Asian countries, especially in the cases of Thailand and Indonesia. But unlike Japan, the USA provided limited amounts of loans to the Asian countries. Furthermore, the Asia-Pacific Economic Conference (APEC) has hardly played any active role to help tackle the financial crisis in Asia. As a consolidated entity in Asia, the Association of Southeast Asian Nations (ASEAN) has almost had no role to play in alleviating the Asian financial crisis. None of the existing organizations are really equipped with instruments to deal with a major economic crisis. Besides, they are consensus-based and thus slow-moving by nature.

If the AMF were to be established, it should play an important role as a separate "IMF" in Asia. In future, the AMF can monitor of supervise economic development of the Asian countries. Member countries of the AMF can mutually keep an eye on each other before a crisis erupts. If a new financial crisis erupts, they can also extend assistance, both financial assistance and remedy measures, promptly and efficiently with immediate results.

In general, Asia has to take more responsibility for Asian affairs. ASEAN, APEC or the IMF cannot take care of Asia alone. An international organization by the Asian countries, for the Asian countries, should be set up. Of late, the USA seems less inclined to object to an AMF and Japan has developed an intention to set up an AMF among the Asian countries through materializing the New Miyazawa Plan. Malaysia gained People's Republic of China's support to push for an East Asian Monetary Fund in Asia. The EMF is no different from the AMF, and the grouping is the same as the East Asian Economic Caucus (EAEC) which was proposed by the Malaysian Prime Minister, Dr. Mahathir Mohamad in December 1990 but which has been dormant, by and large, since.

It would be ideal for the Asian countries, in the time to come, to set up an international institution for strengthening economic cooperation among themselves, adding to the organizations already existing. It does not matter whether the name chosen is the AMF or the EMF, as long as it can prevent another financial crisis from erupting in a country in Asia, or to assist that country effectively before the crisis catches on in the Asia region. To this end, Japan has an important role to play, through implementing the New Miyazawa Plan.

References

Asiaweek, February 21, 2000.

Lian He Zao Bao, 27th December 1999.

Lim Hua Sing, *Japan's Role in Asia*, Times Academic Press, Singapore, 1999.

Noguchi Yukio, Baburu No Keizaigaku (bubble economics), Nihon Keizai Shimbun-sha, 1993, pp. 21–23.

Noguchi Yukio, Nihon Keizai Saisei No Senryaku (Strategies for the Resuscitation of the Japanese Economy), Chukyo Shinsho, 1999.

Straits Times, 27th December 1999.

Tanaka Naoki, Saigo No Jyunen, Nihon Keizai No Koso (Towards the Twenty-first Century — A Vision for the Japanese Economy), Nihon Keizai Shimbun-sha, 1992, pp. 62–64.

CHAPTER 3

CHINA

FINANCIAL CRISIS
AND CHINESE ECONOMY

Dianqing Xu[1]

Department of Economics, Huron College,
University of Western Ontario
1349 Western Road, London, ON, N6G 1H3, Canada.
E-mail: XU2@julian.uwo.ca

1. INTRODUCTION

With all the recent turmoil in Asia, Russia, and Latin America, many people have forecasted that China will be the next victim of the financial crisis. Some called the Thailand crisis in July 1997, the first wave. The second wave hit Russia and Brazil in 1998. And China to be expected as the third wave. Despite attempts by the Chinese government to resist the aforesaid financial crisis (they are committed to keeping the economy stable), many still expect the Chinese foreign exchange rate to collapse very soon. How stable is China's currency?

---

[1] I wish to thank Tzhong-shian Yu, Guoguang Liu, Yuxin Zheng, Xiaochuan Zhou for valuable comments which led to the current revision. I also wish to thank Pamela, Jemmy Berdy, and Taiwo Ajayi for their important research assistance. Financial support from Himalayan Foundation is gratefully acknowledged. Any remaining errors are my own.

After two years from the financial crisis in Asia, the Chinese financial system is still very stable. However, many questions arise: How can China avoid the impending financial crisis? When should China devaluate? Does China still face shock from the financial crisis? And what should China do in order to maintain the stability of the financial system?

Since 1997, there have been thousands research articles regarding the financial crisis in Asia. Relevant to China's situation, there have been numerous intelligent papers published — such as Liu (1998), Wu (1998), Lin (1998), Wang (1999) and so on. Based on the previously mentioned works, this paper is constructed as a framework to study the Chinese situation in the financial crisis and, consequently, to provide suggestions to avoid such a crisis.

A basic framework to study China's predicament in the financial crisis is presented in the second section. The third section discusses China's foreign currency reservation, international trade, foreign debt — and capital inflow and outflow, respectively. All the above variables are quite closely related to China's financial situation. Many indicators reveal that the Chinese currency is still very stable; this is the major reason why China can avoid the shock of the financial crisis in Asia. Moreover, section four will examine the benefits and the costs if China actively devaluates its currency. Considering the game at the current international financial market, there are no strong reasons for China to actively devaluate its currency. And section five will reveal that the huge non-performing loan is the major problem for China's financial security. Because the stock market price increased very quickly in the summer of 1999, the stability of the financial system will be affected negatively. Finally, the sixth section will summarize the lessons available from the financial crisis and will present future suggestions concerning China's fight with the financial crisis.

2. THE BASIC THEORETICAL FRAMEWORK TO ANALYZE THE FINANCIAL CRISIS

2.1 Two Types of Devaluation

Devaluation can be classified into two types: passive and initiative. A passive devaluation is one where the currency is forced down by capital flight. Ensuring capital flight can create chaos to the devaluating country. For example, the collapse of the exchange rate in Thailand, Indonesia, Malaysian, and Korea in 1997 were caused by passive devaluation. Even the governments of the aforementioned countries tried their best to maintain the stability of their currency — but eventually lost the game.

The size of initiative devaluation of exchange rate is usually less than 10% to 15%; however, the scale of passive devaluation is much larger. In the financial crisis the Korean currency devaluated 54%, Thailand 53%, and Indonesia 84%.

The objective of initiative devaluation is to increase the capacity of competition in the international market, and to increase export and market share. Yet passive devaluation is the result of failure in the defense of the exchange rate; the ensuing result of passive devaluation is that exports and imports decrease significantly, contributing to economic depression after the crisis.

2.2 Equilibrium of the Foreign Exchange Market

As pointed out in many articles, the reasons for the financial crisis are both internal and external. In order to describe the reasons for the financial crisis more clearly, the internal and external reasons must be put into a model of foreign currency exchange market. The equilibrium of the foreign exchange market may be interpreted as a level. The demand and supply of foreign exchange are at the two ends of the level. The supply side usually includes the current account surplus and capital inflow. On the demand side there are short-term debt and the capital outflow. Theoretically speaking, the equilibrium between the supply and the demand of foreign exchange determines the exchange rate.

At the beginning of the financial crisis, the international speculator group suddenly sold local currency in large amounts, and in return asked for international hard currency (for example, the U.S. dollar). This places a lot of pressure on the supply side of the local currency. The external shock may cause local residents to lose their confidence in the currency system. Many people forecast that local currency would devaluate very soon — and in order to keep the value of their assets, they rush to buy U.S. dollars using local currency. Conversely, few people like to go the opposite way and sell U.S. dollars to get local currency. Thus the total supply of local currency is significantly larger than the demand for local currency. Because the supply of the U.S. dollar cannot meet the demand, there is always someone who is willing to pay a higher price than the exchange rate to get the U.S. dollar. This puts a lot of pressure on the exchange rate of the local currency. In order to maintain the stability of the exchange rate, the central bank must join the game and buy back the local currency using foreign currency reservation. At that moment, the major players in the market are the central bank and the international speculator: they play on the two ends of the level. If the total amount of local currency held by the international speculator, plus that sold by the local residents, is more than the foreign currency reservation, plus capital inflow and the current account surplus, the exchange rate of the country in question will be in a very dangerous situation. The equilibrium of the foreign exchange market is determined by how much money both sides — the central bank and the speculator — can put into the game and where the pilot point of the level is situated. As known, the financial policy of the country will determine the pilot point for this game.

The basic condition for the security of a country's financial system is:

FR + NL + NX > KO + FD

FR stands for foreign currency reservation, NL for new loans and capital inflow, NX for current account surplus or net export, FD for short-term foreign debt, and KO stands for capital outflow. The left part stands for all funding the country could use to stabilize the foreign exchange system; conversely, the right part stands for the pressure on the banking system. In a country without currency convertibility, the capital outflow will be determined by the possibility for the residents to get foreign exchange. In a system with convertible currency, if the residents have lost confidence in their own financial system, then a large amount of currency will flight away the country. This is an amplified effect of foreign speculation shock.

Even today, everyday, the total transaction in the international exchange market is around $1,600 billion U.S. dollars. It almost equals 80% of the foreign exchange reservation in the world.[2] However, it does not mean all capital flow will affect the exchange rate of a country. The amount of local currency the foreigner can get is the real way to affect the equilibrium of the foreign exchange market. Therefore, the amount of capital outflow can be written as a function of speculator demand (SD).

$$KO = \alpha\ SD$$

SD stands for the maximum amount of local currency the international speculator can get, while α stands for an amplified coefficient which is determined by the structure of the country's financial system and by the confidence of the resident on their financial system. Even we do not have enough data to make a confidential estimation on the amplified coefficient; according to the experiments on Thailand and Malaysia, the size of the coefficient is around 5 to 10 times.

The foreign currency reservation, short-term foreign debt, and current account surplus are measurable. In most cases, we can estimate the amount of foreign capital inflow and the maximum amount of the local currency the foreigner can hold. It is very difficult to observe and forecast the amount of capital outflow. The following sections will quantitatively discuss all these important variables which determine the stability of China's financial market.

3. DETERMINANTS OF THE FOREIGN EXCHANGE MARKET

3.1 Foreign Currency Reservation and Surplus on Current Account (FR+NX)

If a country has a rich foreign currency reservation, of course, the country has a strong capacity to fight any financial crisis. In Table 3.1, we can see that the foreign currency reservation in China has continuously increased over the five years since 1993. The net increase is $123.9 billion U.S. dollars during the period from 1993 to 1998. In China, almost 50% of the foreign currency reservation come from the trade surplus, and 10% comes

---

[2] See IMF, "The Perspective of World Economy", May 1997.

from foreign capital inflow; the remainder comes from the re-investment by the profit of the joint venture in China.[3] The total amount of foreign currency reservation was already over $154.7 billion U.S. dollars at end of 1999.

Table 3.1 Foreign Currency Reservation and Trade in China

	FCR (billion USD)	Total Export	Total Import	GDP (billion yuan)	Exchange Rate	GDP (billion USD)	Supporting Time of FCR
1985	11.91	27.35	42.25	896.4	2.93	305.94	3.4
1986	10.51	30.94	42.91	1020.2	3.45	295.71	2.9
1987	25.24	39.44	43.21	1196.2	3.72	321.56	7.0
1988	17.55	47.52	55.27	1492.8	3.72	401.29	3.8
1989	17.02	52.54	59.14	1690.9	3.76	449.71	3.5
1990	28.59	62.09	53.35	1854.7	4.78	388.01	6.4
1991	42.67	71.84	63.79	2161.7	5.32	406.34	8.0
1992	19.44	84.94	80.59	2663.8	5.51	483.45	2.9
1993	21.20	91.74	103.96	3463.4	5.76	601.29	2.4
1994	51.62	121.01	115.61	4675.9	8.61	545.92	5.4
1995	73.60	148.78	132.08	5847.8	8.35	687.68	6.7
1996	105.03	151.05	138.83	6788.4	8.31	807.60	9.1
1997	139.89	182.70	142.36	7477.2	8.28	890.88	11.8
1998	145.00	183.80	140.20	795.53	8.27	973.72	12.4
1999	154.70	195.00	165.00	831.90	8.28	1004.71	11.3

Data sources: China Statistical Yearbook and People's Daily April 22, 1999, January 12, 2000.

Following from normal cases, a foreign currency reservation in a country should support the import activity for at least three to four months. According to Chinese data, the Chinese foreign currency reservation can support import activity for 12.4 months in 1998 and 11.3 months in 1999, which is much higher than the security line for the currency reservation. Some people say that China has too much foreign currency reservation and needs to use the capital efficiently. Constructing a fence is a good analogy of this: although a well-built fence may be too expensive to build, a good quality fence may

---

[3] See Yang Fan, p. 121, 1999.

deter the thief just the same. Of course, it is still an important research topic to study the relationship between financial security and the efficiency to use the capital.

3.2 Debt Structure and Foreign Debt (FD)

The financial crisis is, in fact, the credit crisis of people relevant to the banking system. A bank's huge debt is one of the major reasons behind the loss in confidence concerning the banking system. Therefore, when we consider the financial security of a country, we must pay attention to the total debt and its structure. Relevant to the Asian financial crisis, the debt ratio in Thailand, Indonesia, Korea and Malaysia was very high, and the financial system collapsed in the crisis. [4]

However, the Chinese government is very conservative and very careful when it comes to the banking system. From 1994 to 1997, the country's deficit was 57.45, 58.15, 52.96 and 55.51 billion yuans respectively. The government deficit was only 1.23% of GDP in 1994 and this ratio decreased to 0.74% in 1997. When the Chinese government made its budget estimation for 1998, it originally tried to reduce the deficit to 46 billion yuan, and hoped to balance the government budget by the end of this century. However, after the financial crisis, China's deficit did not decrease; instead, it increased quite a bit to $96 billion yuans in 1998. The deficit plus the $100 billion newly issued treasury bills represents a total of 1.2% of GDP. If we count the government deficit — according to the rules used in Western countries — when the interest payment of the government debt is added, the total financial debt in China is still lower than the warranty line: 3% of GDP of the country. [5]

In 1997 the total debt of the central government was 8.1% of GDP. At the end of 1998, this ratio increased to 10.3%. If the $270 billion special

---

[4] See Table 3.6 for details on the foreign debts before the financial crisis in Asian countries.

[5] At the same period of time, the financial deficit in U.S was 3.04% of GDP, 6.55% in U.K, 5.13% in France, 10.51% in Italy. Data source: IMF "Government Financial Statistical Yearbook", 1996 and Jia Kang, "The risk of Financial Deficit", Economic Highlight, August 6, 1999.

treasury bills, which were used to increase the asset ratio for the major state-owned banks, are added to the total debt, then the ratio becomes 13.6%. Even this ratio increased very quickly, but it is still lower than the ratio in major industrial countries.

Table 3.2 China's Debt

	Government Debt	SOE Debt	Total Debt	GDP	Debt Ratio
1994	283.12	68.21	351.33	4675.94	7.51%
1995	382.78	64.66	447.44	5847.81	7.65%
1996	494.33	59.77	554.10	6788.40	8.17%
1997	607.24	NA	NA	7477.24	NA

Sources: China Stock and Future Statistical Yearbook, 1997 and 1998.

From Table 3.2, we can see that the debt ratio in China is still maintained at about 8%. In order to increase domestic demand, the Chinese government significantly increased the investment for basic infrastructure in 1999. The budget deficit was 150.3 billion yuans. The newly issued treasury bills were 341.5 billion yuans. Thus that debt ratio is over 10% in 1999. Because the time period concerning the treasury bills is quite long, there is no pressure to pay back the principle and interest over a short period of time.

After the financial crisis in 1997, the international investors concluded Asia to be an area of high risk. Consequently, many foreign investors avoid Asia. This, of course, leads to increased financial difficulty in Asia. Meanwhile, because the Chinese government tries to regulate non-financial institutions and allows for some of them go bankrupt (for example, the Guangdong Trust Investment Company went to bankrupt in 1998), China has much more difficulty getting foreign investment. Table 3.3 shows the structure of the foreign debt. After 1998, among the capital inflows the total amount of loans from the business area and other areas continually decrease. And the government borrowed more from the international financial institutes.

From Table 3.4, we can see that before the financial crisis the total foreign debt was 14.4% of GDP. The domestic debt was 8.17% of GDP. The

Table 3.3 Foreign Debt and Their Structure in China

(Billion USD)

	Total Foreign Debt	Government Loan	Financial Institution Loan	Commercial Loan	Others	Government Loan	Financial Institution Loan	Commercial Loan	Others
1985	15.83	3.63	1.19	6.45	4.56	23.00%	7.50%	40.80%	28.80%
1986	21.48	4.94	2.63	7.60	6.32	23.00%	12.20%	35.40%	29.40%
1987	30.21	5.02	3.74	12.18	9.27	16.60%	12.40%	40.30%	30.70%
1988	40.00	6.65	4.25	18.98	10.12	16.60%	10.60%	47.50%	25.30%
1989	41.30	6.95	5.34	21.67	7.33	16.80%	12.90%	52.50%	17.80%
1990	52.55	8.39	6.29	29.18	8.69	16.00%	12.00%	55.50%	16.50%
1991	60.56	9.51	7.07	31.59	12.39	15.70%	11.70%	52.20%	20.50%
1992	69.32	11.50	8.42	35.48	13.93	16.60%	12.10%	51.20%	20.10%
1993	83.57	14.32	10.46	41.08	17.71	17.10%	12.50%	49.20%	21.20%
1994	92.81	19.59	12.94	47.33	12.94	21.10%	13.90%	51.00%	13.90%
1995	106.59	22.06	14.80	52.63	17.11	20.70%	13.90%	49.40%	16.00%
1996	116.28	22.16	16.74	56.94	20.43	19.10%	14.40%	49.00%	17.60%
1997	130.96	20.78	19.21	64.77	26.20	15.90%	14.70%	49.50%	20.00%
1998	146.04	41.64	41.99	60.74	1.67	28.50%	28.80%	41.60%	1.10%

Data sources: China Statistical Yearbook (1998), Financial Morning Post, April 7, 1998, and People's Daily, April 22, 1999.

Table 3.4 Foreign Debts in Asian Countries

(Billion USD)

	China	Thailand	Indonesia	Malaysia	Philippines
Foreign Debt	116.28	76.5	109.3	36.4	40.2
Ratio of Foreign Debt to GDP	14.40%	43%	48%	39%	48%
Domestic Debt	59.49	286.9	122.4	125.7	70.2
Ratio of Domestic Debt to GDP	8.17%	160%	54%	133%	84%
Total Debt	175.77	355.6	247.2	165.9	108
Ratio of Total Debt to GDP	21.80%	198%	110%	175%	130%

Data sources: Asian Wall Street Journal, August 5, 1997, and China Statistical Yearbook, 1998.

total debt was 21.8% of GDP. All these indicators are much lower than that of the southeastern Asian countries.

According to the international warranty line, the debt ratio (foreign debt over GDP) should not go over 50%. In 1996, such a ratio in Thailand was

50.3% and in Indonesia it was 59.7%. From Table 3.5, we can see that after 1998 the total debt in China became only 15% of GDP; this is a relatively safe situation.

Usually the total foreign debt should not exceed the total amount for exports in a year. This means the foreign debt ratio should not exceed 100%. The average debt ratio in developing countries was 151% in 1988, 126% in 1992, 105% in 1996 and in 1997 around 100%. In European developing countries the debt ratio was 115%, in Africa it was 234%, in Latin America it was 244%. The foreign debt ratio in China was 79.5% in 1998.

Table 3.5 Foreign Debts and Risk Index

(Billion USD)

	Foreign Debt	GDP	Total Debt	Liability Ratio	Debt Service Ratio	Foreign Debt Ratio
1985	15.83	305.94	27.35	5.60%	2.80%	53.40%
1990	52.55	388.01	62.09	14.80%	8.50%	87.00%
1991	60.56	406.34	71.84	15.00%	8.00%	87.00%
1992	69.32	483.45	84.94	14.10%	7.30%	90.70%
1993	83.57	601.29	91.74	14.00%	9.70%	94.50%
1994	92.81	545.92	121.01	17.00%	9.10%	77.80%
1995	106.59	687.68	148.78	15.50%	7.30%	69.90%
1996	116.28	807.50	151.05	14.40%	6.70%	75.20%
1997	130.96	890.88	182.70	14.70%	7.30%	63.20%
1998	146.04	973.72	183.80	15.00%	14.98%	79.50%

Data sources: China Statistical Yearbook (1998), and People's Daily, April 22, 1999.

Normally we use the debt service ratio to measure the capacity to pay back the foreign debt. If the debt service ratio is higher than 20% we need a warning about the crisis. From 1996 to 1998, the debt service ratio average in developing countries was 15%, in European developing countries it was 13%, in Africa it was 28%, and in Latin America it was approximately 40%. In 1996, the debt service ratio was 36.8% in Indonesia and 11.5% in Thailand. Until 1997 the debt service ratio in China was always lower than 10%. In 1998, this ratio increased to approximately 15% but it was still lower than the average in developing countries. Evidently, there is security.

We must not only consider the total amount of the foreign debt but also its time structure. If the short-term debt is less, then the central bank has more ways to deal with the financial crisis. It is very important to avoid the crisis in such a country. Since the 1980s, the ratio of short-term debt in the total foreign debt was around 20% in developing countries. In Thailand the ratio of short-term debt was 41.4% of the total foreign debt in 1996; in Indonesia the ratio was 25% and in Malaysia the ratio was 27.8%. During 1990 to 1993, the short-term debt ratio in Korea was 37%. In 1994 to 1996 the ratio in Korea increased to 62%. Before the financial crisis the ratio of short-term debt ratio to the foreign currency reservation continuously increased in southeastern countries. In June 1997, the average ratio of short-term debt to the foreign currency reservation was around 134% in 1994. From Table 3.6 we can see that in Philippines and Malaysia the ratio of short term debt over the foreign currency reservation is lower than 100%, but in Thailand, Indonesia and Korea this ratio is higher than 100%. This is the reason the impact on the latter countries is stronger than that on the former.[6]

Table 3.6 Foreign Debt Structure in Asian Countries

(Billion USD)

	Total Foreign Debt	Short-term Debt	Foreign Currency Reservation	Ratio of Short-Term Debt to Foreign Currency Reservation
Thailand	90.50	37.60	26.20	143.50%
Malaysia	38.70	9.70	20.80	46.60%
Indonesia	130.20	28.00	16.60	168.70%
Philippines	41.90	7.20	7.30	98.60%
Taiwan	28.40	NA	83.50	NA
Korea	160.70	100.00	20.40	490.20%
China	130.9	18.1	139.89	12.90%

Data sources: BIS, "International Economic Index", 1999, and R. Kumar and B. Debroy, "The Asian Crisis: An Alternative View", Asian Development Bank, Economic Staff Paper, #59.

---

[6] See R. Kumar and B. Debroy, "The Asian Crisis: An Alternative View", Asian Development Bank, Economic Staff Paper, #59.

From Table 3.7 we can see that the short-term foreign debt to the total debt was 22.2% in 1986. This ratio decreased to 11.9% in 1998. From this indicator we can see that the financial security in China is much higher than in most East Asian countries.

Table 3.7 Time Structure of China's Foreign Debt

(Billion USD)

	Total Foreign Debt	Long-Term Debt	%	Short-Term Debt	%
1985	15.828	9.41	59.50%	6.418	40.50%
1986	21.483	16.714	77.80%	4.769	22.20%
1987	30.205	24.485	81.10%	5.72	18.90%
1988	40.003	32.696	81.70%	7.307	18.30%
1989	41.299	37.032	89.70%	4.267	10.30%
1990	52.545	45.779	87.10%	6.766	12.90%
1991	60.561	50.257	83.00%	10.304	17.00%
1992	69.321	58.475	84.40%	10.846	15.60%
1993	83.573	70.027	83.80%	13.546	16.20%
1994	92.806	82.391	88.80%	10.415	11.20%
1995	106.591	94.675	88.80%	11.916	11.20%
1996	116.275	102.167	87.90%	14.108	12.10%
1997	130.96	112.82	86.10%	18.14	13.90%
1998	146.04	128.7	88.10%	17.34	11.90%

Data sources: China Statistical Yearbook (1998), Financial Morning Post, April 7, 1998, and People's Daily, April 22, 1999.

There are other indicators we usually use to measure a country's financial security:

(1) The high foreign trade deficit is not beneficial for financial security. For a developing country, the deficit in current account to GDP ratio should be controlled between 0-5%. When Mexico experienced the financial crisis the trade deficit was 7.8% of GDP. The ratio was 9.7% in Malaysia and 7.7% in Thailand. There is no current account deficit in China and this ratio is negative 2.9%.

(2) From the dynamic point of view, it is good for financial security if the foreign currency reservation increases faster than GDP. The

foreign currency reservation growth rate to the growth rate of GDP in Mexico during 1990-1995 is negative 28%. In Indonesia, Thailand, Philippines, Korea and Malaysia this ratio is negative 30% to 120%. In China, foreign currency reservation increased almost two times more than gross GDP rate from 1994 to 1997.

(3) It is not very easy to attack a country if the ratio between foreign direct investment plus the current account deficit and GDP is high. The international warning line is negative 2.5% and this indicator is negative 5.6% in Mexico; in China this indicator is 5.7%.

In summary, until end of 1999, concerning the foreign debt and the structure of foreign debt, the Chinese financial system is relatively secure.

3.3 The Capital Inflow (NL)

For developing countries that are short of capital, the foreign capital inflow has two effects, both positive and negative. If the foreign capital inflow is targeted towards the productive industrial sector, it will increase productivity and improve technology. This will improve the comparative position of the country in the international market and will increase the foreign currency reservation. If the foreign capital invest into the productive sectors, it usually is a quite stable long-term investment. Suppose the foreign capital does not go to the productive sector, but goes instead into the stock market or the real asset market, of course, the foreign capital lets the country have relatively rich floating capital and reduces the cost to borrow money. This is positive, but, on the other hand, the foreign capital inflow may increase speculation in the stock market and the real asset market. Such an investment will be affected by the external shock from international financial markets at a very short period of time. The size of the stock market and real asset market is relatively small in a developing country, also there is a shortage of well-designed regulations for the capital markets and experienced managers to administrate the capital market. If they open the door to foreign capital in the stock market and the real asset market, the short-term capital inflow will cause a serious bubble economy. When a country is facing financial crisis, a huge amount of foreign capital will leave in a very short period of time, and this will seriously shock the financial system. So we need to pay attention not only to the total amount of capital inflow, but also to where the foreign capital inflow is going in the country.

In Indonesia, Malaysia, and Thailand, huge amounts of foreign capital inflow is going into the stock market and real asset market and is generating economic bubbles. For example, in Thailand in 1994 the total capital inflow was $10.5 billion U.S. This capital inflow increased significantly in 1996 to $30.6 billion U.S. The total amount of the foreign capital inflow is much higher than the capacity of the manufacturing industry in Thailand to absorb. Thus around 25% of bank loans went to the consumption area and 25% entered the real asset market.[7] The burst of bubble economy is one of the major reasons for the collapse of the financial system in that country.

Second only to the United States, China continues to get the most foreign direct investment (FDI) in the world since 1993. From 1993 to 1995, China continuously increased interest rates four times over. For example, interest rates for the one-year fixed-term deposit increased from 7.56% to 12.06%. This is significantly higher than the interest rates for most countries. Meanwhile, because the potential domestic market in China is so large, this introduced a great deal of capital inflow to China.

The foreign capital inflow comes into China through following ways:

(1) joint venture borrow money abroad and exchange for RMB (Renmingbi is the name of the Chinese currency)
(2) the domestic enterprises also borrow foreign loan and receive RMB
(3) some money belonging to the capital account was conversing to RMB under the name of the current account
(4) Some foreign enterprises send money to China using person's name and get RMB.[8]

As Table 3.8 reveals, the total amount of foreign capital inflow was around $64.4 billion U.S. in 1996. During the three years spanning 1994 to

---

[7] See The World Bank, "Private Capital Inflow to Developing Countries", 1997.

[8] See Wu Xiaoling, "International Balance of Payment and Foreign Exchange Policy in China", 1999.

1996, the total capital inflow to China was $129.9 billion U.S. The first part of this number is $81.8 billion U.S., which is a direct investment and which includes some equipment (not including raw material). The second part is $22.1 billion U.S., whereby $10.1 billion U.S. is cash inflow and $10 billion is re-investment from the profit of foreign owned enterprises. The third part is speculative capital around $26 billion U.S. Among this, around $16 billion converted through the trade channel and another $10 billion U.S. stayed in China as RMB profit of foreign joint adventures for financial speculations.

Table 3.8 Foreign Capital Inflow in China

	Total Loans	Foreign Loans	Foreign Direct Investment	Foreign Other Investment
1979-1983	144.38	117.55	18.02	8.81
1984	27.05	12.86	12.58	1.61
1985	46.47	26.88	16.61	2.98
1986	72.58	50.14	18.71	3.70
1987	84.52	58.05	23.14	3.33
1988	102.26	64.87	31.94	5.45
1989	100.59	62.86	33.92	3.81
1990	102.89	65.34	34.87	2.68
1991	115.54	68.88	43.66	3.00
1992	192.02	79.11	110.07	2.84
1993	389.60	111.89	275.15	2.56
1994	432.13	92.67	337.67	1.79
1995	481.33	103.27	375.21	2.85
1996	548.04	126.69	417.26	4.09
1997	644.08	120.21	452.57	71.30
1998	589.00	110.00	456.00	23.00

Data sources: China Statistical Report on National Economy and Social Development (1999) and China Statistical Yearbook (1998).

Until the present, China in general did not open the real asset market to foreign capital. The Chinese government has separated the foreign investment and the domestic investment very clearly and very seriously at the stock market. The domestic stock market is called A share and the foreign investment stock market, which is very small, is called B share. In September

1999, the total amount of B shares were \$2.1 billion U.S. This represents 2.4% of the GDP and approximately 5% of the total value of the stock market in China. This means that most of the foreign capital flows into the productive area in China. It is too small to be considered the reason for a bubble economy. Even if the financial crisis did attack China, the foreign capital cannot run away in a short period of time. A huge amount of foreign capital inflow will generate pressure for RMB's invaluation, not devaluation.

3.4 Capital Outflow (KO)

How much capital flowed out from China during the last few years? Usually we have very clear statistical information regarding capital inflow, because there are some illegal channels for capital outflow, there is no such official published data. Because the Chinese currency still does not have convertibility under capital account, the capital outflow of the data is not easy to retrieve.

We may make some estimates via different methods. In general, the amount of national saving should equal the amount of GDP after deducting the final consumption. Suppose the capital inflow equals the capital outflow, this saving must approximately equal the capital investment. The national savings rate should almost equal the capital investment rate. Suppose the investment rate is higher than the national savings rate, then this would allow for some net foreign capital inflow. Conversely, suppose the investment rate is lower than the national savings rate, then the capital outflow would, of course, be higher than the capital inflow. Although this method is not accurate, we can roughly estimate the size of the capital inflow or capital outflow.

From the national financial balance sheet of 1998, the foreign direct investment to China was \$43.7 billion U.S. At the end of 1998, China's overseas investment was only \$3.78 billion U.S. and other non-trade related investments were \$2.55 billion U.S, the total being \$6.33 billion U.S.[9] Obviously, China's direct overseas investment was much less than the foreign

---

[9] *Data source*: People's Daily, September 6, 1999.

direct investment into China. From this we can know that there is a huge amount of capital inflow. Because the saving ratio in China was very high, including the huge amount of capital inflow, the growth rate of capital stock should be much higher than the saving rate. However, from Table 3.9 we can see that during the five years after 1993, the national savings rate has been continually higher than the investment rate.

Table 3.9 China's Saving and Investment

	GDP	Consumption	Investment Rate	Domestic Saving Rate	GAP
1985	879.2	577.3	37.8	34.3	3.46
1986	1013.2	654.2	37.7	35.4	2.27
1987	1178.4	745.1	36.1	36.8	−0.67
1988	1470.4	936.0	36.8	36.3	0.46
1989	1646.6	1055.7	36	35.9	0.11
1990	1831.9	1136.5	34.7	38	−3.26
1991	2128.0	1314.6	34.8	38.2	−3.42
1992	2586.4	1595.2	36.2	38.3	−2.12
1993	3450.0	2018.2	43.3	41.5	1.8
1994	4711.0	2721.6	41.2	42.2	−1.03
1995	5940.5	3452.9	40.8	41.9	−1.08
1996	6936.6	4103.9	39.6	40.8	−1.24
1997	7625.9	4494.4	37.3	41.1	−3.76
1998	8100.3	4792.2	37.1	40.8	−3.74

Data sources: A Statistical Survey of China (1999), and results of calculation.

Therefore, the only explanation to this contradiction is that the capital outflow is higher than the capital inflow. There is a very serious capital outflow phenomenon in China after the Asian financial crisis.

China's capital outflow has two major parts: (1) the state uses the foreign capital reservation to buy the treasury bills from U.S, Japan and other countries. The total amount of this part is $85.4 billion U.S. And (2) The sum of the Net Error and Omission on China's balance of payment from 1994 to 1996 was as high as $43.2 billion U.S. Excluding the amount of statistical errors and omissions, the major part under this item was capital outflow through various channels.

From 1984 to 1994 the capital outflow from China is estimated at approximately $40.2 billion U.S. — in which almost 50% of such money does not receive permission from the government through illegal channels. Some part of the capital will flow out at first; then; however, it will be reversed back into China in the name of foreign capital, in order to receive a tax break. According to an estimation of the State Statistics Bureau, the capital outflow — which is invested back — is almost 25% of the total foreign direct investment. After the Asian financial crisis the amount of capital outflow from China increased significantly. According to an estimation of the *Economist*, the capital flight from China was $20 billion U.S in 1997 and more than that in 1998.[10] Dr. Gang Fan estimated the sum of capital outflow from China to be around $100 billion, while $48 billion U.S was through illegal channels.[11]

The major way for capital outflow is as follows:

(1) Under the name of joint venture between the SOE and foreign partners, a lot of money is mailed to foreign countries. In many such cases, it is very possible that the fund is already owned by some individual, not continuously owned by the government or by state-owned enterprises.

(2) Some Chinese companies get the foreign currency from the trade, and deposit it into the foreign bank instead of sending it back to China.

(3) Some funds, such as corruption income of government officials and revenue of smuggling, is mailed out through illegal channels to foreign country's under non-trade form.

(4) Some SOE cheats and claim that they import some foreign products. After they get foreign exchange from China's bank, they send it out and deposit it into their personal account. According to a report on China's Customs, around 42% of custom claim forms in 1998 have exaggerated the amount paid for import activity.

---

[10] See *Economist*, September 26, 1998, p. 79.

[11] See Fan Gang, "Debt Ratio and Financial Crisis", *Economic Highlight*, Vol. 350, September 17, 1999.

(5) Some enterprises ask for foreign exchange to pay back the foreign debt earlier than the deadline. After they get the foreign exchange they do not pay back the loan and instantly send the fund out and transfer it to another account.

(6) Some international short-term capital is mixed with the trade and current account; also some SOE use the long-term bank credit to send the money abroad.

Although there is a certain amount of the capital outflow, the Chinese international balance still maintains the double surplus in the current account and capital account from 1994 to 1997. This is the way the foreign currency reservation continuously increases, which, in turn, increases the capacity to fight the financial crisis in 1997. Nevertheless, the currency crisis in Asia generated a very bad effect on China's international balance.

Table 3.10 China's Balance of Payment (1998)

	1993	1994	1995	1996	1997	1998
Current Account	−119	76.6	16.2	72.4	297.2	293.2
Capital and Financial	234.7	326.4	386.7	399.7	229.6	−63.2
Net Error and Omission	−98	−97.8	−178.1	−155.6	−169.5	−165.7
Change in Reserve Assets	−17.7	−305.3	−224.8	−316.5	−357.2	−64.3

Data sources: China Foreign Statistical Yearbook, 1998 and People's Daily June 25, 1999.

On the one hand, the foreign capital inflow to Asia and China decreased significantly. In 1998 China's foreign capital inflow was $58.9 billion U.S.; this represents a decrease of 7.9% compared to 1997. The amount of the foreign direct investment was $45.6 billion U.S.; this represents an increase of 0.7%. Foreign loan was $11 million U.S., represents a decrease of 8.5%. On the other hand, the financial crisis left many people wondering about the stability of RMB and as a result capital flight out increased. After 1998, the international balance payment of China has a $6.3 billion U.S. deficit. This is the first time China has had a capital account deficit. Because the capital inflow decreased while the capital outflow increased, the growth rate of foreign currency reservation decreased. This weakened the capacity for China to successfully avoid the financial crisis in the future. The Chinese government introduced many ways to enforce foreign currency control. To a certain extent, they have decreased capital flight out; however, the Chinese financial sector is still facing a more difficult job in the near future.

3.5 Foreign Speculative Demands (SD)

The stability of the financial sector in China depends, to some extent, on the inconvertibility of the currency in the capital account. As we mentioned before, it does not matter if the foreigner has a lot of money or not. If somebody wants to attack China's exchange system, they need to have a huge amount of RMB. How much money can the foreign speculators get in terms of the RMB? There are four major channels to get RMB:

(1) Borrowing from the bank is the major channel for the international speculator to obtain local currency. Usually the speculator only needs to put some deposit into local banks and then borrow around ten to twenty times the local currency through the future market. In the financial crisis in Thailand and other Asian countries, the speculator first of all borrowed a large amount of the local currency and then suddenly sold all this local currency at the exchange market. Till today, the Chinese government still maintains a very strict foreign currency control over their capital account and the RMB is not convertible in the capital account. Except for a few exceptions, the foreign bank cannot handle the business in terms of RMB. Because of the supervision of foreign currency by the Chinese government it is difficult for the foreign financial institutions to borrow large amounts of RMB. So this cuts the major road for foreigners to obtain RMB.

(2) The profit of foreign owned enterprises is another resource for foreigners to have RMB. According to the current regulation, the foreign enterprises in China can only convert part of their profit to U.S. dollars, and still need to have quite a large amount of this profit reinvested into China using RMB. Until the end of 1998, the total

amount of investment of foreign owned enterprises was around $170 billion U.S. Suppose we place the profit rate at 12% then the total annual profit will be around $20 billion U.S. Suppose 50% is used for reinvestment, then the remaining which is around $10 billion U.S. becomes the short-term capital. Plus there already exists around $30 billion U.S. working capital so the short-term capital in terms of RMB is in total around $40 billion U.S. We predict that only 50% of the short-term capital could be affected by the international speculators. So the total amount of the capital at this point is around $20 billion U.S.

(3) RMB is circulating in Hong Kong and Macao. And it has been estimated to be around 30 billion RMB which is equal to $4 billion U.S.

(4) During the financial crisis in Asia, the international group of speculators usually tried to sell or buy future stock in order to obtain the local currency, however, China currently refuses to open its future market. The foreigner can only have B share of the Chinese stock, and the B share is only $2.5 billion U.S. This is not a significant amount.

In short, the foreign banks cannot obtain shares of stocks in the financial system of Mainland China. They cannot directly handle RMB business, nor borrow RMB from the Chinese banks and neither can they buy/sell future RMB. Because the foreign speculators hold very limited RMB, so in the worst case, if the international speculator attacked China's financial system, the maximum amount of RMB they could obtain would be no more than $30 billion U.S.

3.6 Amplifying Effect of External Shock (α)

Where international currency speculators can exacerbate the crisis is the country's citizens losing confidence in their currency. If the citizens lose confidence in their own financial system, when international speculators sell the local currency, it will generate an amplified effect. Sometimes this effect is very significant. We can not get historical data to support the statistical testing; however, according to the experience in Thailand and Malaysia we can estimate that the amplified effect of the external shock will be around 10 to 20 times. In the financial crisis in Asia, the international speculator group used this amplifying effect and shifted the pilot point of the level of the exchange market close to the side of the central bank. This increased the impact. Suppose the country introduced regulations to control foreign currency, the amplifying effect will be deduced to some degree.

For most Chinese citizens, there are very few options for their investment portfolios. The Chinese government never promised that the local currency would be convertible in near future. As a result, the Chinese citizen never dreamed that they could convert their local currency to U.S. dollars or any other currency except through the black market. Because RMB cannot be freely converted at the capital account, this significantly reduced the amplifying effect of the external impact. In addition, from 1997 price levels in China continuously decreased. Huge amounts of the products were stuck in the domestic market. The people always tried to purchase goods when the price goes up and not down, therefore there is not a great deal of incentive for people to buy the goods immediately. Because the foreign exchange market is still under the regulation of the government and the stock and real asset markets are not well developed, the Chinese citizens have very little choice but to deposit their savings into the banks. [12]

Therefore, a change in the external financial market can only generate a very limited amplifying effect in China.

3.7 Degree of Security of China's Financial System

In summary, we can use an indicator? to measure the security of the system.

---

[12] The financial crisis in Asia had very little effect on China's saving deposit. The total saving deposit continuously increased during the past years. The saving deposit increased 300 billion yuan in 1994, 346.8 billion yuan in 1995, 700 billion yuan in 1996, 750 billion yuan in 1997, and 923.7 billion yuan in 1998. Even the interest rate reduced but the liquidity of financial asset is very low. According to a survey by Chinese Economic Forecasting Center at July 1998, more than 80% people said they will not increase their consumption or investment after government decreased the interest rate. See Zhao Xiaolei, *Economic Highlight*, July 23, 1999.

$$\gamma = \frac{FR + NX + NL}{FD + \alpha \cdot SD}$$

If γ is larger than 1, the ability of the country to resist the financial crisis is higher than the impact caused by international speculators, therefore the financial system of the country is secure.

According to the Chinese data of 1998, at the numerator the foreign currency reservation is $145 U.S. billion, the net export is $43.6 billion, the capital account is −$6.3 billion, the total is $182.3 billion U.S. dollars. At the denominator the short-term debt is $17.3 billion, and the speculators' demand cannot go over $30 billion. Because the Chinese government administrated the foreign exchange, the pilot point of the level is fixed in the middle point. If the foreign speculator wanted to shock the foreign exchange system in China, then they would have to directly put pressure on the level without any amplifying effects. The maximum shock could be $47.3 billion. The parameter γ equal to 3.85.[13] In reality, the capacity of the Chinese central bank to maintain the stability of the current exchange rate is much higher than the shock in the worst case.

Even though some people continuously forecast that China's currency would become devalued, the international speculator does not attack the RMB. The major reason is that the international speculator knows the stability of the Chinese exchange system very well. The conclusion from the data of 1998 is that it is totally impossible to turn down China's foreign exchange system from the outside.

4.   PROS AND CONS OF ACTIVE DEVALUATION

<u>4.1 Benefit and Cost of China to Actively Devaluate Its Currency</u>

The devaluation of the currency can improve the competitive power for exports of this country based on two conditions:

---

[13] The security index in Thailand, Indonesia and Korea was lower than 1 before financial crisis in 1997.

(1) The country can export more and obtain more market share after devaluation.

(2) The profit from the export will be improved instead of being decreased after devaluation.

Suppose after devaluation the profit from export decreases and the country cannot export more, then this exercise is futile. As discussed above, it is impossible to overturn China foreign exchange system from outside. Should China purposefully follow Southeast Asian countries to devaluate RMB?

The major competitors of Chinese export are Indonesia, Thailand, Malaysia and other Asian countries. After passive devaluation, the economic situation was terrible in these countries.

(1) After the exchange rate devaluated significantly it was impossible to increase profits for Malaysia, Thailand and Indonesia and other Asian countries. Because they import the parts and the raw materials, and export the finished manufactured goods, after devaluation the cost to import the material and parts increased very quickly. After the goods were manufactured, there was very little or no profit, because the import costs are too high.

(2) The financial crisis generated a lot of trouble for the macroeconomic environment of these countries. Non-performing loan was very high and many banks could not perform well. This shocked many enterprises leaving them bankrupt. Then, the unemployment rate became very high.

(3) After the financial crisis the interest rate for banking loans increased very quickly. How could we imagine that people would borrow money and invest in Indonesia when the average interest rate was 62.79% in 1998?

(4) After the financial crisis high inflation occurred in some countries and this reduced the comparative advantage in exports that they just received from currency devaluation. For example the inflation rate in Indonesia in 1997 was 6.7%, but it increased to 57.6% in 1998. In the first half of the year in 1999, the inflation rate was 43.8%.

Table 3.11 International Trade of Asian Countries

(Billion USD)

	1997					1998				
	Export	Change (%)	Import	Change (%)	Balance of Trade	Export	Change (%)	Import	Change (%)	Balance of Trade
Japan	420.9	5.3	338.7	–3.1	82.2	388	–7.8	280.6	–17.2	107.4
Korea	136.2	2.4	144.6	–3.8	–8.4	132.3	–2.2	93.3	–35.5	39
Hong Kong	186.7	5	207.1	5.2	–20.4	172.8	–7.4	183.2	–11.5	10.4
China	182.7	4.2	142.4	2.5	40.3	183.8	0.5	140.2	–1.5	43.6
Philippines	25.2	20.9	35.9	10.8	–10.7	29.5	16.9	29.7	18.8	–0.2
Thailand	55.7	22.8	60.3	–12.5	–4.6	52.9	–7.1	40.6	–32.6	12.3
Malaysia	78.9	3.3	79.1	–1	–0.2	73.4	–7.3	58.5	26.1	14.9
Singapore	125	–0.7	132.5	0.9	–7.5	109.9	–12.2	101.6	–23.3	8.3
Indonesia	53.4	0	41.6	–2.9	11.8	48.8	–8.5	28.2	–32.3	20.6
Taiwan	122.1	5.3	114.4	11.8	7.7	110.6	–9.4	104.7	–8.5	5.9

Data sources: Jiang Bingkun, "Asian Financial Crisis and Taiwan's Economy", 1999.

In Asian countries where the exchange rate was devaluated, most of these countries could not increase their exports. After the financial crisis the Korean exports decreased by 2.2% in 1998, Thailand decreased by 7.1%, Malaysia decreased by 7.3%, Indonesia decreased by 8.5%, and Singapore decreased by 12.1%. In the first half of the year in 1999, Korean exports decreased continuously by 1.1%, Indonesia decreased by 10.6%, Thailand increased by 2.6%, and Malaysia increased by 8.6%.

Because of the financial crisis, many Asian countries encountered serious financial problems. In order to pay back the loan, and re-build the necessary foreign currency reserves, they must try every way that they can to obtain hard currency. Then, they have to sell the product in storage, at a low price. In the short term, such a country has already lost the capacity to compete internationally. It requires a huge amount of capital and takes quite a long period of time to let the banking system work normally.

There are two necessary conditions for active devaluation of RMB:

(1) Increase exports and the GDP growth rate and generate more jobs.

(2) Never generate credit crisis for their financial system.

Because competition is going at a different level at the international market, we must study the structure of exports and comparative advantage of the Chinese product in the international market.

The Chinese's exported products could be categorized into three groups according to their degree of labor intensivness. Group one includes some animal products, agricultural products, shoes, toys, china, and some other products. The total amount of these exports is 27% of the total value of Chinese exports.

Table 3.12 Labor Cost in Asian Countries

	Labor Wage Rate (1996)	Relative Wage Rate (%)	Exchange Rate (1997.7)	Exchange Rate (1999.5)	Labor Wage Rate (1999)	Relative Wage Rate (%)
China	26.9	100	8.2	8.2	26.9	100
Indonesia	40.5	151	2432	8030	12.27	45.6
Thailand	92.5	344	25.9	37.1	64.58	240.1
Malaysia	98.3	365	2.52	3.8	65.19	242.3
Philippines	55.2	205	26.37	37.9	38.41	142.8
Korea	318.5	1184	887.8	1188	238.02	884.8
Taiwan	311.9	1159	27.8	32.7	265.16	985.7

Data sources: Cai Qingshan, "Effects of Asian Financial Crisis on China Exports", International Economic Research, Vol. 4, 1998 and the results of calculation.

This group of Chinese products has absolute comparative advantage in the international market. For example, the Chinese export of shoes was 22 times that of other Asian countries in 1997. Almost 85% of Christmas decorations items in the United States in 1997 were made in China because the labor cost per unit of export over there is lower than most countries in the world.

Column 1 in Table 3.12 gives the labor cost per week in some Asian countries in 1996. We use China's labor wage as a basis to calculate the relative wage ratio for other countries in Column 2. From the Table we can see that before the financial crisis the labor wage level in Thailand, Malaysia and Korea was much higher than China. In Korea and Taiwan, the labor cost is more than 10 times higher than that of Mainland China. Even in Indonesia, the labor cost is 51% higher than China. The labor wage rate in India, Pakistan, and Bangladesh is lower than China, but the labor productivity in South Asia is much lower than the township village enterprises and the joint venture in China's coastal area. In order to improve the labor productivity, it will take time to train and educate workers. Also it is not very easy for India and South Asian countries to develop a network to sell their product with low cost. Therefore, in the first group of labor intensive products, China has quite a strong comparative advantage.

The third and fourth column in Table 3.13 provides the exchange rate before and after the financial crisis. According to the exchange rate of May 1999, we calculate the labor wages and list them in column five. The comparative relative labor ratio is listed in the column in the far right. From the table we can see that after the devaluation in Thailand, Malaysia, Taiwan, Korea the labor costs are still higher than that of China's. Because of serious currency devaluation, the labor costs in Indonesia are lower than China. However, in Indonesia the inflation rate in 1998 was as high as 57.6%. The price level increased very quickly and erased the advantage of currency devaluation for export industry. Therefore, for labor intensive products in this category, China's comparative advantage is still very strong. Currently the first group of labor intensive product from China already occupies a large percentage of the world market. The major problem to obtain more market share for Chinese labor intensive products is a non-tariff barrier, for example the quotas of the Multi-fiber Arrangement (MFA) from the United States. Even if China devaluates its currency it still cannot increase exports for this product. Therefore, if China devaluates its currency 10%, the total revenue from this product will decrease by 10%.

The second group of products, for example, textile, chemical products, plastic products, paper products etc. also has a high labor-intensive degree. They are around 38.4% of total exports for China. In this group, China's major competitors are Thailand, Philippines, Indonesia, Malaysia, and some Latin American and East European countries. Unfortunately, most of these countries encountered some serious economic problems and their export ability decreased. Currently only Thailand and Malaysia economies have started to recover. However, the total exports of Thailand and Malaysian are still lower than the level in 1997. Indonesia has a long way to go before recovering the competitive power. Therefore, for the second group it is not necessary to ask RMB to devaluate.

The third group of products (almost 35% of total export in China) includes steel products, mechanical products, vehicles, electronic, and shipbuilding industry etc. After the financial crisis the Chinese product faced heavy pressure from Taiwan, Korea and Singapore. For example, after Korea devaluated, the steel products made in Korea were 20% cheaper than the same product made in China. From January to April 1998, the export of steel product from Korea to Mainland China increased by 40%. If smuggling of steel products were included the figure would be larger. The competitive power of China's product in this category has decreased and this made many steel companies in China turn from profitable to unprofitable enterprises. Also, the shipbuilding industry in Korea is booming now with many new contracts. This means that China's shipbuilding industry will have a very tough time during the next few years. If Chinese currency devalues, of course, they can increase competitive power and gain part of the market. If the Chinese currency devalues, competitive power in the third category might increase, but China will lose in the first two categories.

In addition, 50% of China's imports are used to produce goods for the export industry. If the exchange rate is devalued it will increase the cost of imports. In addition, because in the current year China is meant to pay back the $18 billion U.S. short-term loan, the devaluation of currency will increase the cost to pay back the loan. Also, the devaluation of RMB might generate a big shock to Hong Kong's economy and is not good for the stability of the Hong Kong dollar. So the benefit of currency devaluation is much less than its cost. When all the above reasons are considered, by initiative it is not recommended to devaluate China's currency at this time.

4.2 Two Pressures on China's Exchange Rates

Because the inflation rate in China was higher than in the United States from 1994 to 1996 the RMB had some pressure to devaluate. However, because of the huge amount of foreign capital inflow into China, this puts pressure on RMB to increase the exchange rate. Two effects co-exist together (devaluate and invaluate) which serve as a basis for RMB to maintain a stable exchange rate.

After 1997, China's inflation rate decreased significantly and this caused RMB to increase in value. Meanwhile the capital inflow to China decreased significantly and this generated pressure to devaluate RMB. Therefore there are two other effects occurring simultaneously – increase and decrease of the exchange rate. Therefore there is no significant pressure to adjust the exchange rate currently.

4.3 Shrinking Asian Market Reduces China's Export

Shrinking market in Eastern Asia is the major reason for decrease in China's export. Because of the financial crisis, most Asian countries have a very tough time with their economy. In order to re-build the necessary foreign currency reservation, many Asian countries must cut their imports. So the external market for China is shrinking. This is a fact. Even if China devaluates its currency, in the short term China cannot recover to export products to some Asian countries.

Chinese exports to Japan represent 19.14% of total exports of China in 1996. Korea's is 3.52%, Indonesia 1%, and Thailand 1.3%, Malaysia 1.06%. In May 1997, China's exports to Japan increased by 10.6% compared to one year before, but in the same period in May 1998, exports to Japan decreased by 5.7%. Also, China's exports to most Asian countries decreased by 19%. In 1998, the exports to Korea from China decreased by 35.5%, to Thailand decreased by 32.6%, to Malaysia decreased by 26.1%, to Indonesia decreased by 32.3%, to Japan decreased by 17.2%. In the first half of the year in 1999, Korea and Thailand increased their imports a little bit. Other Asian countries have continuously decreased their imports. Even if China's currency was devalued, it is hopeless to say that Asian countries will buy more Chinese products. Therefore, exports in China really have a tough time in 1999.

4.4 When Should China Adjust Their Exchange Rate?

The shock to Asian countries occurring from the financial crisis is very serious. The job to recover the financial sector, trade, and production sector is very tough and it will take time to recover the economy. If we talk about when China should adjust their exchange rate, the best answer is to wait and see what happens to their neighbors and competitors. If other Asian countries recover their competitive power for exports, of course at that time it will generate pressure on the second group of Chinese products for export. Then we must very seriously consider China's adjusting its exchange rate in order to achieve a comparative advantage for the exports.

5.   NON-PERFORMING LOANS IN BANKING SECTOR

The non-performing loan in the banking system is a major problem for maintaining stability in China's economy. As we discussed before, according to the current economic structure in China, in general, it is impossible to have a financial crisis due to the impact from outside. The real problem is the question on the inside of China's financial system. Especially, if the stock market bubbles generate new non-performing loans to the banking system, it may disturb the stability of China's financial system.

5.1 The Bubble Economy in China

In general the bubble economy in China is not very serious. The history of the stock market and real asset market is short. Compared to the aggregate size of the economy, the sizes of these markets are not very large, even if there is some economic bubble. During the last few years, the Chinese government regulated the stock market and the real asset market and the bubbles cannot significantly disturb the stability of the economy.

Until 1998, the stock market size was only 12.6% of the GDP in China. The total value of stocks which are exchanged at the market is only around 3.8% of the GDP. The GDP of mainland China is six times higher than that

Table 3.13 International Stock Market

	GDP		Stock Market Capitalization		Growth Market Capitalization		Growth in Value Traded	
1	U.S	7434	U.S	8484	Indonesia	133474	Indonesia	1071300
2	Japan	5149	Japan	3088	Russia	16987	Turkey	31927
3	Germany	2365	U.K	1740	Poland	3679	Bangladesh	11933
4	France	1534	Germany	670	Argentina	2841	Morocco	5300
5	U.K	1152	France	591	Philippines	2636	Tunisia	4583
6	Italy	1141	Canada	486	Morocco	2338	Malaysia	4433
7	China	906	Hong Kong	449	Thailand	1720	Namibia	3700
8	Brazil	710	Switzerland	402	Ghana	1679	Pakistan	3637
9	Canada	570	Netherlands	379	Namibia	1589	Poland	3216
10	Spain	563	Australia	312	Malaysia	1558	Egypt	1902
11	Korea	483	Malaysia	307	Peru	1379	Greece	1778
12	Netherlands	403	Taiwan	274	Colombia	1265	Denmark	1712
13	Australia	368	Italy	258	Mexico	1173	Argentina	1646
14	India	358	Sweden	247	Bangladesh	1024	Colombia	1600
15	Russia	356	Spain	243	Iran	998	Ghana	1600
16	Mexico	342	South Africa	242	Hungary	838	Chile	1582
17	Switzerland	314	Brazil	217	Turkey	832	Philippines	1574
18	Argentina	295	Singapore	150	Honduras	745	India	1523
19	Taiwan	275	Korea	139	Singapore	738	China	1432
20	Belgium	269	India	123	Paraguay	733	Hungary	1303
21	Austria	227	Belgium	120	Hong Kong	731	Costa Rica	1300
22	Sweden	227	China	114	India	619	Peru	1164
23	Indonesia	213	Mexico	107	Uruguay	565	Sri Lanka	1118
24	Thailand	178	Thailand	100	Egypt	559	Brazil	1067
25	Turkey	178	Indonesia	91	Tunisia	544	Zimbabwe	1009
26	Denmark	169	Philippines	81	China	523	Nigeria	929
27	Hong Kong	153	Denmark	72	Taiwan	463	Thailand	858
28	Norway	151	Chile	63	Swaziland	453	Venezuela	761
29	Saudi Arabia	137	Finland	63	Pakistan	443	Netherlands	759
30	South Africa	133	Norway	57	Greece	442	Trinidad	723

Data sources: Economists, "World Figures", 1999.

of Hong Kong, but the total value of floating stock (the stock that can be exchanged) is only 10% in the Hong Kong market. In 1998 total number of companies in the stock market were only 740 and they had around 1000 stock. The total value of stock was $113.75 billion U.S. dollars. In 1996, the stock was 3.3% of the total banking deposit savings. It is ranked 22nd in the world. From 1987 to 1996 during this ten years, the total value of China's stock market increased by 523%. The growth rate is ranked 26th in the world. The growth rate of the value of the stock exchange is ranked 19th in the world. From the Table 3.13 we can see the growth rate of the aggregated value of the stock market in some countries is very high for example in Indonesia, Russia, Thailand, Malaysia etc. All these countries meet the financial crisis. Until May 1999, considering the size of the stock market or the growth rate of the stock market in China we cannot conclude that the bubble economy is very serious. Due to the length of the paper we will not be able to discuss the bubble economy in the real asset sector in China, except the Shanghai and Shenzheng areas. The bubble economy in the real asset sector is not very serious.[14]

5.2 Non-Performing Loan in China's Banking System

How much is the non-performing loan in China's banking system? Could these non-performing loans pull China's economy into the financial crisis or the economic deliberation as in Japan?

According to the Xu (1999), the total value of non-performing loan in the Chinese commercial banks is around 28% of the total loans of the banks. Some scholars estimate that the non-performing loan is over 1000 billion yuan in 1997 and grows at 50–80 billion yuan annually. Malay Lunch concluded that because the net assets of the four major commercial banks are lower than the non-performing loan, they are already technically bankrupt. However, according to the President of China People's Bank, Mr. Dai Xianglong, the bad loan in the state commercial bank is only 2.9% of the

---

[14]For more detail please see Tzong-shian Yu, Dianqing Xu and Jinli Wang, "Bubble Economy and Financial Crisis", People's University Press, 2000.

total loan by the end of 1998. The amount of the non-performing loan is only 5% of the total.[15] There are significant discrepancies between the estimations.

One key point is that the definition of the terms is totally different. Malay Lunch headquartered in New York uses the definition most commonly used in the international market. They categorize the banking assets into a total of five categories – Normal, Watch, Substandard, Doubtful loan, and Loss. Non-performing loan includes three categories namely doubtful, substandard and losses. But China uses a different definition. They categorize loans into three categories: Overdue loan, Doubtful loan, and Loan losses. The standard used at the international financial market considers the financial situation of the loan, but China categorizes the loan only according to the time schedule for payback of the principle and interest. According to the Financial Minister in China in 1993, six months after the maturity of the loan, if the enterprise cannot be paid back, it is an overdue loan. If the overdue loan goes beyond two years, then it is a doubtful loan. Only if the borrower dies, disappears, goes bankrupt, or for any other unfortunate reason makes it absolutely impossible to pay back the loan, then the central bank categorizes this loan as loan losses. Only if they obtain permission from the State Council, then the bank can erase the loan as loan losses. Mr. Dai Xianglong's data is based on the loan losses. The data from Mr. Xu includes the all three categories of non-performing loan. The different definitions explain why the discrepancy is so significant for non-performing loans.

According to the official estimation, non-performing loans in China are around 20% to 25% and among this data the loan losses are around 6-8%. The Chinese government is trying to recategorize the non-performing loans according to international standards. In 1997, the Chinese government tried to do that in Guangdong province, but even though the Chinese government asked many people to assist and spent a lot of money, the result was unsatisfactory. In many cases it is very difficult to tell who owes the non-performing loan, the SOE or the government. It may be owned by the local government or owned by the state. This makes it very difficult to recategorize

---

[15] See Dai Xianglong, People's Daily, June 26, 1999.

the non-performing loan. However all the experts and the economists who were involved in the recategorization raised the point that the non-performing loan in the financial sector is much more serious than the data published by the government.

Table 3.14 Non-Performing Loans in Asia

	Indonesia	Malaysia	Philippines	Korea	Thailand
Non-Performing Loan Ratio(%)	30~35	15~25	8~10	25~30	25~30
Debt/GDP	24	36	–	9	4
New Debt/GDP	43	56	–	39	34

Data sources: J. P Morgan, 1999.

Table 3.14 shows the situations on non-performing loans in some Asian countries. According to the Asian development bank, the non-performing loan in most Asian countries is very serious. For example the non-performing loan in Bangladesh is around 60% of the total loans. Large amounts of non-performing loans will destroy the liquidity of the banking system and put serious limitations on economic development. In general we can come to the conclusion, the larger the non-performing loan, the larger the danger for the financial system, and the larger the shock of the financial crisis for the country.

5.3 Non-Performing Loan and SOE Reform

Why is the overdue loan and the doubtful loan in China's system is much higher than the loan losses? This is related to the ownership of the SOE. The SOE use almost 80% of the banking loans in China and generated most of the non-performing loans. Because the SOE and the bank belong to the same owner, when the SOE needs money of course they will ask for the money directly from the state. When the SOE get permission from the government officials, in general it is not necessary to ask the bank to do a feasibility analysis on the project. As we know more than two thirds of

SOEs lose profit in China. For the profit-losing enterprises, if they cannot pay wages and welfare to their employees, why do they need to pay back the loan on time? If the bank asks the SOEs to pay back the loan they will go to the government, and ask for a new loan, therefore, the overdue loan problems become more and more serious.

The loan owned by SOE is a trap for banks. SOEs borrow from the bank and lose profit; if the bank does not provide a new loan then the SOE cannot operate due to shortage of working capital and cannot pay wages to their employees. This is trouble for the government to maintain stability of the society. The officials have to step in and order the banks to issue a new loan to SOE. In many cases, it is hopeless for the SOE to pay back the loan. When the banks give the SOE a new loan they cannot forecast that the SOE will pay back in time because the SOE continuously loses profit. There are only around 20% of SOEs with good credit to pay back the loan. This is a very bad cycle. The SOE borrows more, and there are more and more non-performing loans.

According to regulations, every year the bank should use their profit to get rid of some of the dead loan. However, there is no incentive in China's banking system to do that. If the banks do not get rid of the non-performing loan they can keep a high profit rate. This high profit rate is not only for the achievement of the manager, but the bank can use the profit to increase the bonus and other things pertaining to the welfare of the employees in the bank. No wonder the bank manager prefers to let the non-performing loan exist. The non-performing loan in China's banking system is huge, but the amount that people categorize into losing loans is not very large.

Because of huge amounts of non-performing loans, the asset ratio of China's bank is quite low. If the bank is to use their assets to get rid of the non-performing loan the capital ratio in the bank will continually decrease. The financial system in China is very weak. In 1996 the capital assets ratio in the four large commercial banks was only 3%. It is much lower than the international standard of 8%. After 1997, the ratio improved slightly.

From Table 3.15 we can see that in July 1997 the capital asset owned by the bank was 317 billions yuan in Chinese commercial bank. The total loan is 6620 billions yuan. The bank capital asset is only 4.8% of the total loan. In 1999, the Financial Ministry issued 270 billions yuan special treasury bills and used it to increase the capital asset ratio in the banking system. After the injection of funding the capital asset ratio in four commercial banks it was close to 8% in the later part of 1999.

Table 3.15 Balance Sheet of China's Commercial Banks

(October, 1997)   (Billion Yuan)

Asset		Liability	
Asset Abroad	453	Liabilities Abroad	415
Reserve Funds	1449	Liabilities to Non-Financial Sectors	6876
National Debt	8	Liabilities to Central Bank	1296
Loan to Government	138	Liabilities to Non-monetary Institutions	137
Loans to Others	6433	Bonds	18
Loans to Non-Monetary Sectors	187	Capital	317
		Other Liabilities	−390
Total	8669		8669

Data sources: Statistical Quarterly Report, China People's Bank, 1997.

5.4 The Amount of Dead Loans and an Estimation of the Assets of SOEs

How much is the dead loan in non-performing loans? The key answer to this question is how to estimate the assets of the SOEs? The SOE that has no capacity to pay back the loan can be classified into two categories:

(1) Some SOEs are not able to pay back the loan in the short term but after an adjustment, they can produce an increased profit and pay back the loan.

(2) Other SOEs are not able to pay back the loan at all. These SOEs should go into bankruptcy.

However, these enterprises still have many fixed assets, which could be sold to retrieve some money for the loan. The question is how to evaluate the real assets owned by SOEs. This question has not been solved. If the enterprises in Western countries go bankrupt, it is not very difficult to auction the assets. Because the market economy is very strong, the market will provide the price for the assets. There is always someone who will be willing to buy the asset if the price decreases to a certain level. The bank will get back part of the loan through the liquidation process. After bankruptcy, the manager and the employee can obtain unemployment insurance and find a new job themselves in the labor market. However, it is very difficult for Chinese banks to send an SOE into bankruptcy like the Western bank. First of all it is very difficult to determine the price of the asset because there is no market for them. Secondly, it is very difficult to find buyers because the SOE is usually very large and has many social burdens. Even selling the assets to a foreign company is difficult. Thirdly, it is very difficult for local governments to provide jobs for the unemployed workers from the SOE that is bankrupt. Therefore, many SOEs who are in such a situation cannot pay back the loan but they cannot declare bankruptcy either. Of course, the loan they owe to the bank can only be categorized as a non-performing loan, but neither can it be called a "dead" loan. Because we cannot obtain accurate data for the value of the assets, how can we make a judgement regarding the amount of money the bank will receive back if the SOE goes bankrupt?

Under the central planing system, the SOE received all funding from the government, and at the same time they hand in all the profit to the government. At the beginning of the reform in 1978, the state provided 77.69% of funding for fixed asset investment in SOE. The rest came from the enterprises themselves. In 1983, China tried to change the capital funding system and asked SOEs to get loans from the banks. This was an important reform but the resistance to the reform was very serious. After three years, most enterprises started to change to the new system, and got money from the bank instead of from the government. In 1996, of all the funding of the SOEs, only 6.09% came from the government. The banking loan is around 22.5% and the rest comes from SOE re-investment and foreign investment. In only a few years, the debt owed by SOE became huge. From this case, we can understand that the losing of profit is very serious for SOEs. However, before the government reformed the financial system, the SOEs had already received a huge investment from the state within the last thirty years. The total value of the fixed assets owned by SOEs is huge. For many enterprises, it is not true to simply estimate the assets are less than the debt.

5.5 Different Shocks of Two Kinds of Non-Performing Loan

During the financial crisis, the financial system could not operate when the non-performing loans reached 24% in Korea. The total amount of non-performing loans in China's banking system is more serious than Korea's before the financial crisis. Why does the Chinese financial system work and we are not able to say that it will collapse in the very near future?

The key to this question is that the non-performing loans in China are generated by the profit losses of the SOEs and they are not the result of a bubble economy. Most of the non-performing loans in southeastern countries were the product of the burst of bubble economy. The collapse of the real asset market and stock market can generate huge amounts of non-performing loans in a very short period of time. It will seriously affect people's confidence in the banking system, and will interfere with the normal operation of the banking system.

However, the bad loans generated by the SOEs actually accrue over a long period of time and all questions and concerns have already been addressed. Considering that these loans have not undermined the confidence of the people to date, we cannot say that this will occur in the near future either. Of course such an accumulated non-performing loan will generate big trouble for the operation of the financial system, but it cannot collapse the financial system like the bubble economy.

So we can say till today, the non-performing loan in China's banking system is a "dead tiger". If there is a huge amount of capital being deposited into the bank and the deposit is greater than the amount of withdrawal, then the bank will not have a shortage of working capital. Therefore, it is not really dangerous. However, suppose some day the capital outflow from the bank is greater than the money being deposited into the bank, plus the non-performing loan, the "dead tiger" could become a "real tiger". Stabilizing the financial system is the most important strategic test for China currently.

5.6 Can the Stock Market help China's SOEs or Stimulate the Domestic Market?

A leading article on the *People's Daily* in June 15, 1999 pointed out that China should speed up the development of the stock market in order to stimulate the economy. Immediately, the Chinese stock market began booming. The Shanghai stock index increased from 1045 to 1745 points in only two months. The scale and speed of this expansion was a historical record in China. The stock market has become a very hot point after a long period of depression. One group of economists believes that this would be helpful to provide an incentive to national consumption and investment, and would finally stimulate the economy. In addition, SOE will collect more funding after they issued new stocks. This will be helpful for the reform of the SOE. However, this is not true according to the Chinese situation.

The major problem of SOEs is the shortage of competitive power in the market. Many SOEs do not know where the market for their products is because the style and quality does not meet the requests of the consumers. Without good cooperative governance and qualified managers, inserting more funds into SOE does not help. Because the stock market in China is still at a very preliminary stage the value of the stock has almost no relation with the performance of the enterprise. Therefore, the increase of the stock price cannot solve the problems of SOEs in a short period of time, but will rather damage seriously the stability of the financial system in China.

During this Asian financial crisis, even though there are many shortcomings in the economic system, China is still able to keep the exchange rate and the financial system stable. If huge amounts of capital flow continuously into the banks, and people's deposits are larger than their withdrawals, the banking system will not experience a shortage of funding. In this case, of course, the banking system can work. Even now there are huge amounts of non-performing loans in the banking system, because there were many new deposits entering the bank over the last few years, this funding allows the bank to handle the problem easily, as it is still able to hand out loans. As most people in China have very little choice but to deposit their money into the banks, among other forms of investment, deposit savings always occupies a major portion. Table 3.16 and 3.17 show the continuous increase of banking deposit during last few years. In 1998, the resident deposits increased 713 billion yuan, around 15.4 percent of the total deposits. The huge amount of new deposits entering the banks ensures the banks are able to function.

Table 3.16 Banking Deposit in China

(Billion Yuan)

	1994	1995	1996	1997	1998
Total Deposit	4050.2	5388.2	6859.5	8239.0	9569.7
Enterprise Deposit	1327.9	1732.3	2245.0	2865.6	3248.6
Government Deposit	86.2	100.5	127.4	157.2	218.8
Institution Deposit	85.7	91.7	96.8	85.8	128.5
Resident Deposit	2151.8	2966.2	3852.0	4627.9	5340.8
Rural Deposit	106.3	119.6	136.4	153.3	174.8

Data sources: Statistical Yearbook of China, 1999, p. 68.

Table 3.17 Changes in the Financial Institutions

	Change in Deposit				Change in Deposit (%)			
	1995	1996	1997	1998	1995	1996	1997	1998
Total Deposit	1338.0	1471.3	1379.5	1330.7	33.00%	27.30%	20.10%	16.20%
Deposit of Enterprises	404.4	512.7	620.6	383.0	30.50%	29.60%	27.60%	13.40%
Government Deposit	14.3	26.9	29.8	61.6	16.60%	26.80%	23.40%	39.20%
Institution Deposit	6.0	5.1	−11.0	42.7	7.00%	5.60%	−11.40%	49.80%
Resident Deposit	814.4	885.8	775.9	712.9	37.80%	29.90%	20.10%	15.40%
Rural Deposit	13.3	16.8	16.9	21.5	12.50%	14.00%	12.40%	14.00%

Data sources: Calculation based on Table 3.16.

However, if the outflow from the banks becomes larger than the inflow into them, this, along with the new non-performing loans, will pose a very serious problem for the banking system. Suppose **one-day** a large amount of funding flows out of the bank and into the stock market. This will of course weaken the banks' ability to operate normally. According to a report, in June 25, 1999, the total value of exchange in the stock market was 83 billion yuan. In Shanghai and the Shenzheng stock market during June 14-18, there was an increase of 1.2 million new accounts. In only two days — June 15 and 16, 25 billion yuan was withdrawn from the banks in Shanghai where there are 2.5 million people who became very active in the stock market. In other cities, thousands of people used their mortgages and borrowed money from the bank to buy stock. The savings deposit usually yield an increase of 6 billion yuan in Beijing every month, but in June it only increased by 0.6 billion yuan, a decrease of almost 90 percent.[16] In many commercial banks, the deposit savings decreased, and the amount withdrawn was greater than that deposited. Because there are not any hotpoints for consumers, we can determine that the money outflow from the bank, for the most part, enters the stock market. Now, however, the new deposits are decreasing, as the money goes into the stock market instead of the bank. Thus the banks are not receiving enough funding from household deposits - this is a very dangerous situation for the activity of the banks.

One suggestion is that China should further develop the stock market and allow SOEs to enter the stock market freely, and let the capital of the banking system directly operate the stock. Although this may appear to be a good idea in many other market economies, the Chinese situation is totally different, making this a very dangerous idea.

To begin with, China is still in the transition process from a central planing system to a market economy. The government still plays an important role in the economy. It is estimated that on the stock market almost 65–70 percent of the money comes from the government.[17] During the last few years, some officials used the funding for basic public construction and local tax to play stocks. In addition, officials and SOE managers have also used some of the banking loans to play stocks. Of course, any gains will go into their own pocket, but if they lose, they lose only the government's money. Their losses, in the end, become the bad loans of the bank. It has been forecasted that in early June 1999, the local government and the state

---

[16]See Zheng Jinping, *Economic Highlight*, No. 340, 1999.

[17]See Yang Yiyong, "Over-speculations in China's Stock Market", *Economic Highlight*, No. 261, 1998.

enterprises had used more than 180 to 200 billion yuan in the stock market. Of course, such corruption on behalf of officials should be punished; however, the non-performing loans may continually increase in the banking system. We know that the non-performing loans are already very dangerous to the banking system, if the number of non-performing loans increase, the baking system in China may collapse very soon.

Secondly, rant seeking is a very popular phenomenon in China's transition process. As pointed out by the Chinese government, in 1998, there were over 2.11 million officials punished, among these cases around 80 percent for their corruption, and this were estimated as only 10 percent of the total cases of corruption.[18] In such a situation, if the public funding and the SOEs are allowed to play in the stock market, it is very difficult to forecast what will happen next. Obviously, this is a very dangerous situation, and it presents very serious problems for the Chinese economy.

6.   REQUIREMENTS FOR FIGHTING THE FINANCIAL CRISIS

6.1 Rules of the Game for International Financial Markets

The absence of effective rules causes turmoil in the international financial market. The international monetary market is a current example of market failure due to the lack of sufficient competitive markets and of rules. Not only is there a lack of effective rules for the game, but their absence precludes the presence of an agent to handle the game and, moreover, even a means of determining who that agent should be. Without such a leader, we can not get any verdict telling us that this crisis in the international financial market is short-term.

According to economic theory, the necessary conditions for a general equilibrium is the convexity of the production and the consumption set.

---

[18] According to the report by Mr. Wei Jianxing in June 9, 1999, the number of corruption cases increased continually during last few years. See *Zhengming*, No. 7, 1999, p. 13 for more detail.

Without convexity, it is impossible to have Pareto improvement through market competition. Usually, the production function with diminishing return to scale is the key to this convexity. In order to have convexity, it is important to have the number of players large enough if some of them have production functions with increasing returns to scale.[19] However, current international financial markets cannot meet above basic assumptions for a perfect competitive market.

To begin with, in the current international monetary market the number of players is limited and continually decreases due to mergers of international financial institutes. The economic size of some players in the international financial markets, especially the large hedge funds, is larger than many medium-sized countries. Because such a player can affect or even control prices, the international market is no longer a free market.

Secondly, the larger the financial institute, the stronger their capacity to avoid investment risks. The profit function of large international financial institutes may have increasing returns to scale. The current international monetary market has significant characteristics of a non-convex set.

Thirdly, asymmetrical information between hedge funds and the public is another problem. The lack of transparency of the hedge funds has allowed the appearance of some large hedge funds to distort the international market far from the free market system. This is being unfair to many small and medium sized countries.

Because there is no general equilibrium or optimum solution in the current international monetary market, it is not reasonable to hope that market competition can improve the efficiency of resource allocation in the international financial market. Therefore, market failure is the major cause of the current financial crisis.

The original idea of modern monetary innovation is to improve the efficiency of resource allocation, provide more information and avoid financial risk. However, attempts to avoid risks in the international financial market generate some kind of externality, which accumulates the risk. The welfare

---

[19]See Arrow, K.J. and Debreu, G., 1954, "Existence of an Equilibrium for a Competitive Economy", *Econometrica* 22, 265–90.

transfer happens not only between domestic classes, but also between countries. The transfer of welfare between countries causes serious risk in the international financial market. Furthermore, the development of a financial market in fact moves away from market competition. As the nominal yield in financial markets is much higher than any productive sector, the financial sector becomes the most important profit resource. Increasing amounts of capital shifts from production to financial activity, not only reducing real output but also generating high risk to society. The combination of the foreign exchange market, stock market, future market, and real asset market together, causes current international financial markets to provide much larger room to the speculators than any time before. The international monetary market may fluctuate as a self-enforcement and divergent process. It is impossible to stabilize the international financial market through market competition and the fluctuations on the market will become more enlarged.

Consequently, in order to recover free market mechanisms and to stabilize the international financial market we need both a new declaration of the game as well as some new agent who can supervise the game. The major idea of this new game, then, will be to limit the size of the players and limit the monopoly power of any international financial agent.

6.2 Improvement of the Management of the Capital Flow on the International Financial Market

Learning from the experiences of Thailand, Indonesia, Korea, Malaysia and other Asian countries, victims of the financial crisis in 1997, we see that many countries followed the same process: high speed economic development and the liberalization of the financial sector → larger capital inflow → the increase in the exchange rate → the decrease in exports → a lot of the foreign capital invested into real assets and other speculative sectors → a bubble in the real asset and stock market → imbalance in the economic structure → encountering shock from international speculation → the result: financial crisis. If we can break this chain, risking the fact that there is no guarantee that the country can avoid the shock of financial crisis, at least it is possible to increase the capacity of the country to fight this financial crisis. Sufficient capital is a necessary condition for the bubble economy. Without large foreign capital, even in a developing country where there is a bubble economy, the speed of the growth of the bubble cannot be very quick, nor can its size be very large. The foreign capital is like putting oil into fire, when the bubble economy is forming.

Of the foreign capital flowing into developing countries, the majority goes to newly industrialized countries that have high economic growth rates, as the financial capital can get higher rates of return there. Many statistics show us that there is a positive correlation between the speed of economic development and the inflow of foreign capital. That is to say that the more foreign capital that is achieved, the higher the economic growth rate. In countries with high economic growth rate, it is easy for entrepreneurs to find good investment projects with high economic profits. However, usually the shortage of funding is the major problem for such countries. The entrepreneurs and the countries' banks will try all the ways they can to find funding through domestic and international financial markets.

Foreign capital flowing into the real production sector is very advantageous for the country. The foreign capital merged with rich natural resources and cheap labor generates good economic revalue. It will increase their productive capacity and improve their technology, resulting in an increase of the competitive power of the country in the international market and increase foreign exchange reservation. In the developing countries, considering the limitations of the infrastructure, education, training of labor, market size, and cultural background etc., there is limited capacity for the society to absorb foreign capital. This capacity can only increase step by step with the development of the economy. If the amount of foreign capital exceeds the maximum capacity to absorb the capital in the developing country, of course such capital cannot be used with reasonable risk. It is very easy for foreign capital to enter these markets - the action is very simple because only in the stock and real asset market can the investor have such large capital gains in such a short period of time.

However, if the foreign capital flows into the stock market and real asset market, it can help the circulation of capital. While this is good, the foreign capital, which enters the stock and real asset markets, will increase speculation in these markets. As long as the size of the stock and real asset markets in developing countries is limited and they are still in shortage of management experience and the necessary regulations, if the door to these markets was opened, large amounts of foreign capital will flow into the stock and real asset market. It is very easy to generate an economic bubble.

Therefore, in order to fight the financial crisis, we should manage or cut the short-term foreign capital entering the stock and real asset markets in developing countries. If the size of the stock market is not large enough, the speculation of the short-term foreign capital is very dangerous, and thus we should detach the short-term speculative foreign capital from the long-term investment. In China, the government separates the domestic and foreign capital at the stock market. The foreign capital can only hold B shares in the stock market. In September 1998, the total value of B shares was only 2.1 billion U.S. dollars. This is only 0.4 percent of the GDP and less than 5 percent of the value of the total stock market.[20] The fact that foreign capital can only involve a small part of the stock in China is one of the reasons why China has been able to avoid the currency crisis to date.

6.3 The Tobin's Tax

The Tobin's Tax is an important and efficient way to depress the bubble economy in the developing countries. The objective of the Tobin's Tax is to decrease the speed of the transactions in the international financial market. Of course, the tax rate should be reasonable, and we must be careful to use the Tobin's Tax to fight the financial crisis. On one hand we should decrease the speed of financial speculation, on the other hand, we should not let a high tax rate upstage the regular operation of the stock market and international exchange market. If the Tobin's Tax rate is too small, it can not play an important role in fighting speculation in the international financial market. Currently, in order to stabilize the international financial market, we may need a relatively higher Tobin's tax rate. However, we should be able

---

[20] See Liu Guoguang, "Analysis and Forecast of China's Economy", Social Science Publishing House, 1999.

to fluctuate the tax rate, so that when the international financial market stabilizes, we can decrease the Tobin's tax rate. If we find that the Tobin's tax may hamper normal operation in the international financial market, we can of course stop the Tobin's tax for some period of time.

6.4 Speed of Reforming the State Owned Enterprises

Even in the short term, there is no reason to forecast that the Chinese economy will meet financial crisis very soon. However, if China cannot reform the SOEs, then the Chinese economy cannot avoid the heavy burden of profit-losing SOEs. The profit-losing SOEs will generate large amounts of non-performing loans in the banking system, and finally will turn down the financial system. China must take control or never let the financial sector transfuse blood to profit-losing SOE. The Chinese government must let the profit losing SOE go bankrupt step-by-step, and transfer the productive factor to the market economy.

The reform of SOE is a one-way path because very few of the laid off workers can return to the SOE. The total number of workers in SOEs continually decreased during the reform. However, the bankruptcy of SOE will increase unemployment. We must consider the tolerance of society. In 1997 the total of the unemployed was 9 million. In 1998, add 4.5 million for a total of 13.5 million. This almost equals the 19% of the total number of SOE employees. From the current situation we can estimate that the size of the unemployed could maintain at approximately 13 million. This 13 million is a dynamic number, as some people will flow in and some people will flow out. Because every year the non-state sector can only provide 5 million jobs, the total number of the unemployed must be under control. At the end of 1998, the total employees in SOE were 95 million workers. Suppose we plan to reduce the total number of workers in the SOEs to 50 million. This means every year we should reduce the number by 5 million – it would take 8 years to finish this project. Therefore, the SOE reform is a long-term job, and we cannot try to finish that in a short period of time. Of course if economic development speed is higher than what the society can provide jobs for, then we can let more SOE go bankrupt. If the economic situation is not very good and society cannot provide more jobs, then the speed of the reform of SOE should be slowed down a little.

According to the current situation, even the problem of reform of SOE is very serious, but still China can survive. Suppose in order to solve the problem of the SOE reform and destroy the financial system, then China would have a much more serious problem. The stability of the financial system should receive more attention. The stability in the financial market is very important to China's long-term economic development, and also important to Asia's economic recovery.

6.5 Moral Hazard

During the financial crisis, moral hazards in financial institutions were a very serious problem. It would seriously shock the economy if a large financial institution shuts down. Therefore, if the large financial institution encounters a crisis, the state may bail them out of this financial trouble. Under this forecasting the large financial institution would like to invest in high-risk areas. In Japan and Korea there are some world famous "Chaebol" which include banks and large enterprises. During the economic development process these large business groups exactly showed a very strong competitive power in the world market. But under the main banking system it is easy to have over-investment. And the bank has an over-loan problem because the bank owned stock of enterprises.

If the enterprise losses profit, the effect will spread to the bank. If the stock market collapses after the burst of the bubble economy, it will immediately hurt the bank's capacity of payment. Then the banking system may be very weak during the period when the bubble economy bursts. The managers of the enterprises were not worried about the merging or bankruptcy that followed because they knew only too clearly that, if the large enterprises get into trouble, it will hurt the main bank itself. Therefore, if these enterprises are closed to bankruptcy, they will ask the main bank for help. So the main bank must try everything to save these enterprises. The same logic applies if a large bank is in financial trouble, it will affect the financial stability of the country, and the central bank should do the same and bail out the main bank. Under this mechanism, many important warning signals for the banking system cannot be released. Normally, we see that everything is okay, but if we find some problem, it cannot be solved. So one important lesson from the financial crisis in Asia is we must follow the market economy's regulations. Japan delayed the reform, and tried all the ways it could to maintain the large bank and the large enterprises. This is why the Japanese economy could not recover after the bubble burst in 1990.

The moral hazard in the SOEs is very serious in China. The large amount of non-performing loan is the result of the moral hazard. If the Chinese government cannot stop the moral hazard of the SOEs and always try to save such financial institutions and SOE who is in big financial trouble, then the Chinese economy will face a big financial crisis very soon. In September 6, 1998, the Guangdong International Trust Investment Corporation (GITIC) went bankrupt. This bankruptcy caused a great deal of trouble for the central government as well as for the local government. Also, it reduced the opportunity of China to obtain a loan in the international market. However, this is a good beginning to reduce the moral hazard of the financial sector in China. GITIC is a company, which on behalf of Guangdong provincial government borrows money from abroad and invests in very wide areas. And due to the mistakes for investment and corruption, GITIC had a very high debt. They could not pay back the loan. The provincial government promised to give them financial support, but they could not transfer the local currency to hard currency. At that moment, the Chinese government has decided not to continue the financial support of GITIC and let it go into bankruptcy. Why can GITIC borrow such a huge foreign debt and continuously get new loans to pay back the old loans? Because many foreign banks believed the owner of GITIC was the provincial government and the boss of the Guangdong provincial government was the central government. They believed, according to the planning system, that if Guangdong experienced any financial trouble, then the central government would payback the loan. So therefore, the foreign banks did not worry about the risk of their loan. In general, they made three mistakes: (1) GITIC is only a commercial financial institution and totally different from the government. (2) The foreign bank did not do a feasibility analysis for their loan. (3) When they discovered that GITIC was having difficulties paying back the loan, they asked them to pay up immediately. They did not consider any other opportunity to let allow recapitalizing or get change of the debts to stock and give GITIC some more time to pay back the loan.

In this case, the central government only has two options. The first option is to pay back the loan for GITIC. Because the total debt for GITIC is $2–3 billion U.S., of course, the Chinese government would not have any problem paying back this loan. But if China does that, then the following problems will happen. There are many financial institutions with financial troubles and moral hazards. If the central government pays the debt for GITIC, they should pay for the many other financial institutes. The moral hazard would then induce endless troubles in China.

The second option is to follow the rule of the market economy and let GITIC take responsibility for there mistakes and go bankrupt. Of course, this is correct because it releases very clear information that China wants to follow the market economy in handling the relationship between government and financial institutions. The Chinese government should never guarantee the debt. This is a very good way to fight the bubble economy.

6.6 Open the Financial Market Step by Step

Because the international financial market is not a free competitive market any more, government intervention is necessary and important, especially, during the opening process of the financial market. The government must maintain effective control of the financial market. Sometimes, the Western government and the financial institutions complain that the developing countries do not open their financial sector enough, and that the transparency is not good enough in the developing country.

Opening the financial sector is not only good for international financial sectors but also provides a good chance for the international financial speculators. It cannot be opened too quickly. So opening the financial sector should go step by step.

Firstly, borrow money from the foreign country, then introduce foreign investment into the country, then introduce the foreign capital to have branches in the country, and meanwhile generate the new regulation for the country. After that it is time to open the stock market, the real asset market. When opening the financial market training enough qualified managers and generating rules of the game are most important. Because generating the regulations and training people really takes a long time, therefore, before finishing such a project, government intervention and regulation of the financial sector is necessary.

Currently the Chinese government still has a shortage of experience in supervising the financial sector. In some areas the government did not do a very good job, but in some other areas the government did too much. For example, currently, the government should have more regulations to stop illegal capital flow out of the economy, and generate more regulations against illegal operations of some financial institutions and generate rules to punish illegal operations. However, in some areas the government should speed up the process to open up the financial service sector to good international banking and financial institutions. This would introduce the competition mechanism. If China opens the door to the international financial sector, then the Chinese entrepreneur can learn by doing and avoid the financial crisis and meanwhile maintain a high economic growth rate.

References

Arrow, K.J. and Debreu, G, 1954, "Existence of an Equilibrium for a Competitive Economy", *Econometrica* 22, 265–90.

Cargill, T. Hutchison, M., and Ito, T. "Deposit Gurantees and the Burst of the Japanese Bubble Economy", *Contemporary Economic Policy*, 14:7, 1996.

Chang, Hsin, "The Chinese Economy in the Asian Financial Crisis: The Prospect of the Stability of RMB", Working paper of Harvard Institute for International Development, 1999.

Fan Gang, "Debt Ratio and Financial Crisis", *Economic Highlight*, Vol. 350, September 17, 1999.

Hamada, Koichi, "Bubble, Bursts and Bailouts: A Comparison of Three Episodes of Financial Crisis in Japan", in *The Structure of the Japanese Economy*, (ed.) Okabe, Macmillan, 1994.

Hayakawa, Shigenobu, eds. "Japanese Financial Markets", Cambridge, Woodhead Publishing Ltd. 1996.

Holz, Carsten, "China's Bad Loan Problem" Working paper, Hong Kong University of Science and Technology, Dec 5, 1998.

Jia Kang, "The Risk of Financial Deficit", *Economic Highlight*, August 6, 1999.

Kumar R. and B. Debroy, "The Asian Crisis: An Alternative View", Asian Development Bank, Economic Staff Paper, #59.

Konya, Fumiko, The Rise and Fall of the Bubble Economy: An Analysis of the Performance and Structure of the Japanese Stock Market", in *The Structure of the Japanese Economy*, (ed.) Okabe, Macmillan, 1994.

Merton Miller, "Alternative Strategies for Corporate Governance", in Wen and Xu edited "Reformability of China's State Sector", World Scientific, 1997.

Tobin, James, "Liquidity Preference as Behavior Toward Risk", *Review of Economic Studies*, 25, 1958.

Wu, Jinlian, "Strategic Reform of State Sector", Chinese Development Publishing House, 1999.

Wu Xiaoling, "International Balance of Payment and Foreign Exchange Policy in China", 1999.

Xu, Chongzheng, "Financial Risk in China", *Economic Information*, p. 14, July 1999.

Xu, Dianqing and Ling Li, "Crisis Management in Asian Countries", *Global Economic Review*, Vol. 27, No. 3, 1998.

Xu Dianqing and Li Rui, "Role of the State in Economic Development", Shanghai People's Press, 1999.

Yang Fan, "Fighting with Financial Crisis", China Economic Publishing House, 1999.

Yang Yiyong, "Forecast of the Employment Situation in 1999 and Some Policy Suggestions", in Liu Guoguang (ed.) *Analysis and Forecast of China's Economy*, Social Science Publishing House, 1999.

CHAPTER 4

KOREA

KOREA FINANCIAL CRISIS: THE CRISIS OF A DEVELOPMENT MODEL?

Jaymin Lee[1]

Yonsei University
Seoul 120-749
South Korea
E-mail: leejm@yonsei.ac.kr

1. INTRODUCTION

Korean financial crisis has drawn a worldwide attention. While the East Asian crisis at the end of the twentieth century took the world by surprise, Korean case has been particularly remarkable. Among the crisis-hit countries, Korea, as an early starter in industrialization, had bigger-sized economy, higher *per capita* income, and better macroeconomic fundamentals overall. Before the crisis broke out, Korea was regarded as hardly a place where such a thing could happen.

Korea has also provided a remarkable case of bounce back from the severe crisis. After contacting by 5.8 percent in 1998, Korean economy

---

[1] I am grateful to Cheng-Shu Wu and Teh-Ming Huo and other participants of the conference held in Taipei, January 22–23, 2000 for helpful comments. Remaining errors are mine.

grew about 10 percent in 1999, showing the fastest bounce back among the crisis-hit countries.

The fact that Korean crisis was such an unexpected one does not mean that it cannot be explained. From the beginning, there have been basically two views about the causes of the East Asian crisis. One is that the crisis is a 'structural' one, representing the failure of development model: held by IMF, Korean government, and the majority of neoclassical economists, in and out of Korea. The other represented by Radelet and Sachs (1998), claims that the crisis is short-run panic on a basically sound economy.[2]

This paper will argue that the origins of the crisis are indeed Korea's 'neo-mercantilist' development model. But the neo-mercantilist development model did not cause the crisis *per se* but as a problem of transition there from to a more liberal regime, including proper sequencing in market opening.

The paper will then examine the post-crisis recovery and reform. It will show that, while Korea has managed the short run recovery quite well, the reform so far falls short of making the recovery sustainable: it has not solved the longer run structural problem underlying the crisis. Chapter two will deal with the causes of the crisis, and chapter three the recovery and reform procedures after the crisis broke out. Chapter four will conclude.

2.   THE CAUSES OF THE CRISIS

2.1 Macroeconomic Fundamentals and Crisis

At the onset of the crisis, the macroeconomic fundamentals of Korea appeared to be sound, as shown in Table 4.1. The economy was growing fast, and in 1997, was expected to grow more than six percent. The gross saving rate remained high, well above 30 percent. Throughout the 1990s,

---

[2] For a typical structuralist view of neoclassical economists, see Krugman (1998), and Borensztein Lee (1998). The 'short run panic' view is joined by 'revisionist' development economists, defending as they do the neo-mercantilist development model (see Wade, 1998).

government budget was close to being in balance, and it was not especially deteriorating just before the outbreak of the crisis.

Table 4.1 Macroeconomic Indicators

(Unit: Percent)

	Real GDP Growth Rate	CPI Inflation Rate	Current Account GDP	Fiscal Surplus[1] GDP	Gross Saving Rate
1966	12.2	10.3	−2.8	−	16.6
1967	5.9	12	−4.5	−	15.4
1968	11.3	10.7	−8.5	−	18.2
1969	13.8	11.8	−8.3	−	21.4
1970	8.8	16.3	−7.7	−	18
1971	9.3	13.2	−8.9	0.02	16
1972	5.4	11.7	−3.5	−2.24	17.2
1973	13.5	3.3	−2.3	−0.03	22.6
1974	8.3	24.7	−10.8	−1.88	20.3
1975	7.1	24.9	−9	−2.09	18.2
1976	12.9	15.4	−1.1	−2.9	24.3
1977	10.1	10.2	0.03	−2.6	27.6
1978	9.7	14.4	−2.1	−2.5	29.7
1979	7.6	18.2	−6.7	−1.4	28.4
1980	−2.2	28.8	−8.8	−3.2	23.2
1981	6.7	21.5	−7	−4.6	22.9
1982	7.3	7.1	−3.7	−4.3	24.4
1983	11.8	3.4	−2	−1.5	27.6
1984	9.4	2.3	−1.6	−1.3	29.9
1985	6.9	2.4	−1	−1	29.8
1986	11.6	2.7	4.4	−0.1	33.7
1987	12	3	7.6	0.2	37.3
1988	11.3	7.1	7.9	1.3	39.3
1989	6.4	5.7	2.3	−0.01	36.2
1990	9.5	8.6	−0.9	−0.9	37.5
1991	9.2	9.3	−2.8	−1.9	37.3
1992	5.4	6.3	−1.3	−0.7	36.4
1993	5.5	4.8	0.3	0.3	36.2
1994	8.3	6.2	−1	0.5	35.5
1995	8.9	4.5	−1.7	0.4	35.5
1996	6.8	4.9	−4.4	0.3	33.8
1997	5	4.5	−1.7	−1.5	33.4
1998	−5.8	7.5	12.5	−4.2	33.2

Note: 1) Consolidated public sector.
2) Data before 1990 are calculated at 1990 prices, and data from 1990 at 1995 prices.
Source: The Ministry of Finance and Economy. Various years. *Financial Statistics Bulletin*.
The Bank of Korea. *Monthly Bulletin*.

The only cloudy spot was the current account, mostly in deficit in the 1990s, reaching 4.4 percent of GDP in 1996, though it was being reduced to less than 1.7 percent of GDP in 1997. Overall, from a macroeconomic point of view, Korea looked like a well-managed economy, and this was the reason why the financial crisis in Korea took most observers by surprise in the beginning.

In spite of the sound macroeconomic fundamentals, Korea was vulnerable to financial crisis because of the exposure to external liabilities. As shown in Table 4.2, the amount of external liabilities relative to GDP was rising to above 30 percent by 1996 and 1997. However, the level of external liability as a ratio to GDP around 33 percent in 1997 was probably not a level to trigger the crisis.

Table 4.2 External Liabilities

(Unit: Billion US$, Percent)

	Gross Liabilities (A)	Short-Term Liabilities (B)	GDP (C)	FX Reserves (D)	A/C	B/A	B/D
1992	62.9	37	314.7	17.2	20	58.8	215.7
1993	67	41.5	345.7	20.3	19.4	60.2	198.9
1994	88.7	58.4	402.5	25.7	22	65.8	227.5
1995	119.7	78.8	489.4	32.7	24.5	65.8	240.6
1996	164.3	93	520.1	33.2	31.6	56.6	279.8
1997	158.1	63.2	476.7	20.4	33.2	40	309.8
1998	148.7	30.7	321.3	52	46.5	20.6	59.2
1999	136.4	38.1	–	74.1	–	27.9	51.4

Note: 1) External liabilities include external debts as defined by IBRD, plus offshore borrowings of Korean banks and overseas borrowings of Korean banks' overseas branches.
2) External liabilities and foreign exchange reserves are year end basis.
Source: The Ministry of Finance and Economy.

The problem lay in the relatively high portion of short-term external debt. Throughout the 1990s, short-term liabilities out of total external liabilities stayed at a level of more than 50 percent, and the foreign exchange reserve was not sufficient to cover the short-term external liabilities. The crisis is thus basically a bank-run with foreigners as depositors. While the

Korean government can prevent domestic bank run through implicit and explicit guarantee of deposit, the same does not work with foreigners. Korean government lacked sufficient foreign exchange reserves to insure the repayment of loans denoted in hard currency in a world with a strict hierarchy of currencies (Yotopoulos and Sawada, 1999: p. 426).

The question then is whether the crisis comes from short-run term mismatch of assets and liabilities for basically sound financial and corporate sectors, or it represents a real malady in the economy. The answer to this question by now is rather flatly in favor of the latter. The crisis was not one of illiquidity but of insolvency, caused by non-performing loans (henceforth NPL) of the financial sector.

Table 4.3 shows the performance indicators of bank management. Both the return on assets (ROA) and return on equity (ROE) of domestic commercial banks were low and decreasing. This makes a contrast with the performance of domestically operating foreign banks. Their ROA and ROE are far higher than those of domestic commercial banks, and are not falling between 1994 and 1998.

Table 4.3 Indicators of Bank Management Performance (Average of 20 Domestic Commercial Banks)

(Unit: Percent)

	Return on Assets		Return on Equity		NPL Ratio	
	Domestic	Foreign	Domestic	Foreign	Official	Latent
1992	0.56	–	6.69	–	7.1	22
1993	0.45	–	5.90	–	7.4	26
1994	0.42	1.32	6.09	10.96	5.8	19
1995	0.32	1.17	4.19	10.28	5.2	17
1996	0.26	1.52	3.80	12.51	4.1	22
1997	–0.93	3.89	–14.18	34.79	6.0	26
1998	–3.25	–	–52.53	–	7.4	32

Note: 1) Foreign bank branches operating in Korea.

2) The sum of estimated losses, doubtful, and substandard loans as a percentage of total loans.

3) The ratio of potentially non-performing credit out of total corporate borrowings. Latent NPL ratio is the percentage of borrowings by firms whose interest coverage ratio (EBITDA/Interest payment) is less than one. EBITA denotes earning before interest payment and tax plus depreciation and amortization.

Source: Hahm and Mishikin (1999).

Table 4.3 also presents the NPL ratio for commercial banks according to official statistics. Here NPL does not turn out a special problem. However, official NPL ratio has been calculated by classifying assets according to the judgment by the banks, and probably underestimates the NPL ratio. If the size of latent NPL is estimated from corporate balance sheet, it turns out far higher. Table 4.3 also presents the latent NPL ratio calculated by Hahm and Mishikin (1999) based on the 'interest coverage ratio' with the data of more than 6,000 corporations. It shows that NPL is indeed a serious problem, if not steeply rising just before the crisis.[3]

Korea shares NPL as a potential source of crisis with other East Asian countries like Thailand, Indonesia, Japan and China. While Japan and China have avoided the currency crisis due to large current account surplus, huge foreign exchange reserves, and, in the case of China, a minimal exposure to short run capital inflow, Korea together with Thailand and Indonesia have been unable to do that.

The next question then is where the NPL comes from. It is well known that in Japan NPL has been caused by the burst of the bubble. In Korea, the fact that NPL ratio is already high in 1992, as shown in Table 4.3, suggests that NPL may have come from the burst of bubble after the 'three low' boom in the late 1980s.

The burst of bubble should have produced NPL, but the NPL of Korean financial institutions basically comes from the low profitability of the highly leveraged corporate sector. Table 4.4 shows the profitability, interest rate expenses and debt-equity ratio for the Korean manufacturing sector. After the 'three low' boom ended, from 1989 to 1996 ROE averaged 5.8 percent, falling far short of the opportunity cost of capital, which has been estimated to be about 8.5 percent for the early 1990s (Lee et al., 1993). Five point eight percent of ROE during 1989-96 barely covers the real interest rate actually paid by firms, which is about 4.7 percent. Moreover, ROE falls far short of the real interest paid in 1996 and 1997.

---

[3] The latent NPL ratio has been calculated by using the interest coverage ratio, EBITDA/ (interest payment), where EBITDA denotes earnings before interest payment and tax plus depreciation and amortization. If the interest coverage ratio is less than one, it means that the borrowing firms cannot meet interest payment with its operating cash flow.

Table 4.4 Profitability, Interest and Debt-Equity Ratio (Manufacturing Sector)

(Unit: Percent)

	Net Income to Shareholder's Equity (ROE)	Interest Expenses to Total Borrowings		Debt-Equity Ratio
		Nominal	Real[1]	
1966	16.9	19.3	4.8	117.7
1967	17.0	18.1	2.5	151.2
1968	16.1	14.8	1.3	201.3
1969	13.6	13.4	–1.4	270.0
1970	10.7	14.7	–0.9	328.4
1971	4.5	13.3	0.8	394.2
1972	16.7	12.0	–4.7	313.4
1973	30.0	8.5	–5.1	272.7
1974	16.3	10.5	–20.0	316.0
1975	11.7	11.3	–13.9	339.5
1976	14.9	11.9	–9.3	364.6
1977	12.3	13.1	–3.5	367.2
1978	12.5	12.4	–10.4	366.8
1979	8.8	14.4	–5.2	377.1
1980	–7.3	18.7	–5.3	487.9
1981	–5.2	18.4	1.5	451.5
1982	0.2	16.0	8.9	385.8
1983	9.6	13.6	8.6	360.3
1984	6.8	14.4	10.5	342.7
1985	5.8	13.4	9.2	348.4
1986	10.9	12.5	7.8	350.9
1987	10.7	12.5	9.0	340.1
1988	10.2	13.0	6.1	296.0
1989	6.4	13.6	8.2	254.3
1990	5.6	12.3	2.7	285.5
1991	5.6	13.0	2.2	306.7
1992	3.7	12.3	4.6	318.7
1993	4.2	11.2	4.2	294.9
1994	7.6	11.4	3.8	302.5
1995	11.0	11.7	4.5	286.8
1996	2.0	11.2	7.3	317.1
1997	–4.2	10.6	7.4	396.3
1998	–15.9	13.5	8.2	303.0

Note: 1) Real rate was obtained by subtracting the increase rate of GNP deflator from the nominal rate.
Source: The Bank of Korea, *Financial Statements Analysis*. The Ministry of Finance and Economy, *Financial Statistics Bulletin*.

This is consistent with the evidence provided by the firm-level data. Kim (1998: 16) reports that after accounting for opportunity cost of capital, only 27 percent out of 570 examined non-financial firms listed in Korean stock exchange from 1992 through 1996 were earning net profits. He concludes that Korean firms during that period were 'destroying' rather than adding values.

The low profitability of firms in relation to cost of capital was indeed dangerous given the high debt-equity ratio given in Table 4.4. To help have an idea about the profitability and indebtedness of Korean firms, Table 4.5 presents an international comparison of profitability and debt-equity ratio across Korea, US, Japan and Taiwan. The table shows that Korea in the 1990s has lower profitability and higher debt-equity ratio than all three countries compared. Only Japan up to the early 1980s had comparable debt-equity ratio. While Japanese firms significantly reduced debt-equity ratio thereafter, Korean firms failed to do so.[4]

What is then responsible for the low profitability and high indebtedness of Korean firms? Here the answer is that it comes from the practice of financial and corporate sectors long embedded in Korea's development model.

2.2 Development Model and Crisis

Korea's neo-mercantilist 'developmental state' up to the mid-1980s pursued industrial policy to target particular industries. The government selected the entrepreneur to take charge of the targeted industries, mainly from existing businessmen. Industrial policy thus encouraged the diversification of firms, or the formation of Korean business conglomerate,

---

[4] Korea very much emulated Japan, and in terms of the 'stage' of development, Korea just before the outbreak of the crisis was close to Japan in the 1970s rather than the 1990s. However, Japan in the 1970s had a well-working system to discipline highly leveraged firms by (main) banks (see Aoki et al 1996: Chapter 9). In contrast, Korea in the 1990s had no such system, as will be discussed below. It is also questionable that the replication of the Japanese path of development would have been optimal in the face of the changing international environment, that is, the escalating pressure for market opening from the West in the 1980s and 1990s.

Table 4.5 Profitability and Debt-Equity Ratio: International Comparison (Manufacturing Sector)

(Unit: Percent)

	Korea		US		Japan		Taiwan	
	P/S [1]	D/E [2]	P/S	D/E	P/S	D/E	P/S	D/E
1966	7.7	117.7	–	–	–	–	–	–
1967	6.7	151.2	–	–	–	–	–	–
1968	6.0	201.3	–	75.4	–	320.0	–	–
1969	4.3	270.0	–	83.0	–	335.2	–	–
1970	3.3	328.4	–	86.0	–	365.9	–	–
1971	1.2	394.2	–	86.9	–	395.5	–	–
1972	3.9	313.4	–	–	–	391.4	–	–
1973	7.5	272.7	–	–	–	–	–	–
1974	4.8	316.0	–	–	–	–	–	–
1975	3.4	339.5	–	–	–	–	–	160.3
1976	3.9	364.6	7.8	85.9	–	–	–	–
1977	3.7	367.2	–	–	2.6	474.0	–	–
1978	4.0	366.8	–	–	–	–	–	–
1979	2.7	377.1	–	99.1	–	–	5.7	126.9
1980	–0.2	487.9	6.4	101.4	4.1	412.4	3.8	177.0
1981	0.0	451.5	–	–	3.2	342.0	3.1	175.9
1982	0.9	385.8	5.3	106.2	3.3	320.5	3.1	
1983	2.7	360.3	6.3	–	3.3	–	3.7	158.5
1984	2.7	342.7	7.1	110.1	4.1	293.9	6.7	134.5
1985	2.5	348.4	5.9	121.2	3.9	268.8	6.0	113.6
1986	3.6	350.9	5.8	127.3	2.8	268.5	8.0	101.5
1987	3.3	340.1	–	–	–	–	–	–
1988	4.1	296.0	8.3	138.2	4.5	243.6	13.9	84.3
1989	2.5	254.3	6.9	146.7	4.7	230.4	18.4	71.4
1990	2.3	286.3	–	–	5.2	227.1	4.3	83.4
1991	1.8	309.2	3.7	147.3	3.4	221.0	4.0	97.9
1992	1.5	318.7	–	–	2.6	216.4	3.4	93.0
1993	1.7	294.9	4.0	174.5	1.9	212.8	2.9	88.0
1994	2.7	302.5	7.5	165.5	2.4	209.3	4.9	87.2
1995	3.6	286.8	7.9	159.7	2.9	206.3	5.1	85.7
1996	1.0	317.1	8.3	153.5	3.4	193.2	–	–
1997	–0.3	396.3	8.5	153.8	3.3	186.4	–	–
1998	–1.8	303.0	–	–	–	–	–	–

Note: 1) P/S denotes ordinary profits as a percentage to sales.
      2) D/E denotes debt-equity ratio.
Source: The Bank of Korea, *Financial Statements Analysis*.

chaebol. Chaebol firms formed internal capital and labor market under their diversified firm structure, which facilitated targeting new industries.

Firms were subsidized with various means, including fiscal subsidies, tax exemptions, protection from imports; but the most important means was financial subsidies extended by government-controlled banks. Korea had a severe financial repression, with official real interest rate rarely being positive, as could be inferred from the real interest expense up to the early 1980s appearing in Table 4.4.[5]

Firms under this situation ever had the incentive to expand on borrowed money, not paying much attention to profitability. In other words, they had a tendency to over-borrow and over-invest, showing the well-known behavior of moral hazard "too big to fail". It was believed that the government implicitly guaranteed to bail out firms even when they performed poorly, once they grew beyond some size. Firms that managed to join the rank of *chaebol* could thus eat the cookie and have it: if investment succeeds, it is their achievement; otherwise, the government bears responsibility.

It is incorrect to say that this practice had only dark side. Government guarantee enabled chaebol firms to take risk and do aggressive investment in infant industries.[6] Like Japan in the 1950s and 1960s, Korea through this method succeeded in a transforming industrial structure faster than otherwise. Korea probably compares favorably with other East Asian NIEs in this respect. A few *chaebol* firms have now managed to emerge as effective competitor in global market of intermediate-to-high-technology industries such as steel, shipbuilding, automobiles, and semi-conductors in a short span of time.

The dark side of neo-mercantilist development model lies in its impact on the financial sector. The banks, under the government ownership and control, worked as the window for the government-directed credit rationing.

---

[5] A recent study (Kim, 1999) shows that if the difference between curb market and official interest rate is properly taken into account, redistribution through financial repression at its peak in 1969 amounted to as much as 26.5 percent of GDP.

[6] The behavior of chaebols in this respect has been confirmed by recent empirical study (Hahn, 1999).

They lacked business identity and thus the ability to screen the loans and to monitor the management of the borrowing firms. Neither did they have to, because on their part making loans to *chaebol* believing in the implicit government guarantee was easier way of doing business. Banks themselves were implicitly guaranteed of their survival regardless of their performance. However, during the developmental state era, the government employed various means to contain the tendency to over-borrow and over-invest. While the banks could not screen loans or monitor borrowers, the government disciplined firms directly lest moral hazard should go out of control. Or the government could cope with the outcome of moral hazard somewhat effectively *ex post*.

The disciplining mechanism under the developmental state is summarized in Figure 4.1. The government controlled entry, allocated the amount of

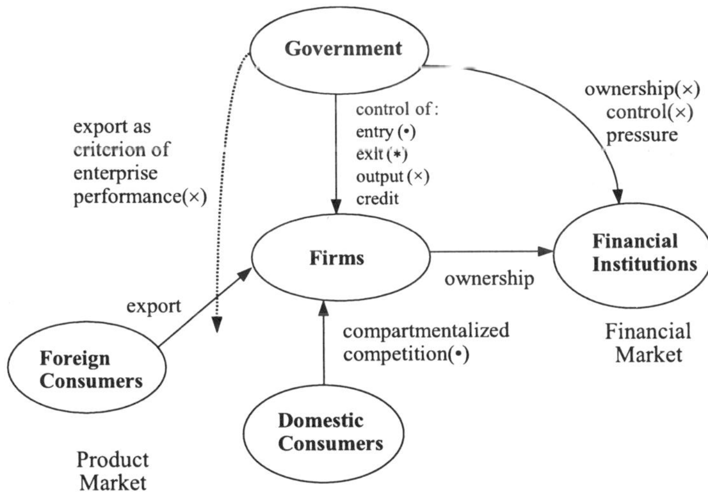

Fig. 4.1 Disciplining Mechanism during Neo-Mercantilist Era and Transition Period

Note:
1) The arrow denotes the way that discipline is exerted, and the dotted arrow denotes the facilitation of discipline by the government.
2) × denotes the disciplining mechanism that worked during developmental state era but was eliminated during transition period.
3) • denotes the disciplining mechanism that worked during developmental state era but was weakened or made unclear during transition period.
4) * denotes the disciplining mechanism that was strengthened during transition period.

investment and output among firms when it saw the necessary. This should have contained the tendency to over-investment, and probably accounts for the high ROE in the 1960s and 1970s shown in Table 4.4.[7] The government ordered large firms to exit when their performance was not proved. Exit was decided rather quickly by the order of the authoritarian ruler, minimizing the burden on financial institutions.[8] The government also tried to control the amount of total credit extended to chaebol through 'credit management'.

These practices often involved unfair and arbitrary wielding of power, intense rent-seeking, symbiotic relationship involving *chaebol*, government bureaucrats and politicians. Hence the name of 'crony capitalism.' But it did work to contain moral hazard from going out of control.

In the product market, the mechanism of 'effective contest', whereby the government was pressing firms to show their performance through exports, was exposing them to the discipline of international market (World Bank, 1993; Lee, 1997). In the domestic market, which was protected from import competition, effective competition among oligopolistic producers, or 'compartmentalized competition' imposed some, if not strong, discipline on firms (Amsden and Singh, 1994).

The critical condition underlying all these disciplining mechanism was the 'hard state' nature of Korean developmental state under the authoritarian rule up to 1987.

2.3 The Problem of Transition

Contrary to usual allegations abroad, on the eve of the crisis Korea was far from being the developmental state that it used to be in the 1960s and 1970s (see Lee, 1999). From the early 1980s, owing to the need to decentralize

---

[7] The ROE figures in 4.4 are for the manufacturing sector as a whole, while the government control of entry, investment and exit is for large firms only. However, ROE figures for large firms provided by the Bank of Korea are about the same as those in Table 4.4.

[8] For example, the change of ownership of current Daewoo Motors was carried out in the early 1970s almost entirely by the will of then president Park. Similarly, the Kukje chaebol, one of the 10 largest chaebols in the 1970s, was dissolved by the order of President Chun in the early 1980s, without drawing any explicit (contemporary) protest.

decision making as the size of the economy grew, neo-mercantilist development model began to give way to more liberal regime. Internationally, developed countries, especially the US, were no longer willing to tolerate neo-mercantilist policy of East Asian countries.

However, the transition was no simple matter. A new industrial-financial system to replace the role of government cannot be built simply by withdrawing the latter. Market mechanism as we see in the advanced countries today is the result of centuries of evolution.

From the mid-1980s, Korean government actually withdrew significantly from intervention. Its brighter side was that protection and subsidy were cut without reducing growth rate. Its darker side was that the government also retreated from the previous disciplining role. As a result, 'over-investment on over-borrowing' practice remained, but the old disciplining mechanism was gone. This should have contributed to the low profitability of firms and prolonged NPL of financial institutions given in Tables 4.3 and 4.4.

Now the government did not target new industries directly and lifted the official restriction on the entry. The task of picking new industries was assumed by private sector, notably *chaebol* firms. But *chaebol*, now often under the control of second generation, showed poor entrepreneurship. Moreover, Korea was over time increasingly under a 'nutcracker' situation between developed countries with high technological capacity and developing countries newly embarking on export-oriented industrialization. Korean firms, including *chaebol*, not daring to challenge advanced countries' multinational corporations head-on in technological capability, and being fully aware of Korea's higher labor cost in relation to latecomers, tried to enter or increase investment in intermediate technology industries with a high capital-output ratio.[9] Fast-rising wage rate and labor dispute with political liberalization after 1987 also prompted firms to do heavy labor-substituting investment. By 1996, Korea's incremental capital-output ratio reached a dangerous level of 6.0 (see Table 4.6).

---

[9] Samsung and Ssangyong's entry into automobile industry and Hyundai's attempt to build steel mill are examples. The decision was allegedly made by the heads of *chaebols* against the advice of professional managers.

Table 4.6 Incremental Capital-Output Ratio

1971	3.1	1985	6.3
1972	4.2	1986	3.1
1973	2.0	1987	2.9
1974	4.0	1988	3.1
1975	3.9	1989	5.7
1976	2.3	1990	4.3
1977	3.4	1991	4.6
1978	3.7	1992	7.5
1979	6.3	1993	6.5
1980	–	1994	4.7
1981	4.3	1995	4.5
1982	5.8	1996	6.0
1983	3.1	1997	7.0
1984	4.2	1998	-3.5

Source: The Ministry of Finance and Economy, *Financial Statistics Bulletin*.

However, now having declared that it was no longer in control of entry officially, the government did not have a well-defined rule concerning the entry. The decision was influenced by lobbying, popular opinion and other political considerations, the outcome often being inconsistent. The government no longer controlled output and investment of large firms either. Exit of large firms, when they went bankrupt, was now determined not by the authoritarian ruler but by the court procedure. It took between five to ten years, during which the debt of the bankrupt firm remained as NPL. The 'credit management' system remained, in an awkward form, but it also did not work consistently enough.

In the product market, the mechanism to ensure the performance of firms with exports as the criterion — a strong discipline previously — was no longer used. Only the opening of product market contributed to somewhat strengthening the discipline.

Now the discipline should have come from financial market. Banks were privatized and financial repression was more or less lifted, real interest rate paid by firms being restored to positive level in the early 1980s, as shown in Table 4.4. Now banks were expected to play the role of disciplining firms. It did not work. Firms believed that there was still the guarantee of bailout beyond some size: too big to fail. *Chaebol* borrowed money through cross-guarantee of loans with their financial structure hardly transparent. Banks lent to *chaebol* simply believing in the implicit government guarantee of bailout. Rather than developing the screening and monitoring ability of their own, banks used the status of *chaebol* as a signal for the safety of their loans. Banks also believed that the government guaranteed their own survival, though they were no longer government-owned. This practice could work for individual firms and banks in the short run, but not for the whole economy in the long run.

The problem would have been alleviated if the government had developed effective supervision or prudential regulation of financial institutions, a necessity as liberalization proceeded. But this could not be done under two consecutive incompetent presidents between 1987 and 1997.

Government not only failed to develop supervisory ability; it still worked as a burden on the banks. There still remained the elements of 'crony capitalism,' though much weakened. The government bureaucrats and politicians were unwilling to release *de facto* control on privatized banks so that the banks were still without an independent managerial entity. Government bureaucrats and politicians often pressured banks to lend money on political kickback, as revealed in the scandal of 'Hanbo' *chaebol* of 1997. Meanwhile, non-banking financial institutions were under the control of *chaebol* itself and worked almost like private chest for *chaebol* heads. Here the disciplining mechanism worked in a reverse way: *chaebol* disciplined financial institutions, not *vice versa*.

The lifting or weakening of the disciplining mechanism during the transition period is summarized in the parentheses in Figure 4.1.

There could be another important source of the discipline by the mid-1990s. As the *chaebol* firms went public, chaebol family of 30 largest chaebols owned only 14.1 percent of stocks by 1996, as shown in 4.7. *Chaebol* heads controlled their empire with minority ownership through the complicated circular investment among the member firms. Under this situation, *Chaebol* families have the incentive to commit moral hazard to benefit themselves at the expense of the general shareholders, which is confirmed by empirical study (Joh, 1999). One result was that *Chaebol* heads did not feel the proper opportunity cost of capital for shareholders' money as well as lenders'. This should have contributed to the tendency to over-invest. But there was no institutional arrangement to check their moral hazard. Continual reform efforts were blocked by *chaebol* resistance.

Table 4.7 Share Ownership of Korean Chaebols

(Unit: Percent)

	Five Largest Chaebols			Thirty Largest Chaebols		
	Family Members	Member Firms	Others	Family Members	Member Firms	Others
1993	11.8	37.2	51.0	13.2	28.9	57.9
1994	9.8	38.4	51.8	12.8	29.2	58.0
1995	9.7	38.7	51.6	14.7	29.2	56.1
1996	9.3	38.8	51.9	14.1	31.1	54.8
1997	8.6	36.6	54.8	11.2	33.5	55.3
1998	7.2	40.7	52.1	7.9	36.6	55.5
1999	4.6	49.8	45.6	5.4	45.2	49.4

Note: 1) The figures are for April each year.
2) Five largest chaebols include Daewoo chaebol as well as Hundai, Samsung, LG and SK because Daewoo went bankrupt later than April 1999.
Source: Fair Trade Commission.

Underlying all these factors was political change. The effectiveness of Korea's hard (developmental) state owed much to the authoritarian rule, but ten years of political democratization much softened Korean State.

The lack of discipline resulted in the 'soft budget constraint' for Korean firms especially *chaebol*s. Krugman's (1994) likening of East Asian economy to that of former Soviet Union is wrong for Korea to the extent that the Korean firms have been under the discipline of product market. But it is right as long as Korean firms lacked the discipline from financial market. This situation could not go forever. By the time the crisis broke out at the end of 1997, eight out of thirty largest *chaebols* had gone out of business, dealing a huge blow to financial sector.

2.4 Market Opening and Crisis

It should be remembered, however, that NPL alone does not precipitate financial crisis. China probably has a more mal-functioning financial and industrial (state enterprise) system, but has managed to avoid the crisis (see Xu, 2000). Over-investment on over-borrowing could precipitate currency crisis only when combined with the exposure to international capital flow. Since the crisis was bank-run with foreigners as depositors, it would not have happened without market opening, which was another aspect of transition from developmental state.

Under the developmental state, capital inflow was strictly controlled, and was supposed to fill the 'two gaps' — current account deficit or domestic saving-investment gap (see Taylor, 1979: pp. 123–26). With the liberalization of capital inflow, however, the mechanism of causation changed: current account began to reflect capital flow through the fluctuation of exchange rate. As a result, the capital inflow, even if not necessarily in the form of short run liabilities, caused complicated problems.

As capital market opening accelerated in the 1990s, Korean won became overvalued. Table 4.8 shows Korea's real effective exchange rate calculated by different agencies. In spite of the divergence in figures, they point to the existence of overvaluation during a few years before the crisis broke out. Once overvaluation began, it was useful for political purposes. Overvaluation of won could keep inflation low without imposing restrictive macroeconomic policies. Capital inflow could keep stock market afloat, which was politically useful in courting the middle class. Overvaluation also helped to attain a high nominal *per capita* GNP in US dollar, which Korean public knew far better than that in Korean won.[10]

The result was, of course, an accumulating current account deficit. Korea accumulated 47.5 billion dollars of current account deficit from 1994 to the third quarter of 1997 before the crisis broke out. Many observers has emphasized the deterioration of the terms of trade in 1996, owing to the adverse

---

[10]For example, achieving per capita GNP of US$10,000 in 1995 was an important topic of political propaganda.

situation in world semiconductor market, as an important underlying factor for the crisis. A much more important fact is that, owing to the overvaluation of won, Korea recorded a current account deficit equivalent to 1.7 percent of GDP in 1995, in spite of the bonanza in semiconductor industries.

Table 4.8 Real Effective Exchange Rate

	KERI[1]	KDI[2]
1990	87.29	–
1991	87.63	93.50
1992	88.67	98.80
1993	89.78	100.90
1994	87.52	98.30
1995	83.74	98.00
1996	84.46	96.00
1997	134.77	104.60
1998	–	131.10

Note: 1) Calculated by Korea Economic Research Institute for the end of each year.
     2) Calculated by Korea Development Institute for the average of each year.
     3) PPP-based equilibrium rate is composed by using the weight of Korea's major trading countries.
Source: KERI data: Jwa and Huh (1998). KDI data: Hahm and Mishkin (1999).

As shown in Table 4.1, the deficit as a percentage of GDP was apparently not a level to undermine the soundness of macroeconomic fundamentals. However, Korean case seems to show that the problem of market opening and ensuing currency overvaluation are more serious than they first look. The overvaluation of won intensified the 'nutcracker' situation of Korean industries, encouraging the over- or mis-investment in capital intensive industries. The probability for currency crisis to break out in emerging countries heavily depends upon the state of current account (Frankel and Rose, 1996; Park and Lee, 1998). Even when the deficit is not mainly caused by short run borrowing, it may well raise the probability of currency crisis.[11] Given Korea's

---

[11] Of course, if current account deficit is caused sorely by the inflow of long-term capital, it will not raise the probability of crisis. However, it will do so when combined with short-term capital inflow.

high domestic saving rate, whether this danger can be compensated by the benefit of capital inflow such as lower interest rate is questionable. In a country like Korea, market opening may reinforce the tendency to over-investment on over-borrowing.

Korea also did an unprecedented amount of 65.9 billion dollars of overseas investment from 1994 to the third quarter of 1997 before the crisis broke out. Overseas investment was mainly the result of capital market opening, given the fact that Korea's domestic interest rate, staying at double digit as shown in Table 4.4, was far higher than overseas interest rate. The government also encouraged overseas investment in order to sterilize the impact of capital inflow in the management of monetary aggregates.

It was dangerous that overseas investment by Korean financial institutions especially newly established merchant banks, which were neophytes in international finance, increased rapidly. The government had hardly any effective supervisory mechanism over the overseas as well as domestic investment by those financial institutions.

Of course, more important than the capital inflow itself was the fact that it was composed mainly of short-term capital. Given the interest rate differential, there was an ever-present demand for overseas borrowing, short or long term, so the real issue here was the sequence of liberalization. The official position of the government, and the consensus among the majority of economists in Korea, was a textbook story: domestic liberalization should precede external market opening; current transaction should be opened before capital transaction; financial industries should be opened in advance of capital movement; long term capital movement should be liberalized before short term capital movement.

The sequence was not kept. The reasons for the reversal are seemingly many, but not yet clearly explicable. The ultimate source of the problem was that domestic liberalization was too slow while external pressure for market opening escalated. The fact that short-term capital had lower interest rate was another reason. More short run reasons include the accession to OECD, which was politically motivated, and the 'segyehwa' drive in the mid-1990s, which could be translated most closely as 'globalization'.

The prevalent deregulation mentality among some economists and government officials should also be responsible. Given the abuses of the neo-mercantilist era, anything close to liberalization tended to be regarded as good. In their deregulation mentality, there was, for example, hardly a distinction between prudential regulation (supervision) and economic regulation (repression) of financial sector. Moreover, over time, some economists and government officials came to think that the vested interests surrounding regulation of the financial sector were so strong that Korea by itself could not generate internal momentum for reform. Only external pressure could prompt the genuine deregulation in financial industry (see Jwa and Kim, 1997, for example).

Through this process, the government officials should have lost sight of the danger of short run capital movement. As a result, short-term capital inflow, which should be the last on the liberalization list, was liberalized almost first.

The question then is how, in spite of the high NPL ratio, foreign financial institutions extended massive loans. Though the high latent NPL ratio was not officially published, foreign lenders should probably have known it. The plausible answer is that with market opening, they joined domestic financial institutions to exploit the implicit guarantee of loans by the government (Dooley and Shin, 1999). In other words, foreign lenders committed moral hazard alongside Korean borrowers. But when the government's ability to guarantee was questioned, they abruptly withdrew, precipitating the crisis.

3.   RECOVERY AND REFORM

3.1 The Road to Recovery

The contraction of the Korean economy in the wake of the outbreak of the crisis was enormous, GDP decreasing by 5.8 percent in 1998 (see Table 4.9). The contraction of GDP was precipitated by the sweeping reversal of capital flow in the last quarter of 1997, when outflow of private capital amounted to 19 percent of GDP. Upon this, the IMF imposed a drastically

Table 4.9 Macroeconomic Indicators, 1997–99: Quarterly Data

		Real GDP[1]	CPI[1]	Currency a/c[2]	Interest Rate[3]	Exchange Rate	Stock Price Index[4]	Nominal Wage[5]	Final Consumption[1]	Investment[1]	M$_2$[1]	Fiscal Expenditure[1]
1997	1Q	5.7	4.7	−7.9	12.4	865.4	684.8	9.9	4.4	0.3	19.5	14.6
	2Q	6.6	4	−2.6	12.1	891.7	724.2	9.3	5.1	0.2	19.3	8.8
	3Q	6.1	4	−2	12.1	898.6	723.1	5.9	5.1	−3.7	19	4.2
	4Q	3.9	5	3.3	17	1143.9	489.5	−2.9	−0.2	−9.8	19.1	6.2
1998	1Q	−3.6	8.9	10.9	20.7	1611.7	507.8	−2.7	−8.4	−20.6	14.5	−5.4
	2Q	−7.2	8.2	11.1	17.5	1394.6	371.2	−3.9	−9.7	−23.7	15.3	17
	3Q	−7.1	7	9.8	12.9	1324.9	317.6	−10.5	−8.9	−22.2	20.6	27
	4Q	−5.3	6	8.7	9.3	1281.2	437.6	4.8	−5.8	−17.9	24.7	10.4
1999	1Q	4.5	0.7	6.2	8.4	1197.6	572.3	9.1	5	−4.3	30	72.2
	2Q	9.9	0.6	6.4	8	1191.8	769.3	13.8	7.3	4.9	30.8	28.2
	3Q	12.3	0.7	6.5	9.6	1194.3	943.8	19.2	8.4	6.9	25.3	−21.5
	4Q	–	1.3	–	–	1174	921.1	–	–	26.4	–	–

Note: 1) Growth rate, percent.
     2) Billion US$.
     3) The arithmetic averages of the yields of guaranteed corporate bonds with maturity of three years.
     4) 1980.1.4 = 100.0
     5) Increase rate based on the monthly earnings of regular employees in manufacturing.
Source: The Bank of Korea, *Monthly Bulletin.*

restrictive macroeconomic policy in order to reverse capital flow by raising interest rate. This plunged the Korean economy deeper into contraction.

The restrictive macroeconomic policy has been controversial. Korea and other East Asian countries are different from other developing countries such as Latin America, it has been argued, where weak macroeconomic fundamentals manifested in fiscal and BOP deficit led to the crisis. High interest rate intended to reverse capital flow was hurting the highly leveraged firms and raising the possibility of bankruptcy so it was rather driving out foreign capital. Indeed, skyrocketing interest rate with firms highly leveraged should have led to sharp contraction. The fact that the restrictive macroeconomic policy was implemented in conjunction with financial and industrial restructuring policy should have added to the severity of contraction.

A recent study (Cho and West, 1999) argues that high interest rate policy was actually effective in reversing the tide of capital flow in the wake of the crisis. It is also argued that the sharp economic contraction resulting from restrictive macroeconomic policy created a large current account surplus, equivalent to 12.5 percent of GDP in 1998 (see Table 4.1), and thus contributed to reversing the flow of capital. The large current account surplus was made possible by the high ratio of exports to GDP in the Korean economy and larger share of the private sector, where adjustment to macroeconomic shock is easier than in the public sector (Cho and Lee, 1999).

The government, under the consent of the IMF, turned to reflationary policy following the stabilization of foreign exchange rate from mid-1998. This brought about the recovery in 1999. Fiscal stimulus began to work and consumption expenditure was coming back. As credit crunch eased over time and firms cut investment, interest rate fell into a single digit first time in history. Low interest rate stimulated the bounce back of the stock market, which in turn facilitated the recapitalization and self-financing of corporations, and thus stimulated investment. Buoyant stock market also stimulated consumption through wealth effect. Lowered interest rate, wages and rental rate on real estate provided a favorable environment for the resumption of investment.

Current account improved sharply as lowered interest rate, wage rate, real estate rental price drastically strengthened the competitiveness of Korean goods. Exchange rate stabilized at about 50 percent higher than the pre-crisis level from summer 1998.

All these led to a V-type recovery. But probably more important than these macroeconomic factors was the injection of the public fund to revive the financial system. The government put public money of 64 trillion won, equivalent to about 14 percent of GNP, to dispose of NPLs, to recapitalize the financial institutions, to close them with payback of deposits. Twenty-one troubled financial institutions and their licenses were revoked, and 71 were suspended in the first round of financial restructuring. Nonviable financial institutions were merged between themselves or with sounder ones. This relieved credit crunches initially, and helped financial institutions function normally afterwards, and contributed to the comeback of foreign capital.

Ultimately underlying this recovery was the quick stabilization of the politics under the new government, which took over power just after the outbreak of the crisis. As Thurow (1996: p. 221) observes, while the largest source of uncertainty in medieval kingdoms or dictatorship is dynastic succession, it is the financial instability in today's capitalist world. Korea actually had dynastic succession as well as financial crisis at the end of 1997: being a developing country still with a virtually omnipotent government, presidential election was like dynastic succession. But once dynastic succession was complete, outlet from the crisis was found. The state was hardened enough to fight at least the short run financial crisis.

Internationally, the boom of the US economy, the high value of Japanese yen, and low price of oil should have helped the recovery. The fact that Korea complied the IMF recipe without raising any objection probably have quickened the resumption of capital inflow, compared, for example, with Indonesia or Malaysia. Moreover, Korea found it easier to reflate the economy by lowering interest rate because G7 countries took concerted action to lower interest rate to avoid financial turmoil after the crisis of Russia and Brazil, and the near-bankruptcy of the Long Term Capital Management. In this respect, it was fortunate for Korea and other Asian countries that the financial crisis spread so quickly to the Wall Street.

By February 2000, Korean economy seems completely out of the crisis. Growth rate is expected to be about 10 percent in 1999 with less than 2 percent rise of CPI. Current account surplus is about 25 billion dollars, well over five percent of GDP.

However, to the extent that the ultimate cause of the crisis lies not in macroeconomic fundamentals but in the structural factors or the development model, short run recovery is not enough. If the recovery is to be sustainable, structural reform or the establishment of a new development model is essential. But the job seems far more difficult than managing the short run recovery.

3.2 Structural Reform

The essence of the structural reform is overcoming the absence of disciplining mechanism characterizing the transition period. Four areas of reform have been declared: firm, finance, government and industrial relations. Essential among them is to build a new system across firms, financial institutions, and government to contain moral hazard that led to over-investment on over-borrowing.

The first effort for structural reform is pushing *chaebol* to reduce debt-equity ratio, that is, to reverse over-borrowing. *Chaebol* has been ordered to reduce the debt-equity ratio to 200 percent or below by the end of 1999. For this purpose, the government has ordered *chaebol* to dissolve the cross-guarantee of loans by the end of March 2000. *Chaebol* has been forced to raise transparency of management through improved accounting system and consolidated financial statement from 1999. The government has also been strongly urging *chaebol* to sell shares to foreign investors to reduce the debt-equity ratio. If *chaebol* fails to meet the expectation, the government then actually puts them into bankruptcy procedure. When Daewoo Corporation, Korea's second largest *chaebol* in terms of assets, failed to reduce debt-equity ratio, it went into bankruptcy procedure in the summer 1999. This may send a signal to the financial sector that "too big to fail" no longer holds. Through this process, the debt-equity ratio of each of four largest *chaebols* — Hyundai, Samsung, LG and SK — has fallen, at least nominally, from about 470 percent at the end of 1997 to below 200 percent by early 2000.

Though the government has heavily intervened to reduce debt-equity ratio, its position is that the intervention has been inevitable to stem the collapse of the financial system. As for the longer run reform, the government has declared that it will completely purge the legacy of the developmental state and build a new system based on 'market economy and democracy'.

The framework of new disciplining mechanism that the government has declared, in piecemeal so far, can be summarized as Figure 4.2. Under the new disciplining mechanism, financial institutions, especially banks, are supposed to discipline borrowers including *chaebols*, by screening loans and monitoring the management. If the firm is expected not to survive, financial institutions will force exit upon them.

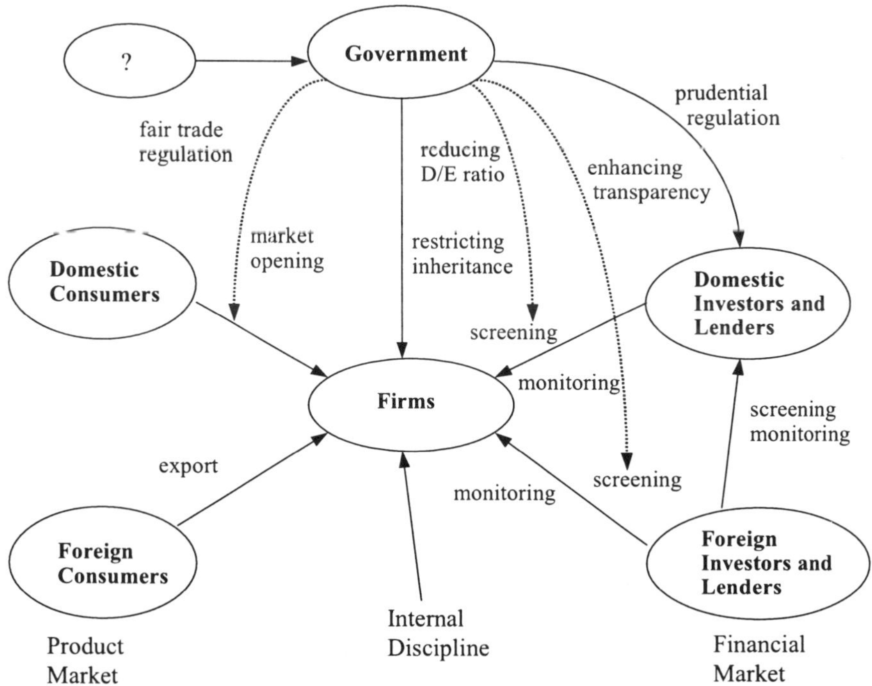

Fig. 4.2 New Disciplining Mechanism

Note: 1) The Arrow denotes the way that discipline is exerted, and dotted arrow denotes the facilitation of discipline by the government.

To carry out the job, financial institutions are supposed to get complete independence from the government and politics. Meanwhile, the government will impose supervision or prudential regulation on financial institutions. Financial Supervisory Service has been created on January 1, 1999 for this purpose by consolidating the existing supervisory bodies for banking, securities and insurance. To reduce the moral hazard by financial institutions, deposit insurance system has been introduced. Instead of the blanket insurance by the government on all kinds of deposit, a ceiling is imposed on the amount of deposit insured by Deposit Insurance Corporation. For example, for accounts opened or deposits made after August 1, 1998, only the principal is to be insured for accounts of 20 million won or more per person. In July 1998 there was a major strengthening revision of the loan classification standards and provision requirement to make them more in line with international standard.

The foreign financial institutions lending money to domestic financial institutions are also supposed to discipline them. When they lend money directly to domestic firms, they will screen loans and monitor the management of the firms.

The discipline on *chaebol* firms is supposed to come from minority shareholders as well as financial institutions. The government, after some turns and twists, has decided to limit the circular ownership of *chaebol* firms, the base of *chaebol* heads' control of assets far beyond their ownership share. Litigation against *chaebol* heads has been made easier for shareholders, domestic or foreign investors, institutional or individual.

The discipline on *chaebol* heads by shareholders is to be institutionalized as the intra-firm discipline within *chaebol* firms by reinforcing board of directors and audit committee. It has been made mandatory for large firms to have outsider directors who are supposed to serve the shareholders' interest.

The discipline through product market is to be strengthened by fair trade regulation and opening market to imports and foreign direct investment. Lastly but most importantly, the government has declared that it will collect the inheritance tax of *chaebol* more rigorously.

In the picture of new disciplining mechanism, there is little direct role left for the government, except for the strengthened supervision of financial institutions. The government is supposed to facilitate the working of the disciplining mechanism by the participants of market. As for the disciplining mechanism in the capital market, the government should enhance transparency to help the financial institution screen loans and monitor management. Reducing debt-equity ratio is also a necessity if the disciplining by banks are to work: if large *chaebol* firms are heavily indebted, it will be the *chaebol*, not the bank, that will have the bargaining power, so that the discipling role of the banks will be out of the question.

The government will also facilitate the discipline through product market by 'leveling the ground': through fair trade regulation and market opening. Lastly but most importantly, the government has declared that it will collect the inheritance tax of *chaebol* more rigorously.

Meanwhile, the government has somewhat slimmed down its own bureaucracy and carried out some deregulation. Politicians have also promised a sweeping political reform to make politics less burdensome to the private sector.

The reform efforts have achieved some declared goals. The new government had come to power from opposition and was relatively less indebted to *chaebol* or government bureaucracy. Moreover, the crisis and the ensuing IMF surveillance were critical. The consensus of public opinion under the crisis together with IMF coercion has made possible otherwise impossible reform. Many of the reform measures, such as the dissolving the cross guarantee of loans, making consolidated financial statement, and reduction of debt-equity ratio were on the reform agenda of the Korean government before the crisis broke out. They would have been simply impossible to implement without the crisis and IMF surveillance. Korean experience in the last two years or so indeed supports Olson's (1982) theme that thoroughgoing reforms can be carried out under the shocks like defeat in a war or foreign occupation.

3.3 Problems in the Reform Process

The reform efforts, however, leave much to be desired. First of all, the NPL remains as a serious problem. In 1999, not only the macroeconomic recovery but also the microeconomic conditions underlying the recovery — lower wages, interest rate, and rental price of land together with higher exchange rate — led to higher profitability. Many firms, including *chaebols*, informally report that they have produced record profit in 1999. However, it is questionable how far the problem of NPL has been resolved. In the depth of the crisis in 1998, the government ordered financial institutions to roll-over the existing loans to small and medium enterprises to avoid credit crunch. In addition, the bankruptcy of Daewoo *chaebol* in the summer of 1999 has left about 30 trillion won of loss to be accommodated by the financial sector.

The Daewoo incident has revealed that Korean financial institutions have little changed their behavioral pattern even after the outbreak of the crisis. For example, trust funds bought the bonds issued by Daewoo in spite of its dangerously high debt-equity ratio, apparently still believing in "too big to fail". The incident also has revealed that the trust funds, which should by definition have no run, need public action and funds. As investors pulled money out of trust funds, which had Daewoo bonds, trust funds sold bonds to raise cash. So bond prices plummeted. The government could not just look this on, because trust funds had promised to pay pre-determined interest rate to investors. In other words, trust funds had gone delinquent in business practice at the consent of the Ministry of Finance and Economy, which was supposed to supervise them. The government set up a fund of about 27 trillion won to buy bonds (similar to a share-buying fund it set up in 1989 after a stock market collapse) by ordering banks to contribute to it. The government also had to guarantee the recuperation value to the investors through putting three trillion won of additional public money. But bond-buying fund is a makeshift measure, and three trillion won is thought to fall far short of the required amount to clean the trust funds.[12]

The result is, notwithstanding the sharp recovery, a persistent instability in financial market. It is simply unclear how much additional public fund is

---

[12]Bond-buying fund is against the principle of the market economy that the government has repeatedly declared. Trust funds need public money because if their assets are evaluated at market price rather than nominal price, their balance sheets will be in a miserable shape. How much public money will be needed has never been studied.

needed to complete the reform of the financial sector. After pretending that public fund besides originally set 64 trillion won is not needed; the government has spent 12 trillion won more by the end of January 2000. The government is planning to spend another 40 trillion won within the year 2000. It is by no means clear whether this is enough. But public fund other than the initial 64 trillion won has been spent without a concerted planning in advance, taking make-shift form. While hesitating to put public fund in a decisive way, the government is coping with the financial instability by supplying more liquidity. The result is the expectation of rising inflation and diminishing current account surplus.

The reduction of debt-equity ratio for *chaebol* is less successful than it appears. The debt-equity ratio for most *chaebols* has nominally been reduced to below 200 percent by early 2000. However, a significant proportion thereof is accounted for by the increase of investment among member firms, made possible by the lift of the ceiling on circular investment in February 1998. As shown in Table 4.7, the circular holding by member firms increased from 36.6 percent to 49.8 percent from April 1997 to April 1999 for five largest chaebols, and from 33.5 to 45.2 for 30 largest chaebols during the same period.

The structural reform so far has also been problematic because of the insufficient scrutiny of responsibility: while public money equivalent to about 17 percent (76 trillion won) of GDP was put and so many people suffered from the crisis so far, many key people who committed moral hazard, either in the government or private sector, have escaped unscathed. This leaves a possibility of the resurgence of moral hazard in the future.

The structural reform with longer-term implications has also left much to be desired. Reform has not been thoroughgoing because of resistance by *chaebol* (and *chaebol*-controlled press), government bureaucrats, and politicians. But the resistance has also been invoked by the choice of wrong agenda or the lack of determination on the part of the political leadership.

As for the *chaebol* reform, the most important should be the issue of the dynastic succession of large *Chaebol Empire* by second or third generation. The fact that the decision making on investment on a national scale was left in the hands of second generation *chaebol* with mediocre ability was indeed responsible for over-investment or mis-investment that caused the current crisis. The succession has been done through various means, sometimes subtle and sometimes outright illegal. The government omitted the issue from the reform agenda in the beginning when it came to power at the end of 1997. The government declared that it would tackle the problem, only after a strong pressure by the public opinion, in August 1999. But it has not taken really effective measures so far.

Meanwhile, the government has been pushing *chaebol* hard to specialize on their core business rather than diversify, through selling, closing, and swapping their peripheral business through 'big deal'. 'Big deal' of affiliated firms among *chaebols* has particularly been the high agenda in the first one and half years of reform. The government still regards ending the 'fleet-style management' as the essence of the reform. However, the relationship between diversification and economic crisis is by no means clear. *Chaebol* firms that went bankrupt during the crisis of 1997 and 1998 are represented more by specialized firms (Lee and Eo 1999). It is also unclear whether the merit of internal market provided by chaebol structure is over for Korea as a developing country. Internal markets of chaebol is often advantageous in the new global competition, especially in emerging markets — contrary to commonly held view. *Chaebol* can make better 'package' deal with customers in emerging markets, where backward and forward linkage industries are not developed.

Diversification or specialization is a longer run problem that should be addressed by the firms themselves, adjusting to the environment formed by the government. This is indeed the spirit underlying the disciplining mechanism described in Figure 2. However, by choosing wrong agenda, the government is losing focus and thus momentum of the reform.[13]

It is questionable whether institutional reform measures newly introduced can work sufficiently as a ground to prevent moral hazard. It is still very difficult for minority shareholders to check the arbitrariness of *chaebol* heads. Outside directors, which government has introduced to enhance the

---

[13]The government drive for specialization should also have added uncertainty to the corporate sector in 1998, and made the contraction sharper.

ability to monitor *chaebol* heads on behalf of shareholders, are appointed by *chaebol* heads themselves. They are generally selected on the basis of their potential loyalty to *chaebol* heads or the ability to lobby the government.

The reform of the financial sector has met much less resistance than the corporate sector. The problem here is that while coping with the short run crisis, the government has strengthened the grip on financial sector. This is legitimate in the short run, considering the urgency of the task of fighting the financial crisis. However, in view of a longer run task of introducing new disciplining mechanism, it surely is a problem.

Now, of the 17 commercial banks, the government owns three biggest and is a majority shareholder in three others. The government has declared that it will privatize them, preferably through overseas selling. It actually sold Cheil Bank to New Bridge Capital in December 1999 at a bargain price after two years of negotiation. The government has promised to privatize other banks and establish their managerial entity.

It is questionable, however, whether the government is living up to its words. Examples of government abuse are many, notwithstanding the intensive talks about building market economy. In September 1998, the government tried to lower interest rate by ordering banks to reduce loan-deposit rate spread; Bank managers are still believed to be selected through political connections, though in a subtle way. Another example is bond-buying fund in the wake of Daewoo crisis mentioned above: when the government urged banks to contribute to the fund, the banks had no choice but to comply.

The lingering possibility that banks may lie under the government control is ominous, since reform of the government has been relatively meager, and politics has not been reformed at all. This raises the question: who will govern the government? — as illustrated in Figure 4.2.

Meanwhile, important non-banking financial institutions are under the control of *chaebol*, and the grip of *chaebol* has been rather tightened after the crisis broke out. As shown in 4.10, the share of five largest chaebols in various financial commodities increased dramatically after the crisis broke out. But *Chaebol*-owned financial institutions remain as a private chest of *chaebol* heads, as illustrated by the case of Hyundai *chaebol* in 1999. After being accused of manipulating stock prices for months, the president of

Hyundai Securities Inc. was arrested on the charges of manipulating stock prices to enhance the value of Hyundai group stocks. This kind of behavior is seemingly prevalent, and cannot be solved just by strengthening prudential and fair trade regulations.

Table 4.10 Market Share of Five Largest Chaebols in Financial Commodities

(Unit: Percent)

	1997.3	1998.3	1999.3
Trust Fund Bonds	6.2	23.7	31.6
Life Insurance Premium	30.5	33.4	36.4
Deposit in Non-Banking Financial Institutions	18.6	29.6	34.0

Note: Five largest chaebols include Daewoo chaebol as well as Hyundai, Samsung, LG and SK because Daewoo went bankrupt later than March 1999.

Source: Data provided by Ministry of Finance and Economy, Ministry of Industry and Resources, Fair Trade Commission, and Financial Supervisory Service, August 25, 1999.

The government declared, through the presidential address on August 15, 1999 that it would restrict ownership of non-banking financial institutions by *chaebol*. But ten days later, facing the resistance of chaebol, the government retreated to only mandatory introduction of outside directors — appointed by *chaebol* heads — without touching the ownership issue.

Entering the year 2000, all attention of the political leadership has shifted to the parliamentary election on April 13, setting aside economic reform. This raises, together with the confusion in the reform process, the question whether the state has been hardened enough to complete the reform.

3.4 Domestic Reform and Market Opening

Korea is in a dilemma where the discipline on the government and *chaebol* is supposed to come only from themselves. Under this situation, a genuine discipline on both of them may come only from foreigners. Korea's current reform agenda is basically that of classical liberalism which Adam Smith saw in his time. Smith's major concern was to contain the power of big privileged company and the government bureaucracy, which was the legacy of the mercantilist era. Korea is struggling with the task of containing the power of *chaebol* and government bureaucracy, the legacy of Korea's neo-mercantilist policy. As Smith noted, market opening can discipline both privileged companies and the government (Smith, 1976: Book 4).

This is indeed the current approach of Korea's political leadership. Korea has, following the demand of the IMF, thrown open all markets. Even the very short term capital movement is to be completely liberalized by the beginning of 2001. Korea apparently has now become a 'star pupil' of the globalization drive by the US and IMF.

The problem is that the discipline introduced by market opening may have widely varying effect. The Foreign take-over of Korean banks may help terminate the government meddling in the management. Increased foreign direct investment will also play disciplining role in the product market, though this does not necessarily justify the 'fire sale' of Korean assets under the crisis.

Under the IMF-imposed reform, market opening has proceeded much faster than Korea had planned before the crisis broke out. As a result, the reversal of the sequence of liberalization and market opening has been institutionalized. Korean government and IMF have never addressed ill-sequenced market opening as a cause of the crisis. They have only addressed the domestic reform. Market opening has been regarded as a disciplining mechanism for the reform, not as a source of trouble.

However, unbridled foreign capital flow when structural reform is miserably incomplete may cause trouble. As foreign capital inflow has resumed, exchange rate has fallen, so current account surplus is shrinking. After recording record current account surplus of 40.6 billion dollars in 1998 and 25 billion dollars in 1998, it is questionable whether Korea will be able to maintain current account surplus in 2000 and beyond.

A more serious problem is that the government, with ascendancy of politics in 2000, seems to look at capital inflow with a similar attitude as the previous government did before the crisis broke out. Falling exchange rate is useful to keep inflation low without imposing restrictive macroeconomic policy. Capital inflow can keep stock market afloat, which is politically useful in courting the middle class.

Of course, the more serious problem is short run capital. The discipline it imposes, due to its volatility, may tend to be too lenient and then too severe. And the severe end of the discipline is not really discipline but crisis. Short run liabilities as a percentage of foreign exchange reserves fell to 57.1 percent by the end of 1999, as shown in Table 4.2. The probability for a bank-run style crisis to recur has been much reduced. However, by the end of 1999, foreigners have come to own about 84 trillion won or 73 billion dollars of Korean stocks. At least some portion of them will move at the sight of crisis. In addition, Koreans themselves will join in the outflow: nobody knows how much this will amount to.

Given the unsound situation of the Korea's financial and corporate sectors, the capital outflow may again assume panic-like rush leading to a free fall of Korean won rather than settling down at a new equilibrium with higher exchange rate (Krugman, 1999: Chapter 5). If the government is forced to spend foreign exchange reserves to stem the outflow, Korea may face another bank-run style crisis.

The next crisis will be more dangerous than the previous one because the government, now under a serious fiscal deficit, will find it difficult to dispose of NPLs, recapitalize financial institutions and bail out depositors. National debt rose to about 23.0 percent of GDP by the end of 1999 from 11.9 percent as of the end of 1996. If the government guarantee of loans is added, national debt is well over 50 percent of GDP.

Koreans cannot also be sure that when another crisis breaks out, IMF and US will be fair towards them in relation to foreign lenders. In the crisis of 1997, Korea had to offer unilaterally high interest rate to reverse the capital flow, though foreign lenders as well as Korean borrowers committed moral hazard. The IMF made it clear to Korean government that it would extend the rescue package only if Korea first obtained the lenders' commitment to roll over the debt. This left Korea without any bargaining power against the lenders, so Korea had to pay high interest rate together with the government guarantee in the roll-over negotiation in January 1998.[14]

---

[14]Korea negotiated the roll-over of about 25 billion dollars of short-term debt in New York, January 1998. Interest with government guarantee was set at 2.25 percent, 2.50 percent, and 2.75 percent plus LIBOR for one, two, and three years of maturity.

The high interest rate paid by Korea at that time seemed natural because Korea was taking high interest policy to reverse capital flow. But, of course, IMF had forced it. The high interest rate policy entailed, as we saw earlier, a sharp contraction of the economy. Korea had to undergo a painful contraction producing 12.5 percent of GDP as current account surplus to get out of the crisis in 1998. Meanwhile, Korea's current account deficit as a measure of macroeconomic 'profligacy' (that is, over-investment) before the crisis was at most 4.4 percent in 1996 (see Table 4.1). This looks hardly fair.[15]

Korea thus ought to restore control at least on short run capital inflow. Furthermore, Koreans should be happy to see a fairer international financial order emerge, whether through changing IMF practices, or by establishing AMF or other international arrangements. Korean government, however, is currently taking an unclear and ambivalent attitude towards these issues.

4. CONCLUDING REMARKS

Korea's current crisis was caused by over-investment on over-borrowing, a practice originating from the developmental state era. However, the practice precipitated the crisis under the absence of a workable system in the process of transition from developmental state to a more liberal regime. Ill-sequenced market opening, another aspect of transition, was also essential.

After the crisis broke out, Korean government has engineered the recovery rather successfully. It has also been pursuing a thoroughgoing structural reform, trying to break the chains of moral hazard that led to over-investment on over-borrowing. However, it is uncertain whether the reform will succeed, while market has been opened completely. This leaves Korea vulnerable to another crisis.

Some important lessons that can be drawn from Korean experience are as follows:

---

[15]Now in the Daewoo bankruptcy negotiation, foreign lenders, with much less bargaining power, are persuaded to be satisfied with 40 percent of recuperation. However, if another crisis breaks out, the relative bargaining power will return to the January 1998 position.

First, while it is impossible to evaluate the performance of Korea's neo-mercantilist developmental model itself, the severe financial repression characterizing Korea's developmental model seems to inflict a cost larger than benefit. The cost is more pronounced in relation to the transition from neo-mercantilist developmental model to a more liberal one.

Second, while the transition from neo-mercantilist model becomes inevitable over time, liberalization should proceed with confirming that disciplining mechanism to replace the government role is installed. Simply withdrawing government intervention does not work.

Third, domestic liberalization and market opening should proceed strictly according to textbook story. Reversing the sequence for whatever reason is dangerous.

Fourth, the transition from developmental state should proceed as far as possible when the state is still 'hard'. If the state can be hard only under some authoritarian regime, economic liberalization should be done before political democratization. Otherwise, the economic decision may become politicalized under newly introduced democracy surrounding the vested interest created by the neo-mercantilist policy. This produce a 'soft' state, and may lead to a financial crisis.

Fifth, when crisis breaks out, the government should be bold enough to put public fund sufficient to solve the crisis. Tinkering with insufficient money and make-shift measures hardly solves the problem. The use of public money of course should be accompanied by strict calling of the responsible persons to account.

Sixth, structural reform should be carried out by setting priority of agenda according to urgency. Avoid concentrating on an issue such as the form of business structure (e.g. diversification or specialization) that should be addressed in the long run.

Seventh, once the financial crisis breaks out, given the current international financial system, complying the IMP recipe seems to help overcome the crisis quickly. However, the rescue method of financial crisis should be reformed. If this is not to be done in global context, probably an individual country should impose capital control after the intense phase of the crisis is over.

These are not the lessons to be learned by only other developing countries. Korea itself falls far short of learning genuine lessons from the crisis. Whether Koreans can do better and avoid the outbreak of another crisis remains to be seen.

References

Amsden A. and Singh, A. (1994) "The Optimal Degree of Competition and Dynamic Efficiency in Japan and Korea", *European Economic Review*, 38: pp. 941–51.

Aoki, Masahiko and Masahiro Okuno-Fujiwara (1996) *The Comparative Institutional Analysis of Economic System*, Tokyo: University of Tokyo Press (in Japanese).

Borensztein, E. and Jong-Wha Lee (1998) "Financial Distortions and Crisis in Korea" a paper presented at the conference on Korean economic crisis and policy evaluation, Koryo University, Seoul, June 13.

Cho, Yoon Che and Changyong Rhee (1999) "Macroeconomic Adjustment of the Asian Economies after the Crisis: A Comparative Study", *Seoul Journal of Economics*, 12(4), Winter, pp. 347–89.

Cho, Dongchul and K. D. West (1999) "The Effect of Monetary Policy in Exchange Rate Stabilization in Post-Crisis Korea", paper presented at the KDI conference on the Korean financial crisis, Seoul, October 15.

Dooley, M. and Inseok Shin (1999) "Private Inflow when Crises are Anticipated: A Case Study of Korea", paper presented at the KDI conference on the Korean financial crisis, Seoul, October 15.

Frankel, J.A. and A.K. Rose (1996) "Currency Crashes in Emerging Markets: An Empirical Treatment", *Journal of International Economics*, 41, pp. 351–66.

Hahm, Joon-Ho and F.S. Mishkin (1999) "Causes of Korean Financial Crisis: Lessons for Policy", paper presented at the KDI conference on the Korean financial crisis, Seoul, October 15.

Hahn, Chin Hee (1999) "Implicit Loss-Protection and the Investment Behavior of Korean Chaebols", paper presented at the KDI conference on the Korean financial crisis, Seoul, October 15.

Joh, Sung Wook (1999) "Does Shareholder Conflict Reduce Profitability? Evidence from Korea", paper presented at the KDI conference on the Korean financial crisis, Seoul, October 15.

Jwa, Sung Hee and Jun Il Kim (1997) "Korea's Economic Reform: Political Economy and Future Strategy", paper presented at the 17th world congress of International Political Science Association, Seoul, August 18–19.

Jwa, Sung Hee and Huh, Chan-kook (1998) "Korea's 1997 Currency Crisis: Causes and Implications", paper presented at the eighth international conference of Korean Economic Association, Seoul, August 18–19.

Krugman, P. (1994) "The Myth of East Asian Miracle", *Foreign Affairs*, 73(6), 62–78.

Krugman, P. (1999) *The Return of Depression Economics*, New York: W.W. Norton and Company.

Krugman, P. (1998), "What Happened to Asia?" mimeographed, Massachusettes Institute of Technology.

Kim, E. Han (1998) "Stock Market Opening and Asian Financial Crisis", paper presented at the eighth international conference of Korean Economic Association, Seoul, August 18–19, 1998.

Kim, Nak Nyeon (1999) "The Role of Government in Korean Economic Development in the 1960s", *Kungje Sahak* (*Review of Economic History*), no. 27, December, pp. 115–50 (in Korean).

Lee, Jaymin (1999) "East Asian NIEs Model of Development: Miracle, Crisis and Beyond", *The Pacific Review*, 12(2), 141–62.

Lee, Jaymin and Woon-sun Eo (1999) "Economic Crisis and Chaebol Bankruptcy" Mimeographed, Yonsei University (in Korean).

Lee, Jaymin (1997) "The Maturation and Growth of Infant Industries: The Case of Korea", *World Development*, 25(6): 1271–81.

Lee, Sung Hwi, Lee, Jisoon, Chun, Young Sub, and Kee Hyun Hong (1993) "Optimal Discount Rate in the Investment for Electricity Development", Mimeographed, Korea Electric Corporation (in Korean).

Olson, M. (1982) *The Rise and Decline of Nations: Economic Growth, Stagflation, and Social Rigidities*. New Haven: Yale University Press.

Park, Dae Keun and Changyong Rhee (1998) "Korean Foreign Exchange Crisis: Procedure and Lesson" a paper presented at the conference on Korean economic crisis and policy evaluation, Koryo University, Seoul, June 13 (in Korean).

Radelet, S. and J. D. Sachs, "The East Asian Financial Crisis: Diagnosis, Remedies, Prospects," *Brookings Papers on Economic Activity*, no. 1, 1998, pp. 1–74.

Smith, A (1976) *The Wealth of Nations*, the University of Chicago Press.

Taylor. L. (1979) *Macro Models for Developing Countries*, New York: McGraw-Hill.

Thurow, L. (1996) *The Future of Capitalism*, London: Nicholas Brealey Publishers.

Wade. R. (1998) "The Asian Debt-and-Development Crisis of 1997–?: Causes and Consequences", *World Development*, August, 26(8), pp. 1535–53.

World Bank (1993) *The East Asian Miracle*, Oxford: Oxford University Press.

Xu, Dianqing (2000) "Financial Crisis and Chinese Economy", paper presented at the workshop on financial crisis in East Asia, Taipei, January 22–23.

Yotopoulos, P.A. and Yasuyuki Sawada (1999) "Free Currency Markets, Financial Crises and Growth Debacle: Is There a Causal Relationship?" *Seoul Journal of Economics*, 12(4) Winter 1999, pp. 419–56.

CHAPTER 5

SINGAPORE

COPING WITH THE ASIAN FINANCIAL CRISIS: THE SINGAPORE EXPERIENCE

Kee-jin Ngiam

Department of Finance & Accounting
National University of Singapore
10-Kent Ridge Crescent
Singapore 119260
E-mail: fbank@nus.edu.sg

1. INTRODUCTION

Since the breakdown of the Bretton Woods system in 1973, the Singapore dollar has come under speculative pressures twice: first in September 1985 when Singapore was facing a recession, and second when it suffered from the contagion effects of the Asian financial crisis which began with the floating of the Thai baht in July 1997. As a small open economy, Singapore is extremely vulnerable to external developments, especially in the region. Thus, the large and adverse economic shocks triggered by the Asian financial crisis could potentially have a devastating effect on the Singapore economy. However, Singapore has withstood the financial storm lashing the region and even managed to maintain a relatively favorable economic performance. Although Singapore has weathered the crisis better than many Asian nations, its close integration with the regional economies means that it could not walk away completely unscathed. Indeed, during the Asian financial turmoil, the Singapore dollar depreciated against the major currencies of the US, Japan and Europe but rose sharply against the currencies in Asia, particularly the Indonesian rupiah, Thai baht, Malaysian ringgit and Korean won.

Singapore's resilience appears to be rooted in strong macroeconomic fundamentals, sound macroeconomic policies, and a willingness to take timely and effective policy measures to counter the adverse effects of the crisis. In response to a weaker competitive position vis-à-vis its neighbours, Singapore initially depreciated the Singapore dollar against the US dollar to maintain its competitiveness. As the crisis became prolonged, Singapore opted not to tinker with the nominal exchange rate but instead worked towards cost-cutting measures to restore its competitiveness. At the same time, the authorities have pressed ahead with financial reforms and liberalisation to ensure its long-run international competitiveness. This should help consolidate Singapore's position as a financial centre after the region has recovered from the economic turmoil. In fact, the Asian financial crisis might even benefit Singapore in the long term as it has reduced the threat some Asian economies pose to Singapore as a financial centre.

This paper is organised as follows. In the next section, we present a simple model of currency crisis. We examine the impact of the crisis on Singapore in section 3. We study the roots of Singapore's resilience in section 4. Section 5 addresses the issue of appropriate policy responses to the loss of Singapore's competitiveness arising from the crisis. In section 6, we analyse Singapore's policy responses to the crisis. The last section provides the conclusions and lessons that can be drawn from the Singapore experience.

2.   A SIMPLE MODEL OF CURRENT CRISIS

In this section, we develop a simple model to describe the kind of currency speculations that has plagued some of the more advanced developing countries such as Singapore. We assume that there is an interest rate ceiling, i_c, beyond which the domestic economy cannot bear. If the domestic interest rate is greater than i_c, the authorities will have to give up defending the exchange rate and allow the domestic currency to devalue. With imperfect substitutability between domestic and foreign financial assets, the following modified uncovered interest parity equation can be used:

$$i = i^* + \pi(E_1 - E)/E + RP \tag{1}$$

where i is the domestic interest rate, i^* is the foreign interest rate, E is the exchange rate (local currency per unit of foreign currency), E_1 is the equilibrium exchange rate, π is the probability of devaluation, $\pi(E_1 - E)/E$ is the expected depreciation of the domestic currency, and RP is the composite risk premium.[1]

Let π be the perceived probability that the government cannot support the current exchange rate. Conversely, $(1 - \pi)$ is the perceived commitment or the credibility of the government to defend the current exchange rate. π is assumed to be an exogenous parameter in the present model and takes on the following values:[2]

$$\pi = 1 \quad \text{when } i \geq i_c \tag{2}$$

$$\pi = \pi^* \quad \text{where } 1 > \pi^* > 0 \text{ when } i < i_c$$

Suppose that the current account and the asset markets are initially in equilibrium, consider the case where there is a large shock such as the regional economic crisis which pushes up the equilibrium exchange rate E_1. From equation (1), this causes the domestic interest rate to rise. As long as the higher domestic interest rate is below the interest rate ceiling (i_c), there will be no currency crisis. Suppose that the shock from the regional economic crisis, perhaps compounded by speculative attacks on the domestic currency,

---

[1] The composite risk premium reflects risk of default, corporate bankruptcy and the like. A similar model is found in World Bank (1998).

[2] Here we assume that π^* is exogenous for various reasons. First, there are so many variables out there that can affect government's credibility that it is better to treat π^* as exogenous. Second, we are more interested in the comparative static results rather than the dynamic interactions of variables which will require the modelling of π^* as a function of endogenous variables. Finally, simplicity and insight can be gained if π^* is treated as a parameter or as a function of some exogenous variables such as an exchange rate appreciation.

is so large that the domestic interest rate shoots above the interest rate ceiling. In this situation, π is equal to unity. The possibility of π equals to unity is therefore self-fulfilling since the government will have to give up defending the exchange rate at a cost much less than the cost of high domestic interest rate. Once the current exchange rate regime collapses, domestic interest rate will fall back to $i^* + RP$ and the exchange rate will depreciate to E_1. The trick for the government is to ensure that the domestic interest rate stays below the interest rate ceiling after a shock.

To see how the authorities can control the domestic interest rate to avert a currency crisis, let us first introduce the following money market equilibrium:

$$R + D/E = M(i), \quad dM/di < 0 \tag{3}$$

where R is the international reserves comprising foreign bonds and foreign money, E is the exchange rate, and D is the domestic credit. The left-hand side of equation (3) is the real money supply, with foreign prices normalised to one and with the purchasing power parity assumed to hold. The right hand side is the real money demand which is negatively related to the domestic interest rate, i.

It can be seen from equation (3) that the government has different ways of managing the domestic interest rate when an unstable situation arises. One way of controlling the domestic interest rate is to run down the secondary reserves (which is the excess of international reserves over and above the monetary base) to retain sufficient liquidity in the economy.[3] The other is for the authorities to increase its holdings of domestic credit, D, thereby injecting enough liquidity into the economy to ease the pressure on the exchange rate. In this case, the government is acting as a lender of last resort. Another way is to appreciate the exchange rate. When the Singapore dollar was under speculative attacks in September 1985, the authorities engineered an appreciation of the Singapore dollar to stem currency

---

[3] The government can also inject liquidity into the economy to stabilise the domestic interest rate by borrowing either locally or from abroad.

speculations and claimed to have inflicted punishment on speculators.[4] An appreciation in itself is self-defeating because it only increases the domestic interest rates with further loss of reserves, as shown by equation (3). To prevent a rise of the domestic interest rate amidst an appreciation of the currency, it is necessary to inject a sufficient amount of secondary reserves into the system.

On its face value, appreciating the exchange rate to stem out currency attacks seems nonsensical. However, there is one important aspect of this policy, which has been widely ignored: It can in fact help the authority to re-establish its reputation as a tough, committed government. Credibility of government during currency crises has been shown to be crucial in the literature on self-fulfilling currency attacks. As emphasised by Obstfeld and Rogoff (1995), speculators do not attack a currency at random; they will attack only when a country's credibility in defending its currency is in doubt. During the recent Southeast Asian currency crisis, policy-makers have learnt the hard way how important credibility was when they tried to reverse market sentiments and restore investors' confidence. The economic impact of a rise in credibility can be illustrated by a lower value of the parameter π^+. From an inspection of equation (1), if the impact of an appreciation on π^* is sufficiently large, offsetting the direct impacts of the appreciation itself, interest rate need not be raised and, perhaps, could even be lowered. This policy of appreciation may help the market agents to focus more on, and opt for, the possibility that the current exchange rate regime will prevail.

If the threat of retaliatory appreciation is fully anticipated by speculators, π^* could be lowered without the need of an actual appreciation. Moreover, the domestic interest rates could be lowered without actual adjustments in the exchange rates. The threat could work as long as there is a chance that it will be applied. However, it remains to be seen whether this policy of appreciation to beat down currency speculators can be repeated in the future, even though Singapore has applied it successfully to avert a currency crisis

---

[4] See Chan and Ngiam (1998) for a more thorough analysis.

in September 1985. During the Asian financial crisis, this policy of appreciation was not tested as the Singapore dollar did not come under speculative attacks. Speculators might have decided not to attack a strong-willed and credible authority. However, Singapore was not completely insulated from the Asian financial crisis as the adverse impact from the crisis was felt by Singapore's financial markets and the real sectors of the Singapore economy.

3.   IMPACT OF THE CRISIS

The Asian financial crisis has adversely affected Singapore through several channels. First, Singapore's exports to the crisis-hit economies were badly affected as a result of severely diminished regional demand due to the collapse of their currencies. Second, Singapore's exports became less competitive against these economies in third-country markets. Third, Singapore's banks were weakened due to their sizeable lending exposure to these countries. Fourth, the large outflow of Singapore's investment to the region in the early in 1990s in response to the regionalisation drive suffered a severe setback. Fifth, Singapore's brokerage firms were hurt when the Kuala Lumpur Stock Exchange (KLSE) imposed a new rule on August 31, 1998 requiring all trading in Malaysian shares to be done on the KLSE. The new KLSE rule, together with the imposition of exchange controls by Malaysia, effectively shut down the trading of Malaysian shares on Singapore's Clob International.[5]

The remainder of this section will examine the effects of the crisis on Singapore's currency and other asset markets, financial and corporate sectors, and economic performance.

---

[5] The controls measures introduced by Malaysia in September 1998 required: the repatriation of all ringgit held abroad and an end to all offshore trading of ringgit, the retention of the proceeds of the sale of Malaysian securities in the country for one year, and central bank approval for the conversion of ringgit into foreign currency.

Currency Contagion

After Thailand's long battle against currency attacks, the Thai baht was finally freed on July 2, 1997 from the peg to the US dollar. It fell by over 15 percent immediately and by about 80 percent by the year-end. The Singapore dollar was not spared the contagion effects. From a high of S$1.43 per US dollar on the day before the float of the Thai baht, the Singapore dollar went all the way down to S$1.75 per US dollar on January 7, 1998, a decline of 18.3 percent over the period. However, the other regional currencies depreciated much more during the same period, ranging from 70 percent for the Indonesian rupiah to 35 percent for the Philippine peso. Although the Singapore dollar depreciated against the US dollar and other major currencies, it appreciated sharply against the regional currencies. As a result, Singapore's nominal and real effective exchange rates were relatively stable both before and during the crisis (See Figure 5.1).

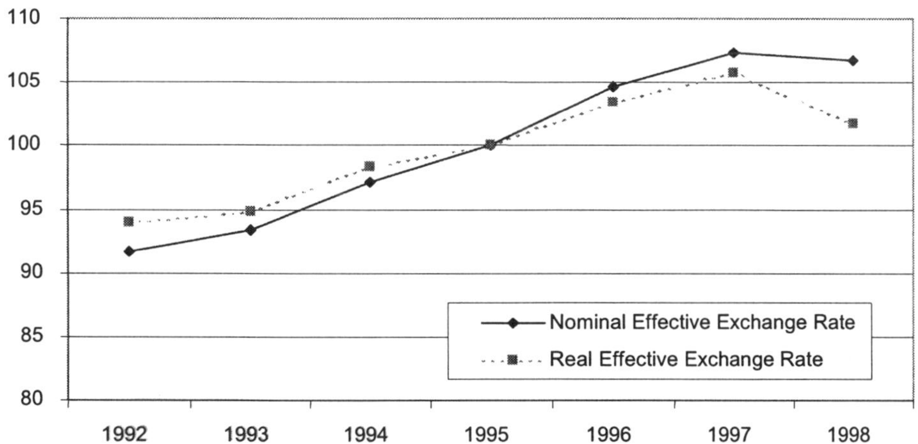

Fig. 5.1 Singapore's Nominal and Effective Exchange Rates

Source: International Monetary Fund, *International Financial Statistics* (October 1999).

Falling Asset Prices

The stock market and the property market in Singapore were badly hit by the crisis. Figures 5.2 and 5.3 show the movements of the stock market and property market price indices. The stock market opened January 1997 with the Straits Times Index (ST Index) at 2,055.44. The ST Index dropped drastically to a 10-year low of 856.43 in September 1998, a decline of some 60 percent over a fourteen-month period. The property market saw the private property price index plunging from 270.0 in the first quarter of 1997 to 163.7 in the fourth quarter of 1998, a drop of about 40 percent over a one-year period. The decline could have been more precipitous had the government not taken drastic measures in May 1996 to cool the private residential property market, which was then showing signs of a bubble.[6]

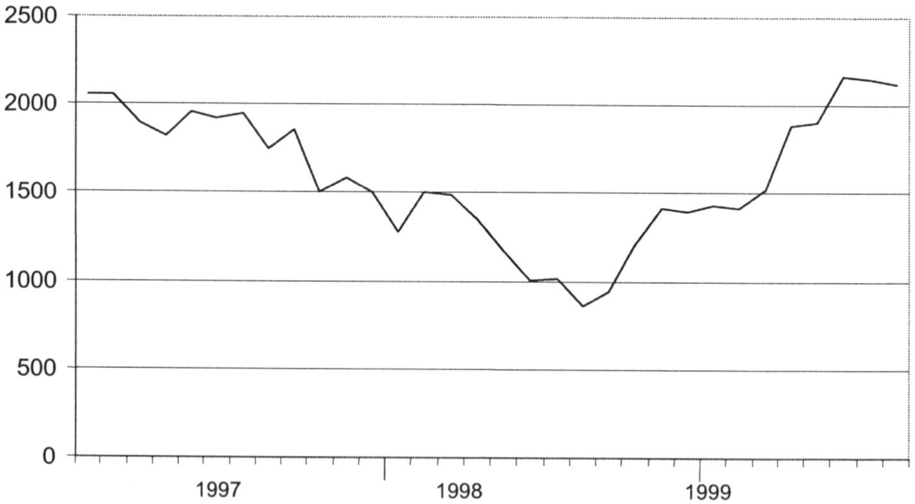

Fig. 5.2 Straits Times Index

Source: Monetary Authority of Singapore, Monthly Statistical Bulletin (September 1999).

---

[6] The measures include capital gains tax and stamp duty on sellers.

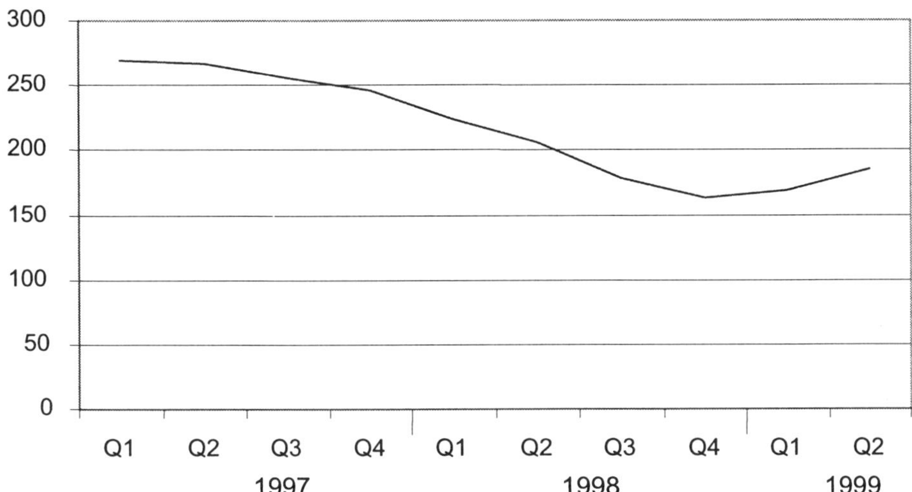

Fig. 5.3 Private Property Price Index

Source: Singapore Department of Statistics, Monthly Digest of Statistics (October 1999).

Weaker Financial and Corporate Sectors

The non-performing loans (NPLs) of local banks operating in the region have gone up.[7] As can be seen from Table 5.1, the local banks' loan exposure to Malaysia, Indonesia, Thailand, South Korea and the Philippines in March 1999 was S$34.7 billion, or 12.5 percent of their total assets. Non-performing regional loans made up 24.3 percent of all loans to these countries, up from 23.3 percent in December 1998 and 17.8 percent in September 1998. If domestic and other global loans were added to these regional loans, the NPL ratio for Singapore banks was only 8 percent in March 1999, up from 7.6 percent in December 1998 and 6.6 percent in September 1998. However, the Deputy Prime Minister, BG Lee Hsien Loong, told Parliament on July 6, 1999 that the NPL levels did not threaten the financial health of any of the local banks because they had set aside substantial provisions and the collateral

---

[7] The local banks are DBS Bank, OCBC Bank, Overseas Union Bank and United Overseas Bank.

backing of these regional loans exceeded the regional NPLs outstanding. The NPLs were high because local banks only wrote them off when all avenues to recover the loans had been exhausted and also because of the broad classification of NPLs.[8]

Table 5.1 Regional Exposure of Singapore's Banks

	Quarter Ending		(S$ billion)
	Sep-98	Dec-98	Mar-99
Gross Exposure to Regional Countries (Rcs)	35.8	34.2	34.7
As Percentage of Total Assets	14.5%	12.5%	12.5%
Inter-Unit*	4.6	4.5	4.4
Net Exposure to RCs:**			
Malaysia	17.1	16.4	17.2
Indonesia	3.6	3.2	3.3
Thailand	8.7	8.4	8.0
South Korea	1.3	1.1	1.1
Philippines	0.5	0.6	0.7
Total	31.2	29.7	30
NPLs Ratios:			
NPLs of RCs as % of Total Loans to RCs	17.8%	23.3%	24.3%
Global NPLs as % of Global Bank and Non-Bank Loans	6.6%	7.6%	8.0%

* Loans to and investment in own banking subsidiaries and branches.
** Gross exposure less inter-unit.
Source: The Straits Times, July 7, 1999.

Slower Economic Growth

The Singapore economy could not be completely insulated from the regional economic turmoil as the country has strong trade and financial linkages with the region. According to Singapore's official statistics (which do not publish figures on Singapore's trade with Indonesia), Malaysia,

---

[8] For example, restructured loans were classified as NPLs. Loans adequately collateralised and not in arrears in interest or principal payments were also classified as non-performing if they had weak financials.

Thailand, and the Philippines combined (the so-called ASEAN-3) accounted for nearly a quarter of Singapore's total exports[9]. The missing statistics are however provided by the Indonesian authorities, which reveal that Singapore exported some US$4 billion worth of goods to Indonesia in 1998.[10] Hence, the ASEAN-4 (which includes Indonesia) accounted for nearly a third of Singapore's total exports. In terms of tourism, Indonesia, Japan and Malaysia are Singapore's top three visitor generating markets in 1999, accounting for 17.4 percent, 12.4 percent and 7.3 percent of Singapore's tourist arrivals respectively.

Because of its regional exposure, Singapore felt the full brunt of the adverse spill-over effects of the Asian financial crisis in 1998, following very strong growth in 1997. As shown in Table 5.2, Singapore's GDP growth slowed down significantly from a positive 11.8 percent in the third quarter of 1997 to a negative 2.1 percent and negative 1.1 percent in the second and third quarter of 1998 respectively. As a result, its GDP growth fell from a robust 8.9 percent in 1997 to a mere 0.3 percent for 1998 as a whole.[11] While admittedly low, Singapore's growth in 1998 was among the highest in Asia.

Given Singapore's role as the business hub of Southeast Asia, three of its services producing industries (namely wholesale and retail trade, hotels and restaurants, and financial services) were severely affected by the crisis. The hotel and restaurant sector registered negative growth for five consecutive quarters starting as early as the first quarter of 1998. The wholesale and retail trade, and financial services sectors had negative growth rates for four consecutive quarters starting in the second quarter of 1998. The manufacturing sector was also hit as it experienced negative growth for three consecutive quarters starting in the second quarter of 1998. Only the transport and communications, and business services sectors continued to show positive quarterly growth despite the crisis.

---

[9] See Ministry of Trade and Industry, 1999 Economic Survey of Singapore.

[10] See International Monetary Fund, Direction of Trade Statistics Quarterly, December 1999.

[11] Singapore was technically in a recession in 1998 as it also had three consecutive quarters of negative seasonally adjusted quarter-on-quarter GDP growth in 1998.

Table 5.2 Gross Domestic Product at 1990 Market Prices (Percentage Change Over Same Period of Previous Year)

	1997					1998					1999				
	Q1	Q2	Q3	Q4	Annual	Q1	Q2	Q3	Q4	Annual	Q1	Q2	Q3	Q4	Annual
Total	5.9	9.9	11.8	7.9	8.9	4.4	0.1	−2.1	−1.1	0.3	0.6	6.7	6.7	7.1	5.4
Goods Producing Industries	−0.9	6.6	12.3	10.8	7.3	9.1	2.4	−3.0	−3.3	0.9	1.9	6.5	7.5	8.5	6.4
Manufacturing	−5.2	4.4	9.8	8.6	4.5	6.6	−0.2	−4.2	−2.6	−0.4	6.7	14.5	16.6	16.1	13.8
Construction	10.2	13.0	19.8	17.4	15.3	15.7	9.0	−0.3	−5.7	4.0	−9.1	−13.3	−15.6	−12.2	−11.8
Services Producing Industries	10.0	11.9	12.0	7.0	10.2	2.4	−1.2	−2.0	−0.4	−0.3	−0.6	5.7	5.3	5.2	3.8
Wholesale & Retail Trade	2.7	8.5	11.1	3.9	6.4	1.9	−4.9	−6.1	−7.1	−4.1	−2.3	6.6	9.3	14.7	7.1
Hotels & Restaurants	2.3	3.6	3.5	−1.5	1.9	−4.3	−2.5	−5.1	−1.4	−3.3	−1.0	2.1	4.1	6.2	3.7
Transport & Communication	8.6	9.8	10.5	8.1	9.2	7.0	5.7	4.0	4.5	5.3	5.7	6.4	7.6	8.4	7.1
Financial Services	27.3	29.2	24.7	12.6	23.4	−6.4	−13.0	−11.8	−3.2	−8.8	−8.6	12.9	4.3	−6.2	NA
Business Services	8.3	7.3	10	8.3	8.5	6.9	5.6	3.4	3.6	4.9	0.6	−0.2	1.2	0.8	0.1

NA = Not available.
Source: Ministry of Trade & Industry, Economic Survey of Singapore, Singapore, various issues.

As a result of the economic downturn, the unemployment rate increased from 2.4 percent in 1997 to 3.2 percent in 1998, the highest since 1989 (Figure 5.4). The number of unemployed persons in 1998 was some 62,100, compared with about 45,500 in the preceding year. The number of unemployed had been accelerating in the second half of 1998 as the seasonally adjusted unemployment rate climbed to a high of 4.5 percent in December 1998 from just 2.3 percent in June 1998. Still, in comparison with other countries in the region, Singapore's unemployment rate has remained low.

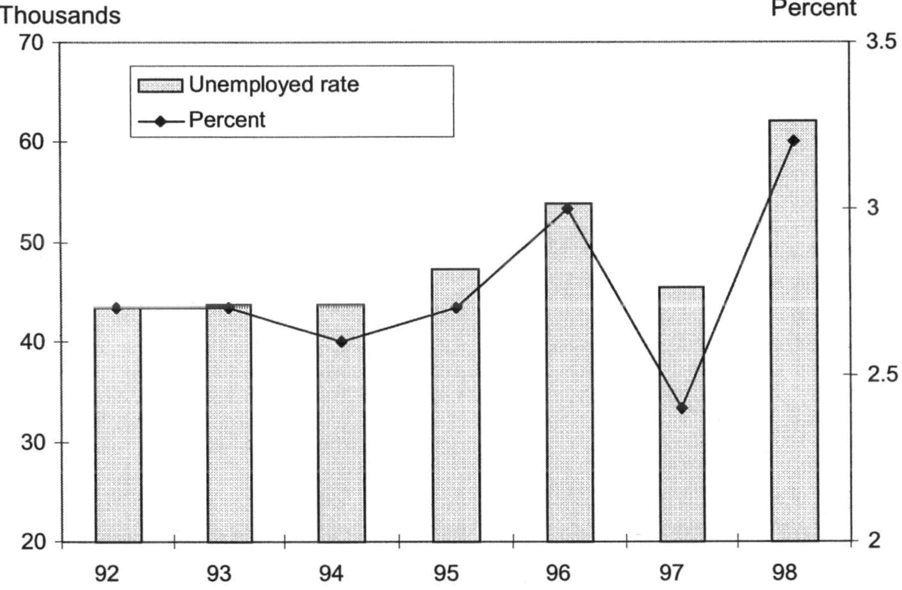

Fig. 5.4 Unemployment

Source: Singapore Department of Statistics, Statistical Highlights, 1998.

4. ROOTS OF RESILIENCE

Singapore's resilience in the face of the large and adverse economic shocks triggered by the Asian financial crisis can be traced to the four "foundations" it has laid over the years. These are: (1) the maintenance of strong economic fundamentals, including a healthy banking sector, (2) the adoption of a managed exchange rate system, (3) the establishment of an adjustable wage system, and (4) controls of bank lending in the Singapore dollar.

Strong Fundamentals

Singapore's strong economic fundamentals are well known. These include low foreign debt, huge foreign exchange reserves, large account surpluses, substantial budget surpluses, high savings rates, strong inflow of direct foreign investment, low inflation rates, prudent government policies and a sound financial system. (See Table 5.3). Good corporate governance and the credibility of policymakers in Singapore have also helped to maintain investors' confidence throughout the crisis.

Table 5.3 Selected Economic and Financial Indicators of Singapore

	1995	1996	1997	1998
Real Economy (change in percent)				
CPI Inflation	1.7	1.4	2.0	−0.3
Gross National Savings (percent of GDP)	51.8	52.9	54.5	54.4
Gross Capital Formation (percent of GDP)	34.5	37.0	38.7	33.5
Public Finance (percent of GDP)				
Revenue and Grants	33.1	36.0	35.8	29.1
Expenditure, Net Lending, and Funds Transfer	21.4	27.6	26.5	29.1
Overall Balance	11.6	8.4	9.3	0
Primary Operating Balance	6.1	4.0	4.0	−0.5
Money and Credit (change in percent)				
Broad Money (M3)	8.7	8.6	8.3	8.0
Credit to Private Sector	20.3	15.8	12.7	8.0
Interest Rate	2.4	3.4	6.6	1.8
(three month interbank rate, in percent)				
Balance of Payments (US$ billion)				
Current Account Balance	14.4	14.5	15.0	17.6
(in percent of GDP)	17.3	15.9	15.8	20.9
Overall Balance	8.6	7.4	8.0	3.0
Official Reserves	68.8	77.0	71.4	75.0
(in months of imports)	7.0	7.5	6.9	9.4

*Overall balance excluding net lending, capital revenue, investment income, debt interest, and fund transfer.
Source: International Monetary Fund, Public Information Notice No. 99/26.

After a brief recession in 1985/86, the Singapore economy has registered continuous strong growth without any sign of macroeconomic imbalances developing. Its current account surplus has grown rapidly from almost zero balance in 1985 to reach a high of 20.9 percent of GDP in 1998. The current account surpluses can be attributed to the surplus in both the public sector budget and the private sector account. As a result, the savings rate has always been exceptionally high, reaching some 54.4 percent of GDP in 1998. The foreign exchange reserves rose to US$75 billion (9 months of imports) in 1998.[12] Monetary policy has been anchored by the exchange rate and directed at price stability. This has helped limit inflation to an average of only 2 percent during the 1990s which was well below the international level.

The sound economic fundamentals of the economy have been reinforced by a well-capitalised and well-supervised banking sector. As shown in Table 5.4, the local banks are well capitalised by international standards. Their capital adequacy ratios increased from 16 percent in 1996 to 18.3 percent in 1998, despite making substantial provisions over the years. They even managed to earn positive profits amounting to some S$1.45 billion in 1998,

Table 5.4 Indicators of Financial Soundness of Singapore's Banks

Variables	1996	1997	1998
Non-Performing Loans to Total Loans (%)	2.8	3.8	11.3
Loan Loss Reserves to Total Loans (%)	2.8	2.8	5.8
Loan Loss Reserves to Non-Performing Loans (%)	92.0	80.5	53.0
Equity to Assets (%)	11.3	12.5	10.5
Total Capital Adequacy Ratio* (%)	16.0	18.5	18.3
Provisions (S$ Millions)	416.0	1,717	3,062
Pre-Tax Profits (S$ Million)	3,239	2,429	1,451
Shareholders Funds (S$ Millions)	20,397	22,426	23,494
Shareholder Funds to Non-Performing Loans (%)	692.1	484.5	184.7

* Sum of tier 1 and tier 2 capital to risk weighted assets.
Source: Gan et al. (1999)

---

[12]This does not include the foreign assets held on behalf of the Central Provident Fund (CPF).

albeit 40 percent below the 1997 levels. Compared to the situation in the region, there was no danger of a banking crisis erupting in Singapore as local banks' exposure to the region constituted less than 20 percent of their total global assets. The bulk of their loans were made domestically where the corporate borrowers were able to absorb the negative shocks in asset prices and demand due to their strong balance sheet positions.

Managed Exchange Rate System

The Monetary Authority of Singapore (MAS) manages the Singapore dollar not against a single currency, but against a trade-weighted basket of currencies of Singapore's major trading partners. In other words, it manages the nominal effective exchange rate (NEER). The NEER is allowed to float (but with frequent intervention to moderate exchange rate fluctuations) within an undisclosed target band, which it assesses to be consistent with Singapore's economic fundamentals. The target band has to be set right as an overvalued exchange rate invites speculative attacks, while an undervalued currency leads to overheating. Singapore has learnt a painful lesson of maintaining an overvalued NEER in the early 1980s. Chan and Ngiam (1998) has shown that the overvaluation of the NEER, coupled with economic recession, led to speculative attacks on the Singapore dollar in September 1985. This episode suggests that Singapore should view currency over-valuation and economic slowdown as warning signs of an impending currency attack on its currency. This finding is consistent with that in Frankel and Rose (1996), which showed that currency crashes in emerging countries tended to occur when their currencies were overvalued and output growth was slow.

Adjustable Wage System

The wage system in Singapore is fairly flexible, as it allows for wage reductions in difficult times such as during the recession years of 1985 and 1998. In Singapore, the National Wages Council (NWC), which is a tripartite body of employers, unions and government, sets non-mandatory annual wage guidelines in the light of external market pressures and domestic inflationary concerns in order to achieve orderly wage settlements consistent with macroeconomic objectives. The NWC was established in 1972 and its guidelines have been generally followed by the public sector and unionised private sectors of the economy. Other employers were also influenced by the guidelines for fear of losing workers (Lim and Associates, 1988, pp. 203). Hence, the NWC guidelines have a definite impact on wages in Singapore.

Following the recession in 1985, Singapore has adopted a more flexible wage system. The NWC has since drawn up a new monthly pay structure, comprising a basic wage and a monthly variable component (MVC).[13] The pay structure also consists of an annual wage supplement (AWS) and an annual variable bonus. However, only the public sector has adopted such a comprehensive pay structure, which allows for more flexible wage cuts in bad times. The private sector has adopted the AWS and an annual variable bonus but not the MVC. Hence, unlike the public sector, it does not have the flexibility to make quick adjustments to wage costs as it would have to wait for cuts in year-end bonus, annual wage supplement or Central Provident Fund (CPF) contribution rates. To make wages in the private sector more flexible, the NWC is advocating that companies should start introducing the MVC into the wage structure. Its aim is to build this component up to 10 percent of total wages over the years. When accomplished, the current structure of 80 percent of basic wage and 20 percent of annual variable bonuses will be altered to this: 70 percent basic wage, 20 percent annual bonus and 10 percent MVC.[14]

Controls of Singapore dollars

The MAS has had a longstanding policy of discouraging the internationalisation of the Singapore dollar, out of fear that a large offshore market in Singapore dollars could destabilise capital flows and cause greater exchange rate and interest rate instability (Ngiam, 1998). Before August 1998, the MAS regulated local financial institutions through regulation "MAS

---

[13] In the public sector, the MVC is known as the non-pensionable variable payment (NPVP) which accounts for about 8 percent of total monthly pay.

[14] See "Employers to receive guidelines on MVC" in The Straits Times, 29 May 1999.

621" (originally issued in 1983 and amended in 1992), which required them to consult the MAS before providing Singapore-dollar credit facilities to non-residents for financial investments, third-party trade or use outside Singapore. Financial institutions were also required to consult the MAS on Singapore-dollar facilities to residents if the proceeds were to be used outside Singapore. To ensure that its regulations were not being circumvented through financial derivatives, the MAS has defined Singapore dollar credit facilities to include a wide range of financial instruments, including foreign exchange swaps, currency swaps, interest rate swaps, facilities incorporating options, and forward rate agreements in Singapore dollars. These restrictions, backed by strong fundamentals and flexibility of the exchange and wages, have helped to mitigate the impact of recent speculative pressures on the Singapore dollar. However, they also have the effect of hindering the deepening and widening of the financial markets in Singapore as well as the growth of Singapore as a financial centre.

5.   ANALYSING POLICY OPTIONS

In this section, we address the issue of appropriate policy responses to the loss of Singapore's competitiveness arising from the Asian financial crisis. After holding steady the Singapore dollar against a basket of currencies for one and a half years, the Deputy Prime Minister Lee proclaimed in February 1999 that "we do not rely on exchange rate depreciation to boost our competitiveness".[15] He went on to say that the MAS would "prefer to do this directly, by reducing business costs, improving labour productivity and enhancing capabilities". The pertinent question is whether exchange rate depreciation can be more effective than cost-cutting measures such CPF and wage cuts in arresting the slide of the Singapore economy during the crisis in 1998.

A convenient starting point for discussion is an equilibrium model of a small open economy, which is depicted in Figure 5.5. In this model, which

---

[15]See "Scenarios for Singapore's future" in The Business Times, February 13–14, 1999.

follows Dornbusch (1996), there are two determinants of output and employment in Singapore: the real wage in Singapore dollars, W/E, and the real money stock, H/E. Obviously, W and H are the nominal wage and money stock respectively, and E is the exchange rate (measured as the number of Singapore dollars per unit of foreign currency). The schedule LL is the combination of real wage and real balances consistent with internal balance. It is upward sloping because an increase in W/E worsens international competitiveness and, thus, requires an increase in H/E to boost spending in order to maintain full employment. Points to its left correspond to unemployment and points to its right reflect over full-employment. The schedule XX is the combination of W/E and H/E that maintain external balance. It is downward sloping because an increase in W/E hurts international competitiveness and, hence, requires an offsetting cut in H/E to reduce spending in order to maintain the external balance. Points to the left correspond to external surplus and points to the right represent external deficit.

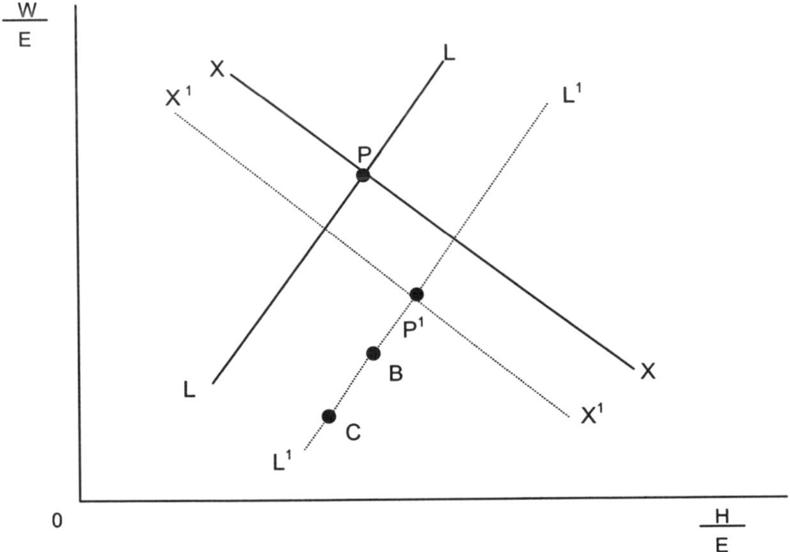

Fig. 5.5 Policies to Bring About Internal and External Balance

Consider now an initial situation at point P and a fall in the regional demand resulting from the Asian financial crisis. The effect is to cause the LL curve to shift to L^1L^1 and the XX curve to X^1X^1. The intersection of the new curves L^1L^1 and X^1X^1 (at point P^1) lies below point P. At point P, the economy is facing unemployment and an external deficit (or an external balance less than the target level). With fully flexible exchange rates and nominal wages, the economy moves to point P^1 where there is both internal and external balance. However, the real wage is lower at point P^1 than at point P because of the negative real disturbances.

With flexible nominal wages but a fixed exchange rate, the economy moves towards L^1L^1 such as at point B. The movement towards point B restores internal balance and improves external balance. As there is an external surplus at point B, real money stock is rising. The economy converges over time to point P^1 where both internal and external balance is restored.

However, if money wages are not fully flexible (or are sticky downwards) and there is no real wage rigidity, then devaluation has a role to play. A devaluation cuts real wages, fosters competitiveness, and in that manner helps create employment and improve external balance. It can bring the economy from point P towards L^1L^1 such as at point C. There is an external surplus, which causes an increase in real money stock. Again, the economy will eventually move to the equilibrium point P^1.

Another extreme case is where real wages are fixed. Suppose, in Figure 5.6, the real wage is fixed at a level shown by the horizontal line ww. The external deficit at point P leads to lower real balances under a fixed exchange rate and, hence, the economy converges to point D. A devaluation can bring the economy to point F, but the sticky real wage implies a rapid adjustment to the line ww at point G. Because of the reduction in real balances, there is a transitory external surplus. The economy will eventually move back to point D. In a world without money illusion a nominal exchange rate devaluation per se will not have any persistent real effects. In this "no money illusion" world, there is also an internal-external conflict as the attainment of external balance at point D (from point P) moves its economy away from internal balance. As a result, real balances will fall (interest rates will rise). High interest rates will worsen the unemployment situation and weaken the banking sector. This state of affairs can make the economy vulnerable to currency attacks as shown in section 2.

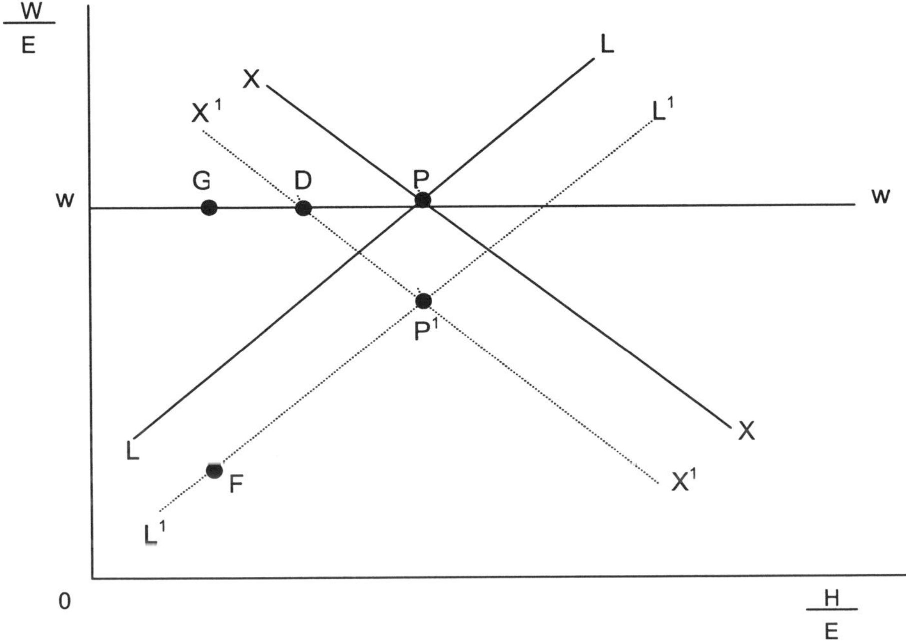

Fig. 5.6 Ineffectiveness of Exchange Rate Changes Under Fixed Real Wages

At this stage, three questions need to be asked. First, is there real wage rigidity in Singapore? Second, are money wages fully flexible in Singapore? Third, is devaluation an effective and useful instrument in the context of Singapore?

Real wages in Singapore are not fixed as workers in general are willing to accept nominal wage cuts and exchange rate depreciation during an economic downturn. With flexible real wages, either exchange rate depreciation or real wage cut can play a useful role in bringing about stimulus of domestic output and correction of external deficit. Singapore has used both of these instruments effectively during the crisis.

Nominal wages in Singapore are fairly, but not fully, flexible. Although the nominal wages can be cut, agreement among employers, trade union and government through the NWC must first be sought before wage guidelines are issued. The guidelines are implemented only by the public sector and unionised private sectors of the economy. Moreover, they are not implemented right away. For example, the wage and CPF cuts recommended by the NWC in mid 1998 were implemented only from January 1999. Months before the implementation, government ministers and traded union leaders, through a series of speeches, have been preparing and exhorting workers to accept wage and CPF cuts to save their jobs and to revive the Singapore economy. When there is unemployment caused by a fall in regional demands (such as at point A) and when the country cannot co-ordinate a drop in wages easily and rapidly, devaluation can provide a quick solution. This has been the strategy of the MAS as it has allowed the Singapore dollar to fall from S$1.43 per US dollar to about S$1.70 per US dollar during the first few months of the Asian financial crisis.

However, when the crisis persisted and further enhancement of export competitiveness was needed to turn the economy around, the MAS argued for direct wage cuts rather than exchange rate depreciation. This is understandable as the MAS has traditionally adopted a strong Singapore dollar policy. The result has been a stable Singapore dollar, low inflation, low interest rate and confidence in the currency and Singapore's financial sector. A large or continuing depreciation to enhance export competitiveness would jeopardise all these achievements. Moreover, as a small open economy, the cost reduction from the depreciation can be quickly eroded through higher inflation. According to studies by the MAS, the bulk of the initial gains in competitiveness arising from a weaker exchange rate are lost within three years through higher inflation.[16] Worse, the higher inflation tends to become entrenched, with adverse consequences for the economy. If the higher inflation is unanticipated, there is also a distribution effect as nominal debtors (in Singapore dollars) will benefit at the expense of nominal creditors.

---

[16]See "Macroeconomic Policies in Singapore: Principles, Milestones and Future Prospects", which was delivered by Dr Richard Hu, Minister for Finance, at the Annual Dinner of the Economic Society of Singapore, 22 March 1997.

6. POLICY RESPONSES

As the Asian financial crisis has eroded Singapore's competitiveness, its policies and costs were adjusted to adapt to the new environment. Singapore's policy responses to the Asian financial crisis have been flexible, timely and pragmatic. As the exchange rate could be adjusted promptly, it was used in the initial stage to prevent the erosion of Singapore's competitiveness. Fiscal and cost-cutting measures, which took a longer time to implement, were employed at a later stage to strengthen Singapore's competitiveness. In addition, Singapore took the opportunity afforded by the lull in regional activity to position its financial sector for the next wave of regional growth by implementing important financial reforms, including the liberalisation of the Singapore dollar. The easing of the use of the Singapore dollar would obviously weaken one of the four foundations for Singapore's resilience discussed in section.4. However, it could be argued that, like a tripod, only three foundations would be enough to ensure Singapore's resilience.

Initial Response: Exchange Rate Depreciation

Following the outbreak of the crisis in July 1997, the MAS took steps to ease its monetary policy to cushion the rapidly decelerating Singapore economy. It has also allowed the Singapore dollar to fluctuate in a flat and wider target band because of the volatility and uncertainty in the financial markets (MAS Annual Report 1997/98, pp. 49). As a result, the NEER has been broadly stable since mid 1997, in contrast to the appreciating trend of previous years. During the crisis, there has been no speculative attacks against the Singapore dollar although some selling pressures caused it to slide against the US dollar. In the absence of domestic inflationary pressures, the MAS has allowed the Singapore dollar to fall against the US dollar in line with the regional currencies in order to preserve its competitiveness. This can be looked upon as a short-term recourse to combat the effects of the crisis. The long-term objective of managing the exchange rate to attain price stability remains unchanged.

With a recovering economy and stable currency markets by mid 1999, the MAS has accordingly shifted its exchange rate policy stance back to neutral and moved the Singapore dollar back to its narrower, pre-crisis exchange rate band.[17] The MAS has also revealed that since early 1999, the value of the Singapore dollar based on a trade-weighted basket of currencies had returned to its pre-crisis levels, even though the economy was still operating below its full potential.

Subsequent Response: Fiscal and Cost-Cutting Measures

In spite of pressures on the currency, and stock and property markets in the second half of 1997, the government has refrained from direct intervention. When the fiscal year 1998 (FY98) Budget was announced in February 1998, the real economy was still robust and growing by 7.9 percent in the last quarter of 1997.[18] Accordingly, the FY98 Budget was not designed to stimulate the economy as it still provided for a budget surplus of some S$2.7 billion (equivalent to 1.7 percent of GDP), down from the surplus of about S$6.1 billion in fiscal year 1997.[19] Clearly, the FY98 Budget was too prudent and underestimated the impact of the regional economic crisis. The authorities might have thought that the impact on competitiveness from regional currency developments would be moderate, owing to Singapore's reliance on higher value-added activities and on industrialised economies for its electronic exports.

When it became clear in mid-1998 that the deterioration of the Singapore economy was more serious and protracted than originally projected, the government unveiled a S$2 billion off-budget package in June with three broad objectives. One was the reduction in business costs through additional property tax rebates as well as rental and utilities rebates by government agencies. The second was the strengthening of economic infrastructure

---

[17]See "Recovery Can Be Sustained" in The Straits Times, 8 July 1999.

[18]FY98 represents the fiscal year which runs from 1 April 1998 to 31 March 1999.

[19]See "Economic Crunch May Cut Budget Surplus In Half" in The Straits Times, 28 February 1998.

through speeding up of development projects as well as providing more funds for skill training and local enterprises. The third was the stabilisation of specific sectors of the economy, in particular the property market, by suspending government land sales until the end of 1999 and deferring stamp duty on uncompleted properties. The government also assisted households by granting them rebates on Housing and Development Board (HDB) charges and rentals as well as helping them with mortgage re-scheduling. As a result, property prices began to stabilise in second half of 1998, as can be seen in Figure 3. The stabilisation of property prices helped prevent more bankruptcies and an increase in non-performing loans.

The June 1998 off-budget package failed to arrest the slide in the real sector of the economy, which registered decelerating quarterly GDP growth rates and rising unemployment. As a result, another cost-reduction package worth S$10.5 billion was introduced in November 1998 which aimed to reduce business cost by 15 percent.[20] The main measures under this package include a 10 percent point reduction in the employers' CPF contribution, wage cut of 5 to 8 percent, 10 percent corporate tax rebate for 1999, and further cuts in government rates and fees.[21]

The two off-budget packages reduced the projected surplus for the fiscal year 1998 to only S$1.1 billion (MAS Annual Report 1998/99, pp. 42). Although the fiscal policy in 1998 was less deflationary than the previous budget surpluses (about 4 to 6 percent of GDP), it could have been more stimulative given that the economy was in recession in the second half of 1998. Nevertheless, the direct cost-cutting measures have improved Singapore's competitiveness. As can be seen in Figure 5.7, the unit labour cost of the overall economy has come down significantly in the first three quarters of 1999. Likewise, the unit business cost of the manufacturing sector has fallen sharply in the first nine months of 1999.

---

[20]The off-budget package introduced in November 1998 was in response to the recommendations of the Committee on Singapore's Competitiveness (CSC), which was originally formed in 1997 specifically to assess Singapore's competitiveness over the next decade and propose strategies for improvement.

[21]For details on the fiscal and cost-cutting measures introduced in 1998 to reduce business costs, see Ministry of Trade and Industry, 1998 Economic Survey of Singapore.

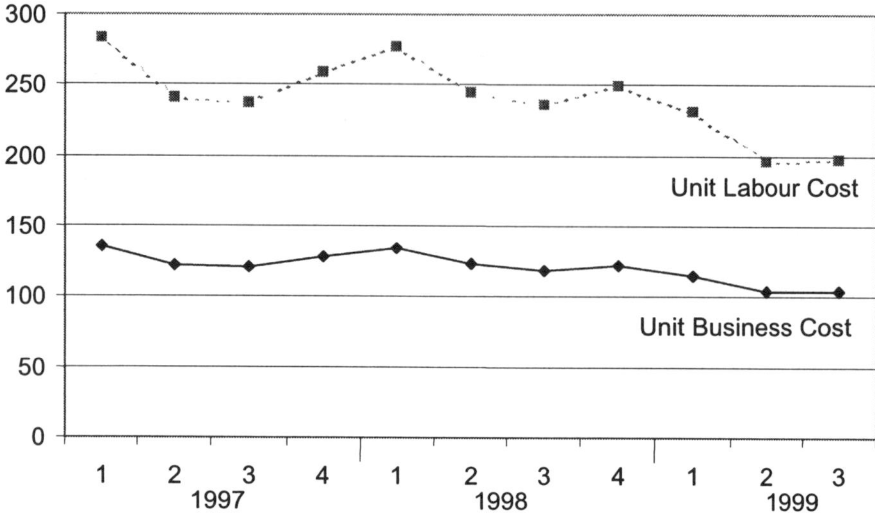

Fig. 5.7 Indices of Unit Business Cost and Unit Labour Cost

Source: Singapore Ministry of Trade and Industry, *Economic Survey Of Singapore* (Third Quarter 1999).

Given the continuing slowdown in economic growth, the government implemented a more expansionary fiscal policy in the FY99 Budget to soften its impact on businesses.[22] For fiscal year 1999, the deficit was estimated at about S$5 billion or 3.5 percent of GDP. The focus of this Budget was on long-term spending in strategic areas like education and infrastructure. Since the announcement of the FY99 Budget in February 1999, the economy has been recovering strongly, registering a growth rate of 6.7 percent for the second and third quarters, and 7.1 percent for the fourth quarter of 1999 (See Table 5.2). For the whole of 1999, Singapore enjoyed a respectable 5.4 percent growth. Its labour market also rebounded sharply as the unemployment rate dropped dramatically to 2.9 percent in December 1999 from a high of 4.5 percent in December 1998. Singapore's V-shaped recovery could be attributed to two main factors. One was the strong growth in global electronics which

---

[22]See "Dr Hu Goes with $5-billion Budget Deficit" in The Straits Times, 27 February 1999.

absorb some two thirds of Singapore's domestic exports. The other was the quick turnaround in the regional economies. With a stronger than anticipated economy recovery in Singapore, the government was able to turn an estimated S$5 billion budget deficit for FY1999 into a surplus of S$3.2 billion.

Financial Sector Reforms

The regional financial crisis laid bare the dangers of over-dependence on manufacturing and entrepot trade. Thus, despite the crisis, Singapore decided to press ahead with liberalising its financial sector because of its resolve to become a leading financial centre. In fact, it can be argued that as a land-scarce nation, Singapore's potential lies in financial and business services rather than manufacturing. The MAS thus took the opportunity afforded by the lull in regional activity during the crisis to position the financial sector for the next wave of regional growth.

To further develop Singapore as a financial centre, the MAS has enhanced financial sector transparency by raising disclosure standards. In view of the strength of the banking sector, higher disclosure standards should reduce the risk of unwarranted contagion. The MAS also decided to take a different approach to financial-sector management by emphasising the need for a "lighter touch", with the focus changing from regulation to supervision. One major outcome of this change in mindset was the introduction of several steps to ease restrictions on the use of the Singapore dollar, including: encouraging well-established foreign entities to issue Singapore dollar bonds in Singapore, allowing Singapore-run firms to borrow Singapore dollars for use outside Singapore, promoting the growth of derivatives based on the Singapore dollar (e.g. Singapore stock index futures and Singapore dollar swaps), and allowing foreign companies to list their shares in Singapore dollars in the local bourse. The new rules allowing a wider use of the Singapore dollar are contained in regulation "MAS 757" issued in August 1998 to replace regulation "MAS 621".[23] Although these changes did not

---

[23] For a detailed description and analysis of the liberalisation of the Singapore dollar, see Ngiam (1998).

amount to a full-fledged internationalisation of the Singapore dollar, they would go a long way towards broadening and deepening Singapore's financial markets. With the internationalisation of the Singapore dollar, the MAS might find it less easy to stabilise the exchange rate as there would be more funds moving in and out of the country. But given Singapore's strong fundamentals and healthy reserve position, the MAS would be well placed to handle this larger movement of funds.

7.   CONCLUSIONS AND LESSONS TO BE LEARNT

As a small open economy, Singapore is extremely vulnerable to external economic developments. Thus, the large and adverse economic shocks triggered by the Asian financial crisis could potentially have a devastating effect on the Singapore economy. Amidst extensive distress in the region, however, Singapore has emerged relatively unscathed. Although its stock and property markets have taken a beating, its economy has performed remarkably well under the circumstances. The economy registered a small positive growth in 1998 and then rebounded with a remarkable 5.4 percent growth in 1999. As a result, pay cuts for public sector employees will be fully restored in January 2000 and CPF cuts for all workers will be restored within five years. Singapore's resilience and quick recovery can be attributed to its strong fundamentals, sound policies, and willingness to take bold and effective measures in response to the crisis.

The Asian financial crisis has taught us several important lessons. The primary lesson is that Singapore has withstood the currency storm lashing the Asian region because of its strong economic fundamentals. With high current account surpluses, substantial budget surpluses, high savings rates, huge foreign exchange reserves, strong inflow of foreign direct investment, almost non-existent external debt, and negligible non-performing loans, it was able to deter currency attacks and to take timely and bold measures to counter the large negative shocks triggered by the crisis. Because of its strong position, Singapore was in a position to promise loans of US$ 1 billion to Thailand and US$ 5 billion to Indonesia as part of the IMF bailout package to these two countries. In addition, Singapore has used its foreign reserves to intervene directly in the foreign exchange markets to help shore up the baht and rupiah in the midst of the crisis.

The other lesson is that the flexibility of both exchange rate and wages in Singapore has enabled it to weather the Asian financial crisis better than most Asian economies. By adopting a managed exchange rate system, it was able to prevent an over-valuation (or under-valuation) of the Singapore dollar. An over-valued exchange rate could invite speculative attacks which Singapore found out the hard way in September 1985. Indeed, the September 1985 episode indicated that currency over-valuation and economic recession were two important warning signs of an impending currency attack. The collapse of the regional currencies during the Asian financial crisis could have left Singapore with an over-valued currency. To prevent currency over-valuation which could trigger a currency attack, Singapore's immediate response was a calculated move to devalue the Singapore dollar against the US dollar and other major currencies.

As the crisis dragged on into 1998, the focus in Singapore shifted to direct cost-cutting measures such as wage and cost reductions to boost its competitiveness because further devaluation of the Singapore dollar would affect investor confidence and thus negatively impact Singapore as a financial centre. Thus, the exchange rate and wage adjustment, coupled with some fiscal and monetary easing to stimulate domestic demand, has enable Singapore to adopt a concerted multi-pronged approach to tackle the crisis. Using a policy mix judiciously, Singapore has not only avoided the worst effect of the crisis but also spread the burden of adjustment across every segment of its society.

Another useful lesson is that Singapore's long track record of prudent fiscal and monetary policies proved to be a great asset as it helped reassure markets that the fiscal and monetary easing taken by the authorities to address short-term problems are less likely to endanger or signal a deviation from commitments to its long-term goals. Singapore has also built up a reputation during the September 1985 episode that it is willing to engineer an appreciation of the Singapore dollar to punish speculators. Speculators might have decided to leave the Singapore dollar alone during the Asian financial crisis because of Singapore's reputation of having a strong-willed and credible government.

Finally, Singapore has shown that financial liberalisation, which will greatly enhance Singapore as a financial centre, can be undertaken despite the crisis. This is because Singapore has built three strong foundations in the form of strong fundamentals, a flexible exchange rate system and an adjustable wage system, which would be sufficient to ensure its resilience against any currency attacks.

References

Bensaid, B. and O. Jeanne (1997) "The Instability of Fixed Exchange Rate Systems When Raising The Nominal Interest Rate is Costly," *European Economic Review* 41, 1461–78.

Bordo, M.D. and A. J. Schwartz (1996) "Why Clashes Between Internal and External Stability Goals End in Currency Crises, 1797–1994," *NBER Working Paper, No. 5710.*

Chan, K.S. and K.J. Ngiam (1998) "Currency Crisis and the Modified Currency Board System in Singapore," *Pacific Economic Review* 3, 243–263.

Dornbusch, Rudi (1996) "The Effectiveness of Exchange Rate Changes," *Oxford Review of Economic Policy* 12, 26–38.

Eichengreen, B., A.K. Rose and C. Wyplosz (1995) "Exchange Rate Mayhem: The Antecedents and Aftermath of Speculative Attacks," *Economic Policy* 21, 249–321.

Frankel, J.A. and A.K. Rose (1996) "Currency Crashes in Emerging Markets: An Empirical Treatment," *Journal of International Economics* 41, 351–366.

Flood, R.P., P.M.Garber and C. Kramer (1996) "Collapsing Exchange Rate Regimes: Another Linear Example," *Journal of International Economics* 41, 223–234.

Glick, R., M. Hutchinson and R. Moreno (1995) "Is Pegging the Exchange Rate a Cure for Inflation? East Asian Experiences," *Pacific Basin Working Paper* PB95-08, Federal Reserve Bank of San Francisco.

Gan, Wee Beng, W.H. Yeo and S.C. Lim (1999) "The Asian Currency Crisis and the Sustainability of Exchange Rate Regimes: The Case of Singapore," paper presented at the Autoridade Monetarie E Cambial De Macau Conference on Central Bank Policies, Macau, May 14–15, 1999.

International Monetary Fund, *Direction of Trade Statistics Quarterly*, Washington, D.C., various issues.

Jeanne, O. (1997) "Are Currency Crisis Self-Fulfilling? A Test," *Journal of International Economics* 43, 263–286.

Krugman, P. (1979) "A Model of Balance-of Payments Crisis," *Journal of Money, Credit, and Banking* 11, 311–325.

Lim, Chong Yah and Associates (1988), *Policy Options for the Singapore Economy*, Singapore: McGraw-Hill.

Ministry of Trade and Industry, *Economic Survey of Singapore*, Singapore, various issues.

Monetary Authority of Singapore, *Annual Report*, Singapore, various issues.

Moreno, R. (1995) "Macroeconomic Behavior During Periods of Speculative Pressure or Realignment: Evidence from Pacific Basin Economies," *Federal Reserve Bank of San Francisco Economic Review*, 3–16.

Ngiam, K.J. (1998) "Liberalising the Singapore Dollar During the Asian Currency Crisis: A Sound Move?" *Malaysian Journal of Economic Studies* 35, 15–28.

Obstfeld, M. (1986) "Rational and Self-fulfilling Balance-of Payments Crises," *American Economic Review* 76, 72–81.

Obstfeld, M. and K. Rogoff (1995) "The Mirage of Fixed Exchange Rates," *Journal of Economic Perspectives* 9, 73–96.

The Straits Times, Singapore, various issues.

World Bank (1998), *Global Economic Prospects and the Developing Countries: Beyond Financial Crisis.*

CHAPTER 6

HONG KONG
FINANCIAL CRISIS IN THE CASE OF HONG KONG: LAST IN, LAST OUT?

Chyau Tuan and Linda F.Y. Ng

Department of Decision Sciences and Managerial Economics
The Chinese University of Hong Kong
Shatin, N.T, Hong Kong
E-mail: LINDANG@CUHK.EDU.HK
Tuan@baf.msmail.cuhk.edu.hk

1. INTRODUCTION

The economic opening of mainland China in the 1980's has served as a pull factor for the Hong Kong's manufacturing industry to conduct cross-border processing in Guangdong and especially in the Pearl River Delta (PRD) region by leaving mainly the service components of manufacturing to be performed in the local Hong Kong economy (Tuan and Ng, 1994). The gradual diffusion of outward investment into the Guangdong province has enabled Hong Kong to evolve into a service-based economy beginning from the 1990's (Tuan and Ng, 1995a).

Alongside with its evolution into a service-dominated economy, Hong Kong has also rapidly expanded its financial market by replacing the gradually outward-relocated manufacturing. The newly developed businesses, such as banks' offshore and syndicate loans, growing futures and other derivatives markets, and bursting freely inflowing capital, have all facilitated Hong Kong in developing into a regional financial center (Tuan and Ng, 1998a). The "passive" industrial policy of the Hong Kong government (Tuan and Ng, 1995b) and together with the linked exchange rate system being adopted since October 1983 in attracting excessive capital inflow have both facilitated the rapid growth and booming of Hong Kong's newly-developed services in finance, insurance, business services, and real estates until the mid-1997. Among the group of 15 high income small-open economies with more than 60% of GDP produced by the service sector in 1993, Hong Kong recorded 83% and was found to rank the top (World Development Report, 1997).

Since the Asian financial crisis beginning in July 1997, the Hong Kong economy has experienced a serious economic downturn. As Hong Kong has transformed from an export-led manufacturing center into a service-oriented state, its economic contractions apparently concentrated mainly in domestic investment and asset markets in particular, and in service exports, such as tourism and its related industries. The Hong Kong dollar (HKD) appreciated relatively to the extensive depreciation of other East Asian currencies due to its linked exchange rate system. The very tight credit market and the soaring interest rates have discouraged investment. Both stock and property prices have adjusted downward accompanying by drastic contracting domestic consumption and record high unemployment rate since the outbreak of the financial crisis.

When almost all other Asian economies except Indonesia, which once suffered the attack of the financial crisis, slowly recovered from the crisis and eventually gained positive growth starting from the last quarter of 1998, however, Hong Kong's GDP growth remained negative not until the second quarter of 1999 at 0.2%. A very interesting question is that why a financially sound and economically healthy economy like Hong Kong has not been among the first to recover from the financial turmoil as boldly claimed by the Hong Kong Government soon after the Asian crisis occurred.

This chapter attempts to review the causes, effects, remedial policy measures, and the process of recovery of the 1997/98 financial turmoil in the case of Hong Kong. It is expected that distinct differences in the causes of the turmoil can be identified for Hong Kong from those most severely attacked economies (such as Thailand, Indonesia, Malaysia, and Korea). A conceptual framework for further analyses was developed. In this connection, policy measures controlling the immediate risk and panic, smoothening the economic downturn, and stimulating recovery will be particularly discussed. This chapter concludes by explanations why Hong Kong is likely one of the last recovered economies in the region in terms of macroeconomic performance.

2. ASIAN ECONOMIES IN CRISIS — A BRIEF LITERATURE REVIEW

2.1 Analytical Framework and Focus

There have been numerous studies proposing explanations to the causes and effects of the Asian financial crisis in mid-1997. To the general public, the Asian crisis was first associated with the Mexican and Latin American financial crises (1994–1995) by relating their similarities and differences. Later, just like the experiences of Russia and East Europe where dramatic currency depreciation has led to severe economic depression and inflation, the 1997–98 Asian financial crisis was considered as an alike phenomenon along the same line. Further, some studies even started to question on the existence of the "Asian Miracle".

However, the Asian economies did not collapse while most of them have seemingly started to recover since 1999. Studies performed in the last two years have tried to emphasize, if any, the uniqueness and differences of the Asian experience. Attention has focused on the financial side of the Asian 97/98 crisis and its contagious effects (Fratzscher, 1998; Kaminsky & Reinhart, 1999). A consensus being reached seemed to be that high performing Asian economies deserved somewhat different explanation for their "crises" being experienced.

In his article "What Happened to Asia?" Krugman (1998) states "i(I)t seems safe to say that nobody anticipated anything like the current crisis in Asia". He argued, amongst some others, that Asian economies had no special immunity to financial crisis and some of them were surprisingly vulnerable to crisis contagion. In thinking of some causes of the recent Asian economic travails, Krugman considered that while there were existing theories through which possible explanations may be offered, further in-depth analyses is needed. The "first generation" model is the conventional currency-crisis theory, which focuses mainly on fiscal deficits, balance-of-payments, and impacts upon overvalued exchange rate. That is, a government with persistent deficits in budget and current account but using limited reserves to peg exchange rate will eventually invite crisis (Krugman, 1979; Flood and Garber, 1984). The "second generation" models (Obstfeld, 1994) are found based on macroeconomic temptation to sustain growth via promoting trade. In this connection, investors always question whether, how long, and how much cost and willingness a government chooses to pay to defend its pegged exchange rate under speculative attacks.

In considering the Asian crisis, a commonly identified element observed among the Asian countries is that financial intermediaries seem to have been the central players in bringing on financial excess and then financial collapse (Krugman, 1998). Such a problem is described by unregulated excessive liabilities or lending perceived to be government guaranteed and then subject to severe moral hazard problem, which consequently lead to high inflation and overvalued asset prices. The proliferation of risky lending creates a vicious circle of further driving up risky asset prices to form asset bubble. When the bubble bursts, the mechanism of crisis is the reverse of the same circular process. Although Krugman's model recognized the over-simplification in explaining the Asian crisis, it seemingly explained closely the 1997 experience of some Asian countries suffering from financial collapse and contagion.

Along the same line but with a different focus, the links between banking and currency crises were analyzed. The findings of these studies suggested that financial liberalization often precedes banking crisis, and then problems in the banking sector typically precede a currency crisis. At the macroeconomic level, it suggested that a prolonged boom in economic activity which was fueled by credit, capital-inflows and accompanied by an over-valued currency could be an ideal environment for the development of financial/currency crises (Kaminsky & Reinhart, 1999).

Based on the observations of the transmission and the evolutions of the 1997 crisis in the following years, Sachs and Woo (1999) suggested that the Asian financial crisis, in fact, is a financial panic involving international creditors, even "Asian specifics in the 1997 crisis" were also reflected at the onset of the panic. That is, "the crisis was built on national weakness that were greatly magnified by a flawed international financial system", but, "the extent of economic devastation in each Asian country differs according to specific national structural conditions and policy reactions" (Sachs and Woo, 1999).

Sachs and Woo (1999) proposed a framework to explain what had happened in the Asian economies since 1996 when the pegged Thai currency was first perceived to be over-valued by investors. At the onset of the financial crisis, the "Asian success" has invited huge capital inflows and international borrowing in such an amount that no financial market in this region was able to allocate the amount of investment efficiently. Weaknesses in the banking system had been accumulated by the end of 1996. Therefore, the financial panic which was ignited in Thailand in the mid-1997 was followed by "creditor panic" with massive capital outflow and sharp domestic credit contraction. The contagion of neighboring country triggered financial panic and "creditor panic" in other Asian countries. The observed sequence was business and production contraction to be followed by economic downtowns of the crisis affected countries.

Along a similar line, Mishkin (1999) proposed a "sequence of events" for the financial crisis in East Asia with special focus on the troubled banking sector and the resultant impacts upon the real economy. He argued that the current Asian economic problems (crises) could be considered as the consequences due to financial instability. In his words, "financial instability occurs when shocks to the financial system interfere with information flows so that the financial system can no longer do its job of channeling funds to those with productive investment opportunities" (Mishkin, 1999). Such a kind of instability has been suggested to occur when asymmetric information problems (moral hazard and adverse selection) worsen due to four factors: (1) deterioration of the balances of financial sector balance sheets; (2) increase in interest rate; (3) increase in uncertainty; and (4) deterioration of the balances of non-financial balance sheets due to changes in asset prices. When external shocks (for example, financial turmoil being happened in the neighboring country) triggered financial panic (such as massive capital inflows turned around rapidly) and herding behavior[1] developed in the domestic market, the resulted currency crisis will easily be further developed into credit panic (short of creditors) and hence contractions of total spending and economic activity.

2.2   Globalization of Asian Financial Market: Imperfections and Speculative Activities

The arguments and research finding summarized by Mishkin (1999) where global capitalism and its impacts, such as instability caused by rapidly turn around of short-term capital flows being focused, might represent the first time that Western mainstream economists to pay attention to the imperfections of globalization in financial market and the opening of capital accounts in the emerging economies.

In 1998, the World Bank proposed voluminous statistics in supporting the imperfections of the international financial market as an exogenous or structural factor to the cause of the prevailing Asian financial crisis (World Bank, 1998). Recent focus of international economic meetings of Central Banks among countries had been observed to shift to pay serious attention to the issues of regulations and/or joint regulations of the huge amount of international capital flows and their operations in the financial markets, including financial derivatives which normally magnified the value of transactions by leverage. The very rapid freely flowing short-term capital into and out of an economy, especially those small-open economies, has

---

[1] "Herding" by investors can be considered as one kind of market failure in contributing to one of the cause of the financial crisis (Krugman, 1998).

created serious fluctuations and impacts in both the foreign exchange and stock markets. If the neighboring country's currency collapsed and domestic macroeconomic situation deteriorated (e.g., persistent inflation, balance of payments deficits, etc.) happened together with investors' coincidental concerns, herding behavior develops, overshooting happens, and financial instability then follows.

The 'liquidity' problem of the U.S. Long Term Capital Management Fund (LTCM) in 1998, which almost paralyzed the whole U.S. banking system and later with the Federal Reserve participating in the rescue action, has indeed served as an illustrating case for the need of the knowledge, understanding, and transparent operations of the international short-term capital flows or hot money and hedge funds. In May 17, 1999, the Chief of IMF restated in Hong Kong regarding such a need and further called for international cooperation in dealing with these off-shore funds. Given asymmetric information, the speedy flows of hot money should have been identified, by experience, as one of the major cause of the current Asian financial crisis.

Summarizing the existing literatures in discussing the causes of the Asian financial crisis facing the East Asian and Southeast countries, some common features being found are:

(1) rapid economic growth attracted huge inflows of foreign capital beginning with direct foreign investment and followed by short-term capital or lending in the form of company bonds;
(2) given the opening of capital market in the Asian economies in the 1990's, easy international borrowing induced over-investment to surpass saving and persistent deficit in the current accounts;
(3) for some Asian countries, over-lending by poorly regulated banks with poor risk management to form illiquidity in the banking system, such as mismatches in the financial system in currencies (denomination in local versus foreign) mixtures lending and its timing of repayment between debtors and lenders. Thus, the problem simulates a 'liquidity' problem which would undermine the whole financial system even with a minor trigger; and

(4) the "triggers" are normally the overvalued local currency, such as Thai Baht, herding behavior or overshooting of regional investors, or just a strategic move of hedge funds (contagion effects). Hence, the currency crisis then financial crisis is the real malady.

3.   BACKGROUND OF THE 1997 FINANCIAL CRISIS IN THE HONG KONG ECONOMY

The experience and transmission process of the financial turmoil in the case of Hong Kong is quite distinct from that of the other Asian countries even though they share the common ultimate phenomenon of economic downturn/recession. Following the literature findings summarized in the above, the experiences of most Asian economies which suffered from financial crisis in 1997/98 can be modeled and constructed as in Figure 6.1 below. Figure 6.1 summarizes the fundamental relations among various macroeconomic activities and depicts the sequence of transmission from financial market operations and banking system to impacts upon the business sectors. Given the existence of managed exchange rate regimes, some weaknesses in the macroeconomy and banking system (such as seemingly overvalued local currency, short-term debts in denomination of foreign currencies in the banking/business sectors, underdeveloped capital market regulations, poor banking risk management, etc.), would have triggered speculators attack in the foreign exchange market. Then, currency crisis and financial crisis followed in terms of full-fledge financial instability represented by sharp contraction in loans and collapse of banks and production firms due to deterioration of their balance sheets. Hence, the channel of transmission of the turmoil in these Asian countries can be presented visually by route (A) in Figure 6.1.

However, the route through which the Hong Kong financial turmoil proceeded was somewhat different. By the mid-1997, Hong Kong has been well known for her healthy economy and prudent banking system in terms of lowest rate of non-performing loans (1.5–3%), highest capital ratio (15–21%) in the region, efficient operations, matured regulations, and

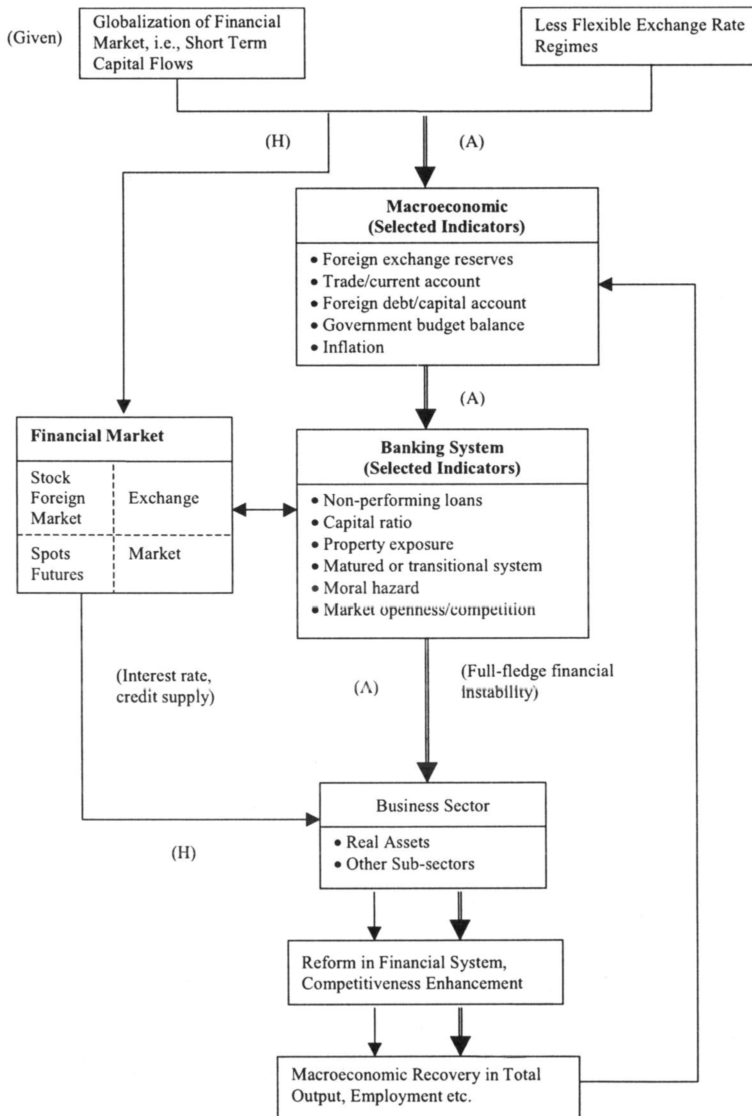

Fig. 6.1 From Financial Crisis to Economic Recovery

Note: (A) Stands for other Asian countries.
   (B) Stands for Hong Kong.
Source: The Study.

developed infrastructure. The reserves to support her linkage exchange rate was (and still is) one of the highest (60% of M_2) amongst all economies adopting Currency Board Arrangement (CBA) in the World. Therefore, Hong Kong was the last Asian open economy being attacked by speculators. Even so, no one doubts until today that their major target by then was in fact realizing profits in the stock/futures market rather than in the foreign exchange market like what the other speculators did in the other countries.

Such financial attacks happened at least three times (October 23, 1997; January-March, 1998; and the most notable in August 1998) in Hong Kong. Hence, the route through which the financial turmoil proceeded in Hong Kong is presented by (H) in Figure 6.1. While the development of such a financial crisis was quite different from the other victims and also without the collapse of the Hong Kong's banking system, the ultimate impacts on her business and macroeconomic downturn were identical. The details of such channels of transmission of the financial turmoil will be discussed in later sections.

In the following sub-section, two of the most critical elements in the Hong Kong economy in the pre-crisis stage will be discussed along with Hong Kong's economic structure: the linkage exchange rate regime and asset market bubble. The former provided incentives for speculators to test Hong Kong's willingness to defend the pegged rate and exploit profits generated from its build-in mechanism. The latter is, in nature, one of the very few remained weakness in the Hong Kong banking system represented by 40% of property exposure in bank loans.

3.1 Hong Kong's Linked Exchange Rate Regime Since 1983

In October, 1983 and just before the Sino-British declaration, Hong Kong has changed from a floating exchange rate to pegging the US dollar in order to stabilize the exchange rate fluctuations arising from the political uncertainty at that time.[2] Hong Kong has adopted a linked exchange rate

---

[2] The first time when Hong Kong adopted a currency board system was in November 1935 and the second in October 1983. For detailed discussion of the development of Hong Kong monetary system since 1935, see Jao (1998).

system ever since. In order to strengthen and stabilize the monetary system preparing for the transfer of sovereignty in the absence of a Central Bank,[3] the Hong Kong Government first established the Foreign Exchange Management Fund in 1988 and later the Hong Kong Monetary Authority (HKMA) in 1993. Since then, the rate has been managed by HKMA[4].

HKMA's management of exchange rate and the money supply in Hong Kong is basically a version of CBA. Jao (1999) used the Cantillon-Hume mechanism to describe this CBA variant in terms of money supply. Given full foreign exchange reserves (e.g., Gold, US$, etc.) and the pegged rate regime, the growth rate of the money supply will approximate the growth rates of foreign reserves and high-power money (Jao, 1999). In principle, sufficient reserves and healthy, prudent banking system, which are required for a successful CBA (Pakko, 1999; Enoch, 1998), are the fulfilled conditions in the case of Hong Kong.

With full backing, the Currency Board (CB) is able to make its commitment by converting local currency to foreign currency at fixed rate. However, like any fixed exchange rate regime, the CB's firm commitment to fixing the value of the domestic currency relating to a foreign currency by such a rigid mechanism also makes the country adopting the CB to lose its independent control on its monetary policy and tie its fate to that of the "hard" currency to which it is pegged. Under a classical CBA, the monetary authority even loses its ability to serve as a lender of the last resort during a liquidity crisis (Pakko, 1999).

As far as the Hong Kong version of the CBA is concerned, the half-a-century accumulation in foreign exchange reserves in Foreign Exchange Fund makes HKMA capable to cautiously provide certain amount of liquidity to the banking system if it is deemed necessary. Such a mechanism was labeled as Liquidity Adjustment Facility (LAF) and later renamed as Discount

---

[3] Outward processing trade is the importation of process goods from China, in particular the PRD region and the Special Economic Zones (SEZs), of which all or part of the raw materials or semi-manufactures are under contractual arrangement originally exported from or through Hong Kong to China for processing.

[4] Money issuance in Hong Kong is conducted by three commercial banks with central clearance performed by one of the bank — the Hong Kong and Shanghai Bank.

Window in the mid-1998. The lost of independence in the monetary policy is mainly observed in interest rates management. From rediscount rate to prime rate, the basic reference lines are their corresponding rates of the US dollar to which the Hong Kong currency pegged. The rate differences between the two currencies usually reflect the level of risk premium in the foreign exchange markets.

From the period of July–October, 1997, the huge currency depreciations of the East Asian countries have made the HKD relatively appreciated due to its pegged rate system. In August 1998, the HKD appreciated 10% in terms of the effective exchange rate (EER) and 7.4% in March 1999 after the stabilization of the East Asian currencies. Such a de-facto currency appreciation would decrease exports and hence retard economic growth.

3.2 The Pre-Crisis Economic Situation: A Service-Dominating Economy

Due to the heavy outflow of outward investment of Hong Kong manufacturing to Guangdong since 1979, in only a decade starting from 1987, the proportion of manufacturing value added to GDP dropped from 22% in 1987 to 7.2% in 1996, and manufacturing employment from 34.1% to 11.2%, respectively. The restructuring of the production from manufacturing to service-dominating was observed starting from 1987 in terms of input-output, labor employment, and industrial structure (Tuan and Ng, 1995c; Ng, 1995).

The outward investment of the Hong Kong manufacturers has also restructured the Hong Kong economy's and contents of tradable goods/services. The outward processing trade[5] derived by the cross-border operations has replaced domestic export trade as a predominate trade component (Ng and Tuan, 1997). Consequently, the evolution of trade activities to emphasize on re-exports and its trade derivatives,[6] given the stagnated growth in domestic

---

[5] The linkage rate is pegged at US$1:HK$7.8 with HKMA managing the rate to fluctuate between HK$7.75 to HK$7.8.

[6] The term "trade derivatives" was first adopted by the authors to describe any further trade activities being "derived" from the traditional or conventional trade activities and operations including offshore trading or transshipment activities developed to supplement and sometimes even to replace the conventional re-exports trade.

exports, has been found as the mechanism in promoting the continuous economic growth in Hong Kong since the mid-1980's (Tuan and Ng, 1998b). Other than the traditional service sector, some newly developed service industries have expanded rapidly in contributing to GDP growth.

In Figure 6.2, the left-hand side of the figure illustrated the significance of industrial production in terms of percentage contributions to GDP by industrial sectors in Hong Kong and the right-hand side depicts the components of total exports. While domestic merchandise exports accounted for only 17.8% of GDP, re-exports was recorded at 99.4% in terms of volume (in dollar value) to GDP. As far as the service exports are concerned, the various service industries together have made significant contributions (24.2% of GDP) in 1996.

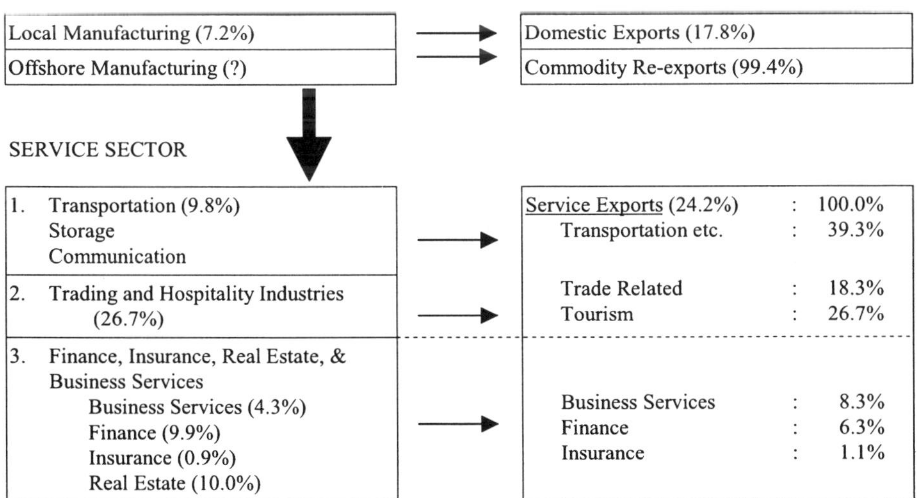

Fig. 6.2 Relations Between Industrial Sectors and Trade Contributions in Hong Kong (1996)

Note: Trading industries include wholesale, retail and import/export trades; figures in parentheses represent percentages of GDP; arrow in bold line represents derived economic activity.

Source: The Study.

The Hong Kong economy has been relying heavily on external demand in its service exports especially since 1987. Figure 6.2 shows that the manufacturing-derived service activities (such as transportation, storage, and trading industries) were sharing a total of more than half of the service exports in 1996 with increasing importance in terms of their dollar values to GDP in all service industry groups. Tourism service exports contributed 26.7% of the total service exports and the newly developed service industries (finance, insurance, and business services) as a whole contributed about 15%.

During the past ten years, among the rapidly growing sectors in services, the traditional (manufacturing related and tourism related) business including wholesale, retail, imports/exports, restaurants, and hotels, had expanded to contribute 26.7% in GDP and 34.7% in employment in 1996 as compared to 24.3% and 24.5% in 1987, respectively. The newly developed business services to include finance, insurance, real estate, and business services have been the most rapidly growing service group. Its respective contributions to GDP and employment were 25.1% and 11.7% in 1996 relative to 17.9% and 6.1% in 1987. Comparing with the performance of export services, the traditional service groups were more outward-led and the newly developed groups were less export-oriented.

Although the regionalization of Hong Kong as a financial center has provided financial investors very limited investment restrictions and debtors adequate sources of funds, the financial intermediaries (market) have given much less priorities to the manufacturing and trade sectors but more to the real estate sector in loans and advances allocations. In this sense, the financial market in Hong Kong has been a less efficient fund provider in facilitating the development of all other industries alongside with its own development (Tuan and Ng, 1998a).

3.3 The Pre-Crisis Asset Bubbles

Given the growth of the financial sector in Hong Kong as a result of regional openness to international capital flows, the economic slowdown of the U.S. economy from the mid-1980 to the mid-1990 and its adoption of a low interest rate as an expansionary policy left Hong Kong with no choice but to follow suit because of its linkage exchange rate with the U.S. currency.

Consequently, an overheated economy with bubble asset prices, double digit inflation, but rapid and continuous money growth due to huge inflows of international capital with low interest rates was observed during the ten-year period before the strike of the Asian Crisis.

Being regionalized as an international financial center, Hong Kong's financial market has attracted vast amounts of foreign funds. In the 1990's, among the international financial activities by types of financial transactions, international syndicate loans ranked top and followed by foreign exchange transactions (after Japan and Singapore). In 1992 and 1995, the daily transaction volume of foreign exchange reached US$61 billion and US$90.2 billion, respectively, holding the sixth and fifth position in the World. Following the Asian financial crisis, the daily contracted transactions of foreign exchange still reached US$78.5 billion in April 1998 and ranked seventh place in the World and after Japan and Singapore in Asia.

Table 6.1 illustrates the growth rates of money supply by M_1 and M_3, real GDP, and consumer price index. Under the currency board system, the growth of money supply has been quite unstable and is basically moving in line with the changes in US dollar reserves. The statistics from Table 6.1 show that since 1989, GDP growth has slowed down to 1-digit but money supply has remained, on average, at the 2-digit level. The growth rates of M_3 were much higher than that of M_1 because of the inflows of international capital.

Table 6.1 Growth Rates of GDP, Money Supply, and Prices (1987–1999)

(percent)

Year	Real GDP (1990 = 100)	M1 (HK$)	M2 (HK$)	Consumer Price Index (A)
1987	13.0	22.1	19.1	5.5
1989	2.6	9.0	19.0	10.1
1991	5.1	16.8	13.0	12.0
1993	6.1	14.2	19.8	8.5
1995	3.9	0.6	16.3	8.7
1997	5.3	11.4	19.0	5.7
1998	−5.1	−12.6	5.1	2.6

Source: Financial Statistics Monthly, Hong Kong Monetary Authority, March 1999; *Estimates of Gross Domestic Products, 1961–1998*, Hong Kong Statistic Department, 1999.

The rapid growth of money supply and high inflation rates, almost zero or negative real interest rates (averaged −0.2% during 1992−97) especially before the turnover of sovereignty in 1997, and together with adequate supply of low cost foreign capital, over-investments and "herding" in the property and stock markets, and overvalued property and stock prices all formed bubble assets. Table 6.2 illustrates the rapidly increasing property (sales and rental) and stock prices for 1991−98. Rental prices for residential as an indicator of actual housing demand was found to increase by 100% from the period of 1989 to July 1997. However, when the sales of residential housing which included speculative demand was used to measure the asset prices, the increase was 333% (Table 6.2). At the same time, stock prices

Table 6.2   Indexes of Real Estate and Stock Prices (1991–1997)

Year		Sales of Private Housing (1989 = 100)	Rental of Private Housing (1989 = 100)	Rental of Offices (1989 = 100)	Hang Seng Stock Price Index[*] (31/7/1964 = 100)
1991		−	−	−	3471.54
1995		272	174	132	9098.47
1996		298	171	112	11646.55
1997	1~3	419	194	115	13294.70
	4~6	429	193	115	
	7~9	433	200	116	16673.00 (August 7)
	10~12	417	198	117	
1998	1~3	354	178	113	
	4~6	322	169	106	6660.00 (June 13)
	7~9	265	153	95	7936.20 (July)
	10~12	258	146	86	13300.00 (October)
1999	1~3	262	146	79	10942.00
	4~6	262	144	73	13532.00
	7~9	255	144	71	12733.00

Note: *Represents day-end transaction average price in December 31 of each year; stock price index in 1989 = 2793; monthly index is the day-end transaction average price in the last day of the month.
Source: *Hong Kong Monthly Statistics*, Hong Kong Government, September 1998; *Third Quarter Economic Report, 1999*, Hong Kong Government, November, 1999.

increased by 480% from 2,793 points in 1989 to a record high of 16,673 immediately after the handover in August 7, 1997.

4. THE HONG KONG VERSION OF 1997–98 FINANCIAL CRISIS: A CONCEPTUAL FRAMEWORK

4.1 Causes of the Crisis

Unlike the Latin American countries, most of the Southeast and East Asian countries as well as the Hong Kong economy were sound and healthy in many aspects during the pre-crisis period and before the 1997–98 financial crisis. In Hong Kong, facts and statistics from Tables 6.3 and 6.4 show that

(1) trade deficits with modest size were only observed in 1995 and 1996 (Table 6.3);
(2) government budget surplus was observed in most years during the past half a century (Table 6.3);
(3) gross domestic savings normally exceeded gross domestic investment before 1995. However, the reverse was true but its size was insignificant as compared to GDP (Table 6.3);
(4) foreign currency assets accumulated by the Exchange Fund was 7.8 times of HKD in circulation, or US$14,028 per capita in 1997. This amount of reserves was equivalent to 14.7 months of retained imports of goods (Table 6.4);
(5) to prepare for the 1997 handover, risk management in the banking system had been strengthened since the early 1990's. Given CBA, the functions of the HKMA had been broadened and its governance over the banking system strengthened;
(6) the banking and business relationship or government-business relationship was comparable to any developed countries.

Following the conceptual framework being depicted by Figure 6.1 in the previous section, it can be further illustrated that, given the maintenance of the pegged exchange rate in the case of Hong Kong and cross country-cross

Table 6.3 Trade Balances, Government Surplus, and Domestic Investment and Savings (1988–1998)

Year	GDP (%)	Trade Balances		Government Surplus	Investment as % of GDP	Savings as % of GDP
		Merchandise	Services			
	(1)	(2)	(3)	(4)	(5)	(6)
1988	8	–8105	48176	16066	28.6	37.4
1991	5.1	–16156	60273	22509	27.2	33.8
1993	6.1	–29460	92583	19164	27.6	34.8
1994	5.4	–84414	96601	10843	31.9	33.1
1995	3.9	–151579	104758	–3113	34.8	30.5
1996	4.5	–141933	124996	25678	32.1	30.7
1997	5.3	–163519	116373	80860	35.1	31.5
1998	–5.1	–84773	88801	–	–	–

Note: Column (1) in 1990 prices; units of columns (2)–(4) in current HK$Mn; units of columns (1), (5)–(6) in percentages. Trade deficits of 1995–97 were 4.3%, 1.4%, and 3.5%, respectively, of the GDP of the corresponding year.

Source: *Annual Digest of Statistics*, 1998, Census and Statistics Department (CSD), 1998; unpublished GDP Statistics of CSD.

Table 6.4 Foreign Currency Assets of the Exchange Fund (1993–1998)

Year (as at end of)	Foreign Currency Assets* (FCA) (US$Mn)			FCA Per Capita (US$)	FCA in Terms of Months of RIG (months)	Ratio of FCA to CIC
	Exchange Fund	Land Fund	Total			
1993	43013	–	43013	7171	10.1	4.7
1994	49274	–	49274	8052	9.9	4.9
1995	55424	–	55424	8840	9.1	5.2
1996	63840	–	63840	9942	10.7	5.7
1997	75341	17482	92840	14028	14.7	7.8
1998	89620	–	89620	13169	17.5	7.4

Note: *Not including unsettled forward transactions; not including Hong Kong dollar assets (7.5% of total value of assets as at end of 1997); RIG represents retained imports of goods; CIC represents currency in circulation.

Source: *HKMA Monthly Statistical Bulletin*, HKMA, March, 1999.

market operations of global short-term capital, how external shocks will be invited and how it can affect the ultimate economic performance. A fundamentally healthy economy like Hong Kong as reflected by the vast foreign exchange reserves, healthy current account, no foreign debt, and sound government budget balances, the linked rate system per sec is possibly the only incentive to attract speculators to come.

In transmitting the external shock to the real economy, it is not necessary to pass through full-fledge financial instability and banks collapse. Interest rate soaring and credit contractions are equally worse. The channel of transmission should not have been via the banking system as demonstrated by the healthy risk indicators, but rather via the financial market.

Without losing the essentials, the cause of the 1997 Hong Kong financial turmoil can only be attributable to the manipulations in the financial market by speculators being initiated by a sequence of devaluation of local currencies in the Southeast Asia region after July 1997. The devaluation of the New Taiwan dollar, a healthy currency of another economically sound economy where managed floating exchange regime was adopted, was considered as the immediate punch (see for example, Tuan, 1997; Tsang, 1998).

It is also a general belief even until the time being that the inflows of short-term capital and their operations in the Hong Kong financial market from October 1997 to mid-1998 were aiming at possible speculative profits from the local stocks and futures market rather than the pegged exchange rate itself. The exchange rate market, at least, was not the primary target (Tuan, 1997; Henderson, 1998). Under a CBA with all necessary conditions being fulfilled, not many investors can question its ability in maintaining the linked rate in the first place.

Then, by what and how the Hong Kong version of the financial turmoil was ignited? A principal way of manipulations of many hedge funds (a major component of short-term capitals during the crisis period) was to raise market interest rates by cross markets (stock-foreign exchange and derivatives) operations and then to settle the HSI futures previously bought at lower purchase price (as an example, see Leung, 1999). The basic procedures of operations were found as follows:

#(1) short the HSI futures at the market a few months in advance (e.g., July or August, 1997) while the financial crisis in Thailand just began and Hong Kong's stock prices was still at its high level;

#(2) short HKD for US dollar in the forward exchange market in order to bid up the forward rate of US dollar against HKD;

#(3) as a signal of speculation in the foreign exchange market, HKMA took a more conservative attitude toward LAF (the Hong Kong version of discount window) operations;

#(4) under the current linkage rate regime (or CBA), operation #(2) also implied a decrease in the supply of HKD;

#(5) consequently, the Hong Kong inter-bank offered rates (HIBOR) increased and soon followed by the market interest rates; and

#(6) the result of operation #(5) was the drop of prices of stocks and HSI futures. Speculators therefore could settle their contracts being shorted before with huge profits.

Such a cross-market operations targeting at earning speculative profits from the financial derivatives (such as HSI futures) market via interest rate manipulations can be illustrated by a flow chart as in Figure 6.3. Relevant financial statistics during the 1997–98 financial turmoil period can be compared in order to identify their associations. The first attack of the HKD by international speculators was experienced on October 23, 1997. Gradual climbing and then soaring risk premium associated with the forward rate (HK$/US$) had been observed since September 1997. Its first peak was further arrived during October–December 1997 when the Thai currency was under attack and in turn was followed by extensive devaluation of other Southeast, East Asian currencies. The second drastic "jump" of the forward rate was recorded during June–September 1998 when the second attack against the HKD was launched. Coincidentally, the daily increase of turnover of HSI futures surged during the two corresponding periods. The subsequent effect was not only the harvesting of speculators in the local stock market via settlement of HSI futures previously shorted for the purpose, but also soaring interest rates in the market.

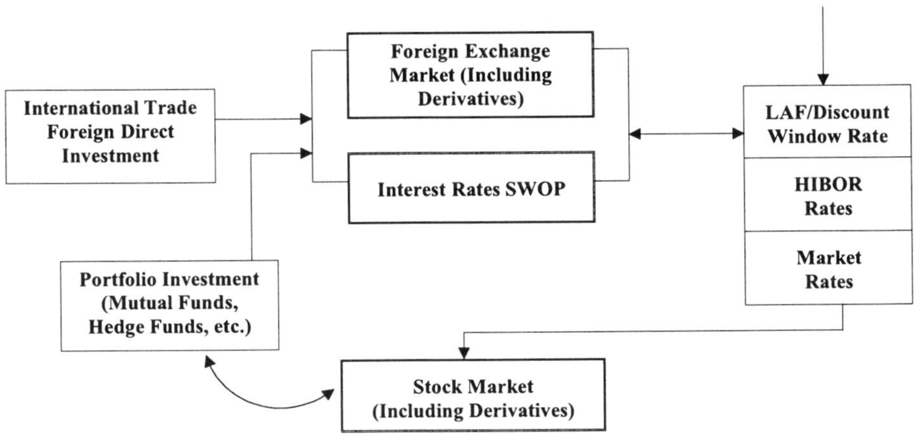

Fig. 6.3 Cross-Market Operations 1997–1998, Hong Kong

Source: The Study.

4.2 Soaring Interest Rate: Effects on Banking System and Real Economy

The immediate result of the crisis on the Asian countries is the extensive depreciations of exchange rates and the collapse of their financial markets. A major impact of the speculators' operations in Hong Kong was a soaring interest rate in the money market. As the HKD relatively appreciated against other Asian currencies due to its pegged rate with the US$, the HKMA has restlessly defended the rate via more rigid operations of the discount window (liquidity adjustment facility by then) whenever the pegged rate was attacked by international financial speculators. The consequence was widely fluctuated and rapidly rising inter-bank rate (at 2-digit until November 1998) to once reached 300% on October 23, 1997 following the speculations against the pegged HKD.

It was clearly observed that the HIBOR once jumped to a record closing high of 100%, 25%, and 20% for the overnight, 3-month, and 12-month rates, respectively, on October 23, 1997. During the period of the second major and obvious attack, the overnight and 3-month rates both surged to a closing high of 19% on August 28, 1998. As far as the monthly averages are concerned, overnight HIBOR recorded its peak at 11.23% in October 1997 and second highest at 9.84% in August 1998. The 3-month and 12-month HIBOR reached their peaks at 11.78% in August 1998 and 12.09% in January 1998, respectively. During the period of October 1997 to September, 1998, the 3–12 month inter-bank rates were kept high (at about 80% higher than at the pre-crisis level), which resulted to extensive contracting inter-bank loans and surging market interest rates.

The best lending rate of the HKD was usually keeping a difference of 0.25 percentage point higher than the U.S. bank prime rate during pre-crisis months in 1997. However, the margin surged since the crisis began on October 23, 1997. Given the reference of the U.S. bank prime rate of 8.5%, the best lending rate in Hong Kong was 9.5% in November, 1997, 15.25% for January-March, 1998, and then gradually adjusted to 10% for April-October, 1998. Until the first quarter of 1999, the margin was still kept at 1 percentage point apart (see Table 6.5).

With high interest rates, the Hong Kong stock market measured by HSI had contracted by 60%, while the monthly turnover decreased to HK$63.7 billion in August, 1997 to only HK$89 billion in July, 1998, and to HK$78 billion in December, 1998. Total market capitalization decreased from

Table 6.5 Hong Kong Dollar Interest Rates

Year	Month	Effective from Day	Savings Deposits Rate	Best Lending Rate	Year	Month	Effective from Day	Savings Deposits Rate	Best Lending Rate
1994	8	22	3.00	7.75	1998	1	12	5.50	10.25
	10	1	3.00	7.75		3	30	5.25	10.00
	11	21	3.75	8.50		10	19	5.00	9.75
1995	1	3	3.75	8.50		11	23	4.75	9.50
	2	6	4.25	9.00		12	7	4.50	9.25
	11	2	4.25	9.00		12	21	4.25	9.00
	12	27	4.00	8.70	1999	1	11	4.00	8.75
1996	2	5	3.75	8.50		4	12	3.75	8.50
1997	3	27	4.00	8.75		5	3	3.50	8.25
	10	24	4.00	9.50		8	30	3.75	8.50
	10	27	4.75	9.50	2000	2	15	4.00	8.75

Source: *Hong Kong Monthly Statistics*, HKSAR Government, December 1999; *Ming Po*, February 16, 2000.

HK$4,607 billion in July, 1997 to its lowest of HK$1960 billion in August, 1998 and to HK$2,661 billion by the end of 1998. The wealth of the Hong Kong stock market thus contracted by more than 40% in 18 months from July 1997 to December 1998.

Along with the tightened credit market with soaring interest rate and sluggish stock market, real estate prices dropped at a two-digit rate. The price level of both offices and residential property dropped drastically for

Table 6.6 Growth Rates of Economic Activities by Sectors (1997.Q1–1999.Q2)

(percent)

	1997				1998				1999	
	Q1	Q2	Q3	Q4	Q1	Q2	Q3	Q4	Q1	Q2
Industrial Production	−1	−3	−1	1	−4	−5	−11	−14	−10	−7
Producers Prices	*	*	*	*	−1	−1	−2	−2	−2	−2
Major Services Revenues										
Imports/Exports	2	3	5	3	−6	−10	−15	−18	−20	−16
Wholesales	1	*	−4	−4	−8	−14	−17	−22	−21	−16
Retails	6	9	7	−2	−13	−15	−19	−19	−14	−8
Hotels	5	7	−15	−26	−28	−34	−25	−20	−12	−9
Restaurants	9	11	6	*	−5	−4	−5	−3	−2	−1
Banking	7	13	10	−12	−5	−9	−13	4	1	6
Finance (except banking)	21	63	68	−4	−25	−41	−47	−23	−20	5
Transports	8	5	1	−1	−13	−11	−10	−12	*	−1
Communications	21	24	21	13	8	−5	−6	−7	−21	−17
Real Estates	37	27	12	−13	−32	−29	−25	−8	−13	−9
Properties										
Residential Sales	18	15	2	−6	−19	−11	−20	−3	6	3
Residential Rentals	6	4	4	−1	−10	−5	−9	−5	*	−1
Office Sales	9	1	−7	−5	−17	−9	−24	−5	−8	*
Office Rentals	2	1	1	0	−3	−6	−10	−9	−8	−8
Overall Real Wages	–	6	–	7	–	5	–	2	–	–
Visitor Arrivals	9	2	−27	−23	−25	−16	10	5	13	10
Bank Loans										
HK Dollar	9.3	6.5	6.4	−2.8	−0.6	0.2	−1.6	−0.7	−1.4	−2.5
Foreign Currencies	−4.6	10.5	−4.5	−4.2	−16.4	−6.5	−11.1	−2.6	−14.4	−8.4

Note: *Represents a change of < 0.5%.
Source: Same as Table 6.3.

four consecutive quarters in 1998, while rentals decreased following a similar pattern (Table 6.6). The bursting of the asset bubbles worsens the balance sheets of banks and non-financial firms. The negative wealth effect, expectations on further spread of the Asian financial crisis, and the uncertainty of the future of Hong Kong dollar and Chinese RMB had all forced the banking system to run it business more conservatively. Loan contractions were observed starting from the fourth quarter of 1997 (Table 6.6).

Even worse, given CBA and a firm commitment to the pegged rate, an obvious spillover long-lasting effects of the Asian financial crisis since 1997 was a persistent high effective exchange rate (EERI) of the HKD, which is partially responsible for the economic downturn in Hong Kong. The high interest rate had damaged not only the financial but also finally the real sector.

5.   PERFORMANCE OF THE ECONOMY DURING 1997/98

The first wave of the Asian financial crisis and its association with the global capital movements in October 1997 were investigated and presented by Tuan (1997). Along with the tightened credit market and the sluggish stock market, the crisis has also affected directly and indirectly the economy in that

(1) a drastic drop in local average property prices at two-digit rate by at least 50% in one year since October 1997. The value of residential property was observed to drop by −19%, −11%, −20%, and −3% for the four quarters in 1998, and the price of office buildings went down even further. Rental for residential buildings declined by −10%, −5%, −9%, and −5% during the same period (Table 6.5);

(2) severe contractions in local consumption and retail sales by record high of 9% and 19%, respectively, in 1998 (Tables 6.6 and 6.7);

(3) decreased tourist visits until the second quarter of 1998 (−16%) and tourists spending until the time being;

(4) all industrial sectors had recorded rapidly decreasing or negative growth in 1998 with the most serious contractions found in finance other than banking, hotels, real estates, and wholesale/retail sales.

Table 6.7 Growth Rates of Output, Prices, and Employment (1996–1999)

(percent)

	1996	1997	1998		1999			
			Q1	Q4	Q1	Q2	Q3	
Changes in GDP								
Private Consumption	4.7	6.7	−6.7	−2.5	−9.1	−4.4	1.3	−
Government Expenditures	4.0	2.4	0.7	2.1	2.5	3.9	3.5	−
Fixed Capital Formation	10.8	12.7	−6.4	−0.8	−19.2	−22.2	−26.4	−
Buildings	8.7	4.7	−4.6	5.3	−17.4	−11.8	−19.9	−
Machinery & Equipments	11.8	13.1	−6.6	−6.3	−21.2	−29.8	−28.3	−
Commodity Exports	4.8	6.1	−4.3	1.4	−9.6	−4.8	−2.0	4.0
Domestic Exports	−8.4	2.1	−7.9	−4.7	−15.5	−9.1	−12.8	−10.0
Re–Exports	7.5	6.8	−3.7	2.5	−8.6	−4.1	−0.3	7.0
Commodity Imports	4.3	7.2	−7.2	−1.7	−13.5	−10.3	−7.9	4.0
Services Exports	9.7	−1.1	−6.5	−10.1	−0.2	0.6	1.7	−
Services Imports	4.9	3.6	−0.6	1.1	−2.0	−0.8	−0.6	−
GDP	4.5	5.3	−5.1	−2.6	−5.7	−3.0	1.1	4.5
GDP Current $ (HK$bil)	1192	1325	1268	307	321	286	302	−
Changes in Prices								
GDP Price Deflator	5.9	5.9	0.9	0.2	−2.3	−3.6	−5.4	−
Domestic Demand Deflator	4.9	4.8	1.0	4.0	−0.1	1.0	−0.7	−
Composite Price Index	6.3	5.8	2.8	5.0	−0.8	−1.8	−4.0	−5.9
Consumer Price Index (A)	6.0	5.7	2.6	4.8	−0.8	−1.5	−3.5	−5.0
Unemployment	2.8	2.2	5.0	3.5	5.7	6.2	6.1	6.1

Source: Computed from Table 6.1, Table 6.2 (Trade, 1999.Q3); Table 6.5 (Unemployment, 1999.Q3); Table 6.1 (Price, 1999. Q3); and p. 1 (GDP, 1999. Q3), *Third Quarter Economic Report, 1999*, Hong Kong Statistics Department, November, 1999.

Even when most of the industries were still adversely affected in 1999, manufacturing production decreased until the second quarter of 1999 (Table 6.6);

(5) continuous contraction of real GDP from −2.6% in the first quarter of 1998, the first negative record in fifteen years, to −3% in the first quarter of 1999;

(6) sustained record high unemployment rate of 6.2% in the first quarter of 1999 and negative inflation rate since the last quarter of 1998 (Table 6.7).

As far as individual industry is concerned, the local property developers were among the most affected groups following the massive withdrawals of Japanese banks and funds from Hong Kong. In order to meet the newly launched international requirement of "liquidity reserves" effective from May 1998, massive funds withdrawal back to Japan since 1995 created loanable fund shortages to the local credit market during the period of the crisis. The local developers' needs for liquidity to repay debt had generated price wars in selling properties in the asset market, which triggered further asset prices to fall sharply. In only five quarters from the last quarter of 1997, the sales and rentals of residential/offices recorded an accumulated decrease of more than 40% and 30%, respectively. Further, the tight money market created shortages in loanable funds, which damaged not only borrowings in the financial/stock/real estate/asset markets but also domestic consumption and investment. It was observed that loanable funds in HKD had reduced by 2–3% and in foreign currencies by 3–16% since the crisis (Table 6.6).

Being a service-dominated economy, the impacts of the Asian crisis have not only generated detrimental effects on the dominant sectors such as financial and real estate industries but also on trade, communication, transportation, tourism/hospitality industries. The contribution of service exports to GDP was 24.2% in 1996 to exceed that of domestic commodity exports by 7% (Figure 6.1). The relative appreciation of the Hong Kong dollar against other extensively depreciated Asian currencies was found to affect Hong Kong trade and especially service exports and alternatively local retail sales (Ng and Tuan, 1998). The commodity and service export trade was among the most adversely affected sectors to record a decrease of −7.9% and −6.5%, respectively, after the crisis in 1998. Re-export trade decreased by −3.7%. Further, domestic expenditures dropped by the same magnitude. Local consumption declined sharply since the fourth quarter of 1999 by −6.7% and capital formation also contracted by −6.4% during the same period (Table 6.7). Such a deteriorating performance had accounted for the economic downturn in the past two years.

A checklist of major chronological events following the Asian Crisis is provided in Appendix I for easy reference.

In summary, given that the Hong Kong Government's decision to defend the prevailing linked exchange rate at any cost, the pressure of adjustment has to be transmitted to the real sector. Aggregate demand and hence GDP growth declined significantly through the following effects:

(a) the soaring interest rate and expectations on possible recession discouraged bank loans, domestic investment, and consumption demand;

(b) the bursted bubble (falling asset prices) deteriorated the balance sheets of banks and non-financial firms, created negative wealth effect and uncertainty of further decreasing household income, and hence, further reduced domestic consumption demand and investment;

(c) the expensive HKD relatively to the depreciated cheap Asian currencies reduced trade in the demands for domestic exports and re-exports, and also service exports and mainly tourism.

6. GOVERNMENT POLICIES: MANAGING THE CRISIS AND STRUGGLING FOR RECOVERY

After reviewing various policies adopted by the Asian countries in coping with the 1997/98 financial crisis, similarities are found as

(1) in the short run along with currency devaluation, government intervention was to be taken in the forms of controls imposed on capital account (as in of Malaysia), or termination of certain type of transactions in the foreign exchange market (as in Taiwan), in order to ease the panicked capital outflows or pressure on the managed exchange rate;

(2) with or without aids from the IMF, liquidity problem was to be eased. However, reforms of domestic banking sector and non-bank enterprises were conducted at the same time with a series of recapitalized financing, debt write-offs or stretch outs;

(3) in the long run, policies were adopted toward the road of recovery. In this connection, expansionary fiscal and monetary policy was

taken for easing the economic downturn. Industrial policy or alike (as further reforming the regulation and supervision of the banking system or financial infrastructure) were adopted in order to restore or raise long-term competitiveness. Sachs and Woo (1999), Mishkin (1999), and Rogoff (1999) also suggested international institutional help so as to slow down the flows of international capital movements and thus prevent the extreme swings between inflows and outflows that have contributed to the last Asian financial crisis. Of no surprise, reform in Asian exchange rate regimes were also suggested (Sachs and Woo, 1999).

In Hong Kong, while CBA and the pegged rate have been upheld, no government intervention was taken until August 1998 when the last visible speculators attack was launched. The then government's purchase of stocks and its futures (HSIF) was the only crisis management measure being taken by the HKSAR government.

In terms of reforming the banking sector, the policy adopted by the HKSAR government mainly concentrated at first, to strengthen CBA so as to increase the transparency of discount window operations, and second, to tighten disciplines in the financial market. Such policies are aiming at the targets to prevent the interest rates from overshooting, to reduce the possibility of herding behavior to develop, and to discourage speculators' cross market operations. Hence, much efforts of the government policy of Hong Kong have been focused at short-run boosting of domestic demand via expansionary fiscal policy and long-term recovery by rebuilding competitiveness.

In chronological order, the policies taken by the HKSAR government in the context of reviewing the 1997/98 financial crisis is presented in Table 6.8 with the details further elaborated in the sections below (and in Appendix I). Major governmental policy measures addressing activities to be taken toward economic recovery since late 1999 are listed in Appendix II.

6.1 The Changing Philosophy of Governmental Economic Policies

During the crisis period, the Government of Hong Kong Special Administration Region (HKSAR) has modified its philosophy by directing

Table 6.8 Post-Crisis Major Events and Corresponding Governmental Policies

Date	Events	Government Policy*
1992–mid-1997	1997 Handover	Strengthening HKMA and banking system
10/1997–2/1998	Financial market attacked by hedge funds	Monetary policy: stabilizing interest rate via fine-tuning HKMA operations
3/1998	Economic downturn	Fiscal policy: deficit budget, increased public investment
6/1998–8-9/1998	Real estate market down financial market attacked by hedge funds	Modifications in housing policy Government purchase of stocks futures
17/9/1998		Fine-tuning HKMA operations and financial regulations
10/1998	1998 Chief Executive's policy address	Strategic policy and plan in financial market reforms and future development
3/1999	Economic downturn continued	Fiscal policy: deficit budget, tax rebate, tax rate reduction
10/1999	Gradual selling of stocks by government Less supply of public housing 1999 Chief Executive's policy address	Restoring image of "free" market Announcing new housing policy More policies addressed toward recovery
11/1999	Scientific Park call for rental	Industrial policy aiming at long run
1/2000	Passing bill on lowering entry salary point of public servants	Speeding up wage (downward) adjustment
2/2000	Passing bill on merging stock exchange, futures exchange, and three clearing houses	Continued reforms on financial infrastructure

Note: *For detailed listings, see Appendix II.
Source: The Study.

economic policies from the "positive non-intervention" being long adopted by the Hong Kong Government under the period of British rule by inclining slightly toward the Singaporean model of government "positive intervention".

A "passive intervention"[7] of HKSAR has been taken as a relatively proactive way of thinking as well as a major direction to formulate economic policies in confronting with the economic challenges generated by the Asian crisis and paving the way to recovery (Figure 6.4).

The typical examples of such practices are, for example, the risk management conducted by HKMA aiming at participation in the financial market and the short-run Keynesian type of fiscal policies including the preparations of two consecutive expansionary budgets in cutting taxation and increasing government expenditures in infrastructural facilities during the last two years. First in 1998, in creating a more attractive investment environment with regard to both software and hardware provision, long-term measures in planning in education, social (welfare and medical), improving transportation networks, regional cooperation, and industrial policies were provided (HKSAR, 1998).

Further, in 1999, policies aiming at establishing high value-added and competitive industries with environmental protection, government directed hi-tech businesses, enhancing financial infrastructures, providing facilities for general services and tourism industries (e.g., among a few, Disneyland is one of the project confirmed recently), education reform in building up quality manpower, immigration preferences provided to the technical expertise, etc., were announced (HKSAR, 1999). Appendix II presents some major selected details of this government's efforts.

The next three sections (6.2–6.4) that follow will further elaborate government's policies in managing the financial crisis and steering the economy toward economic recovery.

---

[7] The authors attempted to describe the existing changing philosophy of HKSAR by using the term "passive intervention" to represent HKSAR Government's moving away from its previous "positive-noninterventionism" toward a state of intervention of being less active than the "positive intervention" of Singapore and Taiwan.

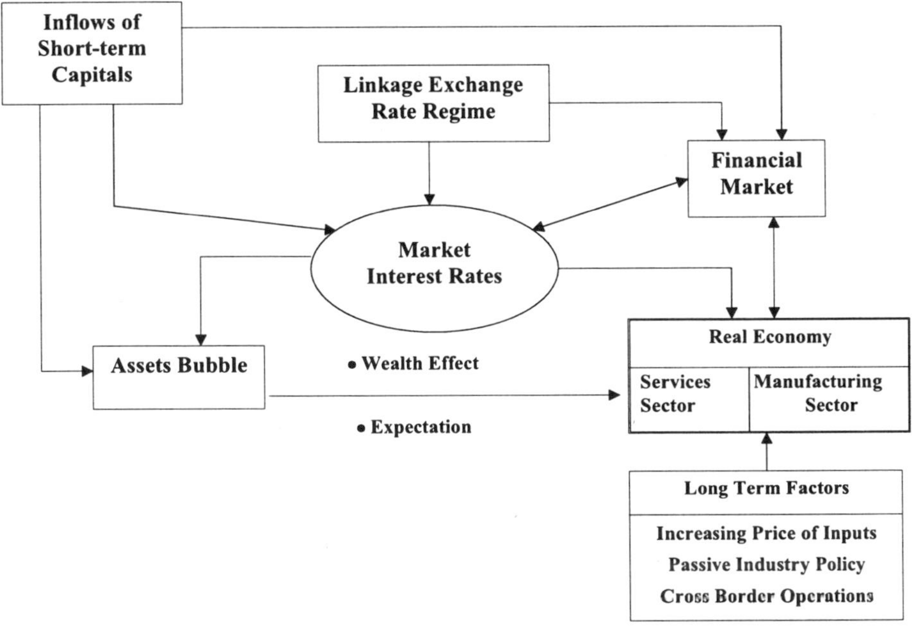

Fig. 6.4 Financial Turmoil and the Real Economy, 1997–1998 Hong Kong

Source: The Study

6.2 Crisis Management

The immediate responses of the Government to the turbulence can be analyzed in terms of two periods from October 1997 to mid-1998 and the period after mid-1998.

6.2.1 Crisis Management During the First Period (10/1997–3/1998)

After the Thai currency devaluation incidence in July 1997, both the Korean Won and New Taiwan dollar devalued in early October of the same year. Given its linked rate regime, the HKD was severely "attacked" by intensive selling of the HKD in the foreign exchange (spot and forward) market in October, 1997 leading to record high HIBOR and drastic contracted bank loans. The major consequences being recognized by the Hong Kong Government during the following half-year time period revealed that both (a) continuous tightened money supply and persistent soaring market interest rates due to the linked rate; and (b) the drastic drop in real estate prices and contracted transaction volumes in the asset market have created chain effect in the banking system because property mortgage loans have constituted a major portion of local bank loans.

In meeting the financial turmoil generated by the October "attack" against the HKD, both HKMA and HKSAR Government have basically adopted three sets of policies as remedial measures to help stabilizing the financial market and the local banking system:

(a) Fine-tune the operations of the LAF (the Hong Kong version of discount window) by increasing its transparency and easier financing in order to release the pressure confronted by the tight inter-bank loan market. The main objective of this policy is to lower market interest rates and to ease the supply of loanable funds;

(b) the HKSAR Government, in fact, postponed the implementations of its expansionary policy in public housing and land supplies (previously announced immediately after the 1997-handover) in order to support prices in the real estate market and ultimately the banking system;

(c) HKMA coordinated with banks in risk management such as announcing guidelines dealing with tightening regulations on the operations of bank system in order to avoid "dominion effect" of risk spreading from a single bank-business problem over to the whole system. The effectiveness of these measures was observed.

6.2.2 Crisis Management During the Second Period (8–9/1998)

After the mid-1998, while fine-tuning and improvements in the banking system were taking effects, the second attack against the HKD in August 1998 was launched again by international speculators. HKMA finally recognized the cross-market operations of inflow short-term capital such as hedge funds were the immediate cause of the local financial turmoil. To preserve the confidence of the general public on the linkage rate and to avoid herding behavior in terms of massive conversion of HKD to US dollar and even a bank run, HKMA decided to intervene directly the stock market in late August, 1998 by government purchases of stocks of valued at about HK$120 billion to support further crash of the stock prices. The battle between speculators and the Government was completed in September 1998 with some hedge funds suffered great loses. Since then, no significant, organized and intensified selling of HKD in the foreign exchange and its derivatives markets has been detected.

To supplement government's intervention in the stock market, HKMA also began to correct two major system defects being detected during the August attack:

(a) To tighten disciplines within the two institutions responsible for trading in the stock market (Stock Exchange and Futures Exchange) in order to reduce the flexibility in leverage of hedge funds and other inflows of short-term capital, and to increase their transaction costs;
(b) To restrain the ability of foreign institutional investors in obtaining HKD from local banks and the bond market by refining the banking regulations and HKMA practices. A series of measures have been taken for the purpose and will be discussed in later sections.

In addition, the influence of hot money in the financial market and on the whole economy was well recognized in the mid-1998. HKMA and government officials began to advocate efforts for international and regional cooperation and legislation in increasing the transparency of hedge funds operations by recording and releasing statistics on international short-term capital flows since then.

6.3 Monetary Policy Measures and Reforms in the Banking Infrastructure

In principle, there is no room for any economy under a rigid version of CBA to undertake independent monetary policy aiming at enhancing macroeconomic stability. However, due to two reasons (1) enough reserves and circulation of Foreign Exchange Fund bills and notes, and (2) imperfect substitution of HKD and USD, a limited policy measures can be taken to stabilize the financial system and interest rate fluctuation in the short run.

In this connection, the major measures of the Hong Kong Monetary Authority (HKMA) being undertaken or officially announced after November, 1997 include: (1) ensuring the perfect operations of the linked exchange rate, such as to publicize the balance of the discount window or its estimates, reduce the pressure on inter-bank rates and the possibility of overshooting, issue 100% U.S. reserves Exchange Fund bills and expand the monetary base; (2) policing rigid banking practices in order to restraint the supply of HKD to potential speculators;[8] (3) developing the bond market and tools for long-term loans; and (4) enforcing risk management of the banking system. Such measures were designed to prevent the chain effects arising from financial problems between banks and firms, which in term may contaminate the macroeconomy.

In order to remove investors and social concerns arising from the Asian crisis and assure the credibility of both the prevailing linked rate and exchange rate regime, HKMA has made a few technical refinements since September 1998. Among the permanent measures being launched to further assure HKMA'S commitment in the convertibility of the HKD to USD: the "defense rate" of 7.75:1 will eventually be replaced by the official rate of 7.8:1 by the middle of year 2000. Such convertibility will apply to all commercial banks and not only be limited to the three money issuing banks as before. Further, to eliminate any room for manipulations, electronic clearing system in the Futures Exchange has been attempted recently.

Along this line, other measures include continuous efforts and careful reforms conducted in

(1) simplification of the three-tier to two-tier banking system;
(2) upgrade of the minimum requirements of capital stock of local banks;
(3) immediate use of the payment system by restricted license banks and deposit-taking financial institutions;

---

[8] Singapore, while adopting a managed floating exchange rate, restricts the supply of Singaporean dollar to foreigners by controlling free exchange of the dollar.

(4) better ruling of HKMA in its role as the lender of the last resort;
(5) reveal of financial information of overseas banks; and
(6) strengthening of risk management as monitor measures.

However, diverse views were found regarding some reforms, such as lifting of interest agreement, adoption of deposit insurance system, and loosening the restrictions of overseas banks in establishing branch offices.

The merger of the Hong Kong Stock Exchange and Futures Exchange by the HKSAR Government will be implemented in the early 2000. It represents a major move to tighten disciplines in the financial market and to restraint effectively and permanently any room for cross-market operations. Also, it is the first immediate step in moving toward a more up-to-date financial infrastructure.

Under the Financial Secretary, the Department of Economic and Finance Affairs (DEFA) is also responsible for formulating, implementing policy related to the financial infrastructure; that is, to facilitate the provision of a healthy economic and legal environment in order to establish an open, fair, and efficient market for businesses. This includes major responsibility such as to maintain and promote Hong Kong as a major international financial center; and at the same time, to attract the international clearing banks to establish the first overseas office in Hong Kong.

Furthermore, to restore the image of a "free market", the Government initiated the selling of the first batch of stocks being purchased in August, 1998 to the general public in October, 1999 under the name of "Traker Fund of Hong Kong".

In summary, HKSAR Government (DEFA with HKMA in particular) has addressed four major policy areas regarding financial/banking affairs to be undertaken from 1998 and onward (HKSAR, 1998 and 1999) to include:

(1) Maintaining the stability of the financial and banking system

The prime and immediate target in maintaining the stability of the financial market and banking system is the maintenance of the CBA as well as the linked exchange rate (HK$7.8:US$1) to be represented by HKMA. Other government units' continuous efforts are as follows:

* to implement the Banking Ordinance and strengthen the regulation on the operations of authorized institutions (banking institutions) so as to ensure a healthy banking system;
* to make reviews on the banking regulations using the international standard and development of local banks as a reference;
* to strengthen the monitor and supervision on authorized institutions (banking and financial institutions) according to the degree of risk involved;
* to promote the fixed interest rate mortgage of the Hong Kong Mortgage and Stock Association;
* to ensure the smooth transitions of banking after its adoption of the Euro;
* to further strengthen the Hong Kong Currency Board system; and
* to further facilitate the transparent operations of the Currency Board and reveal of related information.

(2) Further improvement on the regulations and the management structure

* to propose the banking (amendments) ordains to make the existing regulations to perfectly fit the international standard;
* with reference to the evaluations of individual authorized institutions on risk, to review the existing minimum and effective 'adequate capital ratio';
* to review the existing asset-liquidity ratio requirements with special attention on the quality of the liquidity assets of the authorized institutions;
* to set laws on stocks and futures mergers;
* to make amendments on the regulations of mortgages and loans of stocks, and its implementations;
* to further strengthen the order and transparency of operations of the stock and futures markets;
* to coordinate commercial banks in rescheduling or stretch out syndicate loans extended to businesses;
* to establish laws and regulations governing the Compulsory Superannuation Scheme;

* to strengthen the regulations on the investments of insurance companies on the investment bundles and their related operations regarding the Compulsory Superannuation Scheme, and the prevention of money laundry activities; and
* by means of the "Company Ordinance" and its related bankruptcy laws, to ensure the company related laws and ordinances will benefit investors of local businesses. To pave the way for economic recovery, the following two responsibilities are assigned to DEFA in particular.

(3) Improvement of financial infrastructure to enhance Hong Kong as an international financial center

* to assist the business sector in solving the Y2K problem;
* to assist in merging and improving the systems of the Hong Kong Stocks and Futures Exchange so as to increase the reliability and efficiency and arriving at the ultimate objective of consolidated transactions;
* to examine on the needs of establishing business schools to provide the necessary human resources to the business sector; and
* through the expansion of the liquidation plan to ensure the effectiveness and efficiencies in services to be provided to bankruptcy cases.

(4) Further development of the financial market

* to attract mainland solely-owned enterprises to incorporate in Hong Kong;
* to enhance the development of local bond market via the Hong Kong Mortgage and Loans Association and the Compulsory Superannuation Scheme;
* to strengthen the bilateral relations with other financial centers in remittances and consolidated transactions;
* to expand the joint checking clearing system of Hong Kong and Shenzhen;
* to raise Hong Kong's research abilities in longer-term and more extensive research in financial and banking policies in order to provide

Hong Kong with analytical and policy research in making Hong Kong a leading role in Asia; and

* to adopt the improved statistical system to comply with International Monetary Fund's standard of statistics.

6.4 Fiscal Policy Designed for Economy Recovery

Since the first Chief Executive's Policy Address (1997) of the HKSAR, major efforts in housing, education, and social aspects have revealed the HKSAR government's proactive role, determination, and policy direction. The second Policy Address (1998) announced specific measures in dealing with the economic downturn (unemployment, inadequate demand, and poor economic growth) derived from the Asian financial crisis. The basic strategy was to boost infrastructural investment and aggregate demand by reducing taxes, providing aids to innovation/technology and tourism industry, and increasing efforts to labor training. Some of the measures have been budgeted in the 1999 Government Budget in terms of resource provision. Such efforts represented typical expansionary fiscal policies targeting at economic stability during the period of recession.

Included in the second Policy Address (HKSAR, 1998) were also some discussions in how Hong Kong should adjusting its long-term economic development strategies as a globalizing economy. More detailed discussions were found in the 1999 Address (HKSAR, 1999). Specific directions described in the two reports include Hong Kong to become the center of technology innovation center of South China and Asia via electronic commerce, software development, fashions, communication/information, Chinese herbs, international finance and financing, and culture and entertainment. Specific projects to be implemented included the constructions of the Cyberport and Disneyland. Other than further emphases on the high value-added electronic communications and development of tourism destination, the 1999 Chief Executive's Policy Address also described the Government's emphases in the provision of better investment environment, a World-class business center and long-term planning in environmental protection, housing, and education reform. The details are presented in Appendix II.

The positive participation of the HKSAR Government in economic affairs aiming at enhancing economic recovery and regional competitiveness have committed sizable public spending to be financed by fiscal tools in the next few years. Government expenditures in GDP constituted 14% in 1988-98 and increased to 21% in 1998–99 and 20% (projected) in 2002–03, and together with the two deficit budgets of 1998–99 and 1999–2000, evidence have been provided for the increasing active government role and participation. Fortunately, due to the adequate fiscal reserves of more than HK$200 billion, the ability in financing government-planned projects should not be of great concern in the time being.

In summary, the recent direction of the fiscal policy as reflect by the 1999/2000 Budget is mainly targeting at recovery and competitiveness enhancement as follows.

(1) Spending boosting (tax exemption): lowering corporate income tax (to 16%) and fees and taxes (re-export custom tax, business registration fees, ships parking fees, stamp duties, insurance, etc.), and 10% tax rebate on personal income tax.

(2) Cost reductions: privatization of the MTR corporation; increasing the efficiencies and cost effectiveness of the public sector via the "resource value-added plan" to achieve a target of 5% cost savings; and continuing civil servants reforms by reducing starting points of the salary scales, change of contract terms, savings on fringe benefits and retirement plans.

(3) Economic recovery and sustainable development: new projects mainly include cooperating with land developers on the construction of cyberport to attract international investors on communications and software industries and to create employment during and after the completion of the project; providing loans to the entertainment and amusement parks and cooperating with Disneyland in building a theme park; and to improve infrastructure needed for enhancing the competitiveness of Hong Kong in general.

7. CONCLUSION REMARKS

Now, more than two years after Hong Kong was first attacked by the Asian financial crisis in October 1997, speculations on immediate devaluation or possible de-link of the local currency have disappeared. Soaring market interest rates (until the end of 1998) have been stabilized since early May 1999. The best lending rate set by the Hong Kong Association of Bankers was reduced three times to 8.25% in June 1999.

The Hong Kong economy seems to start escaping from the trough in terms of employment, price level, number of tourist visits, and exports. Unemployment rate declined from its peak of 6.3% in mid-1999 to 6.0% at the year-end. The change in price level improved from −6.1% in August 1999 to −4.0% at the end of the year. Exports picked up its increasing track since mid-1999 and recorded an annual growth of 1.8% in 1999. The size of trade deficit further decreased from $81.4 billion in 1998 to $43.7 billion in 1999. While tourist expenditures were found to decrease by 3.9% from 1998 to 1999, the number of visitors increased by 11.5% from 9.57 million persons to 10.68 million persons during the same period. After five quarters of consecutive contractions in total output, a rebound in GDP was observed since the second quarter of 1999 at 1.1% and 4.5% for the third quarter. The 1999 annual GDP growth rate was estimated by Hang Seng Bank as 1.9% in December 1999 and Professor Lawrence Klein as 1% in January 2000.

Such a macroeconomic performance by the end of 1999 may represent that Hong Kong is not mired in her worst recession on record but likely turned around to the path of recovery. However, the record of recovery seems too modest and less satisfactory when comparing with some other Asian economies such as South Korea, Singapore, and Taiwan showing economic growth in 1999 of more than 5%. Since the Hong Kong economy and its banking sector in particular has not suffered from the financial turmoil as much as South Korea and Thailand, such a sluggish recovery deserves some further explanations.

Based on the conceptual framework presented in Section 2, the possible explanations about the reason why Hong Kong's recovery falls much behind that of many other Asian economies can be summarized.

(1) The first most important factor is that CBA and the maintenance of the linked rate ever since the onset of the financial turmoil. During the turmoil period, the HKSAR government has shown its determination in defending the linked exchange rate regime and the linked rate even at the expense of the overall macroeconomic performance. Many discussions about different possible alternatives in confronting the turmoil have been conducted during the past two years, such as to float the rate, U.S. dollarization, keeping CBA but change to a basket peg, or to re-peg the rate. Nevertheless, maintaining economic, social, and political stability during the early periods after Hong Kong's handover have been considered by the Government as the top priority. Adopting a pegged regime as well as maintaining the pegged rate itself are considered as a test of the Government's determination and ability in maintaining stability. Moreover, the Government has full confidence at the time.

The Government's strict confidence in maintaining the linked exchange rate regime was supported, at least partially, from both theoretical and practical point of views. First, it is still controversial according to literatures that which foreign exchange rate regime is the best for a small open economy (The Economist, 1999). Empirical studies have also suggested that adequate reserves and healthy banking system are the necessary conditions for implementing CBA, which conditions are all being fulfilled in Hong Kong. Hence, to remain status quo will obviously outweigh any change (including rate re-peg or a basket peg of which both consequences are uncertain) in this regard.

(2) RMB went through a pressure of devaluation in the last two years and so as the HKD. Therefore, the consequence of any relative appreciation of HKD and RMB (by 20–50% comparing to the neighboring countries) was the decreases in Hong Kong's domestic exports and re-exports of manufactured (and off-shore manufactured) goods as well as service exports in 1998 and their slow rebound in 1999.

(3) The CBA and linked rate regime have tied Hong Kong's interest rate to that of the U.S. However, the U.S. interest rate has been kept relatively high since the late 1990's and is entering the upturn phase of a cycle representing the Federal Reserve Bank's policy to prevent the U.S. economy

from overheating. The Hong Kong's interest rate has to follow suit regardless of its own economic situation. A prime rate of 8.5% effective since August 1999 and 8.75% in February 2000 have been slowing down the Hong Kong economy's struggling for recovery. Hence, the improvements of the deteriorated balance sheets of banks and non-bank firms will be quite modest and the process to ease credit is time consuming by Mishkin's argument (1999). In fact, negative growth in local bank loans continued until the third quarter of 1999.

(4) Under a pegged rate system, the economic recovery of the Hong Kong economy relies completely on the downward adjustment of factor prices and the general price level (and so as real estate prices) to restore its regional competitiveness.[9] Nevertheless, such a process is painful, lengthy, and resistant encountering when social and political considerations are also taken together with economic rationales. Hence, any drastic government policy in this regard has never been taken in the last two years.

(5) The recovery of the neighboring economies is only at its initial stage. As a regional financial and trading center, Hong Kong is still waiting for the other East and Southeast Asian countries' full fledge recovery from their economic downturns.

(6) After the northward relocation of Hong Kong's manufacturing, re-exports and related services and tourism have become the major exporting sectors. A mini-open economy such as Hong Kong with a narrowing economic base has made stable and sustainable economic growth more difficult. As far as the impacts of the 1997-98 financial crisis are concerned, a full recovery of the Hong Kong economy in view of its service dominance can be a winding and lengthy process.

To review the Hong Kong experiences of the past two years, it is quite clear that the "Asian financial crisis" had attacked only the financial market

---

[9] This argument is supported by the fact that deflation (lasting 16 months) was still observed in Hong Kong by February, 2000 when other crisis-attacked economies have experienced various degrees of inflation since several months ago. Along the same line, HKSAR Government initiated the cutting of salary entry-point for newly recruited employees by the end of 1999 and the corresponding bill was passed in January 2000 (Appendix I).

but left the banking system and most of the business sector from falling in the "storm cycle" as the cases in Thailand, Indonesia, and possibly South Korea in 1997–98. Economic recession during the 1998 to the mid-1999 period has been mainly caused by the Hong Kong version of CBA and the relative appreciation of the local currency. In addition, the restructuring economy has also contributed to the longer and more round about process of recovery than one could anticipate. Given the pegged rate regime, the recovery of a metropolitan economy like Hong Kong would have to depend heavily upon the economic prosperity of the vicinity, that is, the regional and global economy.

To conclude the lessons from the 1997–98 financial turmoil in Hong Kong, while measures in terms of both monetary (within limited content) and fiscal policies (including less passive industry policy) have been explored by the Hong Kong Government during the crisis period in order to provide remedies for managing both the immediate and short run financial panic or economic/societal problems, not much can be done to cope with the side effects arising from financial globalization. To avoid similar attacks or manipulations launched by international speculators as in 1997–98, HKMA should have paid more attention in the following ways: (1) to propose the compilation of monitoring indicators in the context of financial market and financial derivatives in particular, in order to respond timely and quickly to any financial turbulence;[10] (2) to speed up the development of the bonds market in meeting the needs of long-term capital from the business sector; and (3) to continue efforts in addressing the legal and institutional bias in the composition of capital flows to developing countries (Rogoff, 1999), and in seeking regional cooperation and also amongst central banks in regulating short-term capital flows. To any small open economies, these issues are of immediate significance.[11]

---

[10]Tuan (1998) had proposed a few preliminary monitoring indicators on trial basis, such as the ratio of unsettled Hang Seng Index Futures to total volume of HSIF, forward rate of U.S. dollar adjusted by difference in US/HK interest rate, and growth rate of M_2 in HKD/M_2 in USD ratio, etc.

[11]The fact that both the speedy in and out flows of capital causing tremendous impacts on a small open economy can be well observed in the case of Hong Kong. Short-term capital

During the past two years, the trends of evolution of the global economy have seemed to be globalization of financial markets around, rapid development of financial derivatives, and asymmetrically distributed information of the above markets. Given a linked exchange rate regime, Hong Kong will continue to provide incentives to international speculators to realize profits in the local market by new operations developed from financial engineering. Any turbulence from the surrounding region will be contagious to this city as far as Hong Kong is concerned. May be the next hit — the possible devaluation of RMB?

References

The Economist (1999) "Fix or Float?" *Global Finance Survey*, January 30, pp. 15–17.

Enoch, C. (1998) "Currency Board Arrangements and the Banking Systems", International Conference on Exchange Rate Stability and Currency Board Economics, Hong Kong, November.

Flood R. and Garber, P. (1984) "Collapsing Exchange Rate Regimes: Some Linear Examples", *Journal of International Economics*, 17, pp. 1–13.

Fratzscher, M. (1998) "Why are Currency Crises Contagious? A Comparison of the Latin American Crisis of 1994–1995 and the Asian Crisis of 1997–1998", *Weltwirtschaftliches Archiv*, 134(4), pp. 664–691.

Mishkin, F.S. (1999) "Global Financial Instability: Framework, Events, Issues", *Journal of Economic Perspectives*, 13(4), pp. 3–20.

Henderson, C. (1998) *Asia Falling?*, New York: McGraw Hill Publisher.

---

flows is a major component of the item recorded as "Capital and Financial Non-reserve Assets" in Hong Kong's capital account. A net outflow of HK\$71.5 billion (representing 5.6% of GDP) was recorded in 1998 while a net inflow of HK\$142.8 billion (representing 10.8% of GDP) was entered in 1997. Few economies can maintain their economic stability with such a record of in- and out-flows regardless of their adopted exchange regime.

HKSAR (1998, 1999) *Chief Executive's Policy Address, 1998, 1999*, Hong Kong: HKSAR Government.

Jao, Y.C. (1998) "The Working of the Currency Board: The Experience of Hong Kong 1935–1997", *Pacific Economic Review*, 3(3), pp. 219–241.

______ (1999) "Asian Financial Crisis and the Hong Kong Economy", International Conference on China's Economic Reform and Adjustment of Social Structures, Chinese Academy of Social Sciences, China, and Shue Yan College, Hong Kong (in Chinese).

Kaminsky, G.L. and Reinhart, C.M. (1999) "The Twin Crises: The Causes of Banking and Balance-of-Payments Problems", *The American Economic Review*, 89(3), pp. 473–500.

Krugman, P. (1979) "A Model of Balance of Payments Crises", *Journal of Money, Credit, and Banking*, 11, pp. 311–325.

______ (1998) (1998) "What Happened to Asia?" *Chulalongkorn Journal of Economics*, 10(1), pp. 69–87.

Leung, L.H. (1999) "The Battle Between Hong Kong Government and the Speculators", *Hong Kong Economic Times* (in Chinese).

Ng, L.F.Y. (1995) "Changing Industrial Structure and Competitive Patterns of Manufacturing and Non-manufacturing in a Small Open Economy: An Entropy Measurement", *Managerial and Decisions Economics*, 16, pp. 547–563.

______ and Tuan, C. (1997) "Evolving Outward Investment, Industrial Concentration, and Technology Change: Implications for Post-1997 Hong Kong", *Journal of Asian Economics*, 8(2), 315–332.

______ (1998) "The Asian Financial Crisis and its Impacts Upon the Hong Kong Economy: With Special Reference to the Service Exports", International Conference on Asian Crisis: A Global Perspective, Deakin University, Australia.

Obstfeld, M. (1994) "The Logic of Currency Crises", *Cahiers Economiques et Monetaires*, 43, pp. 189–213.

Pakko, M.R. (1998) "Currency Boards: Monetary Magic?" *International Economic Trends*, May, p. 1.

Rogoff, K. (1999) "International Institutions for Reducing Global Financial Instability", *Journal of Economic Perspectives*, 13(4), pp. 21–42.

Sachs, J.D. and Woo, W.T. (1999) "The Asian Financial Crisis: What Happened, and What Is To Be Done?" (Executive Summary), *World Economic Forum*, April.

Tsang, S.K. (1998) "The East Asian Financial Turmoil and Hong Kong's Linked Exchange Rate", BRC paper on China No. 98006, Hong Kong Baptist University (in Chinese).

Tuan, C. (1997) "The October 1997 Financial Turmoil in Hong Kong: Its Causes and Impacts", *Hong Kong-Macau Studies*, 7(11), pp. 1–8 (in Chinese)

______ (1998) *Financial Turmoils in Hong Kong and its Impacts on the Domestic Economy*, Monograph, Taipei: Research Department, Mainland Affairs Commission (MAC).

______ and Ng, L.F.Y. (1994) "Economic Liberalization in China and Structural Adjustment of Hong Kong Manufacturing", *Seoul Journal of Economics*, 7(2), pp. 141–162.

______ (1995a) "Hong Kong's Outward Investment and Regional Economic Integration with Guangdong: Process and Implications", *Journal of Asian Economics*, 6(3), pp. 385–405.

______ (1995b) "Manufacturing Evolution under Passive Industrial Policy and Cross-Border Operations in China: The Case of Hong Kong", *Journal of Asian Economics*, 6(1), pp. 71–88.

_____ (1995c) "The Turning Point of the Hong Kong Manufacturing Sector: Impact of Outward Investment to the Pearl River Delta", *Journal of International Trade and Economic Development*, 4(2), pp. 153–170.

_____ (1998a) "Regionalization of Financial Market and Manufacturing Evolution in Hong Kong: Contribution and Significance", *Journal of Asian Economics*, 9(1), pp. 119–137.

_____ (1998b) "Export Trade, Trade Derivatives, and Economic Growth of Hong Kong: A New Scenario", *The Journal of International Trade and Economic Development*, 7(1), pp. 111–137.

World Bank (1997) *World Development Report*. New York: Oxford University Press.

_____ (1998). *Global Economic Prospect*, New York: Oxford University Press.

Appendix I Listings of Major Chronological Events in Hong Kong Following the Outbreak of the Asian Financial Crisis

DATE	TYPE	DESCRIPTION
Mid-97	**E**	**1997 Handover**
	G	**Strengthening HKMA and banking system**
7/8/97	E	HSI reached all time high of 16,673 points
20/8/97	E	The first signal of effects of the Financial Crisis; HSI dropped by 619.6 points due to the concern on the speculative attack on HK dollar
2/9/97	G	The CEO gave warning about the possible downward trend of the stock market; HSI reached a high of 13,735
Oct 98	**E**	**1998 Chief Executive's Policy Address**
	G	**Strategic policy and plan in financial market reforms and future development**
Oct-Feb 98	**E**	**Financial market 1st attacked by hedge funds**
	G	**Monetary policy: stabilizing interest rates via fine-tuning HKMA's operations**
21/10/97	E	A drop of HSI by 567.8 points to 12,403.1, low in half-a-year
22/10/97	E	A drop of HSI by 765.3 points to 11,637.8, low in 13 months; arising concerns on the maintenance of the linked exchange rate
23/10/97	E	Overnight HIBOR first rose to 100%
23/11/97	G	CEO's revealed in APEC that Hong Kong would be the first to recover reflecting the government's under-estimation of the impacts of the Crisis
15/1/98	G	Government's reassurance of the maintenance of the linked rate
13/2/98	G	Government expenditures announcement to include fighting high unemployment and stimulating the sluggish economy
18/2/98	G	The 98/99 Budget to reduce taxation on 24 items
March 98	**E**	**Economic downturn**
	G	**Fiscal policy: deficit budget, increase public investment**

26/3/98	G	Strategic development of Hong Kong to include land/urban planning in the next 13 years targeting Hong Kong's population to reach 8.1 million
23/4/98	G	Announcing via "Report on Financial Market" regarding the operationally sound linked rate, healthy financial system and stock market; HKSAR would keep oversee any future formation of asset bubbles and maintain effective regulatory mechanism to strive for Hong Kong's long-run competitiveness
18/5/98	E	Unemployment rate reached 3.9% in February–April, 1998; all time high in 13 years
29/5/98	G	To stabilize the real estate/residential market, ease the money market, and stimulate tourism, the Government announced seven ways to stimulate the economy
June 98	**E**	**Real estate market downturn**
	G	**Modifications of housing policy**
20/7/98	E	Unemployment rate climbed to 4.5% from April–June, 1998; high in 15 years and revealed obvious economy downturn
Aug 98	**E**	**Financial market 2nd attack by hedge funds**
	G	**Government purchase of stocks and futures**
3/8/98	E	Estimated GDP of −2.8% in 1st quarter of 1998
13/8/98	E	HSI plunged to 6,544 points
14/8/98	G	HKSAR bought stocks (blue chips and HSIF) in the following two weeks using Foreign Exchange Fund
18/8/98	E	Unemployment rate reached 4.8% from May–July, 1998; high in 15 years
28/8/98	E	Drop in exports by 12.8%; highest in 10 years
5/9/98	G	Government announced 7 new financial policies to strengthen the money supply system in preventing speculators' manipulations
7/9/98	G	Government announced 30 new tactics to tighten up the regulations of stock and futures market to prevent speculators' attack
19/10/98	E	Unemployment rate reached 5% for July–September, 1998

20/10/98	E	Record low −5.2% GDP growth in 2nd quarter, 1998
22/10/98	E	New low record of inflation rate of 2.5%
26/10/98	E	Retail sales contracted by 20%, a record low in 23 years
18/1/99	E	Unemployment rate reached 5.8%; high in 17 years
March 99	**E**	**Economic downturn continued**
	G	**Fiscal policy: deficit budget, tax rebate, tax rate reduction**
3/3/99	G	Government announcing the 99/00 financial budget and the continuation of economic difficulties during the second half of 1999; the need to raise tax; and the cyberport project as a growth locomotive
15/3/99	E	Unemployment rate climbed to 6% in February, 1999
19/4/99	E	20-year high record of 6.2% unemployment rate; further indication of investment contraction
24/4/99	E	Deflation of −2.6% in March, 1999, a continuation in 5 months
26/4/99	E	Continuous contraction of retail sales by 14%
17/5/99	E	All time record high of unemployment rate of 6.3%
25/5/99	G	Bills on immigration skilled labor of quality personnel/Ph.D. holders from the Mainland for innovation and technology development
Aug 99	**E**	**First sign of recovery: GDP growth of 0.2% in Q2 99**
27/9/99	E	Deflation of −6.1% in August, 1999
Oct 99	**E**	**Restoring 'free' market image of Hong Kong: Sale of TraHK Fund**
	G	**Government gradual sale of stocks TraHK Fund (Phase I); less supply of public housing**
	E	**1999 Chief Executive's Policy Address**
	G	**More policies addressed toward recovery**
Nov 99	**E**	**Scientific Park call for rental**
	G	**Industrial policy aiming at long run**
10/11/99	E	Re-exports increased by 8.3% (Sept 99 vs Sept 98)
27/11/99	E	Real GDP growth of 4.5% in Q3 99; estimated average growth in GDP, total exports, re-exports, and consumption of 1.8%, 4.5%, 2.6%, and 1.5%, respectively, for 1999
24/12/99	E	Retail sales increased by 3% (Oct 99 vs Oct 98)

Jan 00	E	**Wage downward adjustments in public sector**
	G	**Passing bill on lowering salary entry points of civil servants**
22/1/00	E	Rapid increase in annual growth (Dec 99 vs Dec 98) of total exports by 15.1% and re-exports 16.4%
Feb 2000	E	**Passing bill on merging Stock Exchange, Futures Exchanges, and three clearing houses**
	G	**Continued reforms on financial infrastructure**
23/2/00	E	Unemployment rate and deflation dropped to −5.3% and −5.1% in January, 2000, respectively

Note: 'E' denotes event and 'G' denotes government policies/strategies; lines in bold represent major events and government responses confirmed during the period.
Source: The Study (compiled by the authors from daily information).

Appendix II Major Policy Addresses by Hong Kong Government in 1999: Toward the Road of Recovery

I. To Establish High Value-Added and Competitive Industries

I.1 Promote Innovation and Technology

*   to establish an Innovation & Technology Fund to finance innovation and technology by establishing a Fund of $5 billion
*   to establish Programs to promote university-business collaboration * to establish an Applied science and technology research institute to support mid-stream R/D
*   to launch new programs to promote collaboration with business/technology institutions on the Mainland
*   to examine the development of an Institute for Chinese Medicine undertaking research, industry support, and commericalization of medicinal products
*   to encourage relevant bodies to foster closer cooperation with the Mainland in technological support infrastructure
*   to aid industries by aiming at improving operating environment in the Pearl River Delta
*   to promote a cultural conducive to technology ventures via the Applied Research Fund

*   to continue supporting the service industry via the Service Support Fund by securing more fund in 1999/2000

I.2   <u>Maximize Access to Hi-Tech Products</u>

*   to implement the Chemical Weapons Convention in HKSAR to achieve international control of chemical products

*   to maintain and improve the effectiveness of enforcement action in combating the unlicensed import and export of strategic commodities

I.3   <u>Develop a World-Class Infrastructure</u>

*   to establish the Science Park (Phase I) in 2001

*   to construct the second industrial technology center in 2001

*   to construct the fourth industrial estate by land provision in 2001 and project completion in 2004

*   to conduct consultancy study on the need of a business park (Stage I by mid-1999)

I.4   <u>Provide Support for SMEs</u>

*   to establish a SMEs Office to help SMEs to gain access to services with a target of achieving 75% user satisfaction

*   to examine the continued need for a credit guarantee scheme for SMEs

I.5   <u>Infrastructural/Transportations Facilities</u>

*   to expand the rail network - West rail (Phase I and II), KCR, MTR, and Spur line

*   to develop and improve the road network — North Coast Road, section of Route 5, and other major road design projects

II.   To Strengthen Hong Kong's Role as International Financial Center

II.1   <u>Maintenance of Monetary and Banking Stability</u>

*   to review the banking supervisory regime in meeting international standard and development of the sector

*   to monitor and supervise authorized institutions on risk-based approach

* to promote fixed rates mortgage to protect against adverse interest rate movements by purchasing $3.5 billion of fixed rate mortgages
* to improve the transparency of the banking sector by implementing a new Guideline to standardize policy and to increase the amount and frequency of disclosure of both foreign and local institutions
* to ensure a smooth changeover to the Euro in the banking sector
* to further strengthen the currency board arrangement by new measures to include convertibility undertaking, technical adjustment of the discount window, removal of restriction on repeated borrowing, issuance of new Exchange Fund paper, introduction of a schedule of discount rates, etc.
* to move toward greater transparency and disclosure on currency board operations

II.2 Improvement of the Regulatory Framework

* to introduce a Banking (Amendment) Bill to bring the framework in line with international requirement
* to review the existing minimum and trigger capital adequacy ratios for assessment of risk profile
* to review the current liquidity ratio system
* to introduce the composite Securities and Futures Bill to remove inconsistencies and improve the regulatory framework
* to introduce and implement legislative amendments for the regulation of share margin financing activities
* to further strengthen the discipline and transparency of the securities and futures markets by new measure such as 30-point program
* to develop the framework for the Mandatory Provident Fund (MPF) Schemes
* to strengthen the regulation of insurance companies with regard to investment portfolio, MPF-related business, and prevention of money laundering activities
* to ensure that the legal framework for companies via review of Companies Ordinance and related bankruptcy and insolvency legislation
* to improve communication between the HKMA and the authorized institutions including the electronic submission of prudential returns

II.3 Infrastructure for a First Class International Financial Center

* to facilitate the integration and upgrading of the systems of various exchanges and clearing systems

* to study the need for a Financial Service Institute to meet the human resource needs
* to ensure the provision of an effective and efficient insolvency service
* to enhance Year 2000 readiness across the whole of the financial services sector
* to monitor the Year 2000 readiness in the banking and insurance industry
* to reduce the pressure and credit expansion of the banking system and payment system from over-subscribed Initial Public Offer of securities
* to study the impact of the development of electronic banking
* to house all major financial authorities under one roof
* to enhance investor education
* to introduce romote, on-line access to key information on companies

II.4 <u>Spearhead the Further Development of the Financial Market</u>

* to attract private enterprises in the Mainland to list in Hong Kong
* to promote the further development of the local debt market through the activities of the Hong Kong Mortgage Corporation and MPF Schemes
* to promote bilateral linkage with other financial centers in Payment vs Payment and Delivery vs Payment transactions
* to expand the joint cheque clearing system between Hong Kong and Shenzhen
* to enhance the research capability of Hong Kong to conduct long-term and wider monetary and banking policy analysis
* to implement an enhanced statistical system to comply with that of IMF

III. To Enhance Local Business Friendly Environment

III.1 <u>Creation of a Friendly Business Environment</u>

* to visit department heads and their directorate to invite suggestions for improvements
* to conduct research into existing regulatory regimes
* to consult more representatives of the business sector

III.2 <u>Commission Studies and Devise Detailed Arrangements</u>

* to study/review licensing requirements for lotteries, tombola, amusements with prizes, and trade promotion competitions; restaurants; and massage establishments

* to promote greater private sector participation in the provision of elderly care services
* to identify and examine possible options for private sector participation in water supplies services
* to conduct departmental business study of Planning Department and review Regulations administered by Transport Department
* to study the feasibility of a copyrights management database; lighting and ventilation regulations for buildings; and licensing requirements for supermarkets

III.3 <u>Improvement of Business Environment</u>

* to fine-tune a scheme for water drainage and supply
* to improve operations by providing better service for the maritime industry
* to streamline licensing procedures for hotels and guesthouse, local vessels; and improve licensing for entertainment and games services
* to improve the application procedures for sales of house development and land leases
* to build a Chinese language index page for public forms on the internet
* to compile a comprehensive practical guide about labor laws and good management practices

III.4 <u>Awareness of Improvement to Business Community</u>

* to devise a comprehensive and coherent publicity program
* to publish regular newsletters and circulate to businessmen

III.5 <u>Appreciation of the Needs of Business Community</u>

* to conduct seminars for and give talks to officers at all levels on deregulation and other areas of the Helping Business Program

IV. To Build Hong Kong as a Pre-Eminent Services Center

IV.1 <u>Strategic Thinking on Future Development</u>

* to organize a forum to facilitate views exchange
* to commission an economic study of Hong Kong's producer services
* to study how Hong Kong in taking full advantage of growth of services in the Mainland and how it may best serve overseas business investing in Mainland

IV.2 <u>Strengthen Institutional Support</u>

*   to develop a strategy to improve dissemination of government information relevant to the business sector through the internet
*   to undertake a study of manpower forecasting and forecasting model for the next ten years
*   to improve the "after-sales" service for overseas businesses in Hong Kong
*   to study manpower training needs of the information technology (IT), travel and tourism sector
*   to study the idea of business parks
*   to establish a mechanism to obtain key information on measures to enhance competitiveness

IV.3 <u>Implement Industry-Specific Initiatives</u>

*   to provide necessary legal framework of electronic commerce
*   to provide logistical support to organize international conferences
*   to promote Hong Kong as Asia's wine trading center and international shipping center

V.   To Maintain Prudent Management of Public Finances

V.1 <u>Prudent and Cost-Effective Government Expenditure Growth</u>

*   to undertake an enhanced productivity program across the Government
*   to conduct fundamental government expenditures reviews to examine cost-effectiveness

V.2 <u>Maintain an Effective Revenue Collection and Protection System</u>

*   to enhance efforts to combat tax evasion and minimize opportunities for tax avoidance
*   to increase efficiency by upgrading the application system for the issue of new business registration certificates

V.3 <u>Provide Sources of Government Finance</u>

*   to seek funding approval for capital investment of railway construction

VI. To Enrich Hong Kong as a Key Tourist Destination

VI.1 <u>Develop and Improve Tourism Infrastructure and Facilities</u>

*   to set up, re-package, and launch programs with regard to sites of specific projects
*   to prepare a Green Guide to Hong Kong covering all natural heritage resources for heritage tourism

VI.2 <u>Improve the Quality of Service of the Tourism Industry</u>

*   to step up "Be a Good Host" Campaign
*   to produce a "Trilingual Taxi Guide"

VI.3 <u>Promote Hong Kong as an Attractive Tourist Destination</u>

*   to commission feasibility studies on new attractions
*   to undertake joint promotion efforts with the Mainland to promote multi-destination tourism
*   to conduct the Disneyland project

Source: Compiled from *The 1999 Policy Address: Policy Objectives*, (Vol. 1 and 2), HKSAR Government, 1999.

CHAPTER 7

TAIWAN

FINANCIAL CRISIS IN EAST ASIA

Teh-Ming Huo

National Chengchi University
64 Tz Nan Rd, Sec 2, Mucha (116)
Taipei, Taiwan
E-mail: dmhuo@nccu.edu.tw

1. INTRODUCTION

The financial turbulence originated from Southeast Asia had spread beyond national borders. Among East Asian countries, it is generally considered that Taiwan is perhaps affected in the least. This conclusion begs more questions. Is it true that Taiwan indeed is least affected? If the crisis ever affected Taiwan, in what capacity is the country affected? How seriously is it affected? Does the crisis have any lingering effect? And finally, how did Taiwan escape from the crisis? These are the questions we intend to explore in the present chapter.

As Taiwan has successfully transformed herself from a developing to newly industrial country, the macroeconomic performance was strong and stable. From 1976 to 1996, the average growth rate of real GNP per capita was 8.1%. The GNP per capita was less than 200 USD in 1950, and was more than 13,000 USD in 1997. The fast growth of the economy was accompanied by mild inflation, high employment and equitable income distribution.

Alternative economic policies were adopted in the process of development.[1] In the 1950s it was the import-substitution policy implemented first, then the export-expansion policy followed. The trade-promotion policy has suited the economy well. Taiwan's balance of trade has been in surplus since 1976 (except 1980). With such a long history of trade surplus, Taiwan has been reforming its financial structure since 1980. Three types of financial liberalization were taken: the interest-rate liberalization, the exchange-rate liberalization, and the capital-mobility liberalization.

The interest-rate liberalization actually started in 1976 when the money market was formally established. The instruments in the money market included commercial papers, bankers' acceptances, negotiable certificates of deposit, and treasury bills. The purpose of establishing the money market is to bridge the gap between the official loan market, which was directed by banks mostly owned by the government, and the non-official loan market, which was dominated by private individuals and institutions.

The initial implementation of interest-rate liberalization was less successful since the government still set the maximum rates on all kinds of deposits while allowing banks set their loan rates, with the provision that the minimum loan rate be higher than the maximum deposit rate. This policy restricted the scope of loans that commercial banks were allowed. However, in November 1980, the Central Bank of China (CBC) allowed the market to determine the rate on NCD and other money-market instruments. This has significant impact on the depth of the money market. The outstanding volumes of bills in the money market grew twice as fast as the corresponding bank loans in the first 18 months. As interest rates in the money market were allowed to reflect the "true" demand and supply of funds, the CBC started to make frequent, usually small, adjustments in the deposit rates of banks.[2]

In 1985, that the "Regulation for Interest Rate Management" prohibiting the maximum deposit rate from exceeding the minimum loan rate was

---

[1] For a succinct summary of those policies, please see Kuo (1997) and Yu (1998).

[2] Within the period of November 1980 to September 1982, the CBC had adjusted the deposit rates 10 times in order to properly reflect the market equilibrium.

abolished. Each commercial bank was allowed to announce its "prime rate" every day as its own minimum loan rate. Moreover, the range of interbank loan rates was allowed to widen gradually from previous 1.25% to 6% spread. This implementation of the second stage of interest rate liberalization was regarded timely as the huge trade surplus and the balanced government budget provided a favorable background for removing all regulations toward controlling the deposit and loan rates of banks. In summary, interest-rate liberalization in the 1980s had paved the way for the revision of the Banking Law in 1989.

The exchange-rate liberalization took place after July 1978. The once fixed exchange rate was allowed to float with intermittent intervention from the central bank. The foreign exchange market was officially established in 1979. Throughout the first half of the 1980s, the exchange rate of NTD remained relatively stable, while Taiwan has accumulated foreign exchange reserves of 23 billions USD at the end of 1985. The depreciation of the USD after the G-5 meeting in September 1985 has resulted in a 40% appreciation of NTD from 1986 to 1987. During the appreciation period, the CBC has also accumulated a whopping reserve of more than 70 billions USD in total. This reserve is enough for the need of three years of Taiwan's imports. In the process of appreciation, it is often said that the CBC did not allow the market to adjust fast enough, so that speculator would profit from the anticipated appreciation of currency. Another consequence of the slow process of currency appreciation is that the CBC was forced to provide an excessive amount of high-power money leading to subsequent asset price inflation.[3]

Both stock prices and real estate prices started to accelerate after 1987. The Taiwan stock index was at 1,100 points in the beginning of 1987; it

---

[3] The annual growth rates of M1a and M1b are 46.14% and 51.42% in 1986; the annual growth rates of M1a and M1b are 32.34% and 37.82% in 1987. These numbers were three times higher than the corresponding average rates in the first half of 1980s. The CBC raised required reserve ratios in 1989, both annual growth rates of M1a and M1b became negative in 1990. The average inflation rate between 1986 and 1990 never did exceed 5%. Yang and Shea (1996) attributed the later fever in the stock and the real estate market as a consequence of high growth of M1 in 1986 and 1987.

climbed to 4,500 points at the end of September 1987, and finally hit the historical peak at 12,495 points in February 1990. The real estate market was also inspired by the oversupply of currency. The housing industry enjoyed fabulous boom until 1991 (Figure 7.1). The busts in the stock and the real estate market in the early 1990s were similar to what had happened in Japan.

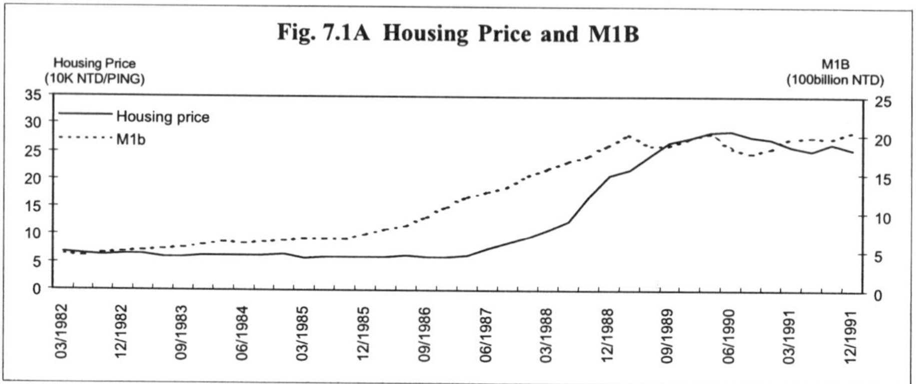

Source: Financial Statistical Monthly Report, Central Bank of China.
Yang (1992) "An empirical study on the determinants of housing price in the greater Taipei area," (in Chinese) master thesis, Tamkang University.

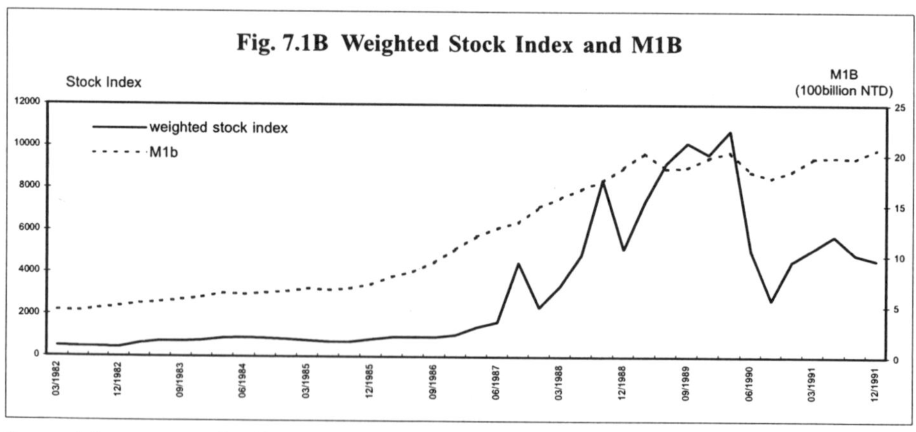

Source: Macroeconomy Profile, Taiwan Economic Journal.
Financial Statistical Monthly Report, Central Bank of China.

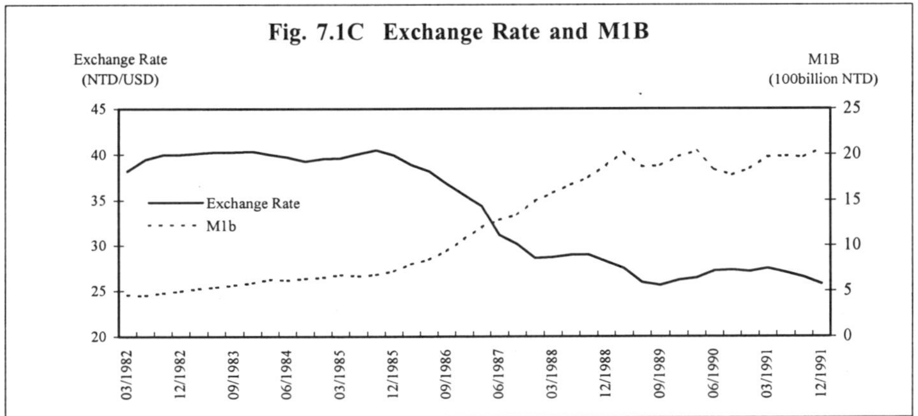

Source: Macroeconomy Profile, Taiwan Economic Journal.
Financial Statistical Monthly Report, Central Bank of China.

The only difference is that Taiwan's stock index fell to around 3,000 points from its highest peak (October 1990), yet most macroeconomic indicators (e.g., consumption, investment and employment) have suffered little. The housing price in Taiwan declined on average 20% to 30%, and yet no serious banking crisis occurred as did in Japan. The bubble economy may be a characteristic of what had happened in the second half of 1980s and early 1990s.

Before 1980, international capital movement in Taiwan was subject to strictly government control. The official channel for capital inflow is for an importer to borrow foreign currency through commercial banks, and to sell his borrowings in the foreign exchange market for NTD. To facilitate the borrowing from importers, commercial banks were allowed to borrow foreign exchange from abroad. During the period of 1986 to 1987, due to the inflexibility of the CBC, NTD gradually appreciated against the USD. However, this policy drew more speculations. With the expectation of further appreciation of NTD, importers started to borrow massive foreign exchange from commercial banks. Banks borrowed foreign exchange from abroad both to relent to importers and to be hoard by themselves. The CBC was forced to freeze the outstanding amount of foreign liability of commercial banks twice in 1987. The appreciation of NTD finally came to a stop and the CBC fell to the victim of its own policy.[4]

As most developing countries, Taiwan's capital outflow was severely restricted. In July 1987, due to the immense pressure of the expectation of appreciation of NTD, the non-bank public was allowed a maximum of 5 million USD of outward remittance per adult per year. The inward remittance was set at 50,000 USD per adult per year in 1987. Starting from 1989, each citizen was allowed the limit of inward remittance of 200,000 USD per year; the sum was raised to 2 million USD in 1990; to 5 million USD in or out in 1995. With strict regulation on the foreign liability of domestic banks, Taiwan's policy has been lenient toward private, small investors. As a consequence, investors from Taiwan have contributed more than 35 billion USD in Southeast Asia and Mainland China. Next to Japan, Taiwan is the second largest capital exporting country in Asia.

The three types of financial liberalization described above set the stage for the passing of the new Security Law in 1988 and the new Banking Law in 1989. Taiwan's financial industry was facing a fresh environment. New security firms and banks were granted licenses as long as they meet the minimum capital requirement. The number of banks more than doubled, and the number of security firms more than quadrupled in three years.[5] The competition between direct and indirect finance was so keen that many banks were forced to take on high-risk loans. This had direct effect on the profit margin of banks. Government supervision of banks was constantly undercut by shortage of manpower. During the second half of 1995 and into 1996, there were several instances where community financial institutions experienced

---

[4] The CBC first froze the outstanding foreign liability of commercial banks on May 31, then lift the ban on October 1, and reimpose the freeze on the next day due to a capital inflow exceeding 3 billion USD on October 2, 1987.

[5] By the end of 1999, there were 212 security firms with 987 branch offices, 36 security investment trust companies and 219 security investment consultant companies. In contrast, there were 38 security firms, 4 security investment trust companies, and 15 investment consultant companies in 1987. By the end of 1999, there were 52 domestic banks, 42 foreign bans, and 364 community financial institutions. In contrast, there were 24 domestic banks, 33 foreign bans, and 381 community financial institutions in 1989.

panic runs. The government subsequently encouraged community financial institutions to either merge with other financial institutions or else convert themselves into commercial banks. The problem with community financial institutions was and is still an unsolved issue in Taiwan's financial system.

Large public banks were entangled with different kind of problems. They were obliged to take administrative orders from the government. Not only the decision on loans cannot be made based on pure profit base, but also they were sometimes forced to invest in the stock market, or to extend loans to enterprises that were considered too important to default.

Taiwan's vibrant stock market attracted speculators from every stratum of society. More than 90% stock transactions were executed by private individuals. In terms of the transaction volume, it ranked the fourth largest market, next to New York, Tokyo and London, in the world. The turnover rate in the stock market ran between 200% to 400% from 1988 to 1999 (except 1992), the highest in the world. Discipline in the stock market was hard to enforce. Insider trading, stock price manipulations, payment default and so on were constantly reported. These fundamental weaknesses exist long before the East Asian financial crisis. With booming stock market, it is socially unpopular to fix the inherent weakness in the system; with busting stock market, it is politically unwise to correct the weakness. The vicious cycle ran from the regulators to regulatees and was well perceived by all participants in the financial market.

2. LITERATURE REVIEW

Most literature on Southeast Asia financial crisis has been focusing on the twin crises: the currency crisis and the banking crisis.[6] Corsetti, Pesenti, and Roubini (1998) developed an interpretation of the Asian meltdown focused on the moral hazard as the common source of over-investment, excessive external borrowing, and current account deficits. To the extent

---

[6] An overwhelming collection of papers can be found on the internet, e.g., http://www.stern.nyu.edu/~nroubini/asia/AsiaHomepage.html.

that foreign creditors are willing to lend to domestic agents against future bail-out revenue from the government, unprofitable projects and cash shortfalls are re-financed through external borrowing. While public deficits need not be high before a crisis, the eventual refusal of foreign creditors to refinance the country's cumulative losses forces the government to step in and guarantee the outstanding stock of external liabilities. To satisfy the solvency, the government must then undertake appropriate domestic fiscal reforms, possibly involving recourse to seigniorage revenues. Expectations of inflationary financing causing a collapse of currency and anticipate the event of a financial crisis. The paper also shown empirical evidence in support of this thesis that weak cyclical performances, low foreign reserves, and financial deficiencies resulting into high shares of non-performing loans were at the core of the Asian collapse.

Yang (1998) discussed the empirical aspect of the impact of the Asian financial crisis on Taiwan. She concluded that the better performance of Taiwan, in the wake of the crisis, could be attributed to various factors, including those linked with the macroeconomic, financial and real sectors. The paper took Taiwan's abundant foreign reserves, low foreign debt, strict financial regulations, and appropriate government reaction as primary causes for the robustness of Taiwan's economy.

Kuo and Liu (1998) have examined the characteristics of Taiwan's economy in the context of the Asian financial crisis. They have focused on the saving-investment imbalance, trade deficits and surpluses, exchange rate policies, the soundness of the financial sector, the order of financial liberalization, and the financial policy of the government. They have found that Taiwan's conditions are significantly different from the troubled countries in the Asia financial crisis.

3.   THE IMPACT OF THE FINANCIAL CRISIS

Table 7.1 summarizes the general performance of Taiwan's economy before and after July 1997. Prior to the East Asian financial crisis, Taiwan's economic fundamentals were relatively sound. The economic growth shows

Table 7.1 Key Economic and Financial Indicators

Year/Month	GDP Growth Rate (%)	Unemploy-ment Rate (%)	Consumer Price Index (%)	Growth Rate Of M2 (%)	Interbank Interest Rate (%)	One Year Deposit Interest Rate (%)	Stock Price Index (1966 = 100)	NTD/USD (end of month)
1988	7.84	1.69	1.28	21.16	4.88	5.25	5.202	28.17
1989	8.23	1.57	4.42	20.42	7.34	9.50	8.616	26.16
1990	5.39	1.67	4.12	12.85	10.49	9.50	6.775	27.11
1991	7.55	1.51	3.63	16.33	6.01	8.27	4.929	25.75
1992	6.76	1.51	4.47	19.94	6.88	7.75	4.272	25.40
1993	6.32	1.45	2.94	16.43	6.41	7.55	4.215	26.63
1994	6.54	1.56	4.09	16.29	6.13	7.35	6.253	26.24
1995	6.03	1.79	3.68	11.59	6.19	6.65	5.544	27.27
1996	5.67	2.60	3.07	9.23	5.44	5.95	6.004	27.49
1997/1	–	2.68	1.96	9.35	5.65	5.95	7.135	27.44
1997/2	–	2.97	2.05	9.88	6.66	5.95	7.642	27.53
1997/3	6.86	2.79	1.10	10.03	6.19	5.95	8.166	27.54
1997/4	–	2.59	0.50	9.76	6.56	5.95	8.506	27.66
1997/5	–	2.51	0.76	8.99	5.66	5.95	8.147	27.85
1997/6	6.34	2.67	1.83	8.35	7.21	5.90	8.605	27.81
1997/7	–	2.85	3.30	7.60	7.11	5.90	9.553	28.70
1997/8	–	3.03	−0.57	7.09	8.11	6.00	9.890	28.63
1997/9	6.91	2.84	0.62	6.50	7.56	6.00	9.112	28.60
1997/10	–	2.63	−0.32	6.52	7.82	6.00	7.983	30.94
1997/11	–	2.60	−0.52	7.29	7.12	6.00	7.732	32.05
1997/12	6.71	2.45	0.26	8.03	6.67	6.00	8.148	32.64
1998/1	–	2.35	1.99	9.78	7.31	6.03	7.850	34.00
1998/2	–	2.57	0.30	8.79	7.22	6.52	8.808	32.10
1998/3	5.67	2.34	2.46	8.32	6.93	6.52	8.976	32.86
1998/4	–	2.29	2.11	8.48	6.80	6.53	8.785	32.97
1998/5	–	2.37	1.66	8.26	6.88	6.53	8.226	33.99
1998/6	5.24	2.7	1.42	8.11	6.84	6.53	7.540	34.35
1998/7	–	2.93	0.84	8.08	6.75	6.53	7.874	34.37
1998/8	–	3.05	0.44	8.39	6.67	6.51	7.218	34.84
1998/9	4.15	2.98	0.41	9.61	6.52	6.55	6.832	34.37
1998/10	–	2.98	2.58	9.19	6.06	6.10	6.886	32.45
1998/11	–	2.93	3.91	9.64	5.40	5.90	7.109	32.44
1998/12	3.36	2.80	2.13	8.56	4.95	5.45	6.832	32.22
1999/1	–	2.76	0.40	6.45	4.85	5.40	6.256	32.30
1999/2	–	2.73	2.08	8.21	4.75	5.20	5.920	33.06
1999/3	4.17	2.84	−0.46	8.65	4.73	5.05	6.677	33.14
1999/4	–	2.75	−0.12	9.38	4.72	5.05	7.390	32.69
1999/5	–	2.84	0.50	9.08	4.70	5.05	7.505	32.73
1999/6	6.55	2.92	−0.83	9.70	4.74	5.05	8.055	32.30
1999/7	–	3.11	−0.82	9.25	4.84	5.05	7.916	32.15
1999/8	–	3.22	1.14	8.83	4.84	5.05	7.656	31.84
1999/9	5.14	3.08	0.59	7.89	4.84	5.05	7.977	31.80
1999/10	–	3.05	0.42	7.26	4.82	5.05	7.697	31.74
1999/11	–	2.94	−0.90	6.57	4.82	5.00	7.670	31.67
1999/12	6.05	2.88	0.13	8.28	4.73	5.00	7.919	31.40

Source: Taiwan Economic Journal Profile: Macroeconomy.

a sign of slight decline mainly due to the economy entering mature stage. The growth has been accomplished with little reliance upon foreign capital. Although the saving rate has steadily declined from a peak of 38.5% in 1987 to 24.4% in 1997, it is still higher than the corresponding investment rate. Private saving continues to be the main source of funds for local investment. Taiwan's current account surplus amounted to 11 billion USD in 1996 (or 4.7 percent of GDP). This surplus is indicative of the excess saving that still exists in the economy.

Just prior to the dramatic collapse of the Thai Baht at July 2, the exchange rate of NTD/USD was 27.8 at July 1, 1997. As Singapore, Malaysia and Indonesia stopped pegging and allowing their currencies to depreciate, many participants in Taiwan's foreign exchange market were anticipating similar depreciation of NTD in mid-July. Trading firms began to short NTD and long USD, foreign portfolio investors withdrew funds from the local stock market. Despite the onslaught of the financial crisis, the CBC initially avowed to maintain the stability of NTD at all costs. Then, suddenly at the end of July 1997, the exchange rate depreciated to 28.8 in four days. The rediscount rate was raised 0.25% on August 1 to quench speculations in the foreign exchange market. With its huge foreign exchange reserves and predicted trade surplus, it seems that the CBC was able to defend NTD, as it desired.

Despite frequent rumors about potential devaluation of NTD, the exchange rate of NTD was pegged between 28.6 to 28.8 by the CBC in August 1997. In the beginning of September 1997, NTD even appreciated to the level of 28.61, but it was apparent that the financial crisis abroad was coming at a stronger pace. In mid-September, many financial institutions were predicting devaluation of NTD against USD. The interest spread between the spot and 3-month forward NTD was only 1% at that time. Due to this speculation, there was a strong surge of demand for USD. To stampede the speculation, the CBC continuously sold 1.7 billions USD in support of NTD even to the extent of mild appreciation of NTD. All attempts were directed to subdue the expectation of depreciation of NTD.

In the process of intervention, the decrease of money supply caused the interest rate to shoot up to 19.8% in the interbank loan market of Taiwan (Figure 7.2). The CBC reduced required reserve ratio of banks' deposits

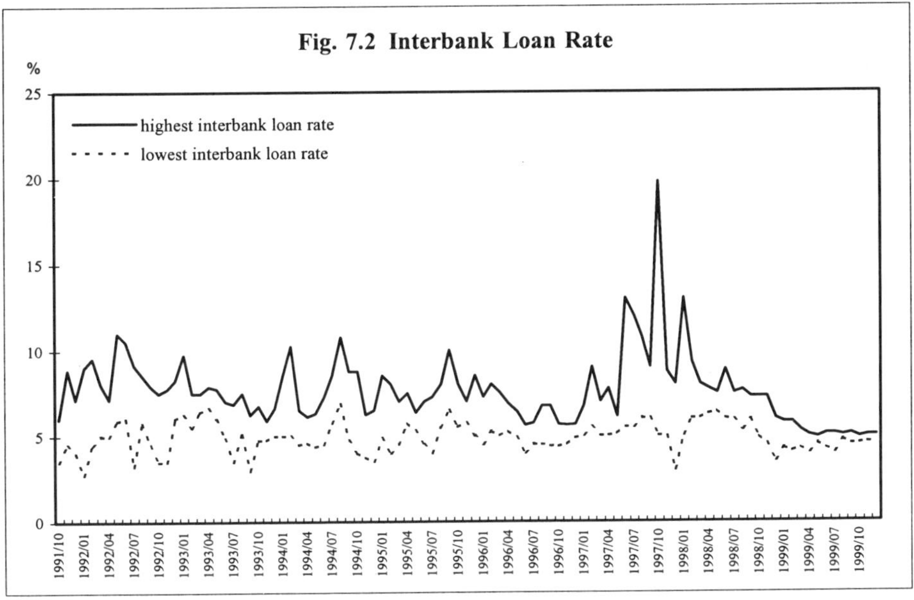

Fig. 7.2 Interbank Loan Rate

Source: Macroeconomy Profile, Taiwan Economic Journal.
Financial Statistical Monthly Report, Central Bank of China.

twice and injected more than 130 billions of high-powered NTD in the market in hope of ameliorate the tension in the interest rate. However, the augmented NTD was again used to exchange USD from the central bank in anticipation of future depreciation of NTD. In the process of defending NTD, it was estimated that the foreign reserves of Taiwan's central bank was reduced from 90 billions of USD in June to 83 billions in October.

Despite the tension in the foreign exchange market, the performance in Taiwan's stock market reached a peak at the end of August, with the stock weighted index of 10,200 points. However, the prosperity in the stock market soon gave way to the pessimistic psychology associated with exiting foreign portfolio investment. The stock index plummeted to 8380 points in the beginning of October (Figure 7.3).

Although the government tried to coordinate public funds in supporting stock prices, both pressures from the depressing investors in the stock market and from the coming election at the end of the year challenged the

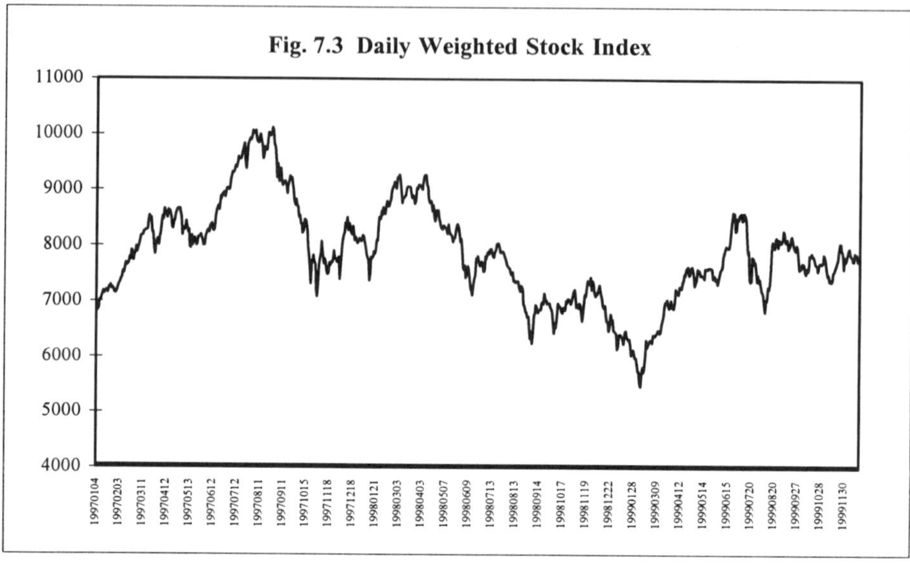

Source: Macroeconomy Profile, Taiwan Economic Journal.
Financial Statistical Monthly Report, Central Bank of China.

determination of keeping NTD from depreciation. On October 3 and 4, the transaction volume between NTD and USD has reached 1.54 and 0.58 billions USD in the foreign exchange market. Those were 5 times the usual transaction volumes. On October 17, 1997, the CBC finally stopped pegging the exchange rate and the market responded swiftly. NTD/USD exchange rate was 28.6 on October 16, 29.5 on October 17, 29.8 on October 18.[7] By January 12, 1998, it was 34.5, a depreciation of 24.1%, relative to its value at July 1, 1997 (Figure 7.4).[8]

---

[7] The stock market did not respond to the depreciation favorably. The stock index fell to 7,316.78 on October 20, 1997.

[8] The depreciation of NTD in October 1997 has another dimension of impact in terms of international politics. The first-round East Asian financial crisis was caused by Thailand, Malaysia, Indonesia and Philippine. With its strong economic fundamentals (ongoing current account surplus, high economic growth prospect and huge foreign exchange reserves), Taiwan was supposed to be able to defend NTD and set a role model for defeating the international

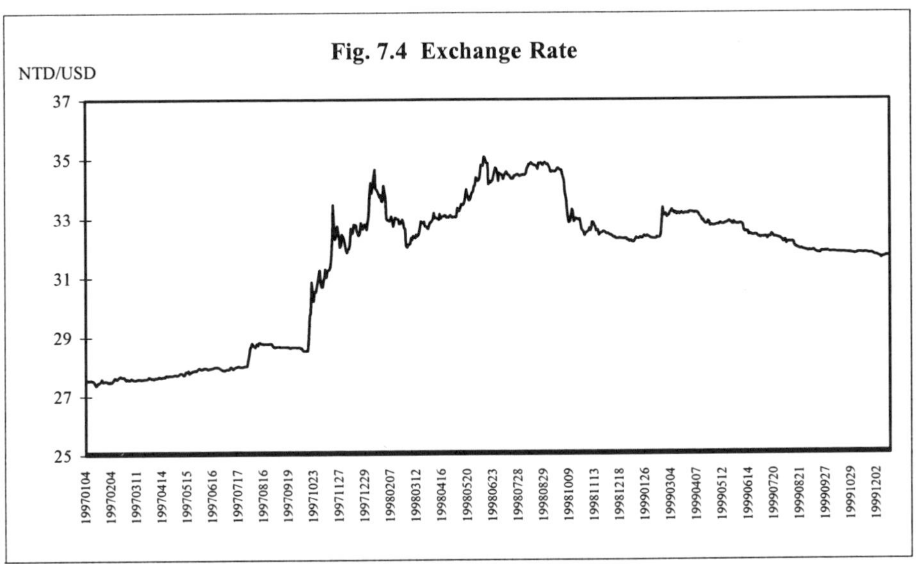

The beginning of 1998 was first greeted by a short recovery in the Southeast Asian countries; NTD climbed back to 32.2 on March 6, 1998. The following crisis in Indonesia caused NTD to fall again to 34.9 on June 10. Between June and September, the exchange rate was bouncing between 34 to 35.[9]

The Asian financial crisis eventually spilt over to Russia and Latin America. Certain large hedge funds, such as the Long Term Capital Management, also suffered big losses. The seriousness of the Asian financial

---

speculators. However, the government of Taiwan succumbed to the pressure from potential international speculators and chose to depreciate its currency as a preemptive strike. This was considered by some as the cause of the second round East Asian financial crisis. By late October 1997, the crisis emanated to Hong Kong; and by November, to Korea.

[9] For fear of further speculative attacks, the CBC greatly reduced the scope of transactions of non-physical delivery forward (NDF) of NTD on May 22, 1998. It caused a furious debate as to whether such policy was warranted.

crisis forced the U.S. government to modify its policy of maintaining a strong dollar. The Federal Reserve Board started to lower the interest rate in late September 1998. Thus NTD/USD exchange rate appreciated from 34.6 on September 23 to 32.47 on October 30, and then stabilize at around that level. The expectations of an appreciation in NTD during the fourth quarter of 1998 seemed so strong that the CBC had to actively intervene in the foreign exchange market in the opposite direction by purchasing a great quantity of USD. As a result, the total amount of foreign exchange reserves held by CBC registered a significant increase of 5.3 billions USD during the fourth quarter of 1998, and NTD exchange rate stood at a steady 32.22 against the USD at the end of 1998.

The immediate impact of the East Asian financial crisis on Taiwan is basically on the financial side of the economy. The real economy did not suffer as much. The economic growth rate was 6.8% in 1997 and 4.9% in 1998, while most other inflicted countries had negative growth rates (Figure 7.5).

The inflation rate was 0.9% in 1997 and 1.7% in 1998. These numbers were low considering the magnitude of the depreciation of NTD. The unemployment rate was 2.7% for both 1997 and 1998, which was a bit high relative high to historical standard (e.g., less than 2% for period before 1996) but extremely low comparing with what happened in Hong Kong, Korea and Japan.

Taiwan's trade was less affected by the financial crisis. In 1997, the export in goods and services was 138 billion USD, a growth rate of 10.5% from previous year; the import was 132 billion USD, a growth rate of 13.6% from previous year. However, the crisis had some lagging effect on the volume of export and import in next two years. In 1998, Taiwan's export was 129 billion USD and imports 126 billion USD; in 1999, Taiwan's export was 97 billion USD and imports 93 billion USD, respectively. The reduction in trade volume should not be taken by surprise. The trade between Taiwan and other East Asian countries accounted for more than 50% of the overall volume of trade of Taiwan. As output of each East Asian countries was reduced by the financial turmoil, their trade volume would be affected in similar ways.

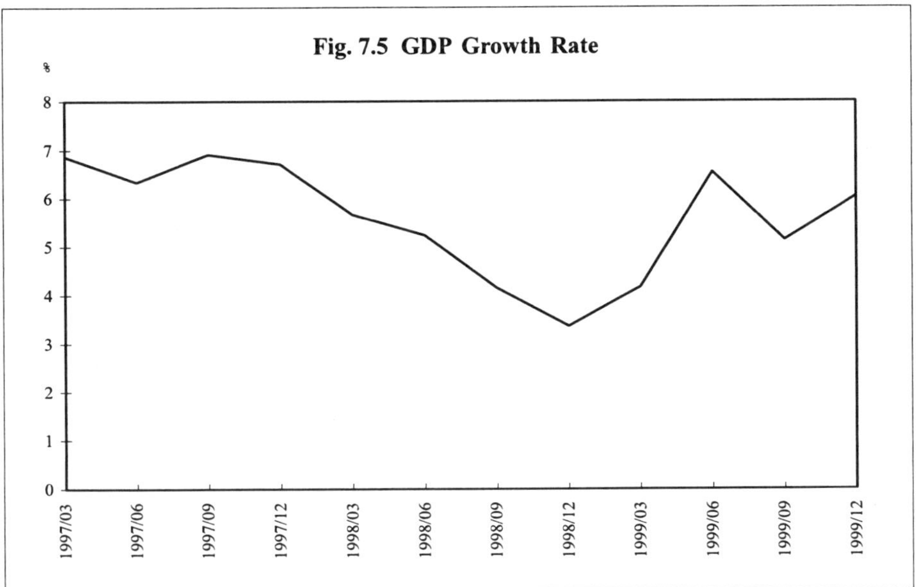

Fig. 7.5 GDP Growth Rate

Source: Macroeconomy Profile, Taiwan Economic Journal.
Financial Statistical Monthly Report, Central Bank of China.

Fig. 7.6 Unemployment Rate

Source: Macroeconomy Profile, Taiwan Economic Journal
Financial Statistical Monthly Report, Central Bank of China

4.   WHY IS TAIWAN HURT LESS?

There are several reasons that why Taiwan was relatively unscathed in the East Asian financial crisis:[10]

• Limited Foreign Debt and Abundant Foreign Exchange Reserves

Public external debt amounted to little more than 100 million USD at the end of 1997. The foreign assets of financial institutions (including OBUs) amounted to 29.7 billion USD at the end of 1997, while foreign liabilities amounted to 29.3 billion USD at the same time. Net foreign assets therefore amounted to only 400 million USD.

• An Improved Financial Structure for Private Enterprises

As stock market trading became more active in 1997, enterprises raised more than 15.3 billion USD in funds from the stock market. As a result, enterprises' capital ratios have also significantly increased, and their dependence on debts has on the whole markedly decreased. Debt-equity ratios for listed manufacturing enterprises averaged 71 percent at the end of September 1997. In this way, the ability of these companies to respond to changing circumstances increased. In addition, in view of the increasing popularity of direct finance as a means of raising funds, banks directed their attention towards lending to small and medium-sized enterprises (SMEs) and consumer loans. As a result, small and medium-sized enterprises have been able to lessen their dependence upon underground financing, and banks' credit risks have become more widely spread out.

The number of SMEs in Taiwan reached more than 1 million in 1997, which accounted for more than 98% of the total number of all enterprises. They have employed more than 7 millions of labor, which accounted for more than 80% of national employment. The gross sales of SMEs were more 200 billions USD, which accounted for 35% of total sales of all enterprises. They exported merchandises worth 60 billions USD, which accounted for more than 50% of the total export of all enterprises. With very

---

[10]Sheu (1998) and Shea (1998) have also expressed similar views.

little assistance from the government, these SMEs are extremely flexible in adapting themselves to the changing environment, they have provided Taiwan a resilient buffer when the Southeast Asian financial crisis hit the economy.

• A Prudent Banking System

Taiwan's commercial banks have traditionally been conservative when evaluating their potential risks. Banks usually try to minimize their currency risk by squaring off their foreign exchange positions. To minimize interest rate risk, the interest on their loans is mostly based on floating rates. To reduce potential loss from credit risk, most of their loans are backed by sufficient collateral. After the bubble had burst in early 1990s and the long recession in the housing market starting, local banks in Taiwan have all along tended to adopt a cautious attitude towards loans backed by either real estate or listed shares. For instance, they only finance up to 60 percent of the value of company stocks, and loans backed by stock shares account for only 2 percent of total bank lending. Similarly, banks in general only extend mortgages for about 70 percent of the purchase price of a house, and all real-estate loans are fully secured. They thereby have the ability to withstand the negative impact of depressed asset market.

Taiwan's minimum requirement of owner's equity for banks is 10 billion NTD. This high equity requirement serves as a shock absorber between assets and liabilities, and has provided a cushion against unforeseen contingencies. The average capital adequacy ratio for banks in Taiwan at the end of 1997 was 11.4%, far exceeding the 8% requirement. The effective functioning of the deposit insurance system and the lender of last resort facility have also helped safeguard the banking system against self-fulfilling panic. This prudential regulatory structure and conservative banking practices together have strengthened Taiwan's overall position in responding to the changing international conditions.

• A Gradual Approach to Liberalizing Movements of Foreign Capital

Since inflows and outflows of speculative capital may exert a significant impact on our local stock and foreign exchange markets, Taiwan has adopted a gradual approach to relaxing controls over flows of foreign capital. The investment of foreign capital in the Taiwan stock market has been prudent. Foreign funds were considered unreliable in the eyes of government officials, thus they were subject to strict regulation. The average volume of daily transactions of foreign funds in the Taiwan stock market has been less than 5%. It is generally considered that the influence of foreign capital is mainly informational, if not psychological.

5.   THE INTERNAL FINANCIAL CRISIS IN 1998

As discussed in the previous section, the East Asian financial crisis did limited damage to the domestic economy of Taiwan. Judging from macroeconomic data, especially growth rate of 6.8% in 1997 and 4.9% in 1998, the conclusion was almost immediate. In November 1998, the *Economist* magazine published a fourteen-page article praising Taiwan's phenomenal performance in the crisis. However, two months later in January 1999, the *Fortune* magazine raised the question that Taiwan could be the last domino in the East Asian financial crisis. How could these respectable magazines have such extreme opposite evaluation of Taiwan's economy in so short period of time? We intend to resolve the issue in this section.

By the end of the first half of 1998, Taiwan was just recovering from the immediate impact of the East Asian financial crisis. It was a general consensus by many local experts that Taiwan did not suffer as much damages as other inflicted countries. Yet, because of the prolonged recession in the real estate market, the construction industry was in serious limbo. Business confidence was extremely fragile. Beginning in August 1998, a number of enterprises encountered financial difficulties due to their misconduct in the fund management.[11] The so-called "land-mine-share" effect started to adversely affect the financial condition of several local financial institutions, which in turn accelerated the downturn in stock prices. The Taiwan stock index fluctuated between 6,500 and 7,500 points in the fourth quarter of 1998.

---

[11] For a list of such companies, please see Appendix 1.

Another key concern of the government has been the steady increase in the domestic banks' non-performing loan ratio. The ratio rose on average from 3.75% at the end of 1997 to 4.36% at the end of 1998 (Figure 7.7). The fragility in the financial market prompted the CBC lowering required reserve ratios on September 29, 1998. It also lowered the rediscount rate on two more occasions (November 11 and December 8), and released postal savings redeposit to inject liquidity into the money market. Its objective was to lower the market interest rates and to supply the medium and long-term funds required for private investment and public infrastructure. As a result, the interbank loan rate fell quickly from an average of 6.52% in September to 4.95% in December 1998, and the commercial paper rate also declined from 6.67% to 5.21% over the same period.

Despite the restoration of stability in the foreign exchange market and the adoption of an easy monetary policy from October 1998 onwards, the

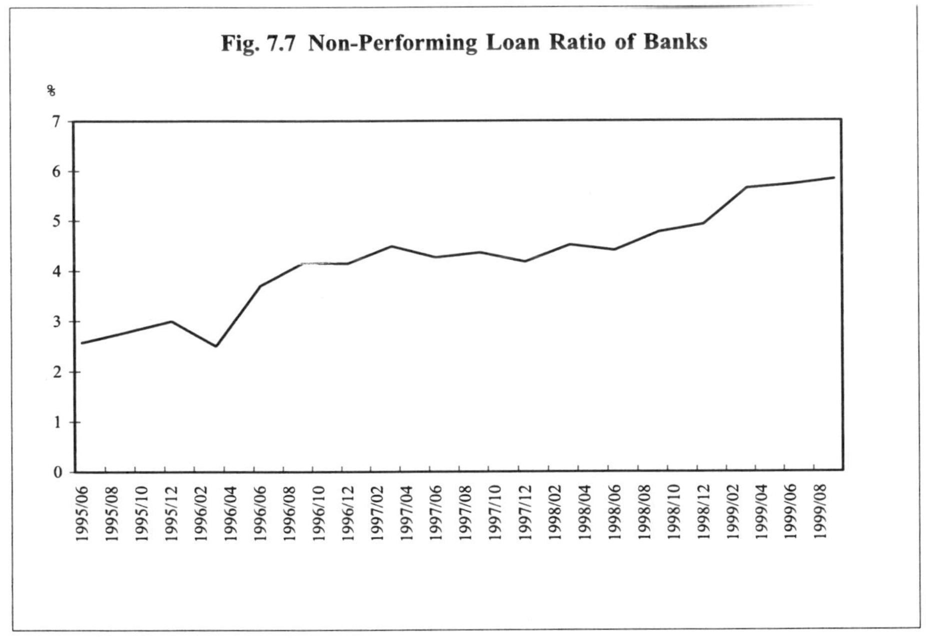

Fig. 7.7 Non-Performing Loan Ratio of Banks

Source: Macroeconomy Profile, Taiwan Economic Journal.
Financial Statistical Monthly Report, Central Bank of China.

performance of both the real economy in the first quarter of 1999 did not seem to be very encouraging. The economic growth rate fell to 3.36% in the fourth quarter of 1998 and recovered a little to 4.17% in the first quarter of 1999, these being the lowest levels recorded since 1983, and significantly below the 5.5% target level for the year as a whole set by the government. The unemployment rate also increased, averaging 2.78% in the first quarter compared with 2.42% a year earlier.

For fear of a meltdown of the financial markets, the MOF in November 1998 required banks to allow for a six-month extension on loans due from companies that were operating normally. Moreover, under certain conditions, fundamentally solvent enterprises but temporarily in financial distress could apply to an *ad hoc* committee set up by the government for financial accommodation. The CBC also teamed up with the MOF to use "moral suasion" to encourage local banks to continue to lend to healthy enterprises which were facing temporary cash-flow difficulties.

In order to prevent a further plunge in the stock market, Taiwan's government also implemented several supporting measures during the fourth quarter of 1998. For instance, a stock stabilization fund was organized by several large banks, government-owned insurance and pension funds to collectively support stock prices. In November 1998, a couple of local financial institutions were threatened by a series of defaults from clients that were heavily involved in highly-leveraged businesses. To maintain the financial stability, the MOF directed its efforts to deal with these particularly distressed financial institutions. It responded by carefully considering the conditions surrounding each case, and then opted for the institutions to be acquired by some healthy banks (Chiu, 1999). In addition, the Taiwan government has also adopted several policies aimed at assisting financial institutions. The interest rate paid by the CBC to account B of the required reserves was raised twice from 2.4% to 3.2%. To improve the quality of bank assets, and to speed up the process of writing off non-performing loans, on February 20, 1999, the CBC lowered the required reserve ratios of banks by an average 2%. The MOF on the same day announced that it would later reduce the gross business revenue tax (GBRT) rate for financial institutions, including banks, securities firms and insurance companies from

5% to 2%. The extra income of financial institutions resulting from the reductions in required reserves and GBRT over the next four years would be used to write off bad loans.

The government has also been concerned with the sluggish housing industry. On December 31, 1998, Taiwan's government approved plans to implement its "Policy to Revitalize the Housing Industry". Central to this directive was the release of NT$150 billion in postal savings to provide low interest loans for the purchase of residential housing. As part of the CBC's selective credit policies, this measure has provided the housing industry with temporary relief.

As a result of these vigorous measures, confidence has been restored among portfolio investors in the stock market. This has been evidenced by the Taiwan stock index rebounding from its low point of 5,474 points on February 5 to 7,572 points on May 5, 1999, an amazing increase of 38.3% in only three months. The economic growth rate has also recovered. The growth rates of GDP per capita climbed back to 5.14% and 6.05% in the third and fourth quarter of 1999 respectively.

6. LESSONS FROM THE FINANCIAL CRISIS

The Asian financial crisis came without premonition. It struck Asian tigers with such force that many experts had predicted a long way to recover. In contrast, the internal financial crisis hit Taiwan with ample forewarnings. It is fortunate that the worst of both crises have come to an end now. The time has come to reflect on the proper role of government.

Although the Asian financial crisis had done only small injury to Taiwan, the structural weaknesses exposed during the internal crisis were similar to the weaknesses pertaining to the financial sector of those countries the Asian financial crisis hit. These include macroeconomic management, sequence of financial liberalization and the regulatory structure of the capital market.

Most East Asian countries share a common goal: grow as fast as one can. They were inspired by the successful experience of Japan in the 1960s.

Some have also attained respectable achievement in the 1980s. Why can't my country become another miracle through proper macroeconomic management? In the case of Thailand, Malaysia, Indonesia and Philippines, economic growth was achieved by running into current account deficits in the 1990s. The inflow of foreign capital would benefit the domestic economy only if it pertains to the long-run nature. Short-term capital has proven to be a non-reliable source of economic growth. In the case of Korea, economic growth was achieved through current account deficits and collusion between government and *chaebols* in the form of debt overhang. Traditionally, Taiwan has based its growth not on short-term foreign capital, but on the SMEs. The choice of macroeconomic management is on how to improve the productivity of domestic enterprises (most of them SMEs). By encouraging international trade, improving the accumulation of human capital, and in particular, fair and non-collusive political environment, Taiwan has weathered through the East Asian financial crisis safely.

Taiwan had also begun its process of financial liberalization more than two decades ago, although the process was not entirely smooth. Interest groups would always be in the way. The slow appreciation of NTD in 1986 and 1987 was thought to be helpful to exporters, yet it turned out that the only significant consequence was the accumulation of huge amount of foreign exchange reserves. The resulting excessive supply of high-powered money finally resulted in bubbles in the stock and the real estate market. After the burst of bubbles in early 1990s, the prolonged recession in the real estate market caused financial depression in the construction and related industries. Had Taiwan be more flexible with its exchange rate policy in 1986, there would not bubbles in the asset market and the long stagnation in the housing market. The liberalization in the capital market (1988) and the banking sector (1989) would have had a healthier environment than what had been in the early 1990s.

Of course, unless a country had a stringent regulatory system, none of the above mentioned would have benefited the economy. A prudential and comprehensive financial regulatory structure should be developed before financial liberalization. One needs to strengthen the financial transparency of enterprises. The accounting practice must conform to the Generally

Accepted Accounting Principles (GAAP). The certified public accountant (CPA) requires serious scrutiny on its due diligence. Other elements of this structure include deposit insurance, minimum capital requirement for banks, independent auditing, risk limitations, close supervision and the central bank's role as a lender of last resort.

Experiences from the Asia financial crisis have highlighted four key aspects for policymakers to reflect on. First, when promoting economic growth a government must adopt consistent macroeconomic policies. The impossible trinity is a good example.[12] A country can only choose fixed exchange rate and free capital mobility, but not concurrently control its money supply independently. In the case of Taiwan, fixed exchange rate and free capital mobility caused money supply run out of control in 1986 and 1987. After that, Taiwan's government was trying to carefully avoid any inconsistency in terms of government policy. In cases of East Asian financial crisis, a country should carefully evaluate the advantages and disadvantages of fixed exchange rates, free capital flows and an independent monetary policy, respectively, according to the country's own conditions before making its choice.

Second, any kind of persistent deficits should be treated with extreme caution. If there were persistent current account deficits, the exchange rate policy should be made to properly reflect macroeconomic fundamentals. If there was persistent imbalance between domestic saving and investment, the interest-rate policy (or other policies) should also be made to properly reflect macroeconomic fundamentals.

Third, asset price inflation and the subsequent deflation always lead to fragility in the financial system and economic slowdown. Although it is hard to quantify, the fever in the asset market lead to excessive investing behavior which took long time to recover. In the case of Taiwan and other East Asian countries, asset price inflation appears to have been the dominant consequence of their excessive monetary expansion. The setting of monetary policy should focus on both the inflation of goods and services and the inflation of assets.

---

[12] See Caves, Frankel and Jones (1996, pp. 564–566).

Fourth, the Asian financial crisis has also highlighted the importance of international cooperation. As intra-regional trade accounts for more than 40% of their total trade, Asian countries depend on each others more closely than before. Due to advancements in technology, financial innovation, and the relaxation of capital control, their financial markets are also more integrated than before. Financial crises are contagious and may easily spread to the rest of the world.[13] To contain a regional crisis, countries in this region should strengthen international cooperation in banking supervision, monitoring international capital flows, standardizing financial transparency and enhancing information exchange. It may be preferable to develop early-warning system for regional financial crisis, and coordinate economic and financial policies among neighboring countries.

References

Caves, R., Frankel, J. and Jones, R., 1996, *World Trade and Payments: An Introduction*, 7th edition, Harper Collins, New York.

Chiu, Paul C.-H., 1999, "The ROC's Strategic Response to the Asian Financial Crisis", a speech delivered at *Conference on Responding to Financial Crisis: Challenges for Domestic Policy and International Cooperation*, Taipei, February 22.

Corsetti, G., Pesenti, P., and Roubini, N., 1998, "Paper Tigers? A Model of the Asian Crisis," working paper, Federal Reserve Bank of New York.

---

[13] Currently, there are between 3,000 and 4,000 hedge funds with an estimated aggregate capital of between 300 billion to 400 billion USD. With leverage, these hedge funds can collectively engage in transactions involving amounts as large as 10 trillion USD. Facing a much wider group of players with more complicated instruments in the global finance, unless a country has a sufficiently large financial market, its short-term capital convertibility might need to be limited to some extent.

Kuo, S., 1996, *Economic Policies: The Taiwan Experience 1945–1995*. Hwa-Tai Publishing Co., Taipei, Taiwan, ROC.

Kuo, S., and Liu, C., 1998, "Taiwan", in *East Asia in Crisis*, ed. By Ross H. McLeod & Ross Garnaut, Routledge, London and New York.

Shea, J.-D., 1998, "Taiwan and the Asian Financial Crisis", Quarterly Journal of Central Bank of China, vol. 20, no. 2, pp. 11–16.

Sheu, Y.-D., 1998, "SEACEN Country Report: Recent Economic and Financial Developments in the Republic of China", speech delivered at the 33rd SEACEN Governors' Conference, Bali, Indonesia.

Yang, Y.-H., 1998, "Coping With the Asian Financial Crisis: The Taiwan Experience," Seoul Journal of Economics, vol. 11, no. 4, 423–445.

Yang, Y.-H. and Shea, J.-D., 1996, "Money and Prices in the 1980s", in *Financial Deregulation in East Asia, NBER-East Asia Seminar in Economics: volume 5*, edited by Takatoshi Ito and Anne O. Krueger, University of Chicago Press, pp. 229–243.

Yu, T.-S. 1998, *The Story of Taiwan: Economy*, Government Information Office, Taipei, Taiwan, ROC.

Appendix 1: List of Enterprises in Financial Crisis from August 1998

1998/8/25	Wan-Yu Paper Co.	Major supplier of industrial paper	1. Excessive inventory 2. Internal financial quarrels
1998/8/27	Pau-Chu Development Co.	Well known construction firm	1. Construction recession 2. Deep in debt
1998/09/09	Hi-Du Development Co.	Electric power plant builder	Stuck with environmental evaluation
1998/09/19	Kuo-Rung Enterprise	Printed circuitry board manufacturer	Financial misconduct of corporate executives
1998/09/20	Yun-Shen Security Co.	Security firm	Financial misconduct of corporate executives
1998/09/22	Len-Pun Food Co.	Largest importer of beef product	1. Failed investment in Wan-Yu Paper Co. 2. Failed investment in finance co.
1998/09/25	Dung-Lung Metal Co.	International top-5 lock manufacturer	Financial misconduct of corporate executives
1998/09/30	Jeng-Chen Enterprise	Printed circuitry board manufacturer	Failed investment in Kuo-Rung Enterprise
1998/09/30	Rei-Lien Enterprise: 1. Rei-Lien Textile 2. Taiwan Construction 3. Rei-Lien Construction 4. Ling-Chuen Construction 5. Jia-Da Construction	Famous construction conglomerate in Taichung (the third largest city in Taiwan)	1. Over expansion 2. High leverage financial operation 3. Business recession
1998/10/03	Chien-Bee Construction Co.	Famous urban developer	1. Over investment 2. High leveraged operation
1998/10/13	Roosa Food Co.	Famous tea drink manufacturer	Financial mismanagement
1998/10/28	Shin-Ju-Chuen Enterprise	Famous construction firm	1. Over leveraged 2. Excessive expansion
1998/10/28	Roger Construction Co.	Famous construction firm in Keelung	1. Failed investment in food industry 2. Construction recession
1998/11/02	Hur-Fung Enterprise	Famous conglomerate	1. Share price support failure 2. Over expansion 3. Deep in debt
1998/11/03	Central Bill Finance Co.	New financial company	Over zealot executive
1998/11/05	Jei-Lien Construction Co.	Famous construction firm in Taichung	1. Construction recession 2. Too much inventory
1998/11/05	Hung-Fu Bill Finance Co.	New financial company	Financial mismanagement
1998/11/09	Kuo-Yang Enterprise	Famous construction company	1. Over expansion 2. Business recession
1998/11/10	Shiou-Mei Food Co.	Famous ice cream manufacturer	1. Competition in food industry 2. Related to Lee-Wei Enterprise
1998/11/10	Lee-Wei Enterprise	Electronic component manufacturer	1. Low dram price 2. Financial mismanagement
1998/11/13	Taipei Airline	Famous helicopter leasing company	Related to Len-Pun Food Co.
1998/11/13	Huang-Chiou Lease Co.	Famous lease company	Related to Len-Pun Food Co.
1998/11/16	Chung-Jin-Jee Enterprise	Largest machinery manufacturer	1. Over expansion 2. Related to failed Central Bill Finance Co.
1998/11/21	Da-Yu Bus Co.	Major public bus operator in Taipei	Financial mismanagement
1998/11/25	Guan-San Enterprise: 1. Guan-San Construction Co. 2. Shuen-Da-Tu Food Co. 3. Guan-San-Sogo Department Store 4. Taichung Enterprise Bank	Famous conglomerate in Taichung	1. Bank audit found mismanagement in Taichung Enterprise Bank 2. Construction recession
1998/11/25	Kuo-Pau Security	Security firm in Taichung	Financial mismanagement
1998/12/01	Young-Rei Computer Co.	Notebook computer manufacturer	Financial mismanagement

Source: Lin, D.-J. (1999) "Financial crisis of domestic enterprises and credit management of banks", (in Chinese) Cooperative Bank Today, no. 290, pp. 15–36.

CHAPTER 8

THAILAND
1997 THAI FINANCIAL CRISIS

Chawin Leenabanchong

Faculty of Economics, Thammasat University
Bangkok, Thailand
E-mail address: chawin@econ.tu.ac.th

1. INTRODUCTION

The collapse of some Asian currencies in the wake of the flotation of the Thai baht on the 2nd of July 1997 is the most recent of several episodes in the 1990s. According to World Economic Outlook[1], the costs of Asia crisis in output losses relative to hypothetical non-crisis output paths range from a minimum of 27 percent in the case of Korea to a maximum of 82 percent in the case of Indonesia. Thailand and Malaysia are in between count 57 and 39 percent of potential output losses. By comparison, particularly for Indonesia and Thailand, these output losses appear to have exceeded those incurred by Argentina and Mexico in the "Tequila" crises in 1994–1995 which cost 15 and 30 percent of potential output respectively.

Lessons from the "Tequila" crisis may provide some common features, but the unusual feature of the Asian financial and economic turmoil is that it was centered in emerging economies which had a record of strong economic

---

[1] International Monetary Fund, (1999), World Economic Outlook, Box 2.6.

growth, moderate inflation and disciplined fiscal policy for at least a decade. What happened to the Asian miracle economies, and why did it happen?

Academic and policy circles are interested in these questions, particularly on the potential causes and symptoms of currency crises. This paper examines the available evidence on currency crises in view of the Thai economic situation. To this end, it first reviews the background of "What happened" before Thailand succumbed to this financial turmoil, which stems from a mix in currency and then banking crises. This might give some clues for the potential causes of this crisis in Thailand.

Second, the paper surveys the theoretical and empirical findings in order to explain "Why did it happen" to the Thai economy. Various approaches used to assess the usefulness of potential causes of currency crises are thereby reviewed. Although there are excellent survey literatures that provide comprehensive discussions of a number of theoretical issues, this paper tries to identify the potential causes under an economic environment that may differ from earlier episodes suggested by an alternative explanation of currency the crisis. As a result, this paper analyses between the traditional approach, which stresses the role played by weak economic fundamentals in inducing a currency crisis, as well as more recent papers, including those that highlight the possibility of self-fulfilling crisis.

An overflow of capital, macroeconomic mismanagement and financial fragility are the hypothetical causes of crisis in Thailand. These causes cannot be directly tested by qualitative methods. Instead, background empirical evidence that had been gathered before might be used.

Third, the paper gives directions on how the Thai economy should move in the future in order to survive the present crisis. What are the "Lessons to be Learned"? With a growing financial integration environment, how can a small open economy like Thailand adjust herself? Controversial issues such as capital control and sustainability are raised and discussed. On the policy issues, the role that government should take and the measures best suited to moving the economy back on track are proposed.

2. BACKGROUND: WHAT HAPPENED?

2.1 Current Account Deficits

Before the currency crisis, the current account deficit was the common macroeconomic instability factor for Thailand and other affected Asian economies. A steady growth in deficit has brought this vulnerability to the creditors' view via the need to borrow in order to finance the deficits, see Figure 8.1.

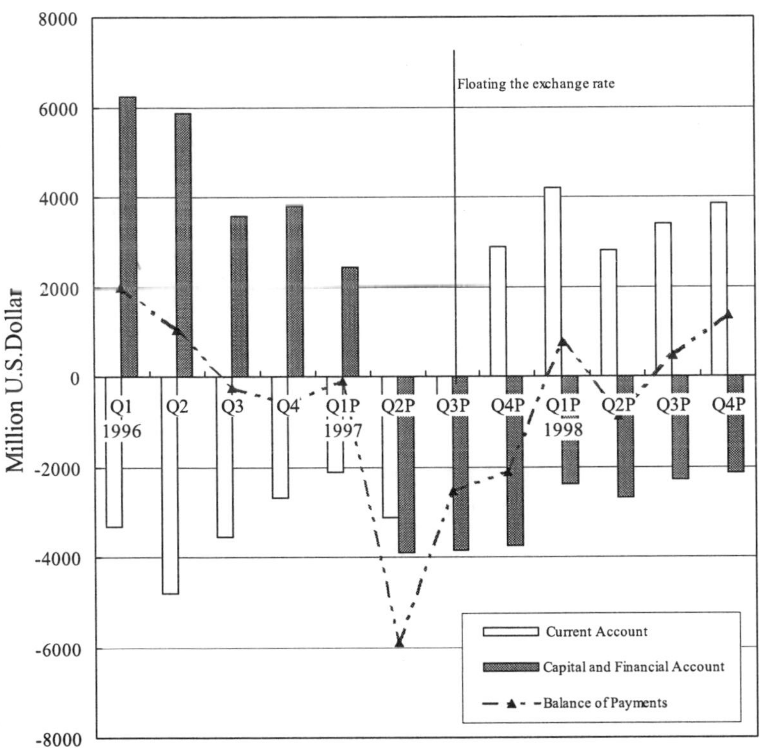

Fig. 8.1 Balance of Payment 1996–1998

However, the level alone may not justify the significance of the current account deficit; the size of deficit relative to GDP may be the better indicator. The larger the share of the current deficit to GDP, the greater the overall macroeconomic adjustment necessary to address pressure on the external account. Between 1994 and 1996, Thailand experienced an average current account deficit of 7.3% of GDP, while Mexico, before the crisis in late 1994, also had a deficit of 7.4% of GDP between 1992 to 1994. From a cross-country perspective, these deficit levels are high but not unprecedented among the successful developing countries.

In assessing the vulnerability of external debt burden to a foreign currency crisis, several points should be taken into consideration.

1) Thailand had long experiences of current account deficits for more than two decades consecutively. Why did the lenders refuse to lend today (before the crisis)? Why not two or three years before?[2]

2) Types of capital flows may be of a more crucial factor than their size, since total debt stock may include hot money, such as portfolio equity investments, rather than cold money, such as foreign direct investment. And, as the record reveals, the currency crises in both Thailand and other Asian economies in 1997 was sparked by the flight of portfolio investment, accommodated by free capital mobility policy under the financial liberalization scheme. Therefore, total figures of external debt are less meaningful than the types of debt of the countries in question, due to the different volatility for different types or characters of capital flow.

Evidence from the behavior of equity markets show how important the volatility of portfolio equity investment was in the period before the crisis. Thai stock prices had fallen sharply from their peak in the end of 1993[3].

---

[2] There were arguments from Sharma (1998) that market participants attached more importance to positive headline macroeconomic indicators such as growth, inflation, fiscal and trade balance than micro information on vulnerabilities that were beginning to emerge in the banking and corporate sector. Moreover, the creditability attached to previous policymakers and past models on why currency crises occur (Krugman's first generation model) still require explanation.

[3] The highest value on December 1993 was 1682.85.

Since equity markets serve as an alternative to bank financing, or as an investment or loan channel by using equities as collateral, the health of the equity market may be regarded as an important barometer of confidence. Additionally, the equity market serves as either an early warning signal or a precipitating factor in many past financial crises in emerging economies.

2.2 Exchange Rates

The most striking commonality was the failure of financial markets to anticipate the crisis. In spite of widely circulated warnings by economists or international agencies, such as the International Monetary Fund (IMF) or the World Bank, the Thai government brusquely rejected these warnings. Like the Latin American experience of late 1994, Thai government officials were adamant that devaluation was not under consideration. In the early period of the currency crisis, the markets believed the government and the current account deficits were easily financed.

The financial markets showed little sign of concern until very late in the game. The main objective indicator was the emergence of very large current account deficits over 8% for two consecutive years, from 1995 to 1996. The slide toward crisis began with slow growth in export value, partly due to an appreciation of the real exchange rate against the U.S. dollar, a response to growing competition from China. Moreover, poor handling of the initial exchange rate adjustment probably exacerbated the crisis that developed.

During the first half of 1997, financial distress appeared to show signs in Thailand, and speculators finally began to take a position in belief that, to re-inflate the economy, devaluation might be necessary. The growing suspicion that such a move was under consideration, despite government insistence that it was not, led to a "self-fulfilling prophecy" situation. Death foretold to a live person is coming true.

The Bank of Thailand used the return of Hong Kong to China on the 1st of July 1997 as a D-day; on July 2nd, the first working day of the second half of 1997, Thailand gave in to the pressures and floated the baht. As in other crises, this led to speculation against other regional currencies and a wave of de-valuations followed. The troubled financial picture revealed by the crisis shook investor confidence, especially given the news that the Bank of Thailand was almost emptied of international reserves from swaps obligation in order to intervene the pegged value of the baht against U.S. dollar. A contagious effect, called Tom Yum Kung Disease[4], spread out to the rest of Asia. The baht was forced to float, and led Thailand to receive an emergency loan from the IMF in August 1997.

The exchange rate crisis episodes in the 1990s consisted of three regional waves, starting from the ERM crises in Europe from 1992–1993, the Latin America crises of 1994–1995, and recently the Asian crises. Several some points merit mention.

In the world of high capital mobility, most of the recent crisis demonstrated the near-irrelevance of foreign exchange reserves. The central banks that abandoned the fixed exchange parity have substantial reserves and also credit lines in support. But are their reserves considered adequate? Britain, in the ERM case, or Korea, in the Asian case, seemed to have a high level of foreign exchange reserves, but they were unable to engage in foreign exchange intervention and then abandoned it after only a short period of time. In the environment of free capital mobility, it became clear that the only way to defend the fixed exchange parity was to contract the size of the monetary base and give in to low interest rates and high employment objectives. Unfortunately, these results were not desired and Britain chose to abandon the fixed parity instead.

Secondly, the consequences of abandoning the fixed exchange parity had different outcomes. As the Bank of England gave in to the pressure, the devaluation of the pound did very well concerning post-devaluation. The confidence in British institutions in general could be restored; though the pound had depreciated substantially, the market responded in a positive way. Markets still had confidence that the British government would continue to allow its debt-free market to function. However, in the Latin American or Asian Crisis, the currency-devalued countries actually did poorly in post-devaluation and thus suffered dramatic catastrophes. Mexico and Thailand suffered incredibly severe recessions, since markets lost confidence and

---

[4] Hot and sour shrimp soup.

both governments had to intervene in free market functions, such as explicitly announcing that all depositors and debtors in financial institutions were fully guaranteed to have their debts honored. The motivation to devalue lies in the perceived need for more, or at least not less, high-powered money in order to evade the discipline of external transaction under fixed exchange rate by drawing on domestic dollar reserves or borrowing dollars from aboard to finance the current account deficits. In the ERM crisis, those countries that abandoned these principles seem to have gone completely unpunished while the followers, Lain America and Asia, suffered serious, adverse consequences on all fronts in the short term. The decision to devaluate currency seems to have led to an even more severe contraction. Why were these experiences so different?

2.3 Exchange Market Intervention

Before July 2nd 1997, the period of capital outflows caused the pressure on the baht exchange rate, since there appeared to be a lot of excess demand for foreign currency, especially the U.S. dollar. As a result of selling dollars and buying back baht by the Bank of Thailand, the liquidity started to disappear and the interest rate went up, see Figure 8.2–8.4. To counter the contraction pressure on money and the foreign exchange market, the Bank of Thailand decided to sterilize these impacts by injecting the money supply back into the system. The central bank's buying of domestic securities in the open market is a straightforward textbook-type intervention policy. However, due to the lack of a well-developed debt market in Thailand, the Bank of Thailand's choice is not simple in implementation. As widely reported, the forward market operations — foreign exchange swaps — were an important element of the Thai's baht defense.

To support the local currency stabilization, in response to less liquidity of local currency, a central bank could sell either spot or forward foreign exchange to compensate for the major source of pressure. If the forward exchange were sold, the seller would be exposed to risk and need to balance its position. To square their position in the inter-bank market, the Bank of Thailand (BOT) would buy on the spot to cover exchange risk and then

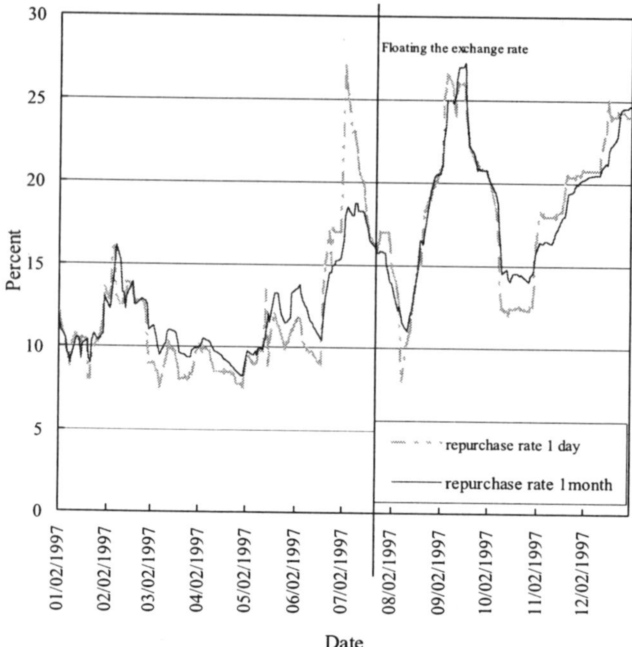

Fig. 8.2 Repurchase Rate 1997

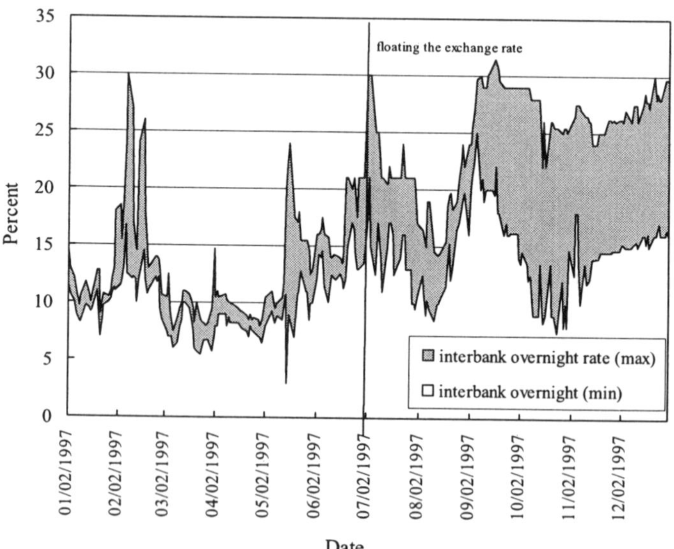

Fig. 8.3 Interbank: Overnight Rate 1997

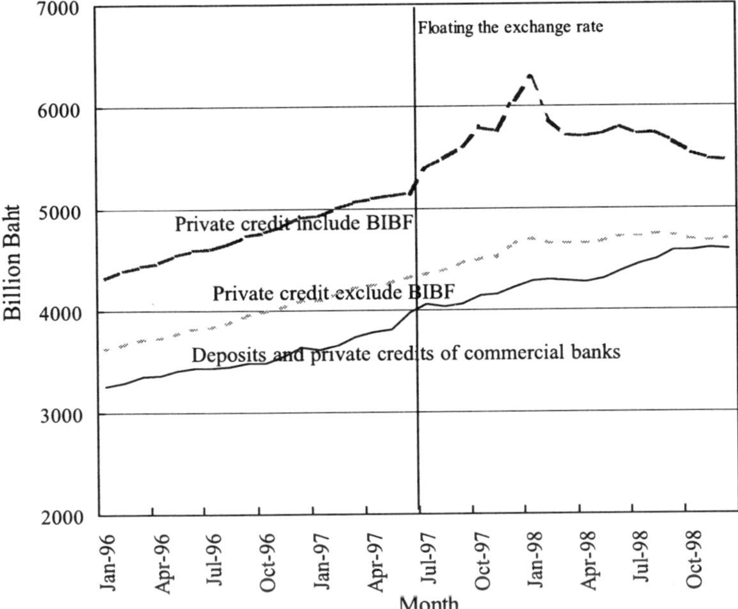

Fig. 8.4 Deposits and Private Credit in 1996–1998

borrow in the local currency in exchange for lending the bought foreign currency for the same duration as the forward contract to cover interest risk. The borrowing in one currency against the lending of another is equivalent to a foreign exchange swap transaction; the Bank of Thailand throws one stone for two birds. This is done in order to release pressure on the exchange for the forward exchange rate so that speculators would not buy forward in hoping that profit will accrue from the spot depreciation of the local currency. Moreover, the swapped transaction also provides an opportunity to inject liquidity back into the system so that upward pressure on the local interest rate is released.

The consequences of the BOT's choice of swaps as a stabilization tool were not as expected. First, the swap transactions used in 1996 to mid-1997 episodes of capital outflows were irrational, given macroeconomic fundamentals at that time. The Thai economy required macroeconomic adjustments to the basic model. The primary function of swap transactions is to stem panic around the stop-loss scale of the Thai baht by foreigners, either investors or speculators. But as the over value of the real exchange rate between baht and U.S. dollar was widely reported in public media, the tool was not the right one for the job. Without sound macroeconomic fundamentals, money and foreign exchange market conditions could not be returned to normal. Fundamentally, an exchange rate needs to be corrected for an over value of the real exchange rate. Markets also anticipated realignment of the nominal exchange rate over restoring it and allowing other macroeconomic variables to adjust. Therefore, swap intervention failed to achieve it objective as evident by the change of exchange regime in the middle of 1997 and the failure of upward pressure on the local interest rate to die down as expected.

Second, the role and objective of the Bank of Thailand, as a central bank, seems to remain within the original scope of works which have been defined by the Bank of Thailand Acct B.E. 2485 (1942). Currency value and fixed exchange rate stabilization may be considered the main objectives and carry on for more than fifty years. Any interventions to restore these two objectives are justified, with less consideration given to any other constraints or objectives. Hence, the policy measures such as swap transactions had been used to restore the fixed exchange rate and resist upward pressure on domestic interest rate at any cost.

The issue of such a liability, in the form of selling forward contract to meet demand for forward foreign exchange, caused the deterioration in international markets' perception. Since markets usually net this liability from a reserve position, the rest of the reserve balance fell drastically from early 1997 and reached critically low levels starting in May, see Figure 8.5. Even the Bank of Thailand claims that there is no implication on foreign reserve, since money from selling forward contract will be matched by buying at spot for the same amount of foreign currency to defy exchange risk that might occur. However, as the situation was aggravated into critical stages, evidence indicated that the Bank of Thailand barely found foreign currency in the spot market to compensate forward contract at the expected exchange rate. As implied from data, such a liability issuance reached its

Table 8.1 Developments of Thailand's Exchange Rate System

Periods	Baht Values	Exchange Rate System
Before World War II	11 baht per pound	Fixed exchange rate with the pound-sterling. Minimal capital controls.
During World War II		**Exchange Control Act 1942**. Thailand was forced to trade with Japan only.
1947	40 baht per pound 9.93 baht per US dollar	**Multiple Exchange Rate.** The market rates were usually much higher than the official rates.
1949	35 baht per pound 12 baht per US dollar	Thailand became the IMF's member. Reserved assets were re-evaluated with the official rate.
1955	56 baht per pound 20 baht per US dollar	Establishment of the Exchange Equalization Fund (EEF). The multiple exchange rate system was abolished due to inflation and trade deficit problems.
1955–1963	20 baht per US dollar	The official rate, used in evaluating the reserved assets, was not related to the market rate.
Oct-63	20.80 baht per US dollar gold 0.0427245 grams per baht	Par Value System or Bretton Woods System. The exchange rates were controlled within the band of 1 percent of the par value (20.59 – 21.00 baht per US dollar).
1973–1978	20.0 baht per US dollar	Revaluation of the baht to 20 baht per US dollar. The exchange rate movements were allowed within a wider band of 2.25 percent of the par value (19.55 – 20.45 baht per US dollar).
1978–1981		Daily fixing with the commercial banks. Changed from the Par Value System to the Basket-of-Currencies system as from 1 November 1978.
1981–1984	23 baht per US dollar	The baht devaluation of 8.7 percent relative to the US dollar on 15 July 1981. The EEF abolished the Daily-Fixing system and became the sole agent determining the exchange rates.
02–Nov-84		Change of the exchange rate system back to the Basket-of-Currencies. The exchange rate of the baht vis-a-vis the US dollar was announced daily by the EEF, which stood ready to buy and sell US dollars with commercial banks at the pre-announced rates from 8.30 a.m. till noon. This new system, with high US dollar weight, resulted in the baht becoming one of the 6 most stable currencies in the world vis-a-vis the US dollar, attracting large amount of capital flows and supported Thailand's rapid growth over the years.
05-Nov-84	27 baht per US dollar	The baht was devalued by 15 percent relative to the US dollar in order to reduce the problem of trade deficits.
30-Jun-97	25.76 baht per US dollar	The last day of the Basket-of-Currencies system.
02-Jul-97	27.383 baht per US dollar	Changed to the managed float system. The baht depreciated by 5.8 percent relative to the US dollar.

Source: Bank of Thailand, Focus on the Thai Crisis.

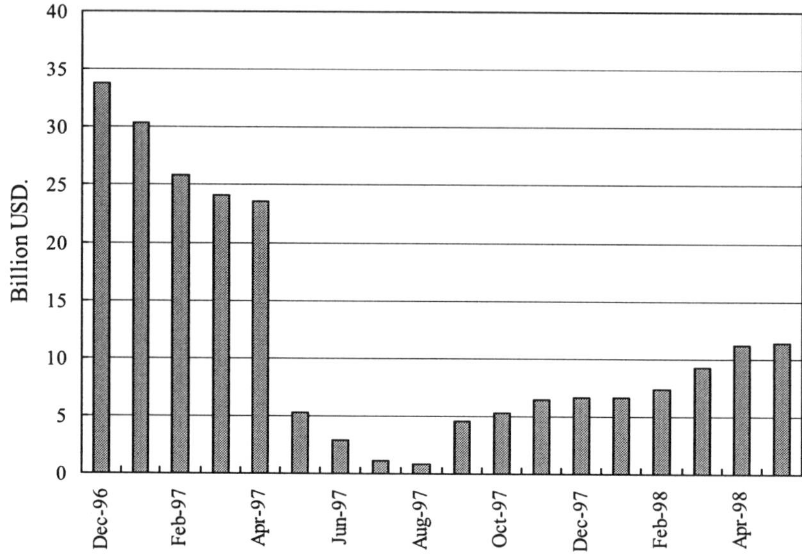

Figure 8.5 Net International Reserves
Note: The date is the end of the time.

Note: 1. Equal to international reserves less net forward position and credit loan International
Monetary Fund.
2. Aid Fund's loan from IMF started on September 1997.
Source: Bank of Thailand.

peak in May 1997 at approximately U.S. $18 billion in one month, implied by the different between previous reserves and present reserves. The proper extent of the intervention in the spot market is a crucial question. The answer was put forward a month later with two options for the Bank of Thailand: (1) continue to issue liability in selling forward contract greater than reserves it had, or (2) abandon the unsustainable project of defending the targeted exchange rate. Historical records reveal that the latter option was chosen. If the authorities continued to issue such a liability in the forward market, this procedure would do harm beyond what the authorities could expect, since the total foreign liabilities would exceed the available foreign assets in the Bank of Thailand's hand.

2.4 Banking Crisis

The recent banking crisis, which illustrated symptoms in early 1998, was not the first such experience for the Thai economy. In the early 1980s, the Thai economy was faced with a large-scale banking crisis. About fifty finance and security companies and five commercial banks, together accounting for about one forth of the total assets of all financial institutions in Thailand, experienced difficulties. Thai authorities were forced to intervene; 24 of 50 finance and security companies were closed and nine were merged into two new companies. The five commercial banks were allowed to continue their operation with a support arrangement from government in the form of "soft" loans. Remedial actions at that time included reductions in capital values – to let owners absorb all losses, manage restructuring, and buildup capital and reserve as directed by authorities.

These scenes from the past repeat themselves about a decade later when the financial authorities use the same remedial actions to cope with about three quarters of Thailand's finance and security companies and basically the same group of ailing banks. However, the recent banking crisis accounts for much greater costs than the earlier crisis. The Fund for Rehabilitation and Development of Financial Institutions (FRDF), set up within Bank of Thailand as a legally distinct entity in order to rehabilitate financial institutions, had lent more than 10 billion baht to assume the non-performing loans from the failing financial institutions in the earlier banking crisis. In early 1998, FRDF had to provide more than 100 billion baht for the same mission, to save the depositors, creditors and the financial system. Do these remedial actions truly solve the crisis, or not? Evidence indicates not, despite the actions of Thai financial authorities, especially the Bank of Thailand.

There appears the undeniable fact that institutional weakness, stemming from the oligopolistic structure of the Thai banking system, was the main reason for the weakening position of banks and financial companies. Concentration ratio on the banking system, either in the size of deposits or loans, did not undergo substantial change for almost the quarter of century. Thai's commercial banks are the main type of financial intermediate institution to mobilize funds. This led the banking industry to be inefficient and encourage bank management and share holder to pay little attention to safety and soundness. Even the authorities acknowledged this shortcoming, and attempted to develop legal, regulatory and supervisory frameworks after problems emerged from the banking crisis in 1980s. However, the legislative frameworks seemed proved fruitless. Some regulations and amendments to the Commercial Banking Act and Financial and Security Company

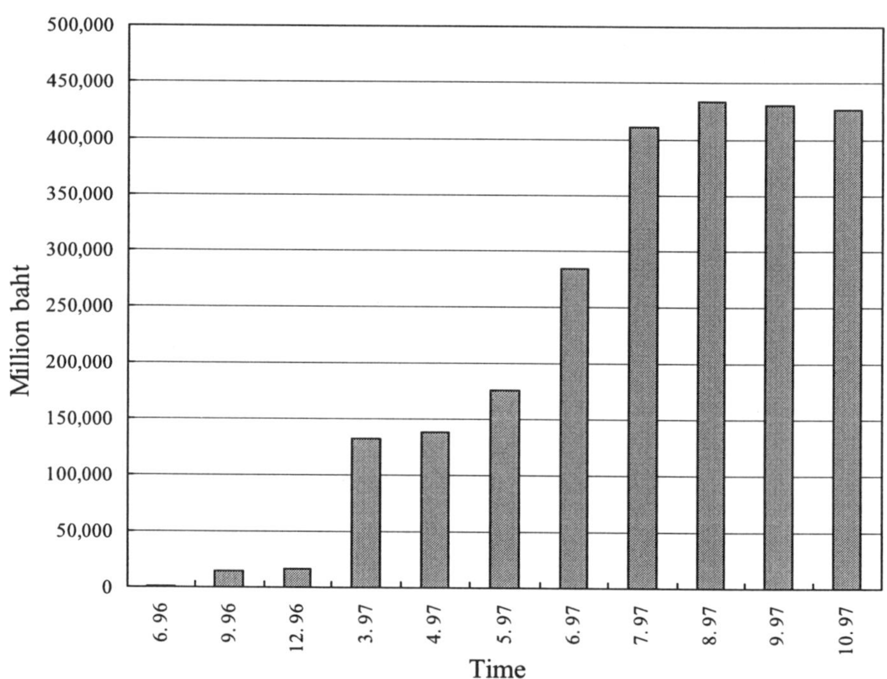

Fig. 8.6 Finance and Security Companies Borrow from FRDF

Table 8.2 Concentration Ratio of 5 Big Banks

	1981	1987	1997*
Deposits	69.00	68.20	64.70
Loans	71.00	67.09	59.30

* As of September
Source: Statistical Data on Commercial Banks in Thailand, Bangkok Bank (public) Co., Ltd.

Legislation, such as concentration of ownership and portfolio, changes in supervisory responsibility, and the expanded supervisory powers and cease and desist arrangements were useless in many cases when the banking crisis of the late 1990s emerged. FRDF became involved in providing loans to both financial and security companies and commercial banks as it had in the 1980s banking crisis with more funds in hand to lend. What was wrong with the experiences the financial authorities had learned from? Why did the reform measures that they tried to implement to improve the weakness of Thai Financial System fail?

In the 1990s banking crisis, FRDF played a major role once again as a rescue arm for the central bank (Bank of Thailand). FRDF's balance sheet reveals the extent of its involvement as of February 19, 1998; of total assets of 1100 billion baht, lending under the purpose of liquidity to financial institutions accounted for more than 770 billion baht, increased from 0.2 billion baht on November 30, 1996. Between mid 1996 and late 1997, finance and security companies were in a difficult period, especially regarding confidence in these companies. A "flight of quality" began, which saw the shift of deposits from the finance and security companies to more safe and sound institutions: the banks. As a result, a shift in deposit or deposit runs to other financial institutions occurred. More cash reserved on hand was needed to meet deposit outflow, leaving two choices, to borrow or sell earning assets. However, the latter choice might create huge fire-sale losses[5] and the economic situation at the time also was stressed. Therefore, most of the financial and security companies had to turn to FRDF to borrow. About half of FRDF's liquidity lending went to financial and security companies. However, six finance and security companies were ordered to close their operations on August 5, 1997.

It is difficult to avoid the implications of the first banking crisis, as it could have been prevented, and second, it could have been defaulted with the flexible powers that the authorities have to intervene with and to restructure the ailing financial institutions. With power under the new

---

[5] The difference between immediate or "fire-sale" market value and equilibrium price which is the highest potential bidder on the market-requires search time.

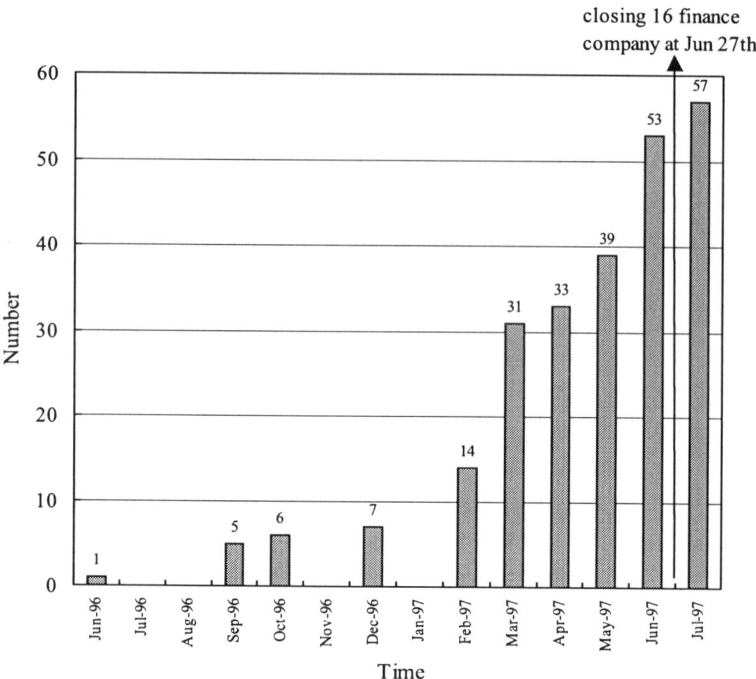

Fig. 8.7 Accumulated Number of Finance and Securities Companies which Asked for Loan from FRDF

legislation, the decision to close the insolvent companies should have come faster than the record illustrates. Consider the first finance and security company, which borrowed from FRDF and was forced to close later; it took a very long time to determine whether this company was insolvent[6] or not. For example, under a closing wave on June 1997, Thai Fuji Finance and Security had started to borrow from FRDF on June 1996 and accumulated more than sixty fold from the initial amount of 200 million baht to 12,249 million baht on the closing date. SITCA Finance and Security is also another example for groups of companies that were forced by financial authorities to close in August 1997. The company began borrowing in September 1996,

---

[6] Generally speaking, when liabilities exceed assets value greater than net worth of shareholders.

beginning with 600 million baht and ending at an amount of 14,447 million baht[7]. Evidence from the earlier crisis in the 1980s, before the authorities decided to close Sayam Bank in 1987, shows that FRDF had provided financial assistance of 3.5 billion baht in 1986 (equivalent to 20% of the bank's asset) after the government took over in August 1984. In most of the cases, the size of the financial assistance from FRDF or other monetary authorities is sizeable and, in fact, greater than the owner's net worth absorbable capacity. Thus, the lag in declaring insolvency affected not only owners, but the depositors, creditors and the general public as well. The longer an insolvent financial institution is permitted to continue to operate independently, the larger its overall losses are likely to be.

3. WHY DID IT HAPPEN?

3.1 Overflow of Capital

There was one argument that the reduced access to foreign savings was once perceived as a major constraint to growth for many developing countries since the investment savings gap in these countries was too wide to be filled by themselves. However, the recent surge in capital inflows has not been taken as an unmitigated blessing as expected. Large capital inflows are often associated with inflationary pressures, real exchange rate appreciation, and the deterioration in current account. The recent Mexican financial crisis at the end of 1994 and also Asia's crisis in the middle of 1997 have triggered a new literature to investigate the appropriate policy response for the recipient countries to manage.

Additionally, Thailand is one of the Asian countries that relied heavily on foreign capital as an important source of growth in the late 1980s era.

---

[7] As a matter of record, revealed recently, most of the financial support from FRDF to these institutions was in the form of direct deposit, not borrowing. The reason for this was the need to meet emergency withdraws from depositors, leaving no time to arrange collateral to borrow. As a result, FRDF was in a high position of exposure to risk from default by these institutions.

Thailand's favorable economic performance was in its peak from 1988 to 1990 with two digits of GDP growth rate. This performance may be due to an important contributing factor — the substantial increase in capital inflows, averaging U.S. $6.6 billion annually. However, less than ten years later, the wind had changed. In 1997, there was a reversal in capital flow and also in growth rate, which was replaced with a minus growth in 1998. What went wrong with our capital inflows?

Characteristics of Capital Inflows

For almost three decades, from 1970 to 1997, capital inflows are the major source of financing the current account deficits as Table 8.1 shows, with the total amount of capital inflows increasing nearly 50 fold from an average U.S. $221 million to more than U.S. $10 billion. The capital inflows started to surge in the period 1987 to 1992, which was associated with the high-income growth period. However, the characteristics behind the inflows in the 1987–92 period are also changed from the majority in medium and long term capital inflows to short term maturity. The net flows of short-term capital have jumped to an average of U.S. $3.2 billion from $376 million.

Table 8.3 Financing of the Current Account Deficits: 1970–92

(Average of Period in Millions of US$)

	1970–74	1975–80	1981–86	1987–92	1993–97
Current Account Deficit (in percent of GDP)	−122 (1.5)	−1249 (5.1)	−1627 (4.3)	−4203 (5.1)	−8784 (5.8)
Medium & Long Term Capital (net)	164	847	1362	3015	N/A.
Short Term Capital (net)	31	222	376	3227	N/A.
Others	26	−38	156	405	N/A.
Change in International Reserves	99	−218	268	2,444	18,903
Total Foreign Capital Inflow (in percent of GDP)	221 (2.3)	1031 (4.5)	1895 (5.0)	6647 (9.0)	10,510

Note: Calculated as the sum of the current account deficit and change in reserves.
Source: Bank of Thailand.

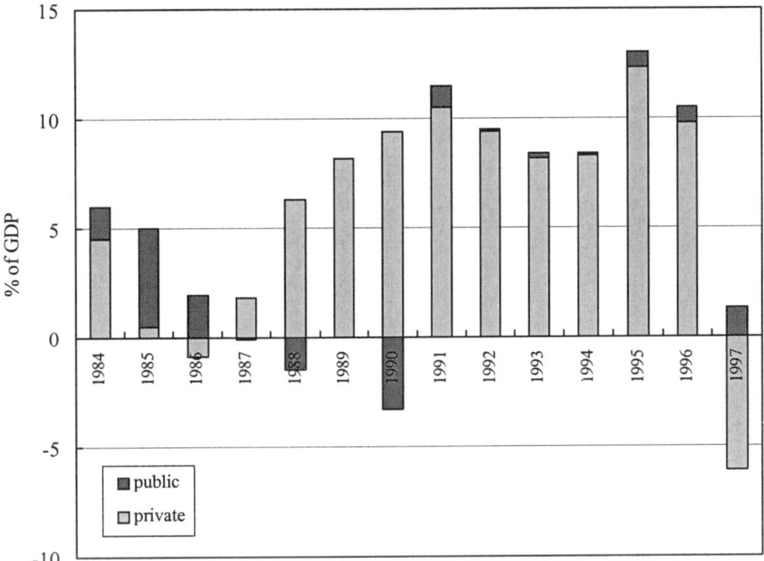

Fig. 8.8 Sources of Finance

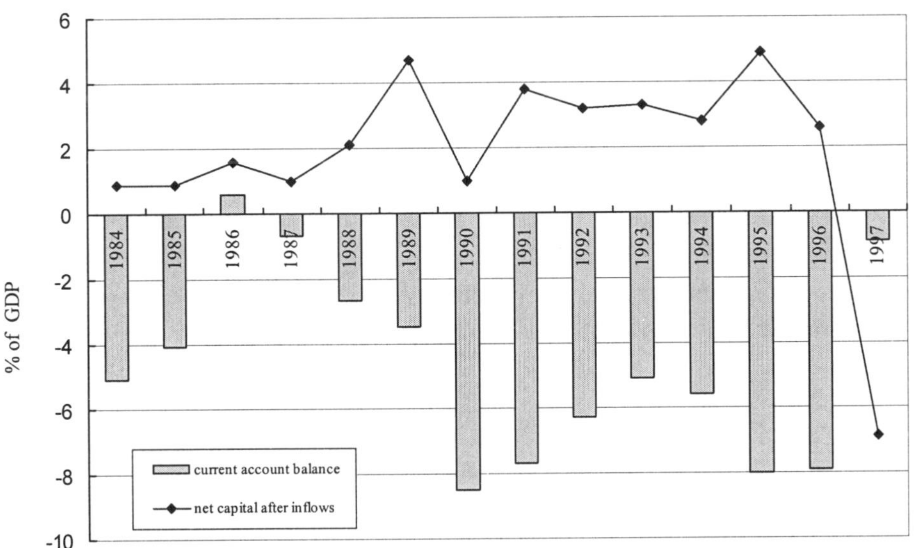

Fig. 8.9 Over Finance Position

Figures 8.8 and 8.9 highlight the importance of capital flow to a country's output as measured by GDP. The size of private capital flows surged from 1.8% of GDP in 1987 to 6.3% of GDP in 1988 which might be due to the relocation of Japanese investments to ASIAN countries from the high value of the yen exchange rate to U.S. dollar. Foreign Direct Investment (FDI) may be contributed as a major factor to these movements. Furthermore, the first concrete sign of financial liberalization was the official acceptance of the obligation under Article VII of the International Monetary Fund's Articles of Agreement announced on 21 May 1990; along with the launching of the first phase of exchange control deregulation. As a result, the composition of private capital flows, which had been dominated by non-banks, was reduced and portfolio investment surged dramatically in 1993.

One of the noticeable features of private capital flows after it surged in 1987 which can be seen in Figure 8.8 is their size, which is always bigger than the size of the deficit in the current account. If the public capital flows are not in a minus, and still has an inflow, then it appears as an over-finance in our current account of a significant size, about 3% of GDP. In other words, the capital inflows may not be a phenomenon of current account deficits financing alone.

3.2 Macroeconomic Mismanagement

Macroeconomic Impact of Capital Flows

The basic principal to creating money supply is to change it in the monetary base. From the simplified central bank balance sheet below, the changes in monetary base may consist of changes in two main items, International Reserves (IR) and Central Bank Credit (CBC).

IR	xxx	Currency in Circulation	xxx
CBC	xxx	Reserves	xxx
Monetary Base	xxx	Monetary Base	xxx

In the closed economy, the money supply is determined solely by the actions of the central bank through the creation (or reduction) of credits. However, in the open economy, part of the money supply is determined outside the actions of the central bank through the balance of payments. Therefore, from either the asset or liability side of central bank balance sheet, the monetary base may be represented by base may be represented by

$$IR + CBC = MB = C + R \tag{1}$$

where C and R refer to currency in circulation and a reserve of commercial banks at the central bank hand respectively. If the relationship between monetary base and money supply can be expressed in the equation as

$$M^s = m \cdot MB \tag{2}$$

where m = money supply multiplier, its changes may be written as

$$\Delta M^s = m \cdot \Delta MB = m(\Delta IR + \Delta CBC). \tag{3}$$

In the closed economy case, the central bank can manipulate money supply directly through the change in CBC, such as an open market operation. A perfectly closed economy is a rare case; an open economy is a more ordinary case. With the fixed exchanged regime, the direct association between monetary policy, in the form of credit creation by the central bank, and changes in the monetary base cannot be made. The control of money supply is not completely in the hands of the central bank because of its link to balance of payments dis-equilibria. The balance of payments is endogenous to the economy because the decisions of the private sector to buy domestic and foreign goods and securities depend on basic economic variables such as income, export or import prices and the interest rate differential between domestic and foreign. All of these variables are determined in the economy and have an influence on the decision of the private sector in their demand for real and financial assets.

Given an economy's international trade in goods and assets, the balance of payment, B, is represented by

$$B = T(q,\ y) + K(i) \tag{4}$$

where trade balance (T) is assumed to depend on relative price of foreign goods in terms of domestic goods (q) and on domestic income (y). The capital account (K) is also determined by domestic interest rate (i).

With access to international financial markets, the countries with current account deficits are not necessarily forced to finance those deficits through losses of international reserves. According to (4), T<0 may be financed through net capital inflows, K>0. In Table 8.4, the deficits in Thailand's current account balance, the net capital inflows help the balance of payment to be in equilibrium and also increase official resources. The openness to international capital movements since 1989 is the major attempt by the Thai central bank at that time to relieve the constraint that obstructed the capital flows.

Before the change in exchange rate regime from fixed to float exchange rate, the massive capital inflows affected the monetary base and also money

Table 8.4 Factors Affecting Monetary Base: 1987–1998 (June)

	1984	1985	1986	1987	1988	1989	1990
Money Supply*	6.93	−3.28	20.46	28.01	12.16	17.65	11.86
Monetary Base*	5.57	8.50	11.31	21.10	14.87	16.92	18.59
Foreign Assets (net)	17.96	2.12	23.76	36.84	48.21	74.76	62.51
Claims on Government (net)	−5.97	10.76	−10.78	−6.32	−43.99	−40.42	−22.69
Claims on Nonfinancial Public Enterprises							
Claims on Financial Institutions	5.63	7.74	12.18	7.03	14.69	−11.26	−6.72
Other Assets (net)	−12.05	−12.11	−13.85	−16.45	−4.04	−6.16	−14.52

	1991	1992	1993	1994	1995	1996	1997	1998 (June)
Money Supply	13.81	12.28	18.60	16.98	12.08	9.12	1.20	−10.99
Monetary Base	13.28	17.85	16.14	14.52	22.56	12.02	4.68	−9.84
Foreign Assets (net)	56.25	35.11	44.35	38.14	52.39	14.59	−12.09	−44.50
Claims on Government (net)	−33.12	−10.43	−8.89	−13.96	−24.90	−2.23	9.53	34.29
Claims on Nonfinancial Public Enterprises						2.35	11.82	0.54
Claims on Financial Institutions	2.47	3.66	−5.29	0.62	−0.77	2.23	−2.41	−34.97
Other Assets (net)	−12.32	−10.50	−14.04	−10.28	−6.72	−3.45	9.19	30.16

Note: *The figures are calculated as a percent change from the previous period. For the factor affecting monetary base, they are calculated by this formula; (change in Xt / monetary base at t−1)*100.

supply. Table 8.4 shows factors affecting monetary base. The net foreign assets, which may represent the IR in (3), have increased rapidly and become the major factor affecting changes in monetary base while the claims on government and financial institutions, the main central bank credits (CBC), have moved in the opposite direction to the change in IR. Whether or not the stabilization operation has been introduced is indeterminate.

Sterilization Operations

By sterilizing the effects of capital inflows to monetary base, it effectively prevents any changes in domestic money supply. From (3) any changes in money supply from the increasing in IR will be offset by the reducing in CBC, so that

$$\Delta M^s = m\Delta MB = m(\Delta IR + \Delta CBC) = 0 \tag{5}$$

if

$$\Delta IR = -\Delta CBC$$

In order to find evidence on the role of sterilization policies in controlling the effects of balance of payment surplus on the domestic money supply, the following equation may be postulated as

$$K = K_0 - b\Delta CBC \tag{6}$$

where K is defined as total capital flows (K>0 represents a capital inflows), b is a parameter called the offset coefficient and K_0 represents the capital flows which are not directly related to domestic credit creation, such as foreign direct investment. If b value is closed to 1, it can be interpreted that there appears the full offset through stabilization operations and vice versa, in which case b value closes to zero. The result, reported below, has b value equal to -0.72[8].

---

[8] Estimated (6) is $K = 206191.3 - 0.73\Delta CBC$, $R^2 = 0.33$ with coefficient and constant are statistical significant at 99% level.

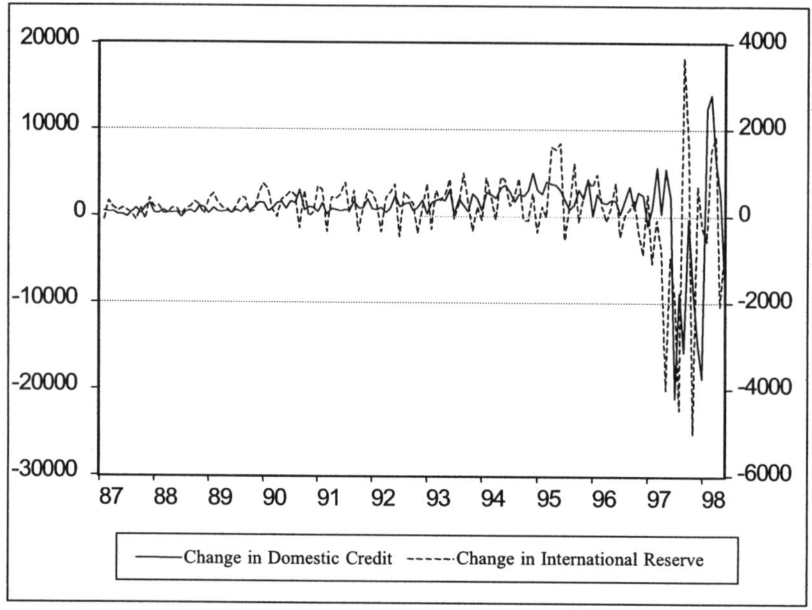

Fig. 8.10 Change in Domestic Credit and International Reserve

From this piece of evidence, the conclusion drawn is that the Thai central bank had conducted the stabilization operation. However, the role of neutralization policies in controlling the effects of surplus of balance of payment due to the massive influx of capital flows has not been fully offset. Therefore, the effect of a surplus in capital inflows over the current account deficits have caused the Thailand money supply to increase as records in surplus of capital inflows as percentage of GDP grow from less than 1% before 1990s to 2–3% after that, which is a substantial figure. This may be called over-financing in current account deficit.

Trilemma

Of the three objectives, (1) free capital movement under financial liberalization schemes, (2) adjustable pegged exchange regime which was used for more than a decade, and (3) independent of monetary policy; any two, but not all three can be manageable. We are compelled to choose. The attempt to have all three objectives is overly ambitious and has produced the external financial crisis, the currency crisis as in Mexico in 1995 and several other cases.

The adjustable pegged exchange rate regime is fundamentally different from the truly fixed exchange regime. For example, the currency board, the traditional type of fixed exchange rate, has a mechanism to correct external dis-equilibrium. If the balance of payments become deficit, domestic money supply will go down automatically, and that brings pressure on the economy to reduce foreign payments and increase foreign receipts. Thus, if you stick with it, the economy cannot evade the discipline of external transactions. By contrast, under the adjustable pegged exchange rate, the Bank of Thailand did not have to reduce quantity of money supply when Thailand had a deficit in balance of payment. The Bank of Thailand could have drawn on its dollars reserves or let the commercial banks borrow more dollars from abroad to finance the deficits and evade the discipline of external transactions. That means it is not immune to infection from currency crisis since it retains an option to terminate the exchange regime, change the fixed rate or introduce the monetary policy at anytime. Such an adjustable pegged exchange regime is like a time bomb, since it is difficult to know whether a deficit in balance of payment is transitory and will soon be reserved or is a precursor to further deficits which needs a major change. For political economic reasons, there are tendencies to allow minor transitory problems accumulate in order to avoid any action that will depress the domestic economy by adjusting the exchange rate. Thus, the minor adjustments in the exchange rate, when they have been done, are not sufficient; major change is required. For the speculator at this stage, the direction is clear. Those speculators who sold shot for Thai baht could lose on commissions and interest if the baht was not devalued. On the other hand, huge profits were the potential reward for devaluation. The situation is practically a sure bet. Speculators are in a position of low risk for enormous benefits.

3.3 Financial Fragility: Impact of A Changing Environment

Growth of Financial Sector

Between the first and second phase of the Financial System Development Plan, the financial sector has grown significantly as the ratio of M2/GDP and M3/GDP have been increased while M1/GDP does not change. That means the role of saving mobilization of the financial institution has also increased during that period. The growth in size of the financial sector compared to GDP is used to measure financial deepening as a phenomenon in which the financial sector grows at a rate faster than the real sector. Hence, the role of intermediary played by financial institutions between savers and investors may be measured by variables such as ratio of M2/GDP or credit/GDP at private commercial banks since commercial banks take a leading role in inter-mediation.

Suchada (1993) used the Granger Causality Test method to answer whether the development of the financial sector after liberalization precedes and induces real sector development, or vice versa. The results indicate that the financial liberalization process in the second period (1986/Q1–1990/Q4) may have helped to increase the relationship between the financial and real sector, since there appears the bilateral causality between M2/GDP and real GDP, as well as credit/GDP and real GDP.

Even though the growth in the financial sector may come from the growth in liberalization and also reform in this sector, the number of commercial bank branches may be another factor that contributes to the growth of the financial sector in Thailand's case. As the banking system in Thailand is a branch bank system, the increase in number of branches suggests, on one side, that the commercial banks are now able to provide more services and also reduce ratio of population per branch. People seem to have easier access to financial services than the period before financial liberalization. That is why M2/GDP or M3/GDP have all increased as branches are expanding. On the other side, newly setup bank branches need to meet some targets, such as deposit and/or loan amounts, in order to make their business survive. Private commercial banks have a tendency to mobilize saving from all their branches but have no requirement to make a loans in the same areas that the deposits are brought up from. Savings from remote areas in small or even large sizes are increasingly collected as the number of branches expand and mobilized to the highest return investment channels.

Banking Sector as a Main Credit Provider

Due to high concentration in the structure of the Thai banking system, the banking sector provided most domestic credits. Even though there are other channels to mobilize funds into the financial system, such as equity markets which developed rapidly in 1990s while bond and other securities markets lagged, all of these channels needed to improve their roles, and the banking system still dominated financial intermediaries. Rapid structural changes in the real economy are required improvements in corporate governance of the firms for which securities markets are important. However, the lack of well-developed capital markets meant that the monitoring of corporations was the unavoidable responsibility of the banking sector and was not fulfilled by other financial institutions. Unfortunately, the banking sector was also faced with weak governance within that often was influenced directly or indirectly by government policies. Under the limited institutional development of banks, much of the lending was done on a collateral basis rather than on a cash flow basis. There were traceable records both in the 1980s and 1990s banking crises that indicate that the flow of credit tended to go to borrowers with relationships to bank owners or favored sectors under government guidance rather than on the basis of creditworthiness[9].

Thus, the oligopolistic structure of the banking sector in Thailand was believed to be the main reason for financial vulnerabilities. However, how can such a structure continue to exist and why did the reforms following the 1980s banking crisis fail to have any changes on the banking structure?

The segmentation of the financial system may be the answer to the above questions. There were rules and other barriers to prevent banks and

---

[9] Even though there is a limit of holding equity to prevent concentration of ownership in other company, but by using nominee or cross holding in equity, banks in Thailand in practice using nominee or cross-holding to circumvent this limit.

non-banking financial institutions, such as financial and security companies, from competing against another. For example, finance companies could not raise funds through deposits as banks could, as a result they had to rely heavily on higher costs of funds, e.g. promissory notes, which created incentives to lend to risky projects to cover high costs and reduce the franchise value of the financial institution. Competition seems to exist within the same segment of the financial system. As a matter of fact, the concentration ratio among commercial banks in the 30-year period did not suggest improvement in competition. Before the crisis, four or five big banks took about two-thirds of either lending or deposit taking share from the 15 banks in Thailand. Profits or other sound measures for the banking sector in aggregate during the 1990s appeared sound, but as individual bank data showed, the weakness and poor performance of small banks was the result of high concentration within the banking sector and uncompetitiveness between segments of the financial system. Therefore, as an industry, the banking sector looked healthy in the lending boom period, since growth in banks' loan portfolio was accompanied by gains in profit measures. Moreover, growth in household savings and capital inflows were factors that allowed banks to roll over their non-performing loans without experiencing liquidity problems in that period.

Close Linkage Between Domestic and Foreign Financial Markets

Under the liberalization process, several measures, such as the establishment of international banking facilities, decline from exchange and capital control or the removal of interest rate ceilings, all supported the increase in openness of the Thai financial market to the rest of the world. Therefore, external factors have an increasing role in the determination of key variables such as interest rates, growth of capital market et cetera.

Domestic interest rates not only seem to move in line with foreign interest rates, but the variability and unpredictability are also the consequences that each participant in domestic market has to adjust for more frequently and with greater magnitude in the 1990s than in the 1980s. Pornpen (1993) suggested that the fluctuation of domestic interest rates, as compared to foreign rates, during the period of one year before and after the removal of each interest rate ceilings increased. Table 8.5 shows the increased ratio of standard deviation between domestic interest rates, represented by time and/or saving, and foreign interest rates, represented by Singapore Interbank Borrowing Rate (SIBOR), in the same maturity indicating the relatively high volatility of the domestic rates during the first year of ceilings relaxation. On the contrary, the volatility of the lending rate as represented by the Minimum Loan Rate (MLR) after the abolition of ceiling rates is measured by standard deviation reduced substantially from 0.75 to 0.014. The ratio of standard deviation between MLR and SIBOR decreased from 3.41 to 0.58. This may

Table 8.5 Standard Deviation of Interest Rates

Interest Rates	Period of 1 Year Before and After Removal of Each Interest Rate Ceiling	
	Before	After
	Jun 88–May 89	Jun 89–May 90
Time Deposit (12–24 months)	0.72	0.84
SIBOR (3 months)	0.79	0.29
TD Rate (12–24 m.)/ SIBOR (3 m.)	0.91	2.9
	Mar 89–Feb 90	Mar 90–Feb 91
Time Deposit (3–6 months)	0.09	1.17
SIBOR (3 months)	0.64	0.49
TD Rate (3–6 m.)/ SIBOR (3 m.)	0.14	2.39
	Jan 91–Dec 91	Jan 92–Dec 92
Saving Deposit	0.82	0.57
SIBOR (3 months)	0.71	0.34
SD Rate/SIBOR (3 m.)	1.12	1.62
	Dec 91–May 92	Jun 92–Nov 92
Minimum Lending Rate*	0.75	0.14
SIBOR (3 months)	0.21	0.24
MLR/SIBOR (3 m.)	3.41	0.58

Note: * Period of 6 months before and after removal of lending rate ceiling.
Source: Pornpen (1993).

suggest why the fluctuation of domestic lending rate was less than the foreign rate. Thus, after being abolished for deposit or lending rate ceilings, the loan rate was much more rarely adjusted in a downward direction than the deposit rate. In terms of the interest rate spread between prime and non-prime rate, the benefits seem to go to prime clients more than non-prime since the widened spread goes to non-prime clients. With an oligopolistic structure in the banking sector, private commercial banks have a tendency to acquire more profit by reducing deposit rates in larger percentages and more quickly as compared to the lending rate. The conclusion arising from the evidences is that the major abolition in ceiling rates under financial liberalization did not help to reduce the oligopolistic power in the banking sector.

Increased Exposure to Risks

As details in Table 8.5 have shown, the two major financial institutions in the Thai system are vulnerable to substantial risk factors at the on-set of the currency crisis in the middle of 1997. Banks seemed to increase external exposures since the ratio of foreign liabilities to capital was increased gradually while the foreign assets compared with liabilities ratio also deteriorated.

Internal exposure showed that in the banking sector, borrowing, either from central bank or other sources, as a ratio to capital did not experience any problem until 1997. On the contrary, finance and security companies relied heavily on loans from the banking sector and also from the central bank via FRDF's[10] loan from 1996 to 1997.

On the uses of funds by banks, loans to the real estate sector data do not suggest or support that there are more exposures to this sector more than any other sectors. However, real estate developers do not have to be an entrepreneur

---

[10] The Fund for Rehabilitation and Development of Financial Institution was set up within the bank of Thailand as a legally distinct entity in order to rehabilitate financial institutions under the Emergency Decree Amending the Commercial Bank Act in 1985. The FRDF's main activities consist of lending (with proper collateral) to placing deposits in, acquiring assets from, and holding equity in financial institutions which the Bank of Thailand is not allowed by its Act to do. For the role of FRDF in crisis, see R. Barry Johnston (1991) for 1985–1987 crisis and Chawin (1999) for 1997 crisis.

Table 8.6 Exposure of Banking Sector and Finance and Security Companies

	1992	1993	1994	1995	1996	1997
Banking Sector						
1. External Exposure						
-FA / FL	0.46	0.45	0.22	0.20	0.14	0.25
-FL / Capital	0.98	1.60	2.55	2.95	2.45	3.53
2. Internal Exposure						
-BOT / Capital	0.21	0.10	0.04	0.04	0.05	0.55
-Other / Capital	0.09	0.09	0.18	0.22	0.17	0.22
3. Allocation of Funds (% of total)						
Manufacturing	23.70	24.00	24.20	25.80	27.10	30.90
Real Estate	11.50	11.30	10.50	9.40	8.80	8.10
Import & Export	9.30	8.40	8.20	7.60	7.10	6.50
Wholesale & Retail	17.00	17.70	18.20	17.80	17.90	17.10
Personal Consumption	12.30	12.60	12.70	12.30	12.60	10.80
Total	73.80	74.00	73.80	72.90	73.50	73.40
Finance and Security						
1. External Exposure						
-FL / Capital	0.61	0.65	0.54	0.64	0.69	1.81
2. Internal Exposure						
-FRDF / Capital	–	–	–	–	0.04	6.27
-Banks / Capital	0.79	0.76	0.74	0.80	0.77	2.12

Note: FA = Foreign assets, FL = Foreign liabilities, BOT = Borrow from Bank of Thailand, FRDF = Borrow from FRDF, Banks = Borrows from Commercial Banks.

in this area. A manufacturer may siphon funds from banks via his loans for production business to invest in real estate in the boom period. With fixed assets, bubble prices on one hand and the huge inflows from cheap capital on the other hand, banks are encouraged to grant more loans to the traceable clients with or without acknowledging that they might misuse loans. As the lending process was done on a collateral basis, loans with fixed assets in the bubble period as collateral seemed be much sounder to bankers than project loans without real collateral.

High external exposure in the banking sector implies that excessive borrowing from abroad may take place. Even the domestic saving rates are high, but investment demand resulting from the high growth period in the late 1980s is higher; borrowing from abroad may be an easier option. These exposures may result from (1) the implicit government guarantees in exchange and deposit, allowing banks to feel more comfortable in borrowing foreign currency and lending domestic currency without any risks in exchange rate being considered. Moreover, any wrong doing which may occur will not be the responsibility of the management of the banks. The explicit paid premium to FRDF as a percentage to total deposits for each bank makes the deposit insurance policy effective. (2) High domestic funding costs may be the push factor for the banks to import cheap money from abroad. This factor reinforces (3) the creation of offshore banking centers, the so-called Bangkok International Banking Facilities (BIBF), providing an important channel for domestic financial sector to raise short term foreign currency dominated funds; "out-in" lending. Historically low international interest rates, especially on Japanese yen and the special incentives such as bilateral tax treaties between Japan and Thailand, and an approval of foreign BIBFs to become full bank branches, made dependent on the volume of loans, were the factors behind the out-in lending boom of Japan's BIBF. Rapid growth of the BIBF out-in lending business which arose from 46 licenses to domestic and foreign commercial banks to operate international banking facilities in 1993 sparked the lending boom period and built up dramatic short term external liabilities exposure of the Thai financial system.

Commercial Banks Efficiency

One objective of financial liberalization is to improve efficiency among financial institutions. Commercial banks seem to be the target of the relaxation of the related competition barriers and allowing more competitors in the market, for example the opening of BIBF, which can do an "out-in" business in mobilized foreign funds for domestic uses. Chaturon (1998) provides evidence to support whether the efficiency of major financial institutions, commercial banks, in Thailand can be improved through the liberalization process or not. The scale efficiency concept is used to estimate the efficiency of commercial banks. It measures the total costs increase as a proportion of

Table 8.7 Scale Economies of KTB, TFB, and BAY During 1981–1996

	1981	1982	1983	1984	1985	1986	1987	1988
KTB	0.8964	0.9486	0.9244	0.9830	0.9636	1.0192	1.0118	1.0434
TFB	0.8561	0.9152	0.8676	0.9029	0.9324	0.9584	0.9454	0.9560
BAY	0.7966	0.7908	0.8317	0.8773	0.8878	0.9307	0.9185	0.9614
	1989	1990	1991	1992	1993	1994	1995	1996
KTB	1.0652	1.0808	1.0922	1.0589	1.0180	1.0646	1.1189	1.1314
TFB	0.9500	0.9458	0.9566	0.9093	0.9093	0.8622	0.8772	0.9190
BAY	0.9830	1.0268	1.0311	1.0097	1.0097	1.0268	1.0778	1.0776

growth in outputs. Hence, a commercial bank will perform efficiently when it has a scale efficiency less than one, which means the costs increase relatively less than the growth of outputs. There is no hard evidence to support any improvement in efficiency after the graduation in financial liberalization and reforms expected to occur.

4. WHAT ARE THE LESSONS TO BE LEARNED?

4.1 Macroeconomic Management with Growing Financial Integration

The air was rife with the idea of financial liberalization in the late 1980s through the early 1990s. Thailand and the new generation of Asia's Tigers were no exception. After a taste of success as a miracle Asian country, Thailand had introduced financial liberalization in many areas, especially on the free capital mobility.

Capital Mobility: To Control or Not Control

Since liberalization allows more flow of capital across the border, a great deal criticism reflects more fundamental doubts about the benefits from free capital mobility to the economy, especially for the recipient economies. The growing integration of financial markets is now shaped by international capital flows. The recent Asian crisis may be said to have close linkages to the IMF-led efforts to encourage capital account liberalization. To be fair to these critics, the financial liberalization process that was undertaken was the process following trade liberalization. Greater openness in the current account should be followed by greater openness in the capital account. However, the freer movement in capital has led to turbulence in international financial markets, especially on the transactions of foreign exchange. As a result, the unregulated financial markets make it too easy for currency traders to buy and sell without regard to fundamentals which introduce unnecessary volatility into foreign exchange markets and capital flows. Their activities may be considered as socially counterproductive and the introduction of barriers, either in price or quantity, on foreign transactions (capital controls)[11] that make it more difficult for investors to speculate against currencies could in principle reduce the incidence of crisis and enhance social welfare. Capital outflows control, as in Malaysia, is a good example of a quantity barrier while the Tobin[12] tax for foreign exchange transaction or Chilean Type[13] for taxing inflows are price barriers.

Barriers to capital mobility, especially on short-term capital inflows, may be an alternative defense against the tendency of domestic financial institutions to take more risks by borrowing abroad. Outflows controls have disadvantages in three main areas. First, they cure the symptoms and not the cause, since the outflow controls cannot prevent the desire for a high leverage position for the bank's owner or its agents. Risks from external exposure

---

[11] An appropriate term would be "foreign exchange controls", since the payments and receipts arising from trade and transaction of financial assets across national borders are involved foreign exchange transactions. Therefore, foreign exchange controls apply not only to trade transaction (in current account) but to financial assets transaction (in capital account) also. In the Malaysia case, suspending the convertibility of domestic currency (ringgit) abroad is a foreign exchange control, and the requirement of portfolio investment to remain in country for at least a year is a capital control. However, capital controls and foreign exchange controls are often taken to be synonymous.

[12] See Tobin (1978) for original argument.

[13] Chile is well known for long required all non-equity foreign capital inflows to be accompanied by non-interest-bearing deposit requirement.

still exist. Second, they create a rent power, which frequently turns into official favoritism or corruption. Third, negligible tax rate levies on outflows may be less effective than a substantial rate, but in the crisis period, high return may be a lucrative enough incentive to disregard the levied tax and creates powerful incentives evasion. All of these outflow controls develop policing costs, which are burdensome for the administration to absorb in the long run. Inflow controls, especially Chilean type inflow taxes, may create less of a problem in these areas. Since it applies equally to all financial transactions, applying both to residents and non-residents, less assets substitution can be expected. Furthermore, by taxing capital at the inflow stage, when the incentive to evasion is less, the opportunity for domestic financial institutes to expose themselves to risk by borrowing more abroad can be reduced.

4.2 Sustainability Issues

The question of sustainability does not move easily by itself to generalization, since the prospects for sustainability vary enormously by country, and also by type of capital flow.

Capital inflows can be measured by the surplus in capital account of the balance of payments. This surplus may have the same meaning as the excess of expenditure over income (current account deficit) plus the change in official holdings of international reserves. Therefore, the increase in capital inflows is usually coincident with wider current account deficits and/or reserve accumulation. The process of over-finance in current account deficits which results in an increasing official reserve accumulation may cause a false signal to policy makers to choose a wrong policy to cope and also to the public regarding their perception of the countries' official reserves. Since foreigners will not finance current account deficits forever, the monetary authorities need to know, as a borrower, how creditworthy the country will be, in order to sustain this deficit.

The traditional measures of creditworthiness are of only limited use in addressing the question of sustainability of capital inflows, since most of the new inflows may take the form of equity. Moreover, traditional creditworthiness ratios measure only the level of indebtedness rather than trends. Therefore, it is hard to judge between two countries with a debt/export ratio of 2 which is better in terms of creditworthiness without knowledge of export trends to compare. The one, which has more growth in export, can sustain the larger current account deficit.

Figure 8.11 shows the traditional measures of creditworthiness in Thailand since 1984. Before the financial crisis in the middle of 1997, all of these indicators gave no reason to policy makers to prepare measures for a reverse in capital flow. Though the deficit in current account in 1995–6 showed the wider gap in deficits, it was hard to tell how much of the deficit level was at an alarming level.

To address this problem, the Asymptotic Liabilities/Export ratio (ALE) by Dadush (1994) should be applied. This technique may be used to track sustainability of capital flows to the recipient countries and can be computed as:

Current Account Deficit / Change in Exports

Let x, m, L and r denote exports, imports, foreign liabilities and return on foreign liabilities, respectively. Given a target of liability/export ratio (k) as follow;

$$L = k\,x$$

Then the sustainable capital inflow (SCF) can be derived as

$$\Delta L = k\Delta x$$
$$m + rL - x = k\Delta x$$
$$(m - x) = k\Delta x - rL$$
$$\frac{(m - x)}{x} = k\frac{\Delta x}{x} - r\frac{kx}{x}$$
$$\frac{(m - x)}{x} = k(\frac{\Delta x}{x} - r)$$

or Sustainable Capital Inflows / Export = k (Export Growth - Interest Rate)

The sustainable capital flow under ALE concept is directly k proportional to the difference between the export growth rate and the interest rate of that country's export value. For example, from 1986 to 1997, the average of K

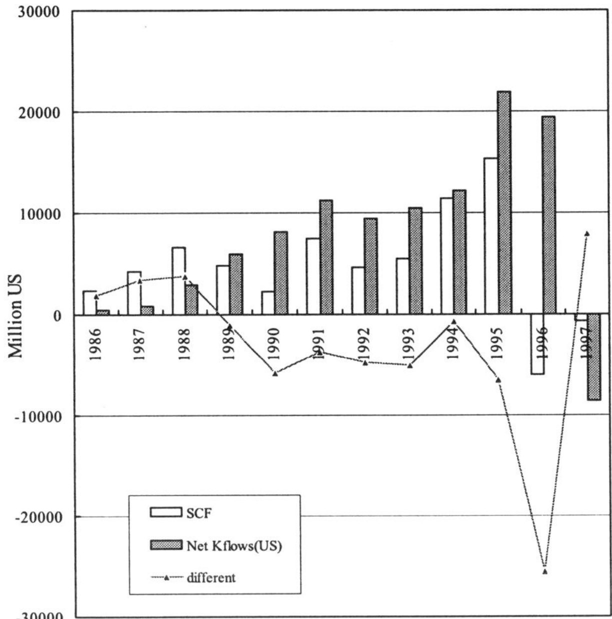

Fig. 8.11 Net Capital Inflows and Sustainble Capital Inflows

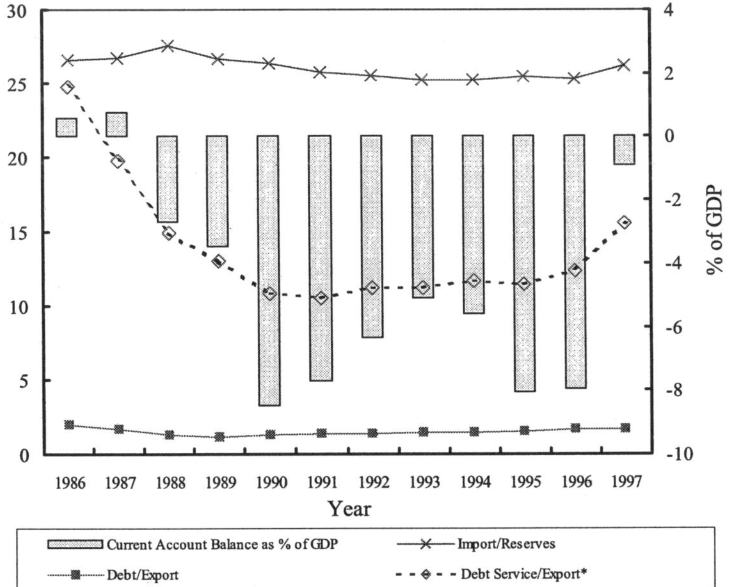

Fig. 8.12 Traditional Measures of Crediworthiness

is about 1.48, while the average growth in export and interest rate is 19.49 and 6.22 respectively. This means that sustainable capital flows (SCF) on average have risen by 1.48 (19.49 − 6.22) = 19.64 per cent of average export USD 32,263.08 or approximately USD 6,337.53 a year.

Figure 8.11 shows the net capital inflows and SCF from 1986 to 1997. From 1989 to 1995, SCF level were lower than net capital inflows, which reflected the over-financing of Thailand's current account deficits beyond a sustainable level. In 1996–7, the negative sustainable capital inflows reflect the fact that the export growth rates were below the interest rates but only 1997 which actual net transfer was also below sustainable level. The evidence in 1997 suggested Thailand's vulnerability to external and/or domestic shocks which induced a reversal of capital flows due to unsustainable current account deficits from the previous periods. The fall in export growth in 1996 signaled the difficulties in servicing external liabilities. Without reforms or adjustment, the reversal of capital flows came quickly in the next year.

4.3 Government Roles

The currency crisis, which turned into a banking crisis and caused severe economic recession in the cases of Thailand and Mexico, or Japan, for a banking crisis only case, could have been alleviated if the government took the appropriate actions. Government has so many possible roles in many situations, but the lessons that we may learn are which courses of action are rational and justifiable to take.

As a Regulator

The financial difficulties which caused banks and non-bank financial institutions, like finance and security company, to fail both affect and are affected by economic activity in the above mentioned economy. With the exception of fraud, bank losses occur primarily from causes such as defaults on loan, increases in interest rates that depress the market values of securities and/or loans more than deposits, and increased competition.

In theory, a bank fails when it becomes insolvent. That means the market present value of the bank's net-worth capital becomes zero. At this point, the present value of the bank's total assets, including balance sheet and contingent items such as forms of "goodwill" or license to operate banking activities are equal to the present value of its deposit and nondeposit liabilities other than equity capital. Effectively, the bank in question no longer belongs to the shareholders, but to creditors (depositors and non-depositors). Any further losses must be charged against creditors' shares in the balance sheet which is a violation to the agreement to repay these claims at face value when due. To protect the creditors not covered by deposit insurance and the insurance agency, so that all shares are equal in the remaining value of the bank's assets, the declaration of insolvency is the important action to do in the appropriate time. If the bank is declared insolvent at the exact moment that the market value of its net worth touches zero and is either merged or liquidated promptly, all losses which may occur go directly to shareholders only. Therefore, no matter how large the bank failures are, no losses accrue to depositors and is unlikely to have consequences on the local economy much different from that of failure of any other non-financial firm of comparable size.

However, to declare insolvency at the right time (when net worth of shareholders reach zero in value) is a problem for the government as a regulator, since the involved parties have a tendency to prolong this kind of action as long as they can. Regulators are often under political constraints to delay declaring banks insolvent because it may be viewed as a blot on their record. On the other hand, as net worth becomes smaller and eventually negative, a bank as a regulatee has progressively less to lose and is encouraged to increase its exposure to more risks in hopes of winning big and staying alive. The timing of the declaration of insolvency affects all of the involved parties. Thus, the longer an insolvent bank is permitted to operate independently, the larger its overall losses are likely to be. The situation is more desperate when the regulatee has a deeper relationship with government, perhaps as a large shareholder by government[14].

---

[14] For example, the case of Krung Thai Bank and the Bangkok Bank of Commerce.

As a Lender of Last Resort

The solvency of individual banks is more fragile than most other types of firms since a large proportion of bank's liabilities are effectively due on demand or are very short on notice while most of the assets are fixed for terms. If depositors and/or creditors doubt the ability of bank to discharge all their claims timely and in full, many are both motivated and able to withdraw their funds quickly. It is rationale to do so. If they do banks face the need to sell assets quickly and incur "fire-sale" losses, or restore their funding through borrowing from the central bank. Fire-sale losses may become sufficiently large to wipe put the banks' capital and make the situation insolvent. If a large number of depositors lose faith in all banks or, more likely, all banks readily available to them, they will not redeposit in other banks but will hold their currency outside the banking system, a situation referred to as "flight to currency". Massive redeposits from Thai banks to foreign banks in late 1997 may be called "flight to quality", but not a "flight to currency".

The situation in the second half of 1997 after the currency devaluation might not be correctly called a financial crisis but perhaps financial distress, since banks and finance companies in difficulty were insolvent but liquid. The entral bank chose not to declare insolvency for these ailing institutions after they lost confidence from depositors and got bank run, but provided liquidity instead. However, the role of government as a lender of last resort was far from justified. After borrowing from FRDF, because the loss is greater than registered capital, the financial institution will have to be closed. Justice requires that an institution should be declared insolvent when capital shortage is discovered and that the failure be resolved on an equitable basis. The Thai financial system seemed to have a short flight to quality situation, but not a flight to currency. Thus, the potential of financial panic to develop in the period after currency crisis, or a large number of solvent institutions likely to be in danger of becoming fire-sale insolvent, was minimal. But the central bank acted as a lender of last resort, routinely assisting insolvent situations whose closing might have saved more money and had less chance of igniting a flight to currency. Moreover, fire-sale losses actually occurred when a large number of financial companies' assets were resumed after permanently being closed by primary creditor-FRDF and the liquidation process by Financial Restructure Agency (FRA) took place, causing a huge loss of these assets.

4.4 Road to Recovery

There are a number of elements to be blamed for causing the crisis. However, the most acceptable cause of financial crisis, which became the economic problem, is the failure of financial institutions. A large part of the credit granted from banks or finance companies become the Non-Performing Loan (NPL) and its value is greater than the capital or shareholder's equity of these institutes can absorb. Money supply and credit in the system decreased because more than half of the financial institutions were closed by the monetary authority after Thailand asked for the financial and technical assistance program from IMF due to insolvency, and for the rest they had to strictly write-off their owns NPLs. This left financial institutions unable to grant more, or even sustain, credit to the economy, since they had to reserve more to cope with NPLs. Furthermore, the central bank, having acted as the "lender of last resort" to the affected financial institutions before the crisis, could not recover loaned money and placed itself in a position which prevented the bank from injecting money supply into the economy when needed. The liquidity situation in Thai economy could only contract further.

Policy Measures

After the government of the Prime Minister Chuan Leakpai had been formed, most economic responsibilities were managed through the various policies measures developed from IMF's technical assistance. These policies were issued to address stability problems, especially the stability of exchange rate and price level while the economic growth problem was given less priority. Therefore, the growth rate of GDP in 1998 was revised from zero level to minus 7% from previous year, while gradually exchange rates and price levels were stabilized.

The authorities had to rearrange the monetary and fiscal targets with the IMF during the preparation of the second and third letter of intent in order to tackle the growth problem. However, the economic recession was greater than expected. The economic growth decreased from 3–3.5% in the second review to 4–5.5% in the third review and eventually to 7% in the fourth review, even though the price level and exchange rate were stabilized.

The central policy of Chuan's regime, at first, is Export Promotion, hoping that by changing the exchange regime to a managed float system (de facto devaluation of baht against US dollar) will produce a switching effect to increase the export value and decrease import value, so that the current balance account will reverse into a plus. Therefore, the availability of credit has been switched to the export related industries — Sectoral Policy. With the surplus in balance of trade and foreign capital inflows, the foreign investors and/or creditor will be more confident. This will make it easier to grant new loans to Thailand for the IMF. Moreover, various policy measures have been imposed to improve the competitiveness of the countries in the medium and longer term, such as export credits and the restructure of production.

The results of Sectoral Policy providing more credit to export oriented industries fell short of expectations. Export revenue in US$ value does not respond to the devaluation of baht as expected. The improvement of the current account does not come from the increase in export but mainly from a large decrease in import.

The argument here is that the unsuccessful nature of the export promotion policy came from the lack of credit granted to exporters so that the exporters cannot purchase raw materials for their production, even though there are orders. This evidence is partly true. However, if we consider the major markets for export of Thailand (see Figure 8.13), there will be (1) North America (2) Europe (3) Japan and (4) within ASEAN. Japan and ASEAN also face the economic crisis as Thailand. So we have another 2 major buyers left. It is not true that export product will be comparatively cheap as a result of baht devaluation since many countries in this region which are our competitors also devalue their currencies. Some currency such as rupiah is devalued more than baht.

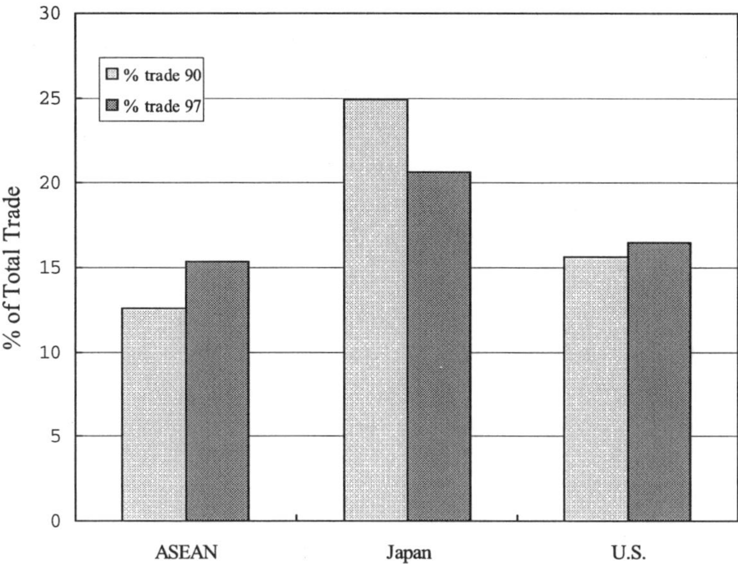

Fig. 8.13 Percent of Internal Total Trade of Thai to ASEAN, Japan and USA

In order to lower the interest rate and increase liquidity in the economy, Chuan's regime introduces the financial sector reform policy. There are many measures but to summarize, there are two areas of concern. First, the government tries to separate, close and liquidate the "bad" financial institutions, which claim to be insolvent. Another is to restore the remaining financial institutions. The measures to increase their capital in order to absorb and able to write-off their NPLs are the main features. However, it appeared that only a few banks and financial companies could raise the capital. Therefore, the Ministry of Finance finally introduced, on the 14th of August 1998, measures that offer to raise the first and second tier of these financial institutes' fund by paying share prices with government bonds to meet the standard at 8.5% of the risky assets. There is little evidence to prove the success of this 14th of August private share to government bond swap measures, since no single banks or finance companies offer to join the program due to the fear of diluting their control.

Fiscal policy may be the last tool that the government can utilize without strictly control from the IMF. The setting of budget deficit as 3% of GDP in the fourth letter of intent and even more in the fifth shows a good sign for the substitute of monetary policy which is strictly controlled. While the financial sector reform has not yet shown any signs of success, one suitable choice for economic recovery is expenditure from government. With the budget deficit tool, the Thai government tries to stimulate growth with expenditure from government. However, the size of the public sector in GDP is quite low and the transmission mechanism in public expenditure is rather inefficient in its impact and its timing. Therefore, like the failing experiences of Japan, which desperately tries to boost its own economy with expenditure in government projects, the outcome is not considered successful enough to recover an economy.

A Road to Economic Recovery: A Domestic Demand View

The economic recovery by stimulating the aggregate demand does not concern only increasing government spending and export boosting, but also stimulation of domestic aggregate demand. Domestic aggregate demand may roughly be defined to includes consumption (c), investment (i), and government spending (g), excluding net export (x−m) or foreign sector (assume current account is surplus).

It has been proven from the record of export revenue more than 10 months ago that "Export Led Growth" policy cannot stimulate the economic growth as the government expected.[15] The short term advantage from the decline in baht value when compared to the US$ is squared or taken over when affected countries such as Indonesia or Malaysia sharply decline their currencies value at the same rate or more than declining baht. Half of the export markets of Thailand such as Japan and Asean are also in trouble. Furthermore, in order to improve the competitiveness of a country's

---

[15] World Bank Advisor, Pieter Bottelier said in Wall Street Journal on 19/06/98, "The previous strategy of export growth is not working". Moreover, the record of export value in USD in 1998 was lower than 1997 about 4%.

production, the restructuring of productivity for export industries is badly needed, but such action takes time and success may be far from immediate reach. More importantly, we cannot wait anymore.

Consider the ratio of private consumption over GDP, its value is about 50% while the government consumption does not show any significant consumers. Within 3 years (1994–1996), this ratio does not change much (See Figure 8.14) as compared to the investment ratio. So the Export Led Growth strategy which has export and import percentage of GDP only 31.64% (average during 1994–1996) is difficult to improve under the current situation. Domestic aggregate demand may be another better choice due to relative importance to other factors.

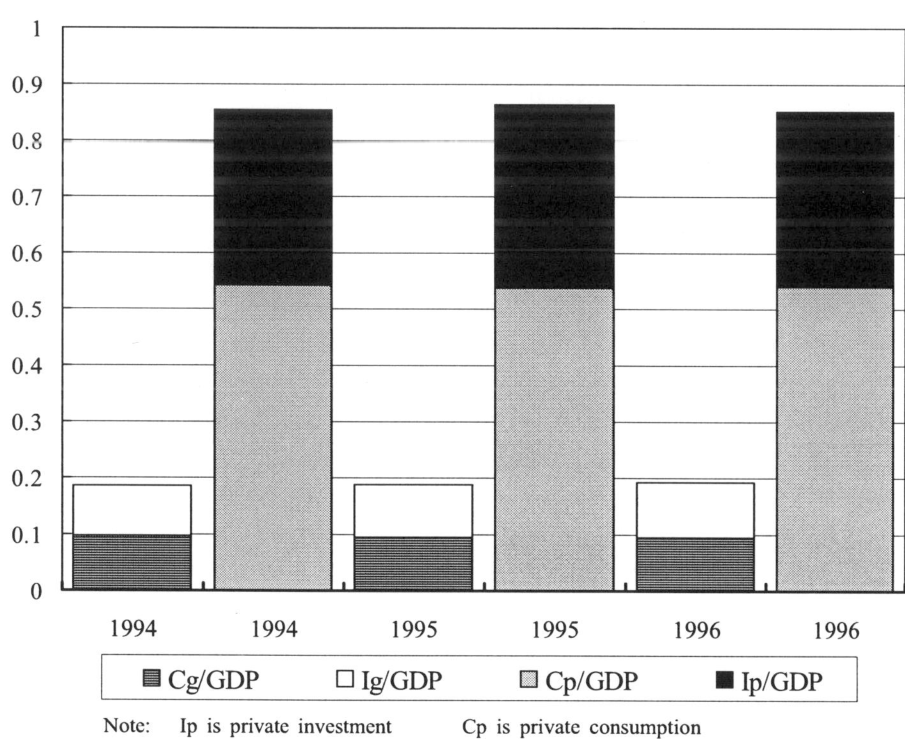

Fig. 8.14 Investment and Consumption of Government and Private Sectors

The idea of relying on ourselves (domestic demand) does not mean that we turn back to the "Autarky" or produce to consume only or live in an agricultural society, but, rather, it is the stimulating policy that the country can do by letting market mechanism such as interest rate works. The producers/entrepreneurs should have a chance to access funds equally with the exporters at the same cost. Because of limited funds, the one who can afford them should get those funds. It is a rate of return, which measure in percentage and no relation with a unit of value either in baht or dollar.

The problem now is in the expectation of people in the future. If people expect that the economy will recess more, the first reaction is to reduce their expenditures, even when their incomes remain the same. Marginal propensity to consume, which ranged from 0.25–0.54, or consumption-income elasticity, which ranged from 0.48–0.92[16] will be affected and then the multiplier effect may not work in full effect. Luxury goods or the less-productive investment will be the result of decreasing in expenditures in the first priority. With the high interest rate situation, the pattern of consumption may not be as easy as before.

According to the composition of domestic demand, the choice of policy measure to use domestic demand as a stimulant should be based on consumption. The rationales for boosting consumption are (1) on its own size and (2) less distorted. Since the government expenditure are far less than private consumption expenditures in size and as many evidences have been shown, the effectiveness of government expenditures are less effective than any policy actions.

To boost domestic consumption, the choice lies between reduction in consumption related taxes and increase in income. However, evidence proves in many countries and time periods that government expenditures that try to increase income have been less effective than other actions, such as monetary policy, especially in the short term. Consumption related tax reduction might be the better policy measure to perform. Value added tax (VAT) may be the

---

[16] See Suchart (1989) for MPC, and June (1992), NESDB (1992) and Wararate (1994) for consumption-income elasticity.

tax in consideration since it has an immediate effect if its rate is reduced[17], easy to access for all, and produce more equality between the rich and the poor. There might be an argument that the reduction in VAT rate might increase in a sharp reduction in VAT revenue. For this argument, it depends on the tax elasticity which most of decision-makers still do not know exactly. Even though the tax rate reduction causes a drop in tax revenue, at present what the decision makers are trying to do is to run a deficit in the government account which can be made either through spending more or receiving less in revenue. Which choice is the better measure?

References

Dadush, Uri, Ashok Dhareswar and Ron Jahannes (1997); "Are Private Capital Flows to Developing Countries Sustainable?", *Policy Research Working Paper (WPS 1397)*, The World Bank, December.

International Monetary Fund, (1999); *World Economic Outlook*, World Economic and Financial Surveys, Washington D.C., September.

Johnston, R. Barry (1991), "Distressed Financial Institutions in Thailand: Structural Weakness, Support Operations and Economic Consequences", in *Banking Crises: Cases and Issues*, edited by V. Sundararajan and Tomas J.T. Balino, IMF.

Kirakul, Suchada, J. Jantarangs, and P. Chantanahom (1993), "Economic Development and the Role of Financial Deepening in Thailand", *Papers on Policy Analysis and Assessment*, Bank of Thailand.

Leenabanchong, Chawin (1999), "In Search of Lessons from Thailand Financial Crisis: A Comparative Approach to Japan and Mexico", Fiscal 1997 Grant for Japan related Research Projects, The Sumitomo Foundation.

---

[17] A temporary 2-year reduction in VAT from 10% to 7% in 1998 is an example.

Leenabanchong, Chawin (1999), "Re-emerging Thailand: Sins of the Past, Shape of the Future", a paper presented at the *7th International Conference on Thai Studies*, University of Amsterdam, The Netherland.

National Economic and Social Development Board (1992), "The Analysis of Private Consumption Expenditure", *National Income.*

Nualtaranu, June (1992), "Household Consumption and Saving", *Thesis*, Faculty of Economics, Thammasat University.

Rungwatthana, Wararate (1994), "The Time Series Consumption Function: ECM", *Thesis*, Faculty of Economics, Thammasat University.

Sharmar, Krishnan (1998) " Understanding the Dynamics behind Excess Capital Outflows and Excess Capital Outflows in East Asia", *Paper for Discussion*, Department of Economic and Social Affairs, United Nations, New York.

Sodsrichai, Pornpen (1993), "An Economic of Financial Liberalization in Thailand", *Thesis*, Faculty of Economics, Thammasat University.

Techaposai, Suchart (1989), "Household Consumption and Saving Pattern in Thailand", *Thesis*, Faculty of Economics, Thammasat University.

Tobin, James (1978), "A Proposal for International Monetary Reform", *Eastern Economic Journal.*

Yindeeyom, Chaturon (1998), "Privatization and Efficiency Improvement: The Evidence of Krung Thai Bank", *Thesis*, Faculty of Economics, Thammasat University.

CHAPTER 9

MALAYSIA

FINANCIAL CRISIS IN MALAYSIA

Mohamed Ariff and Michael Meow-Chung Yap

Malaysian Institute of Economic Research
9th Floor, Menara Dayabumi, Jalan Sultan Hishamuddin,
P.O. Box 12160
50768 Kuala Lumpur, Malaysia
E-mail: ariff@mier.po.my

1. INTRODUCTION

Malaysia's economy grew at an average of almost 9 per cent annually in the period 1988–96. This was achieved at a relatively low average inflation rate of 3.5 per cent per annum. By 1996, the unemployment rate was just 2.5 per cent. Cited by many as a model of successful economic management, the currency crisis of 1997 which sent the ringgit (RM) tumbling thus came as an immense shock.

This chapter examines the currency crisis in Malaysia, which did not seek funding from the International Monetary Fund (IMF), unlike some of the other severely hit countries like Thailand, Indonesia and South Korea. Instead, in September 1998, the Malaysian government chose to implement selective capital controls and fixed its exchange rate against the US dollar; a move that was deemed controversial. This unorthodox policy response allowed the speedy implementation of recovery measures. Since then, the

305

economy has recovered significantly and growth in 1999 is projected at 4–5 per cent.

The chapter is structured as follows: Section 2 lays out the conditions prior to the crisis, in particular the several signs of concern in the economy. The next section details the crisis as it hit the exchange rate and stock market almost simultaneously. Section 4 analyses the initial policy response in terms of fiscal and monetary policies. Section 5 studies the impact of the initial policy response on the economy. The next section examines the change in policy response as both fiscal and monetary policies turned expansionary following the capital control measures. The financial sector-restructuring programme is also discussed. The benefits and costs of capital controls are analysed in section 7. Section 8 talks about the recovery phase of the crisis and this is followed by a conclusion.

2. CONDITIONS PRIOR TO THE START OF THE CRISIS

Following the recession of the mid-80s, Malaysia experienced a period of high economic growth with relative price stability. The economy was a major destination for direct foreign investment (FDI) attracted by its abundant labour (low wages) and political stability. Transparent and liberal policies pertaining to foreign investment also helped. For example, foreign ownership of up to 100 per cent is permitted in manufacturing companies in the export sector. This had spurred growth especially in the export-oriented manufacturing sector.

The Malaysian economy was relatively much less exposed to external debt compared to the other crisis-hit economies. As at June 1997, foreign debt amounted to only US$45.2 billion (42% of GDP). Short-term debt accounted for only 31.1 per cent of this total and this was well backed by foreign reserves (1.97 times). Debt servicing ratio was low at 5.5 per cent of exports while the banking sector had a net non-performing loan ratio of just 2.2 per cent. The country also had a high savings rate of 38.5 per cent of Gross National Product in 1996.

Table 9.1 Malaysia: Critical Economic Indicators

	Dec-96	Mar-97	Jun-97	Sep-97	Dec-97	Mar-98	Jun-98	Sep-98	Dec-98	Mar-99	Jun-99	Sep-99	Dec-99
NPL Ratio (3 months) %	n.a.	n.a.	n.a.	n.a.	n.a.	7.0	8.9	11.4	13.4	13.0	12.4	12.0	n.a.
NPL Ratio (6 months) %	3.7	3.4	3.6	3.7	4.1	7.0	8.9	10.8	7.5	7.9	7.9	7.7	n.a.
RWCR Banking Sector %	10.7	n.a.	n.a.	n.a.	10.5	11.1	11.2	10.1	11.8	12.3	12.7	12.7	12.5
Bank Loan Growth (yoy) %	n.a.	29.6	30.3	28.4	26.5	15.9	10.3	4.5	−1.6	−4.3	−5.0	−5.6	−4.8
Change in CPI (yoy) %	3.5	3.2	2.2	2.3	2.9	5.1	6.2	5.5	5.3	3.0	2.1	2.1	2.5
Change in PPI (overall, yoy) %	2.3	1.5	−1.1	2.1	8.9	11.3	15.4	10.4	1.2	−4.2	−6.7	−1.0	n.a.
Change in PPI (import, yoy) %	0.1	1.0	1.1	3.2	8.3	13.0	11.5	8.1	2.2	−2.4	−0.8	0.0	n.a.
Change in PPI (local, yoy) %	2.8	1.6	−1.7	1.8	9.0	11.0	16.2	11.0	1.0	−4.6	−8.0	−1.2	n.a.
RM/USD Exchange Rate	2.53	2.48	2.52	3.20	3.89	3.64	4.18	3.80	3.80	3.80	3.80	3.80	3.80
KLSE – Composite Index	1238.0	1203.1	1077.3	814.6	594.4	719.5	455.6	373.5	586.1	502.8	811.1	675.5	812.3
3-Mth Interbank Rate %	7.34	7.36	7.71	7.65	8.60	10.91	11.07	7.75	6.48	6.19	3.27	3.14	3.15
7-Day Interbank Rate %	7.28	7.01	7.84	6.68	10.57	10.55	10.71	7.08	5.85	5.49	2.83	2.66	2.62
Overnight Interbank Rate %	7.15	6.43	7.18	5.71	8.30	9.62	10.19	6.64	5.41	5.23	2.81	2.55	2.52
BLR (commercial banks) %	10.65	10.67	10.85	11.28	12.22	14.23	14.49	10.54	9.50	9.48	7.24	6.79	6.79
Average Lending Rate (banks, %)	10.12	10.14	10.68	11.51	13.33	13.51	11.09	9.72	9.56	8.45	8.45	7.89	n.a.
Change in IIP (yoy) %	13.0	11.4	12.9	7.4	9.1	−0.1	−5.7	−10.9	−9.4	2.8	9.3	20.9	16.2
*Change in Import (US$) (yoy) %	0.1	−1.0	11.2	1.4	−8.2	−19.7	−33.8	−29.3	−20.5	−6.8	9.9	21.2	n.a.
*Change in Export (US$) (yoy) %	1.9	6.2	0.1	2.0	−5.7	−11.3	−10.1	−10.8	5.2	4.3	15.6	21.4	n.a.
Net International Reserves (US$ bil.)	27.7	29.1	28.0	19.4	15.2	15.7	13.9	21.4	26.2	27.7	31.1	31.4	30.9
	4Q:96	1Q:97	2Q:97	3Q:97	4Q:97	1Q:98	2Q:98	3Q:98	4Q:98	1Q:99	2Q:99	3Q:99	4Q:99
MIER CSI (points)	129.5	127.2	133.4	122.1	104.7	88.5	79.1	80.0	80.5	84.0	101.6	111.3	117.7
MIER BCI (points)	64.6	63.0	65.5	58.7	49.6	41.0	42.3	41.8	44.7	48.2	60.3	62.2	61.0

Note: NPL — non-performing loans; RWCR — risk-weighted capital ratio; CPI — consumer price index; PPI — producer price index; KLSE — Kuala Lumpur Stock Exchange; BLR — base lending rate; ALR — average lending rate; IIP — index of industrial production; MIER — Malaysian Institute of Economic Research; CSI — consumer sentiments index; BCI — business conditions index; yoy — year-on-year.

Although the ringgit went through a much sharper depreciation than justified by the economic fundamentals of the economy, markets became nervous over several issues that could potentially jeopardise sustainable economic growth. The Thai crisis had shown that aggregate figures could mask underlying vulnerability. Developments in the Thai, Korean and Indonesian financial markets added to these fears.

2.1 Signs of Concern

Prior to early 1997, there were several signs of concern in the economy. These have been analysed in Ariff, et al. (1998), Athukorala (1998) and Yap (1999). Briefly, the main concerns were as follows:

- High growth occurred in the economy above the potential level since 1991, resulting in wage increases above productivity gains. Actual output in 1996 was estimated to have exceeded potential by about 6–10 per cent (Yap, 1997b). The level of actual output above potential output during that period reflects the 'pro-growth' policy of the government. Athukorala (1998) termed this as the "big growth push". Wage increases would probably have been higher had it not been mitigated by the huge influx of (unskilled) foreign labour in the 1990s, who were willing to work for much lower wages than the locals were.

- Declining growth in total factor productivity (TFP) indicating loss of efficiency in the economy. The period of declining TFP growth prior to 1997 corresponded with an investment boom and high loan growth in the banking sector.[1] Growth during this period was driven primarily by capital stock accumulation (Yap, 1997a). The inefficient use of capital

---

[1] The declining growth of TFP in the mid-1990s has also been noted by the National Economic Action Council (NEAC), which was set up by the government in response to the currency crisis in 1997, as well as by the National Productivity Corporation (NPC). Yap (1997a) noted that TFP growth had declined from a range of around 2.5–4.5 per cent in the late 1980s (which corresponded to the beginning of the large influx of foreign investment into the export-oriented manufacturing sector) to a range of about 0.5–1.5 per cent in the first half of the 1990s.

was reflected in a steeply rising incremental capital-output ratio (ICOR) in the period 1995–97. This period corresponded with large infrastructure projects (or the so-called 'mega projects') requiring heavy imported equipment.

- Rapid growth in bank loans resulting in increasing loan exposure to non-tradable sectors such as property development and construction, consumption credit and purchases of stocks.

The high loan growth to the property sector was fuelled by a property boom, which attracted investment, by many property developers. Property prices increased between 12–26 per cent in the period 1991–92 and between 13–18 per cent in the period 1995–96. Urban centres like the Klang Valley and Johor Bahru experienced double-digit property price inflation of between 10–17 per cent yearly in the period 1994–96.[2]

The stock market boom influenced lending for the purchase of stocks in the 1990s. Amidst the investment euphoria in emerging East Asian markets, the Kuala Lumpur Stock Exchange (KLSE) experienced unprecedented boom in the years 1993 and 1996. The composite Index (CI) shot up by a phenomenal 198 per cent in 1993 and by 24 per cent in 1996. Market capitalisation on the exchange had reached dizzying heights of 375 per cent of GDP in 1993 and 323 per cent in 1996. The large capital inflows posed potential risks to financial stability in the event of sudden large reversal of these funds.

Bank loans obtained through collateral in the form of stocks and property also exposed the banking sector to risks should there be a collapse in the prices of these assets. This was especially so in the case of property, as many analysts had predicted that in certain segments of the property market especially high-end residential, hotel and office space, there were emerging signs of excess supply, following rapid expansion for several years.[3]

---

[2] Source: Bank Negara Malaysia, *Monthly Statistical Bulletin*, various issues.

[3] For details, see *Bank Negara Malaysia Annual Report 1998*, pp. 21–22.

- Persistent current account deficits in the 1990s, fuelled by the investment boom and only partly financed by long-term inflows in 1994–95. As Malaysia has one of the highest saving rate in the world, there appears to be no compelling reason why it should run into current account deficit concerns. The current account balance was in deficit since 1990. It was not the result of a drop in the saving rate but rather a rapid rise in the investment rate. The investment to GDP ratio was above 45 per cent from 1995–97.

  Despite the fact that Malaysia continued to attract FDI, in 1994–95 the current account deficit was only partially financed by long-term capital inflows (around 75–79%). The deficit in the current account as a percentage of net international reserves increased sharply from 10–12 per cent in 1992–93 to 22 per cent in 1994 and then 34 per cent in 1995. Reliance on short-term capital to finance the deficit is not tenable in the longer term due to the volatile nature of these funds.

  To compound the problems of the current account deficit, Malaysian FDI abroad (or 'reverse FDI') had been substantial, amounting to RM6 billion in 1996 (Jomo, 1998). Athukorala (1998) noted this as well and both asserted that these FDI outflows were not necessarily in response to market factors but instead the 'hand of government'.

- Sustained appreciation of the real exchange rate since 1995 despite concerns over the current account deficit, indicating overvaluation of the ringgit when the crisis unfolded in 1997.

  In 1995, the current account deficit was sizeable, at RM21.6 billion (US$8.6 billion) or 10.4 per cent of GNP. The basic balance in the balance of payments had recorded a deficit for the second consecutive year, by RM5 billion (1994: –RM3.1 billion). Although many analysts were concerned about the sustainability of this deficit, the ringgit appreciated against the USD. Viewed against a basket of major currencies (in real terms), the ringgit appeared 15–20 per cent overvalued when the currency crisis started in 1997, compared to the period 1994–95. From Figure 9.1, it is obvious that the ringgit had appreciated in real terms not just because of a nominal appreciation but also due to unfavorable price movements compared to its major trading partners.[4]

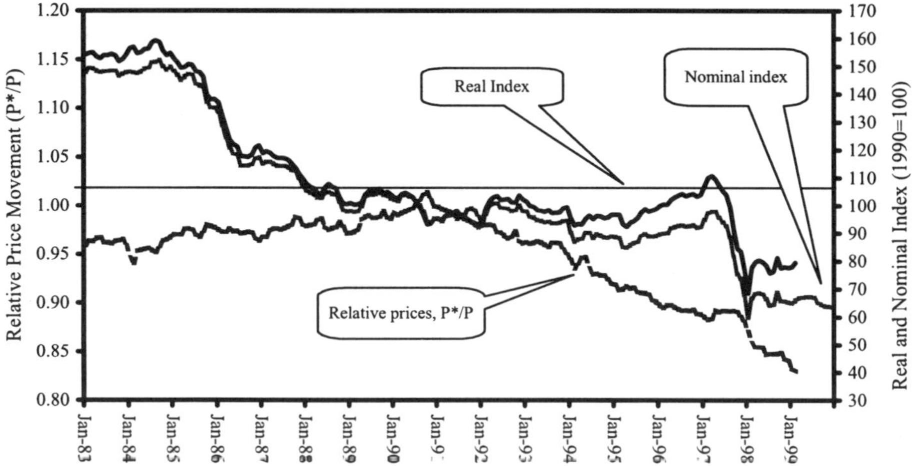

Fig. 9.1 Malaysian Ringgit: Real Effective Exchange Rate and Determinants

2.2 State of the Banking Sector

The banking sector showed little signs of trouble in June 1997, with a net NPL ratio of just 2.2 per cent and a risk-weighted-capital-ratio (RWCR) of 12 per cent, which was significantly above the minimum requirement of 8 per cent.[5] The ratio of loan provisions to NPLs was also close to 100 per cent. However, there was rapid credit expansion and increased exposure to the property sector as well as for stock purchases. This resulted in a highly

---

[4] In Figure 9.1, the ratio P*/P measures the relative movement of foreign prices (P*) against domestic prices (P).

[5] RWCR – The risk-weighted capital ratio is a measure of the capital adequacy of banks, based on the Basle capital framework which weights both on and off-balance sheet items according to their perceived level of risk. It increases the risk sensitivity of banks in the structuring of their balance sheets.

leveraged economy, with the ratio of banking sector loans to GDP rising sharply from just above 100 per cent in the period 1992–94 to 145 per cent in 1997. This posed three potential problems. First, it rendered the economy vulnerable to a currency attack as the authorities are constrained in raising interest rates to defend the exchange rate. Secondly, when there is rapid credit growth over a short time, it may not be prudent, as some borrowers may be less creditworthy. Third, the increasingly high exposure of the banks to the property sector also posed potential risks in view of the mature phase of the property up-cycle. This is especially true of bank loans secured by collateral in property and shares. Despite these growing uneasy signs, the central bank only took corrective action in early 1997, just before the onset of the first attack on the currency. Athukorala (1998) noted the "long silence of BNM" on the issue of rapid credit growth. Bank Negara Malaysia had indeed been guilty of an overly lax monetary policy in the years preceding the crisis. The nervousness of investors over excessive credit expansion by banks and potential bad debt was also prompted by concerns that the corporate sector may be intimately linked to the government. Thus, there could have been some 'connected lending' that is not based on commercial criteria (see Athukorala, 1998; Gomez and Jomo, 1997).

2.3 Exposure to External Debt

A key distinguishing feature of the Malaysian economy from the other crisis-hit economies is that its external debt exposure was low at the onset of the crisis. As at end-March 1997, Malaysia's external debt totalled RM101.2 billion (US$40.5 billion), or 39 per cent of GNP. Of this amount, less than 30 per cent was short-term debt, which was 11 per cent of GNP and had foreign reserves backing of 2.5 times.

But the private sector and the non-financial public enterprises (NFPEs) had increasingly borrowed more from abroad in the years preceding the crisis. Private sector medium and long-term debt rose almost seven times from RM5.4 billion in March 1991 to RM37.7 billion in June 1997. The NFPEs borrowed more from 1993 onwards. Their medium and long-term external debt rose almost three-fold from RM12 billion in March 1993 to

RM32.5 billion in June 1997. The short-term external borrowings of the banking sector increased by about 2.5 times in a short period of 18 months; from RM11.3 billion in December 1995 to RM27.8 billion in June 1997.

This trend had no doubt been facilitated by the stable exchange rate of the ringgit against the US dollar. The exchange rate was 2.44 against the greenback in June 1995 and remained stable until March 1997, when it was 2.48. Domestic interest rates were not too high during that period. Were it not so, there would have been more incentive to increase external borrowings.

3. THE CRISIS

The dramatic collapse of the Thai economy raised serious concerns regarding the Malaysian economy amongst foreign portfolio investors. In the case of Thailand, many foreign investors, analysts and even the international rating agencies had failed to recognise the underlying real risks until it was too late. This influenced their subsequent perceptions of regional economies with some vulnerabilities, such as the Malaysian economy. As such, when the Thai baht debacle was full-blown, the setting was such that self-fulfilling prophecies could happen easily.

The fall of the ringgit exchange rate was swift. From 2.48 against the US dollar in March, it went to 2.57 in July and by year-end, it was 3.77. Bank Negara Malaysia had tried to defend it, unsuccessfully, in mid-year through raising short-term interest rates. The overnight and seven-day interbank rates were increased to a peak of 50 per cent and 35 per cent respectively in July 1997. In spite of this, the RM's slide could not be halted and BNM wisely abandoned the defence to conserve its foreign reserves. Thus, they avoided the mistake made by the Thai central bank, which committed large amounts of its foreign currency in defending the baht in the early stages of the crisis. But there was no respite from the currency markets. In early January 1998, the ringgit went to an all-time low of 4.88 against the dollar. Having recovered temporarily to 3.73 in April that year, it went back down again to 4.20 by August. It became obvious that stability had not returned to currency markets more than a year after the crisis began.

In tandem with the sharp tumble of the exchange rate, the stock market collapsed. Investors began mass selling of stocks on the KLSE amidst concerns about the economy and the exchange rate. The Composite Index of the KLSE fell from 1,216.7 points at the end of January 1997 to 594.4 points in December. In August 1998, just before the capital control measures were imposed, the CI was just 302.9 points. Market capitalisation had shrank to just RM200 billion in August 1998, compared to RM826 billion in January 1997.

The stock market collapse and currency depreciation fed on each other as investors demonstrated typical herding behavior in times of crisis. There was an obvious lack of ability among foreign investors to differentiate country specific factors but the vulnerabilities in the Malaysian economy had reinforced the panic. Hence, whether the similarities that investors see with the other crisis-hit economies were real or perceived, the result was a massive sell-down of stocks and dumping of the ringgit.

These developments quickly took a toll on consumer and business confidence. Starting from the third quarter of 1997, business confidence as measured by the Business Conditions Index (BCI) of the Malaysian Institute of Economic Research dipped sharply for three consecutive quarters. The institute's Consumer Sentiments Index (CSI) also took a battering as it declined sharply for four consecutive quarters beginning from the third quarter of 1997. The CSI hit an all-time low in the second quarter of 1998.

4. POLICY RESPONSE — INITIAL PHASE

The government initially did not expect a recession resulting from the depreciation of the ringgit. When the Minister of Finance presented the 1998 Budget in October 1997, the official forecast of real GDP for 1998 was 7.0 per cent, with the current account deficit projected to be 4 per cent of nominal GNP. Hence the initial policy response sought to stabilise the economy through addressing the current account deficit, keeping inflation down, steadying the ringgit exchange rate and preventing large capital outflows. Policy-makers also aimed at strengthening the banking system.

Table 9.2 Malaysia: Annual Economic Indicators

	1990	1991	1992	1993	1994	1995	1996	1997	1998	1999
Real GDP Growth (%)	9.0	9.5	8.9	9.9	9.2	9.8	10.0	7.5	−7.5	4.3
CPI Inflation (%)	3.1	4.4	4.7	3.6	3.7	3.4	3.5	2.7	5.3	3.0
Change in Housing Price Index (%)	4.1	25.5	12.2	4.9	8.0	16.4	12.9	1.9	−9.4	−12.0*
RM per US$1 (average for period)	2.70	2.75	2.55	2.57	2.62	2.51	2.52	2.81	3.92	3.80
Unemployment Rate (%)	5.1	4.3	3.7	3.0	2.9	3.1	2.5	2.4	3.2	3.0
KLSE Composite Index (end of period)	505.9	556.2	644.0	1275.3	971.2	995.2	1238.0	594.4	586.1	812.3
Current Account Balance (RM)	−2483	−11,644	−5622	−7926	−14,770	−21,647	−10,226	−15,820	36,794	42,010
CA Balance as % of GNP	−2.2	−9.1	−3.9	−4.8	−7.9	−10.2	−4.2	−5.9	13.7	15.0
Long-Term Capital Account (RM)	3473	10,331	10,328	13,864	11,659	16,611	13,525	19,095	10,628	11,470
Short-Term Capital Account (RM)	1356	5135	11,957	13,931	−8484	2529	10,317	−12,913	−20,633	−22,000
External Debt (RM mil.)	45,903	50,969	55,951	69,131	73,635	85,015	97,833	170,757	161,715	161,334
Medium and Long-Term Debt (RM mil.)	41,488	43,798	42,794	51,851	59,391	68,811	72,682	127,500	129,190	132,343
- *Public Sector*	36,545	37,075	32,323	36,353	35,188	40,731	39,709	65,419	68,156	72,495
- *Private Sector*	4943	6723	10,471	15,498	24,203	28,080	32,973	62,081	61,034	59,848
Short-Term Debt (RM mil.)	4415	7171	13,157	17,320	14,244	16,204	25,151	43,257	32,525	28,991
Nominal GNP (RM mil.)	114,017	128,324	142,676	163,928	186,049	212,095	241,931	266,793	269,138	280,932

Note: * Half-year 1999.

4.1 Monetary Policy

Although the International Monetary Fund (IMF) had advised countries hit by crisis at the onset of the crisis to raise interest rates aggressively to defend their currencies, Bank Negara Malaysia did not pursue as tight a monetary policy. The central bank's stance had been to maintain interest rates at relatively high levels, both to contain inflation and to provide adequate returns on ringgit-assets to prevent large capital outflows. The prevailing thinking among policy-makers even then was that raising interest rates excessively would not serve to support the ringgit, given the strong external factors. Instead, it was also important to provide sufficient credit to finance economic activities.

But when the ringgit remained volatile against the major currencies, Bank Negara raised interest rates further, especially after the ringgit exchange rate went past 3.00 against the USD. The 3-month inter-bank rate, BNM's policy rate, was raised from 7.6 per cent in September 1997 (monthly average) to 8.7 per cent by the end of that year. Despite the higher interest rates, the ringgit continued to be adversely affected by external developments (through the so-called "contagion" effect) such as the depreciation of the Korean won in December 1997 and the collapse of the Indonesian rupiah in early 1998. The ringgit fell to an astonishing 4.88 against the greenback on 7 January 1998. Bank Negara responded by further raising short-term rates. The 3-month inter-bank rate rose to 11 per cent in February. Bank Negara Malaysia's 3-month intervention rate in the money market was raised by 100 basis points to 11 per cent on 6 February 1998.

The impact of the ringgit depreciation had started to show up in higher inflation in early 1998. This was evident in both consumer prices and producer prices, with the latter rising more steeply.[6] CPI inflation went up from an average of 2.7 per cent in 1997 to between 3.5–5 per cent in the first quarter of 1998. It peaked at slightly above 6 per cent in the middle of 1998. Producer prices of imported goods responded much faster, rising at between

---

[6] Higher inflation resulting from the sharp depreciation in the Ringgit exchange rate was mitigated to a large extent by the sharp recession of −7.5 per cent in 1998.

9.5–13 per cent in the first three months of 1998. Meanwhile, in the balance of payments, the balance on short-term capital registered a deficit of RM9.2 billion in the first quarter of the year. This was about 42 per cent of the total net outflow of short-term capital for the whole of 1998. The huge net outflow of short-term funds saw liquidity in the domestic financial market tightening considerably.

Quantitative restrictions were also imposed on loans for purchase of shares, non-commercial vehicles and property. These and some other measures are summarised below:

Early Monetary Policy Measures

- April 1997: To curb strong loan growth in the banking system to the "less productive" sectors and the sharp rise in asset prices, BNM imposed a limit of 20 per cent of total outstanding loans for loans extended to the **property sector** (excluding houses below RM150,000); and a ceiling of 15 per cent of total outstanding loans for the **purchase of stocks and shares** for commercial banks and finance companies, and a 30 per cent ceiling for merchant banks.

- August 1997: Following speculative attacks on the ringgit in July, banks were subjected to a US$2 million limit on outstanding non-commercial ringgit offer-side swap transactions with foreign customers. This excludes transactions for trade and direct investment. The objective was to **reduce the supply of offshore ringgit** used to mount speculative attacks on the currency.

- October 1997: Financing on **hire-purchase loans for non-commercial vehicles** was reduced to 70 per cent of the purchase price of the vehicle from the previous 75 per cent. The repayment period was shortened to not more than 5 years from the previous 5–7 years. Banks were also advised to **prioritise lending to productive sectors** such as in the export-oriented manufacturing sector.

- October 1997: Banking institutions required submitting credit plans for the remainder of 1997 and 1998. From the plans submitted, **BNM projected loan growth to moderate** to 15 per cent by end-1998. In order to detect problem loans early, the **classification of NPLs** was reduced from 6-month arrears to 3-month arrears effective 1 January 1998. **Disclosure requirements** for the financial statements of banking institutions were increased to include more information.

- December 1997: Restriction on credit extended to **property projects** which have not started construction (including residential properties costing RM150,000 and below). For on-going property projects, strict selectivity and viability assessment were advised. However, due to slower growth of loans, on 26 January 1998, restrictions on construction and purchase of residential properties costing RM150,000 and below were lifted.

- March 1998: Banking institutions required to publish **quarterly data on financial soundness**. Also required to maintain on a quarterly basis a **minimum 8 per cent risk-weighted capital ratio**.

- May 1998: To allow banks **more flexibility in liquidity management**, the band on required balances to meet Statutory Reserve Requirement was widened to 2 per cent, from previous 0.5 per cent.

4.2 Fiscal Policy

The 1998 Budget proposed in October 1997 showed fiscal restraint, not unlike the IMF-type of recommendation for other affected countries. The recession was still not anticipated at that point; rather a slightly slower growth was projected (7 per cent). Thus the authorities were concerned with maintaining macroeconomic stability, especially in the balance of payments, containing inflation, and maintaining the strength of the public and private sectors' financial positions. With government revenue anticipated to be lower, public expenditures were scaled down. Consumption spending was cut back and non-critical major infrastructure projects were deferred. A fiscal surplus of 2 per cent of GNP was proposed.

The strategy of the 1998 Budget was as follows:

a. strengthening economic fundamentals and stabilising financial markets;
b. maintaining sustainable growth;

c. continuing the process of deregulation and liberalisation of the economy;
d. continuing the social agenda for further overall development.

The overall expenditure allocation increased by 1.9 per cent to RM64.1 billion. Of this amount, RM45.6 billion was for operating expenditure (1.7 per cent rise) and RM18.5 billion for development expenditure (2.6 per cent rise). With revenue projected at RM68.1 billion, the Federal Government fiscal position was expected to show a surplus of RM3.9 billion. Taking into consideration loan repayments and transfers, the overall surplus was projected at RM9.0 billion (3.2 per cent of GNP). The modest increase in operating expenditure was made possible through a 30 per cent cut on overseas travel and a 10–15 per cent cut on daily expenditures.

A summary of the main measures in the 1998 Budget proposals is provided here:

- **Increasing export competitiveness**: To reduce the cost of doing business in the country, especially in the export-oriented manufacturing sector, tax incentives based on the increase in value of exports were given.

- **Reducing imports**: To reduce the dependency on imports of capital and intermediate goods and encourage import-substitution, import duties for several items were raised;

  To discourage the import of consumption goods, import duties on items that are available locally were also raised;

  To encourage the production of local brand names, tax deductions on local advertising expenditure were given;

  To curb excessive private consumption, especially on passenger cars, the import duty on completely built up (CBU) and completely knocked down (CKD) luxurious cars were increased sharply.

- **To help improve the services balance**: Tax measures were used to encourage the domestic life insurance business, discourage international travel by Malaysians, and increase the cost of education overseas.

- **To encourage higher savings**: The tax deduction allowed for employer's contribution to the Employees Provident Fund (EPF) over and above the mandatory contribution was also increased from 5 per cent to 7 per cent.

- **To reduce private sector's cost of doing business:** The corporate tax rate was reduced from 30 per cent to 28 per cent.

- **Deferment of Mega Projects:** To strengthen the balance of payments and ensure that capital is channelled to where it is most productive, several major infrastructure projects were deferred. These include the Bakun hydroelectric project, second phase of the Putrajaya administrative centre, the Kuala Lumpur Linear City project and the Malaysia-Indonesia bridge across the Straits of Malacca.

- **To Reduce Excess Supply of High-end Properties**: The quota for foreign ownership was raised for certain types of property. Certain conditions for ownership were also relaxed. The imposition of property gains tax was also reduced if disposal takes place after the fifth year.

- **To strengthen the banking sector**, the following measures were introduced:
  - Non-performing loans to be classified as such based on 3-month arrears instead of 6 months;
  - Banking institutions be required to disclose more information on non-performing loans, loan exposure by sector, and provisions for bad and doubtful debts including interest-in-suspense;
  - The general provisions maintained by banks be increased from one per cent of total outstanding loans (net of interest-in-suspense and specific provisions) to 1.5 per cent;
  - Requests for foreign borrowing to finance domestic projects to be scrutinised carefully by the central bank.

4.3 December 1997: Further Measures Announced

On 8 December 1999, the Minister proposed further measures in Parliament as the exchange rate continued to be volatile and sentiments on the local bourse worsened in tandem. The Minister announced that the growth forecast of the government for 1998 has been reduced downwards to a range of 4–5 per cent, with the current account deficit projected at 3 per cent of GNP.

The measures are summarised here:

- Ministers and Deputy Ministers took a pay cut of 10 per cent. High-ranking civil servants and political secretaries similarly had their pay reduced by 3 per cent. For officers in the top brackets of the civil service, there was a moratorium on salary increments until the economic situation improves. The private sector was urged to follow suit.
- Federal government expenditure was to be cut back by a further 18 per cent — with an immediate 10 per cent cut across-the-board of both operating and development expenditure and 8 per cent on a selective basis. This was to be over and above the earlier cutbacks announced in the October tabling of the 1998 Budget.
- On-going construction projects, which are not strategic, were deferred and new projects not essential to improving economic efficiency will not be implemented.
- Reverse investments will only be encouraged if it has strategic and significant linkages with the domestic economy and earns foreign exchange.

By the end of the first quarter of 1998, real GDP had contracted by 3.1 per cent (annual rate). The government pursued a less restrictive fiscal policy by trimming the budget surplus down to 0.5 per cent of GNP. An additional RM1 billion was allocated for socio-economic projects as a cushion from the crisis for the more vulnerable segments of society.

Malaysia could have adopted a more stimulating fiscal policy right from the start of the crisis as its accumulated budget surpluses from the previous years could have been used to finance a moderate fiscal deficit. There were perhaps two reasons why this was not pursued. First, the extent of the negative impact of the currency depreciation on the economy was underestimated at that point. Secondly, the financial markets expected a fairly strong fiscal surplus. Thus to a certain extent the initial stance of fiscal policy was dictated to by market expectations. Garnaut (1998, p. 19) noted that there "seemed to be discordance between good policy, on the one hand, and international market perceptions of good policy, on the other". It was almost as if the markets wanted a "cleansing recession", as Jomo (1998) noted.

5.   IMPACT OF THE INITIAL POLICY RESPONSE

Notwithstanding the measures taken by the authorities, the ringgit's external value continue to be affected by external developments such as the riots in Indonesia, the weakening of the yen and the devaluation of the Russian rubble. Higher interest rates and the tight fiscal policy assisted in reducing the current account deficit and kept inflation down to acceptable levels. But together with the plunge in the ringgit exchange rate and the stock market tumble, the end result was that aggregate demand contracted much more than desired and the economy went into a deep recession. The contraction in aggregate demand had to be arrested. Otherwise, the banking sector would have been burdened with increasing bad debt and the financial inter-mediation process would be disrupted.

The large current account surplus in the first half of 1998, which amounted to RM12.6 billion, was not well reflected in an increase in foreign reserves. Reserves declined by almost RM1 billion. This was due to the large net outflow RM13.8 billion in the private short-term capital account.[7] As confidence in the local bourse ebbed, the liquidation of stocks by foreign investors and the outflow of capital put further downward pressure on the ringgit and reduced foreign reserves. The outflow of funds was also due to the high offshore ringgit deposit rates of 20–40 per cent, which was a huge premium over domestic rates of about 10 per cent.[8]

The increase in interest rates had adverse consequences on the real sector as a result of the high level of domestic debt in the country. Borrowers saw their debt obligations rising and, together with the rise in cost of imported inputs, businesses soon experienced financial difficulties. Construction projects with high import content had to be deferred indefinitely. As the

---

[7] Under the item "errors and omissions", there was also a net outflow of RM6.5 billion, which may reflect short-term outflows that were not captured.

[8] Such high offshore rates offered for ringgit deposits were probably by currency traders who had sold the ringgit short and wanted to cover their forward contract obligations. Having made huge profits from the plunging ringgit exchange rate, they could afford to bid high for the ringgit deposits.

number of jobless persons rose, consumer sentiments turned bad. The collapse of the stock market reinforced this following the negative wealth effect. Furthermore, exports did not take off, contrary to what many analysts had expected. This was because external demand suffered as the crisis became more widespread in East Asia. The currencies of competing economies also depreciated, which made their exports cheaper as well.

Apart from the slump in aggregate demand, banks soon became more cautious in extending new loans, as they were concerned with protecting balance sheets. As a result, loan growth slowed down rapidly, further choking off even viable businesses. For the year 1998 as a whole, bank loan growth declined by 1.8 per cent, in sharp contrast to the increase of 26.5 per cent the year before. More loans turned bad as companies suffered cash-flow problems. The banking system's net NPL ratio more than doubled from 4.1 per cent of total outstanding loans as at end-1997 to 9.0 per cent at end-1998.

The impact on the economy was swift. Real GDP slumped to a 5.2 per cent decline (annual rate) in the second quarter of 1998. In the second half of the year the recession deepened. The contraction in real GDP was 10.9 per cent and 10.3 per cent in the third and final quarters of 1998 respectively. Hence for the year as a whole, the economy shrank by 7.5 per cent.

6.   CHANGE IN POLICY RESPONSE

By the middle of 1998, it became evident that the initial policy stance was becoming unsuitable. The exchange rate remained volatile and financial planning continued to be an impossible task under those circumstances. The sharp increase in interest rates raised the cost of capital and obtaining credit became a problem when banks became reluctant to lend. The stock market remained depressed as uncertainties kept investors away. Pursuing the current policy would have exacerbated the recession. Stability was needed but was not obtained from the present policies. It was increasingly clear that both monetary policy and fiscal policy needed to be more expansionary to restore stability. Only then can consolidation and reforms be carried out.

The central bank was faced with a policy dilemma. Due to external factors, exchange rates in the region were still extremely volatile. The capital account was also open, enabling funds to move freely out of the system and thereby contributing to even more downward pressure on domestic currencies. If maintaining or further raising interest rates to support the exchange rate was pursued by Bank Negara, it would have led to more difficulties for the cash-strapped business sector and resulted in a further decline in the economy. There is also considerable doubt that raising interest rates would be successful in perking up the ringgit. Had the economy gone into a steeper recession due to higher interest rates, the impact on sentiments on the ringgit would most likely have been adverse. More firms and individuals would have defaulted on their loan repayments and the banking sector would have had more bad debts. This would have severely constrained the banks' ability to function as financial intermediaries and that would have led to more difficulties for the economy.

On the other hand, had the central bank chosen to aggressively reduce interest rates to boost the economy and leave the exchange rate to the dictates of the market, it would still face potentially damaging consequences. The sharply lower interest rates would have led to capital outflows, putting further pressure on the ringgit's external value. External debt obligations would increase further and the costs of imported inflation grow higher. More investors would have liquidated their investments in the KLSE, thereby contributing further to the ringgit's fall. Expectations of a further plunge in the exchange rate would have driven importers paying in foreign currency to hedge their positions. That action would add further momentum to the plunge in the exchange rate. The end result could well be a major capital flight with foreign reserves rapidly depleted.

To enable interest rates to be reduced aggressively without adverse consequences on the exchange rate, the Malaysian authorities implemented selective capital controls on 1 September 1998. The next day, the ringgit exchange rate was fixed at 3.80 to US$1.00. The use of capital controls for troubled East Asian economies had been given attention by Krugman (1998), who had advocated its use under crisis conditions. Some important features of the capital control measures announced on 1 September are as follows:

a. It relates only to portfolio flows and does not affect foreign direct investment. As it pertains to FDI, foreign investors are free to repatriate profits, interest and dividends.
b. The ringgit was made non-legal tender outside Malaysia.
c. There are various restrictions to Malaysian residents bringing capital out of the country but for purposes of trade, there are no restrictions on the purchase of foreign currency.
d. The current account remains fully convertible.
e. A moratorium of one year was placed on all foreign portfolio funds in the country.

The measures were designed to insulate the economy from the volatile external environment. With the implementation of the measures, the central bank regained some measure of monetary autonomy. Indicating that the measures did not disrupt long-term (real) foreign investment, data for foreign investment applications in the manufacturing sector showed that in 1999, the value of such investment applications amounted to RM9.0 billion

Table 9.3 Malaysia: Gross Domestic Product by Demand Aggregate

(% change; 1987 constant prices)	1990	1991	1992	1993	1994	1995	1996	1997	1998	1999e
Public Consumption Expenditure	5.9	11.7	4.9	8.4	7.9	6.1	0.7	7.6	−7.8	15.3
Private Consumption Expenditure	11.9	9.0	4.7	6.3	9.4	11.7	6.9	4.3	−10.8	4.8
Gross Fixed Capital Formation	27.1	22.4	11.0	17.8	16.1	22.8	8.2	9.2	−42.9	−2.0
Public Investment	n.a.	n.a.	n.a.	n.a.	n.a.	n.a.	0.5	8.5	−8.7	14.1
Private Investment	n.a.	n.a.	n.a.	n.a.	n.a.	n.a.	11.3	9.4	−55.0	−18.5
Exports of Goods and Non-Factor Services	17.8	15.8	12.6	11.5	21.9	19.0	9.2	5.4	−0.2	5.1
Imports of Goods and Non-Factor Services	26.3	25.2	6.4	15.0	25.6	23.7	4.9	5.7	−19.4	4.4
Gross Domestic Product	9.0	9.5	8.9	9.9	9.2	9.8	10.0	7.5	−7.5	4.3

Note: 1999 Figures are official estimates from Economic Report 1999/2000, Ministry of Finance, October 1999.

Although lower than the amount of RM12.6 billion in the previous year, this is still a healthy amount, given the steep economic recession in 1998. Foreign investment approvals in the manufacturing sector for 1999 totalled RM12.3 billion, slightly down from RM13.1 billion in the previous year.

6.1 Monetary Policy Loosened

The capital controls allowed the central bank to loosen monetary policy to spur aggregate demand. This was also facilitated by easing inflationary pressures. The first step towards easing monetary policy was made in July when Bank Negara lowered the statutory reserve requirement (SRR) to 8 per cent. After 1 September, liquidity was augmented through a series of reductions in BNM's intervention rate and the SRR. As part of the expansionary monetary policy, credit terms were relaxed for purchasing property, shares and cars. Easier credit terms were also extended to small and medium sized industries and the lower income groups.

The various monetary measures taken to ease liquidity and encourage spending are summarised below:

- 1 July 1998: Statutory Reserve Requirement (SRR) reduced from 10 per cent to 8 per cent.
- 3 August 1998: Bank Negara Malaysia reduced 3-month intervention rate from 11 per cent to 10.5 per cent.
- 10 August 1998: The 3-month intervention rate further reduced to 10 per cent.
- 27 August 1998: A further reduction of the 3-month intervention rate to 9.5 per cent.
- 1 September 1998: Capital control measures implemented; SRR reduced by 200 basis points to 6 per cent.
- 1 September 1998: The Base Lending Rate (BLR) framework was revised. The BLR will be based on the 3-month intervention rate of Bank Negara instead of the previously used 3-month Kuala Lumpur interbank offer rate (KLIBOR). This is to ensure a more speedy transmission of monetary policy to the lending rates of banks. The flat administrative margin of 2.5 per cent was reduced by 25 basis points and the maximum margin

over the quoted BLR trimmed by 150 basis points to 2.5 per cent.

- 2 September 1998: Ringgit exchange rate with the US dollar pegged at RM3.80 = US$1.00.
- 3 September 1998: 3-month intervention rate cut by 150 basis points to 8.0 per cent; liquid asset requirement of commercial banks reduced by 200 basis points to 15 per cent of eligible liabilities.
- 7 September 1998: To boost the construction sector, various changes were announced to relax credit terms for purchasing property. These pertain to exemptions from loan ceilings and higher margin of financing.
- 16 September 1998: The SRR further reduced by 200 basis points to 4 per cent.
- 23 September 1998: To boost the stock market, the credit ceilings for loans to purchase stocks were raised for commercial banks and finance companies.
- 5 October 1998: The 3-month intervention rate lowered to 7.5 per cent.
- 9 November 1998: The 3-month intervention rate further lowered to 7.0 per cent.
- 20 November 1998: Minimum credit payment on credit cards reduced by 1,000 basis points to 5 per cent.
- 21 November 1998: The margin of financing of 85 per cent for hire-purchase loans for passenger cars was abolished. Banks can fix the percentage of financing based on its own credit assessment.
- 30 December 1998: Maximum finance charge per month for credit cards set at 1.5 per cent; late payment charges not to exceed 1 per cent of amount defaulted, with minimum penalty fee of RM5.
- 5 April 1999: Further reduction of 3-month intervention rate to 6.5 per cent.
- 3 May 1999: 3-month intervention rate cut to 6.0 per cent.
- 9 August 1999: Another cut of 50 basis points for the 3-month intervention rate to 5.5 per cent.

Interest rates dropped significantly following BNM's easier monetary policy. The benchmark 3-month inter bank rate declined to just above 3 per cent in mid-1999, from a peak of 11-plus per cent in May-July 1998. Bank

Negara's 3-month intervention rate, which was at a peak of 11 per cent for much of the first half of 1998, stands at just 5.5 per cent from August 1999. Following this, the base lending rate (BLR) of commercial banks dropped from 12.3 per cent in June 1998 to 6.79 per cent since August 1999. This sharp decline in interest rates to enable the recovery of economic activities without adverse consequences on the ringgit exchange rate would not have been possible without the capital controls.

<u>6.2 Expansionary Fiscal Policy</u>

With the real GDP figures showing a recession for the first two quarters of 1998, it was obvious that a more stimulating fiscal stance was needed. This is to make up for the decline in private sector spending. Thus in July 1998, the government allocated an additional fiscal stimulus package of RM7 billion as well as an Infrastructure Fund worth an initial RM5 billion. This brings the fiscal position of the government to a deficit of RM5 billion (1.9% of GNP), following five consecutive years of fiscal surpluses. Development expenditure increased by almost 15 per cent to RM18.1 billion.

The change in the stance of fiscal policy in 1998 can be seen clearly by analysing half-yearly data. In the first half of 1998, government expenditure fell by 34.4 per cent compared to the previous half-year. This follows the fiscal cutbacks implemented in October 1997 and additional measures introduced in December. However, in the second half of the year, after the change in the stance of fiscal policy, government expenditures rose sharply by 56.6 per cent.

To finance the deficit, the government borrowed RM12.9 billion (net), with domestic sources accounting for 86 per cent. This reversed six years of net repayment by the Federal government. At the end of 1998, the stock of total government debt outstanding was RM103 billion (39% of GNP) compared to RM90 billion (34% of GNP) the previous year. The external component of the debt in 1998 was 14.5 per cent and gross external borrowing of the Federal government totalled RM4 billion. This was financed mostly through multilateral agencies. An amount of US$300 million was obtained from the World Bank under a multilateral arrangement which was to be used to finance projects to revive the economy and as assistance to the more vulnerable groups of society. Another ¥74 billion was obtained from Japan, with a guarantee from the Japanese Ministry of International Trade and Industry. The government also obtained a syndicated foreign currency loan worth US$1.35 billion from 12 locally incorporated foreign banks in Malaysia.

The 1999 Budget proposed in October 1998 targeted a fiscal deficit of 6 per cent of GNP, further building on the fiscal stimulus of 1998. Priority was given to socio-economic and infrastructure projects that stimulate economic activities. Non-essential public spending was curbed to keep the fiscal deficit down. Government debt was kept at sustainable levels.

6.3 Financial Sector Restructuring[9]

Together with the expansionary monetary and fiscal policies enabled by the capital control measures, the government implemented a financial sector-restructuring programme. This programme was built around 3 important vehicles, namely Danaharta, Danamodal and the Corporate Debt Restructuring Committee (CDRC). Danaharta was formed to remove non-performing loans from the banking sector; Danamodal aims to re-capitalise ailing banks; the CDRC's objective is to enable a voluntary workout of corporate debt between borrowers and creditors so that viable companies are able to continue obtaining credit during the crisis.

The banking sector, although appearing strong at the onset of the crisis, nevertheless grew increasingly vulnerable as the crisis wore on. Higher interest rates and increasing import costs caused companies more financial stress. The number of bad loans in the banking system thus went up as the crisis was prolonged. Some banks with large bad debt saw their capital base eroded although the banking system as a whole was always adequately capitalised. Thus the financial inter-mediation process threatened to be disrupted. These problems had to be promptly and firmly addressed to support the economic recovery process.

---

[9] The progress of the various restructuring efforts detailed here is based mostly on Bank Negara Malaysia (1999b) and Danaharta (1999).

6.4 Danaharta

Danaharta performed an important function in cleaning up banks' balance sheets to enable them to continue their role in providing credit to productive economic activities. Having acquired selectively NPLs from banks, it aims to maximise the recovery value of these loans. Banking institutions with a gross NPL ratio of above 10 per cent had to sell eligible bad loans to Danaharta. So too do banks receiving capital injections from Danamodal. Danaharta operates based on market-driven guidelines. It buys NPLs from banks at fair market value. This very often meant that the bad loans were sold by the banks to Danaharta at discounted prices (and the selling bank incurred a loss). Danaharta's financing requirement was estimated at RM15 billion.

Danaharta's work is progressing well and is ahead of schedule. As at 30 June 1999, it had acquired or managed NPLs worth RM39.3 billion. (This compared with RM72.2 billion of gross NPLs, based on 3-months classification, in the banking system as at end-June 1999.) Of this total, RM17.8 billion were acquired NPLs and RM21.5 billion were under management. The Sime group has RM14.5 billion worth of NPLs under management by Danaharta while the Bank Bumiputra group has RM7.1 billion.

Reflecting the fact that these NPLs were purchased at fair market value, the overall weighted average discount on the acquired NPLs up to the end of June 1999 was 57 per cent. To pay for the NPLs, Danaharta issued RM9.2 billion in face value (present value of RM6.7 billion) worth of government guaranteed bonds and paid RM710 million in cash. Another RM173 million payment was still outstanding. Resulting from Danaharta's efforts, the net NPL ratio of the banking system moderated to 7.9 per cent (6-months classification) at end-July 1999, down from a peak of 9.0 per cent as at end-November 1998.[10]

---

[10]Based on a 3-month classification, the NPL ratio as at end-July 1999 was 12.4 per cent, from a peak of 14.9 per cent in November 1998. It has further declined to 11.9 per cent in October 1999.

Danaharta is now very much in the recovery stage of its operations. It has initiated recovery measures with about 60 per cent of the borrowers (based on value) and about RM1.0 billion was recovered. This included 23 accounts where full settlement was achieved. The recovered amount was 13 per cent more than the acquisition cost to Danaharta.

6.5 Danamodal

Danamodal, a wholly owned subsidiary of Bank Negara Malaysia, has a two-fold objective — to re-capitalise and strengthen the banking sector, and to consolidate it. The first of these objectives is met through injecting capital into ailing banks to beef up their capital adequacy ratio. The second objective is achieved through Danamodal's role as a strategic shareholder in re-capitalised institutions. Danamodal facilitates the restructuring process in these banks and serves as a catalyst in merger exercises. To qualify for Danamodal funding, banking institutions must sell their eligible NPLs to Danaharta and must be deemed viable by financial advisors of international repute.

Danamodal has estimated that its funding requirement will not exceed RM16 billion. This will ensure that the RWCR of the banking system will be at least 9 per cent. As at 30 June 1999, Danamodal had injected RM6.2 billion into 10 banking institutions. This was through ordinary shares, irredeemable non-cumulative exchangeable preference shares and long-term subordinated loans. To represent its interest, Danamodal has appointed nominees on the Board of the financial institutions. With the injection of funds by Danamodal, the risk-weighted capital ratio (RWCR) of the 10 banking institutions increased from 9.8 per cent as at end-August 1998 to 15.0 per cent as at end-April 1999.

The operations of Danaharta and Danamodal have no doubt contributed to the recovery process in that the strengthening of the banking system enabled the continued funding of economic activities. The prevention of wide-scale bad debt problems among banking institutions also helped avert possible loss of confidence in the system, which would have been catastrophic during a recession.

Much praise has been heaped on the way Danaharta and Danamodal have gone about performing their functions. Nevertheless, there appears to be certain areas of their operations, which could have been improved to address possible problems related to moral hazard. For example, in publishing details pertaining to its acquisition of NPLs, Danaharta provided only the names of the banks selling these bad loans and its value plus the discount rate. To enhance transparency, the selection criteria of Danaharta in terms of which companies qualify to have their bad debts purchased and the basis of such decisions should have been made public. The same levels of transparency should also be applied to the basis on which ailing banks were given the priority to receive capital injection by Danamodal.

6.6 Corporate Debt Restructuring Committee (CDRC)

The CDRC was set up to ensure that viable businesses facing problems as a result of the currency crisis would continue to have access to funding. The Committee provides an opportunity for borrowers and creditors to work out an amicable solution to debt problems mutually acceptable, without resorting to legal means.

As at end-June 1999, the CDRC had accepted 52 applications. Ten of these restructuring schemes involving debts amounting to RM10.2 billion had been completed and were being implemented. The CDRC expected to complete another 18 cases with total debts worth RM6 billion by end-July.

Special emphasis has been given to assist the small and medium sized companies in the restructuring process, especially Bumiputera entrepreneurs. In this regard, a Rehabilitation Fund for small and medium sized industries was established to provide funding at a lower cost to such companies facing NPLs and temporary cash-flow problems. As at mid-June 1999, the value of loans approved by this Fund was RM139.5 million.

In addition to the efforts by Danaharta and the CDRC, banking institutions have also set up Rehabilitation Units. These were to assist in rescheduling and restructuring loans, which have not been sold to Danaharta or referred to the CDRC.

6.7 Merger Programme for Banking Institutions

Malaysia is regarded by many industry analysts as "over-banked", with too many financial institutions operating and hence not able to tap economies-of-scale which is so essential in modern banking with intensive application of information technology or IT. The central bank has been urging banking institutions in Malaysia to merge in order to better face foreign competition when the financial sector is eventually opened up based on the GATS (General Agreement on Trade in Services) schedule. Nevertheless, progress on this front has been slow.

The slow progress in the banking institutions merger process is a source of concern. As a result, Bank Negara Malaysia had to step in to expedite matters. On 31 July 1999, the governor of BNM announced that six 'mega' core banking groups will be created from the existing domestic financial institutions. Each core-banking group will contain a commercial bank, a finance company and a merchant bank. There are currently 21 domestic commercial banks, 25 finance companies and 12 merchant banks.

Although bigger entities will no doubt be in a better position to compete, nevertheless the point has to be made that bigger does not necessarily mean better managed, which should be the focus of policy-makers. For example, in the recent currency crisis, there were several large financial institutions which ended up with huge NPLs due to weak management, such as Bank Bumiputra, Sime Bank and MBf Finance (see Merill Lynch, 1999). The authorities will definitely have to show more commitment in dealing with the issue of poor management of banks and the related moral hazard problem. In the case of government-owned Bank Bumiputra, it was the third time that the authorities had to step in to rescue it through injecting huge public funds. Although it is acknowledged that bank failures have potentially large negative externalities, it is clear that the lesson has yet to be learned by the respective banks' management. This sort of bad management can only be ingrained by the authorities' demonstrated willingness to step in when a bank was in trouble.

The six core banking groups originally identified by the central bank in the merger programme were Malayan Banking, Multi-Purpose Bank,

Bumiputera Commerce Bank, Perwira Affin Bank, Public Bank and Southern Bank. Despite the government's assertion that the choice of core banks was based on economic or business factors, some analysts remained sceptical, citing political motivations (Nikkei Weekly, 9 August 1999). Moody's Investors Service said that it believed the bank consolidation plan would strengthen the Malaysian banking sector in the long term but warned that "political considerations, which are a paramount factor in Malaysia, will significantly complicate and inevitably delay the process". In particular, some analysts question the choice of some anchor banks, which are much smaller in size compared to the banks that they are to absorb.[11]

Not surprisingly, the choice of the six anchor banks by BNM was met with some resistance (New Straits Times, 5 October 1999). Some banks were reported to be unhappy over the "arranged marriage" and lobbied to be an anchor bank instead.[12] On 20 October 1999, after weeks of speculation within financial sector circles, the governor of Bank Negara Malaysia, acknowledging "some strong objections on certain aspects of the programme", announced that "all banking institutions ... will now be given the flexibility to form their own merger groups and to choose their own leader in each group to lead the merger process".[13]

The banking institutions were then required to report back to the central bank on their respective merger groupings, as well as an agreement in principle from major shareholders, by end-January 2000. Following this, Bank Negara announced on 14 February, that it had approved 10 banking groups (in effect, giving anchor bank status to all 10 parties which had submitted

---

[11]A case in point is Multi-Purpose Bank, a small bank that was to absorb five commercial banks, four finance companies and two merchant banks. This list included RHB Bank, the third largest commercial bank in the country that is four times the size of Multi-Purpose, as well as MBf Finance which is the largest finance company. From its present modest position, Multi-Purpose will become the second largest local banking group after Malayan Banking following the proposed merger (Business Times, 30 September 1999).

[12]These were said to be the larger banks like Hong Leong Bank, Arab-Malaysian Bank and RHB Bank.

[13]Bank Negara Malaysia (1999c).

merger plans).[14] The entire merger plan is to be completed by the end of 2000, with each banking group to attain minimum shareholders' funds of RM2 billion and an asset base of at least RM25 billion.

There are two major concerns following the announced speeded-up merger plan by BNM. The first is the question of redundancy in terms of staff. With the distinct possibility of both the acquiring bank and the acquired bank having branches in the same or nearby locality, some amount of retrenchment of workers will be inevitable. This "branch redundancy" is most likely in major urban centres such as the Klang Valley where most big businesses are located and where bank branches are more heavily concentrated. It has been estimated by the bank workers' union that the number of bank staff likely to be displaced will be around 15,000 although the authorities have been very cautious in the matter and said that the displaced workers should be re-deployed to minimise the adverse impact.

The second concern that the merger process raises is that it may slow down the loan disbursement process of banks, especially those being acquired. Industry observers say that the integration process may take a minimum of two years (Business Times, 30 September 1999). There are already concerns that banks, anxious to protect their balance sheets, are over-cautious in extending credit following the steep recession of 1998. The merger process may accentuate this problem as the banks being acquired are likely to slow down lending activities due to the uncertainty of its future. In fact, the government had earlier noted this problem in the context of the merger programme for finance companies announced in January 1998 by BNM.[15] The government noted that the merger programme, "while intended to rationalise the finance companies to increase their resilience, was untimely". "This policy further restricted the supply of credit, aggravating the liquidity problem as finance companies involved in such merger exercises stopped their lending operations temporarily to focus their efforts on the merger

---

[14] Apart from the original six chosen anchor banks, the additional four are RHB Bank, Arab Malaysian Bank, Hong Leong Bank and EON Bank. See Bank Negara Malaysia (2000).

[15] See *Box 1 — The Wrong Turns Taken During the Initial Stage of the Crisis*, White Paper on the Status of the Malaysian Economy 1999, p. 25.

process." But the problem may be potentially less this time around as the financial institutions are on a better footing with the economy recovering, a large portion of the NPLs having been taken out of the books of financial institutions by Danaharta and Danamodal having injected funds to re-capitalise ailing banks. However, it means that BNM must monitor the situation closely and actively use moral suasion to get banks to lend more. However, as at December 1999, loans in the banking system had declined by 4.8 per cent compared to a year ago.

7. THE PRICE OF CAPITAL CONTROL

The capital control measures imposed in September 1998 will no doubt bring about both positive as well as negative effects. The discussion thus far highlighted the benefits in the short term. These include enabling the RM-USD exchange rate to be fixed, thus bringing about exchange rate stability; restoring a large degree of monetary autonomy and allowing interest rates to be lowered in order to halt the steep economic recession; and enabling a "window of opportunity" or "breathing space" for the authorities to implement reforms and stabilisation programmes in the financial sector. These positive effects restored confidence among Malaysians as well as foreign direct investors in the country.

This section reviews the costs of capital controls. The adverse effects include the immediate dilution of foreign interest in the Malaysian equity market. But foreign fund managers who liquidated their portfolios in the local equity market then were initially prevented from repatriating their funds out of Malaysia by the one-year holding rule for foreign portfolio capital. (This ruling was subsequently relaxed in February 1999 and replaced by a graduated exit levy.) The KLSE was also removed from the MSCI (Morgan Stanley Capital International) indices as the selective capital controls restricted the free movement of capital in and out of the country. There would have been hardly any foreign portfolio inflows between September 1998 to February 1999.

There is also the argument that the sudden implementation of the selective capital control measures and one-year holding rule for foreign portfolio capital demonstrates policy uncertainty which adds to the question of credibility. But economists such as Krugman said that the fact that these measures were implemented under crisis conditions raises the prospect of similar measures being put in place in the future and this in itself should be a deterrent against future (excessive) speculative flows into the country. However, the imposition of such capital controls has also penalised all other funds (even long-term investors) and has left a question mark on the issue of future policy direction. That in itself may mean reduced future portfolio inflows, including the longer-term investors, but only time can tell. Even prior to the end of the one-year holding period for portfolio capital on 1 September 1999, in mid-July up till the end of the year, net outflow of foreign portfolio capital totalled about US$2.4 billion. Nevertheless, this amount was significantly lower than the US$4–5 billion outflow predicted by many.

It is clear that the capital control measures and the fixing of the ringgit exchange rate against the US dollar is only a short-term measure in response to the crisis. In the longer term, keeping the exchange rate fixed will bring about problems such as misallocation of resources, especially with the economic recovery gaining momentum and the economy getting closer to its potential level. The widely perceived under-valuation of the ringgit at 3.80 to the USD will provide the wrong signal to economic agents and exporters may be lulled into a false sense of competitiveness in international markets. The government had said many times in the past that the September 1998 measures were only implemented as a policy response under extreme crisis conditions. It is imperative that it stands by this commitment and, at the opportune time, revert to a market-determined exchange rate as well as allow its residents to freely invest their capital abroad. But some measures need to be retained in containing excessive influence by currency speculators, such as limiting access to the ringgit in international currency markets.

8.   RECOVERY

With monetary policy relaxed following the capital control measures, the lower interest rates saw improved liquidity. Credit cost became lower and business and consumer sentiments improved gradually. The MIER surveys on both business and consumer sentiments showed marked improvement in the since the first quarter of 1999. Other indicators supported this improved outlook in the economy. Private consumption indicators such as sales and production of passenger cars, imports of consumption goods and sales taxes showed improvement after the first quarter of 1999. As conditions in the labour market steadied, retrenchment numbers dropped and job vacancies rose from late 1998. Real GDP contracted by a much smaller 3.1 per cent (annual rate) in the first quarter of 1999. In the second quarter, it turned around after five quarters of decline to register a growth of 4.1 per cent. This was followed by a growth of 8.1 per cent in the third quarter of the year.

The government forecast real GDP growth of 4.3 per cent for the whole of 1999.[16] Growth will be mainly generated by public sector expenditure, both consumption and investment, as well as net exports. The private sector is still expected to remain subdued, except for the export-oriented industries. While private sector consumption is forecast to show a modest growth of 4.8 per cent following a double-digit contraction in 1998, private investment is anticipated to continue dropping by a hefty 18.5 per cent in 1999, on top of the phenomenal slump of 55 per cent in 1998. With the export sector doing well, the current account balance is forecast to register a bigger surplus of RM42 billion in 1999, compared to RM36.8 billion in 1998. This amounts to 15 per cent of nominal GNP (13.7 per cent in 1998).

Inflationary pressures, which peaked around the middle of 1998, moderated significantly by the first quarter of 1999. The consumer price index (CPI) increased by 6.2 per cent (year-on-year) in June 1998 but by March 1999 had slowed down to a growth of 3 per cent. CPI inflation

---

[16]This forecast was made in October 1999, when the Minister of Finance presented the 2000 Budget in Parliament (see Ministry of Finance, 1999). However, most private sector forecasts put growth at a higher range.

declined to 2.8 per cent for the whole of 1999. Producer price inflation showed a similar trend. It peaked around June 1998 at 15.4 per cent before subsiding quickly by year-end to slightly over one per cent, reflecting the weak domestic demand. In 1999, producer prices declined, with the local component dropping at a faster pace compared to the import component.

Following the enforcement of the one-year holding period for foreign portfolio investments and the ban on Malaysians repatriating money abroad (except for trade and other purposes allowed by Bank Negara Malaysia), short-term capital flows stabilised in the final quarter of 1998. The foreign reserve position better reflected the current account surplus, with net international reserves rising from US$20.2 billion in August 1998 to US$31.1 billion in June 1999. At the end of December 1999, foreign reserves stood at US$30.9 billion, sufficient to finance 6 months of retained imports.

The more stable economic environment following the September 1998 measures saw confidence gradually returning among foreign investors and market analysts. This was reflected in the improved credit rating for the country and the sharp upward adjustment in economic growth forecasts for 1999. The sovereign standing of the Federal government was never in doubt as the issuance of US$1 billion worth of bonds in May 1999 showed, with over-subscription by 3 times. Indicative of growing foreign investor confidence, there has also been a sharp improvement in Malaysia's sovereign bond spread, which narrowed to 240 basis points from 330 basis points when the bonds were first launched.[17]

As the economic recovery took root, adjustments were made to the selective capital control measures. When the capital control measures were first implemented, foreign portfolio investments were required to remain in the country for a period of 12 months. On 4 February 1999, that rule was modified. Foreign investors were allowed to repatriate profits subject to a graduated levy (between 10–30 per cent).

There was further change announced on 21 September 1999. The central bank said that the change was in response to feedback from fund managers who complained that the previous format of two-tier levy posed administrative

---

[17]National Economic Action Council (1999).

problems. The former regulation required portfolio funds that came into the country on or after 15 February 1999, to pay levy on any profits made depending on the date of repatriation: 30 per cent if repatriated within a year and 10 per cent if repatriated after a year. This was changed to a flat rate of 10 per cent on profits made through portfolio investments, regardless of when the profits are repatriated. With the change in regulation, all profits from funds brought in on or after 15 February 1999 pay a flat levy of 10 per cent, and there will no longer be any levy paid on the principal.

There was much interest in observing portfolio fund movement on 1 September 1999. With effect from that date, portfolio funds that entered Malaysia on 1 September 1998 or earlier can be repatriated without any levy. Cumulative data on net inflows as of 15 February 1999, showed that by early January 2000, there was a net outflow of some RM4.5 billion. The cumulative net inflow actually started to decline steadily from 16 July when it was at a peak of RM4.7 billion. Thus, between these dates, the net outflow of funds actually amounted to about RM9.2 billion (US$2.4 billion). Bank Negara had estimated that there was possibly a total of US$5–7 billion of foreign funds in the local exchange. Given that, the amount of net outflow is not alarming or destabilising at present, considering the country's foreign reserves of US$30.9 billion as at end-December 1999. However, the situation has to be monitored closely. But the trend appears to be reversing in the first quarter of 2000, as the cumulative net inflow showed a smaller negative number of –RM1.6 billion as at 26 January, indicating some RM2.9 billion worth of net inflow in that month. This is probably due to the foreign interest in the KLSE ahead of its full re-inclusion in the MSCI indices in May 2000.

9. CONCLUSION

Despite early tentativeness and scepticism about the capital control measures, it had brought much stability to the economy. That enabled recovery measures and reforms to the financial sector to be implemented speedily. To complement the expansionary fiscal policy, monetary policy remained easy in 1999, facilitated by the absence of inflationary pressures. Growth in 1999 is estimated to be in the range of 4–5 per cent, spurred mainly by public sector spending and growth in net exports. There is still excess capacity in the economy and as such private investment remained somewhat subdued.

As economic recovery gains further pace, the selective capital controls will need to be further liberalised. This is in line with the country's longer-term objective of further developing and strengthening its capital market and financial sector. Thus Malaysia will need to regain the standing that it once had in the international financial markets. Some form of capital controls relating to short-term flows though will likely remain, probably in the form of taxes.

The present task for policy-makers is to encourage more consumers spending as well as to persuade banks to increase lending to productive sectors of the economy. But to boost private consumption, it should not be done through providing easier credit terms to consumers but instead by augmenting disposable income, for example through tax cuts. Providing easier credit terms may encourage consumers to spend beyond their means and can later result in higher default of loans. While the slow pace of loan growth is a serious concern, nevertheless the banking institutions should not be compelled to increase loans at the expense of prudence.

The currency crisis which began in 1997 showed that there were indeed some weaknesses in the Malaysian economy which resulted in it being vulnerable to a currency attack. This had led to some self-fulfilling panics and also exposed the economy to certain risks as the crisis became protracted. The result was a steep recession and increased stress on the banking sector, given the high loan exposure of the economy at the onset of the crisis. But it is also clear that domestic factors alone cannot satisfactorily explain the extent of the depreciation of the ringgit and especially the speed of its plunge. There are defects in the international financial system. This is particularly so in the area of the lack of an effective surveillance mechanism for short-term capital flows and inadequate transparency regarding the operations of large hedge funds. There is also a need to design an internationally accepted framework for prudential supervision of banking institutions, with common standards across countries. Proper tools and processes are essential in assessing financial risks. That there is, up to this point, a lack of sense of urgency particularly among the developed countries in studying the likely defects of the international financial system with the view of addressing these shortcomings is most distressful. Many noted analysts and economists have cautioned that a repeat of the crisis cannot be ruled out.

On the related important question of moral hazard, it has to be looked at from both the lenders' and borrowers' side. There is little doubt that the issue of moral hazard is at the core of many problems faced by the crisis-hit economies, as government guarantees, be they implicit or explicit, contributed to reckless behavior by the corporate and banking sectors. But the adjustment programmes suggested by institutions such as the IMF should not be tailored towards raising money in the crisis-hit countries to repay foreign banks. These banks acted on their own in extending large sums of credit to the affected economies as they were not able to correctly judge the underlying risks. The response of the IMF is seen as an implicit guarantee to the (mostly developed country) creditors and thus raises the question of moral hazard. Stiglitz (1998) recently highlighted the fact that the moral hazard problem has got worse on the side of the lenders.

Another lesson to emerge from the East Asian crisis is that the heavy involvement of governments in the private sector, while having its benefits, can result in undesirable outcomes if the necessary checks and balances are weak. A worthwhile goal of reforms, therefore, is to create a business environment with a clear division between government and business. A vibrant entrepreneurial class honed through greater competition should be nurtured, not one that is protected instead. Jomo (1998) noted that Malaysia is now "forced by the forces of economic liberalisation to interface competitively with the world economy". Although the currency crisis has shown the need for some form of co-ordinated international intervention in some situations, economic liberalisation involves many benefits. The phenomenon of globalisation cannot be turned back at this point. Together with the benefits will come risks. Countries will have to minimise the likelihood of these risks occurring through pursuing sound policies and enhancing informational flows through greater transparency. Well informed markets have less tendencies for making errors in their judgement and the huge costs to all parties can be averted. Malaysia's future as an open, export-driven economy lies in its ability to take advantage of the opportunities that globalisation affords. This should be done through the correct policies that strike a balance between domestic objectives with options that result in greater openness and encourage keener competition. Only then can the country aspire to be a truly global competitor in international markets.

References

Ariff, Mohamed, Michael Meow-Chung Yap, Wan Abdul Kadir Azidin, Gaik-Ean Ong and Elaine Lae-Imm Tan (1998a), *Currency Turmoil and the Malaysian Economy — Genesis, Prognosis and Response,* by Malaysian Institute of Economic Research; Prinforce (M) Sdn Bhd, Kuala Lumpur.

Athukorala, Prema-chandra (1998), *Malaysia,* chapter in "East Asia in Crisis: From Being a Miracle to Needing One?", eds. Ross McLeod and Ross Garnaut; Routledge, London.

Bank Negara Malaysia, *Monthly Statistical Bulletin,* various issues; Kuala Lumpur.
_______ (1999a), *Annual Report 1998,* March; Kuala Lumpur.

_______ (1999b), *Progress of Banking Sector Restructuring,* Press Release, 14 July; Kuala Lumpur.

_______ (1999c), *Domestic Banking Sector Consolidation Programme,* Press Release, 20 October; Kuala Lumpur.

_______ (2000), *Consolidation of Domestic Banking Institutions,* Press Release, 14 February; Kuala Lumpur.

Business Times (1999a), *Guidelines on Pricing of Mergers,* edition of 23 August; Kuala Lumpur.

______ (1999b), *A Bold Consolidation of the Malaysian Banking Sector*, edition of 30 September; Kuala Lumpur.

Danaharta (1999), *Operations Report, Half-year Ended 30 June 1999*; Kuala Lumpur.

Garnaut, Ross (1998), *The East Asian Crisis*, chapter in "East Asia in Crisis: From Being a Miracle to Needing One?", eds. Ross McLeod and Ross Garnaut; Routledge, London.

Gomez, Edmund T, and K S Jomo (1997), *Malaysia's Political Economy: Politics, Patronage and Profits*; Cambridge University Press, Cambridge.

Jomo, K S (1998), *Malaysia: From Miracle to Debacle*, chapter in "Tigers in Trouble: Financial Governance, Liberalisation and Crises in East Asia", ed. K S Jomo; Zed Books, London.

Krugman, Paul (1998), *Saving Asia: It's Time to Get Radical*, Fortune magazine, edition of 7 September, pp. 33–38.

Malaysian Government (1999), *White Paper on the Status of the Malaysian Economy (1999)*, released 6 April; Malaysian Government Printers, Kuala Lumpur.

Merrill Lynch (1999), *Industry Consolidation — Searching for Order Amidst the Chaos*, 13 August; Kuala Lumpur.

Ministry of Finance (1997a), *The 1998 Budget Speech*, 17 October; Kuala Lumpur.

______ (1997b), *Ministerial Statement on "Strategic Measures to Strengthen the Economic and Financial Stability of the Nation" at the Dewan Rakyat*, 8 December; Kuala Lumpur.

______ (1999), *Economic Report 1999/2000*, October; Kuala Lumpur.

National Economic Action Council (1999), Response to Michael Alan Hamlin's Opinion-Editorial "Myth vs. Reality in Malaysia", *Far Eastern Economic Review, 21 October 1999*, NEAC Statement, 20 October; Kuala Lumpur.

New Straits Times (1999), *Arab-Malaysian, Hong Leong Could Be On Their Own*, edition of 5 October; Kuala Lumpur.

Nikkei Weekly (1999), *Malaysia Orders Banks to Consolidate*, edition of 9 August.

Stiglitz, Joseph (1998), *Boats, Planes and Capital Flows*, Financial Times, edition of 25 March.

Yap, Michael Meow-Chung (1997a), *Sustaining Economic Growth: The Increasingly Important Role of Total Factor Productivity*, Box article no. 1, in "Malaysian Economic Outlook: 2nd Quarter 1997 Update", Malaysian Institute of Economic Research; MIER, Kuala Lumpur.

______ (1997b), *Potential Output of the Malaysian Economy: Initial Estimates*, Box article no. 1, in "Malaysian Economic Outlook: 4th Quarter 1997 Update", Malaysian Institute of Economic Research; MIER, Kuala Lumpur.

______ (1999), *Financial Crisis in Malaysia: Adjustment Through Unorthodox Policy*, paper presented at the "Malaysia Forum", Economics Division, Research School of Pacific and Asian Studies, Australian National University, Canberra, 24 June.

CHAPTER 10

INDONESIA

INDONESIA'S RESPONSES TO THE RECENT ECONOMIC CRISIS

Anwar Nasution

*Faculty of Economics, University of Indonesia
Depok 16240, Jakarta, Indonesia
E-mail: anwarn@bi.go.id*

1. INTRODUCTION

The crisis hitting Indonesia after August 1997 is a combination of political and economic crisis. The economic crisis itself was a mix of banking and external debt crisis mainly centered on debt in the private sector. This paper argues that the recent financial crisis in Indonesia was caused by a number of factors. The first principle factor was the excessive short-term external borrowings in the corporate sector, with greater part not invested in the productive sectors. The distorted product and financial market structures prevented them from being efficiently used. As a result, the external loans were not invested in ways that could have generated stream of export earnings necessary for repayments. The second factor lay in the banking sector. The reform in the financial sector was not carried out with strict implementation of the rules and regulations governing the financial system. Moreover, the liberal 'entry policy' in the financial sector was not accompanied with a clear-cut 'exit policy'. In addition, there was a pervasive lack of confidence in the government partly ignited by the confusing government policies.

The financial crisis broke out in Indonesia at an appropriate time. On the domestic front, the weather-related catastrophe caused by long drought and forest fire in 1997 and 1998 had brought about severe damaging effects in its forestry and agriculture sectors. The crop production fell by 1.8% and the agriculture production growth dropped to 0.6% in 1997. On the external front, there was a combination of negative terms of trade and drain in capital inflows. Fall in oil prices and low demand for Indonesia's exports (such as wood-based products) reduced ita foreign exchange revenues. The price of oil in 1998 was the lowest in the decade. The fall in oil prices reduced Indonesia's export revenues by US$4 billion and the fall in prices of non-oil export commodities by another US$3 billion in 1988. Meanwhile, the economic difficulty and slow growth in Japan and Korea drew away capital inflows from them.

The economic problem was magnified by a political uncertainty and flip-flop government policy. Angered by rising prices and unemployment, violent riots erupted in a number of towns, thus leading to the resignation of President Suharto, who was re-elected for the seventh term in March 1998. However, his departure did not clear away the political uncertainty in the country. The newly appointed President Burhanuddin Jusuf Habibie (and members of his cabinet), known as protege of Mr. Suharto, was a man of no strong political base but a reputation of a big spender. The relatively peaceful general election in June 1999 and a smooth presidential election in 1999 did not put an end to the political instability. It is more difficult for President Abdurrachman Wahid (who came to power on 20 October 1999) to consolidate the power of the present coalition government due to the rigorous transition process to democracy and prevalent sectarian violence and regional tensions.

The IMF should be partly responsible for aggravating the crisis. First, it recommended closing of the banks in November 1997 with no adequate preparations. Sharp devaluation of the rupiah, high nominal interest rates and tight liquidity together pushed the already fragile banks and their customers to bankruptcy. The credit crunch and austere fiscal policy led to economic contraction which brought about high social costs in terms of eroding real wages and high unemployment rates. Second, the IMF made a monumental shift towards recommending fiscal stimulus, creation of social safety net and solution of external debt overhang not until April 1998. Consequently, the slash in the government expenditures magnified the domestic economic recession.

This paper reviews the economic meltdown in Indonesia, its cause and impacts, and the response of the government. Apart from this introduction, the paper is divided into five sections. Section 2 examines the recent macroeconomic development prior to the crises. Section 3 discusses the banking crisis. Section 4 analyses policy responses to cope with the capital inflows since the early 1990s, followed by an analysis of the stabilization and adjustment program in Section 5. Lessons from Indonesia's experience and policy recommendations are dealt with in the last section.

2. WEAK MACROECONOMIC FUNDAMENTALS

Indonesia is indeed in need of adjustment particularly because of its weak economic fundamentals and changes in the international environment that began in 1995. On the domestic front, the massive capital inflows and the change in its composition more towards short-term private sector capital since the early 1990s had caused overheating in the economy of the country. The rapid economic growth had brought about a rise in domestic inflation and interest rates, and widening of current account deficit (Table 10.1). Low inflation rate and high growth of GDP and non-oil exports, often quoted as indicators of sound economic fundamentals of Indonesia, were largely artificial. The government paid expensive subsidies in control of prices of state-vended products and thereby the inflation rate was controlled to below 10% per annum between 1990 and 1996.

The high GDP growth during the 1990s was mostly associated with the 'bubble' industries, including construction, public utilities, services in non-traded sector of the economy. Moreover, the growth of non-oil exports during the 1990s mostly consisted of those sectors which, like electronics, sport shoes and textiles and garments, relied the least on domestic inputs but were associated with firms from East Asia (mainly Japan, South Korea and Taiwan)

Table 10.1 Indonesia: Selected Key Indicators, 1990–1999

(in percent of GDP, unless otherwise indicated)

	Annual Average 1980's	1990's	1990	1991	1992	1993	1994	1995	1996	1997	1998	1999*
Internal Stability												
Gross Domestic Product												
Real GDP (% of growth rate)	6.6	5.2	9.0	8.9	7.2	7.3	7.5	8.1	8.0	4.6	-13.6	-1.7[1]
a. Tradable Goods (%) [2]	n.a.	5.2	8.5	9.3	4.5	6.2	9.5	8.5	9.1	5.2	-8.4	-0.3
b. Non–Tradable Goods (%) [3]	n.a.	3.6	6.4	5.3	7.8	6.7	6.5	7.9	7.3	4.5	-16.6	-2.7
GDP/Capita (USD)	n.a.	697	577	630	686	763	911	1016	1136	672	575	718
Consumption	73.4	67.8	63.7	63.9	62.0	67.5	65.1	69.1	70.3	70.4	78.3	79.6
Private	63.0	59.2	53.9	54.0	52.2	58.5	56.5	61.0	62.7	63.1	70.9	n.a.
Government	10.4	8.6	9.8	9.8	9.8	9.0	8.6	8.0	7.6	7.3	7.4	n.a.
National Saving	n.a.	27.7	27.5	26.9	26.9	27.0	28.4	28.0	29.3	28.0	n.a	n.a.
Private	n.a.	20.5	19.1	19.8	20.5	20.4	22.0	22.4	23.0	17.2	n.a.	n.a.
Public	n.a.	7.3	8.4	7.1	6.4	6.6	6.4	5.6	6.3	10.8	8.0	n.a.
Investment	23.8	29.3	30.1	29.9	29.0	28.3	30.3	31.3	32.7	31.0	20.9	18.9
Private	13.5	22.6	23.5	21.7	20.9	20.9	24.0	25.8	27.4	25.0	14.0	n.a.
Public	10.3	6.6	6.6	7.7	7.8	7.4	6.3	5.5	5.3	6.0	6.9	n.a.
Inflation (CPI)	8.5	16.4	9.5	9.5	4.9	9.8	9.2	8.6	6.5	11.6	77.6	10.6
Fiscal Balance	n.a.	0.1	0.4	0.4	-0.4	-0.6	0.1	0.8	0.2	-0.2	n.a.	n.a.
External Stability												
Current Account Balance	-1.2	-2.4	-2.8	-3.7	-2.2	-1.6	-1.7	-3.6	-3.7	-2.7	0.1	10.9
Real Effective Exchange Rate (1997 =100)	44.1	113.5	95.1	93.2	90.8	85.6	82.5	80.1	78.0	100.0	315.8	101.4
Nominal Exchange Rate / CPI (1997 = 100)	65.1	114.0	111.3	107.7	104.2	97.7	93.2	88.6	85.5	100.0	238.1	431.6
Net Capital Inflows	1.9	-2.3	4.9	5.0	3.8	1.7	2.0	4.0	5.4	-1.1	0.1	-20.6
Of which:												
Net Direct Investment	2.1	1.2	1.0	1.3	1.4	1.0	0.8	1.9	2.5	2.1	-0.7	-4.1
Net Portfolio Investment	0.3	-0.9	-0.1	0.0	-0.1	1.1	2.2	2.0	2.2	-1.2	-14.4	-4.3
Other Capital	n.a.	-1.6	3.3	3.6	3.5	1.4	-0.9	1.2	0.1	-0.2	-26.1	-12.2
Net Error and Omissions	-0.5	-1.0	0.7	0.1	-1.0	-1.9	-0.1	-1.1	0.6	-1.8	-4.6	0.1
Net Resource Transfer / GDP (1997 = 100)	-60.8	-99.5	-100.1	-86.1	-535.6	-749.0	-309.7	396.3	198.5	100.0	190.3	-329.3
Reserves (in months of imports)	5.1	5.1	4.7	4.8	5.0	5.2	5.0	4.4	5.1	4.4	7.3	10.6
Ratio M2 to Reserves (%)	345.7	556.4	514.0	539.0	552.6	602.3	643.4	690.3	638.6	419.9	407.5	289.4
Total External Debt	n.a.	72.0	65.9	68.4	69.0	56.7	55.5	54.8	49.3	101.4	127.1	n.a.
Total External Debt (in percent of exports of goods and services)	n.a.	218.1	222.0	236.9	221.8	211.9	197.4	197.4	188.7	255.0	232.2	n.a.
Short Term Debt (in percent of total external debt)	n.a.	22.1	15.9	17.9	20.5	21.0	19.6	22.2	27.1	27.2	27.2	n.a.
Short Term Debt (in US$ billion)	n.a.	24.9	11.1	14.3	18.1	18.8	21.1	27.6	35.0	37.0	41.0	55.5
Debt-Service Ratio (in percent of exports of goods and services)	15.3	36.4	30.9	32.0	33.0	33.6	32.6	30.3	35.9	40.5	58.6	51.6
Exports of Goods & Services (in percent of GDP)	14.9	25.6	25.1	28.1	30.2	26.8	26.9	27.2	27.1	27.5	11.5	n.a.
Exports of Goods (% of growth rate)	5.9	12.1	15.9	13.5	16.6	8.4	8.8	13.4	9.7	7.5	15.4	-8.7[1]
IM (1997 = 100)	n.a.	122.7	112.0	123.4	131.7	134.6	136.9	165.0	175.4	100.0	24.9	n.a.

Note: * Up to third quarter of 1999.

   1) Compare to that of third quarter of 1998.

   2) Comprise of Non-food Crops, Forestry and Fishery, Mining and Quarrying, and Manufacturing Industries.

   3) Comprise of Farm Food Crops, Livestock & Products, Electricity, Gas, and Water Supply, Construction, Trade, Hotel, and Restaurant, Transportation & Communication, Financial, Ownership & Business, and Services.

Sources: IMF, *International Financial Statistics*, various issues. Bank Indonesia, *Indonesian Financial Statistics*, various issues. BPS, *Statistics of Balances of Central Government*, 1999. BPS, *Indonesian Statistics*, various issues.

with strong currencies. In contrast the domestically owned sectors or sectors that relied heavily on domestic inputs fared poor. The non-traded sector of the economy and 'foot loose' industrial produce were low-value added. The slow down in the increase of export revenue from the export of palm oil and wood-based products was partly due to the quotas imposed on these products. As discussed earlier, the decline of revenues from oil and non-oil exports was also due to the fall in their prices.

2.1 Exchange Rate Movements

The exchange rate is the single most important relative price in the economy. In a more open economy, monetary transmission operates through exchange-rate effects on net exports and interest rates effects on financial portfolio. The exchange rate policy[1] in Indonesia and other policies had traditionally been mainly used to remove distortions in the domestic economy and to help safeguard international competitiveness. Until recently, the authorities have avoided the use of prolonged nominal and real exchange rate overvaluation as a principal instrument for generating fiscal revenues and curbing domestic inflation and interest rates. To offset the 'Dutch disease' effect of the oil boom, in November 1978, the authorities devalued the rupiah by 50 percent against the US dollar and replaced the US dollar as its external anchor with an undisclosed basket of major currencies and moved to a managed floating exchange rate system. Prior to August 1997, the weight of the US dollar in the currency basket had remained substantial. In a normal situation, the authorities targeted nominal depreciation of the rupiah against the dollar between 3–5% per annum. Bank Indonesia, the central bank, intervened in the foreign exchange market by buying and selling the rupiah in an 'intervention band' around the central rate. If the system had been supported by other policies, such an active policy to stabilize real exchange rate would have helped avoid major macroeconomic crises even when the world economic environment proved hostile.

---

[1] The exchange rate policy includes devaluation, speeding up depreciation of the rupiah, widening the intervention band and raising transaction costs in the foreign exchange markets.

Before shifting to the present flexible exchange rate regime, Bank Indonesia had tried to defend the moving band system from the speculative attacks by widening the intervention band to 12% effective from July 1997 (Figure 10.1). Introduced in 1992, such a system was defended through sterilization operations by selling foreign exchange both in forward and spot markets. In theory, such a greater exchange rate flexibility should have induced uncertainty that might have well discouraged part of the purely speculative capital flows and allowed higher degree of freedom for the monetary authorities to exercise control over monetary aggregates. To support these policies, the authorities had also introduced a wide array of tight monetary policy along with administrative measures to limit external borrowings by commercial banks, discourage short-term capital inflows while

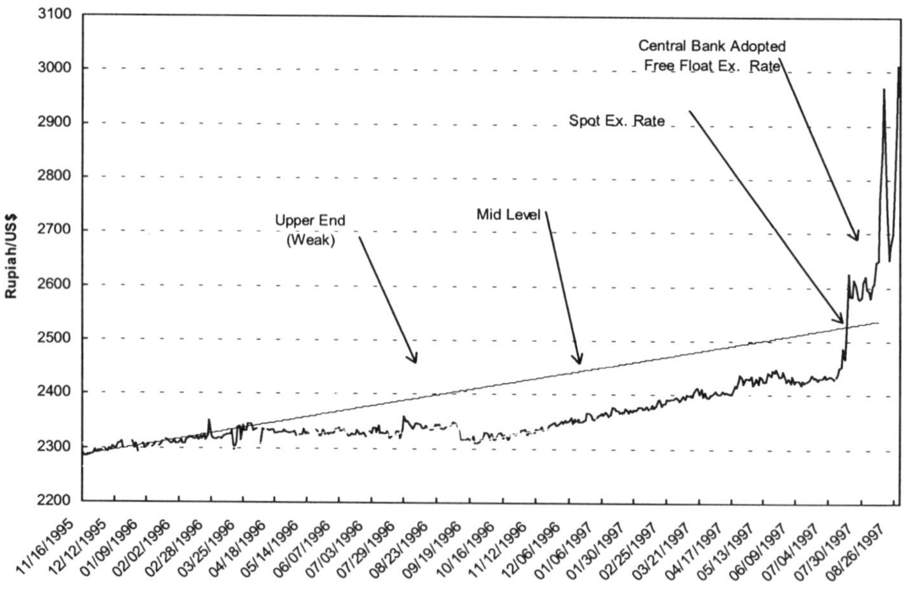

Fig. 10.1 Indonesia: Rupiah Exchange Rate and its Intervention Bands (November 1995–August 1997)

Source: Bank Indonesia, *Indonesian Financial Statistics*, various issues.
University of British Columbia Data Base, Canada.

maintaining open access to the economy for long-term capital, particularly FDI. As the authorities allowed temporary slight appreciation of the rupiah, the policy should also have reduced the need for sterilization of the surge in capital inflows. At the end, the Bank of Indonesia had to abandon the moving band system to defend its foreign exchange reserve position.

Figure 10.2 shows a steady appreciation of the effective exchange rate of the rupiah between 1990 and 1996, indicating a slight change in government policy with respect to exchange rate. The rupiah appreciation was also due to the rising value of its main external anchor, the US Dollar, *vis a vis* the Japanese yen. The rupiah appreciation helped reduce inflation rate and interest rate in 1996. It, however, eroded external competitiveness of the economy, distorted savings and investment decisions, and squandered the scarce savings upon unproductive investment projects to impede the efficiency of the economy at micro level. The decline in inflation rate, on the other hand, had helped stabilize the rupiah appreciation.

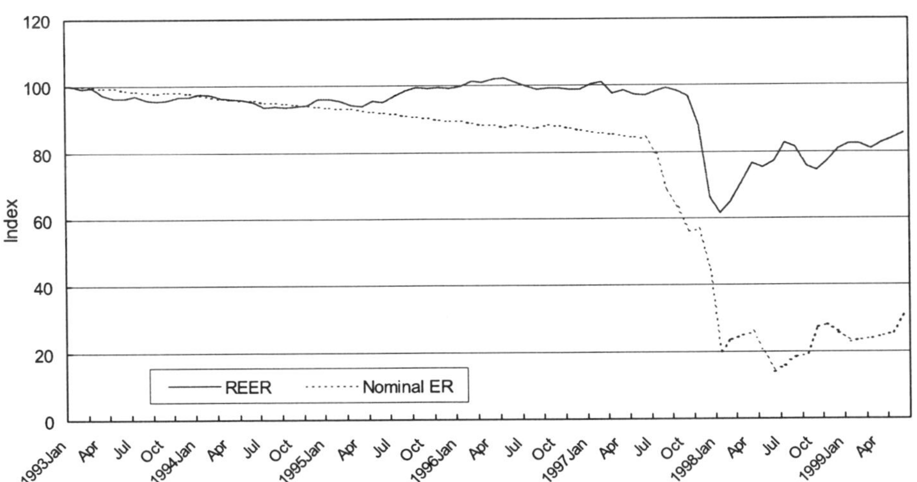

Fig. 10.2 Indonesia: Norminal and Real Effective Exchange Rate 1993–1999 (USD/Rp = 100)

Note: The declining of index means Rupiah depreciates.
Source: JP Morgan Web-site, Real Broad Effective Exchange Rate.
Bank Indonesia, *Indonesian Financial Statistics*, various issues.

2.2 Widening Current Account Deficit

Annual GDP growth in 1993 and 1994 remained below 2% levels and the current account deficit rose to 3.6% in 1995 and 3.7% in 1996. This deterioration did not reflect higher investment alone. Table 10.1 shows that the widening current account deficit between 1990 and 1996 was the result of an increase in overall investment — from 30.1% to 32.7 % of GDP. One of the links was the banking system, which converted part of the increased liquidity into loans to finance investment, including those in land-based industry (hotel and tourist resorts, amusement and industrial parks, real estates, commercial buildings and shopping malls), excessive infrastructure and other non-tradables. Most of the private debt had been directly borrowed from foreign lenders with only a small fraction of it through the banking system.

Part of the capital inflows was, probably, used for financing consumption expenditure. This is partly shown by a slight decline in savings rate in the national account data. In addition, there was a marked increase in the number of credit cards issued and volume of transactions through them. In the fiscal year 1996/97 ending in March, the number of credit cards rose to 1.6 million or up by nearly 30% as compared to 28% in the preceding year. In the same year, the value of transactions handled through credit cards amounted to Rp4.7 trillion or up by over 35% as compared to 22% in the preceding year. As of now there are 17 banks and 84 finance companies (operating with 40,000 merchant outlets throughout the country) are licensed in credit card business.

The widening external deficit was not due to irresponsible fiscal behavior. Greater tax effort, tightening of fiscal policy and improvement in the operation of state-owned enterprises together reduced government budget deficit and increased public sector savings. While formally maintaining the 'balanced budget principle', in reality, the government had been running an annual budget surplus somewhere between 0.2–0.8% of the GDP since the fiscal year of 1993/94[2] . Evidence suggests that the Ricardian equivalence issue —

---

[2] This is lower than the fiscal surplus of 2% of GDP as suggested by the World Bank (1996).

which points to the possibility that the increase in public savings will be offset by a decline in private savings — has been relatively limited in Asean region, including Indonesia (Faruqee and Husain, 1995). The increase in public savings immediately raised national savings, thus helping reduce inflation and interest rate and the current deficit. Lower interest rate differential slowed down capital inflows. As a result, the widening of tax base, removal of egregious marginal tax rates and significant improvements in the efficiency of tax administration and operations of the public companies made an important contribution to enhancing fiscal flexibility, stabilizing domestic aggregate demand and improving external competitiveness.

On external front, the current account balance improved somewhat mainly because of the immediate impacts on the expenditure cut and depreciation of the rupiah on import reduction rather than from increasing exports. The lack of confidence precipitated a rush, panic buying and capital flight that led to both internal and external liquidity crunch and sharp increase in velocity of money. The imports had been restrained, as foreign banks became reluctant over rollover short-term debts and acceptance of letters of credit for Indonesia. The fear for further currency depreciation caused greater pressure on the exchange rate and interest rate. Government decisions to limit access to foreign borrowings and to shift public sector deposits from (mainly state-owned) commercial banks to the central bank squeezed liquidity. With banks suddenly short of liquidity, the risks of default by corporate borrowers and bankruptcies also increased. The fact that Bank Indonesia moved, in mid August 1997, to floating exchange rate system suggests that it had limited external reserves to defend the exchange rate.

The yen depreciation vis a vis the US dollar since 1995, accompanied with continuing weakening of the banking system in Japan slowed down inflow of Japanese foreign direct investment to Indonesia. Capital flows from NIEs also dried up due to slow growth of their exports and strains in their financial system and companies (in the case of Korea). The rise in interest rate and investment returns in the United States further reduced capital inflows, as they made investments in emerging countries, including Indonesia, less attractive. The combination of these internal and external factors began to ignite an interruption and reversal of foreign capital inflows.

2.3 External Debts

Mainly due to the surge in private sector direct borrowings, the total amount of external debts of Indonesia rapidly rose from US$66.9 billion in 1990 to $151 billion in December 1998 (Table 10.2). This level of external debt was alarming by world standards. The World Bank considers a debt to GNP ratio of more than 80% as high risk. In terms of total debt service to exports, the World Bank considers 18% the 'warning' threshold. The stock of external debts of Indonesia in December 1998 amounted to around 308% of export value and 321% of its annual GDP. The debt service ratio was ranging between 30–34% and the interest payment alone amounting to 12% of total exports between 1990 and 1996.

Over 55% of the external debt in December 1998 (US$83.6 billion) was owed by the private sector and over 80% of it was received by non-banking corporate entities. The average maturity of this external debt was approximately 1.5 years (J.P. Morgan, *Global Data Watch*, 16 January 1998, p. 70). In addition, there were short-term external debts denominated in local currency amounting to US$15 billion. Since the late 1960s, the external borrowing strategy of the public sector has been consistently maximizing the inflow of concessionary development aid from its non-socialist Western and Asian creditors. The 'oil boom' in the 1970s did not change this strategy. With the resulting rise in real income, the oil boom only shifted Indonesia's position to a less concessional aid package. When encountering the problem of rising debt repayments following the currency realignment in 1986, Indonesia also turned to its creditors, particularly Japan.

2.4 Inflation Rates

Figure 10.3 depicts the rapid rise in inflation rates since the beginning of economic crisis in August 1997. Following the crisis, the inflationary pressures came from five factors. First, the rapid growth of money supply was partly used for financing the larger budget deficit and propping up the financially distressed banks. Second, the erosion of public confidence in economic management and the fear in banking insolvency encouraged capital flight, panic buying and advance purchase of consumer goods, bank run and

Table 10.2 Indonesia: External Debt Outstanding, 1989–1999

(million USD)

	1989	1990	1991	1992	1993	1994	1995	1996	1997	1998	1999*
External Debt Outstanding	51,974.7	62,820.6	65,697.2	73,358.9	80,591.8	96,500.1	107,831.9	110,170.8	134,794.3	150,886.1	142,415.2
Public Sector	39,576.9	45,100.2	45,724.7	48,768.7	52,461.4	58,615.6	59,588.2	55,302.6	53,865.0	67,328.2	70,786.0
Private Sector	12,397.8	17,720.4	19,972.5	24,590.2	28,130.4	37,884.5	48,243.7	54,868.2	80,929.3	83,557.9	71,629.2
The Structure of Private Sector External Debt (%)											
By Debtors											
1. Banks	**6.4**	**14.8**	**17.1**	**23.4**	**27.6**	**21.7**	**20.9**	**16.5**	**17.7**	**12.9**	**13.4**
- State-Owned Banks	3.4	6.4	7.0	10.3	11.1	7.3	8.0	5.4	7.3	5.7	6.0
- Private Banks	3.0	8.4	10.2	13.1	16.5	14.4	12.9	11.1	10.4	7.2	7.4
2. Non-Bank	**93.6**	**85.2**	**82.9**	**76.6**	**72.4**	**78.3**	**79.1**	**83.5**	**71.2**	**80.8**	**82.1**
- State-Owned Enterprise	26.0	17.6	16.8	18.4	18.0	13.4	10.0	6.8	4.9	5.0	5.8
- Foreign Investment Enterprise	26.4	26.4	25.8	22.7	21.2	25.3	27.0	29.9	29.0	38.8	41.8
- Domestic Investment Enterprise	23.0	23.0	22.5	19.8	18.5	22.1	23.5	26.1	20.4	24.1	21.3
- Financing Institution	3.9	3.9	3.8	3.3	3.1	3.7	3.9	4.4	4.2	2.5	2.2
- Others	14.4	14.4	14.1	12.4	11.6	13.8	14.7	16.3	12.6	10.4	10.9
By Maturity											
- Short term	6.9	6.9	6.9	6.9	6.9	6.9	6.9	6.9	6.1	6.5	6.6
- Long term	93.1	93.1	93.1	93.1	93.1	93.1	93.1	93.1	82.8	87.2	88.9
Memo items :											
1. Share of Government Debt to Total Debt (%)	76.1	71.8	69.6	66.5	65.1	60.7	55.3	50.2	40.0	44.6	49.7
2. Share of Private Debt to Total Debt (%)	23.9	28.2	30.4	33.5	34.9	39.3	44.7	49.8	60.0	55.4	50.3
3. Share of Total Debt to Real GDP (%)	36.7	43.2	44.6	48.4	51.2	59.1	63.6	62.5	99.4	396.2	n.a.
4. Share of Total Debt to Export (%)	234.5	244.7	225.4	216.0	218.9	240.9	237.4	221.2	252.2	308.9	n.a.

Source: Bank Indonesia, Recent Economic Indicators, various issues.
Note: *As of August 1999.

flight from currency to speeding up the velocity of money. Third, the depreciation of the rupiah raised prices of traded goods, including imported goods. Fourth, merchandise was in short supply, including foodstuff due to import compression and harvest failure. Fifth, the prices of state-vended products were adjusted up[3] . The efficiency and productivity gains from the structural reforms were not powerful enough to check these upward inflationary pressures.

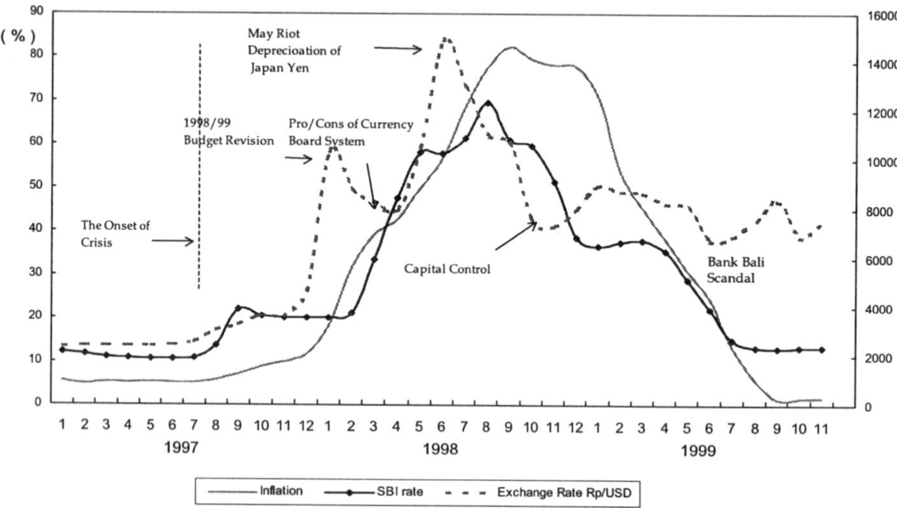

Fig. 10.3 Indonesia: Inflation, One-Month SBI Rate and Exchange Rate 1997–1999

3.   BANKING CRISIS

The indicators of banking system fragility are presented in Table 10.3. In terms of total assets and number of offices, the system used to be the core

---

[3] The increases announced on May 4, 1998 were: gasoline 71%; kerosene 25%; diesel for cars and trucks 58%; diesel for factories 39%; fuel for generator sets 46%; electricity 20%; bus fares (non-airconditioned) 67%; mini-bus fares (metro mini) 50%; and train fares (within Jakarta) 104%; and train fares (inter-city) 50%. Due to widespread demonstration, some of these were reversed on May 15.

of the financial sector in Indonesia (Nasution, 1996). Banking industry played an important role in the economy as the main source of external financing for the corporate sector in Indonesia. Traditionally it adopted a financing strategy of high debt-equity ratio. As a result, the rise in interest rate and credit crunch due to troubles in the banking system had precipitated a collapse in trade and production and aggravated an already unfolding recession as traders and producers could not get credit lines to purchase goods and inputs required in production process.

On the other hand, the faltering economic activity, the sudden depreciation of the rupiah, the high interest rates and bank run dealt a devastating blow to the financial system. Banks were short of liquidity because of client's withdrawals of deposits and Bank Indonesia's policies to support the rupiah by cutting-back base money supply. Indonesian banks, prior to the crisis, had received, borrowed and deposited and made loans denominated in foreign currency (primarily US dollar). The sharp devaluation of the rupiah shifted many of these loans into 'the non-performing category' and yet nothing had been done to relieve them of their foreign currency obligations to their lenders and depositors.

3.1 Surges in Capital Inflows and Lending

The banking reforms caused an 'over-stretching' of the banking system as shown by the rising loan-to-deposit ratio (LDR) and excessive credit expansion by the banking system. Following the reform in the banking sector, LDR of the banking system rapidly rose from 106% in 1988 to 129% in 1992 and peaked at 240% in 1994, 1995 and 1996 (Table 10.3), much higher than the maximum allowable LDR ratio of 110%. On average, credit outstanding of commercial banks rose by over 24% per annum between 1992 and 1997, more than three times over the average annual rate of growth of the economy during the same period. The average annual growth rate of bank loans was also much higher than that of the manufacturing industry, the most dynamic sector of the economy.

The rapid growth of credit expansion of the banking system was induced with the adoption of such measures as lifting restrictions on bank lending

Table 10.3 Indonesia: Banking Sector Indicators, 1985–1999

	1985	1986	1987	1988	1989	1990	1991	1992	1993	1994	1995	1996	1997	1998	1999[a]
Number of Banks	114	110	109	108	145	171	192	208	234	240	240	239	222	222	167
Private Banks	69	65	64	63	88	109	129	144	161	166	165	164	144	130	80
State–Owned Banks [1]	5	5	5	5	5	7	7	7	7	7	7	7	7	7	19
Foreign Banks and Joint Venture Banks	11	11	11	11	23	28	29	30	39	40	41	41	44	58	41
Regional Development Banks	27	27	27	27	27	27	27	27	27	27	27	27	27	27	27
Loan to Deposit Ratio (%)	102,9	96,3	101,9	105,7	112,6	118,2	130,7	129,3	132,4	134,9	137,7	131,0	123,7	129,2	80,7
LGR Minus GDPGR (%)	14,7	19,8	8,8	23,1	31,2	48,1	-9,9	7,7	6,9	5,7	4,0	4,7	12,1	45,5	-42,6
LGR Minus IPGR (%)	29,0	20,8	35,9	34,4	44,2	61,4	9,0	25,9	22,4	16,0	23,1	22,5	16,2	45,1	n.a.
NFL to TBL (%)	-20,0	-23,6	-18,2	-14,1	-10,6	0,9	0,7	2,2	4,9	5,8	3,8	2,8	5,2	2,6	6,4
M2 Multiplier [2]	3,4	3,4	3,8	5,0	5,4	6,7	7,7	7,0	7,8	7,4	8,0	7,5	7,6	7,7	8,2
M2/Forex Reserves (%)	414,2	415,4	367,5	481,5	597,2	596,8	539,0	552,6	602,3	643,4	690,3	638,6	419,9	407,5	549,1
M2/GDP (%)	n.a.	n.a.	n.a.	n.a.	n.a.	43.0	43.6	46.4	44.0	45.7	49.0	54.2	56.9	58.3	n.a.
Non–Performing Loan [3] (%)	n.a.	n.a.	n.a.	n.a.	n.a.	n.a.	9,2	n.a.	14,2	12,1	10,4	8,8	14,0	49.2	39.0
of which: Bad Debt (%)	n.a.	n.a.	n.a.	n.a.	n.a.	n.a.	1,7	n.a.	3,3	4,0	3,3	2,9	2,3	23,4	28,5
Cash Assets to Deposit Ratio (%)	15,9	13,3	12,4	14,5	11,1	6,5	13,7	3,2	2,6	2,5	2,6	4,7	5,8	8,2	7,5
Loans to Assets Ratio (%)	n.a.	53,3	58,2	61,5	65,4	73,4	76,2	73,7	75,4	80,3	79,2	77,0	71,9	70,9	66,7
Credit in USD to Total Credit (%)	n.a.	n.a.	n.a.	n.a.	n.a.	12.2	15.6	17.9	19.4	19.1	19.5	19.9	30.8	35.8	34.2
Dollar Deposits to M2 ratio (%)	n.a.	n.a.	n.a.	n.a.	n.a.	20.6	21.2	20.8	21.7	21.7	19.8	19.5	31.1	24.8	21.3
EL to TL in USD (%)	n.a.	n.a.	n.a.	n.a.	n.a.	9.1	7.4	12.0	12.8	8.3	5.7	4.0	6.1	21.1	11.5

Note: LGR: Loan Growth Rate; GDPGR: GDP Growth Rate; IPGR: Industrial Production Growth Rate; NFL: Net Foreign Liabilities; TBL: Total Bank Liabilities.
EL: Excess Liquidity; TL: Total Liquidity.

1) Including 12 banks take over by IBRA-Indonesian Banks Restructuring Agency, as of June 1999.

2) Ratio of M2 to Reserve Money.

3) As percentage of total loan outstanding of Commercial Banks. Non-performing loan data are tend to be underestimated. The decline of non-performing loan to 8.8 percent of total credit in 1996 was mainly due to write-off of the bad loans at State-owned commercial banks and private 'non-foreign exchange' banks. As end of March 1998, bank non-performing loan reached over 70% of total loan for several banks.

a) Data as of June 1999.

Sources: IMF, International Financial Statistics, various issues. Bank Indonesia, Annual Report, various issues.

and deregulation of asset portfolios, lowering reserve requirements, market opening, privatization, and greater access to offshore markets. The presence of new entrants in a more competitive market environment might well increase the pressures on banks to engage in riskier activities. Yet the bank credit officers reared in an earlier controlled environment probably had no such expertise as needed to evaluate new sources of credit and market risk. When the economy was booming, it was difficult to distinguish between good and bad credit risks because most borrowers looked profitable and liquid. Lifting restrictions on bank lending immediately expanded credits to land-based industry and excessive infrastructure projects. Part of this credit expansion was financed with foreign borrowings. In addition, the surge in private capital inflows relative to the size of equity market drove up the equity prices.

The reform in the financial sector in 1988 relaxed requirements for domestic banks to deal in foreign exchange transactions and open branch offices overseas. It also allowed greater penetration of foreign banks in domestic economy and larger ownership of foreign investors on domestic assets. Moreover, the new rules and regulations replaced the administrative ceilings on offshore borrowings of commercial banks with a more rational system of net open position. Along with privatization, the authorities in 1997 abolished the limits for inflow of FDI and foreign ownership of equities issued in domestic stock markets. Prior to the recent reform, Indonesia, in 1971, adopted a relatively open capital account and managed unitary exchange rate[4]. Under the new system, there was no surrender requirement for export proceeds or taxes or subsidies on the purchase or sale of foreign exchange. Indonesian citizens and foreign residents were free to open accounts either in the rupiah, the national currency, or in foreign currencies at the authorized banks (*'bank devisas'*). These banks were authorized to extend credits in foreign exchange in the domestic market.

---

[4] The open capital account system was partly adopted because Indonesia has no effective and efficient bureaucracy to administer the capital control. Singapore, the regional financial center, is located right in the middle of the archipelagic country of Indonesia which consists of more than 17,000 islands.

To encourage internal foreign investment, between January 1979 and December 1991, a special effective exchange rate was made available to domestic borrowers by providing an explicit subsidy on the exchange rate. The subsidy was extended through the exchange rate swap facility. Under this facility the Bank of Indonesia provided forward cover to foreign exchange borrowing contracts swaps to banks and NBFIs, and to customers with foreign-currency liabilities. The subsidy came about because of the time lag in either an upward adjustment of the swap premium or a nominal depreciation of the rupiah, or combination of both.

Herd behavior of foreign investors also had a role to play in increasing capital inflows and outflows to and from Indonesia. They did buy securities, commercial papers and even real estates and invested in excessive infrastructure projects. The reform, covering nearly all aspects of the economy, combined with the perception of Indonesia as a stable country and one of Asia's success stories, had generated a massive capital inflow since the early 1990s. Demand for securities issued by Indonesian (state-and private-owned) companies rose sharply as foreign investors were allowed to own up to 49% of the listed shares issued by domestic companies (except banks). The latter were also allowed to raise funds by selling securities in domestic and international stock and bond markets.

Capital inflows were encouraged further as domestic interest rates (adjusted for relatively limited actual exchange rate movements) rose and were sustained through the 1990s. Peregrine, a Hong Kong-based investment bank, collapsed in early January 1998 due to a single massive bad loan ($265 million) to PT Steady Safe, a local taxi company in Jakarta. Steady Safe used US$145 million to buy 14% of a toll road building company owned by Ms. Siti Hardiyati Rukmana (Tutut), the eldest daughter of President Suharto. She was then named to Steady Safe's board ("The hunt is over", *Time*, January 26, 1998, pp. 14–16).

During the past quarter of the century since 1969, the economy had grown on average by 6–7% a year, with an annual per capita GDP growth of over 4%. Non-oil GDP (covering the economic sectors toward which most capital inflows were directed) grew by 7.7% annually between 1991 and 1995. Along with this rapid economic growth, the number of population living in absolute poverty fell to 15% in 1990 from 29% in 1980 and 60% in 1970. The rapid economic growth had coincided with a major shift in the structure of the economy from the one highly dependent on a small group of primary commodities, particularly oil and natural gas, to one with a wider range of primary commodities and manufactured products. The development strategy, which promoted investment and non-oil exports, was partly reflected in the large share of capital goods and raw materials as a proportion of total import of goods and services. The increasing openness of the economy to international markets and the broadening base of export raised the capacity of the economy to service external debt as the debt service absorbed a lower fraction of total exports. Moreover, diversification of non-oil export products significantly reduced the vulnerability of its export revenues to commodity price swings.

3.2 Increasing Bank Liabilities with Large Maturity/Currency Mismatches

Liberal capital account, financial sector reform and advances in technology and information processing made it easier for Indonesia to alter currency composition of deposits. A number of indicators pointed to rising percentage of debt instruments denominated in foreign currency, particularly the US dollar. These included the higher ratios of: broad money (M2) to GDP, the dollar deposits as percentage of M2, credit in dollar as percentage of total credit and excess liquidity of commercial banks held in the US dollar (Table 10.3). As emphasized by Calvo (1994) and Mishkin (1997), this makes it more difficult to manage both the banks' portfolio and macroeconomy. Pursuing an expansionary policy, for example, is likely to cause a devaluation of the rupiah and a rise in inflation rate.

When domestic interest rates were high, there was a strong temptation to denominate debts in foreign currency. *Bank devisas* (a licensed bank to deal in foreign exchange transactions) turned to short-term, foreign-currency-denominated borrowing in the interbank market to fund longer-term bank loans. The ratio of external liabilities of the commercial banks to their assets rose from 9.5% in 1993 to over 18% in March 1998. The ratio of net external liabilities to total liabilities rapidly rose from −14.1% in 1988 to

0.7% in 1991, 5.8% in 1994 and 5.2% in 1997. External borrowings of financial sector in Indonesia rose from US$6 billion in 1993 to US$12.1 billion in 1995, and down to US$11 billion in 1996 and to US$10.1 billion in mid-1997[5]. All of them indicate higher exposure of the banking system to foreign exchange risks.

Partly because of historically predictable and low rate of the rupiah depreciation, a large portion of the external debt was hedged. This not only made banks and their customers more vulnerable but also made it more difficult for such problems as banking crisis, rise in interest rate and sharp devaluation of the rupiah to be dealt with. Sharp depreciation of the rupiah had deteriorated the balance sheets of the banks and firms because a greater part of their debts were denominated in foreign currencies. The substantial fall of the value of the rupiah against the dollar rapidly raised the cost of renewing or rolling over the short-term floating rate dollar or yen loans in real terms. The indebtedness of Indonesian banks and firms rose and their networth fell. Vulnerability of banks increased in line with the decline in their capacity to absorb negative shocks because of the mismatch of the currency and maturity. The rise in interest rates caused the rise of the interest payment and deterioration in balance sheets of the banks and their customers as a result.

The risks of maturity mismatches were even higher for the unlisted banks, which had no access to mobilization of long-term sources of funding (by selling bonds, shares and other types of securities) in stock markets. Selling equity in stock markets could spread or cause risk sharing. The risks were higher as most companies in Indonesia had relied exclusively on bank loans for financing with land as the main collateral of the credit. Only a handful of them had supplemented bank finance with equity offerings. The high loan to value ratio of bank loans to companies, such as property developers, exposed the Indonesian banks to sharp decline in real estate prices. This and the plunge in equity prices depressed the market value of collateral and assets of the banks. Thus the liquidity problem became more

---

[5] J.P. Morgan. 1997. *Emerging Markets Data Watch*. July 1. page 3 and *Global Data Watch*, 16 January 1998, p. 70.

serious with no securitisation of mortgages and absence of market for government bonds.

3.3 Weak Financial Positions Of Banks And Highly Concentrated Problem Loans

Liberalization of the banking industry will surely produce long term benefits for Indonesia. In the short run, however, deregulation inevitably presented banks with new risks which, without proper cautions, had led to the current banking crisis. Despite a relatively high economic growth of 6% plus per annum since 1990, the problems of bad loans in the national banks had seemingly deteriorated significantly. Economic crisis and improvements in tbe accounting system had pushed up the ratio of non-performing loan (NPL) from below 10% in 1997 to over 50% in the first quarter of 1999 (Figure 10.4). The rising NPL drove up operating costs of the banks. To cover the immediate losses from the NPL, banks were required to accumulate provisions until they could recover part of the credits or to write them off from the balance sheet. The high NPL also caused a negative spread between lending and deposit interest rates.

The NPL problems were more severe at state-owned banking group and non-'foreign exchange' banks. Traditionally, the state-owned banks (in control of over two-thirds of the assets of the commercial banks) were undercapitalized. The low capital requirements in the past were hardly enforced on this group of banks because of presumption that the state would stand by its banks and insolvency of the state-owned banks would be carried through to the fiscal balance. The state-bank group was the main provider of credit programs with subsidized interest rates during the past long era of financial repression. This group of banks was the main victim of erratic government policies, such as shifting of public deposits from them to the central bank. Each of the four banks (PT Bapindo, PT Bank Bumi Daya, PT Bank Dagang Negara and PT Bank Eksim), now merged into one PT Bank Mandiri, was technically insolvent as the amount of its bad loans was much greater than that of its capital.

Fig. 10.4 Indonesia: The Development of Non-Performing Loan (NPL) 1997–1999

Source: Bank Indonesia

Overstaffing and overextended branch networks were more prevalent for the state-owned banks for their being protected from closure on constitutional ground and their losses covered by the public budget. They were intended for lower incentive for innovation, promptly identification of problem loans and control of cost at an early stage. As risks of state-owned banks were assumed by the state, the lending skills (including risk appraisal) of the officers of these banks were generally weak. Their loan loss performance was usually inferior to that of their private counterparts. Likewise, both physical infrastructure (such as computer system) and human resources of the state-owned banks were inferior to that of their private counterparts.

The financial position of private sector banks was not much better, either. Many of them did not meet the capital adequacy ratio and the legal lending limits regulations, which restricted the aggregate amount of loans and advances to insider, namely, a single borrower (person or firm) or a group of borrowers[6]. It was reported that that, on average, over one half of the loans provided by private banks were given to companies in the same groups. Over 90% of the loans of PT BDNI *(Bank Dagang National Indonesia)* and PT Danamon, two large private banks, were channeled to their own groups. Such large group lending with relaxed monitoring and enforcement of discipline to their customers to stay liquid reduced the franchise value of the private banks.

3.4 Heavy Government Involvement in Selection of Credit Customers

Despite privatization, the six state-owned banks (Bank Bumi Daya, Bank BNI, Bank Exim, Bank Rakyat Indonesia, Bapindo and Bank Tabungan Negara) still retained significant percentage (over 30 percent) of the bank assets in Indonesia. This figure would be even higher if computed under a broad definition of indirect ownership as Bank Indonesia, state-owned banks, line ministries and various branches of the armed forces also owned banks. The banking system with relatively high percentage of state ownership shows greater intrusion of the political objectives of the government on almost all aspects of bank operations including personnel and technology policies. Concurrently, such a banking system also shows greater recourse to the public financing of bank bailouts.

For decades, loan decisions of state-owned banks were subject to explicit or implicit government directions. All too often, creditworthiness of the borrowers received no sufficient weight in credit decision, with the result that loans of the state banks only served as vehicles for extending government assistance to particular industries and a handful of politically well-connected business groups. These groups of large companies - the conglomerates – controlled a large proportion of the GDP and vast range of mainly rent-

---

[6] Through networks of ownership, and business and management interlocking all of domestic private banks are closely connected to large business conglomerates. The collapse of a number of large conglomerates since 1990 indicates that certain sectors within conglomerates could become burdensome, in part because of their strategy of being highly leveraged, which may have been suitable in the past era of subsidized interest rates and highly protected domestic markets (Nasution, 1995, pp. 185–86).

seeking activities. Deregulation did not end the government intervention in lending decisions of state-owned banks and financial companies. This is shown in the direct interventions of the government in providing credits to Mr. Edi Tansil, PT Timor Putra Nusantara and PT Texmaco, which happened even after the banking reform and allegedly it was decided by those that had promoted the reform.

3.5 Bad Governance

Along with the market liberalization, the reform in the financial sector also adopted, in February 1991, a more restrictive CAMEL (capital adequacy, asset quality, management, earning, and liquidity) system to regulate and supervise banks. Indonesia adopted a set of rules and regulations on legal lending limits to limit loans extended to banks' insiders (owners or managers and to their related businesses). The implementation of the prudential rules and regulations was, however, very weak.

The poor implementation of the prudential rules and regulations was partly due to structural weaknesses in the legal and accounting systems. The regulators and bank managers did not have sufficient personnel to supervise and examine the fast-growing number and expanding powers of financial institutions. In an autocratic political system like in Indonesia, there was a principal-agent problem as regulators might operate more in the interest of the rulers than in the interest of the people as their principal. The cases of commercial papers issued by PT Bank Pacific, PT Bank Arta Prima and PT Bank Perniagaan indicate even fraud and collusion were involved with the bank supervisors at Bank Indonesia, the central bank. Four bank supervisors of Bank Indonesia were arrested in early August 1997 for allegedly having received bribes while making inspections during 1993–1996 period (*the Jakarta Post*, August 28, 1997). As indicated earlier, the corrupt officials might have been involved in the use of Bank Indonesia's funds to buy shares of the problem banks. They might have provided low cost and low risk liquidity credits to such troubled banks. Under-regulated banks led to excessive investment by the economy as a whole (McKinnon, R.I. and Pill, H., 1966). Moreover, no private banks, belonging to business conglomerates, exercised tough rules and regulations on affiliated companies, particularly as they could expect assistance from the central bank. Attaching collateral, a costly and time-consuming process, thereby reduced the effectiveness of collateral in solving adverse selection (Mishkin, 1997).

3.6 Lender of Last Resort

At present, there is no deposit insurance scheme in Indonesia. Bailout program to provide support to domestic banks in facing financial problems was introduced in February 1998. Prior to this, however, Bank Indonesia had provided support programs on an ad-hoc and non-transparent basis, including capital injection, liquidity credit and emergency financial assistance. To strengthen primary (Tier I) capital of commercial banks, Bank Indonesia acquired shares of problem banks and provided them with equity capital. The rapid growth of Bank Indonesia's supports to distressed banks was reflected in the rapid growth of claims of monetary system on the private sector, inclusive of claims of the central bank on commercial banks.

Weak market infrastructure, misfeasance, malfeasance and malversation together allowed certain individuals to misuse their banks, such as swindling deposits of the general public, equity share and liquidity credit from the central bank or the public sector, issuing fake commercial papers and obtaining offshore borrowings, without proper back-up, for financing questionable projects owned by bank owners, usually, at inflated prices. Liabilities of such banks were mainly deposits owned by the general public, liquidity credit from Bank Indonesia and unsecured commercial papers sold to the general public (including foreigners) and equity shares owned by Bank Indonesia and other state-related institutions. The latter included state-owned pension funds (*PT Taspen*-civil servants' pension fund) and insurance companies (such as *PT Jamsostek*-workers' social insurance), pension funds and other financial resources self-administered by state-owned enterprises and their cooperatives. Networth of such typical bank (assets minus liabilities) was really negative.

The newspaper reports indicated that financial problems of the recently suspended banks had been existing for a long period of time. Their survival was only based on new injection of financial resources from the central bank. The reports also indicated that Bank Indonesia was only acting as the lender of last resort to state-owned banks and to the politically well connected institutions. Other state-owned enterprises (such as *PT Taspen*, which manages the state pension funds, and *PT Jamsostek*, which manages social security insurance programs) were also under the direction of the government to invest and place deposits in banks and enterprises owned by the politically well connected conglomerates. Providing distressed banks with funding from the lender of last resort (and sources of funding from other public sector) on a continuous basis often committed Bank Indonesia and the public sector to lend money to institutions that had no capital. And yet the owners of such institutions had no incentive to use the new money wisely because they had nothing at risk. Aside from providing equity capital and credit, Bank Indonesia also arranged merger, consolidation, and takeover of problem banks either by stronger institutions or new investors.

To keep the insolvent banks afloat, Bank Indonesia injected liquidity credit to the financially distressed banks during the period of August 1997 to early 1998. The liquidity was sterilized by issuing SBI — Bank Indonesia's certificate of deposit (Figure 10.5). The sterilization operations and the shifting of public sector's deposits from commercial banks to the central bank pushed the interest rate high. As the injection of the liquidity credit was not enough to save the financially weak banks, the authorities provided a blanket guarantee for all (domestic and external) liabilities of the commercial banks.

4.   POLICY RESPONSES

Prior to the fall of President Suharto from power in May 1998, his regime had wasted six months in considering a number of alternative solutions to the economic crisis. Moreover, the quality of government policy response was eroded with the erosion of the quality of technical competence and integrity of President Suharto's cabinet ministers as he had relied mostly on his family members and cronies for advice.

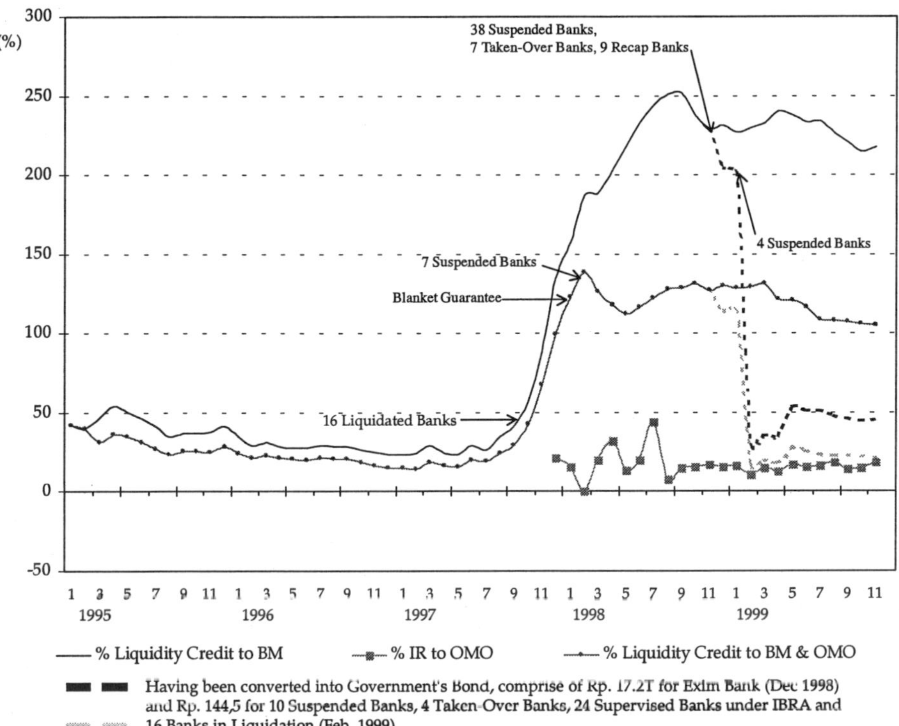

Fig. 10.5 Indonesia: Share of Liquidity Credit to Base Money (BM), Share of Intervention (IR) to Open Market Operation (OMO) and Share of Liquidity Credit to BM and OMO

Source: Bank Indonesia

Note: 1. Liquidation of 16 banks, 1 November, 1997.
2. Blanket Guarantee, 29 January, 1998.
3. The suspending of 7 banks, 4 April, 1998.
4. The suspending of 4 banks, 21 August, 1998.
5. The suspending of 38 banks, taking over of 7 banks and recapitalization of 9 banks, 13 March, 1999.

In the beginning of the crisis, Indonesia signed the Letter of Intent with the IMF in October 1997. The standard IMF Program C consists of the following requirements: (i) short-term stabilization policy to reduce domestic absorption; (ii) medium-term economy-wide reform to remove economic distortions for improving productivity and efficiency, and (iii) measures to strengthen market infrastructure (accounting and legal systems) to improve asymmetry of information and reduce transaction costs.

Unhappy with the slash in their pet projects and the slow results of the IMF program, in February 1998, President Suharto's daughters and cronies brought in Dr. Steven Hanke of Johns Hopkins University to advice him on the use of the currency board system (CBS) as alternative to the IMF program. The CBS, the second alternative, will peg the rupiah to the US dollar and the monetary policy will be constrained in this system as, like in gold standard, the money supply will be directly linked to the balance of payments developments. In such a system, the central bank will stop operating as the lender of last resort.

In the CBS context, the money supply will contract in response to a deficit in the balance of payments. A reduction in external reserves due to the fall in oil exports, rising capital flight and increasing burden of external debt repayments, as now happening in Indonesia, will automatically contract stock of money supply in order to maintain the pegged exchange rate under the CBS. It will also require an adjustment program to suppress domestic expenditures and to encourage non-oil exports. In order to carry out such a policy measure, the price of traded goods must increase relative to non-traded goods. These are traumatic policies that will result in painful consequences in terms of both unemployment and lost output particularly when the share of non-traded sector is relatively high in the economy as in the case of Indonesia. The alternative measure is a combination of a devaluation of a pegged exchange rate and a fall in domestic prices brought about by a domestic recession.

The third alternative is to impose control on capital account transactions, at least short-term capital inflows and outflows. A number of variants have been considered under this proposal. The first mechanism is to control capital flows by using market-based mechanism. This includes Tobin tax, and the Chilean way of taxing capital inflows by freezing them for a certain period of time in non-remunerated deposits at the central bank. Second, by discretionary measures such as foreign exchange control as being adopted in a semi-open economy of the People's Republic of China or controlling certain types of capital inflows to affect both the overall size and structure of capital inflows as recently introduced in Malaysia. At least in the short-run, the control will cut the link between interest rates and exchange rates. This will give more freedom to policy makers to pursue domestic policy objectives.

Indonesia, however, simply does not have the administrative capability to implement the exchange control. The country is big in size with more than 17,000 islands of different sizes. In the middle of the archipelago is Singapore, the leading financial center in the region. Moreover, Indonesia has no adequate legal and accounting systems and efficient bureaucracy to administer the control. The large size of the country, significant role of non-traded sector in the economy, inadequate foreign exchange reserves, distressed banking system, lax discipline and weak market infrastructure (particularly the legal and accounting systems) do not permit Indonesia to adopt the currency board system.

5. STABILIZATION AND ADJUSTMENT PROGRAM

In the end, the new government signed the fourth IMF program in June 1998. This has secured the US$43 billion IMF pledge. The fiscal distress and fragility of the banking system constrained Indonesia from adopting a full-fledged stabilization program. The IMF program has specific targets in (1) monetary aggregates (net domestic credit); (2) fiscal account (public sector borrowing); (3) external sector (external indebtedness); (4) social safety net and (5) strengthening market infrastructure.

5.1 Monetary Policy

By adopting the system of flexible exchange rates on 14 August 1997, the policy objective of the government has shifted to defending its foreign exchange reserve position. This has allowed interest rates to rise precipitously. Moreover, the monetary policy has also been tightened either by tightening domestic credit of the banking system or by the inability of the financially distressed banking system to extend loans. The relaxation in the prudential rules and regulations governing the banking industry has imposed no significant impacts on the ability of the banking system to extend new credits.

In a floating exchange rate system, depreciation of the domestic currency is an effective mechanism to achieve the necessary adjustment. The adjusting factors of an active management of exchange rate policy once adopted in Indonesia have triggered the rise of domestic inflation rate and interest rate. The pressures for the inflation to rise have been partly suppressed by government's policy to run 'budget surplus' or to narrow the budget deficit, the policy to subsidize prices of state-vended products[7] and to adopt a more vigorous trade liberalization program. The trade policy reform and productivity gains generated by the economy-wide reform have helped relax the supply constraint and check the inflationary pressures. The selective credit policy has helped support allocation of resources as set by the authorities, including to projects favored by the remaining import-substitution industrialization (ISI) policy and the executing firms.

5.2 Fiscal Policy

With monetary policy already held tight, the focus of Indonesia's adjustment program is primarily fiscal. The economic crisis has caused fiscal distress (Table 10.4), as government revenues are insufficient to meet the rising expenditure to finance soaring costs of overhauling financial system, social safety net and fiscal stimulus. Extra expenditure is also needed to cover the contingent liabilities falling due because of nationalization of private sector debt[8]. One of the main objectives of the fiscal policy is to redefine the scope of government. Privatization of state-owned enterprises (SOEs) is part of the process to scale back the role of government in providing

---

[7] Include staple foods (such as rice, sugar and wheat flour), building materials (such as Portland cement), energy (such as electricity and petroleum products) and services (such as transportation fares and school tuition).

[8] These include guarantees to protect depositors in (and creditors to) the banking system, guarantees on insured credits to private infrastructure providers (such as tool roads, drinking water and electricity), and obligations for pension payments to civil servants.

Table 10.4 Indonesia : Central Government Budget Summary 1994/95–2000/01

(in billion Rp. or otherwise stated)

	1994/95	1995/96	1996/97	1997/98	1998/99	1999/2000	2000/01
Revenue and Expenditure							
1. Domestic Revenues	66,418	73,014	84,792	108,814	159,135	149,303	140,804
2. Routine Expenditures [a]	44,069	50,435	61,568	84,606	140,535	171,205	134,556
3. Development Expenditures	30,692	28,781	33,454	46,398	65,750	92,683	83,648
4. Budget Deficit (=2+3–1)	8343	6202	10,230	22,190	47,150	114,585	77,400
5. Government Saving (=1–2)	22,349	22,579	23,224	24,208	18,600	–21,902	6248
Borrowing Fund							
6. Program Aid	0	0	0	0	24,926	74,045	47,400
7. Project Aid	9838	9009	11,048	23,817	25,313	40,541	30,000
8. Total Borrowing (=6+7)	9838	9009	11,048	23,817	50,239	114,586	77,400
9. Change in balances (=8–4) [b]	1495	2807	818	1627	3089	1	0
Memorandum Item :							
1. Share of Deficit to Total Expenditure (%)	11.2	7.8	10.8	16.9	22.9	43.4	35.5
2. Share of Government Saving to Domestic Revenues (%)	33.6	30.9	27.4	22.2	11.7	–14.7	4.4
3. Share of Program Aid to Total Borrowing (%)	0.0	0.0	0.0	0.0	49.6	64.6	61.2
4. Share of Project Aid to Total Borrowing (%)	100.0	100.0	100.0	100.0	50.4	35.4	38.8
5. Share of Balances to Domestic Revenues (%)	2.3	3.8	1.0	1.5	1.9	0.0	0.0
6. Share of Balances to Total Expenditures (%)	2.0	3.5	0.9	1.2	1.5	0.0	0.0
7. Share of Balances to Total Borrowing (%)	15.2	31.2	7.4	6.8	6.1	0.0	0.0

Note: a) Including debt service payment.
  b) Positive means increasing.
Sources: Ministry of Finance and World Bank, Indonesia : From Crisis to Opportunity, 1999.

the private goods and services. It is also an instrument for improving the efficiency and productivity of SOEs. The policy has also shifted the role from a tool of resource allocation to a principal instrument of macroeconomic policy and the vehicle for providing public goods.

Prior to the crisis, between 1968–1997, the budget deficit had always been financed by foreign financial assistances, preferably concessionary loans from official sources. Following the crisis, the authorities have to find other sources of revenue to finance the larger unsustainable budget deficit. These include revenues from asset recovery by IBRA — Indonesia Bank Restructuring Agency, proceeds from privatization of state-owned enterprises and flotation of government bonds in domestic market[9]. None of the budget deficit is to be financed through money creation. Early 2000, the stock of government debt amounted to 90% of the GDP, nearly 60% of which was domestic debt. Pressure on repayment of public sector external debt has been partly eased by rescheduling under the auspices of the Paris Club.

The authorities have also introduced various measures to raise revenue from taxation. The efforts have had a limited success, as the tax system in an emerging economy, like in Indonesia, is inflexible, inefficient and less progressive. As a result, the expenditure side of the government budget is expected to carry out multiple tasks, including stimulating economic growth and pursuing equity objective. These objectives can be pursued by increasing the portion of non-debt budget expenditures towards the non-tradable sector of the economy. Such expenditures include public schools, extension and outreach services, and public health care programs and public works programs in rural area.

The growing demand for local autonomy and revenue sharing with local governments has aggravated the fiscal distress. Starting from the fiscal year 2001, local governments will receive 15% of onshore non-tax oil revenue, 30% of onshore non-tax gas revenue, and 80% of forestry revenue generated

---

[9] The process of sales of both SOEs and IBRA controlled assets, however, has been painfully slow. As of January 2000, the authorities only managed to raise Rp6.2 trillion (out of a target of Rp13 trillion) via privatization and generated Rp10 trillion (out of the Rp17 trillion targeted) from sales of IBRA controlled assets.

in the respective regions. By that time, the transfers and shared revenues are expected to double to 6% of the GDP and regional revenue to 7% of the GDP. The arrangement is expected to reduce domestic revenue of the central government by 25%.

5.3 Short-term Program to Protect the Poor from Falling Primary Income

The rise in unemployment and inflation rates has accounted for the rise in the number of people under the poverty line from 22.5 million (11.3% of the total population) in 1996 to 34.2 million (16.7%) in 1998. The poverty issue is more pronounced in non-traded sector of the economy, in the agricultural sector and on Java Island for its heavy reliance on rice and poultry. Rice requires plenty of water and poultry require expensive imported feed. It is estimated that over 45% of the rural population or 56.8 million people now live below the poverty line. Java absorbs more than two-thirds of over 200 million population of Indonesia.

To ease the burden of the poor, the authorities, to some extent, have raised their secondary or social income to supplement the fall in the primary income, i.e. the income derived from labor and assets. As Indonesia has no modern social safety net system, the authorities have tried to raise social income by providing food and other basic necessities at subsidized prices and create labor intensive public works. These require high budgetary subsidies. However, mainly due to the poor administration, in the beginning, the subsidies did not reach the needy. At the same time, the subsidies created a large wedge between domestic and international prices of the state-vended products and provided incentives for their exportation (smuggling) to neighboring countries.

5.4 Dealing with the Debt Overhang

Larger shares of Indonesia's export earnings and GDP are required for the soaring external debt repayments. To ease the pressure, Indonesia is in need of temporary debt relief.

(i) *Public sector debt*

It is true that the bulk of the public sector external debt is long-term in nature. However, the associated principal and interest servicing cost still run high, at some US$9 billion a year. To repay its external debt, the public sector has to accumulate a budget surplus as well as a surplus in the balance of payments. To ease the pressure on the public budget and the balance of payments, on September 23, 1998, the Paris Club creditor nations agreed to reschedule US$4.2 billion in principal repayments of Indonesia's public external debt.

(ii) *The private sector debt*

The crisis hit a devastating blow on Indonesia's economy and damaged its banking and corporate sectors. The move to flexible exchange rate system raised sharply the nominal exchange rate from Rp2599 to US$1 dollar in July 1997 to Rp10,400 in January 1998 and to Rp14,900 in June 1998 (Figure 10.3). The sharp depreciation of the rupiah and the meltdown of banking system once forced a rise (weighted average) in annual lending interest rate from 15.45% in July 1997 to 70% in April 1998 and to nearly 82% in August 1998. Despite large budget subsidy to control prices of state-vended products, the inflation rate rose to 77.63% in 1998 as compared to 11% in 1997 and 6.47% in 1996. The economy (measured as GDP) contracted by −13.6% in 1998 as compared to positive growth of an average over 6% per annum during the preceding 25 years.

The private sector external debt is relatively more difficult to settle as there is a great number of foreign lenders and domestic borrowers. Foreign lenders include foreign private banks, institutional investors and other non-banking entities. It will have to be solved on a voluntary basis based on a combination of Mexico's Ficorca program and the Korea scheme. The Korea scheme includes the restructure of the short-term and non-trade debts of Indonesian banks into loans with one to four-year maturity. Interest rates on the new loans will be paid based on Libor plus margin, ranging between 2.75 and 3.5%.

The non-bank corporate debt is to be rescheduled and restructured along the line of Mexican program. A trust institution, called INDRA, has already been established under the central bank. It is to provide exchange rate risk protection and assurance to the availability of foreign exchange to private debtors that agree with their foreign creditors to restructure their external debts for a period of 8 years with 3 years of grace, during which no principal will be payable. So far, the progress of the program is very slow partly because of the weak bankruptcy law.

5.5 Bank Restructuring Program

The financially distressed banking system is not in a position to lower interest rates and expand credit. The structural weakness of the banking system and the corporate sector has also limited the tightening of monetary policy.

To restructure the banking industry, the authorities are adopting three broad policies. The first element of the bank-restructuring program is to strengthen the capital base of the banks. The risk base capital adequacy ratio (CAR) of the banks which was temporary lowered in November 1998 to 4% will resume the minimum of 8% by 2003. The second component of the program is to improve governance of the banking system. For this objective, Indonesia is now adopting stricter prudential rules and regulations and accounting standards — on par with international standard and improvement on their enforcement and implementations. All the major banks are required to appoint a Compliance Director. Moreover, major shareholders, managers and executive officers of the commercial banks are now required to take proper tests for bank business.

The banking system has practically been nationalized as major private banks are now under the control of the IBRA-Indonesian Bank Restructuring Agency. Established in early 1998, IBRA assumes the function of lender of last resort. It also assumes the responsibility for financially distressed banks and (together with the banks' shareholders) prepares and implements immediate rehabilitation plans by restructuring or by merger with other banks.

On 26 January 1998, the authorities provided a blanket guarantee to all (both domestic and foreign) depositors and creditors of all the banks incorporated in Indonesia. The guarantee scheme will be effective for at least two years and its discontinuation will be announced 6 months in advance and replaced by a deposit insurance scheme.

The Asset Management Unit (AMU) has been established under IBRA, its only role being the purchase of the non-performing loans (NPL) from banks. This allows the banks to focus on their traditional activities of deposit taking and lending. The purchase of NPL will significantly add to resources available for banks for lending purposes. To some extent, IBRA adopts the Swedish model by trying to save both the banks and the borrowers by injecting better management methods and fresh capital into the companies. This is because IBRA also holds equity stakes in corporations and banks.

The bank recapitalization program was announced on 9 December 1998 (the Jakarta Post, 10 December 1998). The objective of the program is to increase the banks' capital adequacy ratio (CAR) to 4% or half of the 8%, the minimum standard as set by the BIS. The program is only available for national commercial banks having a CAR between –25% and +4%. The 40 banks with a CAR below 25% are required to inject fresh capital within 30 days or risk to be closed down. The 10 foreign banks and 32 joint venture banks are excluded from the program.

The government has re-capitalized Bank Indonesia (the central bank) and 126 national commercial banks at a cost of Rp610 trillion (US$87 billion at the exchange rate of Rp7000 per US dollar) or nearly 60% of the GDP (Table 10.5). The would-be re-capitalized banks include seven state banks, 49 private banks (inclusive of the 13 banks taken over by the government) and 15 provincial development banks. Four of the seven state-owned banks (PT Bapindo, PT Bank Dagang Negara, PT Bank Ekspor Impor Indonesia, and PT Bank Bumi Daya) are to be merged with the newly established PT Bank Mandiri. As shown in Table 10.5, the number of banks reduced to 167 in June 1999 from 208 in December 1998. The number of banks under the control of the (local and central) government has increased from 34 in June 1997 to the present 48 with a combined market share of about 73%.

Table 10.5 Indonesia: The Cost of Bank Restructuring (as of December 1999)

(Rp trillion)

	Total Bonds	Percent of Total	Fixed Rate Bonds			Variable Rate Bonds	Index Rate Bonds
			Total	5-year	10-year		
Bonds Issued to Date	500	82	51	22	29	231	218
Bank Indonesia	218	36	0	0	0	0	218
Recapitalized Banks							
State Banks	178	29	43	20	23	136	0
Private Banks (7 Banks)	22	4	3	1	2	19	0
Banks Taken Over in 1998 (BTO 4)	81	13	5	1	4	75	0
Regional Development Banks	1	0	0.4	0.1	0.3	0.8	0
Remaining Bonds to be Issued	110	18	6	2	4	NA	0
Banks Taken Over in 1999 (BTO 8)	12	2	NA	NA	NA	NA	NA
Private Banks (7 Banks)	2	0	NA	NA	NA	NA	NA
State Banks	96	16	NA	NA	NA	NA	NA
Total	610	100	NA	NA	NA	NA	218

Source: Bank Indonesia

To ease fiscal costs of the bank's restructuring program, the authorities have encouraged participation of foreign investors in Indonesia's banking sector. This has been done, among others, by allowing foreign investors to own 100% of domestic banks. Sales of IBRA-controlled assets are also playing a key role in generating cash for the bank re-capitalization program. As of early February 2000, transfer value of those assets amounted to Rp533 trillion or about US$71 billion, more than double of the total credit outstanding of the commercial banks in 1996 (Rp225 trillion). Of this, Rp136 trillion was corporate equity and the rest (Rp397 trillion) stakes in banks including loans and other bank assets.

5.6 Policy Measures to Strengthen Market Infrastructure

A number of policy measures have been imposed to improve governance system and reduce transaction costs: (1) review and dismantle government contracts offered through corruption, collusion, and nepotism; (2) improve domestic competitive policy; (3) restructure, corporatise and privatize state-owned enterprises; (4) speed up trade and policy reforms; (5) strengthen accounting and legal systems and improve both market transparency and contract enforcement; (6) modernize the antiquated bankruptcy codes.

6.   LESSONS AND POLICY RECOMMENDATIONS

The experience of Indonesia shows that sound macroeconomic management and robust banking system are two main pillars of macroeconomic stability. Deregulation of the financial sector, as an integral part of microeconomic reform, should be accompanied with improvements in bank supervision and implementation of the prudential rules and regulations. Close attention should be paid to microeconomic weaknesses of the banks and their customers that can undermine the banks' macroeconomic strength. The microeconomic weaknesses include a financing strategy with high debt-to-equity ratio and over-dependence of banks and companies on unhedged short-term external borrowings. The authorities should also carefully monitor the magnitude and structure of private capital inflows. It is more importance to keep a close watch on warning signs of financial fragility when banks and corporate sector have heavily invested with foreign loans in unproductive sector of the economy. Less distortive prudential measures can be used to discourage destabilizing short-term capital inflows and lending from a particular sector of the economy such as real estate.

The past government policy of free entry into banking industry with inadequate and unclear exit policy was an explosive combination. To reduce the burden of bank recapitalization program, the non-viable banks should be liquidated immediately.

On the macroeconomic side, the massive capital inflows since the early 1990s had slightly appreciated the rupiah in real term, which had reduced external competitiveness of Indonesia's economy on the international market on the one hand and encouraged resource allocation more towards non-traded sector of the economy on the other.

The experience of Indonesia since 1997 has proved that financially distressed banks and relatively large government budget deficit can limit the implementation of strict short-run stabilization measures and long-term economic reform. The inconsistency of government policies and instabilities of political and social systems can aggravate the problems.

Indonesia needs temporary relief from international community, particularly from international financial institutions, to allow for necessary adjustments without a deep economic recession or adverse effects on the mass population, particularly the low-income group. At the outset of the crisis, however, the IMF had aggravated the crisis by prescribing a deep cut in public spending and improper sequence of bank closure.

The availability of financial assistance from the international community, accompanied with progress in the implementation of the IMF program and favorable external factors (such as depreciation of the US dollar against other major currencies and improvement in commodity prices including oil), has helped strengthen external value of the rupiah (*vis a vis* the US dollar), from above Rp15,000 in June 1998 to around Rp7000 as of date (Figure 10.3).

Appreciation of the rupiah, along with the progress of restructuring program of the banking system, has reduced both inflation rate and interest rate. The inflation rate dropped from the extremely high around 70% in 1988 to over 2% in 1999. The average SBI rates steadily dropped from 69% in August 1998 to 38% in December the same year and to 10–12 % in 1999. A combination of positive terms of trade effects, favorable weather condition and expansion of social program has encouraged a positive GDP growth of 0.23% in 1999 as compared to a severe contraction of nearly −14% in 1998. Despite the reduction in interest rates, however, access of corporate sector to bank credit remains very limited. The credit crunch has limited the capacity of corporate sector to increase capacity utilization, production and non-oil exports.

If the country can manage to solve its internal political problems and rebuild its social system peacefully, Indonesia will have stronger fundamentals and therefore can easily resume economic growth. The financial crisis has not seriously affected the basic conditions, which support the long-run growth potential of Indonesia's economy, human and physical capital stock. The high savings and investment emphasis on improvement in human resources are still intact. Deregulation and economic reform that have further integrated the economy to international markets will eliminate economic distortions and enhance productivity and efficiency. Improvements in market infrastructure and economic institution will further enhance productivity with the lowering of transaction costs. They will enable the country to exploit its comparative advantage in labor-intensive sectors and natural resource-based industries. At the same time, they will allow Indonesia to use ample domestic market (with a population of over 220 million) as the engine of growth.

The combination of marked progress in stabilizing the inflation rate, interest rate and exchange rate at low levels (Figure 10.3) and significant progress in bank restructuring has provided Indonesia with a good start to move forward. External factors such as positive terms of trade and favorable weather condition will provide extra push for higher economic growth, which is expected to hover between 3–4% in 2000. Restoration of political stability has improved investment climate and attracted non-oil exports and private capital inflows.

Future growth of the economy will depend on the economic reform inclusive of the financial sector and the tax system. The cost of the recapitalisation of the banking industry does not depend on the speed of the reform alone. Table 10.5 indicates that the fiscal burden on domestic debt also depends on the interest rate and inflation rate. There is a pressure for increasing interest rate in domestic market as the recapitalized banks, starting from 1 February 2000, are allowed to sell 10% of their holding of government bonds in the secondary market. On the other hand, the improvements on bank productivity due to significant progress in bank recapitalization program tend to reduce interest rate. While external debt carries exchange rate risks, debt trap turns into crisis in case the government cannot raise enough revenue to pay the interest rate on the debt. Medium term growth also depends on the ability of the economy to raise the investment productivity (or lower ICOR-incremental capital output ratio) when the fiscal costs of recapitalising financial system partly is passed to the private sector. Historical ICOR of Indonesia was around 4 prior to the crisis in the 1990–1997 period.

References

Calvo, G. 1994. "Comment on Dornbusch and Werner" in *Brookings Papers on Economic Activity* No. 1.

Calvo, G.A., L. Leiderman and C.M. Reinhart. 1993. "Capital Inflows and Real Exchange Appreciation in Latin America: the Roles of External Factors". *IMF Staff Papers* 40(1): 108–151.

Claessens, Stijn, M.P. Dooley and Andrew Warner. 1995. "Portfolio Capital Flows: Hot or Cold?" *World Bank Economic Review* 9(1): 153–174.

Cole, David C. and Betty Slade. 1998. "Why Has Indonesia's Financial Crisis Been So Bad?" *Bulletin of Indonesian Economic Studies* 34(2). August: 61–66.

Dornbusch, Rudiger, I. Goldfajn and R.O. Valdes. 1995. "Currency Crises and Collapse". *Brookings Papers on Economic Activity* 2:995, pp. 219–270.

Eichengreen, Barry, James Tobin and Charles Wyplosz. 1995. "Two Cases for Sand in the Wheels of International Finance". *Economic Journal* 105 (January: 162–172).

Faruqee, Hamid and Aasim M. Husain. 1995. "Savings Trends in Southeast Asia: A Cross-Country Analysis". *IMF Working Paper WP/95/39*. April.

Frankel, J.A. 1994. "Sterilization of Money Inflows: Difficult (Calvo) or Easy (Reisen)?". *IMF Working Paper 159*.

IMF. 1997. *IMF Approves Stand-By Credit for Indonesia*. Press Release No. 97/50. November 5.

Johnson, Colin. 1998. "Survey of Recent Developments". *Bulletin of Indonesian Economic Studies* 34(2). August: 3–60.

"Joint Statement of the Indonesian Bank Streering Committee and Representatives from the Republic of Indonesia". Press Release. 4 June 1998.

J.P. Morgan. 1997. *Emerging Markets Data Watch*. July.

Kaminsky, Graciela, Saul Lizondo and Carmen M. Reinhart. 1997. *Leading Indicators of Currency Crises*. Working Paper No. 36. Center for International Economics, Department of Economics, University of Maryland at College Park. September.

Krugman, Paul. 1998. "Saving Asia: It's Time to Get Radical". *Fortune*. September 7. pp. 32–37.

Lindgren, C-J., G. Garcia and M.I. Saal. 1996. *Bank Soundness and Macroeconomic Policy*. Washington, D.C.: IMF.

McKinnon, R.I. and Pill, H. 1996. "Credible Liberalization and International Capital Flows: The Overborrowing Syndrome". In T. Ito and A.O. Krueger, eds., *Financial Deregulation and Integration in East Asia. Chicago*: Chicago University Press.

Meek, Paul. 1991. "Central Bank Liquidity Management and the Money Market". In G. Caprio, Jr and P. Honohan, eds., *Monetary Policy Instruments for Developing Countries*. A World Bank Symposium. Washington, D.C.: the World Bank.

Mishkin, Frederic S. 1997. "Understanding Financial Crises: A Developing Country Perspective". *Annual World Bank Conference on Development Economics 1996*. Washington, D.C.: The World Bank.

Nasution, Anwar. 1996. *The Banking System and Monetary Aggregates Following Financial Sector Reforms. Lessons From Indonesia*. Research for Action 27. UNU/ World Institute for Development Economics Research (UNU/WIDER). Helsinki.

Perry, Guillermo E. (ed.). 1997. *Currency Boards and External Shocks. How Much Pain, How Much Gain?* World Bank Latin American and Carribean Studies. Washington, D.C: the World Bank.

Radelet, Steven. 1995. Indonesian Foreign Debt: Headed for a Crisis or Financing Sustainable Growth? *Bulletin of Indonesian Economic Studies* 31(3), pp. 39–72.

Reisen, Helmut. 1996. "Managing Volatile Capital Inflows: The Experience of the 1990s". *Asian Development Review*. 14(1): 72–96.

Sachs, Jeffrey, A. Tornell and A Velasco. 1996. "Financial Crises in Emerging Markets: the Lessons from 1995". *Brookings Papers on Economic Activities*, 1:1996. pp. 147–196.

Sachs, Jeffrey and Steven Radelet. 1998. "The Onset of the East Asian Financial Crisis". Manuscript, March. Downloaded from http://www.hiid.harvard.edu/pub/other/asiacrisis.html

Spahn, Paul Bernd. 1995. International Financial Flows and Transactions Taxes: Surveys and Options. *IMF Working Paper* No.: WP/95/60 (June).

Tobin, James. 1979. "A Proposal for International Monetary Reform". *Eastern Economic Journal* 4 (July): 153–159.

United Nations, ESCAP. 1995. *Issues and Experiences in Tax System Reforms in Selected Countries of the ESCAP Region.* New York: United Nations. Part Two: The Case Study on Indonesia, pp. 69–97.

Woo, Wing Thye and Anwar Nasution. 1989. "Indonesia Economic Policies and Their Relation to External Debt Management". In J.D. Sachs and Susan M. Collins. eds. *Developing Country Debt and Economic Performance.* A NBER Research Project Report. Volume 3. Book I. Chicago: The Chicago University Press.

Woo, Wing Thye, Bruce Glassburner and Anwar Nasution. 1994. *Macroeconomic Policies, Crises, and Long-term Growth in Indonesia, 1965–90.* Washington, D.C.: the World Bank.

World Bank. 1996. *Indonesia: Dimensions of Growth.* Report No. 15383-IND. Country Department III, East Asia and Pacific Region. May 7.

CHAPTER 11

PHILIPPINE

THE 1997–1999 PHILIPPINE ECONOMIC DOWNTURN: A PREVENTABLE ONE

Edita A. Tan

School of Economics
University of the Philippines
Deliman, Quezon City 1101
Philippines
E-mail: etan@econ.upd.edu.ph

1. INTRODUCTION

A rich literature has been generated by the economic crisis that hit four of East Asia's highly successful economies — Korea, Thailand, Malaysia and Indonesia. There is a concentration of interest in trying to explain the crisis offering both theoretical underpinnings and political economy analeptics. More recent literature has focused on its social impact. International agencies such as the UNDP and the ILO have sponsored studies on its impact on the poor, especially as a result of loss of employment and reduction in social services. This paper reviews the various explanations of the Asian four's crisis and examines whether they are applicable to the Philippine recession. The Philippines has suffered a serious economic downturn coincident with its neighbors' crisis but it is not clear that the recession could be viewed as a crisis. Indeed there was a downturn but not of the dimension and causes of the neighbors' crisis.

The Philippine GDP growth declined at a much lower rate than that in the East Asian Four (EA-4) from 5.2% in 1996 to −.5% in 1998. Agriculture contributed 241% of the decline in GDP with its output falling by 6.7 in 1996 to 1997. This was largely a result of the drought wrought by El Niño. The economy suffered from contagion effects reflected in capital outflow that led to currency depreciation of more than 50%. Wrong policy responses by the central bank exacerbated the contagion problem. It is noted that major financial and trade reforms had already been undertaken following the 1983–85 economic crisis and these strengthened the economy's ability to avoid a new crisis. The 1983–85 crisis resulted from the accumulated effects of the economic and political abuses committed by the strong dictatorship of Marcos over the 1970–85 period. GDP fell by 15% in 1983 to 1985. His ouster in February 1986 allowed major reforms, especially in trade and in the financial system. The reforms likely avoided much of the problems that caused the crisis in the EA-4. On the other hand, the Philippines continues to suffer from some serious structural problems such as low saving rate, high average inflation rate, poor infrastructure and poor governance. The economy is recovering but to its old slow growth path. Growth rate is projected to rise from about 2.0% in 1999 to less than 4.0% in 2000. The Medium Term Development Plan sets target growth at 5% to 6% in the last 4 years of the Estrada administration, 2000–2004.

The paper is organized into sections covering, successively, a review of the more important hypotheses about the crisis; a brief history of the performance of the economy and reforms prior to the current recession; an analysis of the performance of the external sector and the behavior of the capital account; an analysis of financial development and public finance; an analysis of policy responses, and, finally, the conclusion.

2. HYPOTHESES ON THE ASIAN CRISIS

The hypotheses are grouped into the following: a) market failure arguments, currency and exchange rate mismanagement and premature capital account liberalization. Wrong responses that are largely attributed to IMF prescriptions may be treated as a cause on its own or an exacerbating factor.

2.1 Market Failure in the Financial System

The financial market, which is the market for credit of various forms and maturities, suffers from three inherent problems of market failure and market imperfections — externalities, asymmetric information between borrowers and lenders and moral hazards. Prudential rules and a competitive environment would mitigate these problems, while bad policies and structures would worsen them.

The financial market plays a critical role in smoothing the functioning of the real sector. An efficient financial market pools funds (saving and excess cash inventories) from surplus spending units for lending to deficit units for investment and other uses. The market develops credit instruments with features that vary in liquidity, size and riskiness, and offers financial services such as portfolio advice, insurance, trade credits and most importantly the means of payment through bank checking accounts, credit cards and other payment mechanisms. We refer to the last service as money supply service. While banks earn income from this service, society as a whole benefits from having this relatively efficient means of payment. This benefit is considered an important externality of banks. Some of the information produced in loan processing, services, insurance and other activities cannot all be internalized by its producers and becomes public good. The offering of varied credit instruments allows for greater portfolio diversification that tends to lower risk and the cost of liquidity. The externalities, especially those related to the maintenance of the payment system, have warranted government intervention which has commonly taken the form of central bank guarantees to prevent bank runs and massive financial collapse. Many governments have taken initiatives in establishing deposit insurance and have a central bank that acts as a bank of last resort to failing banks. In some countries, the idea of being 'too big to fail' has been applied.

The rationale for government intervention to prevent massive bank failure may on the other hand foster moral hazard on the part of bank depositors. Central bank support in case of failure may encourage banks to relax their lending criteria and procedures. The insured depositors need not be too careful in choosing the bank in which to place their funds. At the same time, there are inherent moral hazards in banking given the asymmetric information on loan risk that banks and borrowers possess. The borrower necessarily has more information on the prospects of the project for which he is applying for funding than the bank or any creditor at that. That is also true for equities where the issuing corporation has more information about the value of its assets and the expected profitability of its venture than stock buyers. The borrower is faced with the moral hazard of misallocating the borrowed funds since his losses from failure tends to be less than what the creditor bears. Asymmetric information may also lead to adverse selection. The more risky borrowers and equity issuers will have a greater incentive to borrow than the less risky deficit units at any prevailing interest rate which tends to be the market average. Raising the rate for risky borrowers will, however, increase risk since they become less able to meet their debt service (Stiglitz and Weiss 1981). A good summary of market problems is discussed in Mishkin's money and banking textbook (1995).

Note that these problems are inherent to any financial system. Banks are known to minimize the consequences of asymmetric information and the moral hazard of their borrowers by instituting credit evaluation procedures, requiring collateral, monitoring the borrowers' financial conditions during the life of the loan and imposing loan use conditions. Good accounting and auditing standards and practices are a critical minimum requirement for implementing prudent credit rules and evaluation. Financial institutions are trust institutions that need to be monitored and supervised in order to preserve the integrity of the payment system, maximize their development impact and protect the interests of their clients.

The financial systems of the crisis-hit economies are found to suffer from problems other than the problems of market failure that are inherent in all financial system. The international accounting and auditing standards had not been effectively or extensively implemented in Korea, Thailand and Indonesia so there was no reliable financial information to use for assessing loans and equities and the financial condition of banks (White, 1997). At the same time, credit allocation is partly based on special connections and/or government suasion. Connected banking, which takes the form of crony banking in Indonesia, main banking by chaebols in Korea and conglomerated banking in Malaysia and Thailand has impaired the efficiency of credit allocation and the health of the whole financial system. Park (1997) warned about the weaknesses in the prudential practices of Korean banks. These intrusions in credit allocation have resulted in extremely high non-performing loan rates and extensive failures in the banking system and other financial institutions in these countries. The capital account liberalization expanded the sources of loanable funds of these institutions, which could not but be imprudently allocated given the laxed regulatory and supervision environment of the financial system.

2.2 The Currency Problem

Capital account liberalization seriously complicates the management of exchange rate and there are as yet no clear-cut policy tools for doing so. As Krugman would argue, transactions in trade essentially differ from transactions in capital, especially considering the environment in which the latter take place. In trade, the parties to the transaction have fairly good information on the goods and services they are buying and selling. A country's trade deficit or surplus would exert palpable pressure on the exchange rate. An open capital market blurs trade signals. If there is capital inflow for one reason or another, interest rate decreases towards the world level and the currency appreciates. Exports are discouraged and imports encouraged. Income increases, depending on the balancing impact of reduced exports/ increased imports and increased investment. Capital inflows into short-term loans and portfolio investments will have the same negative impact on exports but questionable impact on investments. Short-term inflows increase overall liquidity and credit for financing investment and other expenditures. The appreciation pressure is temporary in nature since short-term capital flows could readily reverse directions. There is asymmetry in currency risk bearing in capital transactions. Short-term creditors could withdraw funds more quickly than debtors could liquidate their assets. Creditors therefore face lower currency risks than debtors. A currency depreciation may be reasonably anticipated but not its precise timing considering the exchange rate policy of the government. Favorable arbitrage could therefore be arranged by a creditor for say a month maturity with little risk of currency depreciation. But an imprudent borrower who uses short-term funds for medium or longer-term investment does not have this advantage and so bears greater currency risk.

The information technology revolution has reduced financial transaction cost to virtually zero. Funds could be invested anywhere at anytime through a few computer entries. But the technology is applied unevenly across countries' financial systems. Most less developed economies have not instituted standard financial reporting system and there is highly imperfect information on the financial position of enterprises, financial and non-financial alike, which are engaged in the capital market. The Basle architecture is yet to be built in most emerging economies, including the Asian NICs. The capital account opening took place in the EA-4 under these defective financial structure. But confluence of policies and events made the EA-4 economies very attractive to foreign capital. Their well-publicized economic success, high domestic interest rate, low inflation rate and stable nominal exchange rate made short-term and long-term investments very attractive. Very large increases in short-term loans and portfolio investments from external sources flowed into Thailand, Indonesia and Malaysia. A vicious circle of capital flow, currency appreciation and high interest rate relative to Libor operated around mid-1990s. Much of the short-term flows went to financial institutions that then lent them on longer maturities to booming sectors like real estate. In Thailand, the inflow happened at a time when the real estate sector was already overheating and it blew more air into the real estate bubble, thus hastening its bursting. Krugman (1998) argued that the very high rate of saving and investment in the East Asian economies implies relatively low marginal rate of return to investment. The capital inflow pushed the marginal rate of return further down. Real estate in Thailand and Chaebol industries in Korea are good examples. On the other hand, they all had relatively small equity market and the surge in portfolio investments meant large demand shifts for equities, hence the equity bubble.

2.3 The Trade Sector

According to Lim (1999), the East Asian economies had relied on the export sector to stimulate and sustain their industrialization efforts until the mid-1990s. This sector expanded the market for their goods and earned the foreign exchange required to finance their capital and intermediate goods imports. Export growth was double-digit for these countries until the first half of the 1990s. Subsequently, the export sector weakened partly because of the competition fostered by industrializing cheap-labor countries (China, India, Bangladesh), the lack of technological capacity for competing in new products/processes, increasing labor cost and the overvalued currency. Thailand and Malaysia were unable to sustain their foreign exchange earning capacity and foreign capital replaced exports as the important source of foreign exchange. The policy of pegging the exchange rate to the US dollar did not help encourage exports but instead encouraged foreign borrowing. Fabella (1999) pointed out that, during the early stages of development, credit allocation favored the export sector and other priority areas. With capital account liberalization, the starved non-tradable sectors like real estate, drew much of the loanable funds. The overvalued exchange rate also made this sector relatively attractive.

2.4 Policy Responses to the Crisis

There is a growing consensus that the IMF policy prescriptions were inappropriate (Stiglitz 1998, 1999, Corden 1998, Hall Hill 1999). Moreover, the measures were not fair in both the economic and political sense (McKinnon, 1998, Stiglitz 1998, 1999). The immediate prescription of the IMF was to deflate the economy as a means of strengthening the exchange rate via high interest rate and low import demand. Restrictive monetary and fiscal policies were prescribed. The capital flow reversal, combined with the restrictive monetary policy, drastically reduced liquidity and put strong pressure on the domestic interest rate. The policy intensified uncertainty and pessimism. Business losses due to currency depreciation and high interest rates led to an over-shooting of non-performing loans. Banks suffered losses from the currency depreciation and the NPLs. An appropriate short-run policy should have been to counter the loss of confidence the deflationary impact of the currency capital outflow by easing the liquidity and interest rate pressure.

The IMF imposed the elements of the now popularized financial architecture on the economies hit by crisis as a condition for its syndicated extended facility (with ADB, World Bank and bi-laterals), possibly because it had failed to get them instituted during normal times. The Basle-IMF architecture consists of international accounting and auditing standards, prudential rules including those on insolvency and financial disclosure and effective supervision and monitoring of financial institutions. Note that these are measures that are essentially long-term in nature. They take time to implement. For instance, establishing good accounting and auditing practice will involve instruction of formal and informal nature (accountancy is a degree program in many countries), institution of the accounting and auditing profession and legalizing the use of audited statements. The practice of these standards has to spread to financial institutions and the business sector. Prudential rules, on the other hand, have to be legislated or written up, the courts have to be acquainted with them and the affected parties educated about them. The central banks and other supervisory bodies need also to be educated and trained in monitoring and supervision.

There is great unevenness in the IMF stance. The architecture is imposed on the crisis-hit economy but the majority of LDCs need it just as badly. The transition economies, for instance, have not yet learned the capitalist accounting system. In addition, McKinnon (1998) pointed out that the US, being the supplier of world liquidity and earning seigniorage from the privilege, should act as a world central bank and take on the responsibility of mitigating currency crises by extending liquidity assistance. US assistance is essential since the IMF resources are inadequate. Fears are expressed that should another region suffer a similar crisis, the IMF would not have the resources to help it. The measures imposed were unfair in another sense. The borrowers were asked to bear all the risks involved in undertaking the loans. The crisis may not have occurred if the short-term creditors were made to share in the risks by rolling-over the credit. This would have reduced the capital flow reversal, reduced the rate of currency depreciation, the business losses and therefore the downturn. A mild recession instead of a crisis would have occurred. Korea's fast recovery might be partly due to its success in rolling-over its short-term loans.

3. PHILIPPINE ECONOMIC DEVELOPMENT BEFORE THE CRISIS

The country's economic performance over the last three decades has been inferior to that of all its East Asian neighbors. GDP grew at much slower rate and exhibited wider fluctuations.

The economy was subjected to more serious interventions and for a longer time than in the other East Asian neighbors (see Note 1). The exchange rate was fixed at P2/$1 in the first 60 years of the last century, the import substituting policy was followed until 1990; financial repression with effective interest rate ceilings and a complex system of subsidized credit was in effect until 1985. The privatization of numerous public corporations has not been completed. The economy was subjected to an abusive dictator for 20 years (1965–1985) where direct and indirect thievery of resources was practiced. It ended in an economic crisis where GDP declined by 7.5% per year in 1984 and 1985.

The major reforms were undertaken only after the dictatorial government was toppled. The new government of Cory Aquino (1986) faced the daunting task of re-establishing a democratic government, servicing a very large external debt, dismantling crony monopolies, privatizing inefficient public corporations, initiating financial and trade reforms and financing the deficits.

Table 11.1 Performance Indicators of the Real Sector 1970–1997

	GNP	GDP	Agric.	Industry	Mfg.	Const.	Services	Expts.
A. Average Annual Growth Rate of GNP, GDP, Sectors, Exports								
1950–54	8.3	8.3	8.3	7.3	13.7	–3.7	9.2	
1955–59	6.0	5.7	3.6	8.5	9.9	4.7	6.1	
1960–64	4.8	3.9	3.9	4.1	4.1	6.6	4.5	
1965–69	5.0	4.9	3.7	5.5	6.1	1.4	4.6	
1970–74	6.2	4.7	2.9	6.5	6.8	5.2	4.8	26.0
1974–79	6.5	6.4	5.6	8.5	4.4	19.9	5.5	12.4
1980–82	3.7	4.1	3.0	3.9	2.6	5.9	5.0	4.1
1983–85	–8.2	–4.2	–0.2	–8.6	–6.1	–19.6	–1.0	–2.2
1986–90	5.4	4.7	2.7	5.0	5.1	7.8	5.7	12.2
1991	0.5	–0.6	1.4	–2.7	–0.4	–15.7	–0.2	8.0
1992	1.6	0.3	0.4	–0.5	–1.7	2.8	1.0	11.1
1993	2.1	2.1	2.1	1.6	0.7	5.7	2.5	15.8
1994	5.2	4.4	2.6	5.8	5.0	8.9	4.2	18.5
1995	4.9	4.7	0.9	6.7	6.8	6.5	5.4	29.4
1996	7.2	5.9	3.8	6.4	5.6	10.9	6.3	17.7
1997	5.2	5.2	2.9	6.1	4.2	16.2	5.4	22.8
1998	0.08	–0.5	–6.7	–1.9	–1.1	–8.5	3.5	16.9
B. Sectoral Shares in GDP								
1950			38.3	21.9	12.5	7.7	39.3	
1960			39.8	22.0	17.4	4.0	43.3	
1970			28.9	29.5	23.2	5.8	41.6	
1980			23.5	40.5	27.6	9.4	36.0	25.3
1985			24.6	35.0	25.2	5.1	40.4	24.0
1990			21.9	34.5	24.8	6.0	43.6	30.2
1995			21.6	32.1	23.0	5.6	46.3	42.9
1998			18.5	33.8	23.8	5.6	43.1	44.9

Source: National Statistical Coordinating Board (NSCB), Philippine Statistical Yearbook, 1980, 1990, 1998.
Bangko Sentral ng Pilipinas (BSP), Selected Philippine Economic Indicators, October 1999.

Excepting the Social Security System, all the government financial institutions[1] that became the vehicle for funneling funds to crony businesses were found insolvent in 1986. The government had to decide whether to close down the Philippine National Bank (PNB) and the Development Bank of the Philippines (DBP) or reduce their size to the level of their performing assets. The latter was chosen. There was no pressure to close the Government Service Insurance System (GSIS) since it could rely on a stable flow of social security contributions. The Philippine Veterans Bank was closed down while the Amanah Bank which operates on Muslim banking principles never developed into a viable bank. Some 180 of the highly subsidized rural banks became bankrupt and closed down. A few private development banks had also to close down. The aggregate impact of the asset value adjustments and bank closure is reflected in the large downsizing of the GFIs. Their share in the total assets of the financial system fell from 25% to 8.7% in 1985 to 1987. It fell further to 7.5% in 1996.

Under pressure from the WB and the IMF, Marcos abolished the interest rate ceilings on long term loans and time deposits in 1981. The remaining ceilings were removed in 1982. The policy change did not have much impact since the credit interventions through subsidized lending and rediscounting continued through the end of the Marcos era. The first important financial reform by the Aquino government in 1986 was to remove the easy/cheap rediscounting facility. Banks, including the GFIs, now have to obtain the bulk of their loanable funds from the market. Other important measures to liberalize the financial system included the relaxation of domestic bank entry and bank branching in 1992–1995. The capital account was liberalized in 1992, foreign banks were allowed entry in 1993 and the CB became independent of the executive in 1995. The last measure was in consonance with the 1986 Constitution which provided for the establishment of an

---

[1] The government financial institutions consisted of The Philippine National Bank (PNB) and the Philippine Veteran's Bank (PVB) are commercial banks; The Development Bank of the Philippines (DBP), the Land Bank of the Philippines and The Amanah Bank are specialized banks; and the Government Service Insurance System (GSIS) and the Social Security System (SSS).

independent central bank. The new Bangko Sentral Ng Philipinas (BSP) includes only two cabinet members on its seven-member Monetary Board.

Drastic reforms had to be implemented in the trade sector. The Aquino government inherited both high and highly differentiated tariff protection and non-tariff barriers that largely protected import-substitute industries. The protection was also used to favor Marcos's crony businesses. The effective rate of protection for the manufacturing industry fell from 70% to 28.3% between 1985 to 1988. The NTBs on some 1800 items which affected 32% of imports were abolished. Tariff rates were reduced to 10% between 1992 and 1998, and then again to 5% by 2003. Exports are provided tax incentives and export facility.

Until 1980, tax effort (tax revenue to GDP ratio) averaged only about 12%. Tax revenue came from import duties, income taxes and indirect taxes plus other taxes. They have about equal shares in tax revenue. Income tax has a progressive schedule, though it is poorly implemented and does not significantly contribute to tax progressiveness. The indirect taxes were, until 1995, largely excise taxes on a few items such as tobacco and alcohol. They have been replaced by value-added tax. The ineffectiveness of tax collection explains much of the low tax effort, though this has been rising and is now at about 18%. Manasan (1998) found that the rate of evasion was about 60% for income and indirect taxes. Corruption is perceived to be prevalent in the Bureau of Customs thus lowering its tax effort. The celebrated government loss of the tax case amounting to 10% of tax revenue against Fortune Tobacco, which is owned by a close friend of President Estrada, adds to the evidence of prevalent tax evasion.

Government expenditures have not been directed at accelerating economic growth.

The share of capital outlay for infrastructure has been very small as compared to the country's East Asian neighbors, averaging 15.7% in the 1986–89 and 16.6% or about 3.0% of GDP in the 1990s. Debt service, which absorbed 39.0%, of the budget in 1986–89, crowded out all expenditures including infrastructure. Debt service has declined since then and is now only 14.4%. The largest allocation has been to social services, mainly education, which averaged more than 20% through the years. The government has

Table 11.2 Indicators of Economic Fundamentals (1986–1999)

Year	S/GDP	I/GDP	CA/GDP	National Government Deficits/GDP	Index of REER 1980=100	Inflation rate
1986	19.0	15.2	3.1	−5.1		0.8
1987	21.0	17.5	−1.4	−2.4		3.8
1988	21.1	18.7	−1.0	−2.9		8.8
1989	21.3	21.6	−6.7	−1.6		12.2
1990	18.7	24.2	−5.8	−0.7	69.2	13.2
1991	16.6	20.2	−1.9	−1.6	68.2	18.8
1992	14.1	21.3	−1.6	−3.1	76.4	8.6
1993	13.8	24.0	−5.5	−1.4	74.7	7.0
1994	14.9	24.1	−4.5	1.1	79.6	8.3
1995	14.5	22.5	−4.3	0.8	84.3	8.0
1996	15.2	24.8	−4.6	0.8	91.4	9.1
1997	15.3	26.3	−5.1	0.6	88.5	5.9
1998	12.4	22.1	1.9	0.6	69.5	9.8
1999	12.1	22.4	4.9	–	75.9[1]	7.4[2]

Note: [1]June 1999.
[2]Sept. 1999 to Sept. 1998.
Source: NSCB, Philippine Statistical Yearbook 1998, BSP Selected Philippine Economic Indicators, 1997, Oct. 1999.

succeeded in enrolling close to about 95% of its young children but the education sector is faulted for producing poor quality education. Advanced science and technology has been badly neglected.[2]

4. THE DOWNTURN AND ITS CAUSE

The economy suffered three downturns over the last two decades. The 1997–1999 economic downturn was much less serious and had different

---

[2] In the Asiaweek rating of the Asia Pacific Region's best universities, the most prestigious University of the Philippines ranked 46 out of 62 in 1997 and 26 in 1998.

causes than the 1989–1991 recession and the 1983–85 crisis: GDP declined from 3.2% to −7.5 in 1980–83 to 1983–84 and to −7.5 in 1984–85 and from 5.2% to −0.5% in 1997 to 1998. A succession of destructive events led to the 1990–1991 recession. A near-successful military coup in December 1989 created uncertainty in the political and economic system and discouraged business investment, stopping short the recovery from the 1983–85 economic crisis. In mid-1990, a strong earthquake badly damaged Baguio, the summer capital and third largest city and its surrounding agricultural area. In 1991, Mount Pinatubo had one of the century's strongest volcanic eruption. It destroyed much of Pampanga, one of the more progressive provinces and hastened the departure of the American military from the Clark Air Base following the termination of the base agreement with the US. The Gulf War added to the problems when oil price shot up for a few months in 1991. All these shifted aggregate supply to the left, resulting in an inflationary downturn. The current downturn may also be seen as a large leftward supply shift, due partly from contagion and all its repercussions and partly from the drought wrought by the El Niño phenomenon. El Niño did not hit all of Asia but mainly North Korea, Indonesia and the Philippines. This section examines in greater details the causes of the 1997–1998 downturn, specifically the macro fundamentals, the external sector and capital flows and the performance of the financial system and the quality of its architecture, and the behavior of the fiscal sector. An outstanding feature of the country's experience is the relative strength of the financial system.

4.1 Growth and Macro Fundamentals in the 1990's

As explained earlier, El Niño reduced agricultural output by 6.7% in 1997–1998 contributing 2.41 times to the GDP decline.[3] The Asian contagion and bad policies damaged the industrial sector which experienced a dive in growth rate from 6.1% to −1.9%. Construction suffered a very large drop, from 16.2% to −8.5%. But export growth accelerated in this period to 1999. The trend in export growth contrasts with the crisis-hit economies, which

---

[3] [(18% to GDP share × −6.7 growth) ÷ −0.5% GDP growth rate].

experienced export slowdown starting in 1994–1995. The up trend may be attributed to the trade liberalization, which reduced the biases against exports (Tecson 1998), and possibly compensated for the declining competitiveness in the garment industry, a major export industry. Exports are increasingly being concentrated in electronics, which now comprise about 60% of the total. This high concentration makes the country's export sector vulnerable to keen worldwide competition and rapid technological changes in this industry. Manufacturing has shown a very modest performance despite the growth of exports.

Saving rate has been low as compared to all the East Asian neighbors. It averaged about 21% in 1986–1990 but began to fall in 1990. There was excess saving over investment in 1986–1989, which went to debt service, but since then the investment/GDP ratio exceeded the saving/GDP ratio by about 8 percentage points on average from 1990 to 1998. This means a high dependence of investment on foreign financing. The current account deficits/GDP ratio (CA/GDP) showed an upward trend rising from −0.7% to 5.1% from 1990 to 1997. The recession drastically brought down imports and led to a surplus in the current account in 1998 up to the first half of this year. There was an upward movement of the real effective exchange rate from 69.2% to 91.4% from 1990 to 1996 which perhaps stimulated exports, albeit not to the maximum considering that the REER index was still less than unity in the 1990s relative to 1980. The REER declined as an aftermath of the Asian crisis as the currency depreciated at a slower rate than its trading partners' did.

The public sector appears not to have contributed to the current problems, since the trend in the cash budget operation was towards a surplus from 1994 onward.

Inflation rate fluctuated widely since 1986 (also in the 1970s to 1985). Supply shocks from oil price inflation; currency depreciation and natural calamities affecting food supply explain much of the upward swings in the price level. The 1989–1991 calamities and political disturbances shifted the aggregate supply curves to the left, thus the inflationary downturn in this period. The supply shifts in 1997–1998 due to El Niño, currency depreciation and high interest rate also resulted in stagflation. Attempts to control inflation through monetary and fiscal policies have had only moderating effects because

Table 11.3 National Government Cash Budget Current, 1986–98

(Billion Pesos)

Year	Revenue	Surplus (Deficits)	Debt Service % share	Other Current Expenditures (% share)	Capital Outlay (% share)	Equity and Net L (% share)
1986	79.2	−31.3	35.2	41.8	23.0	–
1987	103.2	−16.7	45.2	36.9	13.0	4.90
1988	112.9	−23.2	42.6	43.6	10.9	2.90
1989	142.1	−14.6	32.8	50.5	15.8	0.90
1990	179.5	−7.9	41.6	42.6	15.0	0.80
1991	220.8	−19.8	41.1	40.0	16.9	2.00
1992	223.3	−42.3	38.1	48.0	13.1	0.80
1993	260.3	−20.6	36.4	48.4	14.3	0.90
1994	335.3	18.1	24.2	55.8	20.3	0.30
1995	370.0	15.5	19.6	55.3	24.8	0.30
1996	417.2	17.5	19.1	68.4	12.2	0.30
1997	485.1	14.7	16.0	69.5	14.3	0.20
1998	540.9	16.0	14.4	71.1	13.6	0.09

Source: NSCB, Philippine Statistical Yearbook, 1998.

supply shocks occurred before the anti-inflation cycle could be completed. The relatively poor performance of the agricultural sector since the 1980s and its sensitivity to climatic changes tend to set the inflation level at a much higher rate than in the neighboring economies.

4.2 Movement in the Capital Account

The Philippines is known not to be a 'miracle' country and so failed to attract as much capital as the EA-4. (Growth had been much slower and more unstable and the infrastructure, especially communications was inadequate.) Still it experienced capital surges in 1995 to 1997.

The balance of payments (BOP) accounts show net capital flows of less than \$2B until 1992 but increased to \$2.8B in 1993, then to \$4.5B in 1994, and \$4.4B in 1995; it more than doubled to \$11.1B in 1996, but dove down to \$6.6B in 1997 and further to \$0.9B in 1998. The net flow consisted largely of medium and long term loans and direct investments, again in

Table 11.4 Capital Accounts Flows and Gross International Reserves (GIR)

(US$ MN.)

| Year | Net Flows | | | | | | | | Inflow | | | | GIR and Off Period |
	MT & LT Loans	Bonds and Securities	Investments	FDI	Portfolio	S T Loans	Change in KBNFA	Total	Loans MT & LT	Bonds and Securities	Investments Total	Portfolio	
1986	732		114			−824		81	2605		186		2506
87	159		326			80		565	2598		439		2014
88	(519)		986			−303		164	2412		1077		2111
89	381		843			−89		1135	2797		961		2375
1990	674		480			19	603	1776	4575		498		2048
91	835		654			349	40	1878	3622		681		4525
92	633		737			660	289	1850	7432		931		5338
93	2455		812			−148	−299	2820	5205		2135		5922
94	1313		1558			1002	674	4547	4369		2492		7121
95	1276		1609			−56	1574	4403	3927		2944		7762
96	2841	−37	3517	520	2101	540	4214	11,075	6540	4148	3621	1520	11,745
97	4824	−676	762	1249	−406	495	1188	6593	7724	3072	843	1249	8767
98	2850	−1082	1672	2016	206	−1521	−963	956	5791	3308	2016	1752	10,806
99[1]	2898	−439	1022	1244	604	−1163	−214	2104	4562	2594	1244	649	14,575

Note: MT, LT, ST are medium term, long term and short term loans; KB are commercial banks; NFA is net foreign assets.
[1]1999 data is for Jan. to July.

Source: BSP, Statistical Bulletin, 1997, BSP Selected Philippine Economic Indicators, October 1999, December 1997.

contrast to Thailand's largely short-term flows. Both these accounts had positive net flows throughout the critical period of 1996 to 1999. There were fewer fluctuations in the MT and LT loans, which were largely from ODA sources.

The investment flows consisted of FDI that had net inflows throughout the 1997–1999 period and the unstable portfolio flows. Net portfolio investment first reported in 1996 was $2.1 Billion, –0.406B in 1997, $0.206B

Table 11.5 Distribution of External Debt Outstanding by Maturity, by Borrower Type, and by Source

Year	Foreign Exchange Outstanding Liabilities Percent of Total						Non-Bank		MLT & BLT
	Total (US$ Bn.)	MT & LT (%)	ST Non-Trade (%)	ST Trade (%)	To BSP	To KB	To Public	To Private	
1990	28.5	84.6	1.0	14.4	19.2	8.1	57.4	13.3	51.0
91	29.6	83.9	0.8	15.3	17.8	7.1	61.6	13.5	53.5
92	30.9	83.0	1.0	16.0	7.4	6.1	70.3	16.1	59.8
93	34.3	85.3	4.5	10.2	3.8	3.3	72.8	15.4	62.2
94	37.1	86.0	4.9	9.2	2.3	5.9	68.9	18.5	57.5
95	39.4	86.6	6.7	6.8	3.1	10.8	67.7	18.4	61.0
96	41.9	82.8	7.4	9.8	3.3	17.2	54.7	21.8	52.7
97	45.4	81.4	9.6	8.9	5.5	18.0	49.0	27.5	48.3
98	47.8	85.0	9.7	5.3	7.2	16.3	49.8	25.3	52.3
99 Mar.	48.6	86.0	9.1	4.9	6.4	15.9	51.2	25.2	50.9
US$ Bn.									
1997 Dec	45.4	37.0	4.4	4.0	2.5	8.2	22.3	0.5	
1998 Mar	45.7	36.8	4.9	4.0	3.3	7.8	22.1	0.5	
June	45.8	37.6	4.8	3.3	3.9	7.5	21.8	0.5	
Sept	46.4	38.4	5.0	3.0	3.7	7.7	22.4	0.4	
Dec	47.8	40.6	4.6	2.6	3.4	7.8	24.5	0.3	
1999 Mar	48.6	41.8	4.4	2.4	3.1	7.8	25.5	0.3	

Note: ST = short-term, MT = medium-term, LT = long-term.
MLT = multilateral institutions, BLT = bilateral sources.
FCD = foreign currency deposits.
Source: Bangko Sentral ng Pilipinas, Selected Philippine Economic Indicators, December 1998, October 1999.

in 1998 and \$0.604B in 1999. Expectedly, there were net outflows in ST loans and commercial banks (KB) net foreign assets. Large drops in net flows took place in these two accounts for the whole period, turning from positive in 1996 to 1997 to negative in 1998 and 1999. There were always negative net flows for bonds and securities transaction, reflecting resident investments abroad and repayment of government bond issues. The outflows could be inferred as inflow−net flow. Very large outflows took place for bond transactions. Possibly, re-negotiation of MT and LT loans led to lower loan payments beginning in 1997 where outflows show a declining trend despite the rising MT and LT debts.

External debts show a more favorable picture. Medium-term and long-term outstanding liabilities comprise the bulk of the country's external debt averaging about 85% in the early 1990s, falling to 82.8% in 1996, then to 81.4% in 1997 when many short-term loans were coming in. The reversal of short-term flows pushed back the share of medium-term and long-term loans to 86%. About 25% went to the private non-bank sector and 16% to commercial banks or a total of 41% to private. About half of the loans came from multilateral and bilateral sources, which were made largely to MT and LT. Some 35% of the remaining MT and LT loans came from private sources, possibly for private investment in infrastructure through build-operate-transfer (BOT) and similar schemes. These schemes were being encouraged by the government through some risk-sharing arrangements.

Only about 15% of the loans were short-term, half of which were for trade credits, a non-speculative type of loan. Short-term loans as a ratio to gross international reserves was relatively low in 1996 or 61.5% but rose to 95.5% in 1997 when the large inflows took place. The ratio in fact improved from very high levels in the early 1990s.

The debt service burden has been brought down from a very high level −43% of exports in 1990 to 22% in 1997, and 17.2% in 1998. Debt service relative to current account income is much lower, considering that net factor income was generally positive because of the large income from overseas workers. However, overseas workers appear to be quite sensitive to the risk and return of domestic assets relative to those of foreign assets. Foreign income can be readily placed in foreign assets located in the place of work

Table 11.6 Exchange Rate, Debt Service Ratio, Interest Rates, Stock Price Changes 1990–1999

Year	Nominal ER P/US$ Average	Index of REER 1980 = 100	Debt Service as % of			ST Debt/ GIR (%)	Interest Rate					Annual %Δ
			Exports of Goods	Current Acct. Income	GNP		TB 91 days	Lending Rate Average	Lending Rate High	Saving Deposit	Libor Three Months	
1990	24.3	69.2	43.3	25.8	8.1	220.0		24.3			8.2	−12.3
91	27.5	68.2	32.0	18.5	6.2	106.6		23.5			6.0	4.8
92	25.5	76.4	30.0	16.3	5.5	100.0		19.4			3.8	17.4
93	27.1	74.7	28.4	16.5	5.8	84.7	12.3	14.6		8.3	3.3	18.6
94	26.4	79.6	31.1	16.7	6.4	73.2	13.6	15.0		8.0	4.7	25.2
95	25.7	84.3	28.8	15.3	6.6	67.9	11.3	14.6		8.0	6.1	−10.9
96	26.2	91.4	24.5	12.3	5.8	61.5	12.4	14.8		8.0	5.5	−2.6
97	29.5	88.5	22.2	11.3	6.5	95.5	13.1	16.2	19.7	9.1	5.7	−12.9
98	40.9	69.5	17.2	11.5	7.4	66.6	15.3	18.4	19.5	11.0	5.6	−33.5
99	38.5	75.9	18.9	13.1	–	52.7	10.4	12.3	16.6	7.9	5.2	37.6

Table 11.6 (Continued) Nominal Exchange Rate and Nominal Interest Rates, 1998–1999 (Monthly)

Year/ Month	Nominal Exchange Rate P/US$ Ave.	Interest Rate				
		TB 91 days	Lending Rate Average	Lending Rate High	Saving Deposit	Libor 3 months
1998 1	42.7	19.1	21.1	26.8	13.7	5.7
2	40.4	17.8	20.0	26.1	12.5	5.6
3	39.0	16.6	20.1	23.3	12.1	5.7
4	38.4	15.2	18.1	22.0	12.1	5.7
5	39.3	14.4	17.1	21.2	10.3	5.7
6	40.4	14.0	16.1	19.8	10.1	5.7
7	41.8	14.7	16.1	20.4	10.3	5.7
8	43.0	14.1	15.2	19.9	10.2	5.7
9	43.8	13.8	14.6	19.7	10.1	5.5
10	42.9	13.5	14.5	19.8	9.9	5.3
11	39.9	13.5	13.5	19.7	10.0	5.3
12	39.0	13.4	14.8	19.7	10.0	5.2
1999 1	38.4	13.2	14.9	19.5	9.3	5.0
2	38.8	12.7	12.4	19.0	8.9	5.0
3	38.9	12.1	14.0	18.5	8.9	5.0
4	38.2	10.9	12.1	17.2	8.3	5.0
5	37.8	10.0	12.7	16.2	7.6	5.0
6	37.9	9.3	11.5	15.6	7.1	5.2
7	38.3	8.4	10.4	14.9	6.8	5.3
8	39.3	8.4	10.3	14.7	6.6	5.4
9	40.2	8.6	–	14.1	–	5.4

Source: Central Bank of the Philippines (Bangko Sentral ng Pilipinas) Statistical Bulletin, 1990, 1997, Selected Philippine Economic Indicators, June 1998, October 1999.

or anywhere by electronics banking. Remittances declined from $5.7 Billion to $4.9 Billion though the net deployment of workers rose from 747,696 to 755,684 in 1997 to 1998. There is now a fairly permanent stock of workers abroad with only small numbers of new migrants leaving the country each year. As the foreign exchange market stabilized, remittances started to rise again increasing by close to 50% between the first semester 1998 and the first semester 1999. The movement of overseas workers' saving is partly reflected in the foreign currency deposit liabilities of banks.

4.3 The Financial Sector

The reforms undertaken during the Aquino and the Ramos administrations have substantially strengthened the banking system and allowed it to withstand the contagion effects of the Asian crisis. The abandonment of credit intervention and the liberalization of the capital account and bank entry have fostered competition and market discipline. The reforms also encouraged investment in the banking industry and other financial institutions. The number of banks and other types of financial institutions and their branch offices increased significantly, the level of inter-mediation grew substantially, the inter-mediation margin narrowed and a greater variety of instruments and services increased. The banking system manifested a fair degree of stability with rather little insolvency occurring. Only one small bank suffered insolvency in 1998–1999.

The assets of financial institutions/GNP ratio rose from 53.2% in 1987 to 134.1% in 1997 but declined to 123.6% in 1998.

M_3/GNP[4] ratio also had an upward trend from 24.5% to 42.2% over 1986 to 1997, then fell to 41.0% in 1998. The financial assets/GNP ratio grew faster than M_3/GNP ratio, reflecting the increased variety of financial instruments being offered by the proliferating intermediaries. The financial system consists of a very large number of institutions or more than 8000 companies in 1996. Commercial banks (KB) form the most important segment

---

[4] The definition of M_3 is less inclusive than in the US as it consists of only of M_1 and the different types of deposits: saving time, marginal and deposit substitutes.

Table 11.7 Selected Financial Development Indicators (%) 1986–1998

A. Multiplier and Financial Rates

Year	M_1 Multiplier	M_2 Multiplier	Annual Growth of Domestic Credit	Assets of FI / GNP	M_3 / GNP	M_4 / GNP	No. of Bank Offices
1986	1.77	5.98	−15.8		24.5	−	3614
1987	2.10	6.55	11.0	53.2	24.5	−	3547
1988	2.12	7.16	22.7	53.5	25.7	−	3562
1989	1.80	5.93	26.4	58.7	28.5	−	3588
1990	1.77	5.99	24.4	74.6	28.0	29.6	3638
1	1.56	5.36	13.6	73.4	27.7	28.8	3791
2	1.52	5.23	19.9	79.1	28.0	29.2	4296
3	1.46	5.23	32.5	90.6	32.0	33.2	4657
4	1.50	5.99	30.3	94.8	35.0	36.2	5096
5	1.55	6.39	37.2	104.6	38.9	40.2	5564
6	1.62	6.41	47.5	116.6	39.0	40.4	6332
7	1.65	6.62	28.9	134.1	42.2	63.3	7182
8				123.6	41.0	60.7	7696
9							7653[1]

Note: [1] June 1999.

B. Development of Financial Institutions

Year	Asset Share in the Financial System (%) Capital/Asset Ratio							
	KB	EKB	Foreign KB	Gov't KB	FS	KB	EKB	Gov't KB
1986								
7	73.3	38.1	13.9	6.8	13.7	8.7	10.2	30.2
8	74.9	43.1	11.9	6.0	14.4	9.2	10.3	36.5
9	75.8	48.6	9.5	5.0	14.1	8.7	9.1	40.8
1990	76.6	52.1	9.9	6.0	14.0	8.8	9.4	32.9
1	73.6	52.8	8.3	7.6	15.0	10.2	11.2	25.0
2	71.0	52.7	7.0	10.0	15.0	11.3	12.0	18.8
3	68.1	52.2	6.7	12.9	14.3	11.1	11.6	13.3
4	69.4	56.5	6.2	11.2	14.7	11.4	11.7	13.9
5	70.9	57.2	6.4	9.7	15.2	12.5	12.9	13.6
6	82.5	67.3	8.7	−	14.1	11.8	12.6	−
7	74.1	−	−	−				
8	73.2	−	−	−				
9	73.3[2]	−	−	−				

[2] July 1999.

Note: FI = Financial institutions. EKB= Expanded large KB.

KB= Commercial banks. DMB= Deposit money banks.

Table 11.7 (continued) Selected Financial Development Indicators (%) 1986–1998

C. Distribution of Loans and NPL Ratio

Year	% of Loans Granted by KB to Real Estate	% of Loans Outstanding to Real Estate of KB	% MT & LT Loans Outstanding of KB	NPL Ration of DMB
1986	0.6	2.5	30.8	–
7	1.0	2.6	28.5	–
8	1.5	2.8	29.1	–
9	2.6	3.3	25.3	–
1990	2.6	4.0	20.0	7.9
1	1.8	4.3	21.7	7.3
2	1.4	3.7	22.3	6.8
3	0.6	5.5	22.7	5.2
4	–	–	–	4.7
5	–	–	–	4.0
6	6.1	8.0	32.7	3.5
7	7.6	10.4	28.7	5.4
8				11.0[3]
9				

[3]August 1999.

Source: Bangko Sentral ng Pilipinas (BSP) Statistical Bulletin, 1997, Selected Philippine Economic Indicators Dec. 1997, Oct. 1999.

of the financial system and contributed 82% to the system's assets in 1997 and 73% in 1998. There were 49 KBs in 1997 of which 21 were classified as expanded commercial bank (EKB) with larger capital requirement and the authority to make proportionately large investments in equities. Their asset share was 67% of the total. Included among the EKBs are three government banks. Foreign bank branches number 22 from only 4 before the relaxation of foreign bank entry in 1995. The other KBs are much smaller and their assets averaged only P7B as compared to P70B for the EKBs. The other financial institutions are even smaller. They shared only 18% of the system's assets and had an average size of only P56 Million.

The health of the financial system rests on the health of the commercial banks considering their high relative importance. Examined here are their sources and uses of funds and non-performing loan to total loan ratio or NPL. Table 11.8 shows significant improvements in saving mobilization as indicated by the proportion of loanable funds tapped from deposits by both the KBs and the rural banks. The share of their bills and other liabilities which include rediscounting and other borrowings from the central bank gradually declined through 1995. In the Marcos era (before 1986), banks, especially rural banks, relied heavily on this source, since it was given cheaply and they could not attract as many deposits because of the interest rate repression. The share of deposit liabilities was much higher among the KBs than among the government banks and the rural banks; in 1986 the deposit shares were, respectively, 62.3%, 44.0% and 49.2% in 1995–1996, the shares were 69%, 21% and 77%. The share of deposits in KBs fell in 1996 and 1997 because of the increased reliance on short-term foreign loans. The three government banks greatly increased their borrowings in 1995, possibly, in part, from foreign sources as well. Rural banks are too small and little known to be able to issue bills or borrow from abroad.

The banks' portfolios underwent substantial changes. More than 90% of loans went to the private sector (see Table 11.7). The share of medium-term and long-term loans increased from 22.85% average level in 1988–1992 to 27.7% in 1997 and then to 33.7% in 1997. The rise in maturities likely resulted from the growing loans to real estate. The new loans (loans granted accounts) to real estate absorbed 6.1% in 1996 and 7.6% in 1997 from just over 2% in the preceding decade. Other assets in the banking portfolio, such as investment in securities and consumption loans, did not change significantly. No data on car loans is reported, though these became very visible in the late 1990s and could have caused problems.

There was acceleration in the growth rate of gross domestic credits in deposit money banks (DMB) starting in 1993.

Growth rose from an average rate of 21.4% in the preceding five years (1988–1992) to an average rate of 31.4% in the next two years (1993–1994), and then to an average rate of 42.4% in 1994 to 1997. The growth of domestic credit was partly financed from external sources as seen in the rapid acceleration of the growth rate of foreign liabilities. Their growth rate rose from 23.4% to 29.5% and to 60.9% for the same period. The bank's foreign liabilities were not fully hedged, since the foreign liabilities always exceeded foreign assets.

Table 11.8 Sources and Uses of Funds in Banks, 1986–1997

	Commercial Banks				Government Banks			Rural Banks		
Year	Deposits Total Liab.	Bills and Other Liab. Total Liab.	Chattel Mortgage Total Assets	Real Estate Loans Total Asset	Deposits Total Liab.	Bills and Other Liab. Total Liab.	Chattel Mortgage Total Assets	Deposits Total Liab.	Bills and Other Liab. Total Liab.	Chattel Mortgage Total Assets
1986	62.8	35.3	1.9		44.0	55.4	7.9	49.2	49.8	3.9
7	62.4	36.0	1.6		37.9	61.4	4.5	55.7	43.0	3.7
8	66.4	31.6	1.3		53.8	44.9	3.7	58.7	40.5	3.5
9	67.7	30.6	0.9		49.8	48.7	3.3	61.2	37.0	3.2
1990	65.0	33.6	0.8		50.4	47.5	2.5	63.3	34.4	3.0
1	69.4	29.3	0.8		48.8	49.7	1.8	66.7	31.3	2.8
2	71.1	28.2	0.8		47.6	50.1	1.4	70.5	28.2	2.7
3	73.5	24.8	1.1		36.7	62.8	1.1	73.5	25.2	2.7
4	74.8	24.0	1.0		21.3	78.1	1.1	76.1	22.3	2.6
5	75.0	23.7	0.8		21.1	78.2	1.1	76.7	21.8	2.2
6	68.5	29.3	0.6		–		–	75.6	23.5	2.2
7	66.6	32.6	0.8		–		–			–
March 1997				11.9						
Dec. 1997				13.7						
June 1998				12.1						
Dec. 1998				13.1						

Source: Bangko Sentral ng Pilipinas (BSP) Statistical Bulletin, 1997, 1990; Selected Philippine Economic Indicators, Oct. 1999, Dec. 1997.

The 1997–1998 downturn, like the 1983–85 crisis, was preceded by very high ratios of foreign liabilities to foreign assets. The ratio peaked at 478% in 1982 then it gradually declined to 108% in 1988 but rose monotonically until it peaked at 323% in 1996. The capital flow reversal brought it down quite rapidly to 205% in 1997 and 184% in 1998. The reliance on foreign sources of domestic credit is reflected in the ratio of net foreign assets (liabilities) to gross domestic credit. There were modest movements in the money multipliers.

The bank restructuring and reforms appear to have improved the quality of bank loans until the Asian crisis hit the system. The NPL ratio shows a declining trend from 1990 to 1996 for the whole financial system and for the commercial banks (KB).

The high NPL of 7.9% in 1990 was inherited from the financial repression period. The KBs had 7.2% NPL ratio, the thrift banks the same level, but the highly subsidized rural banks 28.5%. The KBs were able to reduce their NPL ratio, which fell to 2.8% and the rural banks to 14.1% by 1996. The improvement in rural banks is partly explained by the closure of some 180 insolvent banks, which contributed a large share of the group's NPLs. The NPL ratio of the whole financial system increased to 11% following the 1997–1998 downturn. The KBs that form a very large segment of the system contributed about 85% to the total NPLs. The KBs' NPL ratio rose first from 2.8% to 4.7% in 1996 to 1997 and then to 10.3% in 1998 and 14.4% in the first quarter of 1999. The large or expanded KBs and the foreign bank branches suffered lower NPL problem than the smaller KBs. The government banks show lower NPL ratios than the private banks, though there could be significant underreporting of their NPLs. The media reported a very high NPL ratio of 26 to 29% for the Philippine National Bank and bankruptcies of some large borrowers of the Land Bank of the Philippines. These banks are reported to have made connected loans.

On the whole, the banking system survived the crisis in 1983–85 and the current downturn with minimal bank failures and no bank runs. There is a core group of large banks that have established prudent practices and a solid reputation. Only one small KB was officially declared insolvent in 1998. The cause was not the currency crisis but violations of the DOSRI

Table 11.9 Foreign Assets and Liabilities of Deposit Money Banks, 1980–1998

Year	Foreign Assets and Liabilities of DMB				Distribution of Gross Domestic Credit of DMB (%)		Net Foreign Assets
	Net (% Δ)	Assets (% Δ)	Liabilities (% Δ)	Liabilities Assets (%)	Loans to Private	ST Loans[1] Total Loans	Gross Domestic Credit (%)
1980				216	78.7	78.2	21.7
81	−9.6	11.7	0.3	194	80.8	73.4	16.7
82	25.0	21.0	23.2	198	79.5	69.0	18.0
83	77.0	19.0	47.1	244	78.2	66.8	24.3
84	21.9	50.3	33.7	217	71.0	60.6	29.0
85	−25.0	−4.8	−15.7	192	68.8	65.9	23.5
86	−63.9	7.8	−26.6	131	62.5	69.2	10.0
87	−35.0	25.0	11.0	116	70.0	71.5	5.9
88	−40.0	26.4	17.1	108	68.1	70.9	2.9
89	73.4	14.0	18.2	112	66.6	74.6	4.0
1990	140.6	35.2	46.1	121	69.6	80.0	7.7
91	49.1	−8.4	1.4	134	66.1	78.3	10.0
92	91.3	15.1	34.2	156	68.7	77.6	16.0
93	39.0	16.8	24.8	166	72.5	72.3	15.8
94	43.8	11.2	24.2	186	71.7	–	18.5
95	63.2	13.4	36.4	223	75.5	–	22.1
96	130.8	28.2	85.4	323	78.2	66.3	34.5
97	−47.4	10.8	−29.5	205	77.7	70.0	14.1
98	−23.3	−4.1	−14.0	184			
99	−2.4	−7.3	−5.5	184			

[1]Commercial banks only.

Source: BSP Statistical Bulletin, 1997, 1990, 1988, BSP Selected Philippine Economic Indicators, October 1999.

Table 11.10 Non-performing Loans of Financial System and Banks

Year	Loan Loss Provision	Non-Performing Loans/Total Loans								
		FS	KB	TB	RB	KB	EKB	NEKB	Gov't.	FX
A. NPL of Financial System 1990–1999										
1990	4.4	7.9	7.2	7.2	28.5					
1	3.8	7.3	6.6	7.6	26.3					
2	3.3	6.8	6.1	7.9	24.4					
3	2.5	5.2	4.7	6.0	21.3					
4	2.0	4.7	3.9	8.4	18.2					
5	1.7	4.0	3.2	7.9	16.1					
6	1.4	3.5	2.8	7.7	14.1		2.4	3.7	4.3	3.3
7	2.3	5.4	4.7	10.7	15.4		4.2	7.2	6.1	4.4
8	4.0	11.0	10.3	16.3	18.0		10.4	13.6	10.1	7.9
March 9			14.4				15.2	18.5	13.3	5.4
B. Percentage in Total NPL										
1998	(P bill)	188.7	160.0	21.3	7.4	160.0	112.4	16.5	18.8	12.2
	%	100.0	84.8	11.3	3.9	100.0	70.2	10.3	11.8	7.6
C. Percentage Share in Total Financial Assets										
		100.0	82.1	7.8	2.0	82.1	67.3	6.1	–	8.7

Note: KB = Commercial banks, EKB = Expanded (large) KB, NEKB = Non-Expanded KB, TB = Thrift banks, government banks, and FX = Foreign banks and branches.
Sources: BSP Selected Philippine Economic Indicator (SPEI) April 1999, October 1999. BSP Fact of Financial System, 1996, 1995.

rule (loans to directors, officers and affiliated individuals). In the 1983–85 crisis, more banks closed down: 3 KBs and some 180 rural banks; 3 GFI's became insolvent but the failures did not lead to a bank run. The rural banks might be the weakest segment of the banking sector, though they form a very small segment of the banking industry, about 5% of its assets. They are small unit banks with an average capital of P56Million ($1.38Million at PP40.1/$1 exchange rate) and likely operate below efficient scale.

While the banking system has exhibited resilience and sound practices, there remains some structural problems that negatively affect its overall efficiency. Too many banks have been allowed to be established as part of the supply-leading strategy of the 1950s to 1970s. There now exist 8000 deposit money banks. The policy that allowed foreign entry has attracted 22 foreign bank branches from the original 4 in 1994. The 10 largest banks dominate the banking system, contributing 67% of its total assets. The banks, in turn, dominate the financial system with an asset share of 73%. The securities' market has not developed fast enough because of weak architecture. A bill is pending in Congress for instituting stricter monitoring and supervision standards. A scandal about connected insider trading is getting much media reporting and flight from the equity market.[5] There is an undeveloped government securities market. The government issues mainly large denominated securities in P100,000 lots which only the very wealthy can afford to hold. The recent issue of P5000 denominated bonds has had little impact in the market since the volume was too small to reach the small savers. Competition is hampered by this structure and possibly contributes to the persistently large inter-mediation margin (lending rate-saving deposit rate) that averaged 7.0 percentage points in 1995–1998. The margin is much higher than in the country's more advanced neighbors.

---

[5] The term connected is used here to mean all forms of politically influenced activities. A gaming company manipulated its stocks that pushed its price from P2.70 to P104 then to P3.0 in one month's trading. The media alleged close friendship between the President and the speculators.

4.4 Policy Responses

Until the end of 1997, the BSP felt confident that its international reserves would be able to fend off attacks on the currency.[6] But by then, the exchange rate had already risen from P26/$1 to P32/$1. Some economists welcomed the depreciation as favorable to exports. The problem in Thailand was initially seen to be limited to its boundaries. The spread to Korea and then to Indonesia at the end of 1997 fanned speculative attack on the peso, and the exchange rate continuously rose by the day, reaching P43/$1 in January 1998.

The BSP's initial response took two forms — "intensified dollar sales and several upward adjustments of its key overnight interest rates" (p. 9 BSP July 1999). The dollar sale was abandoned in July 1997 when the BSP wisely realized it could not effectively move against the assault on the currency. But it continued with the credit crunch by increasing the reserve requirements. The following measures were adopted:

1. The BSP provided non-deliverable forward facility as a hedging facility to cover the risk of eligible borrowers with existing un-hedged foreign liabilities in foreign currency deposits. Under the scheme only the net difference between the contracted forward rate and the market rate was to be settled and paid in pesos. The BSP however also tightened prudential rules on foreign exchange transactions. Banks had to obtain prior BSP clearance for their sales of non-deliverable contracts to non-residents. Restraints on banks' overbought/oversold foreign exchange position from 20% to 5% of unimpaired capital and from $100,000 to $25,000 of over-the-counter sale of foreign exchange.
2. The BSP overnight borrowing rate was raised from 15% in end of June 1997 to 37% in mid-July 1997. Its lending rate was likewise raised from 17% to 34% in the same period. In the following month, its lending facility was temporarily closed "to have a firm grip on liquidity".
3. Liquidity reserves, a new form of reserve requirement, was imposed in July 1997, first at 2% and later raised to 8% in August 1997. The reserves could be in government securities.

---

[6] From a conversation with a Monetary Board member in November 1997.

4. When the NPL rate increased, loan loss provisions were imposed first at 1% in October 1998, then at 1.5% in April 1999 and at 2% in October 1999.
5. The Bankers Association of the Philippines (BAP) agreed among themselves with encouragement from the BSP to transact foreign exchange within a band, initially within 2–4% and later within 4–6%. The band was effective from October 1997 to March 1998.

The deflationary monetary policy did reduce the growth rate of credit from 47.5% in 1995 to 1996 to 28.9% in 1996–1997. The lending rate which averaged 14.5% and 13.5% in 1966 and in the first half of 1997 rose to 19.1% in the second half. The rate reached high levels of 26.8% in November and December of 1997. The drastic rise in interest rate and in the NPL of banks alarmed the BSP and led it to reverse its policy (not without IMF approval). The regular reserve requirement was lowered by 3 percentage points in March 1998, then by another 2 percentage points in May 1998 "to help bring down the cost of money and make more funds available for lending". The BSP lending rate was brought down in January 1998 and the rediscount window was reopened.

Meanwhile, prudential regulations were imposed including the following: (1) portfolio ceiling on real estate loan at 20% of the total, (2) lower loanable value of real estate collateral, (3) a 30% liquid cover on all foreign exchange liabilities and foreign currency deposits, (4) raised the qualification of bank managers, (5) redefined the criteria for past due loans by reducing the number of instalments in arrears to 6- monthly or 2–3 quarterly, and (6) loan loss provisions for NPL loans at 1% in October 1998, 1.5% in April 1999 and 2.0% in October 1999, and (7) increased the minimum capital requirement of the different bank categories from P3.5B to P4.5B for expanded KB and P1.525B to P2.0B for the non-expanded KB. The BSP encourages mergers as a way of raising bank capital.

The deflationary actions of the Bangko Sentral in 1997 exacerbated the uncertainties and pessimism. The large increases in interest rate and the large depreciation of the currency wrought a triple whammy to the banking sector. The higher reserve requirements and the loan provisioning directly increased the inter-mediation cost and reduced credit supply. The banks' un-hedged foreign liabilities amounted to about 22% of domestic credit at end of 1996. The currency depreciation of about 54% implies an approximate loss of 11% on these credits. The tight monetary policy and the rise in NPL arising from the recession reduced the banks inter-mediation volume. Some large banks reported drastic falls in their profit rates. The real sector suffered on two counts. Those who borrowed foreign exchange suffered currency losses and had to pay high interest rates to service their debts. All had to suffer a liquidity crunch and pay high interest rate. The real estate sector and the consumer durable sector were more sensitive to interest rate and so experienced larger output declines.

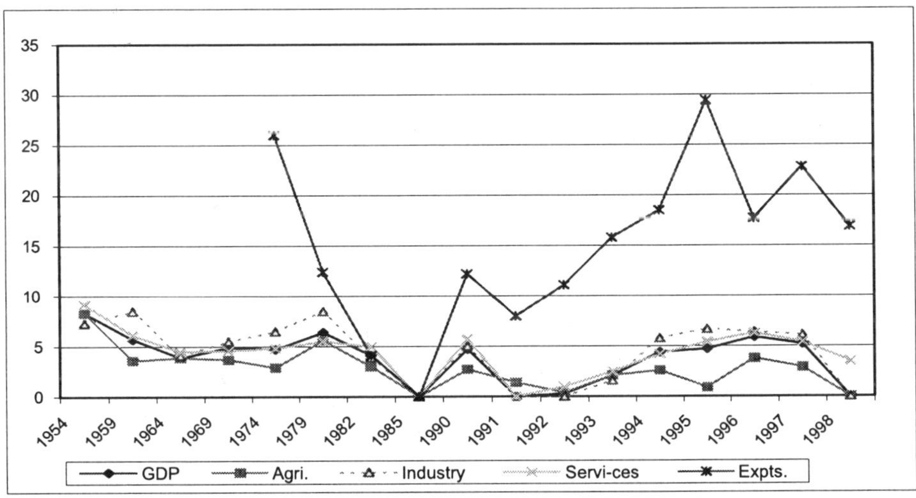

Fig. 11.1 Annual Growth Rate of GDP, Sectors, Exports

5. CONCLUSIONS

The Philippines suffered a serious economic crisis in 1983–1985 of a similar nature to that which Indonesia experiences now. Their problem had a political origin, where the leaders of their dictatorial governments appropriated and misallocated economic resources. The financial system became a channel for economic capture. This sector is vulnerable to abuses since transactions are not physically observable. Misallocation in real resources is not immediately observed and is allowed to accumulate to some substantial dimension before the public becomes aware of the problem. A dictatorship can therefore last for years before it is toppled. External assistance from multilateral agencies helped sustain the Philippines and Indonesian dictators. The Philippines received large increases in ODA from the World Bank and other international agencies after Martial Law was declared in 1972. The Suharto government has also been one of the five largest recipients of ODAs in the world and in Asia 1980s and 1990s. Both the Philippines and Indonesia had large external debt overhang and extensive bank insolvencies when their dictators were removed. Insolvencies in the financial system occurred largely in the GFIs and small rural banks. Fortunately, there was a large enough core of financially strong private commercial banks, which had developed a solid tradition of prudent banking. Their presence prevented bank runs and allowed fast recovery. It also enabled the sector to attract foreign equity without much delay. Indonesia faces a longer struggle with its bank restructuring. It developed its financial institutions later than the Philippines and Indonesia's banking system is dominated by government banks, which may take time to privatize.

The economy began recovering in 1999 as GDP growth reversed from –5% to 2.7%. The growth rate for 1999–2000 is expected to be at about 4%. The manufacturing sector experienced a positive growth of 6% this year, from negative growth in 1998 and 1999. The weather has been favorable, so agriculture is expected to produce above average growth of 3%. The export sector boasts of accelerating growth rate from 16% in 1998 to 19% in the last quarter of 1999. Barring political and other extraneous upheavals, the economy is expected to course through its old low growth path of 5–6%, considering the weak growth fundamentals that have characterized it. There are no new policies and strategies to propel it to a higher growth path. No measures are being taken for raising the saving rate, for intensifying population control, for increasing tax effort, for increasing investments in infrastructure, for raising agricultural productivity, for stimulating tourism, for diversifying manufacturing production, or for strengthening technological capability through advanced ST education and research. The President's promise to pursue poverty alleviation and agricultural growth has not been concretized into operational strategies and measures. Even the rhetoric has been sparse. There are evident signs of a significant deterioration in the quality of governance which creates uncertainties about the direction of policy and how it is to be implemented. The recovery is slower than in the 1983–1985 crisis, possibly because of the uncertainties emanating from a deterioration of governance. Both domestic and foreign investments have been rising, albeit too slowly. A recent survey of 300 of the 700 biggest corporation gave the government a generally poor rating, pointing to its lack of direction and the return of cronyism. A survey of foreign investors gave similar results. In his recent visit, World Bank President Wolfenson warned the administration that it cannot solve poverty at its low target growth given the high population rate of 2.3% (Business World, February 28, 2000).

The three main hypotheses of the causes of the Asian crisis do not strongly apply to the Philippines downturn. The capital account liberalization took place after essential prudential regulations and practices in the banking system have been established. There is much improvement in the BSP data collection detailing the flow of funds from both domestic and foreign sources. More data on foreign transactions are being collected now than before. Goldman and Sachs (1998) in fact gave the country's banking sector fairly high ratings. The banking system was able to absorb their large currency losses and NPLs. Not one major bank became insolvent. The one small bank that failed did so because of violations of BSP rule on DOSRI (loans to directors and related individuals). A 20% ceiling on real estate loans/total loans ratio was imposed in 1996 though the banks' ratio was below this. The capital/asset ratio of banks has always exceeded the Basel standard. The currency depreciation likely prevented the decline in exports and compensated for the slack demand from the region especially Japan.

There were some differences in the problems that led to the crisis in Korea, Thailand, Indonesia and Malaysia. In Korea the concentration of economic power in the chaebols appears to be central to the weaknesses that developed in the financial system and in the allocation of investment funds across industries and companies. The Korean case has its equivalence in Indonesia's crony capitalism. Economic power is more dispersed in Thailand and Malaysia. Thailand had a weaker financial architecture than Malaysia. The role of capital flow also differs significantly across the EA-4. Thailand falls more closely to the stereotype case of short-term capital upsurge that went to create real estate and stock market speculation and over-heating. There were much less short-term flows into Indonesia and Korea than into Thailand. Korea's short-term flows largely went to banks which allowed easier roll-overs. Indonesia's short-term loans went to firms and could not be readily renegotiated. Politics had much to do with the uncertainties and inefficiencies in Indonesia.

The moral hazard in the banking sector are of different nature. Indonesia still has a dominant government banking system which is subject to greater government interventions. Thailand's financial system has always been largely private and their insolvency is the bankers' own doing, permitted by poor prudential environment and over-optimism. Korea's banks are dominantly private but are under the control of the chaebols. According to Park (1997), bank loan officers merely rubber stamp the loan applications that have already been negotiated between the chaebols and the bank heads.

All the EA-4 and the Philippines maintained overvalued currency prior to the crisis. This worsened the loss of competitiveness of Thai exports whose growth began declining since 1994. Thailand had the highest current account deficits among the EA-4, 8% in 1997. Indonesia's export earnings were more subject to oil price movement though oil's share in total export had long declined. Indonesia had the lowest CA/GDP ratio. Korea maintained technological capacity to export higher-tech products. But the inefficiencies in the chaebol-controlled economy offset the advantages from its advanced R&D and high quality manpower.

The IMF imposes the conditions that the EA-4 adopt and implement the prescribed financial architecture, meaning international standards of accounting and auditing, disclosure rules, prudential regulations and effective supervision. The connected banking syndrome has to be broken down. In Indonesia this would require the privatization of banks, in Korea, the break-up of the chaebols, and in Thailand, more effective prudential rules and supervision.

The theory on market failure problems inherent in the banking industry (and other financial sectors) needs to be put in the context of banks' long-run objectives. Central banks do provide some implicit guarantees and last recourse facility to prevent bank runs and the failure of the payment system. In the US the Fed have, in a few cases, also decided to prevent big banks from failing. The banks, in turn, institute mechanisms for reducing moral hazards on the part of their clients. Adverse selection is minimized by good accounting and auditing practices and monitoring. There are unsystematic risk that can be minimized by diversification and prudential procedures. The literature on the market problems implicitly argues that central bank guarantees encourage banks to be imprudent. It does not look at the cost of failure to a bank. A bank is established for a long horizon. As a trust institution, its viability depends on its goodwill which is created by constant good performance over a long time period. Insolvency destroys goodwill so that even if a bank is bailed out by the central bank, it loses goodwill, its most valuable asset. Throughout the world, there are historical banks like the Hongkong Shanghai Bank, Chase Manhattan Bank, Union Bank of Switzerland, etc. In the Philippines, the oldest most respected bank, the Bank of the Philippine Islands, has survived through the Marcos era and the current difficulties. The ten largest banks here, which include the Far East Bank, the Metropolitan Bank, the Rizal Commercial and Industrial Bank, the Philippine Commercial and Industrial Bank and the Allied Bank have remained stable.

The moral hazard problem that is seen to emanate from central bank and other guarantees appears to be exaggerated. From the individual bank viewpoint, they provide a good insurance for temporary problems but they are immaterial as far as the bank's long-run objectives are concerned. The inherent problems of market failure are seen not to be the cause of financial failures. The problems are traceable to direct interventions and abuses in an environment of political-economic concentration.

APPENDIX Note:

As a colony of the US, the country suffered more economic destruction during WWII. The damage from heavy bombing (by America) wrought the heaviest destruction of physical capital and human toll in all of the Asia-Pacific region. America imposed fixed exchange rate at P2/$1 and heavy preferential trading agreement as conditions for its reconstruction assistance to the Philippines. Extensive import controls and conservative monetary policy had to be adopted in order to maintain this exchange rate level. The control package favored import of "essential" goods that in effect provided heavy protection for import substitutes that were largely consumer goods. The import-substitution policy continued until the end of the 1960s although the measures changed from quantitative controls to high and differentiated tariff rates. The currency was devalued for the first time in 1960–63 with the nominal exchange rate doubling to around P4/$1. Gradual trade and industrialization reforms were undertaken intermittently since the 1970s. Tariff rates were reduced for the first time in the early 1970s, then again in the 1980s and the 1990s. But the Marcos government (1965–1985) imposed non-trade barriers on about 1800 items which affected 32.0% of imports. The barriers were used to favor selected crony businesses. Government intervention in the financial market was extensive throughout the first four decades of the post-independence period, 1946 to 1986. Interest rate ceilings were set and subsidized credit were provided to priority sectors by government financial institutions (GFI) and subsidized thrift banks. The government followed the world fashion of supply-leading financial development as it established GFIs and subsidized the creation of private banks. It operated the Philippine National Bank, the largest commercial bank until its restructuring in 1996, the Development Bank of the Philippines and two other smaller banks (the Philippine Veterans Bank and the Amanah Bank), the Government Social Insurance System (for civil servants) and the Social Security System (for private employees). The Central Bank of the Philippines (now called the Bangko Sentral ng Pilipinas or BSP) was established in 1948. Its initial task was to defend the currency, manage the import control scheme and provide subsidized capital and loanable funds to the GFIs and the private development banks and rural banks. These are small unit thrift banks. The Monetary Board of the CB was dominated by cabinet secretaries and was therefore not independent.

The nominal interest rate ceilings originated from the anti-usury law of 1900's. Deposit ceilings were also imposed through 1980. At the same time, CB granted easy and cheap rediscounting facilities for all banks and preferential ones for the government banks and the subsidized thrift banks. The loan rate ceilings meant low real rates which oftentimes turned negative in times of high inflation. The real deposit rates were almost always negative during the 1960s through the 1980s. The policy had the predictable result of repressing inter-mediation activities and the development of the financial system. Banks could not attract as much deposits as they could. The rediscounting facility of the CB was a good substitute source of loanable funds for some banks though the rediscounting volume was restricted by the dictates of general monetary policy. The presence of GFIs and the availability of subsidized credit also permitted inefficient loan allocation. The GFIs are not subject to the discipline of the market since the institutions and their employees enjoyed implicit guarantees of bail-outs and tenure. The subsidized credit created excess demand and encouraged rent-seeking borrowing.

The inefficiencies and disinter-mediation resulting from the financial repression policy are evident. The financial system failed to deepen as reflected in the stagnant and low M3/GNP ratio. From 1960 to the mid-1980s, the ratio remained at around 25%. Inefficient credit allocation resulted in the bankruptcy of almost all GFIs in 1986. The PNB and the DBP had worked as milking cows of the Marcos family and cronies. The term 'behest' loans or those demanded by Marcos were 'front-ended'. The term means that a borrower applies for a loan for purposes other than the reason given to the bank. Borrowing was merely a method for stealing money from the Gifts. The GFIs were largely funded by the Central Bank. They barely tapped deposits and other inter-mediation channels. At the end of the Marcos era (Feb. 1986) an audit of the GFIs showed that 85% of the DBP assets were bad, 65% of the PNB and 50% of the Government Social Insurance System (GSIS).

CHAPTER 12

RECURSIVE DYNAMIC CGE ANALYSIS

THE ROAD TO ECONOMIC RECOVERY IN ASIA

Zhi Wang

Applied Economic Department, Purdue University, U.S.A.
E-mail: zwang@econ.ag.gov

and

Dianqing Xu*

Department of Economics, Huron College,
University of Western Ontario, Canada
E-mail: Xu2@julian.uwo.ca.

1. INTRODUCTION

The terrible financial crisis in Asia is still fresh in our memory, as it only began in 1997. Based on positive indicators observed in Thailand, Korea and other Asian countries since the summer of 1999, many people forecast

---

* We are grateful to Tzong-shian Yu, Sherman Robinson, Huasheng Lim for helpful comments on early drafts. We thank Taiwo Ajayi and Jean McMillian for their helpful research assistance. Financial support from the Himalayan Foundation and other foundations are gratefully acknowledged. Any remaining errors are our own.

a quick recovery of Asian economy. Included in these indicators are: the exchange rates, stock market indexes, foreign currency reservations and economic growth rates, all showing strong increases in many recovering Asian countries.

Firstly, exchange rates in direct crisis-hit countries (Korea, Thailand, Indonesia, Philippines and Malaysia) bottomed in the first half of 1998 and rebounded thereafter.

Table 12.1 Exchange Rates in Asian Countries

	Exchange Rate in 1997.6	Lowest Exchange Rate	Time for the Lowest Exchange rate	Exchange Rate in 1999.9	I	II	III
Indonesia	2432	14,750	1998.6	8360	–83.51%	–70.91%	76.44%
Malaysia	2.52	4.36	1998.1	3.8	–42.20%	–33.68%	14.74%
Philippines	26.4	44.8	1998.9	41	–41.07%	–35.61%	9.27%
Singapore	1.43	1.78	1998.8	1.71	–19.66%	–16.37%	4.09%
Korea	888	1680	1998.1	1218	–47.14%	–27.09%	37.93%
Taiwan	27.9	34.8	1998.8	31.8	–19.83%	–12.26%	9.43%
Thailand	25.3	53.7	1998.1	41.3	–52.89%	–38.74%	30.02%
Japan	114	145	1998.8	107	–21.38%	6.54%	35.51%

I: The ratio between the exchange rate before financial crisis and at the lowest point.
II: The ratio between the exchange rate at September 1999 and before financial crisis.
III: The ratio between the exchange rate at September 1999 and the lowest point.

Secondly, stock markets have shown slow recovery in almost all the Asian economies. Exemplified this is a doubling of index levels over the past 12 months in both the Thai and Malaysian stock markets while the main indexes in Seoul and Singapore are now exceeding those in mid-1997 when the collapse began. Before the Asian crisis, the stock index in Korea measured 705 points. By September 1998, the index had dropped to only 292, a drastic loss of almost 60%. As of September 1999, however, the Korean stock market index had returned to 869 points, a stunning 23% up over that prior to the financial crisis.

Thirdly, the foreign currency reserves in Asian countries have also shown a steady recovery. Take Korea's foreign currency reserve for example. It dropped to US$22.1 billion in January 1998. However, during the recovery, its foreign currency reserve had seen a continuous rise, reaching US$64.9 billion by October 1999, much higher than the reserve of US$30.6 billion before the financial crisis.

Fourthly, after the Asian economies hit the bottom in 1998, their economic growth rates saw much improvement in 1999. Still take Korea for example. By June 1999, the Korean industrial production had risen by almost 30%, allowing some economists to forecast that the economic growth rate in Korea in 1999 would reach 9%. At the same time, Asian exports had increased significantly, with the ratio of current account to GDP in Thailand, for instance, turned around into a surplus of 11% in 1998 from −8% in 1997.[1]

During the crisis of the past two years, most Asian countries had adjusted their financial system. As a result, their exchange rates, foreign currency reserves and stock market indexes had rebounded from the bottom levels,

Table 12.2 Economic Growth Rate in Asian Countries

	1996	1997	1998	1999	2000
Asia	8.2	6.6	1.8	3.9	NA
Japan	3.9	0.8	−2.9	1.0	1.5
Hong Kong	4.9	5.3	−5.1	1.2	3.6
Taiwan	5.7	6.8	4.8	5.0	5.1
Korea	7.1	5.5	−5.8	6.5	5.5
Singapore	6.9	7.8	1.5	4.5	5.0
Malaysia	8.6	7.8	−7.5	2.4	6.5
Thailand	5.5	−0.4	−9.4	4.0	4.0
Indonesia	8.0	5.0	−13.7	−0.8	2.6
Philippines	5.7	5.1	−0.5	2.2	3.5

Data sources: IMF: "World Economic Outlook", December 1998 and the data in 2000 was forecasted by IMF, World Economic Outlook (Oct.1999).

---

[1] See *Economist,* p. 16, Aug. 21, 1999.

helping Asia to attain a relatively stable macroeconomic environment for further development. However, different economic growth rates had been observed among Asian countries.

As described above, it seemed that another economic boom in Asia was impending. But have the Asian economies fully recovered?

In fact, the economic recovery to date appears to have been sadly exaggerated. Asian economic recovery does not rely on supply or production but on demand. To achieve a full economic recovery in Asia, a strong demand for Asian products is crucial. Currently, the domestic demand is still very weak in the two largest Asian economies — Japan and China. In addition, the domestic consumption and investment in other Asian countries have not recovered to their pre-crisis levels yet. As for the external demand, even though Asian countries have attempted to develop markets in North America and Europe, only a limited capacity is available to absorb additional Asian exports. (The trade deficits of both the US and EU with Asian economies have widened in the past two years.) This has resulted in the escalation of competition amongst Asia and other developing areas.

It is very important to study the deeper causes for the insufficiencies in aggregate demand in Asian economies. The domestic demand in Japan has been stagnate since the mid-1990s and yet the increase of domestic demand in Japan is not only crucial for the economic recovery of Japan itself, but also for providing markets for other Asian countries. Japan ought to serve as the engine for Asia's economic recovery. In case Japan devalues its currency, it can increase its exports in the short term, which, however, will further weaken aggregate demand for products from other Asian economies. Thus the Asian market as a whole will shrink again, which will no doubt delay Japan's own economic recovery. On the other hand, in case China devalues its currency, a substantially lower world prices for many manufacturing goods will force other Asia countries to little alternative. In order to maintain their export share in the world market, they will have to devaluate their currency, which will increase the costs of their repayment of foreign debts and their financial system will dip into trouble once again.

This paper deals with the economic impact of currency devaluation in Japan and China and a recovery of private consumption growth in Japan on the rest of the Asian economy, and quantitatively discusses the road to economic recovery in Asia by means of a recursive dynamic Computable General Equilibrium (CCE) model. The paper shows that an increase in Japan's domestic consumption will generate strong positive effects on the economic recovery of other Asian countries whereas devaluation of Japanese yen or Chinese RMB (Renminbi yuan) will likely defer the ongoing recovery process in Asia.

This paper is divided into the following sections: Section II discusses the non-performing loans in Japan's financial system, and their effects on Japanese consumption and investment. Section III describes trade dependence and structure for China and its major trade partners and the possible impact of RMB devaluation. Section IV briefly describes the basic structure of the CCE model used in this study. Section V describes the simulation scenarios and discussion of the simulation results. Section VI or the final section is the summary on the Asian economic recovery.

2. KEY TO RECOVERY: DOMESTIC DEMAND IN JAPAN

2.1 Relation Between Japan and Asian Economy

In general, people believe that the financial crisis in Asia started in July 1997 in Thailand. In fact, the financial crisis in East Asia should be attributed to the bursting of the Japanese bubble economy in 1990, which generated huge amounts of non-performing loans in the financial sector, causing massive capital flight into other countries in this region.[2] The economic boom from 1990 to 1997 in East Asia helped Japan stabilize its economy. However, the financial crisis of 1997 led straight back to Japan, and put its economy into a long-term depression, forcing it to seek economic reform. Considering the fact that Japan's economy is the strongest in Asia, only when Japan's economy fully recovers can the rest of Asia's economy be fully recovered.

---

[2] Japan's investment outflows began in 1965 and increased moderately from the 1960s to the mid-80s. During 1973–85, nearly half of all GDP growth in Japan came from growth in trade surplus.

Japan's economy is very important to its neighbor countries in Asia. Export to Japan accounted for 12% of GDP in Malaysia and 5~7% in Indonesia, Thailand and Singapore. Shrinking of Japanese market has strongly affected the exports from other Asian countries. On the other hand, with closer and closer economic ties between Japan and other Asian countries, Japan's export to them accounted for 31.3% in 1990, 37.7% in 1993, 40.1% in 1994, 43.7% in 1995, and 44.1% in 1996 respectively, seeing a steady rise. However, due to the financial crisis in Asia, Japan's export has been strongly affected, too.[3] Japan's export to five Asian countries (Korea, Indonesia, Thailand, Malaysia and Philippines) has dropped by almost 50%. Japan cannot stimulate its economy through exports as it used to in the pre-crisis years.

2.2 Domestic Demand in Japan Declined

For quick economic recovery, perhaps it is more important or effective for Japan to increase its domestic consumption and investment. Normally, disposable income, wealth and rational expectation are the three major elements to determine the consumption level of the people. Unfortunately all these elements have been found putting negative constraints on the domestic consumption simultaneously.

2.2.1 Income decreased

High unemployment rate

The unemployment rate has been on the rise in Japan, the official unemployment rate in June 1998 reaching a post-war record of 4.3%. The unemployment rate in Japan's statistics does not include "discouraged workers" who only work with jobs available and no initiative to look for jobs. The total number of discouraged workers has been estimated as high as 10% of "people not in labor force".[3] If the statistical methods used in most Western countries were applied, Japan's unemployment rate would

---

[3] See Osamu Nariai, "Japan's Economic Restructuring: The ROE Revolution", 1998.

have measured 9.4% in July of 1998. The high unemployment rate and fall in the resident income together attributed to the drop in Japan's domestic consumption.

Declining wages

During the past few years, resident income has kept falling as companies have tried to cut personnel expenses through wage cuts. Meanwhile, corporations have been curtailing personnel costs by shifting employment from full-time, full-benefit, male workers to lower paid, zero-benefit, part-time female workers.

Declining overtime work

In the past, overtime income accounted for an important part of Japan's resident income, but due to high inventories, many Japanese firms have been forced to significantly reduce overtime working hours. The overall effect has been a further reduction in household income.

2.2.2 Negative wealth effects

Since the burst of the bubble economy, the nominal value of wealth of the Japanese population (stocks, housing and other real estates) has shrunk significantly. These negative wealth effects have reduced the Japanese people's consumption capacity and confidence.

The huge surplus capital accumulated in Japan's financial sector after 1985 was due to the perpetually high savings' rate in Japan.[4] This allowed the banks to actively supply loans to the real asset sector. The total amount of banking loans increased by 10% annually during the 1985–1987 period, fueled by increases in loans to the real estate sector by more than 20%. From 1987 to 1990, the money supplies (M2 + CD) in Japan increased by

---

[4] Japan's national saving rate stayed high, household saving increased to almost 22% of disposable income in the mid-70s. Since 1986, Japan has run a huge current account surplus each year, $80 billion in a peak year, and Yen to dollar rate jumped from 245 Yen in December 1985 to 120 Yen in December 1989.

more than 10% each year.[5] Owing to low interest rate and abundance of money supply, financial speculations became increasingly active.

Since 1986, the scale of price hike in real assets has surprised many people. For example, the 1988 prices of corporate real estate in Tokyo were 350% higher than the prices in 1983. So were the housing prices, up by 300% in many metropolitan areas. Assuming that the average land price per m^2 in 1980 was 100, the price rose to 153.6 in 1985 and 625.9 in 1990 in six major Japanese cities, including Tokyo, Osaka and Nagoya.[6]

The average land price in Japan doubled during the 1986–1990 period. In 1990 the total value of land was almost five times higher than the GDP. Even though the area in the USA is 25 times larger than that in Japan, the land value in Japan was four times higher[7]. Adding to the problem was that more than half of the Japanese families owned property, and so when the price of land rose, most Japanese believed that the value of their assets would double or triple within a few years. Thus, national savings were booming at a very high speed, which stimulated real estate markets and stock market to further attract corporate speculators.

As the real estate market prices soared, the stock market continued to soar on record gains. Beginning in 1985, Japan's stock index was around 12,000 points, which started soaring in 1986 and reached an all time high of 39,000 at the end of 1989. The total value of stocks increased to 890 trillion Yen from 224.2 trillion Yen, having tripled in a brief period of four years. The value of stocks and real estate increased the capital gain almost equaling Japan's GDP during the 1986–1989 period.

In 1987, 40% of Toyota's profit came, not from its auto products, but rather, from the revenues of financial speculation. The ratio of non-operating revenue was even higher in other large corporations, for example, 60% at Matsushita, 65% at Nissan, 63% at Sony and 134% at Sanyo. By the second

---

[5] See Hayakawa, "Japanese Financial Markets", 1996.

[6] Data sources: Oizumi, E., "Property Finance in Japan", *Environment and Planning*, 1994, Vol. 26, p. 200.

[7] The total area is 9.37 million square kilometers in the USA and 0.37 million square kilometers in Japan.

half of the 1980s, Japan was piling up an unprecedented large current account surplus and the recycling of the surplus capital took on additional channels — international portfolio investment and direct investment. 37% of personal savings were channeled to overseas markets.[8]

The Japanese bubble burst in 1990. Using the base price of real assets in 1993 as 100, the price of corporate real estate had fallen from its highest point of 350 in 1990 to 96.3 in 1997, a total decline of 20.3% in 1996, and 14.8% in 1997. Housing prices had dropped from 300 to 135.4 in that period.

2.2.3 Pessimistic income expected

Lifelong employment system has a long history in many Japanese firms. However, when these firms faced bankruptcy in the financial crisis, they had to lay off employees. This significantly shook job security confidence, and future income expectations.

As a result of devaluation of the stock market (decline from its peak 39,000 in 1989 to 14,000 in 1992[9]) and drop in the property prices in 1992, the value lost was equal to 80% of the GDP that year. Since Japanese banks were the largest investors in the stock market, they also became the biggest losers in the burst of Japan's bubble economy. The collapse of the stock market generated many bad loans within the banking system, resulting in very large losses in capital revenue. How many non-performing loans were generated in the Japanese financial system by the bubble economy? The official data on bad loans was ambiguous due to low transparency in Japan's financial sector. The banks were holding somewhere between 87 and 140 trillion-yen in questionable loans. The *Economist* estimated that the bad debts in Japan's bank sector amounted to perhaps 30% of GDP in 1998.[10]

---

[8] See Hayakawa "Japanese Financial Market", 1996.

[9] See Konya, Fumiko, "The Rise and fall of the Bubble Economy: An Analysis of the Performance and Structure of the Japanese Stock Market", in *The Structure of the Japanese Economy*, (ed.) Okabe, Macmillan, 1994.

[10] See Finance and Economics: Japanese Property, *Economist*, August 22nd, 1998, p. 60 and "Time to wake up", *Economist*, September 26, 1998, p. 21.

However, when one major financial institution went bankrupt or a high-ranking official in charge of the financial sector stepped down, the public was surprised to find, usually through newspapers, that the values of bad loans had significantly increased, sometimes by more than ten times. Thus the non-performing loans have become long term headaches for Japan's economy.[11]

Since the burst of the bubble economy in 1990, the Japanese government, corporate firms and financial sectors have continuously released optimistic estimations of quick economic recovery and return to economic boom; however, failed promises have resulted in a complete loss of resident confidence in the government and the financial sector.

Falling prices caused by depressed domestic demand has continued to undermine corporate sales while falling disposable incomes, decreasing values of wealth, increasing unemployment rate, uncertainty over job security, and pessimistic incomes expected have further undermined Japan's domestic consumption.

2.3 Decreased Investment

Japan's investment has decreased due to the burst of the bubble economy. In the late 1980s, over-investment prevailed in Japan. However, with the burst of the bubble economy, many invested projects have lost money. The expected return on investment decreased significantly, forcing investors to become more conservative, resulting in a decline of new investments. Small companies accounted for approx. 50% of Japan's investment. Effected by the financial crisis, many of these firms fell into financial trouble, some even teetered on bankruptcy, resulting in the fall in small enterprise investments by 25.8% in 1998. Of the major components of real GDP, the capital investment fell most drastically by 8.8% in 1998.

---

[11] From 1956–1973, the annual GDP growth rate was 9.3% in Japan, then, the GDP growth rate decreased slowly to 4.1% at 1975–1991. The GDP growth rate continues to decrease 1% from 1992–1999 and shrank to 0.4% in 1999. Japan's economy has fallen into recession.

Since the domestic market was relatively inactive and the overseas markets shrank considerably, inventories in Japan rose to a record high in 23 years. This forced Japanese enterprises to reduce manufacturing production by 18.8% in 1998, and yet the inventories remained unchanged. Also, the construction sector was continuously downsized. The total houses sold in June 1998 decreased by 8.3%, as compared to those sold in the previous year. In July, there was a further drop by another 18%. The Japanese government planned to spend US$16.6 billion to stimulate the economy, of which, 7.7 billion was for public construction, and cut the interest rate at the same time. However, the interest rate cut and the increase of government spending still failed to stimulate the private consumption. Many Japanese were reluctant to spend in order to pay back their loans; thus both monetary and fiscal policies had little effect in stimulating the economy.

2.4 Japan's Deferring Strategy

When the stock and real estate market collapsed in Thailand, Malaysia and Indonesia in 1997, it immediately touched off the collapse of the banking system and induced economic chaos in Japan. However, even though economic bubbles occurred in 1990, the Japanese economy went on operating for quite a long period of time. Why?

Impacts of economic bubbles depend on the tolerance of the society. The stronger the economy, the larger the tolerance. Since huge assets have been accumulated in the past decades, Japan's economy can tolerate strong impacts. Japan's foreign currency reserve was US$213.9 billion in November 1998 and a total value of overseas net assets US$958.7 billion, both the highest in the world. Japan was the biggest debt owner in the world and held more than US$300 billion of US Treasury. The personal savings reached 1200 trillion-Yen (approx. US$9500 billion), equivalent to twice the GDP in 1998, of which the deposit at post-saving system managed by the government was as high as US$1830 billion.[12]

---

[12] See Cargill, T. Hutchison, M. and Ito, T. "Deposit Guarantees and the Burst of the Japanese Bubble Economy", *Contemporary Economic Policy*, 14:7, 1996.

The affluent financial resources have made it possible for Japan to survive for quite a long period before economic collapse. Considering the fact that the Japanese manufacturing industry has been very competitive in the world market, Japan has kept a very high surplus from its exports of automobiles and electronic products. Moreover, the Japanese government, having controlled the bank-dominated system to a large extent, can administer most of the financial resources of the society to support the large banks and enterprises that have encountered financial trouble.[13]

Since 1995, some medium-sized financial institutions have been forced to claim bankruptcy. The Japanese government has tried its best to protect the top 20 banks. Even though the burst of the bubble economy had exposed the risks and the necessity of reform in the financial sector, the Japanese government has tried several ways to defer the reform. It has constantly spread optimism to maintain people's confidence in the financial sector on the one hand, and tried to increase profits generated by manufacturing sectors and inject them into the banking sector to avoid financial crisis on the other.

The Japanese government has deferred the necessary reform to protect the culprits — large banks and corporations. In fact, it has been awaiting next economic boom to come and more contracts to its industry to generate more profits to cover the non-performing loans. Unfortunately, a financial crisis in Asia arrived instead of economic prosperity. When many Asian countries fell into severe financial crisis, Japan's overseas markets shrank significantly. Meanwhile, Japan's investment in these countries was devalued to a great extent, too. The financial crisis attacked Russia and Brazil in 1998 and further narrowed Japan's export market. The uncertainty of the international market worried the Japanese government that had been trying hard to defer the reform of its financial system. Thus it was forced to start economic reform in a very tough domestic and international atmosphere. The delay of the reform in Japan's financial sector had not only held up the economic recovery in Japan but also brought uncertainty to East Asian economies.

---

[13] See Merton Miller, "Alternative Strategies for Corporate Governance", in Wen and Xu eds. "Reformability of China's State Sector", World Scientific, 1997.

There are many prominent economists in Japan who fully understand how severe the problems are. However, the top level of government officials, worrying more about their political frailty, have not paid enough attention to the growing concern. They have always made very optimistic forecasts about the schedule and speed of economic recovery through all kinds of news-medium since 1990. Their dream was the reappearance of economic miracles of the past decades. Although these predications are false in most cases, they do believe in optimal forecasting. At the corporate level, most Japanese do know how to manage the crisis in market competition, but sadly they were not prepared for the impending financial crisis.

2.5 Reform in Japan's Financial Sector

The basic characteristic of Japan's financial sector is the bank-driven governance system. Enterprises are organized like a family. Enterprises hold stocks between each other and emphasize the employment relationship inside the firm by means of the seniority and long-term employment system. This system emphasizes cooperation rather than competition. Of course, this was good for Japan's economic development after World War II and it played an important role in allowing Japan to catch up with Europe and the USA. However, Japan's economy has already matured, and the older system cannot meet the new challenges.

The bank-driven governance system is in fact the cooperation between enterprises, banks and the government. Banks take major responsibilities with regard to enterprises. If the banking system functions normally, its efficiency is high. Under Japan's model, large banks serve both as leading creditors and major controlling shareholders. It is quite possible to induce over-investment under the bank-driven model. The over-investment and over-loan problem in the bank system may easily induce a bubble economy. The performance of Japan's banks in the financial crisis is not as good as that of their counterparts in the USA and some European countries that have adopted a stockholder-driven governance model, a model better suited to resisting financial crisis.

By virtue of the fact that banks own stocks in enterprises, any losses sustained by the enterprises may spread to the banks. In the case of the burst of the bubble economy, the banks will immediately lose much of their capacity for payment. Japan's bank-owned assets are not only small but also short of variety. Also, in the case of financial problems of large enterprises, the interests of the main-shareholding banks will be affected and so they will try hard to protect the enterprises from bankruptcy. Following the same logic, in the case of financial problems in big banks, the financial stability of the country will be affected, and the central bank will have to make every effort to bail out the banks. Of course, under such a system, many warning messages to the financial sector may be distorted. Often behind the appearance of stability lurks severe economic crisis on the horizon.

Moreover, Japan's financial sector lacks transparency and monitoring mechanisms. The central bank of Japan has no power to make independent monetary policy, which in many cases, is controlled by the Japanese government. From the forming of the bubble economy to its collapse, Japan's banks did nothing to tighten the money supply, which was a very serious strategic blunder. All these problems made for a weak banking system.

Even though Japan will have to pay very high cost to reform its banking system, obviously a short-term pain should be preferred to the long-term one. The Japanese government issued huge amounts of bond (equivalent to approx. US$500 billion) in 1999 and used the funds to bailout the financial institutions with heavy non-performing loans. Meanwhile, in order to reduce the pressure of non-performing loans, a new transition bank system has been introduced. All the measures can help the weakened banking system to linger longer, but in no way can they resolve the underlying fundamentals. Not allowing large banks to go bankrupt only works for the short term but not for long-term economic development. Moral hazard may encourage the large banks with a great deal of non-performing loans to take an even higher risky investment strategy, aggravating the uncertainty for the future. How to allow some large banks bankrupt on the one hand and maintain the social stability on the other is a great challenge to Japan's economy. The recovery of the Asian economy needs the success of the reform in Japan's financial sector.

3. STABILITY OF CHINESE RMB

When financial crisis broke out, foreign exchange rates collapsed in many Asian countries with Mainland China and Hong Kong the only exception. The stability of exchange rates in Hong Kong and Mainland China has provided an important condition for the economic recovery in Asia, which, however, has generated heavy pressure on China.

China's exports have seen a continuous decline since December 1998. For example, exports decreased by 1.9% in December 1998, another 10.8% in January 1999, 10.2% in February, 3.6% in March, and 7.3% in April 1999. Some Chinese officials and economists suggested that China should devalue its currency in order to increase exports. A few economists in Taiwan even predicted that if Mainland China had a current account deficit in 1999 and economic growth rate fell below 7%, China would devaluate RMB by around 15%.[14]

Table 12.3 Export Structure of Asian Countries

	China	Indonesia	Thailand	Philippines	Malaysia	Korea	Singapore	Taiwan
Agriculture	2.2	7.2	6.4	2.7	2.7	0.4	0.9	0.5
Processed Food	3.2	6.3	14.2	7.1	7.1	1.6	2.1	2.6
Forest & Fishery	0.2	0.6	0.3	0.3	1.6	0.1	0.1	0.2
Mineral Products	2.3	4.8	3	2.5	1	0.7	0.5	1
Energy	2.4	20.7	0.6	0.9	6.1	1	5.2	0.1
Textiles	21	12.5	9.8	9.8	3.2	12.6	1.4	12.2
Other Light Manufacture	23.8	20.2	11.3	6	12.4	7.2	4.1	9.3
Intermediates	13.4	11.6	7.9	5	8.4	16.1	11.1	19
Motor Vehicles	0.3	0.2	0.3	0.5	0.3	6.3	0.5	0.8
Other Transport Equipment	1.3	0.7	0.8	0.4	2.6	3.4	1.5	2.5
Electronics	8.6	3	11.6	10.7	20.7	9.9	28.5	18.4
Machinery	13.5	3.3	15	22.5	26.3	24.3	23	26.5
Housing & Construction	0	0	0	1.5	0	0.6	0	0
Services	7.9	9	18.8	30.1	7.6	15.7	21.1	6.9
Total	100	100	100	100	100	100	100	100

Data sources: International Economic Statistical Yearbook, 1998.

---

[14] See "Euro-Asia Information", No. 10, October 1999.

Table 12.4 China's Bilateral Trade Dependence With Its Major Trade Partners By Sectors, 1995 (%)

	Taiwan	Hong Kong	Korea	Singapore	Indonesia	Thailand	Malaysia	Philippines	Japan	United States	Western Europe	Rest of the World	Total
Agriculture	4.0	12.7	5.3	4.9	5.0	1.5	1.9	0.7	22.8	4.8	17.3	19.1	100
Forest & Fishery	2.4	24.8	2.3	0.0	0.0	0.0	0.0	–	57.8	0.4	1.9	10.4	100
Energy & Minerals	3.6	3.2	12.1	1.7	1.9	0.8	0.4	0.6	41.0	10.5	12.1	12.0	100
Processed Food	1.0	14.0	5.3	1.7	0.8	0.5	1.1	0.7	44.6	7.9	9.2	13.2	100
Beverage & Tobacco	0.2	37.9	0.2	11.1	0.5	0.1	0.8	18.6	2.7	1.0	1.7	25.0	100
Textile	1.5	13.1	10.7	3.1	1.1	2.1	1.0	1.9	14.8	7.7	12.1	31.0	100
Apparel	0.9	11.6	1.3	0.6	0.0	0.1	0.2	0.1	36.3	12.7	21.9	14.3	100
Other Light Manufacture	1.1	1.4	1.6	1.3	0.3	0.4	0.4	0.3	12.7	38.1	26.1	16.3	100
Wood & Paper Products	4.4	9.0	2.5	1.6	0.5	0.5	0.8	0.3	25.1	25.3	17.9	12.0	100
Manufactured Intermediates	3.7	5.5	7.9	2.3	2.4	3.0	1.7	1.1	15.1	17.5	20.6	19.0	100
Motor Vehicle	1.5	12.8	0.4	1.6	1.2	5.8	0.4	0.7	7.3	34.1	3.3	31.0	100
Other Transport Equipment	1.1	7.7	3.2	5.8	1.8	6.7	0.5	0.6	6.4	26.4	8.1	31.7	100
Electronics	1.5	2.5	1.4	4.5	0.4	1.3	1.5	0.4	10.1	29.9	30.3	16.4	100
Other Machinery	4.2	3.9	2.8	4.1	1.2	1.4	1.5	0.6	14.0	25.0	23.8	17.5	100
Traded Services	0.9	4.2	1.5	1.6	0.3	1.0	0.8	0.4	25.0	12.9	35.6	15.9	100
Total	2.1	6.3	3.6	2.4	0.9	1.2	0.9	0.7	19.7	21.9	22.8	17.5	100

Data source: Author calculated from version 4 GTAP database.

What effect would that have on the Asian economy if China's currency did devalue?

Table 12.3 presents sector structure of exports for Asian developing countries and Table 12.4 the structure of China's exports by destination. They show that China's exports have been concentrated in manufacturing sectors (over 80%), and labor intensive and electronic products have constituted more than 60% of China's exports to industrial countries. Manufactured intermediates and other machinery have also become major export products (accounting for over 25% of China's total exports) in recent years. Other Asian countries export similar goods to the third market but Chinese exports are very competitive as compared to those exported by other Asian countries. Should China actively devalue its currency, it would generate great pressure on the exports of other Asian countries. Therefore, the current economic recovery in Thailand, Korea and some other Asian countries is partially based on the stability of China's RMB. As China has not devalued its RMB, Korea and Thailand have re-gained their competitiveness in the international market since they devalued their currency after the economic crisis. However, if China had devalued its RMB, it would have reduced their competitiveness significantly and forced them to devalue their currency further, which might have triggered another negative cycle of competitive devaluation among these Asian countries. Therefore, it will be of interest to quantitatively estimate the extent of effects on trade performance of other Asia countries if China had devalued its currency.

4. STRUCTURE OF THE CGE MODEL

The global CGE model used in this chapter is an extension of the CGE models used in Noland, Robinson and Wang (1999) to a recursive dynamic setting. It is part of a family of models that have been widely used to analyze the impact of global trade liberalization and structural adjustment programs with focuses on real trade flows, trades balances, world prices, and real exchange rates. It incorporates considerable details on sector output and trade flows — both bilateral and global. However, we obtain the structural details at the cost of not explicitly modeling financial markets, interest rates, or inflation, namely, it is not designed to generate quarterly macroeconomic forecasts. It could be linked to a macro model that includes asset flows and generates macro scenarios. Given a macro scenario by a macro econometric model, our model can then be used to determine the resulting real trade flows and sector structural adjustments for each region in a recursive dynamic framework; given a path of future world economic growth, it can generate the pattern of output and trade resulting from world economic adjustment to the shocks specified in the alternative macro scenarios.

The model uses seventeen fully endogenized regions and sixteen production sectors in each region to represent the world economy. The seventeen regions are: (1) the United States, (2) Canada, (3) European Union (EU) (15 member countries), (4) Japan, (5) Australia, (6) New Zealand, (7) Korea, (8) Taiwan, (9) Hong Kong, (10) China, (11) Singapore, (12) Malaysia, (13) Thailand, (14) Philippines, (15) Indonesia, (16) South Asia (Indian, Bangladesh, Nepal, Pakistan and Sri Lanka), and (17) Rest of the World.

The Sixteen sectors are: (1) agriculture, (2) forestry and fishery (3) processed food, (4) mineral and energy, (5) beverage and tobacco, (6) textile, (7) wearing apparel, (8) other light manufactures, (9) wood and paper products, (10) manufactured intermediates, (11) motor vehicles and parts, (12) other transport equipment, (13) electronic equipment, (14) other machinery, (15) utility, housing and construction, and (16) transportation and services, a portion of which is allocated to international shipping. The correspondence between sectors in our model, GTAP database and ISIC are listed in Table-A1.

There are six primary factors of production: agricultural land, natural resources, capital, agricultural labor, unskilled-labor and skilled-labor. Skilled-labor and unskilled-labor have basic education in common, but skilled-labor usually have more advanced training. While the agricultural labor are with little or no education and work only in farm sectors. Primary factors are assumed to be mobile across sectors, but immobile across regions.

4.1 Production and Demand Structures

In each region, one representative competitive firm is selected for each sector for one product. Production technology is characterized by two-level nested CES functions. At the first level, two types of inputs are used for the firms: a composite primary factor input and an aggregate intermediate input according to a CES cost function. At the second level, the split of intermediate demand is assumed to follow a Leontief specification, with no substitution among intermediate inputs. Technology in all sectors exhibits constant return to scale, implying constant long-run average and marginal costs.

Agents in each region view products from different regions as imperfect substitutes (the Armington assumption). The private household in each region maximizes a Stone-Geary utility function over the sixteen composite goods and savings, which leads to the Extended Liner Expenditure System (ELES) of household demand. Household savings are treated as a demand for future consumer goods with zero subsistence quantity (Howe, 1975). An economy-wide consumer price index is specified as the price of savings and it represents the opportunity cost of giving up current consumption in exchange for future consumption (Wang and Kinsey, 1994). Government spending and investment decisions in each region are based on Cobb-Douglas utility functions, which generate constant expenditure shares for each composite commodity. In each region, firm intermediate inputs, household consumption, government spending and investment demand constitute total demand for the same Armington composite of domestic and imported goods from different sources. A two-level nested CES aggregation function is specified for each composite commodity in each region. Total demand is first divided between domestic and imported goods, and then the expenditure on imports is further divided according to geographical origin under the assumption of cost minimization. Complete trade flow matrices for all regions are part of the model solution.

There is an international shipping industry in the model for transport of products from one region to another. Each region is assumed to allocate a fraction of the output of its transportation and service sector to satisfy the demand for shipping, which is generated by interregional trade. The global shipping industry is assumed to have a unitary elasticity of substitution among supplier sources. The margins associated with this activity are commodity/route specific. In equilibrium, the total value of international transportation services at the world price equals the sum of the export proportions of the service sector's output from each region.

The government in each region is assumed to impose import tariffs, export subsidies, and indirect taxes, all in ad valorem terms. Tariff and tax (subsidy) rates vary by sector and destination.

4.2 Equilibrium, Exchange Rate and Macro Closure

Within each region, the model solves for domestic commodity and factor prices that equate supply and demand in all goods and factor markets. The model also solves for world prices equating supply and demand for sectoral exports and imports across the world economy. In addition, for each region, the model specifies an equilibrium relationship between the balance of trade and the real exchange rate (which measures the average price of traded goods, exports and imports, relative to the average price of domestically produced goods sold at the domestic market), given world prices and regional export supply and import demand functions. An exogenous change in a particular region's exchange rate will reverberate across the world economy, affecting the aggregate trade balances and/or real exchange rates of all seventeen regions, as they will have to adjust their trade flows and structures of production to achieve a new equilibrium. However, as with other CGE models, the model only determines relative prices. The United States is specified as the reference economy, with both its aggregate price level and exchange rate fixed exogenously. All the relative world prices and trade balances are measured in terms of real U.S. dollars. As traded and non-traded goods are assumed to be imperfect substitutes by sectors, changes in relative world market prices are only partially transmitted to domestic markets. The model thus incorporates a realistic degree of insulation of domestic commodity markets from world markets, but the links are still important and provide the major mechanism by which external shocks are transmitted across the regions.

The equilibrium exchange rate determined by the model for each region can be interpreted as the real effective exchange rate (REER) deflating by the ratio of the price index of the regional domestic goods and that of the US domestic goods. It is important to emphasize that the exchange rate variable in the model is not a financial exchange rate since the model has no assets or asset markets. Under appropriate numeraire selection, however, it is equivalent to the real exchange rate defined as the ratio of a price index of all traded goods (imports and exports) to a price index of all non-traded goods (domestically produced goods sold at the domestic market). When the price index of home goods is selected as the numeraire, the percentage change in the real exchange rate is equal to the percentage change of the exchange rate variable in the model. In a multi-region model where all world market prices are endogenous, the equilibrium real exchange rate is affected by changes in the international terms of trade facing a region. Devarajan, Lewis, and Robinson (1993) and Wang (1994) discuss this issue. It represents the equilibrium real exchange rate consistent with a given trade balance.

For each region, the model includes the three macro balances: savings-investment, balance of trade (in goods and non-factor services), and government expenditure-receipts (government deficit). The three balances are not independent and the determination of these macro balances is the subject of traditional macroeconomic models. In terms of our real trade model, which does not include financial markets or variables typical of macro models, the determination of these macro aggregates is specified by exogenously determined rules. The macro adjustment mechanism constitutes the macro "closure" of the model.

The specification of a macro closure is to select rules by which macro balances are brought back to equilibrium when exogenous shocks disrupt the benchmark equilibrium during an experiment. A macro scenario is imposed on the CGE model, which then traces out the sectoral implications of the assumed macro behavior (Devarajan, Lewis, and Robinson, 1990). The macro closure is not based on a specification of optimizing behavior by rational agents in the model, but reflects a simplified description of the results of a macro adjustment process not specified in detail.

In the aggregate, as noted above, there is a functional relationship between the balance of trade (in goods and non-factor services, or the current account balance) in each region and the real exchange rate. If the real exchange rate depreciates, the price of traded goods increases relative to the price of domestically produced goods sold on the domestic market. When exports increase and imports decrease, the trade balance will improve. Given our assumption that aggregate investment is determined as a share of GDP, changes in the trade balance that directly affect foreign savings are assumed to have only a partial effect on aggregate investment in the region. Instead, they lead to an equilibrium adjustment in the domestic savings rate, which partially offsets the change in foreign savings.

4.3 Inter-Period Linkages and Recursive Dynamics

The inter-period linkages are imposed as follows: Along the dynamic path, determinants of growth are given by four factors: rate of labor force growth, accumulation of physical capital stocks, changes of labor force skill composition (migration between rural and urban unskilled labor, increase in the skilled labor force), and the rate of total factor productivity (TFP) growth. We also assume that there is a capital and intermediate goods imports embodied technology transfer among regions, which links a region's TFP growth with its imports of capital and technology intensive products. Technology transfer is assumed to flow in one direction — from more developed regions to less developed regions.

The labor force growth rate is set exogenously. It is calculated from the International Labor Office's population and labor force projections from 1990 to 2010 at five-year intervals. The projection takes into consideration the demographic structure and participation rates of each region.

Capital stock in each simulation period equals the capital stock plus total investment minus depreciation in the previous period. No optimal behavior is assumed for investment and capital accumulation. All net investments in the previous period are assumed to become new production capital in the next period.

Accumulation patterns for capital stock depend upon the depreciation rate and gross investment rate; the latter is set exogenously based on Oxford macro econometric model. However, household savings, government surplus (deficit) and foreign capital inflow (foreign savings) are assumed to be perfect substitutes, which collectively constitute the source of gross investment in each region.

Household savings decisions are endogenous in the model. It represents future consumption goods for the household with zero subsistence quantity (by assuming inter-temporal separable preferences, ELES demand system). Government surplus (deficit) is the difference between government tax revenue and its spending; the latter is fixed as percentage of each region real GDP based on Oxford model's projection. There is no expectation in the model.

Foreign capital inflow or outflow is determined by the accumulation of the balance of trade, which is also fixed as percentage of real GDP in each region (also based on Oxford model) except the United States. The model does not include financial markets and portfolio investment. The trade balance is the only source for foreign savings (can be inflow or outflow). No explicit specification of Foreign Direct Investment (FDI). However, it is counted by trade flows, because in order to convert FDI into production capital stock, technology and equipment have to be purchased via domestic or international trade.

Agricultural labor and urban unskilled labor are not substitutable in production, but are linked by rural-urban migration flows. These flows, endogenous in the model, are driven by the rural-urban wage differentials and structural changes in production and trade. The increase in the skilled labor force is based on the growth in the stock of tertiary educated labor in each region estimated by the World Bank (Ahaja and Filmer, 1995), which provides an indication of changes in the number of those qualified for employment as professional and technical workers. That is, as tertiary education grows, the share of skilled labor force will grow correspondingly.

There is a set of sectoral specific economy-wide TFP growth variables for each region in the model, which is solved endogenously by setting the real GDP growth rate in each region exogenously, based on projections from the Oxford model in the baseline. Then the economy-wide TFP variable is fixed in each region when alternative scenarios are simulated. In such a case, the growth rate of real GDP and the sectoral specific TFP variables that link productivity and imports are solved endogenously.

Table 12.5 Major Assumption for Baseline Calibration

	China	Taiwan	Hong Kong	Korea	Singapore	Indonesia	Thailand	Malaysia	Philippines	Japan	United States	Western Europe	Canada	Australia	South Asia	Rest of the World	World Average
Average annual growth rate, %, 2000–2010																	
Real GDP	*7.2*	*4.5*	*4.2*	*4.9*	*3.4*	*5.9*	*5.5*	*6.2*	*4.2*	*2.4*	*2.5*	*2.4*	*2.8*	*3.2*	*7.1*	*3.0*	*3.0*
Labor Force	*0.8*	*0.8*	*0.2*	*1.1*	*0.3*	*2.0*	*0.8*	*2.7*	*2.4*	*-0.2*	*0.8*	*-0.1*	*0.6*	*1.0*	*2.2*	*2.2*	*1.5*
Skill Labor	*2.7*	*5.1*	*3.5*	*6.3*	*3.6*	*7.7*	*7.0*	*8.6*	*4.6*	*2.2*	*2.6*	*2.8*	*2.3*	*3.0*	*5.6*	*6.1*	*4.4*
TFP	2.7	0.7	1.4	2.1	1.3	1.5	1.4	1.7	1.2	1.1	0.5	1.5	1.0	1.2	3.1	0.5	1.1
Capital Stock	9.9	7.3	4.2	4.3	4.5	6.7	4.9	7.2	3.8	2.9	4.6	2.7	4.2	4.0	5.8	2.6	3.6
Gross Investment	5.5	4.5	5.1	4.3	3.1	4.1	4.6	4.5	2.8	2.5	3.8	2.9	4.3	4.2	6.3	2.7	3.4
Exports	7.5	3.2	3.4	3.8	3.9	7.2	4.7	5.7	5.3	3.3	2.6	2.5	2.8	3.0	7.7	3.1	3.6
Imports	5.5	4.6	4.9	4.5	3.7	4.6	5.2	5.8	3.8	2.5	3.5	3.2	3.2	3.9	7.3	2.7	3.6
HH. Consumption	5.2	5.3	5.8	6.3	2.5	4.2	6.3	7.4	3.2	2.4	2.5	2.4	2.3	3.2	6.5	2.5	2.7
Public Consumption	9.4	4.2	6.1	4.4	3.5	7.0	5.6	6.7	4.5	1.7	1.1	2.3	2.4	2.7	7.5	4.0	2.6
Total Absorption	6.7	5.0	5.6	5.4	2.8	5.1	5.8	6.3	3.5	2.3	2.7	2.5	2.9	3.4	7.0	2.9	3.0
Average annual agricultural labor force migration, 1000 persons, 2000–2010																	
Rural Labor Migration	2505	16	0	26	0	765	328	39	200	12	31	104	-2	1	6719	7144	17,887
Labor composition, %, 2000																	
Agricultural Labor	72.0	9.6	0.9	13.5	0.3	53.8	58.7	22.4	41.0	5.4	2.6	5.0	2.4	4.6	57.0	38.6	46.3
Unskilled Labor	20.6	74.7	78.4	74.0	70.8	41.7	34.6	61.9	51.2	77.2	63.9	65.6	61.7	64.6	38.0	49.3	42.1
Skilled Labor	7.4	15.7	20.8	12.5	29.0	4.5	6.6	15.8	7.8	17.5	33.5	29.4	35.9	30.8	5.0	12.1	11.6
Labor composition, %, 2010																	
Agricultural Labor	70.0	8.2	0.9	12.0	0.3	45.5	50.1	18.2	35.6	5.2	2.4	4.6	2.6	4.6	47.2	32.6	41.4
Unskilled Labor	20.8	67.0	69.2	66.2	58.4	46.4	37.0	52.9	54.5	72.1	56.8	55.2	54.3	57.3	45.6	49.1	42.8
Skilled Labor	9.2	24.8	29.9	21.8	41.3	8.1	12.9	28.9	9.8	22.7	40.8	40.2	43.1	38.1	7.2	18.2	15.8
Gross investment as % of nominal GDP																	
2000	*39.5*	*25.1*	*35.8*	*26.9*	*37.4*	*30.9*	*35.0*	*42.8*	*24.5*	*27.8*	*20.9*	*21.0*	*20.1*	*23.5*	*20.7*	*19.0*	
2010	*38.3*	*25.3*	*37.7*	*27.2*	*37.4*	*30.9*	*35.0*	*42.8*	*24.5*	*29.0*	*24.0*	*22.1*	*23.3*	*26.3*	*21.4*	*19.0*	
Government spending as % of nominal GDP																	
2000	*12.4*	*19.5*	*8.7*	*18.3*	*9.4*	*6.9*	*10.2*	*11.0*	*12.9*	*18.5*	*16.6*	*15.6*	*21.4*	*21.9*	*17.1*	*15.2*	
2010	*13.1*	*18.7*	*10.1*	*17.4*	*9.4*	*6.9*	*10.2*	*11.0*	*12.9*	*17.6*	*14.4*	*15.2*	*20.4*	*19.9*	*16.3*	*15.2*	
Balance of trade as % of nominal GDP																	
2000	*-0.2*	*1.1*	*0.1*	*11.8*	*-4.5*	*4.2*	*12.3*	*16.1*	*-8.9*	*2.7*	*-4.4*	*1.3*	*3.0*	*-1.1*	*2.9*	*-0.5*	
2010	*-0.5*	*-3.6*	*-15.2*	*6.8*	*2.2*	*7.5*	*5.9*	*6.8*	*-9.8*	*3.2*	*-5.2*	*1.1*	*4.4*	*-0.6*	*1.2*	*1.9*	

Note: Numbers in bold Italy face are control variables and fixed exogenously in baseline calibration.

Similar to Hertel *et al.* (1995), the MFA quotas rents are assumed to be captured by exporting countries as export taxes, and these export tax rates are adjusted endogenously to equate with quotas. Such a treatment assumes that all quotas are binding constraints at the equilibrium.

The base year equilibrium data set is constructed around a World Social Accounting Matrix (SAM) estimated for 1995 based on the Global Trade Analysis Project (GTAP) database (version 4, Hertel, 1997). Details of this type of multi-region SAM and its construction from the GTAP Database are described in Wang (1994). The three major macro economic variables (gross investment, government spending and balance of trade) are all specified as percentage of GDP based on projection by Oxford macro econometric model. Major assumptions used to calibrate baseline scenario are summarized in Table 12.5. The model is implemented in GAMS (Brooke, *et al.* 1988) and solved in levels. A detailed algebraic specification of the model is given in the Appendix.

5.   SIMULATION DESIGN AND RESULTS

5.1 Impact of Recovery of Japan's Private Consumption

As shown in Table 12.3, the average private consumption growth rate in Japan was 4.4% during 1985–1990 period. If this growth rate restores to its historical level, it will generate a positive effect on the economic recovery in both Japan and other Asian countries. To show the importance of such a recovery in Japan, the model is first used to evaluate the impact of such a recovery on Asian economies in case Japan maintains an annual growth rate of 4.4% in nominal private consumption during the 2000–2010 period.

Major simulation results are presented in Tables 12.6 and 12.7. Table 12.6 summarizes major aggregate economy-wide effects. The growth in Japanese private consumption will have strong positive impacts on the world economy. The average annual growth rate of world real GDP would roughly be 2 percentage points higher and the total accumulated world real GDP growth would be 35 percent higher at 2010 than that in the baseline scenario. Asian countries would benefit more from such a demand-led growth start in

Table 12.6   Impact of Private Consumption Growth in Japan Recover to the Level of 1985–1990: Aggregated Economic Indicator by Region

	China	Taiwan	Hong Kong	Korea	Singapore	Indonesia	Thailand	Malaysia	Philippines	Japan	United States	Western Europe	Canada	Australia	South Asia	Rest of World	World Average
Accumulated growth during 2000–2010, % change from baseline																	
Real GDP	64.1	43.8	52.6	46.3	40.2	53.4	50.8	53.9	41.8	32.9	33.0	32.2	33.0	38.5	57.8	37.2	35.5
Private Consumption	50.7	47.7	88.8	69.7	18.6	66.9	67.3	60.7	49.5	32.3	33.5	31.7	27.7	40.5	69.3	38.3	35.5
Public Consumption	79.7	40.4	65.3	40.9	37.1	50.0	49.0	54.1	39.6	29.8	28.0	32.0	31.5	36.8	50.5	38.9	33.5
Total Real Absorption	58.1	45.8	75.4	53.4	25.0	57.9	56.7	51.5	45.4	31.8	33.6	32.0	31.6	40.4	62.6	37.8	35.5
Real Export	72.6	38.7	37.1	33.0	44.5	32.4	41.7	52.9	34.1	39.1	33.5	34.6	38.6	31.5	38.9	32.4	37.9
Real Import	49.6	43.9	58.8	44.3	36.8	46.9	51.2	50.1	42.6	28.7	37.6	33.2	34.9	41.6	64.4	35.4	37.9
TFP	31.1	24.5	33.3	29.2	27.6	25.2	23.9	26.5	24.9	25.2	23.0	26.0	23.5	26.8	30.8	23.0	25.2
Gross Investment	46.9	43.8	56.0	42.7	33.4	42.0	44.8	41.4	35.2	32.9	37.2	33.4	38.7	42.4	51.1	34.4	36.1
Capital Stock	30.5	19.6	13.3	10.9	10.8	16.6	13.6	19.0	10.4	8.3	12.0	8.0	11.4	11.2	14.9	8.1	9.9
Average annual growth rate during 2000–2010, % change from baseline																	
Real GDP	2.6	2.3	2.8	2.3	2.3	2.4	2.4	2.4	2.3	2.1	2.1	2.1	2.1	2.3	2.4	2.3	2.2
Private Consumption	2.5	2.3	3.8	3.0	1.2	3.4	2.9	2.4	2.9	2.1	2.1	2.1	1.8	2.4	2.9	2.4	2.2
Public Consumption	2.6	2.2	2.9	2.2	2.2	2.1	2.3	2.3	2.1	2.1	2.1	2.1	2.1	2.3	2.0	2.2	2.1
Total Real Absorption	2.5	2.3	3.4	2.5	1.6	2.8	2.6	2.3	2.6	2.1	2.1	2.1	2.0	2.3	2.6	2.3	2.2
Real Export	2.8	2.3	2.2	1.9	2.5	1.4	2.2	2.5	1.7	2.3	2.1	2.2	2.4	1.9	1.6	2.0	2.2
Real Import	2.4	2.3	2.9	2.3	2.1	2.4	2.5	2.3	2.4	1.9	2.2	2.0	2.1	2.3	2.6	2.2	2.2
TFP	2.0	1.9	2.3	2.0	2.0	1.8	1.7	1.9	1.8	1.9	1.8	1.9	1.8	2.0	1.9	1.8	1.9
Gross Investment	2.2	2.3	2.7	2.3	2.0	2.3	2.3	2.2	2.2	2.1	2.1	2.1	2.1	2.3	2.3	2.2	2.1
Capital Stock	1.0	0.8	0.8	0.6	0.6	0.8	0.7	0.8	0.6	0.6	0.7	0.5	0.7	0.7	0.8	0.6	0.6
Agricultural labor force migration during 2000–2010, 1000 persons, change from baseline																	
Accumulated	602	72	2	175	1	1898	572	42	429	341	251	875	18	30	11,262	21,604	38,187
Annual Average	55	7	0	16	0	172	52	4	39	31	22	80	2	2	1024	1964	3472
Labor composition, 2010, % change from baseline																	
Agricultural Labor	−0.1	−0.7	−0.1	−0.7	−0.0	−1.7	−1.5	−0.4	−1.2	−0.5	−0.2	−0.5	−0.1	−0.3	−1.8	−2.0	−1.2
Unskilled Labor	0.1	0.7	0.1	0.7	0.0	1.7	1.5	0.4	1.2	0.5	0.2	0.5	0.1	0.3	1.8	2.0	1.2
Balance of trade as % of nominal GDP, change from baseline																	
2000	−0.1	0.0	0.0	−0.1	0.3	−0.2	−0.2	−0.2	−0.2	0.0	−0.0	0.0	0.1	−0.0	−0.1	−0.0	0.0
2010	0.4	0.1	−6.1	−1.3	4.1	−2.2	−1.9	0.4	−3.4	0.4	−0.2	0.2	1.4	−0.4	−1.5	0.0	0.0

Japan. The induced additional growth rate is much higher in Asia countries than the world average because of a large market demand for their exports in Japan. Over the whole simulation period, it generates about 73% additional export growth for China, 53% for Malaysia, 45% for Singapore, 42% for Thailand, 39% for Taiwan, 37% for Hong Kong, and about 33% for Korea and Indonesia. It also creates additional manufacturing jobs for agricultural labor in Asian developing countries. There will be 2 million more agricultural labor entering manufacturing sector in Indonesia and 11 million more in South Asian countries during the simulation period.

The gains to economic growth from such a demand-led growth started from Japan are mainly from three sources that reinforce each other: 1) Extended Japanese market that absorbs exports from the rest of the world, especially Asian countries that have suffered from over production capacity since the late 90s, direct increase real GDP and household income for most countries in the world; 2) Higher income leads to higher savings and investment so that more physical capital stock will be available in each regional economy (30% more for China, about 20% more for Taiwan and Malaysia, and 17% more for Indonesia); 3) Higher production level and accelerated capital formation require more intermediate inputs, especially capital and technology intensive products from industrial countries, which will speed up import embodied technology transfer among nations, leading to higher TFP growth.

Table 12.7 presents the impact of an expansion of Japanese private consumption on the trade performance in absolute real terms in different countries each year in the simulation period. It shows that if private consumption in Japan restores to its historical level, it will create a large market for products from other Asian economies and provide a solid foundation for Asia's economic recovery. Japan will also gain significantly from such a process, because in order to export more to Japan market, Asian countries will have to import more from Japan, their largest supplier for intermediate and capital intensive products.

Table 12.7 Impact of Private Consumption Growth in Japan Recovers to the Level of 1985–1990: Trade Performance

(Deviation from baseline, billion of 1995 US dollars)

	2000	2001	2002	2003	2004	2005	2006	2007	2008	2009	2010
					Exports						
Japan	8.7	21.3	38.2	58.0	78.3	98.9	119.6	141.4	169.0	198.8	230.0
China	3.4	8.7	16.6	26.9	39.0	55.8	72.4	92.0	117.8	148.4	183.9
Taiwan	2.0	4.8	8.6	13.1	17.8	22.8	27.7	32.8	39.4	46.6	54.2
Hong Kong	1.4	3.5	6.4	9.7	13.0	17.3	20.7	24.3	28.8	33.7	38.8
Korea	2.4	6.0	11.0	17.0	23.4	30.7	37.7	45.4	55.2	66.1	77.9
Singapore	2.2	5.5	9.9	15.2	20.7	26.4	32.3	38.8	47.0	56.0	65.8
Indonesia	0.4	1.0	1.8	2.9	4.1	5.4	7.0	8.9	11.4	14.5	18.2
Thailand	1.0	2.4	4.4	6.9	9.6	13.0	16.3	20.1	25.0	30.7	37.2
Malaysia	1.3	3.3	6.0	9.5	13.4	18.0	22.8	28.3	35.5	44.0	53.7
Philippines	0.3	0.8	1.5	2.3	3.2	4.5	5.5	6.6	8.1	9.7	11.4
United States	9.7	23.5	41.7	62.7	83.8	104.9	125.7	147.4	174.8	204.3	234.9
Western Europe	14.9	35.8	63.4	95.1	126.8	158.1	188.9	220.9	261.3	304.3	348.8
Canada	3.4	8.2	14.5	21.9	29.3	36.8	44.3	52.1	62.1	73.0	84.2
Australia	0.9	2.2	3.9	5.9	7.8	9.8	11.8	13.8	16.4	19.2	22.0
New Zealand	0.2	0.4	0.8	1.2	1.6	2.0	2.4	2.8	3.4	4.0	4.6
South Asia	0.7	1.7	3.2	5.0	7.1	12.9	16.5	20.7	26.1	32.5	39.8
Rest of the World	8.8	21.3	38.0	57.5	77.5	95.5	115.3	136.6	163.7	193.5	225.4
World Total	61.8	150.3	269.9	410.7	556.4	712.7	866.7	1032.8	1244.7	1479.1	1731.1
					Imports						
Japan	4.8	11.6	21.0	31.9	43.2	54.7	66.3	78.7	94.6	112.1	131.1
China	3.9	9.9	18.3	28.7	39.6	51.2	62.8	75.1	90.5	107.1	124.7
Taiwan	1.9	4.8	8.8	13.5	18.6	24.0	29.6	35.7	43.6	52.3	61.9
Hong Kong	1.3	3.4	6.4	10.2	14.4	18.7	23.9	29.8	37.8	47.3	58.5
Korea	2.1	5.1	9.3	14.3	19.5	25.1	30.8	37.1	45.1	54.2	64.0
Singapore	2.0	4.9	8.9	13.5	18.4	23.4	28.6	34.2	41.2	49.0	57.3
Indonesia	0.8	2.1	3.9	6.0	8.2	10.5	12.8	15.2	18.2	21.4	24.8
Thailand	1.1	2.6	4.9	7.9	10.9	14.1	17.4	20.8	25.1	29.8	34.8
Malaysia	1.3	3.3	6.0	9.4	13.0	16.9	21.1	25.7	31.3	37.5	44.2
Philippines	0.6	1.5	2.8	4.3	5.9	7.4	8.9	10.6	12.6	14.9	17.4
United States	16.0	38.4	68.1	103.0	138.9	179.6	218.2	259.9	313.5	373.1	436.8
Western Europe	10.9	26.3	46.8	70.5	94.7	122.0	147.5	174.9	210.0	248.9	290.8
Canada	2.8	6.7	12.0	18.1	24.3	31.0	37.5	44.3	53.1	62.9	73.2
Australia	1.2	2.9	5.3	8.0	10.9	13.9	17.1	20.6	25.1	30.3	36.0
New Zealand	0.3	0.7	1.2	1.8	2.4	3.0	3.6	4.3	5.2	6.1	7.1
South Asia	1.2	3.1	5.8	9.1	12.8	16.5	20.5	25.0	30.7	37.3	44.5
Rest of the World	11.9	28.6	50.8	76.2	101.7	127.5	152.9	179.8	213.7	250.2	288.6
World Total	64.1	156.0	280.0	426.1	577.2	739.5	899.3	1071.5	1291.3	1534.4	1795.7

5.2 Devaluation of Chinese RMB

The global CGE model is also used to simulate the impact of China's active devaluation of its currency.

Assume China devaluates its currency RMB by 10%, 20% and 30% from the current exchange rate. Suppose China maintains its productivity, government budget, tax rate, labor supply and tariffs at the same level as the other Asian countries during the process of simulation. Also assume non-tariff barriers, that is, the import quotas for textile products (MFP) and other products remain the same and the monetary and fiscal policies of Asian countries remain unchanged after the financial crisis. The result from the CGE simulation is shown in Tables 12.8 and 12.9.

From Table 12.8, we can see that in the case of devaluation of Chinese currency by 10%, China's exports will increase by US$35.7 billion or 17%; imports will decrease by US$16.5 billion or 9.9%; trade surplus will increase by US$52.3 billion. In the case of devaluation of Chinese currency by 20%, its exports will increase by $72 billion or 34%, imports will decrease by $3 billion or 29%, and trade surplus will increase by $102 billion. Evidently the foreign trade situation in China will improve significantly thank to the devaluation, and yet the export market for other Asian countries will shrink considerably with exports reduced by a big margin. Their trade situation will deteriorate.

Table 12.9 shows the results of the simulation and the impact of China's devaluation of its RMB on the exports of the other Asian nations by sectors. Should the latter keep their exchange rates unchanged, exports of light industrial products and textile products will be hard hit. For example, the export of light industrial products by Korea will drop by 6.2% and textile products by 7.2%; the export of light industrial products by Indonesia by 6.9% and textile products by 6%.

In other words, thanks to Chinese currency RMB not devaluated, the Asian countries are capable of restoring their exports. The results of this simulation can be used to measure the contribution to the Asian economic recovery made by China by not devaluating its currency.

Table 12.8 Impact of Chinese RMB Devaluation: Aggregate Results

	China	Taiwan	Hong Kong	Korea	Singapore	Indonesia	Thailand	Malaysia	Philippines	Japan	United States	Western Europe	Rest of the World	World Total
Scenario 1: 10 percent devaluation														
Total Exports (Billion $)	29.2	−3.2	−2.0	−2.3	−0.9	−0.9	−1.2	−1.2	−0.2	−6.0	−5.8	−8.1	−9.2	−12.0
Total Exports (%)	13.9	−2.5	−2.7	−1.6	−0.8	−1.8	−1.9	−1.4	−0.8	−1.2	−0.8	−1.0	−0.9	−0.3
Total Imports (Billion $)	−16.9	−0.4	0.7	−0.2	0.2	−0.0	0.5	0.3	−0.0	0.7	1.2	1.4	0.1	−12.5
Total Imports (%)	−10.1	−0.3	0.7	−0.1	0.2	−0.1	0.6	0.4	−0.1	0.2	0.1	0.2	0.0	−0.3
Balance of Trade (Billion $)	46.1	−2.8	−2.8	−2.1	−1.2	−0.9	−1.7	−1.5	−0.2	−6.7	−7.1	−9.5	−4.5	0.0
Scenario 2: 20 percent devaluation														
Total Exports (Billion $)	58.8	−6.0	−3.8	−4.4	−1.8	−1.8	−2.5	−2.4	−0.4	−11.4	−11.5	−15.7	−18.1	−20.8
Total Exports (%)	28.0	−4.6	−5.0	−3.1	−1.5	−3.5	−3.7	−2.8	−1.6	−2.4	−1.6	−1.9	−1.7	−0.5
Total Imports (Billion $)	−30.6	−0.7	1.3	−0.3	0.4	−0.1	0.9	0.6	−0.1	1.4	2.4	2.8	0.2	−21.7
Total Imports (%)	−18.3	−0.6	1.1	−0.2	0.3	−0.2	1.1	0.8	−0.2	0.3	0.3	0.3	0.0	−0.5
Balance of Trade (Billion $)	89.4	−5.3	−5.0	−4.1	−2.3	−1.8	−3.4	−3.0	−0.3	−13.0	−14.1	−18.6	−8.7	0.0
Scenario 3: 30 percent devaluation														
Total Exports (Billion $)	88.8	−8.4	−5.2	−6.3	−2.6	−2.7	−3.7	−3.5	−0.6	−16.5	−17.0	−23.0	−26.6	−27.3
Total Exports (%)	42.2	−6.5	−7.0	−4.5	−2.2	−5.1	−5.5	−4.2	−2.4	−3.4	−2.4	−2.7	−2.5	−0.7
Total Imports (Billion $)	−41.8	−0.9	1.7	−0.4	0.6	−0.1	1.4	1.0	−0.1	2.3	3.7	4.4	0.2	−28.4
Total Imports (%)	−25.0	−0.9	1.5	−0.3	0.4	−0.3	1.6	1.2	−0.4	0.5	0.4	0.5	0.0	−0.7
Balance of Trade (Billion $)	130.7	−7.5	−6.9	−5.9	−3.3	−2.6	−5.1	−4.5	−0.5	−18.9	−20.9	−27.5	−12.8	0.0

Table 12.9 Impact of 10 % Chinese RMB Devaluation: Changes In Exports By Sector, Percent Division From Base

	China	Taiwan	Hong Kong	Korea	Singapore	Indonesia	Thailand	Malaysia	Philippines	Japan	United States	Western Europe	Rest of the World
Agriculture	30.6	−2.0	1.7	−2.7	−0.7	−1.9	−1.0	−1.4	−2.0	−2.6	−1.9	−2.0	−1.5
Forest & Fishery	73.9	−2.2	0.3	−3.1	−1.1	−3.0	−8.5	−3.4	−4.5	−4.1	−2.0	−3.1	−1.5
Energy & Minerals	26.7	−0.7	−0.3	−1.9	−0.4	−0.8	−2.0	−1.3	−1.7	−1.0	−0.9	−0.6	−0.6
Processed Food	29.0	−1.0	−4.0	−1.5	−1.4	−1.7	−1.9	−2.0	−0.9	−2.5	−1.2	−0.7	−1.1
Beverage & Tobacco	35.1	−2.3	−9.2	−2.5	−4.6	−1.6	−1.7	−4.8	−6.0	0.0	−0.8	−0.8	−0.4
Textile	12.8	−4.4	−4.3	−2.8	−2.9	−1.9	−2.0	−2.6	−1.2	−4.3	−1.3	−2.0	−1.1
Apparel	7.6	−1.5	−2.3	−0.9	−0.9	−1.3	−2.9	−1.1	−0.3	−9.7	−3.6	−5.7	−0.3
Other Light Manufacture	32.2	−6.5	−5.9	−6.1	−3.6	−7.0	−7.1	−5.7	−6.2	−6.0	−5.9	−6.5	−7.1
Wood & Paper Products	27.2	−2.4	−4.5	−3.4	−1.1	−1.8	−1.3	−1.9	−0.7	−1.3	−0.6	−0.4	−0.6
Manufactured Intermediates	21.1	−2.8	−4.5	−1.9	−0.9	−0.7	−1.1	−0.6	−0.7	−1.6	−0.8	−0.7	−0.8
Motor Vehicle	52.5	−0.1	−3.3	−0.1	1.0	0.3	−0.4	0.1	1.0	0.0	0.2	−0.2	0.1
Other Transport Equipment	53.1	−2.4	−2.7	−1.2	−1.6	−1.4	−1.8	−1.8	−1.1	−1.6	−1.3	−1.5	−1.0
Electronics	21.8	−1.1	−3.4	−1.2	−0.5	−1.1	−1.3	−0.9	−0.4	−1.4	−1.1	−1.3	−0.9
Other Machinery	25.7	−2.1	−2.6	−1.1	−0.5	−0.4	−1.1	−0.7	−0.3	−1.3	−0.8	−1.0	−0.7
Traded Services	21.4	−0.1	−2.4	−0.2	−0.1	−0.2	−0.3	−0.5	−0.2	0.1	−0.0	−0.1	−0.1
Utility, Housing & Construction	25.8	−1.0	−1.0	−0.8	−0.3	0.0	−0.7	−0.9	−0.7	−0.6	−0.1	−0.3	−0.7
Total	22.9	−2.4	−2.8	−1.6	−0.7	−1.6	−1.9	−1.4	−0.7	−1.2	−0.8	−0.9	−0.8

In fact, the non-tariff barrier from the Western market to Chinese exports has not been taken into consideration in the above simulation. So the gain from the devaluation of Chinese currency has been somewhat exaggerated because import quotas have been imposed on Chinese textile products. In case RMB did devaluate, this might not increase their exports to North America and European markets. Taking this point into consideration, the non-tariff barrier has been introduced in the model in another simulation. Assume the non-tariff barrier remains at the current level and China devaluates its currency by 10%, 20% and 30% , the results are listed in Tables 12.10 and 12.11.

Since the non-tariff barrier of Western countries mostly exists on the textile market, the import quota imposed on Chinese textile products considered, the impact of China's devaluation of its RMB on the export of textile products from other Asian countries is slight. But the pressure on other light industrial products will rise. For example, the quota imposed on textile exports considered, in the case of China's devaluation of its currency by 10%, the export of the light industrial products from Korea will fall by 6.1% and that from Indonesia by 7%.

Undoubtedly, should China have actively devaluated its currency, great pressure would have been imposed on the other Asian nations. After the financial crisis, in order to rebuild the financial system, pay back the foreign debts, increase foreign currency reserves and restore the financial credibility in the international financial market, it is of foremost importance for Asian countries to expand their exports. Should their foreign trade surplus turn to deficits, it would severely frustrate the people's confidence in economic recovery. As unemployment rate in Asian countries still remains high, the shocks from foreign trade would make the unemployment situation deteriorate further. Of course, under such a situation, in order to maintain their exports, they would have no alternative but to devaluate their currencies.

The next scenario simulates to what degree their currencies should be devaluated if they would like to stabilize their export levels. From Table 12.12, it can be seen that with the devaluation of RMB, all the Asian countries will face pressure to devaluate their currencies.

Table 12.10 Impact of Chinese RMB Devaluation: Aggregate Results With No MFA Restriction In Developed Country Markets

	China	Taiwan	Hong Kong	Korea	Singapore	Indonesia	Thailand	Malaysia	Philippines	Japan	United States	Western Europe	Rest of the World	World Total
Scenario 1: 10 percent devaluation														
Total Exports (Billion $)	35.8	−3.1	−2.2	−2.5	−0.9	−1.1	−1 4	−1.3	−0.3	−5.9	−6.1	−8.5	−11.8	−9.3
Total Exports (%)	17.0	−2.4	−3.0	−1.8	−0.7	−2.2	−2 2	−1.5	−1.0	−1.2	−0.8	−1.0	−1.1	−0.2
Total Imports (Billion $)	−16.6	−0.3	0.8	−0.2	0.2	−0.1	0 5	0.4	−0.1	1.9	1.6	2.0	0.2	−9.7
Total Imports (%)	−9.9	−0.3	0.7	−0.1	0.2	−0.1	0.6	0.5	−0.1	0.4	0.2	0.2	0.0	−0.2
Balance of Trade (Billion $)	52.3	−2.8	−3.0	−2.3	−1.1	−1.1	−2.0	−1.7	−0.2	−7.8	−7.7	−10.5	−6.2	0.0
Scenario 2: 20 percent devaluation														
Total Exports (Billion $)	72.4	−5.8	−4.1	−4.8	−1.8	−2.3	−2.9	−2.5	−0.5	−11.2	−11.9	−16.5	−23.4	−15.2
Total Exports (%)	34.4	−4.4	−5.5	−3.4	−1.5	−4.3	−4.3	−3.0	−2.0	−2.3	−1.7	−2.0	−2.2	−0.4
Total Imports (Billion $)	−29.9	−0.6	1.3	−0.4	0.4	−0.1	1.0	0.7	−0.1	4.0	3.3	4.1	0.5	−15.8
Total Imports (%)	−17.9	−0.6	1.2	−0.2	0.3	−0.3	1.2	0.9	−0.3	0.9	0.4	0.5	0.0	−0.4
Balance of Trade (Billion $)	102.3	−5.1	−5.5	−4.5	−2.2	−2.1	−3.9	−3.3	−0.4	−15.2	−15.3	−20.7	−12.2	0.0
Scenario 3: 30 percent devaluation														
Total Exports (Billion $)	109.8	−8.1	−5.9	−7.0	−2.6	−3.3	−4.2	−3.8	−0.8	−16.1	−17.7	−24.1	−34.8	−18.6
Total Exports (%)	52.2	−6.3	−7.9	−5.0	−2.2	−6.3	−6.4	−4.5	−3.1	−3.3	−2.5	−2.9	−3.3	−0.5
Total Imports (Billion $)	−40.8	−0.9	1.8	−0.5	0.5	−0.2	1.5	1.1	−0.2	6.1	5.1	6.5	0.7	−19.4
Total Imports (%)	−24.4	−0.8	1.6	−0.3	0.4	−0.4	1.8	1.3	−0.4	1.4	0.6	0.8	0.1	−0.5
Balance of Trade (Billion $)	150.6	−7.3	−7.7	−6.5	−3.1	−3.1	−5.7	−4.9	−0.6	−22.3	−22.9	−30.8	−18.2	0.0

Table 12.11 Impact of 10 % Chinese RMB Devaluation: Changes In Exports By Sector With No MFA Restriction In Developed Country Markets

	China	Taiwan	Hong Kong	Korea	Singapore	Indonesia	Thailand	Malaysia	Philippines	Japan	United States	Western Europe	Rest of the World
Agriculture	32.1	−2.1	1.8	−2.9	−0.8	−2.1	−1.0	−1.4	−2.1	−2.8	−2.0	−2.1	−1.6
Forest & Fishery	78.1	−2.3	0.3	−3.3	−1.2	−3.2	−9.1	−3.5	−4.7	−4.3	−2.1	−3.2	−1.6
Energy & Minerals	27.0	−0.8	−0.3	−1.9	−0.4	−0.8	−2.1	−1.3	−1.7	−1.0	−0.9	−0.6	−0.6
Processed Food	29.7	−1.0	−4.3	−1.6	−1.5	−1.8	−2.0	−2.1	−0.9	−2.6	−1.2	−0.7	−1.2
Beverage & Tobacco	35.5	−2.3	−9.8	−2.5	−4.6	−1.5	−1.6	−4.9	−6.0	0.0	−0.8	−0.8	−0.4
Textile	20.1	−2.2	−2.2	−2.2	−3.5	−2.9	−2.6	−3.1	−1.7	−2.8	−2.3	−2.7	−2.3
Apparel	34.9	−6.0	−3.3	−7.3	−0.4	−6.0	−6.8	−5.7	−1.9	−11.8	−6.9	−9.5	−5.3
Other Light Manufacture	32.0	−6.4	−5.8	−6.0	−3.6	−6.9	−7.0	−5.7	−6.1	−5.9	−5.8	−6.5	−7.1
Wood & Paper Products	27.1	−2.5	−4.7	−3.5	−1.1	−1.8	−1.3	−1.9	−0.8	−1.3	−0.6	−0.4	−0.6
Manufactured Intermediates	20.9	−2.8	−4.6	−1.9	−0.9	−0.7	−1.1	−0.6	−0.7	−1.6	−0.8	−0.7	−0.8
Motor Vehicle	51.7	−0.0	−3.3	−0.0	1.0	0.4	−0.4	0.1	1.0	0.0	0.2	−0.1	0.1
Other Transport Equipment	52.3	−2.3	−2.7	−1.1	−1.6	−1.3	−1.8	−1.8	−1.1	−1.6	−1.2	−1.5	−0.9
Electronics	21.5	−1.2	−3.7	−1.2	−0.5	−1.1	−1.3	−0.9	−0.3	−1.5	−1.1	−1.4	−0.9
Other Machinery	25.3	−2.1	−2.7	−1.1	−0.5	−0.4	−1.1	−0.7	−0.3	−1.3	−0.8	−1.0	−0.7
Traded Services	21.2	−0.1	−2.4	−0.2	−0.1	−0.2	−0.3	−0.5	−0.2	0.2	0.0	−0.0	−0.1
Utility, Housing & Construction	25.6	−0.9	−1.0	−0.8	−0.3	0.1	−0.7	−0.9	−0.7	−0.5	−0.0	−0.3	−0.6
Total	27.2	−2.3	−2.9	−1.7	−0.7	−2.0	−2.1	−1.5	−0.8	−1.2	−0.8	−1.0	−1.0

Table 12.12 Impact of Chinese RMB Devaluation: Other Country Exchange Rate, Percent Deviation From Base

	China	Taiwan	Hong Kong	Korea	Singapore	Indonesia	Thailand	Malaysia	Philippines	Japan	United States	Western Europe
Scenario 1: 10 percent devaluation												
Exchange Rate %	−10.0	−1.4	−1.8	−0.9	−0.8	−1.1	−1.1	−1.0	−0.6	0.0	0.0	0.0
Terms of Trade %	−7.8	−0.2	0.1	0.1	0.3	−0.1	−0.2	−0.1	0.4	0.8	0.5	0.5
Scenario 2: 20 percent devaluation												
Exchange Rate %	−20.0	−2.7	−3.4	−1.8	−1.5	−2.1	−2.2	−2.0	−1.3	0.0	0.0	0.0
Terms of Trade %	−14.3	−0.5	0.1	0.1	0.4	−0.3	−0.6	−0.2	0.8	1.4	0.9	0.9
Scenario 3. 30 percent devaluation												
Exchange Rate %	−30.0	−3.8	−4.9	−2.6	−2.2	−3.2	−3.2	−2.9	−1.9	0.0	0.0	0.0
Terms of Trade %	−19.9	−0.7	0.1	0.1	0.5	−0.6	−0.9	−0.3	1.0	2.0	1.2	1.3

After the financial crisis, the financial systems in many Asian countries remain fragile and consumer confidence weak. Should there be any pressure to devaluate their currencies, it could very easily induce another financial crisis. The extent of the devaluation will be far greater than the result in our model in order to keep their foreign trade balance. Evidently, stability in China's currency is very crucial to the economic recovery in Asia as a whole.

5.3 Devaluation of Japanese Yen

During the financial crisis in Asia, the exchange rate of the Japanese Yen decreased significantly, falling to 148:1 as against US dollar, an all time low in August 1998. The devaluation of Yen no doubt has boosted Japan's exports but dealt a heavy blow on the Asian economy. Many economists suspect if the devaluation can bail out Japan's economy. Herein the CGE model is used to simulate the devaluation of Yen to see its effect on the imports and exports of other Asian nations. The results of this simulation are listed in Table 12.13.

From this Table, it can be seen that in the case of devaluation of Yen by 10%, China's exports will drop by US$0.6 billion or 3% of its total exports with very little change to its imports. The effect on Korea will be more severe as exports will drop by US$0.6 billion or 6.3% of its total exports. Exports of all the Asian countries will be affected in different degrees.

Table 12.14 shows the adverse effects generated by the devaluation of Yen on Asian countries by sectors — the hardest hit will be forest and manufacturing sectors in China, trade service and light industry sectors in Korea, and car industry and trade service sectors in Indonesia.

With the devaluation of Yen, Asian countries will have to devaluate their currencies to maintain their exports. Table 12.15 shows the extents of the effects of the devaluation of Yen on respective Asian countries.

Table 12.15 shows that devaluation of Yen has a far stronger impact than that of RMB. It can boost exports and release pressure on unemployment in the short term in Japan. But it will also have very adverse impacts on other Asian nations such as reduction of their export capacity. As a matter of fact,

Table 12.13 Impact of Japanese Yen Devaluation: Aggregate Results

	Japan	China	Taiwan	Hong Kong	Korea	Singapore	Indonesia	Thailand	Malaysia	Philippines	United States	Western Europe	Rest of the World	World Total
Scenario 1: 10 percent devaluation														
Total Exports (Billion $)	79.5	−6.3	−4.1	−1.3	−6.0	−3.4	−1.0	−2.3	−2.0	−0.5	−25.0	−27.1	−19.3	−18.8
Total Exports (%)	16.4	−3.0	−3.2	−1.7	−4.3	−2.8	−1.9	−3.5	−2.3	−2.1	−3.5	−3.2	−1.8	−0.5
Total Imports (Billion $)	−49.4	0.4	−0.4	2.3	0.2	3.4	−0.1	0.9	0.4	−0.2	12.2	11.4	−0.6	−19.4
Total Imports (%)	−11.4	0.2	−0.3	2.1	0.2	2.6	−0.1	1.1	0.5	−0.5	1.4	1.4	−0.1	−0.5
Balance of Trade (Billion $)	128.9	−6.7	−3.8	−3.6	−6.3	−6.9	−0.9	−3.3	−2.4	−0.4	−37.3	−38.6	−6.1	0.0
Scenario 2: 20 percent devaluation														
Total Exports (Billion $)	161.5	−11.7	−7.8	−2.3	−11.4	−6.3	−1.8	−4.3	−3.7	−1.0	−47.1	−51.6	−35.9	−23.5
Total Exports (%)	33.4	−5.6	−6.0	−3.1	−8.2	−5.2	−3.3	−6.5	−4.3	−3.7	−6.6	−6.1	−3.4	−0.6
Total Imports (Billion $)	−87.9	0.9	−0.6	5.0	0.6	6.7	−0.1	1.8	0.8	−0.4	26.0	24.5	−1.3	−24.1
Total Imports (%)	−20.2	0.5	−0.6	4.4	0.4	5.2	−0.3	2.1	1.0	−1.0	2.9	3.0	−0.1	−0.6
Balance of Trade (Billion $)	249.3	−12.6	−7.2	−7.3	−12.0	−13.1	−1.6	−6.1	−4.5	−0.6	−73.3	−76.2	−10.7	0.0
Scenario 3: 30 percent devaluation														
Total Exports (Billion $)	245.3	−16.6	−11.2	−3.3	−16.3	−8.9	−2.4	−6.0	−5.1	−1.3	−67.1	−73.8	−49.9	−16.7
Total Exports (%)	50.7	−7.9	−8.6	−4.4	−11.7	−7.3	−4.5	−9.1	−6.1	−5.1	−9.3	−8.8	−4.7	−0.4
Total Imports (Billion $)	−118.4	1.5	−0.9	8.0	1.0	10.0	−0.3	2.5	1.1	−0.5	41.5	39.5	−1.8	−17.0
Total Imports (%)	−27.2	0.9	−0.8	7.1	0.6	7.6	−0.5	3.0	1.4	−1.4	4.7	4.9	−0.2	−0.4
Balance of Trade (Billion $)	363.6	−18.1	−10.4	−11.3	−17.3	−18.9	−2.1	−8.5	−6.2	−0.8	−108.6	−113.4	−14.0	0.0

Table 12.14 Impact of Japanese Yen Devaluation (10 Percent): Changes in Exports By Sector

	Japan	China	Taiwan	Hong Kong	Korea	Singapore	Indonesia	Thailand	Malaysia	Philippines	United States	Western Europe	Rest of the World
Agriculture	8.7	−3.9	−0.7	−3.6	−4.2	−0.7	−1.3	−0.6	−0.7	−1.5	0.0	−0.0	0.3
Forest & Fishery	30.8	−11.0	−7.9	−5.9	−8.5	−0.6	−3.5	−9.2	−7.0	−6.0	−7.4	−5.8	−1.4
Energy & Minerals	23.6	0.4	1.6	−1.7	−0.2	0.8	−0.4	−2.1	−0.9	1.1	−0.3	−0.5	0.1
Processed Food	21.8	−5.6	−6.1	−2.1	−6.5	−0.8	−3.3	−1.9	−0.3	−2.0	−2.3	−0.7	−1.0
Beverage & Tobacco	37.6	1.6	1.9	−0.4	−4.9	0.4	0.4	1.3	5.3	2.9	−5.6	−1.2	0.6
Textile	26.9	−0.4	−0.9	−2.4	−0.8	−3.2	0.2	−0.3	0.4	−0.2	−1.4	−2.0	−0.5
Apparel	71.5	0.5	0.3	−0.4	0.2	0.5	0.5	0.8	0.6	0.2	−5.7	−7.2	0.2
Other Light Manufacture	44.9	−3.2	−3.1	−2.7	−4.8	1.4	−2.3	−3.1	5.4	−2.4	−4.5	−4.4	−2.4
Wood & Paper Products	32.6	−2.1	−1.7	−0.7	−0.8	−2.1	−3.0	−3.4	−1.6	−1.3	−1.5	−0.7	−0.5
Manufactured Intermediates	20.3	−1.6	−0.8	−2.2	−2.2	−2.9	−2.2	−1.9	−1.3	−2.6	−1.9	−1.4	−1.6
Motor Vehicle	45.4	−9.6	−9.9	−14.6	−7.3	−4.8	−12.7	−6.5	−8.6	−8.3	−8.7	−12.8	−7.9
Other Transport Equipment	61.5	−3.9	−4.1	−13.8	−3.5	−4.8	5.1	−7.6	−4.0	−2.0	−7.2	−6.7	−3.3
Electronics	26.7	−2.0	−3.4	−4.7	−3.2	−0.5	−3.3	−6.0	−2.3	−0.6	−4.5	−4.4	−3.7
Other Machinery	23.9	−4.3	−2.6	−4.5	−4.1	−1.2	−0.7	−4.8	−2.1	0.8	−5.3	−4.7	−4.1
Traded Services	21.5	−3.2	−4.1	−0.9	−6.1	−4.5	−4.1	−4.9	−5.1	−2.5	−1.4	−0.9	−3.2
Utility, Housing & Construction	31.0	2.8	0.9	0.5	1.0	1.9	2.3	1.7	2.3	1.5	0.5	0.1	1.1
Total	28.4	−2.2	−2.5	−1.6	−3.8	−1.9	−1.7	−3.2	−1.5	−1.1	−3.4	−3.2	−1.8

Table 12.15 Impact of Japanese Yen Devaluation: Other Country Exchange Rate When Balance of Trade Fixed At Base

	Japan	China	Taiwan	Hong Kong	Korea	Singapore	Indonesia	Thailand	Malaysia	Philippines	United States	Western Europe
Scenario 1: 10 percent devaluation												
Exchange Rate %	−10.0	−1.4	−1.7	−1.5	−2.0	−1.7	−1.4	−1.9	−1.4	−1.0	0.0	0.0
Terms of Trade %	−7.5	0.2	0.5	0.6	−0.3	0.3	0.2	0.0	0.3	0.5	1.1	1.2
Scenario 2: 20 percent devaluation												
Exchange Rate %	−20.0	−2.7	−3.3	−2.9	−3.9	−3.1	−2.6	−3.6	−2.5	−1.8	0.0	0.0
Terms of Trade %	−14.0	0.3	0.7	1.1	−0.6	0.5	0.3	−0.0	0.5	1.0	2.1	2.3
Scenario 3: 30 percent devaluation												
Exchange Rate %	−30.0	−3.9	−4.7	−4.1	−5.6	−4.3	−3.6	−5.2	−3.5	−2.4	0.0	0.0
Terms of Trade %	−19.5	0.3	0.9	1.7	−1.1	0.6	0.3	−0.1	0.7	1.4	2.9	3.3

the devaluation of Yen will touch off a new round of devaluation in other Asian countries for their survival and exports and the Asian market will thus shrink again. Nevertheless, Japan will sustain the backward effects, as the Asian market is closely linked to Japan's economy and shrinking of the Asian market will bring about severe economic problems for the recovery of Japan's own market.

6.   CONCLUSION

There are three basic characteristics in current economic adjustment and recovery process in Asia: (1) significant decrease of imports; (2) sluggish increase of exports; (3) slow rebound of foreign exchange rate. They have resulted in a sluggish increase of foreign exchange reserves in Asian economies. Since imports by these economies have significantly reduced, the market demand in Asia has by no means restored. Having sustained heavy financial losses due to the economic turmoil, Asian countries are in urgent need to extend their export markets to earn hard currency to pay their debts, rebuild their foreign currency reserves and offset the shrinking domestic market due to decline of income. Increasing exports is a condition necessary for all crises affected Asian economies to recover. As the export structure in Asian countries is quite similar, the competition for market share in Third World countries will be very tough.

Japan's domestic consumption is the largest component of the Asian market and so the recovery of Japan's domestic demand, especially its private consumption and investment, will have a strong positive impact on Asian economies. Only Japan can provide the scale of export market for other Asian countries. Moreover, facts in the past years have shown that such stimulating measures like cutting interest rates and increasing government spending have proved not working for the recovery of Japan's economy because Japan's interest rate is already near zero and government expenditures have already been slashed drastically. The policies so far adopted by the Japanese government have in no way stimulated any rise in domestic consumption and investment. Japan should make more efforts to stimulate and rebuild its domestic market, increase household income and consumption, and rely on demand-led growth. The current stagnation in private consumption growth in Japan is partially due to the large amount of non-performing loans in Japan's banking system. Reforming the financial system and restoring people's confidence are of utmost importance for private consumption and investment to regain steam. Japan should not use devaluation to increase external demand and pass the crisis to other Asian nations, because devaluation of Yen will shrink the Asian market further and thus weaken the foundation of Japan's economy in the long run.

The stability of Chinese RMB has contributed a great deal to the Asian economy. China should continue to maintain the stability of its currency before a full recovery of Asian economy. Should China devaluate its currency, it would bring about a strong substitution effect on the exports from other Asian countries, and thus would reduce the export market for other Asian economies. This would add to the burden of other Asian nations now still facing great difficulties in the struggle for recovery of their economies. Just imagine Asian countries will have to devaluate their currencies again because of the devaluation of RMB, which is very likely to trigger another round of competitive devaluation and financial turmoil in Asia since the tolerance and confidence in many Asian countries are still very weak.

Our simulation results have shown clearly that devaluation of currency, either by Japan or by China, cannot in the least help the economic recovery in Asia as it cannot create the most needed market for Asian products as a whole. Such measures as stimulation of domestic demand, especially private consumption and investment, and development of technology intensive products are main keys to quick economic recovery in Asia.

Some economists hold that the financial crisis in Asia was mainly due to rapid economic growth in Asia in the past two decades; the economic expansion was mainly by way of increasing factory inputs, and such external economic growth was not sustainable in the long run. However, changing the mode of economic growth implies enhancement in productivity, increase of investment in education and R&D, and improvement in operation and management, which cannot be accomplished in a short period of time and should be a long-term objective. In our opinion, two aspects of work of utmost importance can be easily completed. With respect to Japan, measures should be made to speed up its reform of financial system, restore consumer confidence and increase domestic demand to create a market for the Asian economy as a whole. In the case of China, it is necessary to make continuous efforts to speed up the reform of its state-owned enterprises, control the size of the non-performing loans in banks, and maintain the stability of RMB. In this way, the new crisis that may be induced from devaluation of either Yen or RMB can be avoided. As long as the reform of China's state-owned economic sector and Japan's financial system can advance step-by-step, we should be optimistic about the economic recovery in Asia.

References

Brooke, A., David Kendrick and Alexander Meeraus. "GAMS: a User's Guide", The Scientific Press, New York, 1988.

De Melo, J. and David Tarr. "A General Equilibrium Analysis of US Foreign Trade Policy". The MIT Press, Cambridge, MA, 1992.

Devarajan, Shantayanan, Jeffrey D. Lewis and Sherman Robinson, "Policy Lesson from Trade-Focused, Two-Sector Models." *Journal of Policy Modeling*, 1990, 12: 625–657.

Francois, Joseph, Bradley McDonald, and Hakan Nordstrom. "Assessing the Uruguay Round," in Martin, Will, and Alan Winters (eds.) *The Uruguay Round and the Developing Economies,* 1995, World Bank Discussion Paper 307. Washington, D.C.

Harrison Glenn W., Thomas F. Rutherford, and David G. Tarr. "Quantifying the Uruguay Round." in Martin, Will, and Alan Winters (eds.) *The Uruguay Round and the Developing Economies,* 1995, World Bank Discussion Paper 307. The World Bank, Washington, D.C.

Hertel, Thomas W. eds. *"Global Trade Analysis"*, *Modeling and Applications.* 1997, Cambridge, Cambridge University Press.

Howe, H. "Development of the Extended Linear Expenditure System from Simple Savings Assumptions," 1975, *European Economic Review* 6: 305–310.

Krishna, K. and L. H. Tan. "The Multi-fibber Arrangement in Practice: Challenging the Competitive Framework" in D. Roberston (ed.) *Asia-Pacific Trade After the Uruguay Round*, 1995, National Center for Development Studies, Australian National University, Canberra.

Lardy, Nicholas, *China and the WTO*, 1996, Brookings Policy Briefing, No. 10, Brookings Institution, Washington D.C.

Noland, Marcus, Li-Gang Liu, Sherman Robinson and Zhi Wang "Global Economic Effects of the Asian Currency Devaluations" Institute of International Economics, Washington DC, July 1998.

Marcus Noland, Sherman Robinson and Zhi Wang "The Continuing Asia Financial Crisis — Global Adjustment and Trade" The Japanese Economy, 25(5): 70–95, 1999.

Wang, Zhi. "The Impact of China and Taiwan Joining the World Trade Organization on U.S. and World Agricultural Trade: A Computable General Equilibrium Analysis", 1997, Technical Bulletin, No. 1858, U.S. Department of Agriculture, Economic Research Service.

Wang, Zhi, "China and Taiwan Access to the World Trade Organization: Implications for U.S. Agriculture and Trade." 1997b, *Agricultural Economics*, 17: 239–264.

Wang, Zhi and Jean Kinsey, "Consumption and Saving Behavior Under Strict and Partial Rationing", 1994, *China Economic Review — An International Journal*, 5: 83–100.

Wang, Zhi and James Slagle, "An Object-oriented Knowledge-based Approach for Formulating Applied General Equilibrium Models." 1996, *Journal of Economic Dynamics and Control*, 20: 209–236.

Whalley, J., "Trade Liberalization Among Major World Trading Areas." 1985, Cambridge: The MIT press.

Appendix Table 12.1 Exchange Rate in Asian Countries

1997	1	2	3	4	5	6	7	8	9	10	11	12
China	8.29	8.29	8.3	8.29	8.29	8.29	8.29	8.29	8.29	8.28	8.28	8.28
Hong Kong	7.74	7.74	7.75	7.75	7.74	7.75	7.74	7.75	7.74	7.73	7.73	7.75
Indonesia	2372	2390	2398	2419	2443	2432	2585	2880	3000	3610	3660	5445
Malaysia	2.5	2.49	2.48	2.5	2.51	2.52	2.54	2.83	3.06	3.4	3.51	3.81
Philippines	26.3	26.3	26.4	26.4	26.4	26.4	28.7	30.5	33.5	35.1	34.8	40
Singapore	1.41	1.43	1.44	1.44	1.43	1.43	1.47	1.51	1.51	1.58	1.6	1.68
Korea	860	862	889	893	893	888	894	903	914	967	1110	1483
Taiwan	27.4	27.5	27.6	27.6	27.9	27.9	28	28.7	28.6	31	32.4	32.5
Thailand	25.9	25.9	26	26.1	25.8	25.3	31.6	33.9	35.1	39.1	39.7	46.3
Japan	122	122	124	126	115	114	116	121	120	121	127	127

1998	1	2	3	4	5	6	7	8	9	10	11	12
China	8.28	8.28	8.28	8.28	8.28	8.28	8.28	8.28	8.28	8.28	8.28	8.28
Hong Kong	7.74	7.75	7.75	7.75	7.75	7.75	7.75	7.75	7.75	7.75	7.74	7.75
Indonesia	11,800	9450	8600	7950	10,500	14,750	12,300	11,200	11,075	7650	7500	8050
Malaysia	4.36	3.75	3.7	3.77	3.85	3.95	4.12	4.21	3.8	3.8	3.8	3.8
Philippines	42.2	40.3	38.3	38.3	39.1	41.5	42.1	43.6	44.8	40.9	39.4	39.2
Singapore	1.72	1.63	1.62	1.59	1.67	1.66	1.72	1.78	1.73	1.62	1.64	1.66
Korea	1680	1643	1391	1375	1413	1381	1244	1310	1402	1315	1250	1201
Taiwan	34	32.6	32.9	33	33.9	34.4	34.3	34.8	34.7	32.5	32.5	32.2
Thailand	53.7	43.3	39.7	39.3	39.6	41.1	40.8	41.8	40.4	36.9	36.1	36.7
Japan	125	129	133	131	138	141	143	145	136	118	122	115

1999	1	2	3	4	5	6	7	8	9	10	11	12
China	8.28	8.28	8.28	8.28	8.28	8.28	8.28	8.28	8.28	8.28	8.28	8.28
Hong Kong	7.75	7.75	7.75	7.75	7.75	7.76	7.76	7.76	7.77	7.77	7.77	7.78
Indonesia	9125	8885	8725	8515	8135	6873	6840	7675	8360	6825	7135	7195
Malaysia	3.8	3.8	3.8	3.8	3.8	3.8	3.8	3.8	3.8	3.8	3.8	3.8
Philippines	38.7	39.1	38.8	38	38	38	38.3	39.7	41	40.1	40.8	40.2
Singapore	1.69	1.74	1.73	1.7	1.73	1.7	1.68	1.68	1.71	1.67	1.67	1.66
Korea	1175	1229	1223	1179	1186	1158	1198	1185	1218	1200	1162	1135
Taiwan	32.3	33.1	33.2	32.6	32.7	32.3	32.3	31.8	31.8	31.7	31.7	30.7
Thailand	36.8	37.6	37.6	37.4	37.1	36.9	37	38.8	41.3	38.8	38.8	37.2
Japan	115	121	120	119	121	121	116	109	107	104	105	104

Appendix Table 12.2 Stockmarkets in Asian Countries

1997	1	2	3	4	5	6	7	8	9	10	11	12
China	1004	1078	1255	1443	1326	1357	1255	1297	1158	1244	1204	1208
Hong Kong	13,285	13,541	12,833	12,707	14,556	15,065	15,739	14,714	14,205	10,765	10,590	10,692
Indonesia	691	712	657	652	673	713	718	512	553	472	399	369
Malaysia	1213	1265	1217	1110	1096	1070	1034	751	779	663	526	557
Philippines	3374	3349	3204	2913	2722	2829	2636	1994	2077	1814	1799	1797
Singapore	2220	2216	2100	2035	2064	2024	1974	1820	1900	1541	1653	1569
Korea	664	679	639	693	738	705	731	689	656	507	439	419
Taiwan	7149	7730	7843	8577	8058	8956	9381	9461	8994	7089	7698	8347
Thailand	814	739	711	690	563	496	631	514	547	457	402	376
Japan	18,335	18,990	18,439	18,736	20,351	20,679	20,131	18,735	18,420	16,857	16,046	16,541

1998	1	2	3	4	5	6	7	8	9	10	11	12
China	1244	1258	1325	1409	1483	1488	1396	1235	1308	1302	1344	1221
Hong Kong	7252	10,887	11,331	10,978	8983	8197	7809	7834	7504	9927	10,721	10,121
Indonesia	486	483	524	501	417	431	485	361	262	312	387	398
Malaysia	569	713	700	619	552	455	386	325	376	411	502	574
Philippines	1782	2154	2209	2154	2060	1713	1605	1287	1160	1602	1958	1969
Singapore	1260	1583	1600	1476	1296	1075	1054	926	901	1180	1390	1395
Korea	519	516	468	432	314	302	344	318	292	364	464	563
Taiwan	8086	9027	9042	8636	8068	7671	7775	6814	6962	6962	7213	6462
Thailand	434	513	457	437	340	258	264	228	231	331	391	359
Japan	16,974	16,360	16,242	15,762	15,664	15,123	16,158	14,866	13,790	13,516	15,073	13,842

1999	1	2	3	4	5	6	7	8	9	10	11	12
China	1220	1202	1232	1161	1367	1790	1696	1699	1684	1633	1546	1498
Hong Kong	9720	9922	10,940	13,133	12,458	13,532	13,140	13,544	12,835	12,709	15,307	15,946
Indonesia	410	396	394	481	574	662	599	572	527	576	600	678
Malaysia	605	513	499	662	749	811	782	753	684	738	741	816
Philippines	1994	2009	2012	2460	2416	2487	2353	2153	2081	1962	1964	2074
Singapore	1457	1416	1518	1837	1927	2168	2077	2122	2018	1989	2190	2391
Korea	565	535	618	790	775	883	945	906	869	793	969	986
Taiwan	6139	6403	6899	7497	7488	8467	7484	8273	7616	7701	7922	8849
Thailand	373	341	360	423	475	521	462	435	391	379	399	466
Japan	14,450	14,170	15,859	16,942	16,418	17,529	17,579	17,803	17,282	17,382	18,896	18,542

Appendix Table 12.3 Foreign Reservation

($bn)

1997	1	2	3	4	5	6	7	8	9	10	11	12
China	100.9	104.3	104.3	110.6	114.0	114.0	116.3	122.8	122.8	127.8	132.3	136.0
Hong Kong	62.1	62.1	69.6	69.6	69.6	69.6	69.6	76.1	81.9	85.3	85.3	91.8
Indonesia	15.5	15.5	18.3	19.0	19.0	19.0	19.5	20.3	20.2	19.3	20.3	18.9
Malaysia	26.1	26.8	26.8	26.8	26.1	26.1	26.1	26.1	26.1	26.1	26.6	26.6
Philippines	9.6	9.6	10.0	9.7	9.7	10.3	10.4	10.2	10.0	10.0	8.3	9.4
Singapore	74.2	75.0	75.6	76.9	77.3	77.2	78.7	80.4	80.4	80.7	76.8	76.8
Korea	33.1	33.1	31.7	30.5	29.9	30.6	32.7	34.1	34.1	34.4	31.2	31.3
Taiwan	87.7	88.0	88.0	88.0	88.0	88.8	88.8	90.0	87.8	87.8	87.8	82.9
Thailand	38.6	37.7	38.2	37.2	37.1	36.3	32.3	31.4	29.4	34.4	28.6	30.3
Japan	215.9	216.6	216.0	217.0	218.2	218.7	220.6	221.1	221.1	221.1	224.4	227.0

1998	1	2	3	4	5	6	7	8	9	10	11	12
China	139.9	141.3	142.8	143.7	140.6	140.6	140.9	140.9	140.6	141.1	141.1	143.7
Hong Kong	96.5	16.5	75.3	80.3	78.6	96.2	96.2	96.4	96.5	88.4	88.4	88.6
Indonesia	18.9	18.9	18.1	15.5	15.5	16.3	16.9	18.0	18.0	19.0	19.0	19.7
Malaysia	21.7	21.7	21.7	21.7	21.7	21.3	21.3	19.7	19.7	19.5	19.6	20.7
Philippines	9.4	8.8	8.8	8.8	8.8	8.8	7.8	9.3	9.0	9.0	8.5	9.0
Singapore	77.3	74.5	74.4	74.4	74.4	74.4	76.1	71.9	71.9	70.9	69.2	68.0
Korea	20.4	21.1	24.2	26.7	29.8	35.5	38.8	40.8	45.1	47.0	47.0	48.4
Taiwan	83.1	83.1	84.0	84.0	84.0	84.0	84.4	83.3	83.6	83.7	83.7	83.7
Thailand	27.0	26.2	25.9	25.4	26.9	28.7	26.7	26.7	26.0	25.9	26.6	27.8
Japan	227.2	219.6	220.4	222.0	222.0	204.6	205.8	205.8	206.4	208.2	211.2	NA

1999	1	2	3	4	5	6	7	8	9	10	11	12
China	145.0	145.0	149.2	149.2	150.4	150.5	150.7	150.4	150.6	162.3	154.0	154.7
Hong Kong	88.6	90.1	89.8	89.8	89.5	88.9	88.6	89.1	89.2	89.2	90.4	90.4
Indonesia	20.8	23.8	23.8	23.8	23.8	23.2	24.9	26.3	26.3	26.0	26.2	26.2
Malaysia	20.7	23.0	23.0	25.6	27.2	27.2	27.2	30.6	31.6	32.5	31.1	30
Philippines	9.0	9.2	9.2	9.2	9.2	10.7	12.2	12.2	12.3	12.4	12.7	12.7
Singapore	72.4	74.9	74.9	74.0	72.1	71.6	71.6	73.2	73.8	75.1	75.8	75.9
Korea	50.0	53.5	53.5	55.4	59.3	59.3	61.3	61.3	64.9	64.7	65.4	65.4
Taiwan	83.7	91.9	92.6	92.6	95.1	95.1	95.1	98.6	98.6	98.6	98.6	102.3
Thailand	28.2	28.3	28.3	28.0	29.2	29.5	29.9	20.7	31.2	31.5	31.7	31.7

Data sources: *Economist*, varies issues, 1997, 1998, 1999.

APPENDIX

Algebraic Specification of the Global CGE Model

This appendix provides a detailed mathematical specification of the seventeen-region, sixteen-sector recursive dynamic CGE model for world production and trade used in this chapter.

Notation

Regions are defined in set R and indexed by r or s;
Sectors are defined in set I and indexed by i or j;
Agricultural sectors are defined as a subset of I: IAG(I);
Natural Resource based sectors are defined as a subset of I: RES(I);
Primary factors are defined in set F and indexed by f;

Conventions

Uppercase English letter indicates variables, unless they have a bar on top, in which case that variable always set exogenously. Greek letter or lower English letter refers to parameters, which need to be calibrated or supplied from exogenous sources. When multiple subscripts of a variable or parameter come from the same set, the first one represents the region or sector supplying goods; the next one represents the region or sector purchasing goods.

Price Equations

Equations 1–11 are price equations in the model. Equations 1 and 2 define the relationship between border (world) prices and internal prices, while equations 3, 4, 6, 7, and 8 define price indices for aggregate imported goods, Armington goods, composite value-added, and the firm's output with and without production taxes, respectively. In equations 3, 4, 6, and 7, the price indices are the unit cost functions, while in equation 8 they are unit revenue functions, all of which are dual to the corresponding unit quantity aggregator functions. For example, equation 7 is the result of cost minimization by the representative firm in each sector with respect to its aggregate factor and inputs, subject to a CES production function. Since CES functions are used as the building blocks of the basic model, and this quantity aggregator function is homogeneous of degree one, the total costs can be written as total quantity multiplied by unit cost (Varian, 1984, p. 28). This implies that the average cost, under cost minimization, is independent of the number of units produced or purchased. Thus, the unit cost function also stands for the price of the composed commodity. Equation 5 defines the unit price for aggregate inputs, which is the IO coefficient weighted sum of all the value of its contents. Equation 9 states the domestic consumer price is the Arminton goods price plus sales taxes. Equation 10 specifies an economy-wide consumer price index, which is used as price of household savings. Equation 11 defines the numeraire in the model.

$$PWE_{isr} = (1 + te_{isr}) \times (\frac{1}{ER_r}) \times PE_{ir} \tag{1}$$

$$PWM_{isr} = (1 + trs_{isr}) \times PWE_{isr} \tag{2}$$

$$PM_{ir} = \frac{1}{\mu_{ir}} \times \{\sum_{s \in R} \xi_{irs}^{\sigma t_i} \times [(1 + tm_{irs} + tn_{irs}) \times ER_r \times PWM_{irs}]^{1-\sigma t_i}\}^{\frac{1}{1-\sigma t_i}} \tag{3}$$

$$PX_{ir} = \frac{1}{\Gamma_{ir}} \times \{\sum \alpha_{ir}^{\sigma m_i} \times PD_{ir}^{1-\sigma m_i} + (1 - \alpha_{ir})^{\sigma m_i} \times PM_{ir}^{1-\sigma m_i}\}^{\frac{1}{1-\sigma m_i}} \tag{4}$$

$$PN_{jr} = \sum_{i \in I} io_{ijr} \times PX_{ir} \tag{5}$$

$$PV_{ir} = \frac{1}{\Lambda_{ir} \times tfp_r \times ITFP_{ir}} \times \{\sum_{f \in F} \delta_{fir}^{\sigma v_i} \times PF_{fr}^{1-\sigma v_i}\}^{\frac{1}{1-\sigma v_i}} \tag{6}$$

$$PP_{ir} = \frac{1}{A_{ir}} \times \{\lambda_{ir}^{\sigma pi} \times PN_{ir}^{1-\sigma pi} + (1-\lambda_{ir})^{\sigma pi} \times PV_{ir}^{1-\sigma pi}\}^{\frac{1}{1-\sigma pi}} \tag{7}$$

$$P_{ir} = \frac{1}{\chi_{ir}} \times \{\kappa_{ir}^{\sigma eir} \times PD_{ir}^{1-\sigma ei} + (1-\kappa_{ir})^{\sigma ei} \times PE_{ir}^{1-\sigma ei}\}^{\frac{1}{1-\sigma ei}} \tag{8}$$

$$PC_{ir} = (1+tc_{ir}) \times PX_{ir} \tag{9}$$

$$CPI_r = \frac{\sum_{i \in I} PC_{ir} \times C_{ir}}{\sum_{i \in I} PCO_{ir} \times C_{ir}} \tag{10}$$

$$PID_r = \prod_{i \in I} PC_{ir}^{\beta ir} \times CPI_r^{mpsr} \tag{11}$$

Factor Demand and Firms' Supply Equations

Equations 12 and 13 specify the demand functions for aggregate factor and intermediate inputs, while equation 14 gives demand functions of each primary factor. They equal unit demand function multiplied by the quantities of total output, and the unit demand functions are obtained by taking partial derivatives of the unit cost functions (equation 6 and 7) with respect to the relevant factor prices, according to Shephard's lemma.

$$NX_{ir} = (\frac{1}{A_{ir}})^{1-\sigma pi} \times (\lambda_{ir} \times \frac{PP_{ir}}{PN_{ir}})^{\sigma pi} \times Q_{ir} \tag{12}$$

$$VA_{ir} = (\frac{1}{A_{ir}})^{1-\sigma pi} \times [(1-\lambda_{ir}) \times \frac{PP_{ir}}{PV_{ir}}]^{\sigma pi} \times Q_{ir} \tag{13}$$

$$DF_{fir} = (\frac{1}{\Lambda_{ir} \times tfp_r \times ITFP_{ir}})^{1-\sigma v_i} \times (\delta_{fir} \times \frac{PV_{ir}}{PF_{fr}})^{\sigma v_i} \times VA_{ir}$$

$$\sum_{f \in F} \delta_{fir} = 1 \tag{14}$$

Equations 15–18 are the domestic and export supply functions corresponding to the constant elasticity of transformation (CET) function commonly used in today's CGE models. They are derived from revenue maximization, subject to the CET function, in a way similar to the derivation of factor demand functions. Equation 19 aggregates exports by the representative firm in each region, which implies that producers only differentiate output sold in domestic and foreign markets, but do not differentiate exports by destination (foreign markets are perfect substitutes). Equations 15–18 can be partially or entirely turn off in the model, in such case, $PD_{ir} = PE_{ir} = P_{ir}$ will be enforced and exports and domestic sales become perfect substitutes in the model

$$DX_{ir} = (\frac{1}{\chi_{ir}})^{1-\sigma e_i} \times (\kappa_{ir} \times \frac{P_{ir}}{PD_{ir}})^{\sigma e_{sv}} \times Q_{ir}$$

for s sv $\tag{15}$

$$DX_{sv,r} = (\frac{1}{\chi_{sv,r}})^{1-\sigma e_{sv}} \times (\kappa_{sv,r} \times \frac{P_{sv,r}}{PD_{sv,r}})^{\sigma e_{sv}} \times (Q_{sv,r} - TRQS_r) \tag{16}$$

$$EX_{ir} = (\frac{1}{\chi_{ir}})^{1-\sigma e_i} \times \{(1 - \kappa_{ir}) \times \frac{P_{ir}}{PE_{ir}}\}^{\sigma e_i} \times Q_{ir}$$

for s sv $\tag{17}$

$$EX_{sv,r} = (\frac{1}{\chi_{sv,r}})^{1-\sigma e_{sv}} \times \{(1 - \kappa_{sv,r}) \times \frac{P_{sv,r}}{PE_{sv,r}})^{\sigma e_{sv}} \times (Q_{sv,r} - TRQS_r) \tag{18}$$

$$EX_{ir} = \frac{1}{PE_{ir}} \times \sum_{s \in R} \frac{ER_r}{(1 + te_{irs})} \times PWE_{irs} \times X_{irs} \tag{19}$$

Trade and Final Demand Equations

Trade and final demand equations are listed in equations 20–26. Equation 20 is the consumer demand function, which is the Extended Linear Expenditure System derived from maximizing a Stone-Geary utility function subject to household disposable income, which is specified in equation 31. Equation 21 defines household supernumerary income, which is disposal income less total expenditure on the subsistence minimum. Equations 22 and 23 give government and investment demands. Equations 24–26 are demand functions for domestic goods, for aggregate imported goods, and for imported goods by source, respectively. They describe the cost-minimizing choice of domestic and import purchases, as well as import sources. They are derived from corresponding cost functions according to Shephard's lemma in a way similar to the derivation of factor demand functions (taking partial derivatives of the cost function with respect to the relevant component prices). Because of the linear homogeneity of the CES function, the cost function that is dual to the commodity aggregator can be represented by its unit cost function (equations 3 and 4) multiplied by total quantity demanded.

$$C_{ir} = \gamma_{ir} + \frac{\beta_{ir}}{PC_{ir}} \times SY_r \tag{20}$$

$$SY_r = HDI_r - \sum_{j \in I} PC_{jr} \times \gamma_{jr} \tag{21}$$

$$GC_{ir} = \frac{\theta_{ir}}{PC_{ir}} \times GSP_r \tag{22}$$

$$ID_{ir} = \frac{kio_{ir}}{PC_{ir}} \times INV_r \tag{23}$$

$$DX_{ir} = (\frac{1}{\Gamma_{ir}})^{1-\sigma m_i} \times (\alpha_{ir} \times \frac{PX_{ir}}{PD_{ir}})^{\sigma m_i} \times TX_{ir} \tag{24}$$

$$MX_{ir} = (\frac{1}{\Gamma_{ir}})^{1-\sigma m_i} \times \{(1-\alpha_{ir}) \times \frac{PX_{ir}}{PM_{ir}}\}^{\sigma m_i} \times TX_{ir} \tag{25}$$

$$X_{isr} = (\frac{1}{\mu_{ir}})^{1-\sigma t_i} \times \{\xi_{isr} \times (\frac{PM_{ir}}{(1+tm_{isr}+tn_{irs}) \times ER_r \times PWM_{isr}})^{\sigma t_i} \times MX_{ir}$$

$$\sum_{s \in R} \xi_{isr} = 1$$

$$\text{for } s \ r \tag{26}$$

International Shipping Equations

Equations 27–30 describe international shipping industry in the model. Equations 27 and 28 describe the supply side of the international shipping industry. Equation 27 states that at equilibrium, the returns from shipping activity must cover its cost. Like other industries in the model, it also earns zero profit. Equation 28 describes the demand for each region's service sector exports to the international shipping industry, which is generated by the assumed Cobb-Douglas technology in this industry. The next two equations (29 and 30), refer to the demand side of the international shipping industry. The demand for shipping services associated with commodity i in region r is generated by a fixed proportion input requirement (Leontif) coefficient trs_{isr}, which is routine/commodity specific (equation 29). In equilibrium, the total demand of shipping service must equal its total supply (equation 30).

$$TRQ = \frac{1}{PTR} \times \sum_{r \in R} \frac{P_{sv,r}}{ER_r} \times TRQS_r \tag{27}$$

$$TRQS_r = \frac{\tau_r \times ER_r}{P_{sv,r}} \times PTR \times TRQ \tag{28}$$

$$TRQD_{ir} = \frac{1}{PRT} \times (\sum_{s \in R} trs_{isr} \times PWE_{isr} \times X_{isr}) \tag{29}$$

$$TRQ = \sum_{r \in R} \sum_{i \in I} TRQD_{ir} \tag{30}$$

Income and Saving Equations

Equations 31–39 are income and saving equations in the model. Equations 31 and 32 define household disposal income and savings. Equations 33–37 determine government revenue from production taxes, consumption taxes, tariffs and export taxes (its negative equals a subsidy), respectively, while equations 38–39 define government transfer to household and the balance of trade (foreign savings) in each region.

$$HDI_r = \sum_{f \in F} PF_{fr} \times \overline{FS_{fr}} - dk_r \times \overline{FS_{KAr}} + GTRANS_r \tag{31}$$

$$SAV_r = \frac{HDI_r \times \sum_{i \in I} PC_{ir} \times C_{ir}}{CPI_r} \tag{32}$$

$$GR_r = PTAX_r + CTAX_r + TARRIF_r + ETAX_r \tag{33}$$

$$PTAX_r = \sum_{i \in I} tp_{ir} \times P_{ir} \times Q_{ir} \tag{34}$$

$$CTAX_r = \sum_{i \in I} tc_{ir} \times PX_{ir}(C_{ir} + GC_{ir} + ID_{ir}) \tag{35}$$

$$TARRIF_r = \sum_{s \in R} \sum_{i \in I}(tm_{isr} + tn_{irs}) \times ER_r \times PWM_{isr} \times X_{isr} \tag{36}$$

$$ETAX_s = \sum_{r \in R} \sum_{i \in I} te_{isr} \times PE_{is} \times X_{isr} \tag{37}$$

$$GTRANS_r = GR_r - GSP_r - GSVA_r \tag{38}$$

$$BOT_r = \sum_{s \in R} \sum_{i \in I} PWE_{irs} X_{irs} + \frac{P_{sv,r}}{ER_r} \times TRQS_r - \sum_{s \in R} \sum_{i \in I} PWM_{isr} \times X_{isr} \tag{39}$$

General Equilibrium Conditions

Equations 40–43 define general equilibrium conditions of the model, which are system constraints that the model economy must satisfy. For every sector in each region, the supply of the composite goods must equal total demand (equation 40), which is the sum of household consumption (C_{ir}), government purchases (GC_{ir}), investment (ID_{ir}) and the firm's intermediate demand. Similarly, the demand for each factor in every region must equal the exogenously fixed supply (equation 41). In this dual formulation, output in each region is determined by demand. Sectoral equilibrium is determined in equation 42, unit output price equals average cost, which is also the zero profit condition. Equation 43 describes the macroeconomic equilibrium identity in each region, which is also the budget constraint for the investor. Since all agents in each region (households, government, investor and firms) satisfy their respective budget constraints, it is well known that the sum of the excess demand for all goods is zero; that is, Walras's law holds for each region. Therefore, there is a functional dependence among the equations of the model. One equation is redundant in each region and thus can be dropped.

$$TX_{ir} = C_{ir} + GC_{ir} + ID_{ir} + \sum_{j \in I} io_{ijr} \times NX_{jr} \tag{40}$$

$$\sum_{i \in I} DF_{fir} = \overline{FS_{fr}} \tag{41}$$

$$P_{ir} = \frac{PN_{ir} \times NX_{ir} + PV_{ir} \times VA_{ir} + tp_{ir} \times P_{ir} \times Q_{ir}}{Q_{ir}} \tag{42}$$

$$INV_r = dr_r \times \overline{FS_{k,r}} + CPI_r \times SAV_r + GSAV_r - ER_r \times BOT_r \tag{43}$$

There are 19,960 equations and 20,113 variables in the inter-period block of the model. Since the 102 factor endowment variables (FS_r) are determined by initial stock and inter-period linkage equations, three additional sets of variables have to be set exogenously as macro closures in order to make the model fully determinate. They are chosen from following variables for alternative closures: (1) gross investment or government transfer (INV_r or $GTRANS_r$), (2) balance of trade or exchange rate (BOT_r or ER_r), (3) government spending or surplus (deficit) (GSP_r or $GSAV_r$).

<u>Inter-Period and Trade-Productivity Linkages</u>

Equations 44–48 define the recursive structure of the five types of factor endowment (natural resource are sector specific and held constant, it can be modified if more reliable data become available) in the modeled economy. For instance, capital stock in each region at period t equals last period's capital stock plus the region's gross investment minus depreciation. While unskilled labor equals last period's employment multiply by population growth rate, plus rural-urban migration, $MIG_{rt,}$ minus the increase of skilled labor SK_{rt} (set exogenously).

$$FS_{KAr,t} = (1 - dk_r) \times FS_{KAr,t-1} + INV_{rt} \tag{44}$$

$$FS_{RLr,t} = (1 + n_{rt}) \times FS_{RLr,t-1} + MIG_{rt} \tag{45}$$

$$FS_{ULr,t} = (1 + n_{rt}) \times FS_{ULr,t-1} + MIG_{rt} - ds_r \times \overline{\nabla SK_{rt}} \tag{46}$$

$$FS_{SLr,t} = (1 + n_{rt}) \times FS_{SLr,t-1} + ds_r \times \overline{\nabla SK_{rt}} \tag{47}$$

$$FS_{LDr,t} = (1 - dl_t) \times FS_{LDr,t-1} \tag{48}$$

$$\frac{PF_{ALr,t}}{PF_{ULr,t}} = wdf_r^{\,\exp^{-t\varphi\,r}} \tag{49}$$

$$ITFP_{ir} = 1 + ims_{ir} \times \left\{ \frac{NX_{ir}}{NX_{ir} + VA_{ir}} \times \left[\frac{\sum\limits_{j \in IM} \sum\limits_{s \in R} x_{jsr}}{\sum\limits_{j \in IM} \sum\limits_{s \in R} xo_{jsr}} \right]^{\sigma ip_{ir}} + \frac{VX_{ir}}{NX_{ir} + VA_{ir}} - 1 \right\} \tag{50}$$

Equation 49 specifies the wage differential between agricultural labor and unskilled manufacturing labor, which drives the rural-urban migration endogenously and approach to one over time. Equation 50 links import embodied technology transfer (via imports of capital goods and intermediate inputs) and total factor productivity. Where XO_{isr} is the base year real trade flows, IM is a subset of I, including those products embodied with advanced technology. It operates through share parameter and elasticities. An elasticity (ip_{ir}) of 0.1 implies that a 10 percent increase in real imports of capital and technology intensive goods would result a non more than 1 percent increase in total factor productivity in that sector depending the share of intermediate inputs in the sector's total imports. As pointed by Lewis, Robinson and Wang (1995), while there is fairly widespread agreement that linkage between imports of intermediate inputs and productivity gains do exist, there is less evidence of the size of the feedback. In our simulation exercises, the elasticities used for developed countries are at least less that half the values used for the developing countries.

The model is implemented in GAMS (Brooke, et. al. 1988). Readers who are interested in the computer code and related data files may contact the author. Definitions of variables and parameters are list in tables A.1 and A.2. The correspondence between sectors in our model, GTAP database and ISIC are listed in Table-A3.

Table A.1 Definitions of Variables

Variable	Definition	No. of Variables
PWE_{isr}	World f.o.b. price for goods from region s to region r s r	$I \times R\,(R{-}1)\,(4352)$
PWM_{isr}	World c. i.f. price for goods from region s to region r s r	$I \times R\,(R{-}1)\,(4352)$
PM_{ir}	Price of aggregate imported goods in region r	$I \times R\,(272)$
PX_{ir}	Price of composite goods in region r	$I \times R\,(272)$
PD_{ir}	Price of domestic products sold at domestic market in region r	$I \times R\,(272)$
PE_{ir}	Price of domestic goods for exports in region r	$I \times R\,(272)$
PC_{ir}	Domestic consumer price in region r	$I \times R\,(272)$
PP_{ir}	Average output price before production tax in region r	$I \times R\,(272)$
P_{ir}	Average output price after production tax in region r	$I \times R\,(272)$
PF_{fr}	Factor price in region r	$F \times R\,(102)$
PV_{ir}	Price of value added in region r	$I \times R\,(272)$
PN_{ir}	Price of aggregate intermediate inputs in region r	$I \times R\,(272)$
CPI_{r}	Price of savings in region r (consumer price index)	$R\,(17)$
ER_{r}	Exchange rate of region r	$R\,(17)$
PID_{r}	Price index in region r	$R\,(17)$
Q_{ir}	Sector output in region r	$I \times R\,(272)$
VA_{ir}	Variable sector production cost in region r	$I \times R\,(272)$
NX_{ir}	Aggregate sector intermediate input in region r	$I \times R\,(272)$
DF_{fir}	Sector factor demand in region r	$(F{-}3) \times I \times R + (IAG + RES) \times R\,(850)$
DX_{ir}	Sector domestic sales in region r	$I \times R\,(272)$
EX_{ir}	Domestic goods for exports in region r	$I \times R\,(272)$
C_{ir}	Household consumption in region r	$I \times R\,(272)$
GC_{ir}	Government spending in region r	$I \times R\,(272)$
ID_{ir}	Investment demand in region r	$I \times R\,(272)$
TX_{ir}	Composite goods demand (supply) in region r	$I \times R\,(272)$
MX_{ir}	Sector composite goods imports in region r	$I \times R\,(272)$
X_{isr}	Trade flows from region s to region r s r	$I \times R\,(R{-}1)\,(4352)$

TRQ	Total international transportation supply	1
PTR	Price of international shipping service	1
$TRQD_{ir}$	International shipping demand by region r	$I \times R$ (272)
$TRQS_r$	International shipping service supply by region r	R (17)
HDI_r	Household disposable income in region r	R (17)
SY_r	Household supernumerary income in region r	R (17)
GR_r	Total government revenue in region r	R (17)
GSP_r	Total government spending in region r	R (17)
$TARRIF_r$	Total tariff revenue in region r	R (17)
$ETAX_r$	Total export tax revenue (subsidy expenditure) in region r	R (17)
$PTAX_r$	Total production tax revenue in region r	R (17)
$CTAX_r$	Total consumer sale tax in region r	R (17)
SAV_r	Household savings in region r	R (17)
$GSAV_r$	Government saving (deficit) in region r	R (17)
$GTRNS_r$	Government transfer in region r	R (17)
BOT_r	Balance of trade in region r (net capital inflow)	R (17)
INV_r	Gross investment by region r	R (17)
TFP_{ir}	Import embodied TFP shifter by sector in region r	$I \times R$ (272)
FS_{fr}	Factor endowment by region r	$F \times R$ (102)

Total number of variables:

$17 \times R + (2 \times F + IAG + RES) \times R + 21 \times I \times R + 3 \times I \times R(R-1) + (F-3) \times I \times R + 2(20,113)$

Table A.2 Definitions of Parameters

Parameter	Definition
te_{isr}	Sector export tax (subsidy) rate for goods to region r from region s
tm_{isr}	Sector tariff rate for goods from region s in region r
tn_{isr}	Sector NTB for goods from region s in region r
tp_{ir}	Sector indirect tax rate in region r
tc_{ir}	Consumer sale tax rate in region r
trc_{isr}	International transportation cost margin as percent value of f.o.b.
io_{ijr}	Input/output coefficients for region r
kio_{ir}	Sector share of total investment in region r
dk_r	Depreciation rate of capital stock in region r
τ_r	Regional share of international shipping service supply
Γ_{ir}	Unit coefficients in first level Arminton aggregation function
μ_{ir}	Unit coefficients in second level Arminton aggregation function of region r
α_{ir}	Share parameters in the first level Arminton aggregation function of region r
ξ_{ir}	Share parameters in the second level Arminton aggregation function of region r
σm_i	Substitution elasticities between domestic and import goods
σt_i	Substitution elasticities among import goods from different regions
χ_{ir}	Unit coefficients in CET function of region r
κ_{ir}	Share parameters in CET function of region r
σe_i	Elasticities of transformation between domestic sales and exports
A_{ir}	Unit parameter in aggregate cost function
λ_{ir}	Intermediate input share in aggregate cost function
σp_{ir}	Elasticities of substitution between aggregate factor and intermediate input
Λ_{ir}	Unit parameter in value-added function
δ_{fir}	Factor share in value-added function
σv_{ir}	Elasticities of substitution among primary factors in value-added

γ_{ir}	Sector minimum subsistence requirements for private households in region r
β_{ir}	Marginal propensity to consume for private households in region r
mps_r	Marginal propensity to savings for private households in region r
θ_{ir}	Sector share of government spending in region r
tfp_r	General TFP shifter in region r
ims_{ir}	The share of intermediate inputs in sector's total imports
σip_{ir}	Elasticity between intermediate goods import growth with TFP growth
dl_r	Land depletion rate in region r
ds_r	Share of additional tretiry education stock go to skilled labor force at each period
φ_r	Parameter that control the speed of wage convergence between agric. and unskilled labor
n_{rt}	Population growth rate in region r at period t
Wdf_r	Wage ratio of agricultural labor and unskilled labor in region r at base year

Table A.3 Sector in the Global CGE Model and Their GTAP-ISIC Concordance

Sectors in the Model	GTAP[a] 4-Sector Number and Description	ISIC[b] Rev. 3 CODE
Agriculture	1. Paddy rice	01111, 01301, 01401
	2. Wheat	01112, 01302, 01402
	3. Cereal grains nec	01113, 01303, 01403
	4. Vegetables fruit nuts	01121, 01204, 01404
	5. Oil seeds	01114, 01305, 01405
	6. Sugar cane, sugar beet	01115, 01306, 01406
	7. Plant-based fibers	01116, 01307, 01407
	8. Crops nec.	01117, 01122, 1132, 01308, 01408
	9. Bovine cattle , sheep and goats, horses	01211, 01309, 01409
	10. Animal products nec., 11. Row milk	01220, 01212, 013010, 013011, 014010, 014011
	12. Wool silk-worm cocoons	01213, 013012, 014012
Forest & Fishery	13. Forestry, 14. Fishing	0200, 0150, 0500
Mining	15. Coal, 16. Oil, 17. Natural gas, 18. Minerals nec	1010, 1020, 1030, 11101, 11102, 11201, 11202, 1200, 1310, 1320, 1410, 1421, 1422, 1429
Processed Food	19. Bovine cattle, sheep and goats, horse meat p	15111, 15112, 15141, 15142, 1520, 15311, 1542
	20. Meat products nec, 21. Vegetable oils and fats, 22. Dairy products, 23. Processed rice	1512, 1513, 15312, 1532, 1533, 1541, 1543, 1544, 1549
	24. Sugar, 25. Food products nec	
Beverage & Tobacco	26. Beverages and tobacco products	1551, 1552, 1553, 1554, 1600
Textile	27. Textiles	1711–12, 1721–23, 1729–30, 2430
Apparel	28. Wearing apparel, 29. Leather products	1810, 1820, 2430
Leather	42. Manufactures nec	1911, 1912, 1920, 3691, 3692, 3693, 3694, 3699
Wood & Paper	30. Wood products, 31. Paper products publishing	2010, 2021, 2022, 2023, 2029, 3610, 2101, 2102, 2109, 2211, 2212, 2219, 2221, 2222

Manufactured Intermediates	32. Petroleum coal products	2310, 2320
	33. Chemical rubber plastic products	2330, 2411, 2412, 2413, 2421, 2422, 2423, 2424, 2429, 2511, 2519, 2520
	34. Mineral products nec	
	35. Ferrous metals	2610, 2691, 2692, 2693, 2694, 2695, 2696, 2699
	36. Metals nec	2710, 2731, 2720, 2732
	37. Metal products	2811, 2812, 2813, 2891, 2892, 2893, 2899
Motor	38. Motor vehicles and parts	3410, 3420, 3430
Other Transport Equipment	39. Transport equipment nec	3511, 3512, 3520, 3530, 3591, 3592, 3599
Electronic	40. Electronic equipment	3000, 3210, 3220, 3230
Machinery	41. Machinery and equipment nec	2213, 2230, 2911–15, 2919, 2921–27, 2929–30, 3110, 3120, 3130, 3140, 3150, 3190, 3311–13, 3320, 3330
Traded Services	47. Trade, transport, 48. Financial, business, recreational services, 49. Public administration and defense, education, health services	3710, 3720, 4100, 4510, 5010, 5020, 5030, 5040, 5050, 5110, 5121–22, 5131, 5139, 5141–43, 5149–50, 5190, 5220, 5231–34, 5239–40, 5251–52, 5259–60, 5510, 5520, 6010, 6021–23, 6030, 6110, 6120, 6210, 6220, 6301–04, 6309, 6411–12, 6420, 6511, 6519, 6591–92, 6599, 6601–03, 6711–12, 6719–20, 7010, 7020, 7111–13, 7121–23, 7129, 7130, 7210, 7220, 7230, 7240, 250, 7290, 7310, 7320, 7411–14, 7421–22, 7430, 7491–95, 7499, 7511–14, 7521–23, 7530, 8010, 8021–22, 8030, 8090, 8511–12, 8519–20, 8531–32, 9000, 9111–12, 9120, 9191–92, 9199, 9211, –14, 9219–20, 9231–33, 9241, 9249, 9301–03, 9309, 9500, 9900
Utility, Housing & Construction	43. Electricity, 44. Gas manufacture, distribution, 45. Water, 46. Construction, 50. Dwellings	4010, 4020, 4030, 4510, 4520, 4530, 4540, 4550

Note: a. Global Trade Analysis Project, version 4 (Hertel, 1997).
      b. International

CHAPTER 13

CONCLUSION:
LESSONS AND POLICY IMPLICATIONS

Tzong-Shian Yu and Dianqing Xu*

1. INTRODUCTION

No one could have predicted that the economic miracle created in East Asia by the newly emerging economies, and based upon sound economic fundamentals, could have become a myth overnight. And of course, no one could ever have supposed that the countries devastated by the East Asian financial crisis, with their negative growth rates and collapsed financial markets, could have recovered within two years of its initial outbreak in Thailand. The economic performance of Asian countries including the exchange rate, the stock market index, the foreign currency reservation, and the economic growth rate have improved since 1999 from their position at the bottom. Most Asian countries have adjusted their financial system. Even the Indonesia economy, which has been shocked the most in the financial crisis, got the new growth point after the election of the new President in the latter part of 1999. In the overview of this volume, we have pointed out a number of questions about the financial crisis, and attempted to obtain reasonable answers through a careful and comprehensive study of the crisis.

---

*Completion of this chapter is mainly based upon the following authors' papers within this volume: we are indebted to Anwar Nasution, Jaymin Lee, Chawin Leenabanchong, Editu A. Tan, Mohammed Ariff and Michael Meow-chun Yap, Kee-Jin Ngiam, Chyau Tuan and Linda F. Y. Ng, Teh-Ming Huo, and Zhi Wang for their contribution.

493

In this volume, each chapter tells a story of the experiences of the different countries during the period of the financial crisis, and makes an attempt to explain the causes of the crisis, the policy measures used to fight against it, the role played by the various governments, and so on. Accordingly, we intend to summarize and indicate both the lessons we should learn, and the policy implications that should be drawn from the financial crisis, based upon each of these countries' experiences.

Before proceeding, we should attempt to answer questions arising from the experiences of the ten East Asian countries; why some were so seriously hit, why others were less affected, why Hong Kong with strong economic fundamentals was severely affected, and why the Philippines with weak economic fundamentals was less affected. From the answers posed to such questions it may be possible to identify the underlying causes of the financial crisis, and we may also be able to provide reasons for the rapid recovery of the East Asian economy.

2. THE DIVERSE EXPERIENCES OF THE FINANCIAL CRISIS

The East Asian countries, in general, have rich manpower sources, equipped with fundamental levels of education and an industrial nature, high savings ratios, 'export-led growth' strategies, high economic growth over a period of decades and positive policies for the acceleration of industrial development. So why were some of these countries severely affected whilst others were less affected? The less-affected countries include Taiwan and Mainland China, while the most severely affected countries include Indonesia, Korea, Thailand and Malaysia. It is also puzzling that Hong Kong and Singapore, both of which had strong economic fundamentals and well-designed financial systems, demonstrated such disparity in their economic performance during the financial crisis. The Philippines and Japan also had quite different experiences.

Taiwan:

Taiwan was less affected by the financial crisis than most others in the region, and this is mainly attributed to Taiwan's strong economic fundamentals which include moderate economic growth, mild inflation levels, low level of unemployment, minimal external debt, a floating exchange rate system, consistent trade surplus, large foreign exchange reserves and a gradual and orderly sequence in the opening up of its capital account. In addition, there were no conditions present to attract international speculators to seek any advantage.

Mainland China:

Mainland China was one of the less affected economies, and this is mainly attributable to its good economic performance prior to the outbreak of the financial crisis. This included consistent high economic growth, mild inflation levels, trade surpluses, large foreign exchange reserves, small short-term external debt, a restricted capital account and a large depreciation of the RMB in 1994. Under such conditions it was impossible for international speculators to penetrate its financial market in order to seek capital gains.

The following countries, Indonesia, Korea, Thailand and Malaysia, were all seriously affected by the financial crisis, and this is apparent in their subsequent poor economic performance in 1998.

Indonesia:

Prior to the outbreak of the East Asian financial crisis, Indonesia had displayed weak macroeconomic fundamentals. Persistent political instability and natural disasters also served to deepen the effects of the crisis. The high growth rate in GDP achieved during the 1990s, was mostly associated with the "bubble" industries, including construction, public utilities and services in the non-traded sector of the economy, whilst most of the growth in non-oil exports was associated with demand from firms in East Asia with strong currencies. In particular, Indonesia was equipped with a very weak financial system and, as a result, has suffered from a widening current account deficit. The consequence of the overall increase in investment, was that most of the private debt had been borrowed directly from foreign lenders, and not through the internal banking system. With so many non-performing loans extended by the private sector, the excessive levels of heavy external debt continued to increase. Basically, the country operated under a poor financial system in which a large part was dominated by policy-makers' cronies and vested interest groups.

Korea:

Despite its sound macroeconomic fundamentals, Korea was nevertheless vulnerable to the financial crisis due to its heavy exposure to external debt, a high proportion of which was accounted for by short-term external debt. Foreign exchange reserves were insufficient to cover the short-term external liabilities. In fact, the crisis in Korea was not one of illiquidity, but of insolvency, caused by non-performing loans in the financial sector, which basically stemmed from the low levels of productivity in the highly leveraged corporate sector. For many years, Korean government policy encouraged the proliferation of Korean business conglomerates, *chaebols*, and these conglomerates had a tendency to over-borrow and over-invest, demonstrating the behavior of moral hazard, i.e., "too big to fail", or "over investment on over-borrowing". The chaebols were usually characterized by poor entrepreneurial flair, whilst the government also failed to develop appropriate supervisory capabilities.

Thailand:

Why did the East Asian financial crisis break out in Thailand in the first place? This is really a puzzling question to answer. The fact that Thailand became the first target for attack by international speculators could be attributed to its overflows of capital, macroeconomic mismanagement and financial fragility in general, in addition to its burden of excessive external debt and an open capital account which was not accompanied by a particularly sound financial system. Thailand has, in fact, considerable experience of current account deficits combined with insufficient foreign exchange reserves. Most of the total debt had been used for investment in portfolio equity, rather than in foreign direct investment. The oligopolistic structure of the Thai banking sector is generally believed to be the main reason for its financial vulnerability.

Malaysia:

This country had been operating under a persistent current account deficit throughout the 1990s. Fuelled by a high investment boom (partly financed by long-term capital inflow during 1994 and 1995), rapid credit expansion and increased exposure in the property sector and stock purchases, this ultimately resulted in a bubble in both the real estate and stock markets. Many large infrastructure projects suffered from the inefficient use of capital, and demonstrated clear "over-investment and inappropriate investment on over-borrowing." Additionally, external debt amounted to US$40.5 billion, or 42% of the country's GDP, which was much too high in comparison to its foreign exchange reserves. The sustained appreciation of the real exchange rate since 1995, also proved unhelpful in improving its balance of trade.

Singapore:

The East Asian financial crisis could have had a potentially devastating effect on the Singaporean economy. However, Singapore continued to demonstrate favorable economic performance, as a direct result of its very strong economic fundamentals, including high economic growth, mild inflation, low unemployment rate, trade surplus, large foreign exchange reserves and low levels of external debt. In particular, its financial institutions may well be described as the soundest institutions throughout the region, largely because they have been overseen by a well-capitalized and well-supervised banking system. No opportunities existed in Singapore for international speculators, and there is no doubt that Singapore deserves the position of a regional financial center.

Hong Kong:

In a comparison with Singapore, Hong Kong also had financially sound and economically healthy fundamentals, and yet it was seriously affected by the financial crisis in terms of negative economic growth, and high unemployment rate. It should be noted that Hong Kong reveled in rapid growth in its money supply, high inflation rates and almost zero, or negative, real interest rates particularly before the handover of sovereignty in 1997. In addition, Hong Kong was also presented with adequate supplies of low-cost foreign capital, and the subsequent over-investment and herding in both the property and stock markets.

It is clear that the immediate effects of the financial crisis in most other Asian countries were the extensive depreciation in exchange rates and the collapse of their financial markets. However, the major impact of speculators' operations in Hong Kong, was soaring interest rates in the money market; there was neither a collapse of its financial market, nor any depreciation in exchange rates. Needless to say, Hong Kong's firm commitment to the pegged rate should be seen as partly responsible for its economic downturn. In other words, defending the linked exchange rate regime, at the expense of the overall macroeconomic performance, was nothing more than a test of the government's ability and determination to maintain stability. Consequently, the relative consequences of the appreciation of the HK$, were the drop in Hong Kong's domestic exports and re-exports of manufacturing goods, as well as a reduction in service exports during 1998.

The Philippines:

When placed alongside other ASEAN countries during the period of financial crisis, the economic performance of the Philippines was much better. The main causes of the Asian crisis, as applicable to most of the ASEAN nations, such as market failure in the financial system, currency and exchange rate mismanagement, and premature capital account liberalization, did not strongly apply to the downturn in the Philippines. Prior to the financial crisis, the Philippines had undertaken a number of financial reforms, which had substantially strengthened the banking system and allowed it to withstand the contagion effects of the Asian crisis. For instance, its capital account liberalization took place only after essential prudential regulations and practices in the banking system had been established; thus the inherent problems associated with market failure are seen not to be the underlying cause of financial crisis. The problems can be traceable to direct interventions and abuses in an environment of political-economic concentration. Competition and market discipline in the Philippines has been fostered by decisions to abandon credit intervention and to liberalize both the capital account and bank entry. As for the problem of moral hazard, this appears to be somewhat exaggerated in the case of the Philippines.

Japan:

Japan belongs to another category entirely. For many years it stood out as the richest and most modernized country in Asia, nevertheless, during the 1990s, it suffered a total collapse of its bubble economy. Though Japan has possessed the largest levels of foreign exchange reserves, and enjoyed the largest levels of trade surpluses for many years, its financial system is still backward as compared to many other developed countries.

The long entrenchment of Japan's economy in the doldrums of recession and financial despair can be considered an important contributory factor in the breakout of the East Asian financial crisis in July 1997. Japan has invested heavily in other East Asian countries and trading with these countries is very closely linked. There were many reciprocal relationships existing in the region with, on the one hand, East Asian countries purchasing machinery, equipment and industrial materials from Japan, whilst on the other hand, many of their labor-intensive goods were subsequently exported to Japan. Through this channel of trade and capital flows, Japan's economy also suffered from the crisis, not only in terms of its large depreciation in foreign exchange rates and the sharp drop in stock prices, but also in deepening economic recession. The government of Japan pumped in billions of dollar to rescue the country's economy, for instance, public funds were used to bail out banks and finance houses, to expand construction of social and industrial infrastructure, to reduce income taxes and corporate taxes, to give out free tokens to children and the elderly, and so on. Despite mounting numerous economic rescue packages, and providing the massive injection of capital into the Japanese economy, it has nevertheless, remained sluggish.

A recent reform program, introduced by the Japanese government during the 1997 fiscal year, has been undertaken in an attempt to revitalize the financial sector. The program also aims to improve the protective measures for customers and to provide an overall improved mechanism for dealing with financial failures.

3.   RESPONSES TO THE IMF POLICY PRESCRIPTIONS

The IMF policy prescriptions aimed at rescuing the economies of the worst hit countries — Indonesia, Korea and Thailand — have been a controversial issue. Some economists argue that the IMF policy prescriptions were inappropriate and that the measures were unfair in both an economic and a political sense.[1] The immediate aims of the IMF's prescriptive methods, were to deflate the economy in order to strengthen the exchange rate through high interest rates and low import demand, nevertheless, the monetary and fiscal policies, which were restrictive in nature, have served to intensify uncertainty and pessimism.

The country most affected by these policies is Indonesia where, according to the response from local economists,[2] the IMF has been partly responsible for aggravating the crisis. First of all, it made recommendations for the closure of banks in November 1997 without adequate preparation. The combination of the sharp devaluation of the Rupiah, high nominal interest rates, and tight liquidity pushed the already fragile banks and their customers into bankruptcy. The credit squeeze and austere fiscal policy have led to economic contraction that has caused high social costs in terms of eroding real wages and soaring unemployment rates. Secondly, it was not until April

---

[1] See: Stiglitz (1998).

[2] See: Anwar Nasution's paper in this volume.

1998, that the IMF made a monumental shift towards recommending fiscal stimulus, along with the creation of a social safety net and the resolution of the external debt burden. As a result, the severe cuts in government expenditure magnified the domestic economic recession.

Responses to the policies prescribed by the IMF for Thailand,[3] indicate that the recent Asian crisis may have a close linkage to the IMF-led efforts to encourage capital account liberalization, since various policy measures were issued — under the IMF's technical assistance — as a means of addressing problems of stability, particularly stability of exchange rates and price levels, whilst the problem of economic growth was given less priority. Consequently, capital liberalization has become a catalyst for turbulence in the international financial markets, especially in foreign exchange transactions, and due to the unregulated financial markets that existed in Thailand, unnecessary volatility was introduced into the foreign exchange markets and the movement of capital. In 1998, the economic growth rate in Thailand dropped by 7 percent.

Korea appears to have had a rather different response to that of Indonesia and Thailand. The Korean government — with the consent of the IMF — turned to deflationary policies following the stabilization of its foreign exchange rate from the middle of 1998, and this brought about its effective recovery in 1999 as fiscal stimulus was beginning to work and consumption expenditure was returning to some sort of normality.[4] A further disparity lies in the fact that the Korean government had modified the IMF's prescriptive recipe in response to the experiences of Indonesia and Thailand.

In practice, the IMF policy recommendations may provide a good means of maintaining stability in foreign exchange rates, but at the same time, may well be harmful for economic recovery; and they may be good for ensuring the establishment of sound financial systems in the long term, but inappropriate for stimulating economic activity in the short term. For instance, the IMF programs also consisted of the establishment of international accounting and auditing standards, providing prudential rules, including those

---

[3] See: Chawin Leenabanchong's paper in this volume.

[4] See: Jaymin Lee's paper in this volume.

on insolvency and financial disclosure, and the effective supervision and monitoring of financial institutions. All of these measures are essentially long term in nature and take considerable time to implement.[5]

4.   THE ROAD TO RECOVERY

Following their period of coming to terms with the financial crisis, a period which lasted around two years, the East Asian countries noticeably started to recover, and in 1999, all the countries that have experienced economic crisis, with the exception of Indonesia, had re-established positive economic growth, rising stock prices and a slow but steady improvement in foreign exchange rates. Clearly, it would be fascinating to understand how the East Asian economies started to recover so rapidly, therefore, in order to establish the reasons, we have employed a recursive dynamic CGE analysis which provides us with some reasonable answers to the puzzle.

After the financial crisis, the domestic market in most Asian countries is quite weak. There is the need to maintain the aggregate demand. The very weak market demand is the major obstacle, which limits the speed of the economic recovery in Asia. As we already know, Japan, as a giant country within the region, has played a key role not only in its involvement in the outbreak of the crisis, but also in initiating the region's economic recovery. The pursuit of economic recovery depends largely upon the expansion of aggregate demand, both in domestic demand and in exports. According to our findings, the recovery of Japan's domestic demand, especially in its private consumption and investment, would have had a strong positive effect on the Asian economies in general, since only Japan could provide the necessary scale of export market for the other Asian countries. The stability of the Chinese currency also provided a major contribution, and Mainland China had clearly tried in every possible way to maintain the stability of its currency prior to the general recovery of the East Asian economy. If Mainland China had devalued its currency, this would have produced a strong

---

[5] See: E.A. Tan's paper in this volume.

substitution effect, resulting in considerable reduction in the export markets of the other Asian economies. This would also have created the strong possibility of triggering a further round of competitive devaluation and financial turmoil in the Asian countries.

Beyond these findings another important, but largely ignored factor, which has also made a substantial contribution to the recovery of the East Asian economy, is capital movement. During the middle of 1999, stock prices in the United States had soared to an extremely high level, which obviously provided the warning signal for a "bubble phenomenon", such that many international funds were already starting to turn back to the East Asia region. For the Asian Financial markets, this was clearly helpful in building confidence, increasing their investment, and resuming their activities within the region.

5. LESSONS FROM THE FINANCIAL CRISIS

There is an old Chinese saying that goes: "the lessons from past experiences may serve as a master for the future." The East Asian financial crisis is now over, and each of the East Asian countries has gained a different perspective from their experience in combating the crisis. If we can learn something from these shared experiences, it may be helpful for us to cope with any similar challenge in the future.

1. The Current Account Deficit Problem

To many newly emerging economies, their long experiences of current account deficits do not provide a sound indicator of their financial condition. One might argue that the United States has managed to operate under substantial current account deficits for a significant period of time, and yet its financial conditions remain stable. However, the United States is the richest and the strongest country in the world; its currency has been universally accepted, its multinational enterprises have dominated many industries, and their wealth is allocated in many countries. Even though its current account is in deficit, its credit is still the most reliable in the world.

The types of capital inflows may well be more crucial than their size. Total capital inflows include hot money, such as portfolio equity investment, and cold money, such as foreign direct investment. Reliance on short-term capital inflows to finance the current account deficit is untenable in the longer term due to the volatile nature of these funds.

2. Capital Account Liberalization

Currently, the formation of various funds has become universal in nature. By means of channeling their way into the liberalization of the capital account, many large funds have tried to dominate the financial markets of developing countries. If the country has no strong defense against such infiltration, its financial market could quickly form a bubble; the experience of Thailand is a particularly good example. In July 1997, prior to the financial crisis, international accounting and auditing standards in Thailand had not been effectively or extensively implemented, and there was no reliable financial information for use in assessing loans and equities and the overall financial condition of banks.

Usually in developing countries, the stock market and real estate market are relatively small and there is a distinct absence of well-designed regulations for the capital markets, along with a shortage of managers experienced in capital market administration. If the doors were open to foreign capital in the two markets, this would encourage international speculators to take advantage of such an opportunity to dominate the financial markets. Following the bitter experiences of the financial crisis, many banks and economists in the region now insist that governments should follow an appropriate sequence for opening up their capital accounts, that is, the opening up of the current account should be first, followed by the capital account, and when liberalizing the capital account, this should be undertaken in a gradual step-by-step way.

3. Strong Economic Fundamentals

Strong economic fundamentals may be the first line of defense for any country battling against financial attack. Even though the country may be unable to completely avoid such attack, it can instead, significantly reduce the potential damage. Singapore provides a good example in this case. With such strong economic fundamentals, Singapore deterred currency attacks and took bold, timely and appropriate measures to counter the large negative shocks triggered by the crisis. Singapore used its foreign reserves to intervene directly in the foreign exchange markets, in a bid to help shore up both the Baht and the Rupiah in the midst of the crisis. The flexibility of both the exchange and wage rates in Singapore had enabled it to weaken the effects of the Asian financial crisis. By adapting a flexible exchange rate system, it was able to avoid overvaluation (or undervaluation) of the Singapore dollar. An overvalued exchange rate could have invited speculative attacks, whilst the flexible exchange rate system was capable of reacting swiftly to the crisis. The adjustment in wage rates is however, another matter, this would only be applicable in a small-scale country; it is doubtful whether it would be tenable in a larger country.

In short, sound macroeconomic management and a robust banking system may be considered the two main pillars of macroeconomic stability. Hence, the deregulation of the financial sector should be accompanied by improvements in bank supervision and in the implementation of prudential rules and regulations.

4. Over-Investment in Real Estate

Most of the East Asian countries prefer to invest heavily in real estate in order to make substantial capital gains. Around the 1990s, both Japan and Taiwan had suffered seriously from the sluggishness of the real estate markets, due mainly to enterprises having built a substantial number of properties with high prices, most of which had been beyond the purchasing power of the middle-income class. Inevitably, these enterprises were unable to recoup sufficient capital to repay their loans to the banks, which in turn led them in to financial crisis. During the past decade, mainland China, Hong Kong, Thailand, Malaysia and Indonesia have each had similar problems; they have built many high priced residential properties, hotels and department stores, even though there was no effective demand for them. This has not only caused bankruptcy amongst many constructors, but has also resulted in financial difficulties within many of the banks. Due to the widespread policy of low interest rates, many Japanese enterprises also undertook speculative real estate activities in many East Asian countries, such that these Japanese enterprises suffered losses on their investment in real estate, not only in Japan itself, but also in many other East Asian countries. It is therefore regarded as reasonable to say that the underlying cause of their losses is attributable to their over-investment in real estate.

5. Government Intervention vs. Laissez-Faire

In July 1997, as the financial crisis broke out, the immediate effect within the East Asian countries was the collapse of their financial markets. When faced with such a catastrophic event, all the governments within the region adopted some form of policy measures aimed at combating the crisis. Even Hong Kong, the so-called model of the free market, also adopted measures to fight against the activities of international speculators, and then took some of the blame from the monetary school. The result is that there is now some controversy between the appropriateness of government intervention as opposed to a more laissez-faire approach.

Theoretically, a free market means that no individuals can influence price determination; if the market is strongly dominated by a few speculators, the market is no longer free. Under such a condition, there is a requirement for some form of policy measures capable of eliminating monopolistic or oligopolistic power, whilst facilitating effective resumption of the market.

No economist in the world believes that the current financial international market is a perfect competitive market. Market failure in the international financial market is very clear. If the size of the international financial group increases, the ability to avoid the risk is strong. Because the total number of players in the international financial market has been reduced step by step, many assets have been focused into few large groups. The merger of the large financial institutions leaves them with the power to influence the price in the international financial market. Therefore, performance of the financial group follows the increasing return to scale and the international financial market has no convexity. Definitely there is no competitive equilibrium in the international financial market. Without rules of the game in the international market is one of the major reasons for the financial crisis in the world. However, until today no one knows who has the authorization to reform the rules of the game for the international financial market. Also, there is not one institution that will take the responsibility to change the rules. Therefore, there is not any reason to make such a judgement: the financial crisis in the international financial market is only a short-term problem. Of course, the responsibility for protecting the market from speculator control lies with the government.

6. The Moral Hazard Problem

The so-called moral hazard problem, as a cause of the financial crisis in East Asia, has been discussed in many relevant papers and books. Although there is not, as yet, any general agreement, it really is an economic issue that has to be dealt with. The moral hazard problem indicates that private banks were implicitly encouraged to finance favored companies on the assumption that the government would guarantee their favors.[6] If the favored company was to incur losses through financial crisis, due to the following causes: (i) rapid expansion of scale through its borrowings; (ii) over-play of the principle of financial leverage through investment in the financial market; (iii) the use of short-term loans for investment in real estate; or (iv) failure in the adjustment of its liquidity; then the government would act as the last resort of lenders, that is, the government would try to protect the depositors of the bank on the one hand, whilst on the other hand, rescuing the troubled company, through some special measure.[7] For the troubled company, such a policy would encourage it to borrow even more from the banks, because it comes to believe the myth "too large to fail."

---

[6] See: William H. Overholt, "China's economic squeeze", in China's Reform, 2000, pp. 13–33.

[7] Several public banks, or private banks, which have large amounts of public shares, form a team, which takes over the management of the troubled company; once the troubled company recovers, the management is handed back to the original owners under some conditions.

This moral hazard problem took place in many of the East Asian countries, the most severely affected country being Korea. Indeed the formation of the Korean *chaebol*, should be directly attributed to this myth. Even in Taiwan, the government also adopted this special measure ever since the early 1980s, the main purpose of the government being to avoid the domino effect. However, it seems that if a company temporarily experiences disequilibrium of its liquidity, then the government should consider rescuing it; but if the company has completely lost its ability to fulfill its repayment liability, then insolvency should be the destiny for that troubled company.

6. POLICY IMPLICATIONS

A number of constructive policy implications can be drawn from the many lessons learned by the East Asian countries from their recent experiences; these are as follows:

1. "Prevention is better than cure". Governments should provide in-built early warning systems which indicate changes in the financial conditions, in order to enable a timely response to any future financial turbulence.

2. Capital account liberalization should proceed, under the condition that a strong disciplinary mechanism is installed to replace the government's role. The simple withdrawal of government intervention does not work.

3. The design of an internationally acceptable framework for prudential supervision of banking institutions is of paramount importance, and this should clearly demonstrate common standards across the different countries. Proper tools and processes are essential in assessing financial risks.

4. To meet the requirements of economic liberalization, governments should pursue sound policies, along with enhanced informational flows, facilitated through greater transparency.

5. Domestic liberalization and the opening up of markets should proceed strictly in accordance with the textbook. Reversing the sequence for whatever reason is dangerous.

6. Moral hazard, based on government sympathy for specific enterprises, has the potential to fuel further financial crises.

7. Financial enterprises should not become deeply involved with the provision of loans to affiliated enterprises that have acquired real estate throughout the country. Once unpaid loan interest and bad debt are amassed, this would affect the survivability of the affiliated enterprises, finance companies and banks.

8. Governments should speed up the development of bond markets to meet the needs of long-term capital from the business sector.

9. When drastic depreciation takes place in neighboring countries, the adoption of either a fixed exchange rate system, or a policy of pegging the exchange rate to the US dollar, discourages exports and causes a reduction in the country's economic growth rate.

10. Long-term capital inflow is good for direct investment. If short-term funds are used for direct investment, clearly the result will be dangerous, by virtue of the very short maturity period of such loans.

11. The combination of economic crisis and improvements in accounting systems has substantially increased the ratio of non-performing loan (NPLs). The rise in NPLs can drive up banks' operating costs, and also cause a negative spread between lending and deposit interest rates.

12. Heavy governmental involvement in the private sector, whilst having clear benefits, can also result in undesirable outcomes if the necessary checks and balances are weak. A worthwhile goal of reform is the creation of a business environment with clear divisions between government and enterprises.

INDEX